The Diplomacy of Annexation

The Diplomacy of Annexation

TEXAS, OREGON, AND THE MEXICAN WAR

DAVID M. PLETCHER

UNIVERSITY OF MISSOURI PRESS

ISBN 0–8262–0135–0

Library of Congress Catalog Number 72–88573

Copyrght © 1973 by

The Curators of the University of Missouri

University of Missouri Press, Columbia, Missouri 65201

Printed and bound in the United States of America

To Ellen and Ralph,
Jean and Katie

Acknowledgments

A project as long-lasting and complex as this one raises a mountain of debts for aid and advice. I first conceived the idea of studying Anglo–American rivalry in Mexico, while holding a Fulbright Senior Research Fellowship at University College, London, in 1953–1954. Nearly a decade later, in 1962–1963, a grant from the Social Science Research Council, combined with sabbatical leave from Hamline University, enabled me to spend a year in concentrated research on the 1840s in Mexico City, London, Paris, and Madrid. During the 1960s several summer research grants from Hamline University and Indiana University aided my work in Washington, D. C., and London and gave me leisure in which to write and revise.

Many archives and libraries have courteously opened their manuscript resources to me. For public papers I should like to express appreciation to the National Archives, Washington; the Public Record Office, London; the Archives du Ministère des Affaires Étrangères, Paris; and the Biblioteca de Asuntos Exteriores and the Archivo Histórico Nacional, Madrid. I regret that the Mexican government did not see fit to allow me similar access to its foreign affairs archives, despite the kind intercession of Daniel Cosío Villegas. I have made extensive use of transcripts from the Mexican archives, prepared decades earlier under the direction of Eugene C. Barker and Justin H. Smith and photostats made by France V. Scholes. These materials are now on deposit at the University of Texas Libraries and the Library of Congress (Division of Manuscripts), respectively. I have also been permitted to consult private manuscript collections at the Library of Congress; the Massachusetts Historical Society, Boston; the New York Public Library; the New York Historical Society; the Historical Society of Pennsylvania, Philadelphia; the University of Delaware Library, Newark; the British Museum and University College, London; and All Souls College, Oxford.

My "headquarters" libraries for this research were those at Hamline University and Indiana University (Bloomington). I am

vii

deeply indebted to the staffs of both institutions for obtaining books on interlibrary loan and for many other favors. Other libraries in which I have spent many hours consulting books, newspapers, and other printed materials are the University of Minnesota Library, Minneapolis; the Minnesota State Historical Society and the St. Paul Public Library, St. Paul; the Library of Congress; the British Museum; and the Bibliothèque Nationale, Paris. It is impossible for me to list the many libraries which have lent me individual volumes from time to time, but I thank them as a group. I am also grateful to the following universities for making available highly useful unpublished dissertations: University of California (Berkeley), University of Chicago, George Washington University, Indiana University, University of London, University of Minnesota, Université de Paris, University of Pittsburgh, Stanford University, University of Texas (Austin), and University of Virginia.

Individuals have helped me in many ways, such as by reading part or all of the manuscript, offering advice and encouragement, and suggesting materials or avenues of approach which had not occurred to me. I am especially grateful to Maurice G. Baxter, Shirley A. Bill, Robert H. Ferrell, Charles Hayden, R. A. Humphreys, Cecil Alan Hutchinson, Ralph W. Marsden, John A. Munroe, Irene D. Neu, Robert E. Quirk, Martin Ridge, Marie V. Scholes, and Walter V. Scholes. William H. Listerud drafted the maps. I have also enjoyed the valuable services of Gene Frickey, John F. Kessler, and Lynn Ruark as research assistants in such tasks as preparing bibliography cards and checking footnote citations.

Bloomington, Indiana, January 1973

D. M. P.

Contents

Footnote Abbreviations

BM, AM: British Museum, Additional Manuscripts. London.

Dublán and Lozano, *LM*:   Manuel Dublán, José María Lozano, Adolfo Dublán, and A. A. Esteva, eds., *Legislación mexicana, ó Colección completa de las disposiciones legislativas expedidas desde la independencia de la Republica* [etc.] 50 vols. México, 1876–1912.

France, MAE, CP: France, Archives du Ministère des Affaires Étrangères, Correspondence Politique. Paris.

Garrison, *DCRT*:   George Pierce Garrison, ed., *Diplomatic Correspondence of the Republic of Texas*. Annual Report of the American Historical Association for the Years 1907, 1908. 3 vols. Washington, 1908–1911.

GB, A 1/5568:   Great Britain, Admiralty, Series 1, Volume 5568. Public Record Office, London.

GB, CO 43/100:   Great Britain, Colonial Office, Series 43, Volume 100. Public Record Office, London.

GB, FO 50/200:   Great Britain, Foreign Office, Series 50, Volume 220. Public Record Office, London.

HSP: Historical Society of Pennsylvania. Philadelphia.

LC: Library of Congress. Washington.

Manning, *CR*:   William R. Manning, ed., *Diplomatic Correspondence of the United States: Canadian Relations, 1784–1860*. 4 vols. Washington, 1940–1945.

Manning, *IAA*:   William R. Manning, ed., *Diplomatic Correspondence of the United States: Inter-American Affairs, 1831–1860*. 12 vols. Washington, 1932–1939.

Manning, *LAI*:   William R. Manning, ed., *Diplomatic Correspondence of the United States Concerning Latin-American Independence*. 3 vols. New York, 1925.

MHS: Massachusetts Historical Society. Boston.

NNR: *Niles' National Register*. Baltimore.

NYHS: New York Historical Society. New York City.

PRO: Public Record Office. London.

Rdh-m: Javier Malagón Bárcelo, Enriqueta Lópezlira, and José María Miquel i Vergès, eds., *Relaciones diplomáticas hispano-mexicanas (1839–1898). Documentos procedentes del archivo de la Embajada de España en México. Serie I, Despachos generales.* 4 vols. México, 1949–1968.

Spain, AHN: Spain, Archivo Historico Nacional. Madrid.

Spain, BAE: Spain, Biblioteca de Asuntos Exteriores. Madrid.

SRE: Mexico, Secretaría de Relaciones Exteriores. México.

US, 28C, 1S, *CG*:   United States, 28th Congress, 1st session, *Congressional Globe*. Washington.
Citations of the *Congressional Globe* follow this form, with variations to indicate the session of Congress.

US, 27C, 3S, HED 166: United States, 27th Congress, 3d session, House Executive Document 166. Washington.
Citations of House documents follow this form, with variations to indicate the session of Congress and the number of the document.

US, 30C, 1S, SED 52:   United States, 30th Congress, Senate Executive Document 52. Washington.
Citations of Senate documents follow this form, with variations to indicate the session of Congress and the number of the document.

US, DN, LCS: United States, Department of Navy, Letters Received by the Secretary of the Navy from Commanding Officers of Squadrons. Record Group 45. National Archives, Washington.

US, DN, OL: United States, Department of Navy, Letters Received by the Secretary of the Navy from Officers below the Rank of Commander. Record Group 45. National Archives, Washington.

US, DS, D: United States, Department of State, Despatches from United States Ministers. Record Group 59. National Archives, Washington.

US, DS, CD: United States, Department of State, Consular Despatches. Record Group 59. National Archives, Washington.

US, DS, I: United States, Department of State, Instructions to United States Ministers. Record Group 59. National Archives, Washington.

US, DS, SA: United States, Department of State, Special Agents. Record Group 59. National Archives, Washington.

US, DS, SM: United States, Department of State, Special Missions. Record Group 59. National Archives, Washington.

US, LC, /46:   United States, Library of Congress, Division of Manuscripts, Photostats, H/252 (73:72)/46. Washington.

The Diplomacy of Annexation

Introduction

For well over a century Americans have been studying the history of their great territorial acquisitions during the 1840s. The annexation of Texas, the Oregon compromise, and the occupation of California have become chapters in the epic that Theodore Roosevelt called "the winning of the West." It is easy to understand this heroic view of American expansion. The events themselves have grandeur, and their results—possession of the Southwest and the Pacific Coast—assured America's destiny as a Great Power.

The annexations of the 1840s reached their climax in a military conflict whose causes and justification have stimulated never-ending argument. The Mexican War, through which the United States gained possession of California and New Mexico, appealed to a strain of moralistic exaggeration in the American character. To some the war was eminently right, "a monument more lasting than brass,"[1] and it came about "as logically as a thunderstorm."[2] To others it was "wholesale butchery" carried on by "presidential despotism,"[3] the greedy action of "a quarrelsome people seeking a cause for hostility, . . . [and] an ambitious and selfish government envying her neighbor her possessions, and watching an opportunity to despoil her of them."[4] Extremists saw the war either as the culminating act of bravery in the western epic or as the great stain on the American shield, the curse of the house of Atreus.

These opposite views of the Mexican War developed from certain conditions of the postwar environment. At first, in the late 1840s and 1850s, many writers about the war tried to prove a case for the Democratic party or for the Whig party. Some insisted that President James K. Polk undertook an honorable conflict only as a last resort; others replied that he brought it on deliberately for partisan advantage. After the Civil War and Reconstruction a

---

1. US, 30C, 1S, CG, p. 499. Speech of Senator Jefferson Davis.

2. Justin H. Smith, *The War with Mexico*, II, 310.

3. Anonymous, *The Mexican War*, pp. 1, 3.

4. Charles T. Porter, *A Review of the Mexican War*, p. 95.

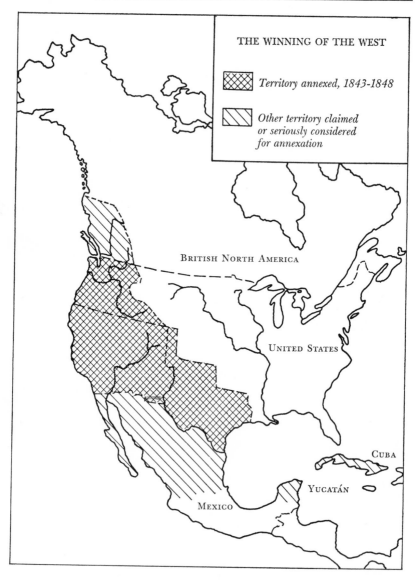

THE WINNING OF THE WEST

Territory annexed, 1843-1848

Other territory claimed
or seriously considered
for annexation

BRITISH NORTH AMERICA

UNITED STATES

CUBA

YUCATÁN

MEXICO

group of Northern historians explained the conflict with Mexico as the result of a gigantic slaveholders' conspiracy to add new plantation lands and proslavery states and thus restore their faltering grasp on the United States Government.[5] At about the time of

5. Hermann Eduard von Holst, *The Constitutional and Political History of the United States*, III, Chaps. 9–12. James Ford Rhodes, *History of the United States from the Compromise of 1850*, I, 87–93. For brief surveys of Mexican War historiography from the American view, see Peter T. Harstad and Richard W. Resh, "The Causes of the Mexican War: A Note on Changing Interpretations," *Arizona and the West*, 6 (Winter 1964), 289–302; and Roberto

World War I, when other historians reexamined the evidence, their conclusions were influenced to some degree by the anti-Mexican prejudice that had grown out of the friction between Woodrow Wilson and Venustiano Carranza. Holding a low opinion of Mexicans and a high, patriotic view of American expansion, these historians repeated the case of Polk's Democrats and used scholarly evidence to demonstrate that Mexico was really the aggressor and that the American victory had served the cause of humanity.[6]

Less sure of these conclusions, many twentieth-century writings have indicated some shame at what their authors try to avoid calling American aggression.[7] (None of them, of course, suggests that the United States should have returned the conquered territory to Mexico.) Some historians have explained the war as part of a general land hunger that affected the North and the West as well as the South and involved Oregon as well as California and New Mexico.[8] Others have preferred to emphasize commercial expansionism rather than land hunger as motivation and focus their attention upon San Francisco Bay and Puget Sound rather than upon the Southwest and the Columbia Valley.[9]

The reputation of President Polk has risen and fallen in this controversy like a cork bobbing on a whirlpool. He has appeared as victorious leader, master planner, Machiavellian intriguer, and hack politician responding to forces too great for him to understand. At the turn of the century he was deemed too insignificant for inclusion in J. T. Morse, Jr.'s biographical series, *American Statesmen*, but within a generation or two he had become the forerunner of the dominant, self-assured executive of the twentieth century and a vital link in the chain from Jackson to Lincoln, Theodore Roosevelt, and Wilson. More recently, biographers and other analysts have qualified their admiration for his decisiveness

---

Esquenazi-Mayo, "Historiografía de la guerra entre México y los EE. UU.," *Duquesne Hispanic Review*, 1 (Fall 1962), 33–48; (Winter 1962), 7–35. Mexican historiography, much less known in the United States, is set forth in Homer C. Chaney, Jr., "The Mexican-United States War, As Seen by Mexican Intellectuals, 1856–1956," Ph. D. diss., Stanford University, 1959.

6. The classic example of this approach is Smith, *War with Mexico*, cited in note 2, which won the Pulitzer Prize for 1920. For later echoes of his judgments, see Alfred Hoyt Bill, *Rehearsal for Conflict, the War with*

Mexico, 1846–1848, especially pp. vii–viii; and Seymour V. Connor and Odie B. Faulk, *North America Divided. The Mexican War, 1846–1848*.

7. A good example is Richard W. Van Alstyne, *The Rising American Empire*, pp. 135–46.

8. See, for example, William E. Dodd, "The West and the War with Mexico," *Journal of the Illinois State Historical Society*, 5 (July 1912), 159–72.

9. The outstanding example of this interpretation is Norman A. Graebner, *Empire on the Pacific: A Study in American Continental Expansion*.

with regret that he did not realize more clearly the internal reper-
cussions of external conflict or anticipate the effect of the Mexican
War on North–South sectionalism.[10] Nevertheless, in the early
1960s historians were still so much impressed with Polk's accomplishments that in a poll conducted by Arthur M. Schlesinger, Sr.,
they ranked him eighth among Presidents—between Theodore
Roosevelt and Harry Truman. And that man of action, John F.
Kennedy, is said to have felt that even this rating was too low.[11]

Perhaps Polk's reputation will undergo further change if we
abandon considerations of right and wrong and examine the expansionism of the 1840s and particularly the Mexican War as diplomatic problems. Let us start with the assumption that the duty
of those who determine or carry out foreign policy is to secure their
country's best interests in the most efficient and the safest manner
available to them—by peaceful means if at all possible, since wars
are costly and dangerous, but by war if it cannot be avoided. Further, if they can, it is their duty to use honorable means, as this
term is understood by their generation.

An analysis of the Mexican War based on this view of diplomacy will approach questions that are rather different from those
raised by most historians in the past. One question involves the
whole cost of the war to the United States in men, in money, in
morale, and in later disunion. It will be important to inquire
whether the policy makers of 1845 and 1846 fully counted these
costs (within the limits of their knowledge) before undertaking
war. Could they have hoped to secure all or most of the advantages
obtained in the war without actually fighting an all-out conflict?
Were there any points at which they might have turned the course
of events in another direction, or was the Mexicans' will for battle,
as they later maintained, insuperable?

Insofar as these questions can be answered, the answers require analysis of more than United States–Mexican relations of
1845 and 1846. The Mexican War had its roots in the American
annexation of Texas, which raises questions as knotty as those of
the war itself—for example, American responsibility for the Tex-

10. The first scholarly biography of
Polk was Eugene Irving McCormac,
James K. Polk, a Political Biography.
It is now being replaced by another
politically oriented study, even more
detailed: Charles Grier Sellers, *James
K. Polk, Jacksonian: 1795–1843*; and
*James K. Polk, Continentalist, 1843–
1846.* At this date the third and final
volume is unpublished. For a historiographical study of Polk, see James Van
Horn, "Trends in Historical Interpretation: James K. Polk," *North Carolina
Historical Review,* 42 (October 1965),
454–64.

11. *New York Times Magazine,* July
29, 1962, pp. 12–13. Arthur M. Schlesinger, Jr., *A Thousand Days,* pp.
675–76.

ans' revolt from Mexico and the nine-year delay of annexation. How did the supporters of annexation finally bring it about, and did their methods best serve American interests, broadly defined? In a similar manner we must examine the Anglo-American quarrel over Oregon, for it is unreasonable to suppose that the United States could sustain two simultaneous diplomatic crises in separate, sealed compartments. We may wonder whether the Oregon crisis continued longer than necessary and why the two countries yielded just as the Mexican War began. Finally, we need to go beyond the actual declaration of war with Mexico and examine the bases of Polk's decision to launch an invasion of central Mexico, the negotiation of a peace treaty, and Polk's reluctance to accept that treaty.

A basic assumption of this study is that the Mexican War, Texas, and Oregon were not simply family quarrels in the Western Hemisphere. Instead, they formed a truly international question of first importance in which Britain, France, and occasionally even Spain played lively roles, both political and economic. The governments of these three nations did not intervene openly, for reasons that will become apparent, but certain individuals in each government wanted to intervene. If the United States had not won the war decisively, the power of Britain and France might have increased in the Atlantic and the Caribbean. Thus, the war was a turning point, not only in the internal history of the United States and in its relations with Latin America but also in the relations between hemispheres. Victory in the Mexican War did not launch the United States as a Great Power—this would require another half-century of growth—but it certainly helped to promote the nation from a third-rate to a second-rate power that would have to be reckoned with in its own neighborhood.

The diplomats and warriors of the 1840s thus furthered many American interests. The questions remain: Were these the only interests worth furthering, and did the United States government promote them in the best possible way?

I

The Growing Tensions
1815-1842

1

The Special Relationship: Britain and the United States

In twentieth-century international affairs the term *special relationship* has usually meant the unique Anglo–American friendship, setting off the two nations from the rest of the world. During the nineteenth century such a term could only have represented a more complex connection between the two countries—a mixture of attraction and repulsion, admiration and disdain, cooperation and competition. At that time the joint motto of the two countries might well have been that cliché of the romantic movie: "I cannot live with you or without you."

Examples of this Anglo–American ambivalence abound. The American people had derived many of their political and legal institutions from the English Parliament and common law, and British liberals hoped that the Old World would adopt some ideals of American democracy. Most upper-class Britons, however, looked on the American cult of equality as a social disease. For their part, many upper-class Americans admired the stability and grandeur of Westminster, but Anglophilia seldom appealed to the masses, and in 1841 the British minister complained of the malignant hatred animating most American politicians who had visited England.[1]

Social contacts produced the same contradictory reactions. British travelers flocked to America to see the new society, and some returned home to denounce Southern slaveholding and Yankee materialism and boorish manners. Americans' visits to Britain also generated mixed emotions. Nathaniel Hawthorne, for example, arrived in England with "a singular sense of having been there before" but soon recoiled before British haughtiness.[2] British intellectuals sneered at Americans' cultural pretensions; as Sydney Smith, dean of St. Paul's, put it bluntly, "Who reads an American

1. Henry S. Fox to Earl of Aberdeen, October 26, 1841, No. 117, GB, FO 5/364, p. 34. The foundations of these ambivalent attitudes in the years after 1812 are well set forth in Bradford Perkins, *Castlereagh and Adams: England and the United States, 1812–1823*, especially Chaps. 10, 12; and George Dangerfield, *The Era of Good Feelings*, especially Part IV.

2. Quoted in R. B. Mowat, *Americans in England*, pp. 159–62, 171. See also Allan Nevins, ed., *America through British Eyes*.

book?"[3] Americans deeply resented such slurs, but at the same time publishers in the United States pirated English novels and essays, thereby building up resentment in Britain.

But more influential in the diplomatic relations of the two countries was the mixture of interdependence and rivalry between their economic systems. Since colonial days, except for a few unusual years, each nation had been the other's best customer.[4] Economic interdependence, however, brought little desire for cooperation. Despite the influx of British capital, Americans delighted in boasting of their material expansion as having been achieved through their own, unassisted efforts. On their side the British resented American trade competition in Latin America and the Pacific and did not repeal the protective British Navigation Acts until 1849.[5]

*   *   *   *

In large part, this ambivalence in Anglo–American feelings between 1815 and 1840 resulted from the fact that both countries were changing rapidly in somewhat the same direction but at varying rates. During the 1830s the Jacksonian revolution, in Henry Clay's words, "swept over the [American] Government . . . like a tropical tornado," shattering aristocratic precedents and spreading democracy and demagoguery indiscriminately.[6] England was somewhat more gravely undergoing political and social changes too— the Reform Bill of 1832 and the factory, municipal reorganization, and poor laws passed by the Whigs in following years.

Political radicals in England, who felt that these reforms were too limited, regarded Jacksonian America as "an incandescent example," the hope of the world, their personal discovery and possession, where republican institutions were solving the social problems of mankind. Benthamites, Chartists, Socialists, Dissenters, all

3. The question was part of a long diatribe reprinted in John Bach McMaster, *A History of the People of the United States, from the Revolution to the Civil War*, V, 328–30. See also Chap. 48, *passim*.

4. During the 1830s and 1840s the United States sent between one third and one half of her exports to Britain; Britain sent between one sixth and one fourth of her exports to the United States. For a convenient summary of Anglo–American trade figures in the middle period, see H. C. Allen, *Great Britain and the United States, a History of Anglo-American Relations (1783–1952)*, p. 59.

5. In 1841 a committee of the Boston Chamber of Commerce complained that British duties and regulations threatened to extinguish the direct American trade with the British West Indies. *Merchants' Magazine*, 5 (December 1841), 509–13.

6. Quoted in Glyndon G. Van Deusen, *The Jacksonian Era, 1828–1848*, p. 90.

visited the United States, some to be disillusioned but many to bring away ideas and inspiration for reforms at home. As a result of this cross-fertilization, the great humanitarian movements of the 1830s and 1840s—women's rights, temperance, world peace, and educational and prison reform—were truly Anglo–American in character.[7]

The most explosive of these joint humanitarian movements was that for the abolition of slavery. After a long campaign, in 1833 British reformers secured freedom for slaves in British possessions and turned their attention to slavery in the United States. The British government was well aware that open interference in American domestic institutions would be deeply resented, so it merely proposed a joint patrol over the mid-Atlantic to wipe out the slave trade. Unfortunately, this proposal aroused in Americans bitter memories of impressments and violations of neutral rights that had led to the War of 1812. More directly, Southern cotton and sugar planters suspected that their British rivals in the West Indies wanted abolition in the United States only in order to disrupt the American labor supply. This distrust, perhaps not entirely baseless but certainly unfair to most British humanitarians, produced a groundswell of resentment throughout the American South during the 1830s.[8]

Even these suspicions of Britain, however, could not destroy the Anglo–American economic ties. From 1805 to 1835 British imports of cotton multiplied about seven times, to almost 200,000 tons a year. The United States supplied nearly all of this cotton and bought in return textiles, iron goods, and many other British manufactures. By the mid-1830s several dozen British merchants had established themselves in New York as agents for British business and prosperous outposts of British influence. A few American businessmen similarly migrated to Liverpool or London.[9]

Much capital from both countries was invested in the shipping that plied the Atlantic sea lanes, and a number of successful British merchants also expanded into banking and finance. A

7. Frank Thistlethwaite, *The Anglo–American Connection in the Early Nineteenth Century*, Chaps. 2–5, *passim*. Alice Felt Tyler, *Freedom's Ferment: Phases of American Social History from the Colonial Period to the Outbreak of the Civil War*, pp. 346, 417–19, 428, 446, *et passim*.

8. A good sample of this sort of thinking is a letter from Francis P. Blair to Andrew Jackson, September 10, 1840, Andrew Jackson, *The Correspondence of Andrew Jackson*, ed. John Spencer Bassett, VI, 75–76. On the slave trade question, see Hugh G. Soulsby, *The Right of Search and the Slave Trade in Anglo-American Relations, 1814–1862*.

9. Thistlethwaite, *Anglo–American Connection*, Chap. 1, *passim*, and especially pp. 18–19.

powerful influence in Anglo–American finance influence was the British house of Baring Brothers and Company, which came to specialize in American investments and accounts. By 1840 two of the most important figures behind the Anglo–American economic scene were Thomas Wren Ward, the firm's principal American agent, and Joshua Bates, originally of Weymouth, Massachusetts, who moved to London and became one of Baring Brothers' three managing directors.[10]

Until the late 1830s the most serious problem which the new economic developments seemed to pose in Anglo–American relations was that of the tariff. As early as 1820, a Parliamentary committee had reported that British industry and capital needed only equal treatment in international trade in order to prosper.[11] Cotton planters of the American South, who sold their crops through middlemen to British textile mills and sought to buy manufactured goods as cheaply as possible, were equally interested in keeping the American tariff low. During the 1820s this tariff crept upward, but the nullification crisis of 1832 resulted in a compromise act that scaled down duties generally over the next decade and permitted considerable import of British manufactures.[12]

For its part, however, Britain maintained an oppressive duty on tobacco and some other American raw materials. The most notorious of these agricultural tariffs, the "corn laws," imposed a sliding scale of duties on wheat and other small grains, which the British lumped under the general term "corn." Thus, when crops were good and prices fell, the American wheat and flour exporters faced a daunting obstacle in the rising British tariff. The rate could change by as much as one fourth in a matter of weeks, often while shipments were on the high seas. Some American farmers evaded the corn laws by sending their wheat to Canada for milling, since Empire foodstuffs enjoyed a lower duty, but many were too far from the border to use this device profitably.[13]

By the mid-thirties many British manufacturers and mer-

10. Ibid., pp. 19–20. Ralph Willard Hidy, *The House of Baring in American Trade and Finance, English Merchant Bankers at Work, 1763–1861*, pp. 82–84, 98, *et passim*. In 1842, out of 22 recently elected directors of the Bank of England, 6 were connected with Anglo–American trade and considered generally friendly to the United States. Samuel Allenson to Duff Green, May 31, 1842, Duff Green Papers, box 2, LC.

11. Robert Livingston Schuyler, *The Fall of the Old Colonial System, a Study in British Free Trade, 1770–1870*, pp. 102–3. J. H. Clapham, *An Economic History of Modern Britain*, I, 495 ff.

12. Ibid., p. 482. Edward Stanwood, *American Tariff Controversies in the Nineteenth Century*, II, 3–4.

13. For a sample of how the British corn laws operated, see *Merchants' Magazine*, 6 (April 1842), 326–32.

chants were reaching the conclusion that the corn laws had out-lived their purpose. High food prices at home set off demands for higher wages. Furthermore, the British knew that industrialists in the American North were complaining more and more loudly against the Southern-inspired decline in tariffs. At any time a po-litical alliance between interests in the Northeast and the North-west might reverse the tariff policy of the United States and force a protective bill through Congress.

*   *   *   *

During 1837 two major upheavals shook the precarious bal-ance of Anglo–American political and economic relations. A finan-cial panic put an end to the booming prosperity of the mid-thirties, raising fears of canceled orders and repudiated securities. At al-most the same time revolutions broke out in Canada, arousing the covert sympathy of many Americans and the overt support of hot-heads along the New York frontier. For the next four or five years a depression and several border controversies drove Britain and the United States toward a crisis.

The policies of both countries had helped to cause the panic of 1837. In America, Jackson's war on the United States Bank and his brusque, ill-considered handling of government deposits and the currency aggravated regional shortages of coin and scuttled the hitherto buoyant confidence. In Britain, after railway speculation and bank loans had been allowed to exceed prudent limits, the Bank of England suddenly raised the rediscount rate. The abrupt change in financial climate threatened particularly a flourishing Anglo–American trade in the securities of American states, which were trying to imitate the success of the Erie Canal with state-financed public works of all descriptions.[14]

After an initial fall of prices and curtailment of British invest-ments in 1837, economic conditions appeared to recover for a time, but bad harvests in 1838 and 1839 tightened the money market again, and in October 1839 the United States Bank (now a pri-vately chartered institution) suspended specie payments, ruining a series of lesser banks and plunging the country into a severe de-pression. Some sections, especially the West, suffered more acutely

14. Reginald Charles McGrane, *The Panic of 1837, Some Financial Problems of the Jacksonian Era*, Chaps. 1–3, pp. 91–94, 99. Bray Hammond, *Banks and Politics in America from the Revolution to the Civil War*, pp. 445–50, 455–57. Clapham, *Economic History of Britain*, I, 513–18.

from the second panic than from the first, and many discouraged farmers were impelled to leave the more settled areas and move to the Far West.[15]

Britons now became alarmed for the safety of American state bonds. In August 1840, to the general dismay of investors, the state of Pennsylvania, whose securities were regarded as the best risk of all, postponed its semiannual interest payment. During succeeding months, as defaults and excuses followed each other across the Atlantic, British investors learned a bitter fact about the American federal system—that neither the national government nor individual taxpayers regarded themselves as responsible in any way for the financial misdeeds of the states. The house of Baring, deeply involved in American securities, worked mightily to quiet complaints in Britain, but the chorus of lamentations rose steadily for the next three or four years.[16]

The loss of returns on American securities affected only the investing minority of the British public. American aid to Canadian revolutions, however, was viewed generally as a direct affront to the British flag and thus aroused the anger of all nationalists as well as the British government. In 1837 uprisings for more local autonomy broke out among the French Canadians of Quebec and the English, Scottish, and American settlers on the Ontario Peninsula. The latter movement attracted much support in the United States, for Americans had long assumed that Ontario was destined for annexation. The majority opposed overt action, but many pressed for recognition of the rebels' independence and for their invitation into the Union as a counterpoise to the newly independent Texas (see Chapter 3).

Across the Niagara River and Lake Ontario from the Canadian rebels impetuous upstate New Yorkers organized mass meetings, public subscriptions, volunteer troops, and secret societies to plan filibuster expeditions. One of these expeditions promptly came to grief, for in December 1837 a Canadian raiding party attacked its supply ship, the *Caroline*, on the American side of the Niagara

15. George Rogers Taylor, *The Transportation Revolution, 1815–1860*, pp. 342–46. McGrane, *Panic of 1837*, Chaps. 4, 6. Hidy, *House of Baring*, Chaps. 8, 9. Hammond, *Banks and Politics*, pp. 467–71.
16. Reginald Charles McGrane, *Foreign Bondholders and American State Debts*, Chaps. 1, 2, pp. 70–71. Hidy, *House of Baring*, Chaps. 8, 9. British conservatives naturally blamed the shortcomings of American finance on "the licentious, disorderly, and unstable character of democratic institutions." London *Times*, April 14, 1841, p. 4. Americans reciprocated with attacks on the Bank of England as a tyrannical monopoly. *Merchants' Magazine*, 3 (September 1840), 236–37.

River and sank it, killing an American in the action. The United States government protested, and when no immediate answer arrived, belligerent patriots demanded war. Alarmed, President Van Buren sent the prudent, dignified General Winfield Scott to restore order along the Great Lakes and urged Congress to strengthen the feeble neutrality laws. Gradually, by a mixture of firmness and promises of reforms, the British government pacified the rebels.[17]

Meanwhile, more trouble was appearing along the border of northern Maine. Here the vague definition of the international boundary in 1783 had left in dispute large areas containing little but pine trees and Indians. During the mid-thirties, as the timberlands of Maine attracted speculators, the state began to survey the disputed area. At the same time the British government decided to establish an all-weather military road from Halifax to Quebec. Canadian and American lumberjacks made contact with each other after their fashion. By 1839 the press was referring ominously to an "Aroostook war," and the United States government sent General Scott to arrange an informal truce.[18]

Late in 1840 another event intensified the Anglo–American crisis. On the New York border, where public belligerence had almost entirely subsided, the New York police arrested a Canadian named Alexander McLeod on a charge of murder for taking part in the *Caroline* raid. The British government demanded his immediate release without trial as a point of honor, arguing that he had acted under orders. Van Buren, about to leave office, could do nothing but temporize and reprove the British for their long silence on the *Caroline* question. The McLeod case was in the hands of the New York courts, where the United States government had no jurisdiction. Once again the American federal system seemed about to deny the British what they deemed to be justice.[19]

Repeatedly between 1837 and 1841 the press and people of both countries discussed the possibility of war, some eagerly, some with alarm and foreboding. At the end of 1839, for example, a British agent investigating public opinion in New England found re-

17. This summary is based on Albert S. Corey, *The Crisis of 1830–1842 in Canadian-American Relations*, Chaps. 1–8. For the American protest of 1838, see Manning, *CR*, III, 48–51, 449–67.

18. Eugene Irving McCormac, "John Forsyth," in Samuel Flagg Bemis, ed., *American Secretaries of State and Their Diplomacy*, IV, 329–36. Thomas LeDuc, "The Maine Frontier and the North-

eastern Boundary Controversy," *American Historical Review*, 53 (October 1947), 30–41. By 1840 the British had about 20,000 troops in Canada. Corey, *Crisis of 1830–1842*, p. 151.

19. Ibid., Chap. 9. Alastair Watt, "The Case of Alexander McLeod," *Canadian Historical Review*, 12 (June 1931), 145–67.

spect for Britain mingled with self-confidence and the conviction that Canada must be annexed: "Even when there is no proximate or remote cause of rupture they deem, in obedience as it were to an instinct, to be forever reckoning their chances in the *next* war with Great Britain." Admitting their initial weakness in war, the Yankees were sure of ultimate victory: "We should be 'whipped' for the first two or three years, we know. . . . We only begin to prepare at the moment when we ought to be ready; but we then make up for lost time—we are never tired of 'holding on,' and our energies are inexhaustible." The agent also found many pacifists, but he added that they had no conception of the British side of the argument and little confidence in their ability to restrain the jingoists.[20]

A year or so later, when the agitation over McLeod had further inflamed the Anglophobes, the New York *Herald* summed up their case for a defensive war that would add Canada to the United States:

> The progress of British aggrandizement in every part of the world, savage and civilized, ought to alarm all independent nations. . . . Her ambition is as active on this continent as in the old world. She has for half a century held possession of a large tract of American territory in Maine, and now refuses to give it up. She is making the same encroachments on the northwest. . . . Under the plea of suppressing the slave trade, she seizes our merchant vessels in the African seas, and sends them for abjudication [*sic*] and confiscation, wherever she pleases. Not content with these encroachments, her minister at Washington, Mr. Fox, most insolently demands the liberation of McLeod, . . . while in Canada across the line, every preparation seems to be making to invade our soil. . . .
>
> In one view, our vessels are seized—our territory held—our waters invaded—our citizens murdered—our property outraged by British agency and British subjects.[21]

In Britain the news of McLeod's arrest and the defiant American reaction threw the country into an uproar. For several weeks in March the British press speculated on the chances of war. Stocks fell; textile mills began to lay in supplies of cotton; and a special squadron of warships was reported to be sailing west. With some exaggeration the London correspondent of the New York *Journal of Commerce* reported

20. Stewart Derbishire to General Sir John Harvey, Portland, Maine, December 13, 1839, GB, FO 5/348, ff. 284–329, *passim*.

21. New York *Herald*, January 19, 1841, quoted in *NNR*, 59 (February 13), 370.

one universal feeling of anger and indignation upon every lip and feature. . . . I have never beheld, or read of, anything at all equal to the manner in which the whole community from the highest to the lowest . . . were so completely convulsed. . . . England has felt herself insulted, outraged, and menaced, and . . . in the language of the *Times*, "without the especial interference of the ALMIGHTY, any human means of averting war" does not seem to be entertained for a moment.[22]

Other issues of the *Times*, however, assured the British that many moderate Americans opposed war, the United States Navy was weak, the nation's frontiers vulnerable, and its Negroes ready to revolt.[23]

*   *   *   *

At this point a different group of policy makers came to power in each country. On March 4, 1841, a new administration took office in the United States, and before the year was out, a general election had changed the cabinet in Britain. Fortunately, both of the new governments, the American Whigs and the British Tories, were more conciliatory in purpose and manner than their predecessors. While the outgoing President, Van Buren, had been friendly to Britain, the general unpopularity of his administration had increased his natural caution and encouraged him to maintain strict neutrality in the border crisis.

Anglophiles expected little of William Henry Harrison, but they were pleased that Daniel Webster was to be the new secretary of state—the "godlike Daniel" of the beetling brow, cavernous eyes, booming voice, and an oratorical style at its best like a "great cannon loaded to the lips." Unfortunately, the great man's fondness for whiskey and fat retainers detracted somewhat from his grandeur. Britain could indeed count on Webster's good will, for he had many friends in that country whom he had visited as recently as 1839, and he had served many years as legal counsel to Baring Brothers. Also, like most Whigs, Webster was not a confirmed expansionist. However, the British minister thought him deplorably timid in his anxiety about domestic political reactions, especially in New England.[24]

22. Quoted in Corey, *Crisis of 1830–1842*, p. 138. The report was dated March 9, 1841. See also summaries of the British press in *NNR*, 60 (April 10), 81–82, 96.

23. London *Times*, March 10, pp. 3–4;

April 1, p. 5; August 18, p. 5.

24. Fox to Palmerston, September 7, 1841, GB, FO 5/362, ff. 253–55. See also Arthur M. Schlesinger, Jr., *The Age of Jackson*, pp. 83–84. Hidy, *House of Baring*, p. 100. After Webster left the State

One month after his inauguration President Harrison died, and within the next six months the new President broke irrevocably with the Whig party and set himself adrift as a leader almost without followers. John Tyler was a Virginia gentleman, courteous and suave, irresolute yet stubborn, and a consistent states'-righter in a party that preached economic nationalism. As far as relations with Britain were concerned, he opposed the Whigs' desire for a higher tariff and shared the concern of Southern slaveholders for cotton sales and their suspicion of British abolitionism. Differences on domestic issues, especially that of the National Bank, caused his break with Clay and the Whig party. Webster chose to remain in the cabinet for a time, hoping to improve Anglo–American relations, and Tyler let him stay, having no good candidate to put in his place.[25]

When Tyler took office, the British Whig party was sliding toward defeat after more than a decade of power with only brief interruptions. The prime minister, Viscount Melbourne, took little direct interest in international affairs, but two younger members of his cabinet made up for his seeming detachment by their dashing, impetuous speeches and attitudes, which were to be the hallmark of Whig foreign policy for the next generation. The first of this impulsive pair, Lord John Russell, had served briefly as colonial secretary in 1839 and 1840. Russell was a small, baldheaded man with a bookish manner and a thin voice, devoted to political liberalism but little interested in economic matters.[26]

Melbourne's foreign secretary was even more a political maverick than Russell. The redoubtable Viscount Palmerston, already an *enfant terrible* in British politics, "half hornet and half butterfly," was an Anglo–Irish peer, who could thus sit in the House of Commons. The Queen eventually came to detest him for his high-handed actions and overbearing manner, but his gaiety, his eye for good horses, his bumptious optimism, and above all his pride in being an Englishman suited the dynamic, confident England of the thirties. He was an efficient foreign secretary, but his subordi-

---

Department, Thomas Wren Ward wrote that because of their close association he could have Webster's services and influence whenever he needed them. Thomas Wren Ward to Joshua Bates, December 1, 1843, Letterpress, Thomas Wren Ward Papers, MHS.

25. Van Deusen, *Jacksonian Era*, pp. 153–54. Robert Seager, II, *and Tyler Too, a Biography of John & Julia Gardiner Tyler, passim.*

26. E. L. Woodward, *The Age of Reform, 1815–1870*, pp. 93–96. For a slightly different characterization of these two men, see Élie Halévy, *The Triumph of Reform, a History of the English People, 1830–1841*, pp. 193–95.

nates in the Foreign Office grumbled under his discipline and feared his withering tongue. In the short range his instructions were always clear and usually practical, but he found it difficult to define long-range goals and to plan how to reach them with consistent, patient, logical policies. As a result, foreign governments mistrusted him for his tactlessness and unpredictability, and when the Whigs fell from power in 1841, they left through Europe a trail of insults, wounded feelings, and developing crises. In opposition, "Lord Pumicestone" continued to play the role of jingoist, attacking the new government savagely in Commons and inspiring denunciations in the more nationalist newspapers.[27]

Since he sympathized with most liberal reform movements, Palmerston probably did not disapprove of United States policies on ideological grounds, but like most members of the British upper classes, he sneered at the Americans' bad manners and resented the expansion of their influence as a threat to Britain's interests in the New World. During the early 1840s he was not yet prepared to extend a blanket guarantee of protection to British trade and investments, and he gave little comfort to British holders of defaulted American state bonds. "British subjects who buy foreign securities," he declared, "do so at their own risk and must abide the consequences."[28] But legal rights to territory and the personal protection of British subjects were different matters, and Palmerston took a strong stand in the New York and Maine border quarrels. When Alexander McLeod was arrested, he instructed the British minister, Henry S. Fox, to leave the country at once on McLeod's execution.[29] For his part, Fox made no effort to mitigate

27. Woodward, *Age of Reform*, pp. 212–15. A. W. Ward and G. P. Gooch, eds., *The Cambridge History of British Foreign Policy, 1783–1919*, II, 163. Philip Guedalla, *Palmerston, 1784–1865*, Chaps. 2–5. Donald Southgate, *"The Most English Minister . . . ," the Policies and Politics of Palmerston*, pp. xvii–xxix *et passim*. For the nickname "Pumicestone," see Herbert C. F. Bell, *Lord Palmerston*, I, 372.

28. McGrane, *Foreign Bondholders*, p. 202. Much later, Palmerston issued a detailed pronouncement explaining Foreign Office policy concerning such debts—that it was entirely up to the British government to determine the support it would give to frustrated creditors and that each question of support would be settled "entirely on British and Domestic considerations."

Draft circular letter, January 17, 1848. Copy sent to Percy W. Doyle in Mexico City, GB, FO 50/218, ff. 1–3. For a fuller discussion of this subject, see Leland H. Jenks, *The Migration of British Capital to 1875*, pp. 119–25.

29. Palmerston announced to Commons that the execution of McLeod would mean war. Privately, he urged Stevenson to press on Van Buren the necessity of releasing him. Southgate, *Most English Minister*, pp. 173–74. Corey, *Crisis of 1830–1842*, p. 137. When Tyler took office and learned that Fox was instructed to leave in the event of McLeod's execution, he declared that he would refuse to issue him passports. Fox to Aberdeen, October 12, 1841, No. 112, GB, FO 5/363, ff. 181–95. By this time, however, everyone expected McLeod to be acquitted.

the crisis through personal approaches to responsible officials.[30]

Sir Robert Peel, who led the Tories into office after a general election, planned a program of economic reforms which would relieve some of the lower-class distress in the factory towns while at the same time increasing foreign trade. Vigorous, hard-working, and businesslike, Peel gathered about him an able cabinet that included six former and future prime ministers and five viceroys of India. Keen of mind and strong-willed, he had a deliberate, restrained manner and a chilly smile—"like a silver plate on a coffin." Most men respected him; few really liked him. While he did not attempt to dominate the work of the Foreign Office, his preoccupation with the corn laws and free trade naturally influenced foreign policy. For many years Peel had been convinced that maintenance of good trade relations with the United States should be a cardinal British policy.[31]

Such a policy met the approval of Peel's foreign secretary, the Earl of Aberdeen. A Scottish laird, studious and fond of his secluded country house, Aberdeen regarded his office more as a duty than as a pleasure. His shyness and courtesy contrasted sharply with Palmerston's bluntness, and his wide travels on the Continent made his views more cosmopolitan than those of his predecessor. He got on well with Peel, who answered his questions and gave him advice in short, trenchant notes. Since the prime minister had little time for long conferences, Aberdeen was accustomed to meet him at Euston Station whenever Peel came up to London from his country estate, and the two transacted much business while rattling through the city streets in a cab.

Unlike his chief, Aberdeen was little interested in economic matters, and his primary concern on coming to office was to restore friendly relations with France and the United States, especially the former. He was better acquainted with the government and public of France than with those of the United States and was apt to risk American criticism in order to maintain the French *entente*. Throughout Peel's administration Aberdeen had to resist the truculence of more nationalistic colleagues, such as the Duke of Wellington, who kept up a cry for rearmament and loudly resented any

30. Herbert Gambrell, *Anson Jones, the Last President of Texas*, p. 151.

31. Sir Robert Peel to Aberdeen, July 28, 1830, Peel Papers, BM, AM, vol. 40312, ff. 116–17. On Peel's character and policies, see Woodward, *Age of Reform*, pp. 103–8; Élie Halévy, *The Age of Peel and Cobden, a History of the English People, 1841–1852*, p. 10; and Blanche Cecil Woodham-Smith, *The Great Hunger, Ireland 1845–9*, pp. 42–43.

slights—real or imagined—from France or the United States.[32] Although Aberdeen was aware of the coolness existing between Fox and the Tyler administration, he left Fox for a time at the Washington legation while by-passing him in important matters.[33] Just as the British government changed, however, Tyler appointed as minister to Britain Edward Everett of Massachusetts, a friend of Webster and a fortunate choice. Having been professor of Greek at Harvard and editor of the *North American Review*, Everett could establish an easy rapport with Aberdeen, who always treated him with courtesy and genuine friendship. Everett impressed even the Yankeephobe Dean Sydney Smith as "an amiable American[,] republican without rudeness, and accomplished without ostentation. . . . I am sure we owe to the Americans a debt of gratitude for sending us such an excellent specimen of their productions."[34]

*   *   *   *

The two new administrations in the United States and Britain needed only a little over a year to solve the most serious problems that divided them. Webster sent the attorney general to New York to look after Alexander McLeod's interests and tried to persuade the Whig governor, William H. Seward, to drop charges or transfer the case to the state supreme court. Fortunately, when McLeod finally appeared before the lower court, he was able to establish an alibi, and the jury acquitted him after deliberating only twenty minutes. With rather ill grace the British press and public admitted that justice had been done.[35]

32. Wilbur Devereux Jones, *Lord Aberdeen and the Americas*, pp. ix–xii, Chap. 1. Arthur Hamilton-Gordon Stanmore, *The Earl of Aberdeen*, passim. George Lockhart Rives, *The United States and Mexico, 1821–1848*, I, 537–38. A. B. Cunningham, "Peel, Aberdeen, and the *Entente Cordiale*," *Bulletin of the Institute of Historical Research*, 30 (November 1957), 190–93.

33. Beckles Willson, *Friendly Relations, a Narrative of Britain's Ministers and Ambassadors to America (1791–1930)*, p. 149.

34. Beckles Willson, *America's Ambassadors to England (1785–1928), a Narrative of Anglo-American Diplomatic Relations*, pp. 229–34.

35. Corey, *Crisis of 1830–1842*, pp. 133–35. Watt, "Case of Alexander McLeod," passim. After the verdict was known in England, the London *Times* conducted a rather academic discussion on how best to go about invading the United States. London *Times*, October 12, 1841, p. 4; October 13, p. 4; October 20, p. 4. In America an interesting by-product of the McLeod affair was a group of Irish-American associations to promote Irish freedom. Fox to Palmerston, March 15, 1841, No. 30, GB, FO 5/360, ff. 51–53. These survived for many years.

But if the Tyler administration had escaped from one Anglo–American crisis, it soon faced another, almost as troublesome. Less than a month after McLeod's acquittal, the American ship *Creole*, bound from Virginia to New Orleans in the legal interstate slave trade, put in at Nassau under the control of its human cargo, who had mutinied, killed a passenger, and forced the crew to sail to the nearest British territory. The authorities at Nassau arrested the murderers but, over the protests of the American consul, set the other Negroes free. As soon as the news of the mutiny and the liberation reached the United States, a violent argument broke out in Congress and the press between the abolitionists and the proslavery men, who demanded the return of the fugitives and an apology. Tyler supported the Southerners' demands, but Webster pointed out that in the absence of an extradition treaty the United States had slight legal basis for action. For the time being the stew was left to simmer.[36]

Near the end of 1841 Tyler decided to send an unofficial agent to Europe to report on the international situation and put out feelers for a loan, since the new administration faced a rising deficit. For this delicate task he made an odd choice—Duff Green, an old Jacksonian warhorse who had supported the Whigs in 1840 but was now principally guided by loyalty to his friend John C. Calhoun and by bitter hatred of abolitionism. Green complicated his stay abroad by combining his public mission with several private business ventures.[37]

The new envoy fancied himself a master manipulator, but he accomplished much less than he thought. British financiers, sullen over the defaults on American state securities, greeted him coldly, and in Paris no less a person than Baron James Rothschild informed him, "You may tell your government that . . . the man who is at the head of the finances of Europe . . . has told you—that they cannot borrow a dollar, not a dollar."[38] Led by his own prejudices

---

36. David Hunter Miller, ed., *Treaties and Other International Acts of the United States of America*, IV, 458–59. Jesse S. Reeves, *American Diplomacy under Tyler and Polk*, pp. 47–48.

37. James C. N. Paul, *Rift in the Democracy*, pp. 41–42. Fletcher M. Green, "Duff Green, Militant Journalist of the Old School," *American Historical Review*, 52 (January 1947), 247–64. Among his other projects Duff Green was trying to obtain a contract with Russia for the supply and repair

of railroad engines and a concession for a Franco–American packet line. See Green Papers, box 2. LC.

38. Duff Green to John C. Calhoun, Paris, January 24, 1842. John C. Calhoun, *Correspondence of John C. Calhoun*, ed. J. Franklin Jameson, Annual Report of the American Historical Association for the Year 1899, II, 842. See also an unidentified letter apparently by Green, London, January 1, Green Papers, box 1, LC.

and by Calhoun's views, Green concluded that Britain had undertaken a huge conspiracy to wipe out American commercial competition. First, the British would repeal the corn laws, thus lowering the cost of home labor; then they would develop a supplementary cotton supply in India and force the United States into a destructive war. He embodied some of these inflammatory ideas in articles that he later published in *Le revue des deux mondes* and the *Great Western Magazine*.[39]

Green's nightmares might bring smiles or irritated frowns in Europe, but in the United States they produced alarm, for the South faced a real if less melodramatic danger—the possible union of the free-trade and the abolitionist movements in Britain and the northern United States. Both movements sprang from the economic and social liberalism of the rising middle classes, which could easily identify the British landed gentry with Southern planters. The hard times following 1837 had driven many reformers toward political action, and by 1840 the Liberty party in the United States, the British and Foreign Anti-Slavery Society, and the Anti-Corn Law League were reaching out to join hands. In July 1840 an American abolitionist newspaper warned: *"If England desires America to be freed from slavery, England must receive the products of our free labour, instead of the products of our slaves. . . . Let, then, every Abolitionist in England . . . strive in every lawful way to open your ports for the corn of our country, which grows upon free soil and is cultivated by free men."* This combined free-trade and abolitionist agitation continued through 1841 and 1842, as the Liberty party sought to extend its roots in the American Northwest.[40]

Seeing the South thus threatened, Green did his best to divert British free-trade sentiment into channels more acceptable to the cotton growers. For a time he thought to combine tariff reform with a loan, but he soon gave up hope of securing financial aid. Through the summer and fall of 1842, however, he continued to

---

39. Letter of Green, Paris, January 18, 1842, enclosed with Green to Edward Everett, January 20; Green to Nicholas Biddle, January 24; Green to Daniel Webster, January 24; Green to John Tyler, [January], Green Papers, box 1. F. Green, "Duff Green, Militant Journalist," pp. 259–60. Frederick Merk challenges Green's accuracy as a reporter of British events. Frederick Merk, *The Monroe Doctrine and American Expansionism, 1843–1849,* pp. 11–15.

Green's *magnum opus,* "England and the United States," is reprinted in *Proceedings of the American Antiquarian Society,* n.s., 40 (October 1930), 218–76. See also a long introduction by St. George L. Sioussat, pp. 175–218.

40. Thomas P. Martin, "The Upper Mississippi Valley in Anglo–American Anti-Slavery and Free Trade Relations, 1837–1842," *Mississippi Valley Historical Review,* 15 (September 1928), 204–20, especially pp. 214–15.

exchange ideas on the tariff with members of the Anti-Corn Law League and a minor government official or two. His most attractive lure was trade with the American South and West and an alliance between these two sections to lower the American tariff. In this effort Green got little support from Webster or Everett, who were both Northern protectionists, but he managed to arrange interviews with Aberdeen and Peel. At first he made little impression on them, but he continued his efforts, and eventually some of Peel's policies came to harmonize with Green's views.[41]

While Green explored the possibility of Anglo–American reconciliation by way of free trade, the two governments were accomplishing much more through conventional diplomacy. In the spring of 1842 Peel and Aberdeen sent a special envoy to take over negotiations from the ineffectual Fox—Alexander Baring, first Baron Ashburton. He had obviously been chosen to conciliate the Americans, especially the Whigs and Northeastern businessmen, for he was the retired head of Baring Brothers and a personal friend of Webster, the firm's onetime legal counsel. Furthermore, Ashburton had an American wife, and he held extensive Anglo–American investments, including lands in Maine. He came to America with broad diplomatic powers and the optimistic hope of adjusting all unresolved problems.[42]

Through the spring and early summer of 1842 Webster and Ashburton negotiated cordially and so informally that there are no detailed records to guide the historian. In England the nationalist Duke of Wellington and his allies in the cabinet prevailed on Aberdeen to send new instructions to Ashburton, limiting permissible boundary concessions. Nevertheless, the Webster–Ashburton Treaty, which was signed on August 9, drew a compromise line across the disputed territory in the northeast, giving the United

41. Green to C. A. Wickliffe, London, May 18, 1842; Green to Abel P. Upshur, May 18. Richard Cobden to Green, Manchester, May 28; Green to John MacGregor, London, August 9, 10/11; Green to Elizabeth Green [wife], August 16, September 1, 17; MacGregor to Green, October 6, 18, Green Papers, box 2. British free traders such as Cobden and Nassau Senior advised Green to soft-pedal the slavery issue and suggested that repeal of the corn laws might give the American states more revenue with which to pay their debts. Thomas P. Martin, "Free Trade and the Oregon Question, 1842–1846," in *Facts and Factors in Economic History: Articles by Former Students of Edwin Francis Gay*, pp. 477, 480. For Everett's opinion of Green's activities, see Everett to Upshur, August 17, 1843, Confidential, US, DS, D, Great Britain, LI.

42. Reeves, *American Diplomacy under Tyler and Polk*, pp. 38–41. Hidy, *House of Baring*, pp. 28–29, 45–48, *et passim*.

States over half of it, which Webster estimated to be worth at least four fifths of its total value.[43]

The treaty also contained long-overdue extradition provisions between the two countries. The list of extraditable crimes did not include mutiny on the high seas, as Tyler and the Southerners had hoped, but in a separate letter Ashburton stretched his instructions by assuring Webster that henceforth the British government would prevent "officious interference with American vessels driven by accident or by violence" into West Indian ports. Since the two men were no more able to agree on a statement of responsibility for the *Caroline* case, Ashburton wrote another letter expressing regret that "some explanation or apology was not immediately made"—a comfortable rationalization, for it placed all blame on Palmerston. While not entirely satisfied with these left-handed assurances, the United States government allowed the incidents of the *Creole* and the *Caroline* to fade from official concern.[44]

Some historians have regarded the Webster–Ashburton Treaty as an American defeat, since Webster surrendered about five thousand square miles of land in Maine to which the United States had an excellent claim, without obtaining clear-cut satisfaction on other major points at issue.[45] This was also the view of expansionist Democrats in his own day. For example, in the Senate

43. Wilbur Devereux Jones, "Lord Ashburton and the Maine Boundary Negotiations," *Mississippi Valley Historical Review*, 40 (1953), 477–90. The text of the principal instructions to Ashburton may be found in Manning, *CR*, III, 688–94n3, and 711–13n1. The story of the negotiations is greatly complicated by the fact that each side discovered a map supposedly drawn by Benjamin Franklin in 1782 that confirmed the claims of the other side. Webster received his map from the historian Jared Sparks, who had found it in the French archives; he used it skillfully to keep the New England commissioners quiet. The English map turned up in the British Museum in 1839 and was impounded by Palmerston. Apparently Ashburton did not know of either map until after the treaty had been signed. Historians now generally accept the British map—and thus the American claim—as genuine. For a detailed discussion of this "battle of the maps" and other technical cartographical problems involved, see Miller, *Treaties and Other International Acts*, IV, 403–13. See also Richard N. Current, "Webster's Propaganda and the Ashburton Treaty," *Mississippi Valley Historical Review*, 34 (1947), 187–200; and Frederick Merk, *Fruits of Propaganda in the Tyler Administration*, pp. 39–92.

44. Corey, *Crisis of 1830–1842*, pp. 169–82. Miller, *Treaties and Other International Acts*, IV, 443–69. The text of Ashburton's letter on the *Caroline* appears in Manning, *CR*, III, 766–71.

45. The most extreme criticism of Webster on this score is Samuel Flagg Bemis, *John Quincy Adams and the Foundations of American Foreign Policy*, pp. 479–81. In this connection it might be worth noting that Ashburton described the disputed territory to Aberdeen as "this miserable region which will not be cultivated to any extent for the next century." Ashburton to Aberdeen, April 25, 1842, No. 3, Manning, *CR*, III, 708.

Thomas Hart Benton proposed to "mark all the new boundary of Maine with black stones, and veil with black the statue of tthe god Terminus, degraded from the mountain which overlooked Quebec, to the humble valley which grows potatoes." Andrew Jackson wrote angrily of "that odious treaty . . . not only disgraceful, but humiliating to our national character and humbling us in dust and ashes." Nevertheless, the Senate approved it at once by a vote of 39 to 9.[46]

In Britain criticism of the treaty was equally bitter and more enduring. Since Parliament was not in session, Palmerston attacked what he called "Ashburton's capitulation" with anonymous articles in the *Morning Chronicle*. After Parliament convened, the Whigs' criticism so stung the Peel government that the Tories went to the unusual length of giving Ashburton a vote of thanks for his services.[47] Palmerston's attack undoubtedly made Aberdeen more cautious later in making concessions to the United States, but perhaps the freely expressed dissatisfaction in both countries was a true measure of the treaty's fairness. At least it removed several areas of friction from Anglo–American relations.[48]

Unfortunately, the two countries could not extend their *rapprochement* into the field of tariff policies. In 1842, against strong Whig opposition, Peel managed to lower many duties on raw materials and set a maximum duty of 20 per cent on all manufactures, but he made only minor changes in the corn laws and maintained tobacco and sugar duties, on the grounds that reduction would encourage slave labor in parts of the New World and cut too deeply

---

46. Benton is quoted in Reeves, *American Diplomacy under Tyler and Polk*, pp. 44–45. See also Thomas Hart Benton, *Thirty Years View; or a History of the Working of the American Government for Thirty Years, from 1820 to 1850*, II, 421–23. Jackson to Blair, August 7, 1842. Jackson, *Correspondence*, VI, 162. However, *Niles' National Register*, always on guard against British wiles, praised two minor articles supporting joint action against the international slave trade. *NNR*, 63 (February 4, 1843), 360–62. Charles M. Wiltse gives primary credit to Calhoun for the Senate's approval. Charles M. Wiltse, *John C. Calhoun, Sectionalist, 1840–1850*, pp. 72–73.

47. Clyde Augustus Duniway, "Daniel Webster," in Bemis, *American Secretaries of State*, V, 45–47. Everett to Webster, August [September?] 19, 1842;

March 28, 31, 1843, Nos. 24, 34, Manning, *CR*, III, 782–83, 797–803. Lord Palmerston to Sir John Russell, September 1842. G. P. Gooch, ed., *The Later Correspondence of Lord John Russell, 1840–1878*, I, 58–59. See also Southgate, *Most English Minister*, pp. 174–75. On the vote of thanks, see an unpublished dispatch of Everett to Webster, May 1, 1843, No. 37, US, DS, D, Britain, L. Although usually anti-American, the *Times* approved the treaty, declaring, "A speedy settlement was *necessary*." London *Times*, September 21, 1842, p. 4.

48. Halévy, *Age of Peel and Cobden*, pp. 11–20. Woodward, *Age of Reform*, p. 107. For American comments on these developments, see *NNR*, 58 (April 4, 1840), 71–72; 60 (May 1, 22, August 7, 1841), 130, 179–80, 353–54.

into government revenues. Meanwhile, the United States was moving in the opposite direction, for the declining government revenues reinforced the protectionist demands of the Whigs, who also blamed the hard times on the low tariff and denounced Britain for her meaningless reforms. Reluctantly, Tyler recommended higher duties for revenue only.

Congress needed weeks of debate and maneuvering to put together a tariff bill, and on August 30—ten days after the Senate approved the Webster–Ashburton Treaty—Tyler signed the bill into law. It represented a return to the moderate protection that had prevailed before the nullification crisis of 1832. An average duty of 30 per cent was levied on gross imports, but the schedules were so much more detailed than ever before that the duties seemed heavier and more numerous. The new law may have hastened the nation's recovery from the depression, but it deeply displeased Britain and the South.[49] Many British liberals, such as Richard Cobden, blamed passage of the law on Parliament's failure to admit American grain, sugar, and tobacco on generous terms. They deplored the narrow-mindedness it represented—a limitation that would continue to threaten the Anglo–American partnership.[50]

On the American side of the Atlantic there was also much dissatisfaction at the prospect of increased commercial rivalry. Slight as they were, the British concessions aroused some spirit of conciliation in the Middle West, and low-tariff Democrats won the fall elections in New York, Pennsylvania, and Ohio. Webster, who supported the higher tariff, instructed Everett to press the Peel government for less restricted trade with the British colonies, telling him to warn the Board of Trade that "we shall be after them by acts of Congress, unless they will come to some reasonable relaxation of their present system of colonial intercourse."[51] But Calhoun and his supporters never became reconciled to the "black tariff." Their opposition to it helped to counterbalance their fears of British abolitionism and gave them a bond of sympathy with the Peel administration that was to prove important within a few years.[52]

---

49. Stanwood, *American Tariff Controversies*, II, 8–37. Wiltse, *Calhoun, Sectionalist*, Chap. 6. For anti-British statements on the tariff question, see *NNR*, 61 (November 6, 20, 1841), 153–54, 183–87; 62 (March 26, August 20, 1842), 53, 389–90.

50. Ibid., 63 (September 3, November 19, 1842), 3, 187.

51. Webster to Everett, November 28, 1842. Fletcher Webster, ed., *The Private Correspondence of Daniel Webster*, II, 154–55. Martin, "Free Trade and the Oregon Question," pp. 478–79.

52. For contrasting views on the tariff act in the North and South, see *NNR*, 63 (December 3, 1842), 216–18.

* * * *

No account of Anglo–American relations before and after 1840 would be complete without some discussion of France, a country that often formed a kind of diplomatic or economic triangle with Britain and the United States. During the first half of the nineteenth century France was evolving in much the same direction as the other two, but her economy lagged far behind England's, and her political and social framework was in some ways more conservative than that of either Britain or America. In 1830 the "citizen king," Louis Philippe, attained the throne through revolution. For almost two decades he used every resource of shrewdness and calculation to establish a permanent dynasty, basing his power on the middle class. Despite the suspicions of nationalists in both countries, France and England drew cautiously together in the mid-thirties and established a fragile understanding—ostensibly to regulate affairs in Spain and Portugal but, the French hoped, possibly to cooperate in other areas as well.

This *entente peu cordiale,* as it might well be called, was threatened by almost every diplomatic change that involved either country. In 1840 a serious quarrel between them over Near Eastern affairs brought demands for war in the French press and legislature. Stocks fell on the Bourse, and the French government readied its navy in the Mediterranean and its army in the North. Fortunately, in both countries there was a strong desire for peace. In England the *Times* and most of the Tory opposition denounced Palmerston for his brusqueness; in France popular unrest and an attempt to assassinate the King warned the government that war abroad might touch off revolution at home. France withdrew its demands in the Near East, and an Anglophile, François Guizot, became premier just as the Whigs and Palmerston were resigning their posts in London. Nevertheless, the war crisis and its humiliating resolution left a residue of bitter memories among French nationalists.[53]

Franco–American relations were never subjected to such severe strain during the 1830s. After 1815 a certain coolness prevailed between the restored Bourbons and American republicans,

53. *Cambridge History of British Foreign Policy,* II, Chap. 3, pp. 177–82. James Edgar Swain, *The Struggle for the Control of the Mediterranean Prior to 1848, a Study in Anglo–French Relations,* Chaps. 8, 9. Southgate, *Most English Minister,* Chap. 7. Beckles Willson, *The Paris Embassy, a Narrative of Franco-British Diplomatic Relations, 1814–1920,* pp. 160–71. John Hall, *England and the Orleans Monarchy,* Chap. 8.

but much of this chill disappeared in 1830, when Americans exuberantly welcomed the monarchy of Louis Philippe. In trade, each country furnished about one sixth or one seventh of the other's imports, but the United States held a somewhat stronger position, since it enjoyed a wider market for its raw materials than France for its luxury items such as silks and wines. This rather limited commerce produced the usual grievances, which were, in this situation, minor. Americans resented French tariffs, differential charges on American shipping, and the fact that their corporations had no legal status in France; French manufacturers were alarmed at the growth of the textile industry in New England and the Whigs' demands for higher tariffs.[54]

The only Franco–American quarrel of the 1830s was provoked by the refusal of the French Chamber of Deputies to ratify and carry out a treaty made in 1831 that provided for the payment of claims dating back to the Napoleonic era. Instead of being patient and trusting to the good faith of Louis Philippe's government, Jackson reacted with literal-minded myopia. At the end of 1834 he sent a hot-tempered message to Congress; both countries recalled their ministers, and the departing French diplomat predicted a thirty-year war that would lead to a stalemate. Fortunately, although belatedly, reason prevailed. Jackson was persuaded to apologize indirectly for his blunt words, and the Chamber voted the money for the claims.[55] But younger American nationalists learned—and were to remember—that direct demands sometimes bring results.

The Franco–British crisis of 1840 over the Near Eastern question aroused a desire in some French circles for closer relations with the United States, and when the McLeod affair stimulated talk of Anglo–American hostilities during the following year, a Paris correspondent of the *Courier des États Unis* declared, "Should a war break out between the American eagle, and the British lion, the first will not long have flapped its powerful wings,

54. Henry Blumenthal, *A Reappraisal of Franco–American Relations, 1830–1871*, pp. viii, 7, 87–89, 91–93, 100–103, 108, *et passim*. In the mid-thirties French trade with the United States accounted for about 15% of the total French trade and American trade with France for about 17% or 18% of the total United States trade.

55. Ibid., pp. 73–77. Richard Aubrey McLemore, *Franco-American Diplomatic Relations, 1816–1836*, Chaps. 5–7. In addition to Jackson's personality, French fear of a Russo–American alliance and British mediation were undoubtedly important factors in the outcome. See also Charles K. Webster, "British Mediation between France and the United States in 1834–1836," *English Historical Review*, 42 (1927), 58–78.

before the French flag will be seen floating by its side."[56] However, the "black tariff" of 1842 prevented a further *rapprochement*, for French industrialists regarded the new duties as "an act of violent commercial aggression against the commerce of France."[57]

When Aberdeen entered the British Foreign Office late in 1841, he placed a full reconciliation with France high on his agenda—such a reconciliation as would forestall any future Franco–American alliance against Britain without alarming the rest of Europe. He and Guizot were personal friends and much alike in temperament and outlook: reserved and formal, scholarly and a bit withdrawn, and confident that the world was large enough to satisfy the ambitions of both countries. Each had his *bête noire* in opposition—Palmerston in England, the ex-premier Adolphe Thiers in France—and each had to restrain patriotic subordinates who could not understand why the old defiant tones must be muted. Peel and Wellington did not share Aberdeen's esteem for Guizot, and indeed, even Aberdeen's patience was much tried by French evasions and wavering.[58]

Nevertheless, during the next five years Aberdeen and Guizot picked their way cautiously around one diplomatic pitfall after another in Tahiti, Greece, Spain, and elsewhere. Partly in order to develop the habit of cooperation and partly to commit the French government to a policy of resisting American expansion in the New World, Aberdeen took the lead in laying out areas of joint activity: intervention in a dispute between Argentina, Brazil, and Uruguay; encouragement of Texan independence; and even, very briefly, opposition to American expansion into California.[59] When Aberdeen finally retired from office in 1846, it was a measure of his abilities that he had managed to uphold the Anglo–French *entente* while avoiding an open break with the United States.

56. Quoted in *NNR*, 60 (April 17, 1841), 104. The London *Times* professed to see a direct correlation between such journalistic predictions of Franco–British hostilities and American intransigence in the McLeod case during the first part of 1841. London *Times*, February 19, 1841, p. 4.

57. Quoted in Blumenthal, *Franco–American Relations*, p. 88.

58. Stanmore, *Aberdeen*, Chap. 7. Jones, *Aberdeen and the Americas*, Chap. 1, especially p. 7. Peel was accustomed to send Aberdeen angry letters about France, hoping to stiffen his backbone, but as a rule he was careful to moderate his public statements. Cun-ningham, "Peel, Aberdeen, and the *Entente Cordiale*," pp. 196–97.

59. The Plata intervention, which falls outside the area of this study, is discussed fully in Jones, *Aberdeen and the Americas*, Chap. 4; and in John F. Cady, *Foreign Intervention in the Rio de la Plata, 1838–1850*. A comprehensive account of Anglo–French relations in the 1840s, emphasizing European and Near Eastern affairs, is Gordon Wozencroft, "The Relations between England and France during the Aberdeen–Guizot Ministries, (1841–6)," Ph. D. diss., University of London, 1932. Wozencroft regards Aberdeen as the dupe of Guizot in much of the diplomacy.

2

The Sick Man of North America: Mexico

The "special relationship" between nineteenth-century Britain and the United States was due to jostling between two similar yet changing peoples. The same could not be said for the relationship between the United States and Mexico. Mexico of the 1820s and 1830s was essentially a static society in which complacent conservatives and frustrated liberals argued over political theory and fought over the right to govern. Meanwhile, foreigners dominated the stagnant economy, and a great mass of ill-assimilated Indians performed the manual labor and filled the ranks of the army, with little hope of ever bettering their lot. Mexico was a sick country, with the national equivalents of dropsy, intermittent fever, and creeping paralysis. In the cruel world of nineteenth-century *Machtpolitik* her illness inspired in her ambitious neighbor more cupidity than sympathy.

When Mexico achieved independence in 1821, she superficially resembled the United States. The two countries occupied about the same area, and Mexico's population was six or seven million, compared to perhaps eleven million in the United States.[1] Both countries were rumored to contain vast natural resources; each had inherited a great European culture and had then seized freedom from the mother country. The newly independent Mexicans, filled with tropical fantasies, considered their country a potential member of the Great Powers, and during the 1820s many European and American visitors agreed that the nation had a brilliant future.[2]

Unfortunately, Mexico and the United States were more different than similar, and the differences were nearly always to the disadvantage of Mexico. In the first place, the population of the United States was increasing by 30 or 35 per cent every decade,

1. George Lockhart Rives, *The United States and Mexico, 1821–1848*, I, 51–53. Francisco López Cámara, *La estructura económica y social de México en la época de la Reforma*, pp. 14–15.

2. José C. Valadés, *Santa Anna y la guerra de Texas*, pp. 72–73. Examples of early optimistic writings by foreigners are Joel Poinsett, *Notes on Mexico, Made in the Autumn of 1822*; Henry George Ward, *Mexico*; and C. Harvey Gardiner, ed., *Mexico, 1825–1828, the Journal and Correspondence of Edward Thornton Tayloe.*

that of Mexico very little. Then, too, the population of European descent, better trained and more progressive, amounted to over four fifths of the total in the United States but less than one fifth in Mexico.[3] Mexicans had cut out the canker of Negro slavery, to be sure, but a great many nominally free Indians lived in virtual serfdom. At the other end of the social scale the aristocracy monopolized the best lands and official positions, and the Church's hierarchy inveighed against change.

Many of Mexico's troubles were due to unfortunate inheritances from Spain or to an unfriendly environment. From its beginning the colonial political and social system had emphasized differences of race and class and had failed to train native Mexicans adequately in government. Eager for mineral wealth, the Spaniards had left Mexican agriculture backward and inefficient. Nature, for its part, had not bestowed on Mexico rich farmlands comparable to the Ohio and Mississippi valleys.

Perhaps the most formidable environmental obstacle to Mexico's well-being was difficulty of communication. Jagged mountain ranges and fever-ridden coastal plains separated the populous central plateau from the Gulf of Mexico and the Pacific. Through much of Mexican "national" history, the government, isolated on the central plateau, held only precarious control over the remote coasts and borders. Even relatively close to the national capital, populous states like Jalisco, Michoacán, and Puebla lived to themselves as much as they could. The Spaniards had built good roads between Mexico City and Veracruz, the principal port, but these began to deteriorate soon after independence. As the stagecoach jolted over potholes and floundered through quagmires, its passengers shaken like dice in a cup, bandits might appear at any moment, especially in the forests and passes between Puebla and Mexico City. Sometimes for months on end not one diligence got through unscathed.[4]

The uncertainties and perils of transportation inhibited trade and weakened the whole Mexican economy. Almost isolated from

3. Rives, *US and Mexico*, I, Chap. 3 and especially p. 54. As late as 1843 a French consul, traveling across Mexico, was impressed by the emptiness of the country. A. Guérolt to Ministère des affaires étrangères, May 24, 1843, No. 2, politique, France, MAE, CP, Mexique, XXIV, ff. 81–96. See also Vicente Fuentes Díaz, *La intervención norteamericana en México (1847)*, pp. 31–34.

4. *A Sketch of the Customs and So-ciety of Mexico, in a Series of Familiar Letters; and a Journal of Travels in the Interior during the Years 1824, 1825, 1826*, pp. 227 ff. Charles J. Latrobe, *The Rambler in Mexico*, pp. 237, 282, 284, 294–97, *et passim*. Frances Calderón de la Barca, *Life in Mexico during a Residence of Two Years in That Country*, pp. 28, 52, 176–77, 210, 339–43, *et passim*. Waddy Thompson, *Recollections of Mexico*, pp. 20–25.

the Atlantic world by mountains, yellow fever, and Gulf storms, Mexico had always funneled most of her imports through Veracruz to the capital and then distributed them in the interior at great expense and delay. High freight rates meant that only the most valuable exports, such as silver, were worth sending abroad. Poor roads, lack of adequate rainfall in many areas, and a scarcity of skilled farmers perpetuated the weakness of colonial agriculture, so the economy rested insecurely on silver mining.[5]

Such a backward economy in turn starved the government of income, so its budgets were never balanced and salaries usually in arrears. The poorly managed Treasury quickly fell into the slough of chronic debt. During the early days of the Republic a class of professional money-lenders (*agiotistas*) sprang up in Mexico City and Veracruz—merchant-bankers, some Mexican and some foreign, including many of the higher clergy, who advanced funds to the government for operating expenses on usurious terms. Many of these lenders also carried on trade, bought and sold government contracts, and pulled wires among contending Mexican political factions. As they were well aware, revolutions required arms, and these in turn required more loans.[6]

*　　*　　*　　*

Mexico's unhappy political history during her first two decades of independence is soon told. She had leaders enough, but unfortunately the revolutionary heroes and the bemedaled generals could give her neither stability nor reform. The few men of vision, whether conservative or liberal, were usually civilians with little popular appeal who had to work through the generals or behind their backs. As the years passed, the habit of revolution became more ingrained.

The first ruler of independent Mexico was Agustín de Iturbide, a creole (native white) army officer who had forced Spain's last viceroy to negotiate peace. Iturbide might have set some of the

5. López Cámara, *La estructura económica y social de México*, pp. 20–25. Fuentes Díaz, *Intervención norteamericana*, Chap. 6.

6. Ibid., Chap. 5. Agustín Cue Cánovas, *Historia social y económica de México (1521–1854)*, pp. 246–48, 288–90. Juan José del Corral, *Exposición acerca de los perjuicios que ha causado al erario de la República y a su administración, el agiotaje sobre sus fondos, y reflexiones sobre los medios de remediar*

aquellos males, *passim*. The clergy enjoyed an advantage over other *agiotistas*, for their great wealth enabled them to lend at lower rates of interest than secular loan sharks. López Cámara, *La estructura económica y social de México*, pp. 164–68. A classic survey is [Mariano Otero], "Consideraciones sobre la situación política y social de la República Mexicana en el año 1847," in *Obras*, ed. Jesús Reyes Heroles, I, 99–137.

same firm, peaceable precedents as George Washington in 1789. Instead, he preferred Napoleonic pomp, had himself crowned Emperor Agustín I, and squandered both the money in the Treasury and the patience of his followers. In 1823, after a series of barracks revolts, he was overthrown and a republic proclaimed. The new government declared him an outlaw, and a few months later, when he attempted to return from exile, he was captured and shot—a violent precedent for a nation that needed peace and stability.[7]

Meanwhile, a constitutional convention sought to draw up the framework of a republican government that would somehow reconcile the interests of property holders with the popular will. Conservatives looked to the aristocratic precedents of Europe and favored a powerful president and a highly centralized government. Liberals were more inclined to follow the model of the United States, citing as reasons not only the abstract virtues but also the material prosperity of their northern neighbor. To the dismay of conservatives, the resulting Constitution of 1824 established a federal system and gave the states much power over local affairs. During the confused factional struggles of the next three or four decades most conservatives continued to be centralists, while the terms *liberal* and *federalist* referred to loosely the same groups of people. Even while American plans for aggression grew more obvious, the liberals' admiration of the United States persisted, thus producing an ambivalence not unlike the "special relationship" between the United States and Britain. When the nations finally went to war, this ambivalence exposed some liberals to charges of disloyalty and splintered the existing factions.[8]

Two out of the first three presidents under the new constitution were revolutionary heroes of limited abilities. The only real guiding force in the government during the late 1820s was a con-

---

7. The standard biography is William Spence Robertson, *Iturbide of Mexico*.

8. This ambivalence, little understood in American–Mexican relations, is well outlined in Charles A. Hale, *Mexican Liberalism in the Age of Mora, 1821–1853*, Chap. 6, especially pp. 193–209. One modern interpretation of the Constitution of 1824 attributes Mexican federalism largely to derivation from the provincial organization of the late Spanish Empire. Nettie Lee Benson, *La diputación provincial y el federalismo mexicano*, pp. 11, 21, 121, et passim. A sample of the usual conservative interpretation is Lucas Alamán, *Historia de México desde los primeros movimientos que prepararon su independencia hasta la época presente*, V, 589–90. See also Wilfrid Hardy Callcott, *Church and State in Mexico, 1822–1857*, pp. 52–54; and Fuentes Díaz, *Intervención norteamericana*, pp. 87–88. There is a little evidence that Mexicans reacted strongly against what they saw of race prejudice in the United States just before the Mexican War. Gene M. Brack, "Mexican Opinion, American Racism, and the War of 1846," *Western Historical Quarterly*, 1 (April 1970), 161–74.

servative congressman and cabinet member, Lucas Alamán—an energetic little man with a bulging forehead, thick black hair, rosy cheeks, and piercing eyes behind gold-framed spectacles. Although he appeared timid and irresolute, he was actually a hard worker with a headful of political, business, and intellectual interests.

Privately, Alamán hoped to see a monarchy restored; publicly, he accepted the Republic and worked to strengthen the central government, the landowners, and the Church. Convinced that economic development was fundamental to Mexico's survival as a political entity, he strove to revive mining with the aid of British capital and to stimulate agriculture, trade, and manufacturing with tariffs and subsidies. It was sometimes hard to distinguish between Alamán's public program and his private business interests, and his view of economic diversification utterly ignored its effect on the common people. Nevertheless, he saw Mexico's problems more clearly than most of his contemporaries and might have ranked among the great policymakers of Latin America if he had enjoyed a decade of peace in which to inaugurate and stabilize his programs.[9]

Instead, Mexico suffered a series of revolutions and an ill-advised attempt to liberalize a regime that needed continuity above all else. At the end of 1832 an oddly matched pair took office—an opportunistic army officer and an idealistic civilian reformer. The new president, General Antonio López de Santa Anna, a man in his late thirties, had risen to power through the postrevolutionary campaigns. For almost a quarter century he was to dominate Mexican politics, both in and out of office. Santa Anna could be ruthless, and he was prone to sudden passions; usually, however, he was courteous in manner. Tall and wiry, with a mobile face and a vibrant voice, he exercised enormous charm. His pale, melancholy countenance, his large eyes, and his high forehead gave the impression that here was a philosopher or a scholar, but his principal nonpolitical interests were cockfights and women.

The gaps in Santa Anna's general information were many and deep. For example, years after the Mexican War, when he examined an accurate map of Mexico—apparently for the first time—he was amazed and bitter at the extent of territory which Mexico had lost to the United States. During that war he sometimes made up for his tactical errors with energy, organizing

9. *L'Illustration*, 2 (December 9, 1843), 226–27. José Vasconcelos, *Breve historia de México*, pp. 315–16. Moisés González Navarro, *El pensamiento político de Lucas Alamán*, Chap. 5, pp. 94–95, *et passim*.

ability, and sheer nerve. Above all, he knew his people better than any other mid-nineteenth-century Mexican leader and played on their hopes, fears, and pride with a virtuoso's skill. In and out of office he attracted a shifting, variegated group of followers (*santanistas*), distinguished more for self-seeking than for principles or consistency.[10]

Santa Anna's vice president was Valentín Gómez Farías, his antithesis in almost every respect: an honest, unpretentious, peace-loving physician, something of a scholar and devoted to the ideal of a liberal nation freed from Church and landed aristocracy.[11] What followed the inauguration of the two men was, in conservative eyes, a parody of the French Revolution, with Gómez Farías as would-be Robespierre. First, Santa Anna retired to his great tropical estate near Veracruz, whether from laziness, caution, or genuine sympathy with what he must have known to be his subordinate's ideals. Gómez Farías and a supporting majority in Congress, knowing their time to be short, rushed through a series of reform laws aimed primarily at Church powers. Compulsory tithes were abolished, education secularized, and Indian missions liquidated. In addition the army was reduced, and officers lost their special legal privileges, such as the right to be tried for all offenses in separate military courts.

Predictably, the measures aroused strong protest from churchmen, army officers, and all other conservatives. Their curses reinforced by a terrible cholera epidemic, they incited a general uprising against "French atheism." In April 1834 Santa Anna, who was now convinced that reform was not the key to power, journeyed in triumph from his estate to Mexico City, proclaimed a dictatorship, and dissolved Congress. Gómez Farías fled, to plot for reform from exile in New Orleans. When the federalist state government of Zacatecas ventured a sympathetic revolt, Santa Anna marched north at once, scattered the state troops, and turned Zacatecas City over to his soldiers for looting. Thereafter, liberal federalism was usually restricted to local flare-ups. In December 1836 the conservatives imposed a new constitution (the "Siete Leyes"), which reduced the states to administrative units or departments and established property qualifications for voting.[12]

10. Wilfrid Hardy Callcott, *Santa Anna, the Story of an Enigma Who Once Was Mexico*, pp. 81, 139, 151, 181–82, 185, 193–94. *L'Illustration*, 1 (July 20, 1843), 337–38. Valadés, *Santa Anna y la guerra de Texas*, p. 122.

11. Hubert H. Bancroft, *History of Mexico*, V, 129–30. C. Alan Hutchinson, "Valentín Gómez Farías: a Biography," Ph. D. diss., University of Texas, 1948.
12. Callcott, *Church and State*, pp. 86–108.

Santa Anna was not on hand to inaugurate this constitution, for earlier in the year the Texans, alarmed at these centralist tendencies, had launched their own revolution (see Chapter 3). At the Battle of San Jacinto, Santa Anna managed to lose his command, his liberty, and—temporarily—his reputation. When he was finally allowed to return to Mexico, he retired to his hacienda for a decent period, leaving the presidency to General Anastasio Bustamante—kind-hearted and reasonably honest, but vacillating and given to relying on bad advisers.[13]

For the next two years Bustamante's attention was monopolized by the French, who tried to collect debts and claims against Mexico by blockading two Gulf ports and seizing the fort of San Juan de Ulúa, off Veracruz. In the course of the fighting Santa Anna, who had dashed to the scene, regained much of his reputation for heroism by losing a leg. While he was recovering from his injury, a rash of revolutions broke out all over the country to plague the uneasy Bustamante administration. Their climax was an uprising in Mexico City during July 1840. Here Gómez Farías, who had returned from New Orleans, and the principal surviving federalist leaders spent twelve days in street fighting and artillery duels with the government troops before fleeing once more into exile.[14]

To the right-wing conservatives and monarchists the uprising of 1840 was the last straw, the final proof that Mexico could not govern herself as a republic with elected officials. In October one of their number, José María Gutiérrez de Estrada, a former cabinet minister, published a provocative pamphlet in which he decried the degraded condition of the country and called for a European prince to "renovate the social machine." Many Mexicans agreed with his diagnosis of the country's ills, but he had underestimated the strength of republicanism in prescribing so drastic a remedy. A large part of the press rejected all thought of a monarchy; the latent hatred of the Spaniards rushed to the surface; Bustamante came forward in opposition; and Gutiérrez escaped to Europe, to continue his intrigues there. But if his premature effort did nothing else, it revived the idea of a Mexican monarchy in Spanish minds.[15]

13. Bancroft, *Mexico*, V, 235–36.

14. Callcott, *Church and State*, pp. 123–27. Calderón de la Barca, *Life in Mexico*, pp. 226–47.

15. Jaime Delgado, "España y el monarquismo mexicano en 1840," *Revista de Indias*, 13 (1953), 57–80. Gutiérrez de Estrada himself was a native Mexican from Yucatán, but the idea of monarchy was always closely associated with the Spanish residents in Mexico.

By mid-1841 Bustamante had come to the end of his resources, and Santa Anna had recovered his health sufficiently to make another bid for power. After a brief campaign he entered Mexico City on October 7 to the ringing of bells and salvos of artillery. Soon he was surrounded by his usual crowd of *santanistas*. He first appointed a middle-of-the-road cabinet, including moderate liberals and a few conservatives. Then he set out to revise the law codes, created a mercantile court, reestablished the old mining tribunals, granted a few concessions, and in other ways encouraged business. At the same time he strengthened the army and juggled the tax system so as to give an impression of economy. Pressed for money, he called on the Archbishop of Mexico to mortgage Church property for one million pesos and settled for a fifth of that amount plus a rich Jesuit estate. Meanwhile, he diverted the populace with fiestas and spectacles. The most absurd and cynical of these occurred on September 27, 1842, when, with magnificent ceremony, he staged the Christian burial of the severed leg he had lost at Veracruz.[16]

Santa Anna's brilliant improvisations, his knowledge of the Mexican people, and his shrewd timing were to keep him in office for over three years, but the most serious Mexican problems lay beyond his power to solve. Texas remained independent, and her successful example stimulated secessionism in the northeast and in Yucatán, where Santa Anna was forced into a long and expensive war. The Treasury remained nearly empty; most of the customs revenues were mortgaged to creditors; and the foreign debts mounted with each year. There were limits to what the most unscrupulous ruler could squeeze out of landowners or Church without driving them to rebellion. Last but not least, diplomatic relations with France, Britain, and especially the United States were moving irresistibly toward a crisis which the exhausted, impoverished Mexico of the 1840s was ill prepared to meet.

*   *   *   *

During the Mexican war for independence foreign observers gave the rebels little effective aid, but when Iturbide set himself up as ruler of the new nation, Britain and the United States paid closer attention to his activities. The British concern was primarily

---

16. Callcott, *Santa Anna*, pp. 174–78. Bancroft, *Mexico*, V, 236–41, 245–46. Manuel Rivera Cambas, *Los gobernantes de México*, II, 243–44. Niceto de Zamacois, *Historia de Méjico desde sus tiempos mas remotas hasta nuestras días*, XII, 280–83.

economic and focused on Mexican markets, mines, and raw materials. A second basis of British interest, which grew steadily with the years, was the desire to make Mexico a barrier to the southward expansion of the United States. In the 1820s George Canning, foreign secretary and later prime minister, was especially anxious to prevent the growth of hemispheric unity, "the drawing of the line of demarcation which I most dread—America *versus* Europe." But, he added hopefully, "Mexico and they are too neighbourly to be friends."[17]

Since the United States had only a partly matured economy and the great West to develop, Mexican trade and mining were less immediate attractions to Americans than to Britons. The principal announced motive of the United States for friendship with Mexico was a desire to spread the blessings of democracy and to exclude European political influence from Mexico in accordance with the Monroe Doctrine of 1823. As will become clear in the next chapter, however, behind these innocent-seeming expressions of friendship lay inchoate territorial ambitions that were to give further substance to Britain's fears.

During the first year of Mexican independence the United States recognized the new nation, but by failing to appoint a resident minister at once missed an opportunity to gain a head start in friendly relations with Mexico. In December 1824 Britain finally recognized Mexican independence, and during the following May ministers from both Britain and the United States presented their credentials in Mexico City. The American, Joel Poinsett, was cosmopolitan and fluent in Spanish, but also "a flaming evangel of republicanism" with a penchant for impetuous intrigue. The British minister, Henry George Ward, was also aggressive and apt to exceed his instructions. Ward managed to ingratiate himself with Lucas Alamán and most of the conservatives in the government. To offset this advantage Poinsett organized the liberals of the country into a cohesive political force, using as his agency the York rite lodges of Mexican Freemasonry. Before long the two ministers were waging spirited guerrilla warfare against each other, employing paid propaganda, banquets, and personal influence with more flourishes and less tact than diplomats are supposed to display.[18]

17. George Canning to William A' Court, December 31, 1823. Augustus Granville Stapleton, *George Canning and His Times*, pp. 394–95. *Quarterly Review*, 30: 156. British interests and Anglo–American rivalry in Mexico were revealingly debated by Parliament in May 1830. *Hansard Parliamentary Debates*, 3d series, XXIV, cols. 875–907.

18. J. Fred Rippy, *Rivalry of the United States and Great Britain over Latin America (1808–1830)*, Chap. 7, especially pp. 253–61. Clay's original instructions are printed in Manning,

The immediate goal of both men was to negotiate a satisfactory commercial treaty with the Mexican government. After much preliminary work by Ward, Britain and Mexico signed an acceptable treaty in London at the end of 1826. Ward took great pleasure in revealing its terms to Poinsett, for Britain had obtained complete reciprocity of trade and other privileges which Mexico had denied to the United States. The British minister strove to sabotage Poinsett's negotiations, but on two occasions the American signed limited commercial treaties. Despite Poinsett's carefully cultivated friendship with *Yorkino* liberals, however, the Mexican Congress rejected both agreements.[19]

Eventually, Poinsett's intrigues made him generally unpopular in Mexico, and with his consent Andrew Jackson recalled him late in 1829. A year and a half later his successor finally negotiated an adequate commercial treaty for the United States. As a later British minister, Richard Pakenham, remarked, Poinsett's meddling in Mexican politics not only frustrated his own plans but imperiled those of all foreigners.[20] In later years, angered by their humiliating losses to the United States, Mexican nationalists made Poinsett the scapegoat for all their woes and a symbol of ruthless imperialism. As some recent Mexican historians have recognized, this was scarcely fair to him, but in partisan intrigue the only real protection is anonymity, and Poinsett had never made any effort to cover his tracks.[21]

LAI, I, 229–33. Canning's original instructions to Ward appear in Charles K. Webster, ed., *Britain and the Independence of Latin America, 1812–1830*, I, 459–62. For a perceptive comparison of British and American policies in Mexico during the early 1820s, see Carlos Bosch García, *Problemas diplomáticas del México independiente*, pp. 274–75.

19. Rippy, *Rivalry of the US and Britain*, pp. 261–65, 275–76, 277–79, 282–85, *et passim*. James Morton Callahan, *American Foreign Policy in Mexican Relations*, pp. 47–49. Ward to Canning, September 9, 1826, No. 103, GB, FO 50/23, ff. 78–83. Webster, *Britain and the Independence of Latin America*, I, 485–93.

20. Callahan, *Mexican Relations*, pp. 55–59. Richard Pakenham to Earl of Dudley, June 28, 1828, No. 74, GB, FO 50/44, ff. 1–6. Ward was recalled in 1827 for extravagance. Apparently Canning did not disapprove his other actions. After Poinsett's departure, Alamán sounded out Pakenham on a European protectorate, but Pakenham discouraged the idea. Rippy, *Rivalry of the US and Britain*, pp. 301–2.

21. For extreme anti-Poinsett interpretations, see Vasconcelos, *Breve historia*, pp. 298–99, 304–11; and José Fuentes Mares, *Poinsett, historia de una gran intriga*, *passim*. The Spanish historian Jaime Delgado accepts most of this view, declaring that Poinsett was trying to destroy Mexico's unity and weaken it for American absorption. Jaime Delgado, *España y México en el siglo XIX*, I, Chap. 7, especially p. 305. A moderate Mexican interpretation is Luis G. Zorrilla, *Historia de las relaciones entre México y los Estados Unidos de América, 1800–1958*, I, Chap. 3, especially pp. 71–73. Zorrilla suggests

Unlike Britain and the United States, France faced an uncomfortable dilemma in her early relations with Mexico. French agents in the New World reported brilliant opportunities for French capital in Mexican trade and mining, but the Bourbon king refused to recognize the independence of an empire claimed by his Spanish relative.[22] Only on strong pressure from merchants in the seaports did the French government finally establish a commercial agent in Mexico City and draw up a set of "provisional declarations" (dated May 9, 1827), to regulate trade. These declarations embodied broader concessions by the Mexicans than either the British or the American commercial treaties—for example, they granted reciprocal free trade and expressly exempted French residents from forced loans—but the Mexican Congress never approved the agreements.[23] After the July Revolution of 1830 the government of Louis Philippe established formal relations without insisting on the ratification of the declarations, and throughout the 1830s France obtained no commercial treaty.[24]

The last of the Atlantic powers to recognize Mexico's independence was the mother country, Spain. The delay was due to natural chagrin and to several fundamental misconceptions about the New World. Spanish conservatives and reactionaries, led by the stubborn Ferdinand VII, refused to grant the slightest concession to their former colonies; in the case of Mexico the covert monarchism of Alamán and other centralists encouraged them to believe that if they remained adamant, the errant colony might return home. Spanish liberals focused their attention on the struggle for rights and privileges in Spain, assuming that if these were won, they would satisfy liberals in Mexico as well. Neither group appreciated the growing national pride of Mexicans or the threat which

that Mexican representatives in Washington should have encouraged American initiatives for boundary and commercial treaties (pp. 54–55). See also Poinsett's account of his mission in a dispatch of March 10, 1829, to Martin Van Buren, Manning, *LAI*, III, 1673–85.

22. William Spence Robertson, *France and Latin American Independence*, pp. 201–3, 220, 341–42, *et passim*. Delgado, *España y México*, I, Chap. 10.

23. For pressure on the French government by commercial interests and Mexican agents, see Luis Weckmann, ed., *Las relaciones franco-mexicanas*, I, 21, 23, 27, 69, 74, 76, *et passim*. On the

provisional declarations, see I, 115–16, 131–35; and Robertson, *France and Latin American Independence*, pp. 395–97.

24. On the negotiations leading up to French recognition, see Weckmann, *Relaciones franco-mexicanas*, I, 163–68; and Robertson, *France and Latin American Independence*, pp. 542–46. On treaty negotiations in the 1830s, see France, MAE, CP, Mexique, VI, ff. 173–74; VIII, ff. 243–52; IX, ff. 33–37, 41–45, 122–26; and Weckmann, *Relaciones franco-mexicanas*, I, 208–10. Jorge Flores D., *Lorenzo de Zavala y su misión diplomático en Francia, 1834–1835*, pp. 78–79, 96–97.

Anglo–American expansionism in the New World posed to Spanish institutions there.[25]

Accordingly, Ferdinand repudiated the treaty in which his last viceroy had recognized Mexican independence. Until 1825 his troops occupied Ulua, the fortress dominating Veracruz harbor, and his agents encouraged the conservatives' intrigues against the Mexican government. On their part, the Mexicans persecuted Spanish-born residents, especially those with property, and on two occasions passed laws expelling them from the country. Many left, taking with them capital and skills that Mexico could ill afford to lose. In 1829 Spain retaliated with a military expedition from Cuba, which landed at Tampico but was soon stranded and forced to surrender to the Mexicans.[26] The principal effects of this fiasco were to breed implacable hatred of Spain among Mexican liberals and to weaken and embarrass Mexican conservatives. In later years both government and people intermittently harassed the remaining Spanish residents of Mexico, many of them wealthy landowners or merchants, who were scattered throughout the country as involuntary hostages.[27]

Even in the 1820s a few far-sighted Spaniards had urged a *rapprochement* with Mexico, hoping to substitute economic and cultural ties for the lost political unity. Reconciliation developed slowly, but after the failure of the Tampico expedition and the death of Ferdinand VII in 1833, negotiations were undertaken. On December 28, 1836, the two nations signed a peace treaty, and nearly three years later the first Spanish minister, Ángel Calderón de la Barca, arrived in Mexico City to a warm and somewhat sentimental welcome.[28] Thereafter, Spanish ministers customarily allied themselves with Mexican conservatives or reactionaries. Their principal problems were to avoid alienating liberals altogether, in the interests of Spanish residents, and to find some basis of cooperation with British and French diplomats to offset the force of American expansionism.

25. Delgado, *España y México*, I, 4–19. Carlos Bosch García feels that Spanish and Mexican liberals essentially agreed on Mexican independence; I, 30–33. Bosch García, *Problemas diplomáticas*, Chap. 2, p. 278.

26. Vicente Riva Palacio, ed., *México a través de los siglos [etc.]*, IV, 158–60, 194–97. Alamán, *Historia de México*, V, 308–12, 628, 639–41. Francisco de Paula de Arangoiz y Berzábal, *México desde 1808 hasta 1867*, II, 97, 163–64, 191–96. Delgado, *España y México*, I, Chaps. 9, 11, *et passim*.

27. Arangoiz, *México desde 1808*, II, 214, 221–22.

28. Delgado, *España y México*, II, Chaps. 12, 13. Calderón de la Barca, *Life in Mexico*, pp. 24–25, 50–59, *et passim*.

*   *   *   *

Long before the complicated diplomacy of recognition and treaty making had come to an end businessmen and mere adventurers from both Europe and the United States had begun to knit complex economic ties between their countries and Mexico. Between 1820 and 1840 the three fields of economic activity that exerted greatest influence on diplomatic relations were loans to the government, mining, and trade. British capital entirely dominated the first field and most of the second, while Mexican foreign and domestic trade became a tangle of British, French, Spanish, German, American, and domestic interests.

If the independent Mexican government had managed to take over intact the elaborate revenue-raising machinery of the viceroys, the young nation might have established a firm footing without needing to borrow money. Unfortunately, the Spanish system of taxes and fees broke down early in the revolutionary period. After independence, many fruitful sources of income, such as Indian tributes, excise and sales taxes, and the tobacco monopoly, were relinquished or drastically reduced, as symbols of Spain's tyranny. At the same time, Iturbide's extravagance created an immediate financial crisis.

Inevitably, he and the republican government which followed his overthrow had to cast about for loans, but in view of the competition from other Latin American nations and the uncertain status of Mexican politics, British capitalists exacted hard terms. In 1824 Goldschmidt and Company issued a thirty-year Mexican bond issue of £3,200,000 at 5 per cent. The interest rate was favorable enough, but what with discounts, commissions, and other payments, Mexico received less than $6 million cash in return for assuming an indebtedness of $16 million.[29] Within a year the government had run through the entire amount. In 1825 Barclay, Herring, Richardson and Company put out a similar issue, this time at 6 per cent, for which Mexico received about $11 million in cash. For a time the Mexican economy seemed to flourish, but in 1827 the Mexican government suspended payments, and a long cycle of recriminations began.[30] While the fruitless correspon-

29. Edgar Turlington, *Mexico and Her Foreign Creditors*, pp. 4, 6, 16–21, 27–30. Jan Bazant, *Historia de la deuda exterior de México (1823–1946)*, Chap. 1. Riva Palacio, *México a través de los siglos*, IV, 116–21. In this study the symbol $ will be used to designate both dollars and pesos, since during the first half of the nineteenth century they circulated at about the same value.

30. Turlington, *Mexico and Her Foreign Creditors*, pp. 41–45. Bazant, *His-*

dence mounted, so did the foreign debt; by 1840 it was said to have passed $80 million.[31]

The second field in which foreign capital dominated the Mexican economy was mining. During the decade of revolutionary fighting and uneasy truces that began in 1810 the mining industry, already backward and inefficient, disintegrated except in a few fortunately stable areas. Deserted mine shafts filled with water; machinery rusted or broke; labor forces scattered in all directions; and the contending armies confiscated any silver they could lay hands on. After about 1818 conditions stabilized somewhat, and the independent Mexican government immediately liberalized the mining laws so as to attract foreign capital.[32]

Investors responded readily, for the British had long panted for access to what they imagined to be the riches of Golconda. The glowing reports of Baron Alexander von Humboldt on the mines of New Spain were translated into English and reprinted in many editions; pamphleteers and journalists improved on his descriptions and statistics. Only a few prudent souls observed that the average yield of Mexican ores was low, so that mines would have to be carefully selected and worked with great economy and diligence.[33]

By the mid-1820s the newly accessible mines of Latin America and the aggressive, self-confident British capitalist who emerged from the Napoleonic Wars combined to produce a speculative boom in Mexico. Alexander Baring, head of Baring Brothers (later Lord Ashburton), warned the public that the wealth of the Spanish–American mines might prove a delusion, for British mining companies would need much time to adapt their methods to

toria de la deuda exterior, pp. 29–32. By the time the suspensions began, both the British lending houses had gone into bankruptcy and the ever-present Baring Brothers had taken over the Mexican accounts. For the history of the debt question in the next two decades, see Turlington, Mexico and Her Foreign Creditors, Chap. 3; and Bazant, Historia de la deuda exterior, Chap. 3.

31. López Cámara, La estructura económica y social de México, p. 171.

32. Cue Cánovas, Historia social y económica, pp. 241–45, 291–92. William Jackson Hammond, "The History of British Commercial Activity in Mexico, 1820–1830," Ph.D. diss., University of California (Berkeley), 1929, pp. 108–10.

Robert A. Potash, El banco de avío de México, pp. 29–30.

33. John Taylor, Statements Respecting the Profits of Mining in England Considered in Relation to the Prospects of Mining in Mexico [etc.], p. 3 et passim. See also Taylor's Introduction in his Selections from the Works of Baron de [sic] Humboldt, Relating to the Climate, Inhabitants, Productions, and Mines of Mexico, pp. i–xxxiii. A good example of more optimistic publicity is An Inquiry into the Plans, Progress, and Policy of the American Mining Companies. On the effects of Humboldt's works in England, see Cue Cánovas, Historia social y económica, pp. 293–94.

unfamiliar conditions.[34] All in vain. Late in 1825 the boom collapsed, and most of the tissue-paper companies disappeared over night. A generation of British investors learned a temporary lesson, but the silvery image of Spanish America was forever tarnished. Baring Brothers, enjoying an enhanced reputation for financial wisdom, used the occasion to divert investors' attention to United States securities, unable to predict that the next swing of the economic cycle would bring these into disrepute as well.

When the dust of the stock-market crash had cleared, somewhat over a half dozen large British mining companies remained in Mexico, along with uncounted small outfits whose records have been lost. For the next thirty or forty years the large companies formed the nucleus of the Mexican mining industry and one of the most important blocks of British capital in Mexico. A decade after the crash of 1825 the six largest British companies operating in Mexico reported a total paid-in capital of £4,231,631.[35]

If the Mexican mines had been half as rich as their reputation, skillful management controlling that amount of capital should have produced dependable profits. Instead, the bad years outnumbered the good, and the British companies faded away until by 1870 only one or two were operating. A number of factors, some of them difficult to anticipate, accounted for the decline of British mining in Mexico. First, communications were so slow that the directors in London often did not know what was happening in Mexico until it was too late to prevent trouble. Perhaps more important, the companies too readily substituted English methods and machinery for the simpler techniques which the Spanish had found better adapted to the environment. For example, to pump out the flooded shafts, the British hauled in cumbersome steam engines, only to discover that Mexico had no usable coal and, at many sites, little timber in the vicinity of the mine.[36]

34. J. D. Powles, *A Letter to Alexander Baring, Esq., M.P., on the Subject of Some Observations Reported to Have Been Made by Him . . . in Relation to the Foreign Mining Associations*, pp. 63–65 et passim.

35. *Quarterly Mining Review*, 3 (1835), 6. The six principal companies and their paid-in capital, 1835, were: Anglo–Mexican Mining Co., £1,050,000; United Mexican Mining Co., £1,320,-000; Real del Monte Mining Co., £900,-000; Mexican Co., £340,000; Bolaños Mining Co., £516,631; and Tlalpujahua Mining Co., £105,000.

36. Charles O'Gorman to John Bidwell, July 15, 1826, No. 9, GB, FO 50/27, ff. 91–94. A good contemporary summary of the problems confronting the British companies is Edward James, *Remarks on the Mines, Management, Ores, &c &c of the District of Guanaxuato, Belonging to the Anglo–Mexican Mining Association, passim*. Much information can be gathered in small bits from annual reports of the principal companies and from the dispatches sent to the British Foreign Office. For a recent, scholarly account, see William Frederick Cody, "British

Many of the British difficulties arose from their dealings with individual Mexicans and the Mexican government. Since the Mexican Indian changed slowly, the English overseers must needs resign themselves to losses and delays occasioned by everything from outright theft to a plethora of saints' days. Some of the companies spent years in lawsuits with mineowners who were technically their partners under Mexican law. When the ore had been mined and its silver smelted, the companies then had to devise some way to get it out of Mexico. If they chose to have it minted into coins, they must deal with the local mint, usually leased from the government and worked for a profit.

The climax of their troubles was often the *conducta* or convoy of mules loaded with several hundred thousand pesos' worth of bars or bullion, winding its way along mountain trails to a port on the Gulf or the Pacific, where company agents would load the silver onto a British warship or a merchant packet. From the ore vein in the mountain to the numbered bar in the ship's hold, silver mining in Mexico was a risky business. At almost any point the local or national government might intervene with a sudden new tax or fee, or civil war might create a rebel army to loot the smelter or demand "protection money." Even a stable, friendly government was no guarantee against bandit raids on the slow-moving *conducta*.[37]

There can be little doubt that the Mexican government and the mineowners welcomed the influx of British capital, and in many areas the inhabitants regarded the British promoter as a kind of Messiah, able to dispense all kinds of blessings.[38] Such a welcome was sure to give way to envy and suspicion as misunderstandings developed, but the British mining companies, for all their inefficiency and disappointments, revived industry and agriculture in

---

Interest in the Independence of Mexico, 1808–1827," Ph.D. diss., University of London, 1954, pp. 302–33, 344–52, *et passim.*

37. These problems are best studied in the history of the three largest companies, the Anglo–Mexican, the United Mexican, and the Real del Monte companies. Good summary accounts appear in Henry English, *A General Guide to the Companies Formed for Working Foreign Mines, With Their Prospectuses, Amount of Capital, Number of Shares, Names of Directors, &c.,* pp. 4–8, 53–56, 67–70, 96–99; and Hammond, "British Commercial Activity,"

pp. 123–33. An excellent monographic study, based on intricate company records, is Robert W. Randall, *Real del Monte, a British Mining Venture in Mexico.* For contemporary descriptions, see Isidore Löwenstern, *Le Mexique, Souvenirs d'un voyageur,* pp. 220–43, 325–37. See also the sources cited in note 36.

38. Statement by General Arthur G. Wavell, quoted in Ward to Canning, July 12, 1825, GB, FO 50/13, f. 152. A fuller statement of the value of British capital to Mexican mining is found in *Quarterly Review,* 42: 349–50.

many districts, built roads, restored deserted towns, and set an example of enterprise and initiative badly needed in the stagnant Mexican economy.

The role of foreign capital and residents in the development of Mexican commerce was more complex than in mining. The revolutionary disturbances that had begun in 1810 destroyed the Spanish commercial monopoly—already undermined by widespread smuggling—and for a time they interrupted all but local trade. The newly independent government, bewildered by conflicting commercial policies and hampered for years by Spain's occupation of Ulua, failed to restore centralized control over trade.[39] Tampico, Alvarado, Matamoros, and the Pacific coast ports began to compete with Veracruz, and the federalist constitution of 1824 and United States influence on the northern border reinforced the centrifugal economic trend.

As with mining, Britain was the first foreign nation to realize the potential value of Mexican trade. British merchants pressed for recognition and a commercial treaty which would open "that incalculably extensive mart to the operations of our commerce." They even predicted that with Latin America as an economic satellite Britain could make herself entirely independent of Europe and the Holy Alliance.[40] George Canning and William Huskisson, the economic brain of the Tory cabinet, outlined a policy of reciprocal free trade with the new nations comparable to that which they were urging in Anglo–American relations.[41]

Despite the optimistic expectations of British merchants, they avoided the mistakes made by the mining companies in attempting too much, too fast. Instead, they sent out agents to examine the market, experimented with small shipments, and prepared from the beginning for long-range competition with other foreign merchants. At first they chose Veracruz and other ports for their operations, but yellow fever soon drove them inland to establish their

39. López Cámara, *La estructura económica y social de México*, Chap. 4. Cue Cánovas, *Historia social y económica*, pp. 246–48. Hammond, "British Commercial Activity," Chap. 6. John E. Baur, "The Evolution of a Mexican Foreign Trade Policy, 1821–1828," *The Americas*, 19 (January 1963), 225–38.

40. Quotation taken from William Bullock, *Catalogue of the Exhibition, Called Modern Mexico . . . Now Open for Public Inspection at the Egyptian Hall, Piccadilly* (London, 1824), pp. 3–4, as quoted in Hammond, "British Commercial Activity," p. 163; William Adams, *The Actual State of the Mexican Mines*, [etc.], p. 50. However, there were those who felt that the Far East offered a better market to Britain than Latin America.

41. Rough draft of a memorandum from Huskisson to Canning, dated October 28, 1822. William Huskisson Papers, BM, AM, vol. 38,766, ff. 20–23.

headquarters in Mexico City. Here they introduced fine textiles, ironware, machinery, and a great variety of other manufactured goods, both British and Continental in origin, intended chiefly for the middle and upper classes. Poor transportation greatly raised the price of these imports in the interior and forced the merchants to keep large stocks on hand. In addition, the competition of rival ports, the decentralization, and the generally unsettled conditions of the country made it impossible to predict trends accurately or to place orders very far in the future.[42]

Nevertheless, British trade flourished and expanded until in 1830 total British exports to Mexico considerably exceeded a million pounds.[43] The most important British mercantile houses of Mexico City imported goods of all countries, sent out to London regular shipments of Mexican coin, lent money to the government and to mining companies, owned or leased mines, and carried on daily confidential relations with officials of the Mexican government and with the British legation. Although their trade continued to grow during the 1830s, the British never achieved the near-monopoly in merchandising they enjoyed in mining. Some of them explained self-righteously that this was due to their refusal to deal in shoddy goods or to imitate their competitors' shady business tactics. A more likely explanation was that they put most of their capital into wholesale houses in the principal cities, whereas other merchants concentrated on retail trade, content to establish only a few wholesale firms.[44]

This explanation becomes more plausible when one examines the French merchants' trading practices in Mexico. Although the French government did not recognize independent Mexico during the 1820s, French exporters managed to increase their sales of luxury products until in 1831 they sold goods worth 34 million francs in Mexico—more than in all the rest of Latin America combined and more than in all the French colonies in the New World. After the revolution of 1830 the commercial bourgeoisie who had brought Louis Philippe to power pressed for still greater trade as

42. Hammond, "British Commercial Activity," Chap. 6, *passim.* For a good contemporary description of the merchants' problems in Mexico of the 1820s, see *Sketch of the Customs,* pp. 68–72, 183–85. On the quasi monopoly of Veracruz, see López Cámara, *La estructura económica y social de México,* pp. 110–22.
43. See annual tables in R. A. Humphreys, ed., *British Consular Re-*

ports on the Trade and Politics of Latin America, 1824–1826, pp. 348–51. These figures are based on merchants' declarations rather than on official valuations. Among the fragmentary and estimated statistics of the time these are probably as reliable as any. Cody, "British Interest," pp. 269–73.
44. Hammond, "British Commercial Activity," pp. 186–87.

part of general French expansion into the Far East, the Pacific, and Africa.[45]

At the heart of French commercial enterprise in Mexico were the small-scale retail merchants of the interior who obtained their goods from both British and French wholesalers in the large cities. These merchants were sometimes nicknamed "Barcelonnettes" after a town in eastern France from which some of the earliest arrivals had come. Scattering through central and eastern Mexico, these prudent, vigilant storekeepers set up their one-room shops—windowless, whitewashed, divided in two by a long counter, and closed at night by a massive iron barricade reinforced by wooden beams. The French *patron* lived on the premises, surrounded by his family and Mexican employees. He seldom mingled with the native population but spent his days in his store and his evenings with friends in a café or at a *jeu de boules*.[46]

Like the French, the Spanish-born merchants in Mexico concentrated on retail trade, although they also maintained a few wholesale houses in Mexico City and the principal ports. They had the advantage of similar language, religion, and culture, but during the first fifteen years of Mexican independence they faced constant hostility without the aid of a minister or consuls. Since they could not obtain a regular supply of Spanish products, they had to deal in French wines, British ironware, and British and French textiles. After Spain and Mexico finally established diplomatic relations in 1836, Spanish exporters made an effort to regain the Mexican market, but this proved to be a long, slow process.[47]

Because much of the trade from the United States traveled across Texas and New Mexico, it became involved in the border quarrel (to be discussed in Chapter 3). Outside of the border area most American merchants concentrated their activities in the ports on the Gulf of Mexico. Here they were readily able to sell American flour and raw cotton for consumption in the coastal areas because the high freight rates on the wretched roads raised the costs of transporting Mexican products from the farmlands of the in-

45. Baron de Deffaudis to Ministère des affaires étrangères, July 31, 1833; May 15, 1834, Nos. 16, 31, France, MAE, CP, Mexique, VIII, ff. 90–92, 212–15. Jean-Paul Favre, *L'expansion française dans le Pacifique de 1800 à 1842*, pp. 337–38.

46. Etienne Micard, *La France au Mexique, étude sur les expéditions militaires; l'influence, le rôle économ-*ique de la France au Mexique, pp. 245–48. Auguste Génin, *Les français au Mexique du XVIe siècle à nos jours*, pp. 365–67. For material on French experiments with agricultural colonies, see Weckmann, *Relaciones franco-mexicanas*, I, 185–90. Génin, *Les français au Mexique*, pp. 386–87.

47. Delgado, *España y México*, II, 184–92.

terior.[48] The number of American ships plying to Mexican ports may have been as great as four times that of British ships during the 1820s and 1830s, but the American ships were smaller, and they brought many British goods to Mexico from New York or New Orleans. During this period perhaps as much as two thirds of Mexican imports were of British origin.[49]

*   *   *   *

It was not to be expected that during two decades of internal unrest the Mexican government could follow a consistent policy toward foreign capital, trade, and residents. At times, the mere appearance of foreigners aroused virulent hostility, for the more ignorant, superstitious natives looked upon the British and Americans as heretics with tails who plotted to enslave honest Mexicans or lead them off to Hell. Even the Roman Catholic French and Spanish residents were alienated from the Mexican common people by language, wealth, or memories of the Wars of Independence. The impatience of foreigners at easy-going Mexican ways and the native resentment against foreign managers and creditors widened the gap. When European or American businessmen resorted to sharp practices or took sides in local politics or revolutions, they brought popular or governmental retaliation on themselves, which they often blamed on Mexican institutions rather than on their own dishonesty or ineptness.

Again and again conservative, proclerical nationalists played upon their countrymen's xenophobia by issuing inflammatory propaganda. To be sure, some far-sighted statesmen like Lucas Alamán saw in foreign capital and skills the only hope for Mexican progress, but an unstable government often could or would not control the popular whim. Since the foreigners in Mexico were never sure of just where they stood, most of them risked only short-term investments and returned home as soon as possible.[50]

One source of the chronic uncertainty was Mexican tariff policy, which often reflected the xenophobia of the Mexican people and their conservative leaders. After independence, some mem-

48. *Texas Historical Quarterly*, 2 (January 1899), 192–93.

49. Cody, "British Interest," p. 273.

50. As a German observer put it: "Foreigners in this country are without defense and without protection. . . . The representatives of their govern- ments do little or nothing for them, but confine themselves to polite protests to the president, protests which usually remain unnoticed." A. R. Thümmel, *Mexiko und die Mexikaner, in physischer, sozialer und politischer Beziehung*, [etc.], p. 68.

bers of Iturbide's government were inclined to let down all the trade bars, and the first tariff of 1821 imposed a revenue duty of only 25 per cent, along with lists of duty-free and prohibited imports. Each new administration during the twenties tinkered with the tariff, however, until that of 1827 taxed 543 articles and forbade the import of most cereals, tobacco, sugar, cane brandy, and many kinds of clothing and textiles. The last-named prohibition made no sense whatsoever, since the preceding tariff, which forbade the import of cotton, had virtually destroyed what little textile industry existed in Mexico. By 1833 it was again permissible to import textiles and brandy, but only on payment of duties ranging from 100 to over 300 per cent.[51] Needless to say, smuggling flourished. Between 1825 and 1827, for example, it was thought to be over twice as extensive as legal trade.[52]

The only shred of systematic thinking behind this experimentation was Lucas Alamán's conviction that Mexico would never develop manufacturing as long as she imported all but her simplest necessities. For over a decade the Mexican government attempted to subsidize development of a textile industry, but revolutions and graft opened such drains on the Treasury that officials had to abandon the program as a failure.[53] Nevertheless, and despite spirited resistance from free traders, the almost prohibitive tariff policy continued, for it had the support of Alamán and other conservatives—as well as that of smugglers, who wished to avoid legitimate competition, and loan sharks, who did not want the government to develop a reliable source of income. In 1836 and 1837 new laws raised import duties and increased prohibitions, and two years later Congress added a consumption duty of 15 per cent on the few remaining imports. During much of this period the government

51. Hammond, "British Commercial Activity," pp. 172–75. Cue Cánovas, *Historia social y económica*, pp. 278–84. Potash, *Banco de avío*, Chaps. 2, 3, *passim*. Sample duties from the tariff of 1833 are cited in *Esposición del ayuntamiento constitucional de Tampico de Tamaulipas, al Congreso de la Unión, sobre reforma del arancel de aduanas y de todas las leyes comerciales*, p. 21. Baur, "Mexican Foreign Trade Policy," pp. 238–53.

52. Ibid., pp. 254–56. One type of smuggling that especially disturbed Anglo–Mexican relations was the shipment of silver bars on British warships without payment of the export tax. Eustace Barron to Charles Bankhead, Tepic, January 10, 1846, GB, FO 50/203, ff. 80–90.

53. Cue Cánovas, *Historia social y económica*, pp. 298–304, 355–57. Robert Crichton Wyllie, *Mexico, Report on Its Finances under the Spanish Government; since Its Independence, and Prospects of Their Improvement; with Calculations on the Public Debt, Foreign and Domestic*, pp. 63–65. In 1843 Mexico was estimated to have 53 textile mills with 131,280 spindles, the United States 1,250,000 to 1,500,000 spindles. Rives, *US and Mexico*, II, 103.

forbade or hampered the export of gold and silver, the nation's only means for correcting a chronically unfavorable balance of trade.[54]

This short-sighted economic nationalism stifled the import trade and aggravated the effects of the depression during the late 1830s. Between 1835 and the early 1840s American exports to Mexico fell from a high of $9 million to about $2 million, and in 1842 the United States consul at Veracruz reported that business was languishing and textile mills closing for lack of raw cotton.[55] It was reported that British textile shipments to Mexico had fallen from 26,000 pieces in 1824 to 19,000 pieces in 1841, valued at a little over a third of the former unit price.[56] Two facts, however, somewhat lighten the gloom of these figures: In Mexico statistics were seldom accurate, and smugglers were always active.

Since the framing of tariff laws is an incontestable right of a sovereign state, foreign merchants and diplomats could do no more than try to argue Mexicans into reductions when they saw their trade ruined by exorbitant duties. On many other occasions, however, the xenophobia, the greed, or simply the carelessness of the Mexican government or the Mexican people supplied just grounds for complaint. These grievances may be divided into two general categories: those arising from the failure of the government to grant a reasonable minimum of protection to life and property and those arising from capricious or corrupt actions of the government itself.[57]

54. México, Cámara de diputados, *Dictamen de la comisión de industria . . . sobre el nuevo arbitrio para dar un gran aumento a la hacienda federal* [etc.], pp. 8–10 *et passim*; and *Esposición del ayuntamiento de Tampico*, pp. 9–31. González Navarro, *Pensamiento político de Alamán*, pp. 74–83. Cue Cánovas, *Historia social y económica*, pp. 282–83. Potash, *Banco de avío*, pp. 192–204. Delgado, *España y México*, II, 169–70. López Cámara, *La estructura económica y social de México*, pp. 179–88.

55. Imports from Mexico also fell in the same period but not so far. United States, Bureau of the Census, *Historical Statistics of the United States, Colonial Times to 1957*, pp. 551, 553. Dispatches of Consul F. M. Dimond in 1842 and 1843 are in US, DS, CD, Veracruz, IV. Another source indicated that between 1839 and 1842 American exports to

Mexico fell from $2,787,362 to $1,534,233 and imports from $3,147,153 to $1,995,696, the greatest fall occurring in the last year. Some American exports, however, increased during the period—for example, rice, breadstuffs, and provisions. *NNR*, 67 (October 5, 1844), 68–69.

56. Memorandum of a Mr. Sheppard, June 16, 1842, to Sir Robert Peel, forwarded by him to the Earl of Ripon. Earl of Ripon Papers, BM, AM, vol. 40,863, f. 354. A survey of reports by British merchants in 1842 on effects of Mexican restrictions may be found in GB, FO 203/87, *passim*.

57. A convenient survey of American claims cases may be found in Clayton Charles Kohl, *Claims As a Cause of the Mexican War*, pp. 80–90. A similar memorandum of British claims is in GB, FO 50/121A, ff. 184–208. For a summary of the principal French

Life and property were never entirely secure in a country where revolution might break out at a moment's notice, bringing crowds surging into the streets with the cry "¡Mueran los extranjeros!" ("Death to the foreigners!") According to the French minister, this meant that the people wanted to loot.[58] At the beginning of December 1828 occurred the most notorious of these uprisings, when troops quartered in the center of Mexico City fought four days against the government troops, and the rabble, taking advantage of the disorder, sacked and burned Spanish and some other foreign shops in the Parián market, the largest in the capital. Damages were estimated at perhaps $2 million—mostly foreign property—and resulted in claims cases that smoldered for over a decade.[59]

Out in the countryside foreigners were no safer from sudden outbursts of hatred than in the city. During the cholera epidemic of 1833, a mob in a little village near Puebla, maddened by a rumor that foreigners were poisoning the wells, lynched five Frenchmen and one American. Several years later the people of Orizaba, disturbed by the government's abrupt inflation of the currency, accused foreigners of stealing all the local supply of silver and barricaded a group of Frenchmen in their small cotton mill. Fortunately, on this occasion the authorities restored order before anyone was killed.[60]

The harassed Mexican government might have been able to explain away some of these isolated outbursts of antiforeignism in time of revolution or some other general disturbance, were it not for the perils to be encountered along the principal highways, where even escorts of government troops were sometimes unable to fight off bandits. Also, the government seldom made serious efforts to track down the assailants of foreigners, and if it happened to catch them, the courts all too often released the offenders with light punishment. The notorious corruption of Mexican courts was a special grievance of foreign businessmen, for the Spanish-

claims, see Richard S. Coxe, *Review of the Relations between the United States and Mexico and of the Claims of Citizens of the United States against Mexico*, pp. 69–72. Except where noted, the ensuing discussion of grievances is based on these cases.

58. Deffaudis to Ministère des affaires étrangères, June 11, 1833, No. 13, France, MAE, CP, Mexique, VIII, ff. 70–75.

59. Naturally, foreign representatives played up the damages as much as pos-

sible, and the conventional modern view of the Parián outrage is that of Henry Bamford Parkes, *A History of Mexico*, p. 194. Poinsett's contemporary report, however, suggests that the actual damage was much less. Poinsett to Van Buren, March 10, 1829, Manning, *LAI*, III, 1683–84.

60. For details of the lynching, see France, MAE, CP, Mexique, VIII, ff. 110–12. On the Orizaba case, see XI, ff. 67–68.

based code of commercial law was primitive, vague, and vulnerable to all kinds of distorted interpretations which the Mexican citizen could easily obtain through influence or bribery. A British firm complained that one of its debtors in Durango admitted owing $35,000, which he was quite able to pay. The debtor stated, however, that he had bribed the local judges; in effect, he defied the company to attempt collection.[61]

In addition to denying the foreigner security or justice, from time to time the Mexican government itself added to his distress by arbitrary restrictions and levies of money. For example, it refused to grant foreigners the right to engage in retail trade. In practice many foreigners, especially Frenchmen and Spaniards, were retailers, but the government carefully avoided recognizing their status officially and usually required them to become permanent residents with families.[62] While frequent changes in the tariff laws, though unsettling, were not in themselves open to legitimate objection, the government sometimes showed bad faith by enforcing the new (and usually higher) duties so promptly that large consignments were caught in mid-ocean and eventually forced on the market at a loss.[63]

Probably the most fertile ground for the foreigners' discontent, however, was the "forced loan," a type of special, impromptu tax to which both government and rebels resorted in time of revolution. Under Canning, the British government took the position that such loans were unobjectionable if levied on natives and foreigners alike. During the early 1830s, when the loans had become more frequent and were obviously being levied only on wealthy foreigners, British Minister Pakenham tried to shield his complaining countrymen behind an ambiguous phrase in the English translation of the commercial treaty of 1826, which seemed to exempt them from unusual levies. He failed, for the Mexican government was able to prove that both sides had recognized the

---

61. G. M. Murray to Pakenham, Mexico City, April 14, 1837, GB, FO 50/117, ff. 31–33. On the inadequacy of Mexican commercial laws, see GB, FO 50/38 ff. 192–97. A particularly egregious instance of trouble in local courts involved the United Mexican Mining Company, which became involved in an interminable suit with the Marquis de Rayas and his heirs. See the company reports in *Mining Review*, July 1835, pp. 131–35; and John Easthope to Viscount Palmerston, London, January 27,

1834; Pakenham to Duke of Wellington, February 14, June 2, 1835, Nos. 5, 33, GB, FO 50/89, ff. 43–45; 50/91, ff. 50–56, 135–40.

62. Palmerston to Pakenham, May 9, 1831, GB, FO 50/65, ff. 15–16.

63. An outstanding case of this sort was the sudden imposition of the 15 per cent consumption duty in 1839, against which the principal foreign diplomats in Mexico protested for years. Delgado, *España y México*, II, 169–76, 254–61.

Spanish version as official. It is true that the unwilling lenders received customs certificates in return for their money, but their redemption required valuable time and often involved a considerable discount, especially if the government had changed hands meanwhile.[64]

Since the government handled ordinary business transactions in this arbitrary manner, it is not surprising that during this period it failed to liquidate the British loans of 1824 and 1825. For a decade after 1827, when it ceased payment of regular installments, it improvised with short-term loans, usually from *agiotistas*. In the hope of realizing some return on their investments, the British creditors banded together to elect the Committee of Mexican Bondholders and pressed the British government for satisfaction. The Foreign Office would give only the lukewarm promise of "friendly support" by the British minister. In April 1837, after long negotiations, the Mexican government announced a complicated conversion arrangement whereby the old 6 per cent bonds were to be exchanged for new ones yielding only 5 per cent, plus special "deferred bonds" bearing interest beginning in 1847. If the bondholders chose, they could exchange these latter bonds for public lands in Texas and along the border.[65] The conversion settlement of 1837 silenced the complaints of British creditors for a time, but by offering land in the border area, it aroused American suspicions of an Anglo–Mexican "deal."

* * * *

Although foreigners exaggerated some of their grievances against Mexico, there can be little doubt that they had many reasonable claims against a government which, however weak and corrupt it might be, had assumed the responsibilities of sovereignty. Between 1835 and 1842, as complaints mounted in the

64. Pakenham's principal correspondence on his negotiations with the Mexican government concerning forced loans appears in GB, FO 50/55, ff. 49–52; 50/80A, ff. 47–50; and 50/85, ff. 27–30. See also Byrns Hooton and Company to Pakenham, Mexico City, April 18, 1838, GB, FO 50/117, ff. 37–39.

65. Turlington, *Mexico and Her Foreign Creditors*, pp. 49–79. By a decree of December 13, 1843, the Mexican government recognized a total "London debt" of $54,573,730. The hopelessness of the Mexican financial situation is shown by the fact that in the same year the total net revenue was only $28,819,083 and total expenditures were $29,220,119. Turlington remarks that this was a comparatively favorable record (p. 79). See also Jenks, *Migration of British Capital*, pp. 109–12; and Lester D. Engelson, "Proposals for Colonization of California by England in Connection with the Mexican Debt to British Bondholders, 1837–1846," *California Historical Society Quarterly*, 18 (June 1939), 136–37.

American and European capitals, the three governments most concerned reacted in different ways. The United States blustered and threatened and finally submitted its claims to a mixed commission. France blustered, threatened, sent over a military expedition to exact satisfaction, and obtained a modest settlement. Britain did what it could to restrain the other two, argued, persuaded, and awaited future events.

Joel Poinsett and his successor, Anthony Butler, presented a few claims to the Mexican government, but neither of them pressed very hard for payment, being more concerned with negotiating a commercial treaty and settling the boundary question. During 1835, however, the Jackson administration began to lose patience. This change in attitude was partly due to Jackson's success in obtaining claims payments from France, partly to the increasing anti-Americanism among Mexican conservatives in the mid-thirties, and partly to Americans' rising interest in Texas, with which the claims question was to be thereafter entangled. At the end of the year Jackson sent Powhatan Ellis, a minor Southern lawyer–politician, to Mexico as chargé d'affaires with instructions to call for immediate examination of American claims.[66]

After several encounters with the "light-hearted and meaningless" excuses of the Mexican foreign ministry, Ellis advised Jackson that only force would make the Mexicans see reason. Probably encouraged by the victory at San Jacinto (which was reported in Washington several weeks before Ellis' dispatches began to arrive), Jackson supported his envoy's demands, but in December, after more than six months of fencing with the Mexicans, Ellis gave up in disgust and returned home.[67] Hitherto, Jackson had made only moderate public statements concerning the Mexican claims question, but after he had talked with Ellis, he sent a stern message to Congress, in which he declared that "the repeated and unavailing applications for redress, [and] the wanton character of some of the outrages . . . would justify in the eyes of all nations im-

66. The most detailed treatment of the American claims is Kohl, *Claims As a Cause*. Other briefer accounts are Rives, *US and Mexico*, I, 417–33; Callahan, *Mexican Relations*, pp. 91–98; and Carlos Bosch García, *Historia de las relaciones entre México y los Estados Unidos, 1819–1848*, pp. 53–56, 61–66, 70–73.

67. A dispatch from Ellis, dated May 28, advising the use of force is quoted in Rives, *US and Mexico*, I, 421, but does not appear in Manning, *IAA*. The phrase quoted in the text appears in Rives, *US and Mexico*, I, 423. Similar advice appears in Ellis' unnumbered dispatch of August 26, Manning, *IAA*, VIII, 343–46. A note on the back signed "A.J." directed that Ellis be instructed to remonstrate strongly and ask for his passports if he got no satisfaction.

mediate war." In the end, however, he asked Congress only for an act authorizing him to use the Navy to reinforce new demands for a settlement.[68]

The severity of Jackson's language doubtless owed something to a heated debate he was then carrying on with the Mexican minister, Manuel Gorostiza, over the entrance of American troops into eastern Texas, ostensibly to fight Indians (see Chapter 3). In both cases, Congress recommended more negotiations, and Jackson left office soon thereafter. With a little less bluster, his successor, Martin Van Buren, continued the policy of applying strong pressure. He sent a special agent to Mexico to present a new list of claims, reported in gloomy language to Congress on Mexican relations, and solemnly received from Congress its recommendations for peaceful settlement. In June and July 1838, John Quincy Adams, now become an outspoken abolitionist, engaged in a marathon debate in the House on antislavery petitions, Southern expansionist plots, and many related subjects. He accused Jackson and Van Buren of stirring up the claims question so as to have a pretext at hand for annexing Texas. Most recent historians discount this charge, for, about two months after Adams made it, the United States and Mexican governments finally signed a convention setting up a mixed commission with an umpire to judge the outstanding claims.[69]

The actions of the mixed commission, which functioned from August 1840 to February 1841, raised charges of bad faith on both sides. The Mexicans tried to bring before the commission claims involving American support of the Texan revolution, but the Americans managed to wave these aside as vague or affronting national honor. For their part, they objected that the Mexican commissioners and government used every available excuse to delay hearings, withhold evidence, and waste time in procedural squabbles. Nevertheless, the commission covered much ground, although the harassed umpire, Baron Roenne (appointed by the King of Prussia), eventually had to decide most of the cases. In all, claims amounting to $11,850,589.49 were presented to the commission, of which $5,201,776.61 were left undecided. The total awards

---

68. James D. Richardson, ed., *A Compilation of the Messages and Papers of the Presidents, 1789–1897*, III, 278–79. See also Kohl, *Claims As a Cause*, pp. 13–16.

69. Adams' tirade is extensively quoted, paraphrased, and refuted in Kohl, *Claims As a Cause*, pp. 21–29. George T. Tade, "The Anti-Texas Address: John Quincy Adams' Personal Filibuster," *Southern Speech Journal*, 30 (Spring 1965), 185–98.

were $2,026,139.68, mostly to American claimants.[70] A precedent of peaceful adjudication had been set, but the question remained— would Mexico pay the amounts declared against her?

In the late thirties the government of Louis Philippe decided that only force would ensure a favorable answer to this question. French diplomats in Mexico had a lower boiling point than the British or the Americans, and, as early as 1830, just before the July Revolution, there had been indications that the tottering Bourbon government was seriously considering armed intervention in Mexico.[71] Louis Philippe's policies relieved this belligerent pressure for a time, but after five years of mounting complaints from French residents in Mexico, the Franco–Mexican correspondence again took on an angry tone. At the end of 1837 the French government sent a naval squadron to Veracruz to back up the negotiations. In March the French minister, the impetuous Baron Deffaudis, withdrew to the deck of a French warship and sent an ultimatum to the Mexican government. Here he listed his government's grievances and demanded an indemnity of 600,000 pesos, the removal of certain objectionable Mexican officials, commercial reciprocity, and exemption of French residents from all forced loans. The Mexican government refused to discuss any of these matters while the French squadron threatened her shores. In response, on April 16 the squadron's commander declared a blockade of the Mexican Gulf coast.[72]

The French soon realized that it was much more difficult to maintain a blockade than to declare it. The fever season was approaching, and although the American consul in Veracruz described the epidemic of 1838 as unusually mild, by September 343 French sailors and officers out of about 500 had been or were sick. The tiny squadron contained barely enough ships to intercept trade at Veracruz and Tampico, ignoring the rest of the coast. Indeed, one of the largest ships had to sail off to Havana for over a month to renew the water supply.[73] The blockade, being incom-

70. Kohl, *Claims As a Cause*, pp. 30–44. Figures on pp. 38–39. See also sources cited in note 66 and Ivor Debenham Spencer, *The Victor and the Spoils, a Life of William L. Marcy*, pp. 118–19. Marcy was one of the American commissioners.

71. France, MAE, CP, Mexique, V, ff. 61, 146–52, 193, 268–71; VI, ff. 52–55.

72. William Spence Robertson, "French Intervention in Mexico in 1838," *Hispanic American Historical Review*, 24 (May 1944), 222–52. Except where noted, the present summary of French actions is based on this account.

73. P. Blanchard and A. Dauzats, *San Juan de Ulua, ou rélation de l'expédition française au Mexique sous les ordres de M. le Contre-amiral Baudin*, pp. 51–52, 68–75. The blockading squadron also had to withstand a hurricane in September. On the relative mildness of the fever season, see L. E. Hargous to John Forsyth, Veracruz,

plete, at once drew the attention of the British. Although hounded by protesting merchants, Palmerston was reluctant to complicate Anglo–French relations, so he confined his actions to delicate inquiries and advice behind the scenes. British Minister Pakenham happened to be at home on leave, but at the request of the French, Palmerston gladly instructed his chargé d'affaires to press the Mexicans for negotiations.[74]

At the end of October 1838 Rear Admiral Charles Baudin arrived off Veracruz with sizable reinforcements (26 ships and 4,300 men) to find both blockaders and Mexican government almost at the point of collapse. With some aid from the British chargé, Baudin and Foreign Minister Luis Cuevas arranged conferences at Jalapa, where the two argued for several days, Baudin demanding a larger indemnity and even more concessions than Deffaudis. Undoubtedly, the major issue was the right of the French to engage in the retail trade, which Cuevas absolutely refused to recognize.[75] On November 21 the conference broke up, and a week later the French squadron bombarded and attacked the crumbling island-fortress of San Juan de Ulua, which surrendered after a gallant but utterly futile defense.[76]

The French capture of Ulua did not bring the Mexicans to agreement. Instead, the Mexican government at once declared war on France and ordered all French residents to leave the country on impossibly short notice and under unnecessarily harsh conditions. Baudin raided Veracruz in an effort to capture Santa Anna, who had rushed to the scene to repel the invader, but Baudin succeeded only in making a hero of him by shooting off his leg. The French admiral had no desire to occupy the port or to move inland. As the winter wore on and a new fever season approached, he even resorted to the humiliating expedient of sending a secret emissary to federalist rebels at Tampico, an intrigue which failed to win him any dependable support and only infuriated the Mexican government further.[77]

In the end the British helped Baudin and his troops out of their predicament. First, the chargé in Mexico City interceded with the Mexican government to soften the harsh orders against

August 25, 1838, No. 98, US, DS, CD, Veracruz, III.

74. Robertson, "French Intervention," pp. 234–37. A full account of Anglo–French negotiations behind the scenes can be put together from dispatches in GB, FO 27/561–65, 580–81, *passim*.

75. Robertson, "French Intervention,"

p. 242. Charles Ashburnham to Palmerston, December 10, 1838, No. 98, GB, FO 50/116, ff. 33–44.

76. Blanchard and Dauzats, *San Juan de Ulua*, pp. 295–338.

77. Blanchard and Dauzats, *San Juan de Ulua*, pp. 457–62.

the French residents. At the end of December Pakenham arrived off Veracruz with a British squadron and went to Mexico City to serve as liaison until bases of negotiation could be set down on paper. On March 9 a peace treaty was signed. The French won the promise of a 600,000-peso indemnity, a future commercial treaty (mentioning no stipulations), and most-favored-nation treatment for their nationals in the meantime. Within the next two years Mexico paid the whole indemnity, but the treaty was not forthcoming, so the intervention won no permanent advantages for French interests in Mexico.[78]

The official French press made a great show of Napoleonic glory at the capture of Ulua and proclaimed that a dose of French discipline was necessary to revive the degraded Mexicans and forestall British and American competition: "France is the leader and guide of the southern peoples of Europe and America, of all those Latin races which have been least effaced by the Germanic invasion."[79] Many of the opposition pointed out, however, that few material gains accompanied the glory, and that the French attack on Ulua would prove only to have created "a Western question" to match that of the East.[80] Much of the British press agreed with the French opposition that French grievances did not justify armed intervention, that it had interrupted trade without accomplishing anything of value, and that it would undoubtedly arouse the Americans.[81] But in the United States, Congress did no more than pass a resolution of inquiry, and opinion in the American press was divided.[82]

78. Robertson, "French Intervention," pp. 247–48. Blanchard and Dauzats, *San Juan de Ulua*, pp. 482–89. Antonio de la Peña y Reyes, *La primera guerra entre México y Francia*, pp. 215–29, 239–55.

79. *Le journal des débats*, March 17, 1839, pp. 1–2; July 31, 1838, p. 1.

80. Joseph-Gabriel-Marie, Baron de Beaumont, *Lettre à M. le Comte Molé sur la question mexicaine [etc.]*, *passim*; and *Résumé et solution de la question mexicaine, pour servir à la discussion sur les crédits supplementaires*, *passim*. For the French government's defense of the peace terms, see Blanchard and Dauzats, *San Juan de Ulua*, pp. 500–513.

81. See, for example, London *Times*, June 2, 1838, p. 5; August 22, p. 4; August 28, p. 4; September 11, p. 4. London *Courier*, n.d., as quoted in *Le*

national, February 19, 1839, pp. 1–2. The *Courier* described the whole affair as "a coup de théâtre . . . a commercial speculation . . . from which in return a great cargo of popularity is expected in Paris." (Retranslated from French.)

82. Robertson, "French Intervention," pp. 245–46. Some American newspapers defended the French action, since Mexico admitted the legitimacy of French claims but refused to pay. Philadelphia *Herald and Sentinal*, n.d., as quoted in *Le journal des débats*, February 19, 1839, pp. 2–3. Another American newspaper expected a British counter-intervention and a division of Mexico between Britain and France. New York *Morning Herald*, n.d., as quoted in *Le constitutionnel*, February 7, 1839, p. 2. Still another foresaw Anglo–French cooperation but advised the United

In contrast to the American and French policies toward Mexico, that of Britain often seemed mild and passive. Throughout the 1830s letters and petitions flowed into the Foreign Office, calling for naval demonstrations, blockades, and other evidences of British might. In 1836, after the French minister had obtained the refund of a forced loan by means of a very stiff note, a British merchant wrote: "This is what our own Government ought to have done long ago, and not have left its subjects to receive protection from France—We cut a pitiful figure in the eyes of the Mexicans and other nations." During the French blockade of 1838, even the British chargé, Charles Ashburnham, for all his skillful liaison work, was privately convinced that in the long run only armed intervention would compel the Mexican government to pay its just debts.[83]

And yet, with the full approval of the doughty Palmerston, Pakenham carefully avoided any statement that might hint at an ultimatum and contented himself with notes of protest, interviews with officials, vague warnings, and persuasion. Why did Britain stop short of force in Mexico? Several circumstances explain her discretion. As Palmerston had shown in his response to the American states' defaults, he was not yet ready to commit the British government to automatic, full support of British investments abroad, although he always maintained that it had a legal right to protest officially if it chose to do so.[84] Britain also observed a variety of deterrents to armed intervention in the French experience of 1838–1839—Mexico's formidable natural defenses, the expenses of a military expedition, and the resulting commercial losses. If these reflections were not enough, the Foreign Office could take warning from Pakenham's gloomy report in 1839 that the French action had cast the Mexicans in the role of martyrs:

> The moral effect of the operation undertaken by the French Government has been entirely lost. Instead of conveying to this People a salutary respect for the power of European Nations which would have made them for the future more cautious in their proceedings

States to stay out. New Orleans *Courier*, n.d., as quoted in *Le national*, February 26, 1839, p. 2.

83. Charles Whitehead to M. Penny, Mexico City, January 6, 1836; Ashburnham to John Backhouse, July 26, 1838, GB, FO 50/103, ff. 64–65; 50/114, ff. 200–206.

84. Foreign Office draft to Pakenham, June 6, 1829, Circular, GB, FO 50/52,

ff. 22–24. McGrane, *Foreign Bondholders*, p. 202. Jenks, *Migration of British Capital*, pp. 119–25. In 1836 Palmerston considered a formal joint protest with the United States and France against Mexican forced loans, but apparently he never made an open proposal. Palmerston to Henry G. Fox, November 1, 1836, No. 5, Copy in Palmerston Papers, BM, AM, vol. 48495, ff. 51–54.

towards Foreign interests, the result appears to have been an uni-versal conviction that they have distinguished themselves by an heroic resistance to unjust oppression, and that they have come out of the conflict with far more honor than their assailants.[85]

This quixotic pride in defeat was to reappear many times during the Mexican War.

While rejecting the use of force, the British concluded that peaceful coercion was equally impracticable. On one occasion the Foreign Office asked the Board of Trade for an opinion on the wis-dom of placing heavy duties on Mexican products in retaliation for Mexican tariff exactions. The dismal reply was that Britain needed Mexican silver, and that all other imports from Mexico were vital raw materials that could not be easily obtained elsewhere.[86] As for establishing a mixed commission on the order of the American–Mexican group, Pakenham pointed out in 1842 that, since Mexico had already recognized most British claims, the main problem was to obtain payment. He added that it would be impracticable to as-semble such a commission in Mexico anyway, since all British resi-dents with sufficient information to serve on it would undoubtedly themselves be involved with claims, and he did not know of any Mexicans honest or brave enough to decide a case in favor of a foreigner.[87]

Another reason why Britain continued to prefer conventional bilateral negotiations without overt action was that such negotia-tions were often successful. When he learned that British petition-ers were impugning his devotion to duty, Pakenham replied:

I cannot recollect any general grievance to British Trade, which could have been resisted upon international principles, that has not been successfully and steadily opposed by His M's agents in this country. There has not been a session of the Mexican Congress, since I have been in Mexico, in which some vexatious or objectionable measure with regard to Trade has not been proposed and afterwards abandoned upon Representation of the Foreign Agents, . . . [in which] His Majesty's servants invariably take the labouring oar.[88]

Samples of British diplomatic correspondence during the 1830s show Pakenham successfully protesting against an illegal military

85. Pakenham to Sir Thomas Harvey, July 20, 1839, GB, FO 50/126, ff. 5–11. For an account of the material effects of the French intervention on Mexico, see Cue Cánovas, *Historia social y económica*, pp. 349–53.

86. Denis Le Marchant to Backhouse, London, April 2, 1840, GB, FO 50/141, ff. 90–92.

87. Pakenham to Earl of Aberdeen, January 31, 1842, No. 14, GB, FO 50/153, ff. 111–17.

88. Pakenham dispatch of November 23, 1834, quoted in memorandum by Palmerston, March 13, 1836, GB, FO 50/103, ff. 70–73.

service tax in 1832, arranging for mining companies to export bar silver in 1834 despite a prohibiting law, spurring the Mexican government to counterpropaganda against xenophobes in 1835, and getting five British mining companies exempted from a forced loan in 1836. A great tribute to his effectiveness was a letter from a representative of the United Mexican Mining Company in 1838, while he was on leave, expressing the company's full satisfaction with Mexico's liquidation of a claim after several years of Pakenham's correspondence and exertion of personal influence.[89]

Finally, it is probable that Britain preferred quiet diplomacy to open defiance in its relations with Mexico because of the growing American threat on the northern border. From 1837 to 1841 Britain faced major crises in her relations with the United States, and in 1842 the Webster–Ashburton Treaty established only an uneasy peace, which might be broken at any time. American expansionism westward and southward became more alarming to the British with the passage of each year. An ultimatum from Great Britain to the Mexican government, arousing American jealousy and suspicions, might bring about a compensatory attack on northern Mexico, or a renewed Anglo–American crisis, or both. So Pakenham stayed on in Mexico City, protesting and exhorting, while the British Atlantic and Caribbean squadrons kept their distance. Meanwhile, all Britons in Mexico watched the border provinces to see how far and how fast the Americans would advance.

89. Correspondence on these subjects may be found in GB, FO 50/73, ff. 53–54, 121–22; 50/86, ff. 139–42; 50/91, ff. 27–29; 50/92, ff. 201–3; 50/98, ff. 22–24; 50/99, ff. 261–62. For the letter from the United Mexican Mining Company, see J. N. Shoolbred to Ashburnham, Mexico City, March 10, 1838, GB, FO 50/113, ff. 129–31.

3

The Border Provinces: Texas

By the 1840s some far-sighted Europeans and Latin Americans had been anxiously speculating on United States expansionism for more than half a century. As early as 1787 the Spanish intendant of Louisiana foresaw that the Anglo–Americans to the north would try to extend their domains to the Pacific. In 1812, after the Louisiana Purchase and American feints at Florida, Luis de Onís warned the viceroy of New Spain from his post at Washington that the United States intended to fix its southern border on a line west from the mouth of the Rio Grande taking in Texas, New Mexico, Chihuahua, Sonora, the Californias, and parts of other provinces. He added, "This project will seem delirium to any rational person, but it certainly exists."[1]

The new government of Mexico inherited this fear, and in 1821, the first year of independence, a committee on foreign affairs predicted that the United States would overrun their land like the Visigoths descending on the Roman Empire. Seven years later General Manuel Mier y Terán, the military commandant of the northern provinces, completed the picture with a description of what a later generation would call fifth-column activities:

Instead of armies, battles, or invasions, which make a great noise and for the most part are unsuccessful, these men . . . begin by . . . making ridiculous pretensions based on historical incidents which no one admits. . . . In the meantime, the territory against which these machinations are directed, and which has usually remained unsettled, begins to be visited by adventurers and *empresarios*. Some of these take up their residence in the country, pretending that their location has no bearing upon the question of their government's claim or the boundary disputes. Shortly . . . complaints, even threats, begin to be heard, working on the loyalty of the legitimate settlers,

1. Quoted in Agustín Cue Cánovas, *Historia social y económica de México (1521–1854)*, p. 339. On the prediction of 1787, see Charles Gayarré, *History of Louisiana, the French Domination*, III, 182–83.

discrediting the efficiency of the existing authority and administration; and the matter having arrived at this stage . . . diplomatic maneuvers begin.[2]

The Mexican fears were only too well justified. Three years after the United States won its independence an article in the *American Review* declared that two thousand brave men, properly led, could clear the Spaniards out of Louisiana and West Florida and "carry the war into the very heart of Mex[ico]."[3] After the Louisiana Purchase, some Americans felt that the Mississippi Valley would provide sufficient room for generations of growth. In 1819, however, when a treaty with Spain fixed the southwestern boundary at the Sabine River, a thwarted expansionist declared that "the great Engineer of the Universe" had reserved Mexico for the United States. Even the negotiator of the treaty, John Quincy Adams, told the Monroe cabinet that he considered "our proper dominion to be the continent of North America. From the time when we became an independent people it was as much a law of nature that this should become our pretension as that the Mississippi should flow to the sea."[4]

Beginning in Jackson's time, the idea of expansion tended to be concentrated in the Democratic party, as the Whigs, wishing to build national authority in a relatively limited area, warned against too much dispersion of population and resources.[5] In 1835 the expansionists received widely publicized liberal support when Alexis de Tocqueville predicted that "the Anglo–Americans will alone cover the immense space contained between the polar regions and the tropics, extending from the coasts of the Atlantic to the shores of the Pacific ocean."[6] Four years later an article in the

2. Mier's statement is quoted in Eugene C. Barker, *Mexico and Texas, 1821–1835*, pp. 8–9. See also Joseph Carl McElhannon, "Relations between Imperial Mexico and the United States, 1821–1823," in Thomas E. Cotner and Carlos E. Castañeda, eds., *Essays in Mexican History*, p. 128.

3. Quoted in John Douglas Pitts Fuller, *The Movement for the Acquisition of All Mexico, 1846–1848*, pp. 12–13.

4. *Memoirs of John Quincy Adams*, ed. Charles Francis Adams, IV, 438. The earlier statement is quoted in Albert K. Weinberg, *Manifest Destiny, a Study of Nationalist Expansionism in American History*, p. 55.

5. In the Twenty-eighth Congress (1843–1845) party voting on three expansionist issues (Texan annexation, Oregon, and admission of new states) was as follows: In the House of Representatives 75.6% of the Democrats were proexpansionist, while 87.5% of the Whigs were antiexpansionist; in the Senate 95.7% of the Democrats were proexpansionist on the same questions, while 93.1% of the Whigs were antiexpansionist. Joel H. Silbey, *The Shrine of Party: Congressional Voting Behavior, 1841–1852*, pp. 60–62.

6. Alexis de Tocqueville, *Democracy in America*, trans. by Henry Reeves, I, 469.

Democratic Review, modestly entitled "The Great Nation of Futurity," proclaimed: "Its floor shall be a hemisphere—its roof the firmament of the star-studded heavens, and its congregation an Union of many Republics, . . . governed by God's natural and moral law of equality." [7] In the same year an Illinois newspaper declared that if the Americans could secure Oregon, that "grand thoroughfare to Asia, . . . nothing but the power of Omnipotence could prevent the United States from becoming the leading nation of the world." [8]

Heady rhetoric that, but many Americans believed it, at least with a part of their minds. It was apparent to all, dreamers and skeptics alike, that realization of the vision depended on the early acquisition of the lands bordering the western frontier—Texas, California, and Oregon. When the 1840s began, the Americans were already directing their potent magnetism toward these vital provinces.

*   *   *   *

Americans' serious interest in Texas dated from the beginning of the nineteenth century, when such adventurers as Philip Nolan and Aaron Burr had plotted filibusters against the Spanish dons. For years after the Louisiana Purchase of 1803 some Americans had argued that the lucky deal with France included Texas as well as the lower Mississippi Valley. The Adams–Onís treaty of 1819 recognized Spanish sovereignty over that province, but even before the treaty was ratified, the American occupation of Texas had begun. In 1820 a Connecticut wanderer, Moses Austin, obtained a colonization concession from the Spanish provincial governor that was confirmed a year later by the viceroy with the easy stipulations that the colonists be reputable Catholics and take an oath of allegiance to Spain. After independence, the government of Iturbide approved the transfer of the concession to Austin's son Stephen. In 1824 the new republican regime further encouraged immigration into Texas with a lenient colonization law, and the federalist constitution of the same year yielded extensive control over local affairs to the state of Coahuila y Texas. [9]

Although the panic of 1819 and the refusal of the United

---

7. "The Great Nation of Futurity," *The United States Magazine and Democratic Review,* 6 (November 1839), 427.

8. Alton (Illinois) *Telegraph,* November 9, 1839, quoted in James C. Bell, *Opening a Highway to the Pacific, 1838–1846,* pp. 86–87.

9. George Lockhart Rives, *The United States and Mexico, 1821–1848,* I, 130–47. On other colonization proposals of the same period, see *Southwestern Historical Quarterly,* 32, *passim;* 47: 253–54.

States government to continue selling public lands on credit had created discontent on the Southwest frontier, only a few thousand American residents emigrated from the area into Texas during the 1820s. These settlers organized municipalities under Mexican law and were soon sending a small delegation to the state legislature. Despite these evidences of political compliance, they retained their character as Americans. Their language, culture, and frontier self-reliance contrasted strongly with the Mexicans' way of life, and few if any of them conformed to the stipulation that they be Roman Catholics. Also, many immigrants brought Negro slaves with them, as part of their property, to work the low, malarial coastlands, for nothing in the Austin concession forbade slavery although the Mexican Constitution of 1824 proclaimed all men equal.

Given the differences in customs and the confusion of the Mexican national government, conflict between Mexico and the Texan settlers was probably inevitable. In 1827 an abortive local uprising, the Fredonian revolt, warned the Mexicans of future crises. The Anglophile Lucas Alamán put through Congress the law of April 6, 1830, which forbade further immigration and directed the military commandant of Texas to construct a chain of defensive forts. At about the same time the Mexican government imposed high tariffs on most of the imports needed by the Texan settlers and abolished slavery. These two actions were part of general policy and may not have been aimed particularly at the Texans. Unfortunately, they ignored the realities of the settlers' situation, especially the fact that trade with central Mexico was difficult and expensive.[10]

Being both too late and badly enforced, the new restrictions irritated the Texans without strengthening the government's control. During the next years more immigrants arrived from Arkansas and Louisiana, despite the prohibition of 1830, and another abortive rebellion occurred on Galveston Bay. The Texans organized a convention and petitioned the state and federal governments for redress of grievances, while Stephen Austin, anxious to carry out the oath of allegiance which he and his colonists had taken, served as intermediary between the settlers and Mexico City. But the federal government, torn by revolutions and disor-

10. Barker, *Mexico and Texas*, Chaps. 2, 3. See also Rives, *US and Mexico*, I, Chap. 8. On the law of 1830, see Alleine Howren, "Causes and Origin of the Decree of April 6, 1830," *Southwestern Historical Quarterly*, 16 (April 1913), 378–422; and Ohland Morton, *Terán and Texas: a Chapter in Texas-Mexican Relations, passim.*

ganized by the reforms of the liberal Vice President Valentín Gómez Farías, could pay little attention to remote border problems. At the same time anti-American conservatives saw Jacobinism in the Texan convention and liberals winced at Texan slavery.

Perhaps at this point Mexico might have slowed the Texans' drift toward independence by granting them separate statehood. Austin journeyed to Mexico City and proposed this solution to Gómez Farías without success.[11] In 1835 leaders of the conservative reaction destroyed the last hope of a peaceable solution by drawing up a new centralist constitution which abolished most local autonomy. When federalists in Zacatecas revolted, Santa Anna brutally suppressed the rebellion and sacked the state capital. Alarmed at the turn of events, the Texans organized troops, ostensibly to defend the old federalism, whereupon Santa Anna led a force northward to subdue them in turn. News of this action fed the already growing secessionism, and in January 1836 another special convention declared the independence of Texas.[12]

The Mexican punitive expedition faced a more stubborn adversary in Texas than in Zacatecas. First of all, Santa Anna further unified the Texans by capturing the Alamo and Goliad without giving quarter to their defenders. Then he advanced eastward and seemed on the point of driving the ragged Texan forces across the Sabine River into the United States. But on April 21 the Texan general, Sam Houston, suddenly turned on him at San Jacinto. Caught in the midst of a siesta, his camp virtually unguarded and without a line of retreat, Santa Anna surrendered ignominiously. To avoid being lynched, he signed a treaty with Houston that rec-

11. Austin, disappointed at his failure, warned that Texas might take matters into its own hands. When Acting President Gómez Farías received evidence that Austin was organizing a movement for separate statehood, he arrested him and kept him in jail through most of 1834. Oddly enough, after Gómez Farías' fall from power, he and his group of federalist exiles in New Orleans supported the Texans for a time, believing most of them to be federalists rather than secessionists. The federalist General José Antonio Mejía launched an abortive attack on Tampico in 1835, partly to aid the Texan cause. As soon as it became obvious that the Texans were bent on independence the New Orleans federalists broke all connections. Gómez Farías' disillusionment undoubtedly stimulated his Yankeephobia, so influential on his policies and actions a decade later. C. Alan Hutchinson, "Valentín Gómez Farías and the 'Secret Pact of New Orleans,'" *Hispanic American Historical Review*, 36 (November 1956), 471–89; "Mexican Federalists in New Orleans and the Texas Revolution," *Louisiana Historical Quarterly*, 39 (1956), 1–47.

12. Barker, *Mexico and Texas*, Chap. 5. Rives, *US and Mexico*, I, Chaps. 11–12. William Campbell Binkley, *The Texas Revolution, passim*. For modern Mexican accounts of the revolution, see José C. Valadés, *Santa Anna y la guerra de Texas*, Chaps. 8–13, and Luis G. Zorrilla, *Historia de las relaciones entre México y los Estados Unidos de América, 1800–1958*, I, 101–8.

ognized Texan independence. Then Santa Anna was taken to Washington and finally allowed to return home.

What influence did the United States have on the Texan revolution? Mexicans naturally professed to find in the whole sequence of events a gigantic American plot to steal Texas—a plot directed by Andrew Jackson, the spearhead of frontier imperialism.[13] It is certainly true that during the late 1820s Joel Poinsett worked impetuously and tactlessly in Mexico City to further his country's influence and that some Western newspapers and congressmen kept up a steady clamor for Texas. Also, Jackson had a reputation for chauvinism and was a personal friend of the Texan general, Sam Houston.

Beyond these facts, however, the evidence of a concerted plot is less impressive. There is good reason to believe that Jackson favored the boundary treaty of 1819.[14] To be sure, Adams and Clay had instructed Poinsett to offer the Mexican government $1 million for Texas, but he did not press the matter, thinking the offer too small and the times unfavorable. When Jackson took office in March 1829, he ignored the Texas question for five months, and then, probably influenced by his friend Anthony Butler, he told Poinsett to offer $5 million for part of the desired territory. This offer undoubtedly gave some substance to Mexican fears. Jackson seems to have been taken in by the loud-mouthed, dishonest Butler, for after Poinsett's recall he appointed Butler minister to Mexico—a far less reputable choice than Poinsett—and left him there, almost entirely unsupervised, for nearly five years. At long last, Butler's bluster, intrigues, and clumsy efforts at bribery overcame Jackson's loyalty to his friend, and he was recalled to Washington.[15]

13. For examples of this sort of Mexican writing, see Alberto María Carreño, *La diplomacia extraordinaria entre México y los Estados Unidos, 1789–1947*, I, 240–41; José Vasconcelos, *Breve historia de México*, pp. 327–30; and Carlos Pereyra, *Tejas, la primera dismembración de Méjico, passim*. Some Mexican suspicions undoubtedly arose from the fact that one of the Texan leaders was Lorenzo de Zavala, a former Mexican official who had deserted. W. S. Cleaves, "Lorenzo de Zavala in Texas," *Southwestern Historical Quarterly*, 36 (July 1932), 29–40; and Raymond Estep, *Lorenzo de Zavala, profeta del liberalismo mexicano, passim*.

14. Adams, *Memoirs*, IV, 239. Andrew Jackson, *The Correspondence of Andrew Jackson*, ed. John Spencer Bassett, III, 28.

15. Rives, *US and Mexico*, I, Chap. 10. James Morton Callahan, *American Foreign Policy in Mexican Relations*, pp. 63–76. Eugene C. Barker, "President Jackson and the Texas Revolution," *American Historical Review*, 12 (July 1907), 788–803. Jackson, *Correspondence*, VI, 94–95, 227. Correspondence in the Butler Papers suggests strongly that Jackson was originally more amenable to bribing Mexican officials than he later indicated. Glenn W. Price, *Origins of the War with Mexico: the Polk–Stockton Intrigue*, pp. 20–23. See also Zorrilla, *Relaciones*

Suspicions of Houston's motives are a little more difficult to allay, for his personality has always presented problems to the historian. On the surface he seemed a Western political stereotype: a tall, strong-featured, forceful extrovert, courtly in manner and elaborate in speech, fond of eccentric costumes and liquor. Behind this façade, however, he was sometimes irresolute and devious, devoted to Jackson and the Union, but moved also by impulse and his insights into his fellow Westerners and their desires.[16] It is quite possible that he went originally to Texas with some wild idea of reviving the Burr Conspiracy, but when Jackson heard rumors to this effect in 1829, he wrote Houston that he must be insane. The fact that Jackson received the news of San Jacinto with almost childlike glee does not prove in itself that he had actively supported Houston beforehand.[17] Indeed, Jackson later declared that he did not seriously consider any sort of negotiation with the rebels until after the battle.[18]

The reaction of the American people and some government officials to the events of 1836 lends somewhat more substance to the Mexicans' charges. Press and public all over the country and especially south of the Ohio River enthusiastically supported the rebels. Sympathizers openly collected funds for their aid in the cities and towns, and several thousand volunteers formed regiments and began the long march toward the Sabine River. Public declamations about freedom and Mexican tyranny thinly concealed a mounting greed for the cheap, fertile Texan lands.[19] Jackson's of-

entre México y Estados Unidos, I, 93–94, 97–100.

16. Llerena Friend, *Sam Houston, the Great Designer*, pp. 13–14, 35, 67, 88, 90–92, 103, 106, 111, 287, 291, *et passim*. Another modern biography, less analytical and relying heavily on Houston's writings, is M. K. Wisehart, *Sam Houston, American Giant*.

17. The story of a plot between Jackson and Houston can be traced as far back as 1829. John Quincy Adams publicized it through speeches in 1838, and it has survived to the present. See, for example, Richard R. Stenberg, "The Texas Schemes of Jackson and Houston," *Southwestern Social Science Quarterly*, 15 (December 1934), 229–50. The most outspoken arguments against Jackson's involvement are in Barker, "Jackson and the Texas Revolution," pp. 788–809; and Justin H. Smith, *The Annexation of Texas*, pp. 20–33 *et passim*. Friend has summarized the evi-

dence for Jackson's involvement and reached the most reasonable verdict—accusation unproved. Friend, *Houston*, pp. 38–41, 50–53. Considering the influence of land speculators in the later annexationist movement, one might naturally assume that they played an important role in the coming of the revolution. Barker has examined this subject carefully and concluded that they did not. Eugene C. Barker, "Land Speculation As a Cause of the Texas Revolution," *The Quarterly of the Texas State Historical Association*, 10 (July 1906), 76–95.

18. Jackson to W. B. Lewis, September 18, 1843, cited in Smith, *Annexation of Texas*, p. 27.

19. James E. Winston, "The Attitude of the Newspapers of the United States towards Texan Independence," *Proceedings of the Mississippi Valley Historical Association for the Year 1914–1915*, 8:160–75; "New Orleans Newspa-

ficial posture of neutrality was correct but not very effective, for American laws were full of loopholes, as the Canadian revolutions of the following year were soon to demonstrate. The Mexican minister in Washington, Manuel de Gorostiza, did not greatly exaggerate when he wrote to his government: "[American] neutrality consists only in words, and does us a thousand times more harm than declared enmity."[20]

The most discreditable American breach of neutrality was an impetuous act by General Edmund P. Gaines, the commander of troops on the Louisiana frontier, who had a reputation for flightiness and insubordination. Like most other Westerners, he sympathized with the Texans but would probably have done nothing if a wave of refugees fleeing from Santa Anna's advance across central Texas had not brought rumors that the Indians had joined forces with the Mexicans. In the apparently sincere belief that American settlements were in danger, Gaines, on his own initiative, issued two calls for volunteers. Finally, three months after the Battle of San Jacinto, he ordered a small body of troops to occupy Nacogdoches, about fifty miles west of the Sabine, for a few weeks.[21] Gorostiza vehemently protested to Jackson's government that Gaines' action was clear evidence of American bad faith in the Texas–Mexican crisis, and when the State Department objected to

pers and the Texas Question, 1835–1837," *Southwestern Historical Quarterly*, 36 (October 1932), 109–29. Eugene C. Barker, "The United States and Mexico, 1835–1837," *Mississippi Valley Historical Review*, 1 (June 1914), 3–8. For the Mexican view of this American reaction, see Carlos Bosch García, *Historia de las relaciones entre México y los Estados Unidos, 1819–1848*, pp. 173–78. Three or four months after San Jacinto an incomplete set of muster rolls showed 14 companies (672 men) in the Texan army composed largely of bona fide Texans and 39 companies (1,813 men) composed of persons who had arrived in Texas since the battle. Joseph Milton Nance, *After San Jacinto, the Texas–Mexican Frontier, 1836–1841*, p. 18. On land speculation, see especially Elgin Williams, *The Animating Pursuit of Speculation: Land Traffic in the Annexation of Texas*, Chap. 2. On financial connections, see Joe B. Frantz, "The Mercantile House of McKinney and Williams, Underwriters of the Texas Revolution," *Bulletin of the Business Historical Society*,

26 (March 1952), 1–18. It does not appear that the American election campaign of 1836 played a significant part in determining American attitudes on Texas or vice versa.

20. Gorostiza to Ministerio de Relaciones Exteriores, October 4, 1836, quoted in Bosch García, *Relaciones entre México y los Estados Unidos*, p. 193. Earlier, however, he had recognized the sincere desire of the United States government to maintain neutrality despite its inability to control the Westerners (p. 188). At any rate, the United States Navy acted with complete neutrality in the Gulf of Mexico. K. Jack Bauer, "The United States Navy and Texan Independence: A Study in Jacksonian Integrity," *Military Affairs*, 35 (April 1970), 44–48.

21. James W. Silver, *Edmund Pendleton Gaines: Frontier General*, Chap. 9. Charles Winslow Elliott, *Winfield Scott, the Soldier and the Man*, p. 422. Jackson apparently acquiesced in the occupation at first but quietly relieved Gaines and withdrew the troops during the autumn.

his strictures, he published the whole correspondence and left for home in disgust.[22]

Whether funds and volunteers from the United States provided the margin for the Texans' victory, as Mexicans have always believed, the revolution produced outbreaks of anti-Americanism all over Mexico and embittered Mexican–American relations for years afterward.[23] British and French diplomats reported the revolution in varying tones of alarm to London and Paris. Most of them attacked the United States for partisanship and some predicted an American invasion of northern Mexico, but the home governments refused to take action. Palmerston did no more than instruct Fox in Washington to encourage the United States government to remain neutral and avoid premature recognition of Texan independence, while the French government dryly assured a consul in Mexico that it would not be necessary at that time for France to seize Texas in order to keep it out of American hands.[24]

*   *   *   *

From the beginning of the independence movement Texan leaders realized that their best chance of success lay in prompt recognition of the new state by foreign nations, especially the United States. At one point some of them proposed a flag which combined thirteen stripes, a miniature Union Jack, and a picture of Washington as an open appeal to both the United States and Britain. By the end of 1835 three sets of Texan agents had arrived in the American capital.[25] Before the news of San Jacinto had reached the East Coast, Congress was receiving petitions for prompt recognition of Texas, and these increased throughout 1836. At the suggestion of Congress, Jackson sent an agent to inspect the new republic; the resultant report described Texas as so weak in population and finance that "without foreign aid, her future security must depend

---

22. Antonio de la Peña y Reyes, *Don Manuel Eduardo de Gorostiza y la cuestión de Texas, passim.* Thomas Maitland Marshall, *A History of the Western Boundary of the Louisiana Purchase, 1819–1841,* Chap. 10.

23. M. Burrough to John Forsyth, Veracruz, December 3, 1835; May 29, June 14, 1836, Nos. 35, 39, 40, US, DS, CD, Veracruz, II.

24. Viscount Palmerston to Henry S. Fox, November 14, 1836, No. 6, Palmerston Papers, "To North America," BM, AM, vol. 48495, pp. 54–55. Ministère des Affaires Étrangères to Def-

faudis, November 21, 1835, No. 26, France, MAE, CP, Mexique, IX, ff. 188–90. For other French reactions, see IX, ff. 140–45; X, ff. 70–74, 164–67; and Abraham P. Nasatir, *French Activities in California, an Archival Calendar-Guide,* pp. 148–49.

25. George Pierce Garrison, "The First Stage of the Movement for the Annexation of Texas," *American Historical Review,* 10 (October 1904), 73–74. Stanley Siegel, *A Political History of the Texas Republic, 1836–1845,* p. 44.

more upon the weakness and imbecility of her enemy than upon her own strength."[26]

In December Jackson delivered two cautious messages to Congress on the Texas question, urging delay lest the world suspect the United States of annexationist intentions. Historians have variously attributed this sudden reluctance on his part to fear of a complete break with Mexico (since Gorostiza had left for home in October), to a vain hope that Mexico would sell her province (a solution he seems to have proposed to the captive Santa Anna in January), and to the restraining advice of Secretary of State John Forsyth and President-elect Van Buren, who were concerned over rising Northern opposition to annexation.[27] Jackson's message somewhat subdued the friends of Texas for a time, but by the beginning of March Texan agents, land speculators, and other expansionists had prevailed on Congress to pass resolutions in favor of recognition. On March 3, 1837, the last day of his term, Jackson appointed a chargé d'affaires to Texas and formally received the Texan agents over a glass of wine. His change of policy may have been due to reports that Mexico had no strength for immediate invasion, to rumors of British interest in Texas, or to concern lest the tottering republic collapse without this modicum of encouragement.[28]

Most expansionists regarded recognition of Texas as simply the first step toward annexation. During the preceding session of Congress the Texan agents had broached the subject unofficially. John C. Calhoun, always eager to expand Southern influence in national affairs, had declared himself in favor of it, and the increasing numbers of Americans who held bonds or land scrip from the Texan government formed an approving chorus, since they assumed that the United States government would take over all obligations of the Texan Republic upon annexation. Hard pressed by other problems, however, Van Buren did not allow the Texan minister to present a formal proposal for annexation until midsummer of 1837. On August 25 Secretary Forsyth gave him a chilling refusal. The Constitution, Forsyth said, made no provision for annexing an independent state, and the United States government

26. Henry M. Morfit to Forsyth, Velasco, Texas, September 10, 1836, No. 9, Manning, *IAA*, XII, 114–16. Rives, *US and Mexico*, I, 389–92.

27. James D. Richardson, ed., *A Compilation of the Messages and Papers of the Presidents, 1789–1897*, III, 237–38, 265–69. Rives, *US and Mexico*, I,

395–97. On Jackson's offer to Santa Anna, see Valadés, *Santa Anna y la guerra de Texas*, p. 240.

28. William H. Wharton to J. Pinckney Henderson, March 5, 1837. Garrison, *DCRT*, I, 201–2. Rives, *US and Mexico*, I, 398–401. Smith, *Annexation of Texas*, pp. 56–63.

would not look for a formula to surmount this obstacle as long as Texas remained at war with Mexico.[29]

Van Buren's rejection was not surprising, for the Texans had chosen the worst possible time to present their proposal. By January 1837 Americans had acquired scrip for over a million acres of Texan land, usually in return for loans or other favors, but the panic of that year deflated investors' confidence and cast uncertainty over every kind of speculation. Even more serious, years of abolitionist agitation had convinced many Northerners that the bitter struggles over the admission of Missouri in 1820 and over nullification in 1832 as well as the more recent quarrels in Congress about antislavery petitions and the "gag rule" were part of an immense conspiracy by Southerners to expand their domain and thus force the nation to accept their views on slavery and the tariff. During the spring and summer of 1837 petitions against the annexation of Texas poured into Washington.[30]

William E. Channing, the great New England Unitarian, lent his prestige to these views by writing an open letter to Henry Clay, in which he marshaled evidence and rhetoric to prove that the Texan revolution was not justified by grievances against Mexico and that its real causes were land speculation and proslavery expansionism. The annexation of Texas, declared Channing, would involve the United States in war with Mexico and Britain, corrupt American domestic institutions, and lead to dissolution of the Union: "We cannot consent, that the South should extend its already disproportionate power by an indefinite extension of territory."[31] Channing supplied the arguments; John Quincy Adams, a curmudgeon turned crusader, rasped them forth day after day in Congress; and the Democratic party seemed likely to split into sectional factions. No wonder Van Buren wanted to avoid the annexation question!

29. Garrison, *DCRT*, I, 157–200, *passim*. Forsyth to Memucan Hunt, August 25, 1837, Manning, *IAA*, XII, 11–13. Rives, *US and Mexico*, I, 406–11.

30. Williams, *Animating Pursuits*, p. 83. Gilbert Hobbs Barnes, *The Anti-Slavery Impulse, 1830–1844*, Chaps. 11–13.

31. William E. Channing, *A Letter to the Hon. Henry Clay, on the Annexation of Texas to the United States*, *passim*. The sentence quoted appears on p. 50. Smith, *Annexation of Texas*, pp. 14–19. For an answer to this argument, see Garrison, "First Stage of the Movement for Annexation," pp. 82–84. Many in the South also opposed annexation or even recognition. See, for example, Thomas H. O'Connor, *Lords of the Loom: The Cotton Whigs and the Coming of the Civil War*, pp. 60–61. The early opposition to recognition and annexation in Massachusetts, the heart of the movement, is set forth in Kinley J. Brauer, *Cotton versus Conscience: Massachusetts Whig Politics and Southwestern Expansion, 1843–1848*, Chap. 3. As Brauer points out, Channing emphasized moral arguments, Adams constitutional.

*　　*　　*　　*

Indeed, the annexation of Texas remained an open question for the next eight years, and its settlement was to depend on political conditions within the United States. Until June 1838 Texas continued its initial offer, but by then Houston was casting about for other expedients. Support from any source was vital, for the ramshackle Republic of Texas was teetering on the edge of bankruptcy. Its population, about 30,000 in 1836, nearly doubled during the next four years, but its settlements were either concentrated along the humid, fever-stricken Gulf coast or thinly scattered in the interior. To be sure, the lands of eastern Texas were ideal for growing cotton; farmers with their slaves were constantly arriving from the East, and a flourishing trade focused on New Orleans.[32] Like the United States, Texas had great expectations for the future, but in the meantime an almost penniless government migrated from one frontier village to another as the Treasury Department juggled its account books and Congress echoed with fulsome oratory and grandiose plans. By 1840 the Republic of Texas had issued over $3.5 million in paper money, valued at 16.6 cents on the dollar, and the entire national structure rested on a speculative foundation of land grants and promissory notes.[33]

Under these circumstances it was fortunate for Texas that the faction-ridden Mexican government, deep in debt and facing a diplomatic crisis with France, could manage only an occasional military raid northward. One historian has estimated that the reconquest of Texas would have required a well-drilled army of twenty thousand and a navy capable of blockading three or four hundred miles of coast.[34] Since Mexico had no prospects of marshaling such forces, it might have seemed wise to recognize Texan independence and then to concentrate on defending what remained of the northern frontier. At the beginning of 1839, indeed, Palmerston instructed Pakenham to urge this policy on the Mexican government, pointing out that prompt action might prevent annexation of Texas to the United States and furnish Mexico with a barrier against further American encroachment.[35] Unfortu-

32. James E. Winston, "Notes on Commercial Relations between New Orleans and Texan Ports, 1838–1839," *The Southwestern Historical Quarterly*, 34 (October 1930), 91–105. A British report on Texan trade is reprinted in *The Quarterly of the Texas State Historical Association*, 15 (January 1912), 205–9.

33. Rives, *US and Mexico*, I, 464–70. Smith, *Annexation of Texas*, pp. 39–42. Siegel, *Texas Republic*, pp. 31–32, 56–57, 61–62, 68–70, 120, *et passim*. Williams, *Animating Pursuits*, Chap. 3 *et passim*, probably overplays the importance of this factor.

34. Rives, *US and Mexico*, I, 478.

35. Palmerston to Richard Paken-

nately, the Bustamante government, though weak, was proud and stubborn. Refusing to admit a parallel between the Texan revolution and the Mexican struggle for independence from Spain, it would not or dared not recognize the *fait accompli*.

Soon after the Republic of Texas gave up its hopes for immediate annexation by the United States, Houston yielded the presidency to his political enemy, Mirabeau Buonaparte Lamar, an activist with ambitions for his country as grandiose as his name. For two years, from 1839 to 1841, Lamar tried to persuade or compel Mexico to recognize the independence of Texas. In succession he sent Barnard E. Bee, James Treat, and James Webb to negotiate for recognition, offering to pay Mexico $5 million in one form or another. On instructions from the Foreign Office and in the hope that at least some of the indemnity money would find its way to British bondholders, Pakenham did all he could to support the three envoys, but in vain. Bee arrived just too late to exert much leverage, since the French intervention was nearly at an end. The Mexican government dallied for a time with Treat before rebuffing him for his lack of proper credentials, and when Webb arrived at Veracruz, officials would not allow him to disembark for the journey up to Mexico City.[36]

A good reason for the envoys' failure was that Lamar was threatening the Mexicans with offensive action at the same time. The most sensitive area under dispute was the lower valley of the Rio Grande, a land which Stephen Austin had called "the poorest I ever saw in my life" but which Texas claimed, as far as the river, on somewhat dubious grounds.[37] Here legitimate trade, smuggling, and Indians created an atmosphere of great confusion. Soon after Lamar became president he obtained authorization from Congress to start a line of defensive forts through the disputed area. By 1839 the chronic federalism of northeastern Mexico had produced a

ham, April 25, 1839, No. 9, GB, FO, 50/122B, ff. 17–26.

36. For the correspondence of the three Texan commissioners, see Garrison, *DCRT*, II, 431–766, *passim*. Asa Kyrus Christian, *Mirabeau Buonaparte Lamar*, pp. 135–55. Vicente Riva Palacio, *México a través de los siglos*, IV, 442–43. Siegel, *Texas Republic*, pp. 121–36, 151–54. The course of Pakenham's supporting negotiations may be followed in his dispatches: GB, FO, 50/125, ff. 71–75, 156–58; 50/126, ff. 180–85, 241–44; 50/127, ff. 193–97, 201–2; 50/134, ff. 7–9, 157–64; 50/135, 152–

54, 244; 50/136, ff. 83–86; 50/137, ff. 79–83; 50/138, ff. 64–71, 146–51. For his pains, a Mexico City newspaper accused Pakenham of having accepted a Texan bribe to tender his good offices. GB, FO 50/145, ff. 319–22. Ephraim Douglass Adams, *British Interests and Activities in Texas, 1838–1846*, Chaps. 1–2, *passim*.

37. Quoted in Nance, *After San Jacinto*, p. 6. For a concise account of the early stages of the Rio Grande boundary question, see William Campbell Binkley, *The Expansionist Movement in Texas, 1836–1850*, Chap. 1.

secessionist movement that proclaimed the Republic of the Rio Grande, with an indefinite boundary and a migratory capital, part of the time located within the limits of Texas. Lamar did not formally recognize this would-be republic, lest he imperil further his own negotiations with Mexico, but the secessionists recruited men, money, and supplies in Texas. Unfortunately, their generalship against Mexican forces was as bad as that of Santa Anna at San Jacinto. After a disastrous defeat or two the Republic of the Rio Grande disintegrated, and the surviving Texan volunteers straggled back across the border.[38]

A second theater of Texan operations was the Gulf of Mexico. During the revolution a few Texan ships had operated out of American ports, most of them carrying reinforcements and supplies, for Mexican merchant ships were too few and too poor to attract privateers. After San Jacinto the independent government managed to outfit a miniature navy, led by ambitious American commodores who had resigned their regular commands. Because of the French blockade and attack on Veracruz in 1838 and 1839, the activities of the Texan navy probably impressed the Mexicans more than its strength warranted. In September 1841 the Texan government negotiated a defensive alliance with the secessionist state government of Yucatán, which agreed to pay $8,000 a month for the use of three Texan warships as raiders. In the following spring, however, an adventurer from Havana, Francisco Sentmanat, obtained control over the Yucatecan government and signed a truce with Santa Anna, the new president of Mexico, on the basis of practical state autonomy. In spite of the truce, Yucatán and Texas maintained friendly relations, and the Texan warships, hovering like mosquitoes off the Mexican coast, were an irritation to the Mexican government, if not a real threat.[39]

Lamar's most ambitious assault against Mexico and his most disastrous failure was his attempt to capture Santa Fe, the principal Mexican settlement of the upper Rio Grande Valley. Here Texan expansionism cut across the interests of the United States, for overland trade with Santa Fe had formed one of the principal subjects of Poinsett's negotiations with Mexico until the commercial treaty of 1831 legalized it. By that time caravans of traders were regularly plying between Independence, Missouri, and Santa Fe, and during the 1830s and early 1840s the trade grew steadily,

38. Nance, *After San Jacinto*, Chaps. 5–6, 9–14, *passim*.

39. Jim Dan Hill, *The Texas Navy in Forgotten Battles and Shirtsleeve Diplomacy*, pp. 40, 101–2, 123–58, *et passim*. Hubert H. Bancroft, *History of Mexico*, V, 217–19.

despite attacks by Indians and the rapacity of Mexican customs collectors. Until 1844 the total value of American exports probably averaged under $130,000 a year, but the growing population of the Ohio Valley looked on Santa Fe as a promising secondary outlet for its products.[40]

Soon after independence various Texan leaders made plans to claim the Rio Grande as boundary, to the source of the river, and to divert the Santa Fe trade down the Colorado or some other Texan river to ports on the Gulf. When Bee and Treat failed to obtain from the Mexican government recognition of the desired boundary, Lamar decided to establish it by force. Operating on vague authority from his Congress and on the dubious assumption that the inhabitants of Santa Fe would prefer Texan to Mexican rule, he sent out a combined military and trading expedition in the spring of 1841—over three hundred men with twenty-three wagons, loaded variously with supplies and merchandise. From the beginning everything went wrong. Crossing a little-known, arid country, the expedition fell behind its schedule and then divided into two parts. Indian attacks and hunger weakened the men; discipline slackened. As both parties neared Santa Fe, a guide betrayed one of them to the Mexican garrison, and eventually both surrendered ignominiously. Proclaiming a great victory over the ambitious Texan adventurers, the Mexican commander executed some of the prisoners and sent others off to Mexico City in chains.[41]

When news of the disaster reached the capital of Texas, Lamar had already turned the presidency back to Sam Houston. The collapse of the expedition discredited Texas before the world and encouraged Mexico to continue its unprofitable policy of nonrecognition and border skirmishes. In March 1842 a small Mexican force drove the even smaller Texan garrison out of San Antonio and held it for two days; in September, during another raid on San Antonio, the Mexicans took several dozen prisoners. These pinpricks naturally goaded the Texans to retaliate, and with some private aid from Americans Houston marshaled troops along the

40. Callahan, *Mexican Relations*, pp. 45–47. Cardinal Goodwin, *The Trans-Mississippi West (1803–1853)*, pp. 139–45. Josiah Gregg estimated American exports to Santa Fe at $450,000 in 1843 and the total North Mexican trade from all sources at about $5,000,000. For a description of this trade and its influence on the Texans, see Noel M. Loomis, *The Texan–Santa Fe Pioneers*, p. 167. For evidence of contemporary enthusiasm about the trade with northern Mexico, see *NNR*, 59 (October 31, 1840), 130–31; 62 (March 12, 1842), 19.

41. Binkley, *Expansionist Movement*, Chaps. 2, 4. Loomis, *Texan–Santa Fe Pioneers, passim*. Thomas Maitland Marshall, "Commercial Aspects of the Texan Santa Fe Expedition," *The Southwestern Historical Quarterly*, 20 (January 1917), 242–59.

frontier. The Texans made some raids across the Rio Grande and then, disobeying their commander, attacked the town of Mier, where the Mexicans beat them off with heavy casualties and took over two hundred prisoners, many of whom they later executed. Other border actions during early 1843 led to an impasse. Neither Texas nor Mexico could conduct a successful invasion; neither would admit defeat.[42]

*　*　*　*

During the difficult years after San Jacinto, while the Texan government was trying to achieve stability at home, it kept agents busy in Europe seeking formal recognition and loans. In addition to these ostensible goals, many Texans undoubtedly hoped that success in Europe might induce Mexico to recognize their independence or the United States to reconsider annexation.

Late in 1837 J. Pinckney Henderson tried to persuade Palmerston to grant British recognition to Texas, holding out the lure of trade in Texan cotton and British manufactures. Palmerston realized the danger of Texan annexation to the United States, but the uprisings in Canada made him reluctant to condone any other revolution. Also, British holders of Mexican bonds, newly refunded on the security of public lands on the northern frontier (see Chapter 2), urged the government not to weaken their chances of repayment, and abolitionists argued loudly against opening relations with another slaveholding nation. Consequently, Palmerston postponed judgment while promising to admit Texan ships to British ports on a temporary basis.[43]

In the spring of 1838 Henderson extended his mission to Paris. The government of Louis Philippe, already at swords' point with Mexico, was not restrained by bondholders or abolitionists, and it was eager to gain advantage over British trade. Being uncer-

42. On the effects of the Santa Fe expedition, see Binkley, *Expansionist Movement*, p. 96; and Nance, *After San Jacinto*, pp. 519–20. The ensuing border skirmishes are briefly related in Rives, *US and Mexico*, I, 485–94, and almost day by day in Joseph Milton Nance, *Attack and Counter-attack, the Texas–Mexican Frontier, 1842, passim*.

43. Mary Katherine Chase, *Négociations de la République du Texas en Europe, 1837–1845*, pp. 18–23. Joseph William Schmitz, *Texan Statecraft, 1836–1845*, pp. 63–66. Garrison, *DCRT*,

III, 1241. The whole course of Texan negotiations for European recognition may be followed in this volume. See also Carlos Bosch García, *Material para la historia diplomática de México*, p. 201. For comments on the Mexican debt conversion plan and the position of the abolitionists, see Mary Lee Spence, "British Interests and Attitudes Regarding the Republic of Texas and Its Annexation by the United States," Ph.D. diss., University of Minnesota, 1956–1957, pp. 13–20, 136–40.

tain of Texas' survival as a sovereign state, however, France also contented herself with a temporary commercial arrangement while sending the secretary of the Washington legation to inspect the new republic. This man, the young, ambitious, and impetuous Count Alphonse de Saligny, reported favorably on Texan independence and economic conditions; observations by Admiral Charles Baudin, visiting on his way home from the occupation of Veracruz, confirmed this impression. Therefore, France formally recognized Texas with a commercial treaty, dated September 25, 1839.[44]

By this time Texas had sent another diplomat to the Continent to reinforce Henderson's efforts. This was James Hamilton, aggressive and able, a former governor of South Carolina and an eager promoter of Texan securities. The best example of Hamilton's methods is a memorandum which he submitted to Palmerston on October 14, 1840, outlining in shrewd, realistic terms what Britain would gain from close relations with Texas: new trade, a neutral source of cotton in case of war with the United States, the probability of peace between Texas and Mexico, repayment by Texas of part of the Mexican debt, and a check against further American expansion. If England withheld recognition, he warned, Texas might blockade the Mexican coast, support revolutions in northern Mexico, levy a differential tariff against British goods, and come to terms with "some continental nation."[45]

Apparently Palmerston was impressed, for during the following month he and Hamilton signed three treaties.[46] These treaties constituted formal recognition, but the weakening Whig cabinet made no immediate move to ratify them. In addition to this disappointment, Hamilton failed to obtain a European loan. In February 1841 he managed to sign a preliminary agreement with the

---

44. Chase, *Négociations du Texas*, pp. 23–43. Schmitz, *Texan Statecraft*, pp. 66–80. On French negotiations and the decision to recognize, see France, MAE, CP, Texas, I, ff. 76–95, 247–53, 329–37, 338–43; II, ff. 4–21, 69–71. On Baudin's visit, see P. Blanchard and A. Dauzats, *San Juan de Ulua*, pp. 522–72. On the commercial treaty, see Henderson to D. G. Burnet, October 16, 1839, Garrison, *DCRT*, III, 1271–75.

45. Chase, *Négociations du Texas*, pp. 43–44, 53–60. Adams, *British Interests*, Chap. 2, *passim*. Hamilton's memorandum to Palmerston is reprinted on

pp. 53–54. He wrote similarly urgent letters to British ministers Fox in Washington and Pakenham in Mexico City. Garrison, *DCRT*, III, 867–70, 881–84.

46. Adams, *British Interests*, pp. 54–60. For the reports of the Mexican minister in London, Tomás Murphy, and a British memorandum of March 11, 1841, explaining the treaties and offering mediation, see US, LC, /53. Hamilton also signed a commercial treaty with Holland on September 18. Chase, *Négociations du Texas*, pp. 65–66.

French banking house of J. Lafitte et Cie. An international paper of such importance required approval by the French government, however, and several chilly articles in the official journals frightened off the bankers.[47] In England Hamilton tried to persuade the new foreign secretary, Lord Aberdeen, to guarantee a Belgian loan in return for commercial concessions. Unfortunately, Aberdeen was less susceptible to Hamilton's dashing manner than Palmerston and more eager for peaceful relations with the United States, where Lord Ashburton was even then carrying on delicate negotiations. He therefore rejected the proposal, and Hamilton returned to Texas.[48]

Meanwhile, both Britain and France sent minor diplomats to live in Texas (or in New Orleans when they needed relief from sickness or frontier crudeness). At the beginning of 1840 Saligny arrived at the capital of Texas as French chargé d'affaires, with a wagon train of gilded furniture, carpets, tapestries, paintings, and fine wines. Characteristically, he paid off his teamsters in counterfeit notes. His reports to Paris complained about the Texan officials, whom he treated with much condescension, and about British machinations.[49]

With some support from the pro-Houston faction, which was then out of power, Saligny got a bill introduced in Congress for the incorporation of the Franco–Texienne Colonization Company and a grant of three million acres in western Texas for the introduction of eight thousand French families, as a nucleus of future influence. Colonization projects were commonplace in Texas of the 1840s, but the Franco–Texienne grant was unusual for its size and provisions for autonomy, and it naturally aroused British suspicions. To Saligny's great indignation, President Lamar stifled the project, largely for political reasons. At about this time the French chargé became involved in an undignified quarrel with a neighbor over the killing of some pigs that had been eating Sali-

---

47. Chase, *Négociations du Texas,* pp. 77–82. Schmitz, *Texan Statecraft,* pp. 152–61. Herbert Rook Edwards, "Diplomatic Relations between France and the Republic of Texas," *The Southwestern Historical Quarterly,* 20 (January 1917), 233–35.

48. Chase, *Négociations du Texas,* pp. 82–98. Adams, *British Interests,* pp. 67–72 *et passim.* On Hamilton's loan negotiations in Holland and Belgium, see Chase, *Négociations du Tex-*

as, *passim,* and Schmitz, *Texan Statecraft,* pp. 143–47, 162–67. Aberdeen's rejection was partly based on an unfavorable analysis of the Texan economic situation by Chancellor of the Exchequer Henry Goulburn, GB, FO 75/2, ff. 151–52, 154–56.

49. Herbert Gambrell, *Anson Jones, the Last President of Texas,* pp. 187, 220. France, MAE, CP, Texas, II, ff. 273–92; III, ff. 39–42, 95–101, 216–18, 246, 247. Garrison, *DCRT,* III, 1329–30.

gny's corn. When the Texan government failed to support him as he had expected, Saligny stomped off to New Orleans in a rage and remained there for months.[50]

Britain's representatives were somewhat less temperamental. Late in 1841 Aberdeen appointed as consul in Galveston William Kennedy, a publicist who had written an enthusiastic book promoting colonization in Texas. Because of rivalry with other promoters and bad publicity from fraudulent projects, however, Kennedy had little success in attracting British immigrants.[51] A more influential British agent was the chargé d'affaires, appointed in the following year, Captain Charles Elliot, R.N. Elliot was a rangy, weather-beaten man who usually wore a flopping white hat, smoked a great pipe, and looked more like a cattleman than a sailor or a diplomat. Drifting about in the British Foreign Service, he had acquired a strong dislike for slavery in British Guiana and a reputation for independent action as Senior Superintendent of Trade in China during the Opium War. The British government had recalled him with disapproval and probably intended his assignment to Texas as cautionary exile.[52]

Elliot has been described as combining the characteristics of "the political dreamer and the honest philanthropist with . . . strong underlying patriotism," but as lacking a grasp of practical details.[53] He arrived at his post in ill health, from which he suffered intermittently thereafter, but despite this handicap, he soon won the friendship of President Houston. He began to weave together his instructions from Aberdeen, his observations in Texas, and his own predispositions into a set of ambitious and incompatible goals. In order to strengthen Texas against American expansion, he would increase British influence and encourage the Texan government gradually to incorporate northern Mexico as far as Tampico. At the same time he hoped to stimulate abolitionism in Texas —a movement that was, naturally, unpopular with Texan landowners. As a result of his plans he hoped that foreign merchants

50. Christian, *Lamar*, pp. 112–13. Bernice Barton Denton, "Count Alphonse de Saligny and the Franco-Texienne Bill," *The Southwestern Historical Quarterly*, 45 (October 1941), 136–46. Edwards, "France and Texas," ibid., 20 (April 1917), 342–44. On British suspicions, see William Kennedy to Aberdeen, September 22, 1841, Aberdeen Papers, BM, AM, vol. 43126, ff. 88–89. Correspondence on the pig episode is in Garrison, *DCRT*, III, 1303–4, 1344–51.

51. Spence, "British Interests and Attitudes," pp. 7–8, 70–75, 86–95, 101–4. Adams, *British Interests*, pp. 72–78.

52. Gambrell, *Jones*, p. 277. Clagette Blake, *Charles Elliot, R.N., 1801–1875, a Servant of Britain Overseas*, Chaps. 1–4. Adams, *British Interests*, pp. 106–8.

53. Adams, *British Interests*, pp. 115–16.

and capital would soon infiltrate the rich Texan regions peacefully and offset the power of the United States in North America gradually and without open provocation.[54]

Elliot's ambitions were further advanced than those of the British government, for Peel and Aberdeen were still trying to decide on a policy toward Texas. Many conflicting considerations were involved: British desire for trade and a secure source of cotton, the agitation of British abolitionists and British investors with interests in Mexico, the desire to follow a parallel policy with France in the New World, and the hope of restraining the expansion of the United States without reviving its Anglophobia.[55]

Signs of indecision were unmistakable in British policy toward Texas through much of 1842. In the spring, for example, it became known that British shipyards were constructing two modern steam warships for Mexico, clearly intended for use against Texas. When the Mexican minister requested permission to have the ships armed, Aberdeen refused, but he offered no objection to a separate purchase of armaments. Despite the protests of Ashbel Smith, the newly arrived Texan chargé d'affaires in Britain, the first of the ships sailed for Mexico at the beginning of July, heavily armed, and manned by British sailors and a commander on leave from the Royal Navy. For a time Texan agents, working through the British customs office, were able to delay the sailing of the second warship. By the time it too departed in September, the British government had ordered it stripped of arms and had canceled

54. Charles Elliot to H. U. Addington, November 15, 1842, Ephraim Douglass Adams, ed., *British Diplomatic Correspondence Concerning the Republic of Texas, 1838–1846*, pp. 125–30. The quotation is on p. 128. However, Elliot felt that for the time being Texas should follow a strictly defensive policy toward Mexico and deplored the Santa Fe expedition. Elliot to Aberdeen, November 2 (pp. 121–24). On Elliot's fears of American expansion, see same, January 28, 1843 (pp. 154–56). Elliot believed Houston to be the only man who could save Texas from the United States. Adams speculates on the possibility that Houston may have helped to develop the abolitionist part of Elliot's project. Adams, *British Interests*, pp. 109–20.

55. Rives, *US and Mexico*, I, 536–38. Britain was willing to publicize and

encourage the Texan cotton industry in order to relieve herself from dependence on the United States but was less anxious to develop the Texan sugar industry, lest it compete with that of the British West Indies. Evidence of the connection between British holders of Mexican bonds and the Texas question is found in the activities of Robert Crichton Wyllie, an Anglo–Mexican merchant and member of the Committee of Spanish American Bondholders, who returned to London in the late 1830s and helped to sponsor Nicholas D. Maillard's unfavorable *History of Texas*, published in 1842. However, Wyllie's motivation may have been to stimulate British influence in California rather than to strengthen Mexican finances. Spence, "British Interests and Attitudes," pp. 110–11, 113, 119–20, 146–55.

leaves from the navy for its intended crew. British Consul Kennedy warned Aberdeen that these ships would drive Texas into the Americans' arms, but the foreign secretary gave Smith a full defense of British actions.[56]

While the argument over the warships was going on, Aberdeen and Smith were amicably exchanging ratifications of Palmerston's treaties and establishing regular diplomatic relations. During the summer the Texan minister proposed joint mediation by Britain, France, and the United States between Mexico and Texas. After consultation with Guizot, Aberdeen decided that he preferred independent action, and later in the year Pakenham presented a British mediation proposal in Mexico City without success. It is possible that Aberdeen's action was due to his disappointment at the limited scope of the Webster–Ashburton Treaty and to a resulting belief that he must encourage Texas more than heretofore.[57] If so, he was beginning to move in the same direction as Elliot. In any case, at that point both Santa Anna and Houston had some reason to hope for British friendship and support.

*   *   *   *

Throughout the period between the Texan revolution and the end of 1842 the relations between Texas and Europe produced varying reactions in the United States. A rumor that Britain intended to purchase the province from Mexico had circulated in Washington as early as 1837, but it did not prevent the Van Buren administration from declining the Texans' proposal of annexation to the United States.[58] For a time, the rejected suitor felt strong

56. Adams, *British Interests*, pp. 83–93. Spence, "British Interests and Attitudes," pp. 159–66. Kennedy to Aberdeen, London, June 25, 1842, Aberdeen Papers, BM, AM, vol. 43126, ff. 94–97. Aberdeen to Elliot, July 16, 1842. Adams, *British Correspondence*, pp. 91–92. The first ship, the *Guadalupe*, was the first iron-hulled steam warship in the world to be launched and the largest iron vessel up to that time. Tom Henderson Wells, *Commodore Moore and the Texas Navy*, p. 118.

57. Adams, *British Interests*, pp. 94–96. Rives believes that Aberdeen was genuinely undecided, being too little acquainted with American affairs. Rives, *US and Mexico*, I, 541–45. Aberdeen to Lord Cowley, October 15, 1842, No. 147; Cowley to Aberdeen, October 24, No. 349, GB, FO 27/646, 27/652 (no

pagination). At the time, Ashbel Smith suspected that Britain was following a "soft" policy toward Mexico partly because she would need Mexican aid if war developed with the United States and partly because she wanted to preserve her commercial monopoly in Mexico. Smith to Jones, November 30, 1842. Garrison, *DCRT*, III, 1401–2. A factor working against Mexico was the discovery in November that the official government agent in London had made an unauthorized issue of Mexican bonds.

58. Garrison, "First Stage of the Movement for Annexation," pp. 85–87. J. L. Worley, "The Diplomatic Relations of England and the Republic of Texas," *The Quarterly of the Texas State Historical Association*, 9 (July 1905), 2–3. Norman E. Tuterow, "Whigs

resentment against the United States government, and the Lamar administration opposed any renewal of the offer.

For their part, the American people lost interest in Texas, and discussion of the new republic virtually disappeared from northern newspapers for weeks at a time. Van Buren, who as Jackson's secretary of state had supported early efforts to purchase Texas from Mexico, probably favored annexation, but, realizing the strength of the opposition, he kept quiet and awaited developments. In 1839 Secretary of State Forsyth made a half-hearted attempt at mediation between Texas and Mexico. A year later, however, when the Texan agent James Treat appeared in Mexico City to negotiate for recognition, American Minister Ellis refused to meet him publicly, lest he offend the Mexican government and prejudice Ellis' negotiations for payment of claims.[59]

Nevertheless, since blood and business are often more potent than diplomacy, behind the appearance of indifference solid connections were developing between the United States and Texas. From the beginning, New Orleans was the center of Texan business affairs, and as the city recovered from the panic of 1837, its trade with Texas rose sharply, while that with Mexico declined. Between 1837 and 1839 American exports to Texas increased from $1,007,928 to $1,687,086, and imports from $163,284 to $318,116.[60]

Even more powerful was the silver cord made up of loans and speculation in Texan lands. As early as 1835 Stephen F. Austin and William H. Wharton visited the United States to sell lands, and as soon as the Republic of Texas came into existence it began to peddle bonds and land scrip on almost any available terms. Many prominent Americans were soon taking a financial interest in the new country, among them Samuel Swartwout, who was collector of the port of New York, a son of DeWitt Clinton, ex-governor Thomas W. Gilmer of Virginia, and Duff Green, the Jacksonian editor who later became Tyler's special emissary in England. Gilmer and Green in particular combined their Texan speculations with political agitation for annexation, since both

of the Old Northwest and Texas Annexation, 1836–April 1844," *Indiana Magazine of History*, 66 (March 1970), 56–62, 67.

59. Smith, *Annexation of Texas*, pp. 68–72. McCormac, "Forsyth," in Samuel F. Bemis, ed., *American Secretaries of State and Their Diplomacy*, IV, 327–28. Rives, *US and Mexico*, I, 533. Callahan, *Mexican Relations*, pp. 90–91.

Powhatan Ellis to Forsyth, March 9, 1840, No. 14, US, DS, D, Mexico, IX. However, between 1837 and 1841 the United States and Texas managed to trace their common boundary. Marshall, *Western Boundary*, Chap. 11.

60. *The Economist*, No. 34 (April 20, 1844), pp. 713–14. Winston, "Notes on Commercial Relations," pp. 91–105, *passim*.

had many friends in the Jackson and Calhoun wings of the Democratic party.[61]

The Texas question crossed all factional lines. Perhaps the principal American speculator-annexationist between 1837 and 1841 was Nicholas Biddle, president of the United States Bank and no great friend of either Jackson or Calhoun. Biddle and his business associate, the Texan loan commissioner James Hamilton, both invested heavily in Texan paper, and in 1839 the United States Bank agreed to advance $400,000 in return for £94,000 of Texan 10 per cent bonds. Biddle used his connections with both parties in behalf of Texas—on one occasion he tried in vain to get Van Buren to insert a "kind word about Texas" in an annual message, and on another he asked Webster for the Austrian legation in order to be able to support Texan loans abroad.[62]

After 1841 an increasingly important "contact man" for Texas was Robert J. Walker, a senator from Mississippi who was usually up to his ears in debt but by skillful borrowing and the use of political influence carried on active speculation in Western lands. Both Biddle and Walker favored annexation, but Walker went beyond Texas and built up fond expansionist dreams of an American empire stretching across prairies and mountains to the Pacific.[63]

"Texas fever" was beginning to break out here and there in Congress by 1840, but it did not spread to the Executive until the following year, when John Tyler succeeded to the Presidency. After his break with Clay and the Whigs over the Bank and the tariff, friends directed Tyler's attention to the issue of annexation. As he put it to Webster: "Could the North be reconciled to it, would any thing throw so bright a lustre around us?"[64] Knowing the strength of abolitionism in New England, Webster could not give an enthusiastic answer. As 1842 began, however, he could not deny that American interest in Texas was reviving. This interest arose partly from sympathy for the plight of the Texan prisoners captured at Santa Fe and Mier and partly from a fear "that the

61. Williams, *Animating Pursuits*, Chap. 5, especially pp. 140–49.

62. Williams, *Animating Pursuits*, pp. 100–108, 147–48. Siegel, *Texas Republic*, p. 114. Thomas Payne Govan, *Nicholas Biddle, Nationalist and Public Banker, 1786–1844*, pp. 353–54, 389.

63. H. D. Jordan, "A Politician of Expansion: Robert J. Walker," *Mississippi Valley Historical Review*, 19 (1932–1933), 363–68. James Patrick

Shenton, *Robert John Walker, a Politician from Jackson to Lincoln*, Chap. 3. James C. N. Paul, *Rift in the Democracy*, pp. 26–27.

64. Paul, *Rift in the Democracy*, pp. 27–29. John Tyler to Daniel Webster, Washington, October 11, 1841. *The Letters of Daniel Webster from Documents Owned Principally by the New Hampshire Historical Society*, ed. C. H. Van Tyne, pp. 239–40.

poverty of Texas would ultimately gain Great Brittain [*sic*] a pretext to claim the country." On March 17 the New Orleans *Commercial Bulletin* advised Texas to "call to her standard the thousands of impatient, daring, and ambitious spirits in the South West, by whom a march to the city of Montezuma would be embraced as an adventure full of fun and frolic, and holding the rewards of opulence and glory."[65]

At this point Tyler and Webster decided to replace Ellis as minister to Mexico with a more energetic man. They chose Waddy Thompson of South Carolina—reluctantly, since he was a Clay Whig who had been promised the post by the late President Harrison—and instructed him to do all he could for the release of the Santa Fe prisoners. Thompson also determined of his own accord to work for the annexation of Texas.[66] When he arrived in Mexico City, he found an atmosphere of bitter resentment against Americans for supporting the Texans' forays across the border. On May 31 Mexico's Foreign Minister José María Bocanegra denounced American influence in a dramatic letter to the diplomatic corps. The note may have been inspired by European diplomats, as Thompson suspected, or by Santa Anna's desire to save face and offset the effect of the Webster–Ashburton negotiations. Thompson stoutly defended his government, insisting that American aid to Texas had been private and irrepressible. Webster backed Thompson with renewed assurances of United States neutrality, but the incident increased tensions and made American mediation in Texas unthinkable for months thereafter. When Houston offered to discuss the annexation question in July, Tyler showed no interest.[67]

There were other reasons for Tyler's caution. American claims against Mexico were still unpaid. Furthermore, on September 17 John Quincy Adams delivered a fiery anti-Texan speech to his constituents at Braintree, Massachusetts, declaring scornfully

65. New Orleans *Commercial Bulletin*, March 17, 1842, as quoted in Smith, *Annexation of Texas*, p. 49. Joseph Eve to John White, Austin, December 29, 1841, reprinted in *Southwestern Historical Quarterly*, 43 (October 1939), 220. On American opinion regarding Texas during 1842, see Smith, *Annexation of Texas*, pp. 72–74.

66. Lyon G. Tyler, *The Letters and Times of the Tylers*, II, 268. Waddy Thompson to N. B. Tucker, Edgefield, March 13, 1842, reprinted in *William and Mary Quarterly*, series 1, 12 (January 1904), 152–54. For Webster's instructions to Thompson, see Manning, *IAA*, VIII, 105–8. Many prisoners were eventually released at the instance of European diplomatic representatives in Mexico.

67. Manning, *IAA*, VIII, pp. 110–21, 491, 493–96, 503–10. Most of the correspondence is conveniently summarized in Rives, *US and Mexico*, I, 509–16. Jesse Reeves, *American Diplomacy under Tyler and Polk*, p. 118. Zorrilla, *Relaciones entre México y Estados Unidos*, I, 157–59.

that "land-jobbing—stock-jobbing—slave-jobbing—rights of man-jobbing were all hand in hand sweeping over the land like a hurricane" and denouncing "the slave-breeding conspiracy against the freedom of the north."[68] Intemperate though it was, the speech appeared widely in the press and gave the annexation of Texas a persistent ideological taint. Later in the fall Houston tried to reopen the question with Tyler, but the President would not listen. To be sure, a few Southerners, led by Calhoun, were working quietly for annexation and trying to raise the specter of British meddling in the Western Hemisphere, but even in the South, pro-Texas sentiment was far from unanimous.[69]

In December 1842 the Mexican minister, Juan N. Almonte, wrote home that, on the evidence of expressions in the press, American opinion had never been so favorable to Mexico.[70] Thanks to a more active British policy, pro-Texan propaganda, and the shifting pattern of American politics, this condition would soon change. Even while Almonte wrote, the opposing forces were organizing for a showdown, and the new year was to thrust the Texas question to the fore in American public affairs.

68. Reprinted in *NNR*, 63, 136–40.
69. Reeves, *American Diplomacy under Tyler and Polk*, pp. 119–22. Charles M. Wiltse, *John C. Calhoun, Sectionalist, 1840–1850*, p. 151. Charles S. Sydnor, *The Development of Southern Sectionalism, 1819–1848*, p. 322. For an example of Southern anti-Texas sentiment, see a quotation from the Macon (Georgia) *Telegraph*, n.d., in *NNR*, 62 (April 9, 1842), 83.
70. Juan N. Almonte to Ministerio de Relaciones Exteriores, December 12, 1842, No. 26, Barker transcripts, vol. 569, p. 3. At this time, of course, Almonte had not yet learned of Jones' seizure of Monterey (see Chapter 4). Contrast the wary, suspicious attitude of Elliot at the same time, commenting from Texas on Tyler's annual message. Elliot to Addington, December 28. Adams, *British Correspondence*, pp. 145–48.

4

The Border Provinces:
California and Oregon

By the early 1840s two other border areas, somewhat less developed than Texas, had attracted the attention of American expansionists. Although Spain had once claimed both areas, she renounced her interest in Oregon just before Mexico became independent, and Mexico inherited both Upper and Lower California intact. As soon as the Texans declared their sovereign state, however, they argued that its western boundaries included San Francisco Bay, the Pacific coast to the south, Lower California, and Sonora. At one point in Sam Houston's imperial reveries he suggested the possibility of a union between Texas and Oregon, along with the Californias and a large area of northern Mexico.[1]

There was not much likelihood that the Texans could make good their claims unaided, but behind them the government and people of the United States were moving westward with irresistible momentum. By 1841 Sir George Simpson, the territorial governor of the Hudson's Bay Company, was writing: "The only doubt is whether California is to fall to the British or the Americans."[2] In Oregon Britain and the United States were competing for possession too, but without concern for the rights of any third party but the Indians.

Until the late 1830s events in California and Oregon followed clearly separate lines of development. At that time the problems of the two border areas began to converge, as American settlers trickled westward into both of them, arousing alarm in Mexico and in Europe. The stakes were high—fertile lands, rich deposits of minerals, and the fine harbors in San Francisco Bay and Puget Sound. Even more abundantly than Texas the provinces of California and Oregon offered to an ambitious United States the ingredients of future greatness.

1. William Campbell Binkley, *The Expansionist Movement in Texas, 1836–1850*, Chap. 2. See especially a map opposite p. 38. Sam Houston to William S. Murphy, May 6, 1844, *The Writings of Sam Houston*, ed. Amelia W. Williams and Eugene C. Barker, IV, 320–

25. In this study the name *California* will be used to designate the area which the Spaniards and the Mexicans called *Upper California*.

2. Sir George Simpson, *Narrative of a Journey Round the World, during the Years 1841, and 1842*, I, 408–9.

*   *   *   *

Settled during the eighteenth century, Upper California was tied to New Spain mainly by the missionary activities of the Jesuits and the Franciscans. At the beginning of the nineteenth century foreigners rarely visited its shores, although a few trading vessels from New England, Britain, and Russia were beginning to take sea otter skins from the northern part of the coast for sale in China.[3]

After the Mexican war for independence, California was wretchedly neglected—the mission economy disintegrating, the Indians disease-ridden, and the integrity of the territory threatened by Russian expansion from the north. With much reluctance the population of thirty thousand (nine-tenths of them Indians) accepted Mexican authority. To encourage secular colonization and thus frustrate the Russians, the Mexican governments of the 1820s planned to divide the landholdings of the missions. These plans were not actually carried out until 1833–1834, coincident with the liberal reforms of Valentín Gómez Farías. Since few of the Indians were ready for the responsibility of landownership, the mission lands became *ranchos* and passed into the hands of the Mexican creole minority.[4] The projected large-scale colonization failed to develop, and in the long run the disappearance of the missions probably loosened California's ties to Mexico.

By 1835 the export of sea otters from the northern coast was declining, and a flourishing trade in cowhides and supplies for Pacific whalers was taking its place. British and New England ships brought hardware, clothing, boots, furniture, and other manufactures from the eastern United States. These ships often spent months in California ports or trading along the coast, and they departed, loaded with hides, which doubled in value by the time they arrived at Boston or New York. The trade reached its peak with the export of 200,000 hides in 1838 and then declined as the missions broke up and the Mexican government raised tariffs and added new fees. Imports continued, however, for the Yankee and other

3. Except where noted, this general summary is based on Hubert Howe Bancroft, *History of California*; Irving Berdine Richman, *California under Spain and Mexico, 1535–1847*; John Walton Caughey, *California*; and Robert Glass Cleland, *From Wilderness to Empire: a History of California, 1542–*

1900. On the sea otter trade, see Adele Ogden, *The California Sea Otter Trade, 1784–1848*, pp. 151–52 *et passim*.
4. C. Alan Hutchinson, *Frontier Settlement in Mexican California: the Hijar–Padres Colony and Its Origins, 1769–1835*, Chap. 10 *et passim*.

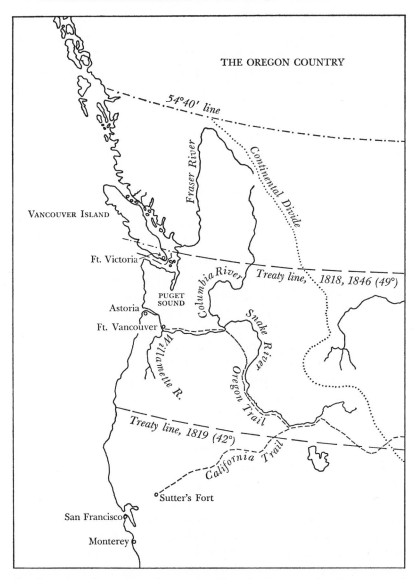

THE OREGON COUNTRY

54°40' line

Fraser River

Continental Divide

VANCOUVER ISLAND

Ft. Victoria

Columbia River   Treaty line, 1818, 1846 (49°)

PUGET SOUND

Astoria

Ft. Vancouver

Snake River

Willamette R.

Oregon Trail

Treaty line, 1819 (42°)

California Trail

Sutter's Fort

San Francisco

Monterey

foreign captains resorted to smuggling, bribery, and other ways of evading the law.[5]

The first nuclei of American influence in California were

5. Eugène Duflot de Mofras, *Travels on the Pacific Coast*, trans. by Marguerite Eyer Wilbur, ed., I, 260–65. Ogden, *Sea Otter Trade*, p. 146. For a sample of the New England trade to California, see Adele Ogden, "Alfred Robinson, New England Merchant in Mexican California," *California Historical Society Quarterly*, 23 (September 1944), 193–202. Sister Magdalen Coughlin, "California Ports: a Key to Diplomacy for the West Coast, 1820–1845," *Journal of the West*, 5 (April 1966), 153–72.

small colonies of New England merchants and shopkeepers at Monterey, Los Angeles, and other points along the coast. Acting independently or as agents of Eastern firms, these men lived quietly on good terms with the local government and with the Spanish-Mexican *rancheros,* for the merchants were, in the main, nonpolitical and interested only in making a reasonable profit.

The most important of these American traders was Thomas O. Larkin, "el Bostoño," who had migrated from Massachusetts to North Carolina as a storekeeper and arrived at Monterey in 1832 to set up a trading post with $500 of borrowed capital. Through hard work and Yankee shrewdness Larkin expanded his business steadily until he was dealing in hides, lumber, sugar, brandy, and New England goods at ports from Oregon to Hawaii and along the whole Pacific coast of Latin America. Soon he was lending money as well—the last two Mexican governors of California never paid their debts to him. There is no evidence that he worked for United States rule in California during the first decade of his residence there, although he declined to become a Mexican citizen and it was noticed that he always celebrated the Fourth of July lavishly.[6]

American interest in the interior of California developed more slowly. Between 1826 and 1828 Jedediah Smith led the first major American exploring expedition across the Sierras to central California and southern Oregon, and during the next decade hardy bands of mountain men crossed the ranges and deserts of the West and Southwest in all directions, usually searching for furs and incidentally filling in blank places on the maps. Their descriptions of the Sacramento and San Joaquin valleys reinforced what Yankee sea captains and writers such as Richard Henry Dana and Hall Jackson Kelley were saying about the California coast. After about 1839 a severe economic depression in the Middle West made farmers more receptive to such publicity. Although most of the resulting migration of the 1840s moved to Oregon, several dozen pioneers under the leadership of a former schoolmaster, John Bidwell, branched off the Oregon Trail to California in 1841, beginning a new generation of American settlers.[7]

6. John A. Hawgood, ed., *First and Last Consul, Thomas Oliver Larkin and the Americanization of California, passim.* See also Rayner Wickersham Kelsey, "The United States Consulate in California," *Annals of the Academy of Pacific Coast History,* 1 (June 1910), 161–267. For a refutation of the common belief that Larkin was an American agent from the beginning, see John A. Hawgood, "The Pattern of Yankee Infiltration in Mexican Alta California, 1821–1846," *Pacific Historical Review,* 27 (1958), 27–30.

7. William H. Goetzmann, *Army Exploration in the American West, 1808–*

The strongest non-Mexican influence in the interior and, generally speaking, a counterpart to Larkin on the coast, was a German Swiss, John A. Sutter, who fled from his creditors to America, crossed the continent by stages, and obtained a land grant on the upper Sacramento River from the California government in 1840. After building a fort and stockade, Sutter founded a quasi-feudal settlement, New Helvetia, comprising Indians and whites of all nationalities, and in the mid-forties welcomed many parties of exhausted, half-starved American emigrants who had straggled across the Sierra. As a suspicious official of the Hudson's Bay Company observed, the fort was admirably situated to challenge Mexican control of all central California. Unlike Larkin, Sutter was a poor businessman, always in debt. After the discovery of gold in 1849, for which he is best known, emigrants overran his holdings, and he lapsed into bankruptcy.[8]

During the late 1830s American and other foreign settlements in California were as yet small, scattered, and generally peaceable, but dissension broke out among factions of native leaders in the north and south. During 1836 a relatively able clique led by Juan Bautista Alvarado, Mariano Vallejo, and José Castro seized power, and American trappers began to talk of another revolution on the pattern of Texas, but Alvarado silenced these mutterings and managed to maintain his rule for a few years. In 1840 he arrested about a hundred American and British residents of the coastal area on unproved charges of conspiracy to revolt and shipped them off to Mexico, where they were imprisoned for a time but eventually released. This incident created a flurry of alarm in Mexico City, and officials issued orders forbidding immigration into California, but there was no way of enforcing them.[9]

In 1842 the Mexican government replaced Alvarado with General Manuel Micheltorena, who brought along with him a bodyguard of three hundred ill-equipped, undisciplined troops. Alvarado, Castro, and their supporters retired northward to bide

1863, passim; Exploration and Empire, the Explorer and the Scientist in the Winning of the American West, Chaps. 2, 4, 5. Rockwell D. Hunt, John Bidwell, a Prince of California Pioneers, passim.

8. James P. Zollinger, Sutter: the Man and His Empire, Pt. II et passim. Richard Dillon, Fool's Gold. The Decline and Fall of Captain John Sutter

of California, Chaps. 2–8. Reuben L. Underhill, From Cowhides to Golden Fleece, pp. 39–41, 51. Simpson, Narrative, I, 326–27, as quoted in George Lockhart Rives, The United States and Mexico, 1821–1848, II, 36.

9. Bancroft, California, IV, 6–41, 108. Richard Pakenham to Viscount Palmerston, July 8, 1841, No. 63, GB, FO 50/145, ff. 306–9.

their time, while foreigners split their allegiance between the two cliques or tried to remain neutral. For all practical purposes, by this time the central government in Mexico City had lost control of affairs in California. Micheltorena maintained a show of defense in the southern area around Los Angeles, but in the north the port of Monterey was garrisoned by fewer than a hundred poorly trained soldiers, with a dozen dismounted, useless cannon, a few muskets and carbines, and three thousand rounds of ammunition. The regular army in the whole of California numbered less than six hundred.[10] Not only were its forces weak, but the central government had also alienated natives and foreigners alike with crippling tariffs and other restrictions that threatened the commercial basis of the economy.

Apparently official United States interest in California began in 1835 with a suggestion from Jackson's unscrupulous minister to Mexico, Anthony Butler, that he might be able to purchase it along with Texas. Jackson authorized Butler to bid for the San Francisco area. During the following year, while Santa Anna was in Washington following his capture at San Jacinto, Jackson offered him $3.5 million for the Bay region, but the matter rested there. Van Buren did not renew Jackson's offer, although Congress published Hall Jackson Kelley's descriptive account of the area in 1839.[11] Under pressure from New England commercial interests, the Navy sent Lieutenant Charles Wilkes on a long reconnaissance of the Pacific coasts and islands between 1838 and 1842. When Wilkes visited California and Oregon in 1841, he pronounced San Francisco Bay and the Strait of Juan de Fuca "two of the finest ports in the world" and predicted that California would free itself from Mexico, annex Oregon, and "perhaps form a state that is destined to control the destinies of the Pacific."[12]

By this time the favorable reports of sea captains, fur traders, and other visitors were beginning to affect the American public, and a groundswell of annexationist sentiment developed. In 1840 and 1841, for example, John J. Warner, for years a resident of California, visited the East Coast to lecture and to publish articles urging the annexation of California and construction of a transcontinental railroad. He warned that England was negotiating with Mexico to purchase San Francisco or the whole province and

10. Robert Glass Cleland, *A History of California: the American Period*, pp. 161–62.
11. Rives, *US and Mexico*, I, 259–60. Binkley, *Expansionist Movement*, Chap. 2, *passim*. Manning, *IAA*, VIII, 33–34.
12. Bancroft, *California*, IV, 257. Richard W. Van Alstyne, *The Rising American Empire*, pp. 126–27.

asked, "Is it not important, then, that instead of permitting it to fall into the hands of our most dangerous rivals, it should be united to our own territory?"[13]

*   *   *   *

European nations were interested in California largely because of its strategic location on the eastern edge of the Pacific basin, where the principal island groups had become the scene of developing colonial rivalries during the 1830s. British and French traders, missionaries, and naval officers established friendly relations and even protectorates over the islanders. In these activities they were supported erratically by their governments, for the Whigs in London lacked the steady imperialist drive and Louis Philippe in Paris the necessary power for a consistent push into the Pacific. For example, the French coveted New Zealand but would not openly challenge the British-sponsored company that had established a base there. France was even more interested in Tahiti, where George Pritchard, a fanatic missionary and consul, almost singlehandedly maintained British influence over the native Queen Pomare, despite Palmerston's categorical refusal to sanction a formal protectorate. In Hawaii, the influences of Britain, France, and the United States were evenly balanced, and although the French created a flurry in 1839 with a naval demonstration and a commercial convention negotiated at cannon's muzzle, they were careful to go no further.[14]

Another factor that drew world attention to the Pacific basin was the rising importance of trade with China. By the 1830s the business dealings of the British East India Company and many less powerful British concerns had been increasing steadily for nearly half a century despite many onerous Chinese restrictions. The basis of this trade was Indian products such as cotton and opium, which merchants smuggled into Chinese ports. Americans, French, Portuguese, and others engaged in this trade, but the British far outstripped all competitors. When Chinese opposition to foreign trade in general and to opium imports in particular reached the flash point in 1839, British ships and troops fought the Opium War and, after three years, forced China to open certain ports on a permanent basis.[15]

13. Quoted in Bancroft, *California*, IV, 259n5.

14. Jean Ingram Brookes, *International Rivalry in the Pacific Islands, 1800–1875*, p. 48, Chaps. 4, 5.

15. Michael Greenberg, *British Trade and the Opening of China, 1800–42*, passim. Edgar Holt, *The Opium Wars in China*, Chaps. 1–12.

International rivalries in the Pacific islands and the Far East enhanced the value of San Francisco Bay and other harbors along the California coast. During the 1830s the principal European threat to California seemed to be Russia, which had held Fort Ross, north of San Francisco, since 1812 and was rumored to be negotiating with Mexico for the purchase of the whole province. Communication lines between colony and homeland were too long, however, and by the end of the decade Russian fortunes in the Western Hemisphere were declining. In 1841 the officials at Fort Ross sold their rights to John A. Sutter.[16]

After the mid-thirties British designs on California seemed far more menacing. At Tepic in western Mexico, for example, the British merchant-consul Eustace Barron was eager to expand British interests on the Pacific. In 1837 the Mexican government refunded the British debt on the mortgage of public lands in the northern provinces (see Chapter 2). Two years later Barron's partner, Alexander Forbes, published an enthusiastic account of California's resources, in which he proposed a quasi-political organization modeled on the British East India Company to administer any bondholders' lands that might be located there. The proposal received polite approval in London, and William Kennedy, the publicist of Texan lands, praised it, but the bondholders preferred land nearer Texas.[17]

In 1840, as has been mentioned, the California officials deported a number of American and British residents to Mexico City on suspicion of plotting rebellion. This action drew the attention of the British minister to Mexico, Richard Pakenham. Probably influenced by Barron and Forbes, he drew up a formal proposal for the establishment of a British colony in California along the lines of Forbes' book, and presented his plan to the Foreign Office. Aberdeen, now foreign secretary, referred it to the Colonial Office, which replied that it had little interest in "the formation of new and distant Colonies, all of which involve heavy direct and still heavier indirect expenditure, besides multiplying the liabilities of misunderstanding and collisions with Foreign Powers." It had even less interest in "a Company of Adventurers, with more or less of the powers of Sovereignty and of Legislation." Pakenham

16. Caughey, *California*, pp. 191–92, 208–10, 247.

17. Lester G. Engelson, "Proposals for the Colonization of California by England in Connection with the Mexican Debt to British Bondholders, 1837–1846," *California Historical Society Quarterly*, 18 (June 1929), 138–39. Alexander Forbes, *California: a History of Upper and Lower California from their First Discovery to the Present Time, Comprising an Account of the Climate, Soil, Natural Productions, Agriculture, Commerce, passim.*

promptly dropped the matter. Since Aberdeen later wrote to Peel confidentially that he could find no records in the Foreign Office of any dealings between the preceding Whig government and Mexico over California, one may assume that American suspicions of the British government at this time were entirely groundless.[18]

There remains to be considered one other source of British influence in California—the Hudson's Bay Company, which was actively expanding its fur-trading operations north of the Columbia River. During the late 1820s and 1830s the Company sent out reconnaissance expeditions into the unsettled parts of northern California, and between 1838 and 1840 its agents began to negotiate with Governor Alvarado for the purchase of livestock and for a license to hunt furs in the area of San Francisco Bay and as far south as the Gulf of California. An amicable arrangement seemed in the offing, and Company officials in Oregon were optimistic, but further reconnaissance showed the furs of the interior to be few and poor in value. When Sir George Simpson inspected California during a world tour in 1841–1842, he commented favorably on the commercial opportunities of San Francisco. Nevertheless, since the Company got no support from the British government, its officials decided to liquidate its interests in California and concentrate its efforts on Oregon. The Company sent a final expedition into the interior in 1842–1843 and maintained an office at Yerba Buena on the Bay until 1846, thereby unintentionally sustaining the Americans' fear of British encroachment.[19]

During the same period French agents were also interested in California but enjoyed no more support from their home government than the British. In the late 1830s several French exploring expeditions cruised along the California coast on their way to or from the central Pacific. Their reports praised the land and resources and expressed some suspicion of British and American influences. In 1840 a young attaché of the French legation in Mexico City, Eugène Duflot de Mofras, arrived in northern California on

18. Engelson, "Proposals for the Colonization of California," pp. 139–40. Ephraim Douglass Adams, "English Interest in the Annexation of California," *American Historical Review*, 14 (July 1909), reprinted in Adams, *British Interests and Activities in Texas, 1838–1846*, pp. 234–64. The communication from the Colonial Office, dated November 23, 1841, is reprinted on p. 240. Earl of Aberdeen to Sir Robert Peel, March 7, 1845, Peel Papers, BM, AM, vol.

40455, f. 7.

19. John S. Galbraith, "A Note on the British Fur Trade in California, 1821–1846," *Pacific Historical Review*, 24 (August 1955), 253–60. Engelson, "Proposals for the Colonization of California," p. 141. Sir George Simpson to Sir John H. Pelly, Honolulu, March 10, 1842. Reprinted in *American Historical Review*, 14 (October 1908), 88–90, 92.

reconnaissance. De Mofras went as far north as Oregon, where agents at the Hudson's Bay Company received him cordially. Their manner cooled, however, because of his loose talk about French power and his general haughtiness. Since his expedition produced only another voluminous description of the California landscape, which for a time was widely read in France, French interest in California declined.[20]

Although European activities in California were mostly sound and fury, they kept American expansionists in a lather of anxiety as the propaganda of Kelley and others began to demonstrate the value of the province. *Niles' National Register* and other nationalistic journals published full details about the debt conversion plan of 1837, reprinted passages from Alexander Forbes' book, and spread fantastic rumors, often contradictory, of Hudson's Bay Company monopolies, Anglo–Mexican purchase treaties, and foreign naval expeditions to seize San Francisco. An editorial from the Baltimore *American*, widely reprinted during 1840, epitomizes the feeling in the States:

> The policy of the British government looks toward nothing more favorably than to the acquisition of territory in different parts of the world. The possession of California would strengthen her in carrying out her pretensions to the Oregon country. . . . The whole coast of the Pacific would thus be in the grasp of a powerful nation—a nation that never lets slip an occasion of extending the limits of her domains. To make the Rocky Mountains the boundary of the United States on the west; to hold the spacious valley between that ridge and the ocean, . . . thus possessing the seaboard, by means of which the commerce with China and the East Indies would be secured to British interests—this would be an attainment worthy of no small effort on the part of Great Britain.[21]

When Daniel Webster became secretary of state in March 1841, he did not share these extreme suspicions of Britain, but as a native of commercial Massachusetts, he had observed European expansion in the Pacific and the Far East with much interest and

20. Abraham P. Nasatir, *French Activities in California, an Archival Calendar-Guide*, pp. 4–19 *et passim*. Rufus K. Wyllys, "French Imperialists in California," *California Historical Society Quarterly*, 8 (June 1929), 116–29.

21. Reprinted in *NNR*, 58 (March 7, 1840), 2. For other samples of anti-British warnings, mostly reprinted from other newspapers, see ibid., 58 (April 4, 1840), 70; 59 (February 13, 1841), 369; 62 (April 30, 1842), 144; 63 (December 17, 1842), 242–43. However, the New York *Courier* retorted that reports of the British purchase of California were based on no solid evidence—simply an assumption that cession was the only way in which Mexico could pay for the two warships she had ordered. Ibid., 63 (January 28, 1843), 337.

was determined to facilitate American trade there. In the following year, therefore, he warned European powers that the United States wanted Hawaii to remain independent and neutral, its commerce open to traders from all nations. Webster also appreciated the potential value of ports in California, but, since he was not a continental expansionist, he could not decide whether they ought to belong to the United States or become part of an independent Pacific nation.[22]

During his negotiations with Ashburton in 1842 he briefly considered ways of acquiring the area around San Francisco Bay. In May his interest in the Pacific coast sharpened after he received a dispatch from Waddy Thompson, in which the new minister to Mexico praised San Francisco and California as "destined to be the granary of the Pacific." Although Thompson was then engaged in a dispute with the Mexican government over American interference in Texas, he was optimistic enough about its outcome to suggest to Webster that Mexico might be willing to exchange Texas and California for the cancellation of her debts to the United States. In a confidential letter to Tyler, Thompson also pointed out that acquisition of California might reconcile the North to the annexation of Texas.[23] Tyler and Webster reacted favorably to this suggestion. The secretary of state authorized Thompson to sound Santa Anna about the possibility of purchasing San Francisco, at least, but he prudently urged Thompson not to let the Mexicans expect a high price: "The cession must be spoken of, rather as a convenience to Mexico, or a mode of discharging her debts. . . . Endeavour to hear, more than you say, to learn more than you communicate."[24]

Meanwhile, news of Thompson's dispute with the Mexican government aroused such anti-British suspicions in the United States that Ashburton felt compelled to present Tyler with an explicit denial that Britain had brought about the dispute as part of

22. Richard W. Van Alstyne, "International Rivalries in the Pacific Northwest," *Oregon Historical Quarterly*, 46 (September 1945), 205–6.
23. Norman A. Graebner, *Empire on the Pacific: a Study in American Continental Expansion*, pp. 70–71. Waddy Thompson to Daniel Webster, April 29, 1842, No. 1, Manning, *IAA*, VIII, 483–84. Thompson to John Tyler, May 9, John Tyler Papers, LC. Jesse Reeves, *American Diplomacy under Tyler and Polk*, pp. 100–101.
24. Webster to Thompson, June 27,

1842, Webster, *Letters*, pp. 269–70. Reeves, *Diplomacy under Tyler and Polk*, pp. 101–2. Six months later, Webster repeated his instruction, suggesting that Mexico would do well to give up her "projects of war, & aggrandisement, & turn her thoughts to peace, & the improvement of her own resources." Webster to Thompson, December 30, Waddy Thompson Papers, University of Texas, as quoted in Glenn W. Price, *Origins of the War with Mexico: the Polk-Stockton Intrigue*, p. 27.

a scheme to acquire California. Perhaps because of this suspicion or because the Webster–Ashburton discussions on Oregon had reached an impasse, the American secretary made a remarkable proposal. He suggested that, if Britain would use its influence to persuade Mexico to cede San Francisco or even the whole coast line from 36° to 42° North latitude, the United States would accept the Columbia River as the Anglo–American boundary in Oregon. Lacking instructions, Ashburton merely remarked that Britain could not take part in the negotiations with Mexico but would not object to the cession of San Francisco. His calm contrasted strongly with the British attitude a year or two later, for in 1842 he exaggerated the strength of the Indians there and doubted that the Americans would soon make "any considerable lodgment on the Pacific."[25]

Webster had little prospect of purchasing San Francisco in 1842 because of Mexican resentment over American aid to Texas. Furthermore, during the autumn occurred a comic-opera incident which raised Mexican Yankeephobia even further. The commander of the American naval squadron in the Pacific, Commodore Thomas ap Catesby Jones, while cruising off the Peruvian coast, received reports of the Thompson–Bocanegra argument in Mexico City. These convinced him that war was about to break out at any moment between the United States and Mexico. Observing the sudden departure of the British squadron from its nearby station, Jones assumed that it had been ordered to intervene in California, so he raced northward to forestall it. On October 19 he entered Monterey harbor with two warships and called on the surprised garrison to surrender. Being utterly defenseless, the commandant complied at once, and Jones raised the United States flag over the Mexican fort. On the next day reliable dispatches informed him of his mistake; he solemnly ordered the flag to be lowered and apologized to the authorities. The incident concluded with banquets and dances given by Larkin and Jones to cover the general embarrassment.[26]

25. Ashburton to Aberdeen, April 25, 1842, No. 2, GB, FO 5/379, quoted in Frederick Merk, *The Oregon Question, Essays in Anglo-American Diplomacy and Politics*, pp. 205–6. Merk argues that the "deal" would never have won American approval (pp. 206–11). On Ashburton's assurances to Tyler, see Ashburton to Aberdeen, July 13, Aberdeen Papers, BM, AM, vol. 43123, ff. 141–44. Van Alstyne, *Rising American Empire*, pp. 107–8. C. A. Duniway, "Daniel Webster and the West," *Minnesota History*, 9 (March 1928), 13–14.

26. George M. Brooke, Jr., "The Vest Pocket War of Commodore Jones," *Pacific Historical Review*, 31 (August 1962), 217–33. G. G. Hatheway, "Commodore Jones's War," *History Today*, 16 (March 1966), 194–201. James High, "Jones at Monterey, 1842," *Journal of the West*, 5 (April 1966), 173–86. To

On the whole, the ridiculous "vest pocket war" caused less harm than might have been expected. Since Jones had treated the Mexican garrison with courtesy, the inhabitants of Monterey undertook no reprisals against American residents. Governor Micheltorena stormed and blustered a bit but finally contented himself with submitting an inflated claim for damages. In Mexico City the government accepted Thompson's explanation that Jones had acted without instructions, but dark suspicions remained, and the nationalist press beat the drums against American aggression for months afterward. European diplomats in Washington and Mexico City found it difficult to believe that even an American naval officer would go so far on his own initiative, but they kept their opinions to themselves. Soon after Jones' war had ended, the commander of the British Pacific squadron visited the Mexican coast, and Britain established a vice consulate at Monterey as a listening post.

Authorized or not, Jones' attack on Monterey clearly showed American intentions toward California.[27] As with Texas, Mexico could neither defend the region effectively nor sell it honorably. Six months after the Monterey incident had become generally known, Alexander Forbes told a representative of the British bondholders, "If some wise plan of colonization is not adopted, and that speedily, California will cease to be a province of Mexico."[28]

* * * *

Another border area the Americans coveted was Oregon, a vaguely defined territory that stretched along the Pacific coast from California to Alaska. In the case of Texas and California the

soothe Mexico, the American government recalled Jones but never officially censured him. Reports by Jones and other official communications about the episode are conveniently collected in US, 27C, 3S, HED 166.

27. Cleland, *California: American Period*, pp. 150–52. Frank A. Knapp, Jr., "Preludios de la pérdida de California," *Historia mexicana*, 4 (October-December 1954), 238–45. Thompson to Webster, January 15, 1843, US, DS, D, Mexico, XI. For European reactions, see *Rdh-m*, II, 177–80; GB, FO 5/391, ff. 73–77, 231–37; 50/155, ff. 224–28, 233–35; 50/167, ff. 18–20.

28. Letter of Alexander Forbes, Tepic, July 1, 1843, in Robert Crichton Wyllie, *Mexico*, pp. 77–79. There is some evidence that about this time Santa Anna offered to cede California to Prussia. Early in 1845 the Prussian minister to Britain told Everett about the proposal and added that the Prussian government had declined the offer because the province was too remote to defend and Prussia had no desire to risk a collision with the United States. Edward Everett to John C. Calhoun, March 28, 1845, No. 284, Letterbooks, LI, 417–19, Everett Papers, MHS. See also John A. Hawgood, "Friedrich von Roenne—a German Tocqueville, and His Reports from the United States in 1848 and 1849," *University of Birmingham Historical Journal*, 3 (1951), 88.

chief obstacle to American annexation was weak Mexico, but the United States had no shadow of title to these areas or had yielded whatever claim it once possessed through the treaty of 1819. In the case of Oregon the Americans faced the more formidable rivalry of the British government and the Hudson's Bay Company, but here they held some sort of legal title to part of the disputed territory.

Both Britain and the United States claimed rights along the Oregon coast on the basis of explorations conducted late in the eighteenth century. On their voyages, James Cook, John Meares, and George Vancouver had produced maps of Puget Sound, the Straits of Juan de Fuca and Georgia, Vancouver Island, and most of the coast between the straits and northern California. The sole American discovery was a stroke of luck. In 1792, two weeks after Vancouver had sailed past the mouth of the Columbia River without bothering to investigate it, a New England fur trader, Robert Gray, boldly steered through heavy breakers and over a sandbar into the lower river. Thirteen years later, Meriwether Lewis and William Clark explored the valleys of the Snake River and the lower Columbia River for the United States. However, the British explorers Alexander Mackenzie and Simon Fraser did far more to strengthen the British claim by mapping the whole interior area around Puget Sound and the straits and by establishing forts and fur-trading posts for the North West Company.

In 1811 the American fur-trading magnate John Jacob Astor founded the first important American settlement in the disputed territory—Fort Astoria at the mouth of the Columbia River. Upon the outbreak of the War of 1812, Astor sold all his property in Oregon to the North West Company in order to prevent seizure by the British. After the war Astor made no effort to reenter the area, but the United States government claimed sovereignty over it, and in 1818 the British government sent a warship to the Oregon coast to protect the North West Company's rights. The ship's captain recognized American political sovereignty as he established the company's rights, and his government absent-mindedly failed to correct the error, thus providing the United States with another frail prop for its claim.[29]

During the same year, Albert Gallatin and Richard Rush met

29. Joseph Schafer, "The British Attitude toward the Oregon Question, 1815–1846," *American Historical Review*, 16 (January 1911), 273–85. Merk, *Oregon Question*, pp. 1–29. A good modern survey of early Oregon history is Dorothy O. Johansen and Charles M. Gates, *Empire of the Columbia; a History of the Pacific Northwest*, Chaps. 1–12.

with British diplomats in London to settle some of the international disputes remaining from the recent war. When the Oregon question was introduced, Gallatin and Rush proposed to run the northern boundary of the Louisiana Purchase, already fixed at 49°, straight west to the Pacific Ocean, bisecting Vancouver Island. This line would have excluded the British from the Strait of Juan de Fuca, at the southern end of the island. (The Strait of Georgia, north of the island, was difficult to navigate.) The British representatives countered with a proposal to run the line down the Columbia River to its mouth. At this point in the negotiations the Americans might have accepted a compromise line along the watershed between the Columbia River and Puget Sound, so it was fortunate for the later claims of the United States that a stalemate developed.

In order to reach some resolution of the dispute, the diplomats agreed on a joint occupation of the whole territory for ten years, during which time the governments would observe developments. The negotiations had clarified several matters. The real "Oregon dispute" centered in a rectangle of territory between the Columbia River and the forty-ninth parallel; neither side as yet fully appreciated the importance of Puget Sound and its harbors, being chiefly concerned with fur trading and the rights of settlement in the river valley.[30] Already the British were becoming anxious about American immigration, and Lord Castlereagh, the foreign secretary, is said to have commented ruefully to an American negotiator, "You need not trouble yourselves about Oregon, you will conquer Oregon in your bedchambers."[31]

During the 1820s the impasse continued, and both nations sought to improve their positions. In the Florida treaty of 1819 John Quincy Adams obtained the shadowy Spanish title to the southern half of Oregon for the United States, and in 1824 and 1825 Russia negotiated treaties with the United States and Britain which fixed the southern boundary of her Alaskan claims at 54°40', leaving the two nations to negotiate for possession of the intervening area. The merger of the North West Company and the Hudson's Bay Company in 1821 infused new energy into British fur-trading activities north of the Columbia River, and Parliament extended Britain's jurisdiction over her subjects in the area.

30. Merk, *Oregon Question*, pp. 30–71. While Gallatin attached little importance to ports on the Sound, there were some Americans who did, even at this early time. Graebner, *Empire on the Pacific*, p. 27.

31. Quoted in Charles Grier Sellers, *James K. Polk, Continentalist: 1843–1846*, p. 384.

Alarmed at these developments, a Virginia member of the United States House of Representatives, Dr. John Floyd, took up the Oregon question and almost singlehandedly set off a noisy expansionist debate that continued through several sessions of Congress. "Sir, our natural boundary is the Pacific Ocean," declared one of his followers. "The swelling tide of our population must and will roll on until that mighty ocean . . . limits our territorial empire."[32] It is worth noting that the speaker seemed to value Oregon less for its lands or resources than as a stepping-stone for commerce with the Orient. Floyd and his cohorts tried in vain to pass a bill authorizing the construction of a fort in the disputed territory. (Interestingly, James K. Polk, then a member of the House, voted against the measure.)[33] The only visible result of more than five years of American agitation over Oregon seems to have been that the Hudson's Bay Company decided to abandon its trapping activities south of the Columbia River, where furs were poor and scarce anyway, and moved its headquarters from the mouth of the Columbia upriver to Fort Vancouver, where it prepared to dig in and resist further American claims.[34]

Anticipating the end of the ten-year joint occupation, the British and United States governments initiated further efforts to settle the Oregon question in negotiations that lasted from 1825 to 1827. Again the diplomats met in London, and again Gallatin represented the United States. Apparently, he and some of the British negotiators were willing to split the difference somewhere between the Columbia River and the forty-ninth parallel, but Gallatin was restrained by explicit instructions, and representatives of the Hudson's Bay Company were on hand to stiffen the resolution of the British government.

The result was an interesting show of diplomatic gymnastics. When the British objected that the 49° line would bisect Vancouver Island, Gallatin offered to cede the whole island (thereby anticipating the eventual settlement nearly twenty years later). He

32. Quoted in Albert K. Weinberg, *Manifest Destiny, a Study of Nationalist Expansionism in American History*, p. 57.

33. [George] Verne Blue, "The Oregon Question—1818–1828," *Quarterly of the Oregon Historical Society*, 23 (September 1922), 193–219. Charles Grier Sellers, *James K. Polk, Jacksonian: 1795–1843*, pp. 117–18. Floyd's interest in Oregon arose largely from his friendship with the explorer William Clark

and with members of the Astor colony. Thomas Hart Benton also had some influence on his thinking. Charles H. Ambler, *The Life and Diary of John Floyd*, pp. 53–54. See also Chap. 3.

34. The decision was made in 1824 by Sir George Simpson as part of several operational changes in the Columbia River area to cut the Company's losses. Merk, *Oregon Question*, pp. 73–74, 236–37.

also offered free navigation of the Columbia River. When he argued that the United States needed better seaports than the obstructed river mouth, the British offered several harbors on the Olympic Peninsula as enclaves, well knowing that their naval bases in Puget Sound would make them useless to the Americans in case of war. At the end, the diplomats could only sign a treaty that renewed the joint occupation indefinitely and required a year's notice for abrogation.[35]

For a time after the signature of the 1827 treaty the Hudson's Bay Company enjoyed an expanding and almost unchallenged control over the Oregon country. An able chief factor, Dr. John McLoughlin, respected by the Indians as the "Great White Eagle," strengthened the Company's organization and set out to build a chain of forts from the Columbia River to Alaska. During the 1830s the Company crowded individual American operators out of the fur trade, one after another. For diversification the Company also turned to agriculture, and in 1838 a subsidiary, the Puget's Sound Agricultural Company, marked out 167,040 acres of grazing grounds at the southern tip of the Sound. By 1842 the subsidiary was packing nearly four thousand pounds of wool a year, and it seemed possible that enough British settlers might be attracted to keep the Americans out forever.[36]

At this point, however, the tide began to turn. The Opium War and the opening of Chinese ports by treaty in 1842 diverted the attention of many British traders and businessmen from Pacific furs to trade with the Far East, while New Zealand and other developing colonies competed with Puget Sound for British settlers. As early as 1841 Sir George Simpson of the Hudson's Bay Company was complaining to the British government that the sandbar at the mouth of the Columbia River complicated the defense of Fort Vancouver and was suggesting that the district headquarters be withdrawn northward to Vancouver Island.[37]

As British appreciation of Oregon began to decline, American interest in the area was rising. At the height of the British monopoly the writings of such publicists as Hall Jackson Kelley and Nathaniel Wyeth kept alive Dr. Floyd's enthusiasm, and groups of missionaries, mostly Methodists and Presbyterians, arrived to work

35. Merk, *Oregon Question*, pp. 107–88, *passim*. On John Quincy Adams' insistence that the United States obtain adequate harbors, see Graebner, *Empire on the Pacific*, pp. 29–30.

36. Oscar Osburn Winther, *The Great Northwest, a History*, Chaps. 4, 5. John S. Galbraith, *The Hudson's Bay Company as an Imperial Factor, 1821–1869*, pp. 81, 101, 193–94, 198–99.

37. Galbraith, *Hudson's Bay Company*, pp. 210–13.

among the Indians. McLoughlin received them hospitably, despite his superiors' misgivings, but at the same time he tried to keep them away from those Indian tribes which supplied the best pelts to the Company. The missionaries founded several missions in the central Columbia Valley, but their conversions were less significant than the reports they sent back to the States about a fertile rolling country of "oak openings" and well-watered lands, much like those of Ohio and Michigan.[38]

The missionaries' reports found willing readers, for the Middle West had been struggling in an economic depression since 1839. In Cincinnati, for example, the price of flour fell from about $6.25 a barrel in January 1839 to $2.51 in October 1842; in the same period Illinois corn fell from about 30¢ to 14¢ a bushel and hogs from $4.20 to $1 a hundredweight.[39] A group of eleven men left Peoria, Illinois, for Oregon in 1839, the vanguard of a small army. By 1842 the well-defined Oregon Trail extended from Independence, Missouri, to the Columbia River, and emigrant trains of as many as sixteen or eighteen covered wagons were making the long, wearing trip. It is worth emphasizing that the emigrants did not drive the British northward but settled south of the Columbia River, especially along its lovely tributary, the Willamette, for the specific reason that no one was there to hinder them. Indeed, McLoughlin and other Company agents rescued many an emaciated, half-dead emigrant. Through loans and other aid they exercised a type of control over the American settlers and prevented them from infiltrating north of the Columbia.[40]

Meanwhile, the Oregon question reappeared in the United States Congress, where Senator Lewis F. Linn of Missouri, who had taken up Dr. Floyd's monomania, brought up the subject at every opportunity. In 1838 Linn introduced bills and resolutions for the military occupation of the Columbia River, the abrogation of the 1827 treaty, the extension of United States law to the area, and the grant of free land to American settlers. During the next four years he hammered at his prediction that if the United States postponed acting, Britain would occupy the whole territory down to the border of California. Eventually he won support from expansionists of all sections, including Thomas Hart Benton and John C. Calhoun, although, unlike Linn, these two statesmen were

38. Winther, *Great Northwest*, Chaps. 6, 7. On the attitude of the Hudson's Bay Company toward the Columbia Valley, see *American Historical Review*, 14 (October 1908), 70–94.

39. James C. Bell, *Opening a Highway to the Pacific, 1838–1846*, pp. 124–25.

40. Merk, *Oregon Question*, pp. 236, 239–41. Winther, *Great Northwest*, pp. 127–29.

inclined to limit the American claim at 49°. The expansionist press reprinted the congressional debates on Oregon and borrowed ideas for editorials.[41]

At this period the executive branch of the government had not yet adopted a consistent policy toward the Oregon question. Robert Greenhow, a minor functionary of the State Department, compiled a memoir on the geography and history of Oregon, incidentally setting forth the American claim to the territory.[42] When Charles Wilkes' exploring expedition, dispatched by the Van Buren administration, visited the Oregon coast, Wilkes was so much impressed with the area's resources and the excellence of harbors in the Sound that he drew up a special report on Oregon, urging the government to push its claim to the whole territory as far as 54°40'. Otherwise, he warned, "we should give up what may be considered a storehouse of wealth in its forests, furs, and fisheries."[43]

Briefer and milder references to Oregon in Wilkes' other writings reached the public during 1843 and 1844, but the Tyler administration suppressed his enthusiastic special report; it was not published until sixty-nine years later. Political jealousy may explain Tyler's action, for Wilkes and his supporters were mostly Democrats. Another reason may be that Benton was displeased at Wilkes' insistence on claiming all territory to 54°40'. The most powerful reason, however, seems to have been fear that the report might arouse widespread Anglophobia, for in 1841–1842, when Wilkes submitted his report, Webster and Ashburton were just beginning negotiations to settle all outstanding Anglo–American quarrels.[44]

Despite Tyler's caution, however, the two negotiators were unable to settle the Oregon controversy. Ashburton's instructions, hastily prepared by a member of Britain's 1826 commission, repeated the demand for the Columbia River as boundary and

41. *NNR*, 59 (October 3, 1840), 68; 61 (December 11, 1841), 226–27; and 62 (May 21, 1842), 184–87. *Merchants' Magazine*, 3 (September 1840), 204. Michael B. Husband, "Senator Lewis F. Linn and the Oregon Question," *Missouri Historical Review*, 66 (October 1971), 1–12, *passim*.

42. Robert Greenhow, *Memoir, Historical and Political, on the Northwest Coast of North America, and the Adjacent Territories.*

43. Charles Wilkes, "Report on the Territory of Oregon," *Quarterly of the*

Oregon Historical Society, 12 (September 1911), 269–99, especially pp. 293–94. David B. Tyler, *The Wilkes Expedition: the First United States Exploring Expedition (1838–1842)*, Chaps. 17, 18, *et passim*.

44. John E. Wickman, "Political Aspects of Charles Wilkes's Work and Testimony, 1842–1849," Ph.D. diss., Indiana University, 1964, pp. 20–50, *passim*. Wilkes' *magnum opus* was his *Narrative of the United States Exploring Expedition during the Years 1838, 1839, 1840, 1841, and 1842.*

omitted all mention of enclaves on the Olympic Peninsula. Although the inadequate records do not indicate exactly how Webster reacted to this proposal, he seems to have protested that its provisions would deny to the United States any adequate port on the Pacific. Then or in a later discussion he suggested a three-way exchange, involving the two principals and Mexico, by which the United States might obtain San Francisco Bay instead of Puget Sound. Although Ashburton had no objections to this proposal, he could not promise Britain's aid in obtaining Mexico's consent. Clearly, neither man regarded the Oregon question important enough to risk a disagreement over the northeastern boundary settlement, and they finally agreed to leave it out of the treaty.[45]

There was considerable regret in both countries that Webster and Ashburton had not settled the Oregon question. In October, therefore, Aberdeen instructed Fox to make a formal proposal to Webster that he authorize fresh negotiations by Edward Everett in London. In a private letter to Everett, Webster professed to see no hope for a compromise, since Britain insisted on the Columbia River line, which would shut the United States off from the only good harbors in the Northwest. At the same time he hinted that the United States might accept most of the Columbia River boundary if the agreement included a narrow strip of Pacific coastline from the mouth of the river to the Strait of Juan de Fuca.[46] Fox suspected that the secretary was marking time, hoping to end his service to the State Department with a special mission to Britain. Since Webster clearly regarded most of the disputed territory north of the Columbia River as negotiable, it was probably just as

45. Merk, *Oregon Question*, pp. 189–215. Ashburton to Aberdeen, April 25, June 29, 1842, Nos. 2, 10, Manning, *CR*, III, 703–5, 744–45. Wilbur Devereux Jones, *Aberdeen and the Americas*, p. 27. On pressure from the Hudson's Bay Company for a favorable Oregon settlement, see Pelly to Palmerston, London, February 26, 1840, GB, FO 115/72, ff. 137–42. Aberdeen might have agreed to a three-way arrangement for Oregon and San Francisco. See his private letter to Ashburton, July 18, Aberdeen Papers, BM, AM, vol. 43123, pp. 148–50.

46. *NNR*, 63 (November 19, 1842), 185. Aberdeen to Henry S. Fox, October 18; Edward Everett to Webster, No-vember 18, No. 28, Manning, *CR*, III, 786–87. Webster to Everett, November 28, *The Private Correspondence of Daniel Webster*, ed. Fletcher Webster, II, 153–54. Everett communicated Webster's hint to the British government, where it met some support. Ashburton to Aberdeen, January 1, 1843, as quoted in Jones, *Aberdeen and the Americas*, p. 27. Jones suggests that the British government might have accepted a boundary at 49° as early as the beginning of 1843. However, he has mistaken a reference to Fort Vancouver (on the Columbia River) for Vancouver Island. Actually, Aberdeen did not reconcile himself to the 49° boundary until late in 1843.

well for long-range American interests that he never received the assignment.[47]

Contrary to the hopes of Peel and Aberdeen, Tyler not only failed to authorize negotiations but even suggested in his annual message of 1842 that it was the United States rather than Britain which wished to see the question settled. This deceptive hint at British stubbornness, together with British attacks on the Webster–Ashburton Treaty, weakened the effectiveness of Anglophiles in Congress. When Linn introduced his expected belligerent resolutions for the political and military organization of Oregon, he won much support, especially from Western and radical Eastern ("locofoco") elements in the Democratic party. This time, however, Calhoun and the Southern wing opposed Linn, on the grounds that it would be only honorable to abrogate the joint occupation treaty before taking action and that time was working for the Americans anyway. The true policy toward Oregon, declared Calhoun, was "a wise and masterly inactivity."[48]

The British regarded Linn as "a foolish and unprincipled demagogue" and his proposal as a silly attempt to add more acres to an already land-rich nation. To them, the American campaign for Oregon was typical of the "extravagant demands, reckless assertions, disingenuous conduct, and . . . all those things which have on so many previous occasions tended to place American statesmen so low in the scale of morality." But the British also recognized "the blind, unsparing haste" of the westward movement and foresaw that if international trade continued to shift in the direction of the Far East, the Americans would not rest until they had at least one first-rate port on the Pacific.[49] As early as March 1842 Sir George Simpson predicted that the Oregon boundary would prob-

47. Fox to Aberdeen, November 15, No. 37, GB, FO 5/377, ff. 174–79. Webster planned to send Everett on a mission to China, but Everett did not want to make the change. See also Samuel Flagg Bemis, *John Quincy Adams and the Union*, pp. 482–84.

48. Charles M. Wiltse, *John C. Calhoun, Sectionalist, 1840–1850*, pp. 107–8. Husband, "Linn and the Oregon Debate," pp. 13–16. For British correspondence on the message and the debate, see GB, FO 5/377, ff. 201–5, 240–41; 5/391, ff. 50–54, 81–83, 89–91, 177–84, 191–96; 115/81, ff. 4–7, 13–15. Aber-

deen instructed Fox that if Congress passed the Oregon bill, he should warn Webster that the British government "would feel themselves at full liberty to take such steps as they might think fit for the assertion and maintenance of . . . [its] claims." Aberdeen to Fox, February 3, 1843, No. 5, GB, FO 115/81, f. 15. In diplomatic language this would be regarded as a moderately stern warning.

49. London *Times*, January 31, 1843, p. 4; February 27, p. 4; March 7, p. 4. *Dublin University Magazine*, 21 (March 1843), 394.

ably be drawn close to the forty-eighth parallel. After Calhoun's speech advising "masterly inactivity," Simpson's subordinate in the Hudson's Bay Company, James Douglas, wrote to him that "the wily old lawyer" was correct: "It would appear from the rush of emigration to this quarter, that his words have produced their effect, and there can be no doubt of the final success of the plan, if the country remains open a few years longer."[50]

50. Sir George Simpson to Governor and Committee of Hudson's Bay Company, March 1, 1842. James Douglas to Simpson, October 23, 1843. E. E. Rich, ed., *The Letters of John McLoughlin from Fort Vancouver to the Governor and Committee: Third Series, 1844–46*, pp. xxx–xxxi.

II

The Annexation of Texas
1843-1845

5

Tyler's Campaign for Texas

As the year 1842 ended, relations between the United States, her neighbors, and the Great Powers of Europe rested in precarious balance. The weak Tyler administration had managed to resolve the dangerous Canadian border crisis with Britain by a compromise treaty. But Peel and Aberdeen, though anxious for peace, could afford no further compromises because of hot criticism from the opposition and general disgust over American debts and tariffs. As revolutions, corruption, and irresponsibility bled away Mexico's strength, the inheritance of her great resources worried both London and Washington. The French had used force on the exasperating Mexicans without obtaining satisfactory redress of grievances. Observing their failures, the British temporized, advising Mexico to improve its domestic administration and resist American expansion.

The focus of American, British, and Mexican policy was Texas, which had become too strong and self-confident to submit again to Mexican rule. Instead of recognizing a *fait accompli*, the Mexicans persisted in jabbing at the Texan border, thereby strengthening the position of those Texans who favored annexation to the United States.[1] Seeing the danger more clearly than Mexico, Britain worked to create a buffer state west of the Sabine River. Behind the fate of Texas, the British knew, lay that of California, even richer in resources and equally beyond Mexico's power to protect or to hold. Here Britain had fewer immediate interests than in Texas, but rising European rivalries in the Pacific made San Francisco a prize worth negotiation if not war. American migration was beginning to threaten British interests also in Oregon, which both countries occupied jointly under a stopgap agreement.

1. The Mexican minister to the United States was advising his government to crush the Texans before they recovered from their defeat at Mier and gained effective aid from the United States. Juan N. Almonte to Ministerio de Relaciones, February 7, 15, 1843, Nos. 13, 19, México, SRE; US, LC, /46. For an example of the effect of Mexican raids on Texas opinion, see Joseph Eve to John J. Crittenden, Galveston, December 22, 1842, John J. Crittenden Papers, LC.

The peace of the Atlantic world and the future of western North America were at stake when the year 1843 began. They rested on the answers to several questions. Could Mexico swallow the bitter dose of reconciliation with Texas before it was too late? Would Britain and France risk war with the United States to prevent American expansion into Texas, California, or Oregon? Most perplexing of all, could any faction in the United States summon up enough support in both North and South to put through a general expansionist program?

*   *   *   *

The obvious person to lead American expansionists in the Texas question was John Tyler, a Southerner often sympathetic with the annexationist Calhoun and a President badly in need of an issue on which to seek reelection. He had shown interest in acquiring Texas as soon as he entered the White House. To be sure, he had rejected two overtures from Sam Houston during 1842. At the end of the year, however, the Texan minister in Washington reported home that Tyler, supported by most of his cabinet, favored annexation and would negotiate a treaty as soon as he was sure of the Senate's approval, "believing it would render him omnipotent in the South and West" for the approaching campaign.[2]

Another indication of Tyler's interest was the publication in mid-January of an open letter by his friend, ex-Governor Thomas W. Gilmer of Virginia, an active agent for Texan bonds and lands. In his letter Gilmer bid for Northern support with the argument that annexation would benefit Northern trade and further a reconciliation between North and South.[3] Since Gilmer had the reputation of a moderate, his letter created a greater sensation than the usual expansionist declamations, but most of the American public soon forgot it. One who did not was Andrew Jackson, who took alarm at Gilmer's casual references to British intrigue in Texas and dashed off a letter to a mutual friend, in which he declared that a dastardly plot loomed over the American West unless Texas were annexed:

2. Isaac Van Zandt to G. W. Terrell, December 23, 1842, No. 93, Garrison, *DCRT*, I, 633. Justin H. Smith, *The Annexation of Texas*, pp. 103–5, 130.

3. *Madisonian*, January 23, 1843, as cited in Smith, *Annexation of Texas*,

pp. 131–32. Elgin Williams, *The Animating Pursuits of Speculation: Land Traffic in the Annexation of Texas*, p. 144. Samuel F. Bemis, *John Quincy Adams and the Union*, pp. 427–28, 434–35.

Great Britain keeps the north western boundary as a peg to declare war against us, whenever she may find to her interest to do so. . . . [She] enters into an alience [*sic*] with Texas—looking forward to war with us, she sends to Texas 20 or 30,000, organizing her army near to the Sabine, . . . marches thro Louisiana and Arkansa [*sic*], makes a lodgment on the mississippi, excite[s] the negroes to insurrection, . . . and a servile war rages all over the southern and western country. In the mean time great Britain moves an army from canady [*sic*], along our western frontier to cooperate with the army from Texas. what mischief and havock would be inflicted upon us before we could organize an army to repel this egression [*sic*].

Gilmer soon saw this letter, realized its value as propaganda, and filed it away for future use.[4]

At the opposite end of the Texas question Gilmer's arguments touched off the equally explosive John Quincy Adams, who was his bitter political enemy. On March 3 Adams and eleven other abolitionist Representatives issued a memorial declaring that any effort to introduce into the Union "such *misbegotten and illegitimate progeny*" as Texas would lead directly to secession by the North.[5] Adams then turned detective, using his prestige as former President to consult the State Department's archives in the hope of finding evidence that Jackson had plotted to purchase Texas. On March 25 the irascible old man buttonholed the uncomfortable Webster for three hours, demanding to know the government's stand on the right of search, the Oregon question, the seizure of Monterey, and, of course, the annexation of Texas. All these, he wrote in his diary, "were parts of one great system, looking to a war for conquest and plunder from Mexico, and a war with England and alliance with France."[6] Naturally, the aboli-

4. Jackson's letter to Aaron V. Brown, Hermitage, February 9 [12], 1843, appears in *The Correspondence of Andrew Jackson*, ed. John Spencer Bassett, VI, 201–2. James C. N. Paul, *Rift in the Democracy*, pp. 82–83. Smith, *Annexation of Texas*, p. 108. In his letter Jackson remarked incorrectly that before the signature of the 1819 treaty the American minister in Madrid had informed John Quincy Adams that Spain was willing to cede Texas as well as Florida to the United States. This statement started a long, bitter controversy with "that lying old scamp," as Jackson called Adams. (Jackson to Fran-

cis Blair, November 29, 1844. Jackson, *Correspondence*, VI, 332.) This collateral quarrel undoubtedly raised the temperature of the central conflict over Texas by several degrees.

5. Washington *National Intelligencer*, as reprinted in *NNR*, 64 (May 13, 1843), 173–75. For Gilmer's reply to the memorial, see *NNR* (July 1), 284–85. Kinley J. Brauer, *Cotton versus Conscience: Massachusetts Whig Politics and Southwestern Expansion, 1843–1848*, pp. 55–57.

6. *Memoirs of John Quincy Adams*, ed. Charles Francis Adams, XI, 344–47, 357, *et passim*.

tionist press and Mexican newspapers were glad to broadcast Adams' suspicions.[7]

Adams believed that Tyler and Webster were deliberately inflating American claims against Mexico in order to create a situation in which Mexico would be forced to sell Texas or California or both. Actually, Webster opposed the annexation of Texas, but when Adams asked him pointblank if he had instructed the American minister, Waddy Thompson, to negotiate for the purchase of California, Webster faltered and refused to answer, whereupon Adams declared triumphantly that his hesitation was answer enough. Nine months earlier, Webster had indeed sent such instructions to Thompson. Seeing no chance of executing them, Thompson had signed instead a preliminary convention by which Mexico promised to pay already arbitrated claims in cash within five years—another vain hope, but one that momentarily improved relations between the two neighbors.[8]

Under these circumstances it was not surprising that Tyler should avoid open discussion of annexation during the early months of 1843. Texan Minister Isaac Van Zandt continued to suggest that Houston was still interested in annexation. As a stimulus Van Zandt even hinted that Britain might intervene to bring about the abolition of slavery in Texas.[9] On one occasion, soon after a rebellious Senate had rejected two of his appointments, Tyler told Van Zandt: "Sir, I wish you to be assured that I feel the deepest interest in the affairs of your country, and wish . . . if possible to annex you to us; *but you see how I am situated.*"[10] This encouraged the Texan minister, but it was not enough for the impatient Houston, who grumbled to the British chargé, Charles Elliot, that the United States regarded Texas as a mere appendage. Houston suggested that if Britain could induce Mexico to recognize Texan independence, annexation might never take place. However, he did not withdraw his offer to the United States until July.[11]

7. See, for example, a pamphlet entitled *The Complaint of Mexico and Conspiracy against Liberty* (Boston, 1843). Frank A. Knapp, Jr., "John Quincy Adams, ¿Defensor de México?" *Historia mexicana*, 7 (July–September 1957), 116–23.

8. Clayton Charles Kohl, *Claims As a Cause of the Mexican War*, pp. 47–50. George Lockhart Rives, *The United States and Mexico, 1821–1848*, I, 507–8.

9. James Norton Callahan, *American Foreign Policy in Mexican Relations*, pp. 118–19. Van Zandt to Anson Jones, March 13, 1843, No. 97, Garrison, *DCRT*, II, 135–36.

10. Van Zandt to Jones, April 19, 1843, ibid., pp. 164–67. Same, March 15. Anson Jones, *Memoranda and Official Correspondence Relating to the Republic of Texas, Its History and Annexation*, pp. 211–14.

11. Sam Houston to Elliot, May 13, 1843, Ephraim Douglass Adams, ed.,

Since the time was not yet ripe for annexation, plans for foreign mediation between Mexico and Texas served to keep the diplomats busy. As stated earlier, Aberdeen had vainly offered mediation to Mexico during the summer of 1842. After Houston had failed in his first two bids for annexation during the summer and autumn, he appealed formally for American mediation in December.[12] Unfortunately, the confusion in Texas had created a bad impression in the United States, so the Senate would not even approve a Texan–American commercial treaty.[13] Rebuffed by the United States, Houston wrote to Elliot in January, suggesting again that if Britain wanted to prevent annexation, the best way would be to persuade Mexico to recognize Texas. But by this time Aberdeen had come to the conclusion that the border clashes indicated a stalemate, and he hoped that Texas would retreat from her demand for outright recognition.[14]

The principal effort toward mediation early in 1843 was based on just this assumption. Its starting point was a letter dated January 9, which Santa Anna received from a minor Texan official who had been captured in the recent raids. This man declared that, in order to obtain peace, the Texans would consider formally rejoining Mexico under some special arrangement for local autonomy. He proposed that the Mexican government send him and his companions home to arrange for a preliminary armistice. Santa Anna may have suspected that the Texan was merely trying to talk his way out of prison; the Mexican president may also have been trying to gain time or to impress his people. Whatever his motives, he had nothing to lose by listening to the proposal. Calling the Texan into his presence, he heard him out, drew up a draft agreement, and sent him back to Texas.[15]

Santa Anna's opposition in Mexico at once suspected him of planning to sell out to the Texans, but the proposed compromise gained immediate support from the diplomatic corps in Mexico City. British Minister Pakenham was on leave, but his chargé, the optimistic, aggressive young Percy W. Doyle, promptly sec-

British Diplomatic Correspondence Concerning the Republic of Texas— 1838–1846, pp. 208–13.

12. Van Zandt to Daniel Webster, December 14, 1842, Manning, *IAA*, XII, 256–59.

13. Smith, *Annexation of Texas*, p. 71.

14. Blake denies that the American rebuff greatly affected Houston's policy, since he had already assured Elliot

that he intended to maintain Texan independence. Clagette Blake, *Charles Elliot, R.N., 1801–1875, a Servant of Britain Overseas*, pp. 79–80. Wilbur Devereux Jones, *Lord Aberdeen and the Americas*, p. 21.

15. Rives, *US and Mexico*, I, 548–51. Dennis E. Berge, "Mexican Response to United States Expansionism, 1841–1848," Ph.D. diss., University of California (Berkeley), 1965, pp. 79–81.

onded the proposal of the Texan prisoner. The French minister volunteered to act as mediator, and even the pro-Southern American minister, Waddy Thompson, offered to persuade the Texans to accept nominal Mexican sovereignty as the price of peace.[16]

Probably nothing short of crushing military defeat could have made Houston agree to such humiliating terms, but he did not at once commit himself. Elliot and the French chargé in Texas both argued that negotiations with Mexico, once begun, might lead to recognition of Texan independence.[17] Also, at that moment Houston was exasperated at Tyler's inaction and may have wanted to goad the American government. Whatever his reasoning, on June 13 he proclaimed an armistice—obviously a prerequisite to negotiations. When word of Houston's action reached Santa Anna, he promptly ordered all troops on the Texan frontier to cease fire, but although Doyle tried to persuade him to take further conciliatory steps, he showed no disposition to consider recognition.

As long as both sides refused to yield on this point, no mediation could take place. Aberdeen seems to have realized this, for he was not impressed by the *démarche* and warned Ashbel Smith, the Texan minister to Britain, not to expect too much from the armistice. Nevertheless, Elliot urged the Texans to accept Santa Anna's proposals at least as a basis for negotiations and relayed to them Doyle's assurances that on every point except recognition Santa Anna was growing more conciliatory toward Texas.[18] Houston eventually sent commissioners to Mexico City without formal mediation from abroad, but by that time conditions had radically changed, and their negotiations came to nothing.

*   *   *   *

During the spring and summer of 1843, even while Santa Anna and Houston were declaring a cease-fire and considering

---

16. Berge, "Mexican Response," pp. 81–84. Percy W. Doyle to Aberdeen, April 24, 1843, Aberdeen Papers, BM, AM, vol. 43126. Alleye de Cyprey to François Guizot, March 20, No. 152, France, MAE, CP, Mexique, XXIII, ff. 299–302. On Thompson's offer, see a report of the Spanish minister, who witnessed the interview. Pedro Pascual Oliver to Primer Secretario de Estado, March 13, No. 234, Jaime Delgado, *España y México en el siglo XIX*, III, 551–53.

17. Elliot to Jones, June 10, 1843, Garrison, *DCRT*, III, 1090–91. Rives, *US*

and Mexico, I, 552.

18. Adams, *British Interests*, pp. 128–37. Rives, *US and Mexico*, I, 552–53. Aberdeen to Elliot, May 18, June 3, 1843, Nos. 5, 6, Adams, *British Correspondence*, pp. 194–95, 200–202. Ashbel Smith to Jones, London, June 16, Garrison, *DCRT*, III, 1094–96. See also Aberdeen's instructions to Doyle, July 1, GB, FO 115/81, ff. 149–50. Elliot to Jones, Galveston, August 17, 28, Jones, *Memoranda*, pp. 246–48. For a slightly different interpretation of Elliot's actions, see Blake, *Elliot*, p. 83.

negotiation, several developments raised the hopes of annexationists on both sides of the border. For one thing, the American State Department received a new secretary, bringing to Tyler's side another annexationist, more determined than he. Also, the ceaseless pendulum of European–Mexican relations swung from cordiality to ill-feeling, thereby lessening the likelihood of a united stand by the European powers concerning Texas.

On May 8 Webster submitted his resignation as secretary of state. He had kept his awkward position in Tyler's cabinet of ex-Democrats and political mavericks largely in order to complete his negotiations with Britain and to enhance his prestige. Possibly, also, he hoped to move to the congenial legation in London. Now, however, that hope was dead, and Tyler's expansionism, which Webster had never supported enthusiastically, was becoming less possible to reconcile with the views of his abolitionist constituents in New England.[19]

To succeed Webster, Tyler would probably have preferred John C. Calhoun, but Calhoun would not tie himself to another man's administration at that time. The President therefore appointed *ad interim* another South Carolinian, Hugh S. Legaré. When Legaré died after serving only a month, Tyler promoted his secretary of the navy, Abel P. Upshur, to head the State Department. Like Webster, Upshur possessed a strong legal mind—also a powerful physique, a bald head, and a beetling brow. Here the resemblance stopped, however, for Upshur regarded slavery as a positive benefit to the country and a strong national government as the chief threat to the well-being of the states. He was a Virginian first and foremost and had probably entered Tyler's cabinet primarily to combat the economic nationalism of the Whigs. Whether Calhoun had been actually grooming him as Webster's successor, he persuaded Upshur to accept the office. Texan Minister Van Zandt thought his appointment "one of the best . . . that could be made for the interests of Texas. He is devoted in his attachment to our country . . . and has the nerve, as the Venerable Sage of the hermitage would say, to 'take the responsibility' and act with decission [*sic*]."[20]

A second set of circumstances, which less directly encouraged

---

19. Brauer, *Cotton versus Conscience*, pp. 52–53.
20. Lyon G. Tyler, *The Letters and Times of the Tylers*, III, 181, 198. Charles M. Wiltse, *John C. Calhoun, Sectionalist, 1840–1850*, pp. 138, 504.

Randolph G. Adams, "Abel P. Upshur," in Samuel F. Bemis, ed., *American Secretaries of State and Their Diplomacy*, V, 67–68. Van Zandt to Jones, April 19, 1843, No. 99, Garrison, DCRT, II, 164.

the annexationist movement was a new series of arbitrary measures by the Mexican government restricting the rights of foreigners. Angry at British and French colonization projects in Texas, Santa Anna informed members of the diplomatic corps that unauthorized colonists there would be "treated as real invaders and enemies of Mexico" and warned land purchasers that Mexico would not recognize any titles from the "rebel" government.[21] At this moment of hopeless deadlock Santa Anna's timing and language were most imprudent, and he made matters worse by refusing to recognize the official status or privileges of foreign consuls in Texas. The diplomatic representatives of the United States, Britain, France, and Spain protested long and loud; and Waddy Thompson, hitherto friendly to the mediation proposal, quietly withdrew his support.[22]

At the same time Santa Anna levied a special "temporary" tariff of 20 per cent to finance an invasion of Texas and abandoned his earlier promises to Pakenham that he would repeal the heavy duties on cotton textiles. He also decreed a forced loan of $500,000 but did not dare apply this levy to foreigners, since the British, French, and Spanish representatives let it be known that if he did, they would ask for their passports.[23] In June Foreign Minister Bocanegra and the French minister quarreled over the collection of another forced loan, and Aberdeen sent protests reviving a long-standing claims case and opposing a Mexican law that forbade British residents to act as brokers.[24] In August the Mexican government retaliated by announcing a long list of prohibited imports and by ordering that stocks of these goods already in Mexico must be sold within a year.[25]

*   *   *   *

A third and the most important circumstance favoring annexation was the increasing interest of British abolitionists in

21. Hubert H. Bancroft, *History of Mexico*, V, 331–32.

22. México, SRE, *Memoria, 1841–1843*, Appendix, pp. lxxi–lxxxvi. *Rdhm*, II, 231–32, 257–58. Waddy Thompson to José María Bocanegra, April 16, 1843, US, DS, Mexico, XI. Thompson to Abel P. Upshur, October 2, Manning, *IAA*, VIII, 562–63.

23. Dublán and Lozano, *LM*, IV, 411–12, 413–19. Wilfrid Hardy Callcott, *Church and State in Mexico, 1822–1857*, p. 163. Doyle to Aberdeen, April 24, 1843, No. 7, GB, FO 50/161, ff. 215–

21. Cyprey to Guizot, April 20, 22, 23, Nos. 156–58, France, MAE, CP, Mexique, XXIV, ff. 4–5, 7–10, 15–16.

24. Cyprey to Guizot, June 18, 20, Nos. 167, 168, ibid., ff. 111–16, 124–28. Aberdeen to Doyle, June 1, July 1, Nos. 4, 2, GB, FO 50/160, ff. 43–45, 53–55.

25. Doyle to Aberdeen, August 29, 1843, No. 60, GB, FO 50/163, ff. 161–66. Cyprey to Guizot, August 27, No. 184, France, MAE, CP, Mexique, XXIV, ff. 291–95. Dublán and Lozano, *LM*, IV, 510–11.

Texas. The British antislavery movement had been linked with that for free trade, despite the efforts of Tyler's confidential agent, Duff Green, to dissociate the two issues in British opinion. Both Peel and Aberdeen had expressed interest in lower tariffs, and after Webster left the cabinet, he too proposed a "commercial arrangement" under which Britain would admit American rice, cotton, tobacco, Indian corn, and bacon at lowered rates, although retaining the corn laws unchanged for the time being. American protectionists asked suspiciously what concessions to British manufactures would be expected of the United States in return.[26] Nevertheless, since Tyler, Upshur, and Calhoun all supported tariff revision as sincerely as Peel and Aberdeen, patient diplomatic probing between London and Washington might have led to formal negotiations during 1843.

Unfortunately, British abolitionism, the *bête noire* of the Southerners, was becoming involved in the Texas question. British support of the antislavery movement was nothing new. Since the government had freed the slaves in the West Indies the planters there had found it difficult to compete with planters in slaveholding areas, as Peel had admitted in Commons during the preceding summer. British Quakers and other abolitionist humanitarians held many Mexican bonds, had helped to finance Mexico's purchase of warships, and might, therefore, strengthen Mexico's antislavery policy if she reconquered Texas. British abolitionists had tried to prevent the recognition of slaveholding Texas, and the British chargé d'affaires, Charles Elliot, who disliked slavery, had encouraged the Foreign Office to believe that Britain might safely oppose it there. Clearly Peel and Aberdeen could not afford to ignore the abolitionist bloc.[27]

In the spring of 1843 a young Texan set out for Europe to appeal for funds with which to buy and free slaves held in Texas. Stephen Pearl Andrews, a stenographer and lawyer originally from Massachusetts, had migrated to Texas and organized a small group of abolitionists there. On his way abroad Andrews stopped in New England to receive the blessings of John Quincy Adams. In July Andrews and other Americans attended a world conven-

26. Edward Everett to Hugh S. Legaré, July 1, 1843; Everett to Upshur, August 1, 30, September 1, Nos. 44, 49, 55, US, DS, D, Britain, LI. *NNR*, 64 (June 3, 10, 17, 24, July 16, 22), 219–22, 231–32, 234, 252–54, 264–65, 319, 329; 65 (October 21, November 4, 25), 114–15, 150, 204–5.

27. Smith to Van Zandt, undated (probably January 25, 1843), Garrison, *DCRT*, III, 1107–8. Elliot's encouragement arose partly from his natural optimism and partly from his misunderstanding of Houston's attitude. Elliot to Aberdeen, June 8, Adams, *British Correspondence*, pp. 205–7.

tion of the British and Foreign Anti-Slavery Society in London, spreading the glad but mistaken tidings that Sam Houston favored their cause and that a loan from the British government would provide an entering wedge for British abolitionist influence in Texas. A number of them talked to Aberdeen, the Whig leader Lord Brougham, and other British politicians; later, they exaggerated the polite remarks of these gentlemen. Aberdeen did not grant the proposed loan, but he reaffirmed the official British position supporting the principle of abolition. In August, when Brougham asked him pointblank in Parliament for information about a reported plan to compel Mexico to recognize Texas if Texas would abolish slavery, Aberdeen avoided a direct answer. But he was well aware that he had instructed Doyle to suggest this arrangement to Mexico about six weeks earlier.[28]

The menace of effective British intrigue for abolition among Texan slaveholders does not seem alarming, with the perspective of time, but rumors about Aberdeen's devious policy lent themselves admirably to exaggeration and propaganda in 1843. At the center of the gossip was the Texan minister to Britain, Ashbel Smith, a physician turned politician, who reported it in considerable detail. During July his dispatches home described the anti-slavery convention and warned against too ready acceptance of British arguments for abolition. At the same time he told Aberdeen that Andrews had no official status in Texas and that the Texan government would never accept British interference with slavery. Aberdeen assured him that, while Britain favored abolition, she had no desire to interfere improperly in Texas.

The Texan government sent Smith's dispatches to its minister in Washington, Van Zandt, who undoubtedly showed them privately to members of the Tyler administration. However, Smith had also written directly to Calhoun in June, informing him that Elliot was corresponding with the Foreign Office on abolition. Smith added, "I sincerely believe that the ultimate purpose is to make Texas a refuge for runaway slaves from the United States, and eventually a negro nation, a sort of Hayti on the continent, to be more or less, according to circumstances, un-

28. Harriet Smither, "English Abolitionism and the Annexation of Texas," *Southwestern Historical Quarterly*, 32 (January 1929), 193–205. Rives, *US and Mexico*, I, 562–67. Adams, *British Interests*, pp. 137–39. Spence, "British Interests and Attitudes," pp. 44–58. For Aberdeen's instructions to Doyle, dated July 1, 1843, see GB, FO 115/81, ff. 148–50.

der the protection of the British Government."[29] This was exactly what Calhoun wanted to believe.

Tyler's agent Duff Green was an even more irresponsible rumor-monger. He had returned to England in the spring of 1843, hoping to continue his campaign for commercial reciprocity, only to find that reviving prosperity, coupled with British landowners' continuing fears of cheap American wheat, had made the Peel administration cautious about continued tariff reform. Lacking the scruples and restraint of a more conventional diplomat, Green turned to the Whig opposition. He discussed with Palmerston and others the possibility of a general Anglo–American agreement encompassing both free trade and the unsettled Oregon boundary. He seems also to have encouraged the Whigs to attack the Peel administration on the slavery question.[30]

Naturally, he kept Calhoun and the American government informed about the Anglo–American antislavery movement. At the end of May he warned Tyler of Elliot's abolitionist activities in Texas. During July he wrote to Upshur of Andrews' approach to the British government and declared that Aberdeen had promised Texas a loan on condition that her government abolish slavery. A little later he warned Calhoun that Britain might foment a war or intrigue against slavery in the States in order to save the West Indian sugar planters. Green suggested that if the United States government could be brought to take a strong stand for the annexation of Texas, Whigs and other free traders would support noninterference in that question, and this opposition would force the Peel government to meet American demands.[31] Thus he managed to link the annexation of Texas with tariff reform.

Calhoun replied to Green, agreeing that the British Tories must resort to force against slaveholding countries or yield to the free traders. His agitation at Green's diagnosis is shown in a letter which he wrote to Secretary Upshur on August 27, urging him

29. Smith to John C. Calhoun, June 19, 1843, quoted in Smither, "English Abolitionism," pp. 199–200. Smith to Jones, July 2, 31, Nos. 41, 43, Garrison, *DCRT*, III, 1099–1103, 1116–19.

30. Thomas P. Martin, "New Alignments in Anglo-American Politics, 1842–1843," Louisville *Courier-Journal*, April 15, 1923, section 3, pp. 11–12. Duff Green to John Tyler, May 17, 31, 1843; Sir Robert Peel to Green, June 20; Nassau W. Senior to Green, September 8; Joseph Hume to Green, September 12, Green Papers, box 2. Green to Calhoun, August 2, September 29, Calhoun, *Correspondence*, pp. 834–35.

31. Green to Tyler, May 31, 1843, Green Papers, box 2. Rives, *US and Mexico*, I, 569. Green to Upshur, August 3, US, DS, SA, XIII. Green to Calhoun, August 2, September 2, Calhoun, *Correspondence*, pp. 846–49, 871–72.

not to underestimate Britain's wiles in Texas: "Her object is power and monopoly, and abolition but the pretext. . . . No nation, in ancient, or modern time, ever pursued dominion & commercial monopoly more perseveringly & vehemently than she has. She unites in herself the ambition of Rome and the avarice of Carthage." He advised Upshur to demand an explanation of British behavior, to warn France and Texas, and to frustrate British designs in Mexico.

Meanwhile, Calhoun was suggesting that the State Department start a propaganda campaign for annexation in the Richmond *Enquirer* and other friendly Southern newspapers. "Would it not also be well," he concluded, "if the West should push the Oregon question, to unite with it the annexation of Texas, in the shape of an amendment of the bill and make them go hand in hand?"[32] He soon ceased his urgings, especially on the subject of Oregon, but this letter foreshadowed some of his own impetuous actions when he succeeded Upshur in the State Department.

During the summer of 1843 information about Texas from Europe played a larger part in the councils of the Tyler administration than direct information from Texas. The reason was that earlier in the year the American chargé in Texas had died of fever, and his successor, William S. Murphy, did not reach his post until early June. At first the new chargé merely observed that Elliot was advocating mediation proposals, which were generally unpopular, but in September Murphy assured Upshur that his suspicions of the British were correct. As evidence he sent the secretary copies of correspondence between Elliot and the Texan secretary of state. However, by the time these letters arrived in Washington, nearly two months later, Upshur had already begun to make overtures for annexation.[33]

While Smith, Green, and other individuals worked on official minds, the American press spread the alarm more widely, motivated by devotion to slavery, hatred of Britain, or both. In the spring, New Orleans newspapers described Andrews' little abolitionist clique, scolded the "imbecile administration" of Texas, and published a letter from one A. J. Yates, accusing Elliot of intrigue. The letter was widely reprinted, to Yates' discom-

32. Calhoun to Green, Fort Hill, September 8, 1843, Calhoun, *Correspondence*, pp. 545–47. Calhoun to Upshur, August 27, quoted in St. George Leakin Sioussat, "John Caldwell Calhoun," in Bemis, *American Secretaries of State*, V, 141–44.

33. William S. Murphy to Upshur, July 6, September 24, 1843, Nos. 3, 7, Manning, *IAA*, XII, 292–94, 299–309.

fiture, for he realized that his charges were exaggerated. The loudest outcries on the Texas question came from the Southwest, but in the North the New York *Journal of Commerce*, the Boston *Daily Mail*, as well as the *Globe*, the *National Intelligencer*, and other Washington newspapers took up the cry that the redcoats were coming. In June, Tyler's own administration organ, the *Madisonian*, proclaimed:

> If Great Britain, as her *philanthropists* and blustering presses intimate, entertains a design to possess Mexico or Texas, or to interfere in any manner with the slaves of the Southern States, but a few weeks we fancy, at any time, will suffice to rouse the whole American People to arms like one vast nest of hornets. The great Western States, at the call of "Captain Tyler," would pour their noble sons down the Mississippi Valley by MILLIONS.[34]

* * * *

It is difficult to determine how much these private and public communications shaped the policies of the Tyler administration and how much Tyler and Upshur used them as rationalizations.[35] Certainly it is unfortunate that the two men did not have at hand in the summer reports from the American minister to Britain, Edward Everett, like the two he sent home in November, describing the suspicions of British plots as greatly exaggerated.[36] Regrettably also, increasing tension between the American and Mexican governments during June and July served to divert attention from Mexico's quarrels with European nations and to start rumors that the British were intriguing in Mexico too.

34. For a summary of American press opinion, including the quotation from the *Madisonian*, June 24, 1843, see Smith, *Annexation of Texas*, pp. 111–15. *NNR*, 44 (June 10, July 8), 229–31, 293. Yates later confirmed Elliot's statement that the Foreign Office had instructed him not to interfere in Texan domestic affairs. A. J. Yates to Elliot, July 12, Adams, *British Correspondence*, pp. 229–32.

35. Upshur's latest biographer concludes, for example, that while he did not trust Duff Green, the corroborating information from the Texan representatives convinced him of the nefarious British aims against the South. Claude H. Hall, *Abel Parker Upshur, Conservative Virginian*, pp. 198–99. Wiltse, *Calhoun, Sectionalist*, pp. 153–56. A recent account attaching much significance to the news from abroad is Frederick Merk, *Slavery and the Annexation of Texas*, pp. 11–35.

36. Everett to Upshur, November 3, 16, 1843, No. 62, private, Manning, *IAA*, VII, 246–48, 251. Wiltse suggests that Tyler did not have much faith in Everett's judgment, believing him sympathetic with abolitionism. Wiltse, *Calhoun, Sectionalist*, p. 155. This explanation does not jibe with a later statement by Tyler to Calhoun that it was Everett's dispatches which convinced him and Upshur that Britain was intriguing for abolition in Texas. Calhoun, *Correspondence*, p. 1173. See also Frederick Merk, *The Monroe Doctrine and American Expansionism, 1843–1849*, pp. 18–22.

As late as mid-June the Mexican minister, Almonte, had reported to his government that public opinion in the United States was unusually well disposed toward Mexico, but almost at once he sent home a story—probably retailed to him by his friend John Quincy Adams—that Waddy Thompson was a Texan agent in disguise, reporting Mexican troop movements and other useful information to the rebels.[37] Santa Anna's government may not have believed this accusation against Thompson, but it was alarmed and outraged by the rash of pro-Texan articles in the American press. Late in July, Foreign Minister Bocanegra reopened the provocative question of American aid to the Texans. A month later, on August 23, he wrote to Thompson that the Mexican government had learned of a proposal for Texan annexation to be submitted to the next Congress. Without mincing words, he declared, "The Mexican Government will consider equivalent to a declaration of war against the Mexican Republic, the passage of an act for the incorporation of Texas with the territory of the United States."[38]

In midsummer of 1843 the rumors of British schemes and the reports of Mexican defiance spurred Upshur to action. On July 25 and 27 he sent off two strong protests to the Mexican government, one concerning Mexican obstructionism in settling claims and the other against an announcement by Mexico that all prisoners of war taken in Texas (including many American citizens, of course) would be shot at once.[39] On August 8 he wrote to Chargé Murphy in Texas that information recently received from London seemed to verify his suspicions of British intrigues in Texas. He described the disastrous effects which these intrigues would produce in the South and declared that the United States would make "the most strenuous efforts" to frustrate abolitionism in Texas.[40] Two days later he discussed the same subject with the

37. Almonte to Ministerio de Relaciones, June 16, July 6, 1843, No. 75 with enclosure, Barker transcripts, v. 569, pp. 11, 19-22.

38. Bocanegra to Thompson, July 21, August 8, 23, 1843, Manning, *IAA*, VIII, 547-48, 551-53, 555-57. The passage quoted appears on p. 557. Bocanegra's strong language arose at least in part from rumors about a Texan raiding expedition in the vicinity of Santa Fe led by Colonel Jacob Snively in the spring of 1843. The Mexican government assumed that the United States

had furnished men and supplies. Actually, American troops had intercepted and disarmed Snively's men. Berge, "Mexican Response," pp. 87-90. Hubert Howe Bancroft, *History of the North Mexican States and Texas*, II, 371-72.

39. Upshur to Thompson, July 25, 1843, No. 42, US, DS, I, Mexico, XV, 232-46. The second note urged Mexico to reconquer or recognize Texas. Same, July 27, No. 43, Manning, *IAA*, VIII, 132-38.

40. Manning, *IAA*, XII, 44-49. The quoted phrase is on p. 45. See also

Texan representative, Van Zandt, who told him that if he suspected undue British influence in Texas, the best preventive would be "to act promptly and efficiently."[41]

By August 14 the questions in Upshur's mind were apparently resolved, for he wrote to Calhoun in positive terms that Britain was determined to bring about abolition throughout America in order to destroy competition against her tropical colonies and that she planned to flood the Texan market with British goods. If Texas threw herself on the protection of the United States, as seemed likely, the American government would have to receive her as a slaveholding state. He anticipated "a burst of repugnance" in the North but added, somewhat optimistically, "To the South, it is a question of *safety*; to the North, it is one of interest. . . . I have never known the North to refuse to do what their interest required."[42] Soon after this, administration newspapers in the North began to echo these sentiments.[43] During the next two months Upshur outlined his fears about British intentions in even greater detail to Everett and published two series of Anglophobe articles anonymously in the *Madisonian*. All of these writings showed how clearly he had accepted the ideas of Green and Calhoun about the commercial basis of British abolitionism.[44]

Upshur's next step was to sound out the intentions of the Texan government, since in July Houston had formally withdrawn his annexationist feeler of the preceding winter. After several informal conversations, on September 18 Upshur formally told Van Zandt that he would make a definite proposal for annexation if Houston would authorize Van Zandt again to negotiate. He also instructed Murphy to convince the Texans, if possible, that annexation would meet with support in the North.[45] On October 16, having received no reply from Van Zandt for four weeks, Upshur renewed the offer to negotiate, and Van Zandt reported to

Smith, *Annexation of Texas*, pp. 119–21. It is not certain that this note was inspired by Green's July letter, as the exact date of its receipt is not known.

41. Van Zandt to Jones, August 12, 1843, Jones, *Memoranda*, pp. 243–44.

42. Upshur to Calhoun, August 14, 1843, *William and Mary Quarterly*, series 2, 16 (October 1936), 554–57.

43. For example, the New York *Aurora*, which was supposed to represent Tyler's views, began a series of articles on Texas on August 23 and 24. Smith,

Annexation of Texas, pp. 133–35.

44. Upshur wrote twice to Everett on September 28, Manning, *IAA*, VII, 6–17. Tyler also wrote privately to Thompson urging him to be alert. Tyler, *Letters and Times*, III, 118. See also Hall, *Upshur*, p. 199.

45. Van Zandt to Jones, September 18, 1843, No. 107, Garrison, *DCRT*, II, 207–10. Murphy to Upshur, July 8; Upshur to Murphy, September 22, Manning, *IAA*, XII, 51–52, 295–96.

Houston that congressional and public opinion in the United States had never been more favorable to annexation.[46]

This time, however, the capricious Houston decided to give the Americans a taste of frustration. In a public speech at Huntsville he declared that England had no designs on either Texas or Texans' slaves, since it was obvious that slave labor could develop the agriculture of the area eight times as fast as could free farmers.[47] When Van Zandt's October dispatch arrived, Houston showed it to Elliot and in a long conversation assured him that if Mexico should recognize Texan independence, he and the Texan people would never approve an annexation treaty with the United States.[48]

During the autumn, anxiety within the Tyler administration mounted, as reports of British plotting continued to reach the State Department; within the country, the propaganda campaign in pro-Texan newspapers revived the animus of Northern abolitionists. In mid-October Upshur received a copy of Bocanegra's threat that annexation would mean war with the United States, and he sent off a firm dispatch to Thompson to reinforce his stiff reply. Thompson later wrote that, in his opinion, the threat was designed mainly for home consumption, since Santa Anna was about to run for reelection.[49] However, on November 3 Minister Almonte also warned Upshur that annexation would mean war. He, too, received a blunt reply.[50]

October brought a sudden but brief crisis in Anglo–Mexican relations, which Tyler and Upshur might have put to good use for American interests if they had learned of it in time. Late in September Santa Anna allowed a British flag to be displayed at a banquet among trophies captured from the Texans. No one knew how

46. Van Zandt to Jones, October 16, 1843, No. 109, Garrison, *DCRT*, II, 221–24.

47. Houston's speech is quoted in Herbert Gambrell, *Anson Jones, the Last President of Texas*, p. 294.

48. Elliot to Aberdeen, Galveston, October 31, 1845, Adams, *British Correspondence*, pp. 271–78. Adams, *British Interests*, pp. 151–52.

49. Upshur to Thompson, October 20, 1843, No. 51; Thompson to Upshur, October 29, No. 31, Manning, *IAA*, VIII, 139–40, 565.

50. Almonte to Upshur, November 3, December 11, 1843; Upshur to Almonte, November 8, December 1, Man-

ning, *IAA*, VIII, 140–42, 144–48, 566–67, 575–76. Almonte's reaction was largely bluff, too, for at the same time he advised his government not to break relations until Tyler had actually signed an annexation bill into law. Almonte cited the precedent of the bill for occupying the disputed territory in Oregon, which had passed only the Senate and had not provoked Britain to action. Almonte to Ministerio de Relaciones, November 4, No. 120, US, LC, /86. John Quincy Adams seems to have assured him that Congress would not approve annexation. Callahan, *Mexican Relations*, p. 114.

it had come to be there, but the Mexican government refused to hand it over to the British chargé, Percy W. Doyle, who inflated the incident into a mortal insult to his country.[51] Because of this quarrel, European diplomats foresaw a *rapprochement* between Santa Anna and Thompson, and indeed the two did discuss the possibility that Britain might seize California. Thompson took advantage of the crisis to maneuver Bocanegra into signing a claims convention, but before he could obtain further concessions, Aberdeen formally accepted the Mexican explanation of the flag incident, and the crisis subsided.[52] For a time Santa Anna was more deferential than usual to Britain, but Thompson felt that the Mexicans were nevertheless extremely jealous of British influence in Texas and California. He was sure that Mexico would cede no territory to Britain voluntarily and that Santa Anna was not deeply concerned about the slavery question in Texas.[53]

By the beginning of December Tyler and Upshur were committed to the annexation of Texas, but their campaign had made little progress outside of the American press. Early in November Upshur had approached Van Zandt for a third time, but received no encouragement.[54] As the month wore on, he could do nothing but support Thompson in various protests to Mexico and advise Murphy to counteract British influences in Texas by cultivating good personal relations with government officials.[55] The increasingly bitter arguments over Texas in American newspapers aroused much speculation about Tyler's treatment of the question in his annual message, but it contained no positive recommendations about Texas—nothing beyond a strongly worded denunciation of Mexico's border war, which was weakening both nations

51. Doyle to Aberdeen, September 29, October 30, 1843, Nos. 74, 79, GB, FO 50/164, ff. 198–211; 50/165, ff. 14–21. Doyle suspected that Santa Anna had deliberately provoked the crisis so he might station troops around Mexico City during the approaching election and also sell cattle to the government for feeding the troops. Jones, *Aberdeen and the Americas*, p. 32. Antonio de la Peña y Reyes, *Incidente diplomático con Inglaterra en 1843, passim*.

52. Oliver to Primer Secretario de Estado, October 12, 1843, No. 311, Delgado, *España y México*, III, 561–64. Thompson to Upshur, October 3, November 20, Manning, *IAA*, VIII, 563–

64, 570–75. The American Senate never approved the convention. Aberdeen to Tomás Murphy, November 1, 20, T. Murphy to Aberdeen, November 13, GB, FO 50/168, ff. 144–70.

53. Thompson to W. Murphy, November 25, 1843, Manning, *IAA*, XII, 322, note. This remained Thompson's opinion when he returned home and wrote his memoirs. Waddy Thompson, *Recollections of Mexico*, pp. 236–38.

54. Van Zandt to Jones, November 4, 1843, No. 110, Garrison, *DCRT*, II, 225.

55. Upshur to Thompson, November 18, 1843, No. 53, Upshur to W. Murphy, November 21, No. 11, Manning, *IAA*, VIII, 142–44; XII, 55–58.

and exposing them to outside interference. This, of course, was a slap at Britain.[56]

Reactions to the message were mixed. The *National Intelligencer* and some other Whig journals concluded that administration newspapers had exaggerated the President's desire for Texas. Andrew Jackson praised Tyler for his prudence in not showing his cards before he had signed a treaty.[57] In Europe one French newspaper called the message an indirect attack on British commercial ambitions in Texas, but the London *Times* scornfully dismissed it as "a mere flourish of trumpets to honour Mr. Tyler's *exit* from the Presidential throne of the Republic."[58] Aberdeen strongly resented the President's imputation of British interference in Texas, but the effects of his indignation did not appear for a time.

*   *   *   *

For over a month after Tyler had presented his annual message the Texas question seemed dormant. In the United States the President's reticence bewildered even the most enthusiastic annexationists. In Texas, public reaction to his position was still very much divided. Hard times, the fear of renewed hostilities with Mexico, and innumerable personal and economic ties to the United States had apparently converted the majority of Texans to annexation, but an inchoate national pride had asserted itself here and there, and uncertainty about American intentions impelled an undetermined number to look to England for support. One Texan wrote to Senator J. J. Crittenden, "We wish sincerely that the U. States would plainly mark the line she intended to pursue towards us. If she would let us alone, we can soon settle our affairs in a manner to suit us, but . . . the first moment we engage in negotiations with any other power to give us peace, she forbids it, and then leaves us to our fate. This is neither just or generous."[59]

Houston, never entirely sure whether he wanted annexation or independence, easily matched his actions to the public indeci-

56. James D. Richardson, ed., *A Compilation of the Messages and Papers of the Presidents, 1789–1897*, IV, 260–63.

57. Smith, *Annexation of Mexico*, p. 137. Jackson to William B. Lewis, December 15, 1843, Jackson, *Correspondence*, VI, 249.

58. *Le constitutionnel*, January 1, 1844, p. 1. The official French organ accused Tyler of courting the mob. *Le journal des débats*, December 31, 1843, p. 2. See also London *Times*, December 29, p. 4.

59. "Texas" to editor of Houston *Citizen*, published December 30, 1843. Clipping in GB, FO 75/10, f. 21. James Jones to J. J. Crittenden, Galveston, February 1, 1844, Crittenden Papers, IX, 1656–57. On general public opinion in Texas, see Stanley Siegel, *A Political History of the Texas Republic, 1836–1845*, pp. 228; and Llerena Friend, *Sam Houston, the Great Designer*, p. 127.

sion. In his opening message to Congress on December 5 he dismayed all pro-Americans by contrasting the do-nothing policy of the Tyler administration with the open friendliness of Britain. About a week later he sent a delayed and chilly reply to Van Zandt's two autumn reports of American overtures, saying that European mediation between Texas and Mexico offered more solid chances of peace than "the very uncertain prospect of annexation to the United States however desirable that event." He expressed fear that if Texas agreed to negotiate for annexation, Britain would withdraw her support, and that if annexation did not succeed, Texas would then be left without a friend in the world.[60]

Behind the appearance of inactivity in Washington, Upshur had been busily lobbying among senators in behalf of a Texan annexation treaty, tactfully parrying abolitionist complaints and soothing those who feared war with Mexico. By January 16 he felt certain enough of his two-thirds majority to send new instructions to Chargé Murphy. In his dispatch he explained Tyler's failure to advocate annexation openly in his annual message and declared that sentiment in its favor had now so increased that the Senate would now approve a treaty. He warned that British influence would Europeanize Texas and that when the inevitable Anglo–American war came about, Texas would "find herself between the upper and the nether millstones, ground to powder in their revolutions."[61] Three days later Van Zandt also reported that in his opinion the Senate would approve an annexation treaty and that Mexico would not grant unconditional recognition.[62] Also, at the urging of Robert J. Walker and others the aged Jackson wrote several letters to his erstwhile protégé, Houston, exhorting him to resist the British threat.[63]

Even before these various communications arrived from the United States, annexationist pressure was building up against the susceptible Houston. Murphy had little sophistication or diplomatic training, but with the persistence and personal contacts of

60. Siegel, *Texas Republic*, pp. 225–26. Jesse Reeves, *American Diplomacy under Tyler and Polk*, p. 135. Jones to Van Zandt, December 13, 1843, Garrison, *DCRT*, II, 232–35. Jones, *Memoranda*, pp. 278–79.

61. Upshur to W. Murphy, January 16, 1844, No. 14, Manning, *IAA*, XII, 59–65. The quoted phrase is on p. 63. Hall, *Upshur*, pp. 204–5. Jackson also assured Houston of a two-thirds majority. Tyler, *Letters and Times*, II, 284–85. Smith, *Annexation of Texas*, p. 159n14.

62. Van Zandt to Jones, January 20, 1844, No. 113, Garrison, *DCRT*, II, 239–43.

63. Robert J. Walker to Jackson, January 10, 1844; Houston to Jackson, February 16, Jackson, *Correspondence*, VI, 255–56, 260–64.

the lobbyist, he helped to induce members of the Texan Congress to bring in bills for annexation and to call for information on current negotiations. Unfortunately for Elliot, illness had taken him from Texas to Washington, where he was commenting on the American campaign, like a dog growling in front of the wrong gopher hole. On January 20 Houston gave way before the accumulated pressure and in a secret message to Congress recommended that if the delegates insisted on negotiating, they should act quickly and secretly in order not to antagonize Britain more seriously than necessary. In familiar fashion the Texan Congress did not get around to appropriating money for a special envoy until just before adjournment on February 5. Nine days earlier, however, Jones sent Van Zandt a list of points relevant to annexation that he might discuss with Upshur if he were certain the American Congress would ultimately approve the measure.[64]

Houston insisted on one prerequisite—an American guarantee of protection against a possible attack by Mexican forces during the negotiations. When Van Zandt first broached this subject to Upshur in a note of January 17, the secretary replied that under the Constitution he could not commit the United States to war with Mexico, but he promised to assemble a large naval squadron off the Texan coast and send troops to the Texan border.[65] Before Van Zandt's dispatch (dated January 20) could have reached Texas, Houston asked for a similar guarantee from Murphy. In a note of February 14, acting wholly without instructions, the American chargé promised flatly that "neither Mexico nor any other power, will be permitted to invade Texas, on account of any negotiation which may take place, in relation to any subject upon which Texas, is, or may be invited by the United States to negociate[sic]."[66] This reassurance had the desired effect, for Houston replied that he would send J. Pinckney Henderson, an experienced diplomat, as special envoy to assist Van Zandt with the negotia-

---

64. Smith, *Annexation of Texas*, pp. 160–62. Rives, *US and Mexico*, I, 593–95. Jones to Van Zandt, January 27, 1844, Garrison, *DCRT*, II, 248–50. The instructions provided that Texas should be admitted as a state if her population qualified her, that the United States should assume the Texas public debt, estimated at about $20 million, and that all remaining public lands in Texas should go to the American government.

65. Van Zandt to Upshur, January 17, 1844, Manning, *IAA*, XII, 324–25. Van Zandt to Jones, January 20, No. 113, Garrison, *DCRT*, II, 242.

66. Murphy was later reproved for going so far. Jones to W. Murphy, February 14, 1844; W. Murphy to Jones, February 14; John Nelson to W. Murphy, March 11, No. 15, Manning, *IAA*, XII, 70–71, 326–29. The passage quoted is on p. 328.

tions. On February 25 fuller instructions for the envoys left the Texan State Department.[67]

After Houston had made his decision, he wrote a long reply to Jackson, weighing against each other the advantages of close relations with the United States and with Britain and explaining the need for protection during the crucial period ahead. He closed by describing Texas as a "bride adorned for her es[p]ousals" and expressing his hope that she would not be jilted at the altar.[68] Texas was certainly more coy than most brides, for while Houston considered the American blandishments, he carefully kept open his lines of communication to Britain and Mexico. On February 17 Elliot, who was presumably receiving occasional information from his friends in Texas, reported to Aberdeen from the United States that all prospects of annexation had dissipated; as late as March 22 he wrote to Jones that he could not believe that Houston would sacrifice Texan independence.[69] During the preceding September Houston had sent two commissioners to Mexico to negotiate under the armistice. Now he allowed them to continue their discussions without any hint that their government's policy was changing. On February 18 they signed a tentative agreement with Mexico.[70]

Two days earlier, Upshur called Minister Almonte to the State Department and explained to him why the United States government felt it necessary to annex Texas. He laid great stress on the dangers which British influence in Texas posed to the United States: endless litigation over smuggling and fugitive slaves, meddling in the American South, and attacks on American trade in wartime. Upshur offered support for Mexican neutral rights and "full justice" if Mexico registered a damage claim for the loss of Texas.

67. Smith, *Annexation of Texas*, pp. 165–66. Jones to Henderson, February 15, 1844; Jones to Van Zandt, February 24; Jones to Henderson and Van Zandt, February 25, Garrison, *DCRT*, II, 252–53, 259–60.

68. Jackson, *Correspondence*, VI, 260–64.

69. At least part of Elliot's statement of February 17 rested on assurances from Henry Clay that the Senate would never approve an annexation treaty. Rives, *US and Mexico*, I, 599. Elliot to Jones, Galveston, March 22, 1844, Jones, *Memoranda*, pp. 329–30. In a letter to

Elliot, Houston explained that he had decided to negotiate for annexation because of the breakdown of negotiations with Mexico for an armistice and for the release of the Mier prisoners. Houston to Elliot, March 1844, *The Writings of Sam Houston*, ed. Amelia W. Williams and Eugene C. Barker, IV, 288–92. This explanation must have been largely rationalizing after the fact.

70. Rives, *US and Mexico*, I, 597. Houston to G. W. Hockley and S. M. Williams, February 3, 1844, Garrison, *DCRT*, II, 786–89.

The secretary's arguments and his hint of an indemnity did not produce the intended effect on his hearer. For some time John Quincy Adams and others had been telling Almonte that Congress would not approve annexation and that Tyler did not command enough popular support to turn sensible persons against Mexico. The Mexican minister favored playing for time by letting the American government think that a negotiated settlement was possible. Consequently, he told Upshur that reasons of personal honor prevented Santa Anna from recognizing Texan independence; he also pretended to agree with Upshur's strictures against Britain. But Almonte reported to his government that Upshur's veiled offer of remuneration constituted recognition of the basic Mexican claim to Texas and that the American government, facing a split between North and South, wanted to avoid war and would be willing to negotiate. Thus, Mexico would have time to prepare for hostilities. Clearly, Upshur and Almonte took away from the conversation only what each wanted to believe.[71]

Meanwhile, what of Britain and France? Reports of American outbursts against British abolitionism and intervention in Texas so alarmed Aberdeen that he determined to clarify British policy. On December 26 he instructed Pakenham that, while Britain wished to see Texas independent and slavery abolished, she would not use improper means to achieve these ends and, in particular, had no intention of establishing any dominant influence in Texas; her objects there were entirely commercial and not at all political. He denied any desire of producing dissension within the United States over the slavery question.[72] When Aberdeen learned of Tyler's annual message, with its imputation of British intrigue, he became angry and suggested to Guizot that France take a stand on the American annexation of Texas. Louis Philippe personally informed the British ambassador, Lord Cowley, that France wished to set a barrier to American expansion, and Guizot informed his

71. Manning, *IAA*, VIII, 577–79. Almonte to Ministerio de Relaciones, February 17, 1844, No. 4, US, LC, /86. According to Upshur, Almonte conceded that Mexico's reconquest of Texas was impossible. According to Almonte, he told Upshur that Mexico would overrun half of Texas before the United States could complete annexation negotiations with the Texan government, whereupon Upshur replied that the Americans would rather see Mexico conquer Texas than have it become a British satellite! See also Rives, *US and Mexico*, I, 599–601.

72. Aberdeen to Pakenham, December 26, 1843, No. 9, GB, FO 115/83, ff. 182–86. At this time Aberdeen had not yet read Tyler's annual message. Adams, *British Interests*, p. 156. It seems clear that Aberdeen's new interest in Texas also reflected an accumulation of disgust at Mexican commercial restrictions. Smith to Jones, Paris, January 29, 1844, Jones, *Memoranda*, pp. 304–5.

minister in Washington that France could not watch with indifference even voluntary Texan annexation to the United States.[73] Neither Aberdeen nor Guizot, however, proposed any further action at this time.

Thus, late in February the way seemed clear for negotiations between Upshur and the Texan envoys. At this point a trick of fate further postponed the annexation treaty. On February 28 the President and members of his official family visited the U.S.S. *Princeton* for an official demonstration of a great new cannon, sardonically nicknamed "Peacemaker." After displays of artillery and a pleasant lunch, most of the company went on deck for more firing, but Tyler remained below. Since the United States had no vice president at the moment, his pause was fortunate, for this time "Peacemaker" exploded like a huge grenade. When the smoke cleared, five men lay dead on the deck. One of them was Secretary Upshur.[74]

*   *   *   *

To most friends of Texas the logical man to replace Upshur in the State Department was his mentor John C. Calhoun, the leader of the Southern bloc in and out of Congress and the most avid annexationist of all. With his powerful, probing mind, his colossal self-righteousness, and his steel-like will, the gaunt, forbidding Calhoun might be expected to overshadow the more pliable Tyler. The President need not fear opposition from the South Carolinian in his campaign for reelection, however, since Calhoun had formally withdrawn from the presidential contest in December 1843.

Even so, Calhoun hesitated for a time before accepting the appointment.[75] His annexationist friends (three of whom died on

73. Aberdeen to Lord Cowley, January 12, 1844, No. 16; Cowley to Aberdeen, January 15, No. 33, GB, FO 115/85, ff. 9–12. Guizot to Alphonse Pageot, February 10, No. 10, France, MAE, CP, États-unis, C, ff. 34–35. In addition to Aberdeen's overture to France, the foreign secretary wrote a direct protest against Tyler's message but decided not to send it to Pakenham. Adams believes that at this point Aberdeen was quite prepared to join France in directly prohibiting annexation. Adams, *British Interests*, pp. 156–60.

74. Seager, *and Tyler Too*, pp. 204–6.

75. Some historians accept the statement of Tyler's close friend, Henry Wise, that he committed his chief to the appointment by sounding out one of Calhoun's lieutenants without consulting Tyler. See, for example, Paul, *Rift in the Democracy*, pp. 105–7. Wiltse, however, doubts that Wise acted without consulting the President and submits evidence that on two earlier occasions Tyler had tried to persuade Calhoun into the cabinet. Wiltse, *Calhoun, Sectionalist*, pp. 87, 138, 161–63, 504. If Tyler did want Calhoun in the cabinet to handle the Texas question, it is odd that he should have urged Van Zandt to rush through the treaty ne-

the *Princeton*) had long been urging him to take up the Texas question actively, if only as a political move. He had replied with restatements of the strategic and economic arguments for annexation, which he compared in importance to the union of England with Scotland and Ireland. When he learned of his appointment, his first desire was to limit his responsibilities to the actual negotiations with Texas. Nearly a week later he agreed to accept a full-scale appointment, with the proviso that he could resign when the Texas and Oregon questions were settled.[76] As yet he had little interest in California.

The settlement of the two principal expansionist problems would bind together the South and the West in the kind of political alliance for which Calhoun had long worked and which might further his own presidential chances in 1848. However, he had in mind two very different diplomatic campaigns—active negotiations for Texas and passive delay in Oregon to give American settlers time to occupy the territory. The difference in Calhoun's methods, his reputation for stubborn sectionalism, and his bad judgment in defending the Texan treaty were to turn much of the Northern press against him, but at the time of his appointment the leading Northern newspapers welcomed his choice, confident that he would not yield any part of Oregon or take any "rash step" in Texas.[77]

At the time of Upshur's death, he and Van Zandt had reconciled all but minor differences in their drafts of the annexation treaty; as soon as Calhoun and J. Pinckney Henderson, the new Texan envoy, arrived in Washington at the end of March, the negotiations continued. Apparently neither newcomer made any substantial changes in the draft before the signature of the treaty on April 12. The treaty provided that Texas enter the Union as a territory, with the rights to control her own domestic institutions (that is, slavery) and to apply for statehood under the Constitution. No boundaries were specified. Texas agreed to surrender her public lands, and the United States agreed to pay the Texan public debt, but in the latter provision, to Van Zandt's dissatisfaction, no distinction was made between the original purchasers of Texan bonds and those who had bought them later at cut rates. Also, he

gotiations with the acting secretary, Attorney General John Nelson, before Calhoun's arrival in Washington. Van Zandt to Jones, March 5, 1844, No. 115, Garrison, *DCRT*, II, 262.

76. Wiltse, *Calhoun, Sectionalist*, pp. 163–65. Calhoun, *Correspondence*, pp. 552, 555, 559–60, 573–77, 896–97, 900–908.

77. *NNR*, 66 (March 23, 1844), 49–50.

objected to having an American-appointed commission pass on individual claims.[78]

In view of its later importance, the question of interim protection against Mexico deserves special attention. After Upshur's death and before Calhoun's arrival in Washington, Acting Secretary John Nelson had disapproved Murphy's pledge of February 14, on the grounds that it exceeded the constitutional powers of the President. In response to pressure from the Texan envoys, Calhoun now assured them orally that Tyler would concentrate troops at Fort Jesup, near the Sabine River, and order a naval force of ten or twelve ships to the Gulf. In the event of a Mexican naval demonstration, Tyler would inform the Mexican government that the United States would repel an attack on Texas. It was hoped that Texas could fight off mere border raids.[79] For strict constructionists like Tyler and Calhoun, these assurances stretched to the limit the President's powers as commander-in-chief of the Army and Navy.

While Van Zandt objected to some provisions of the treaty, he reported to the Texan government that its terms were as favorable as could reasonably be expected, since they would have to be approved by the United States Senate. When Houston saw the completed treaty and Van Zandt's report, he grumbled that the guarantee of protection and the method of paying the Texan debt were inadequate, but on the whole he seemed fairly well satisfied. One reason for Houston's agreement may have been that at about this time the Texan armistice commissioners returned from Mexico, proudly bearing a document which extended the truce but also formally designated Texas as a department of Mexico. This provision was totally unacceptable to Houston; it demonstrated once again the hopelessness of mediation or direct negotiations with Mexico.[80]

Nevertheless, Houston was still afraid that the bride might be left waiting at the altar. On accepting the treaty draft, he wrote to

78. Smith, *Annexation of Texas*, pp. 174–76. Rives, *US and Mexico*, I, 606–10. For the text of the treaty, see US, 28C, 1S, HED 271, pp. 5–8. Van Zandt to Jones, March 5, 20, 25, April 12, 1844, Nos. 115, 116, 118, 119, Garrison, *DCRT*, II, 261, 263–65, 269–73.

79. Nelson to Murphy, March 11, 1844, No. 15, Manning, *IAA*, XII, 70–71. Van Zandt to Jones, April 12, No. 119, Garrison, *DCRT*, II, 270–72.

80. Houston to Van Zandt, April 29,

May 10, 1844, Garrison, *DCRT*, II, pp. 274–76, 279. Smith, *Annexation of Texas*, p. 172. At this time both Murphy and Elliot were hovering around Houston, seeking to influence him in one way or another. Elliot to Aberdeen, Galveston, April 7, enclosing Elliot's correspondence with Anson Jones, Adams, *British Correspondence*, pp. 304–15. Smith, *Annexation of Texas*, p. 178.

Van Zandt: "I again declare to you that . . . [this] is the last effort at Annexation that Texas will ever make, nor do I believe that any solicitation or guarantee from the U. S. would at any future day induce her to consent to the measure." In a private letter he instructed his envoys that, if Congress refused any sort of action toward annexation, they must approach the British and French ministers and the State Department with a proposal for a triple guarantee of Texan independence and peace with Mexico.[81]

The issue was now squarely before the Senate. With their party already partly split on Texas, could Tyler, Calhoun, and the Southern bloc of Democrats obtain a two-thirds vote in favor of the treaty?

81. Garrison, *DCRT*, II, 275. Houston to Van Zandt and Henderson, April 16, 1844, Houston, *Writings*, IV, 298–99.

6

Annexation Defeated, Polk Elected

Unfortunately, the negotiations with Texas had reached their climax at the beginning of a United States presidential campaign —that quadrennial ritual of incantations, ceremonial dances, and burnt offerings during which no politician's behavior can be fully relied on. Generally speaking, the annexationists divided into two groups: those speculators and other expansionists who tended to value Texas as land to be bought or sold and others like Tyler and Calhoun for whom annexation was principally a means toward their political ends. In both groups the differences were blurred and the alignments constantly shifting. A little withdrawn from the friends and foes of annexation was another group of practical politicians such as Clay and Van Buren, who hoped somehow to keep the Texas question in the background until the election was over.

Both men had good reasons to avoid discussing Texas. Despite the Whigs' victory in 1840 the party was weak and loosely organized, with only shallow roots in the American political soil. While the Democrats held a basically stronger appeal to the mass of American people, they were also more divided internally than the Whigs. Van Buren still held the party's titular leadership and expected nomination in 1844, but behind the scenes many others had ambitions to overturn the "Red Fox."

Sensing the explosive sectionalism inherent in the Texas question, Clay and Van Buren appear to have agreed confidentially as early as 1842 that they would not raise the question in debate.[1] At the end of 1843 there was no reason to believe that they had changed their views. Early in that year, however, Van Buren made one important concession to his rivals. At the urging of Robert J. Walker and a small group, mostly Southerners, he agreed to postpone the Democratic convention from November 1843 to May 1844. Some guessed that Calhoun, still hoping desperately for the nomination, had inspired the change. More likely Walker was only

1. James C. N. Paul, *Rift in the Democracy*, pp. 87–88. Henry Clay to J. J. Crittenden, December 5, 1843, Crittenden Papers, IX, 1610–12.

playing for time in which to force the Texas question upon the public and make it a leading issue of the approaching campaign.[2]

*　　*　　*　　*

If such was Walker's intention, he made good use of the time gained. During the fall and winter of 1843–1844, while Tyler and Upshur feinted with the Texan government, Walker kept in close touch with friends in Texas. One of these was William S. Murphy, the American chargé d'affaires—like Walker an avid land speculator—who warned him about British intrigue for abolition. Early in January Walker composed a letter, ostensibly in reply to an annexationist petition from Kentucky. The Washington *Madisonian*, Tyler's spokesman, printed it as a pamphlet and eventually published fifty thousand copies. On February 3 it appeared in the Washington *Globe*, and from here it ricocheted all around the country.[3]

Walker's letter was a masterpiece in which he set forth and reconciled all the arguments for annexation. There was something in Texas, it seemed, for every American. Appealing to the legalist, Walker argued that the United States had not really given up Texas by the treaty of 1819. To the merchant he offered new Gulf harbors and trade, to the farmer broad, fertile acres. To slaveholders he offered freedom from abolitionist plotting and from the loss of runaway slaves. To humanitarians he offered a warmer climate for slaves to work in and a chance for them to slip away into Mexico, become free, and rise in the social scale. To the South he offered more territory; to the North he suggested the annexation of Oregon as compensation. Above and beyond all other arguments, however, was fear and hatred of England—her growing empire, her trade competition, her plans to colonize Texas, undermine the American tariff system by smuggling, close her markets to American cotton, and flood the New World with cheap manufactures:

> We can yet rescue Texas from her grasp, and, by reannexation, insure at least the command of our own great sea, and the outlet of our own great river. And shall we neglect the reacquisition, and throw Texas, and the command of the gulf, into the arms of England? Whoever would do so, is a monarchist. . . . He is also an

2. Paul, *Rift in the Democracy*, pp. 63–65.

3. Paul, *Rift in the Democracy*, pp. 96–100. William S. Murphy to Robert J. Walker, Galveston, October 10, 1843; A. C. Allen to Walker, Houston, November 13, Walker Papers, Nos. 037, 039, LC.

Englishman in feelings and principle, and would recolonize the American states.[4]

Opponents of annexation took alarm at Walker's letter. As early as January, Webster had written an open letter to the citizens of Worcester, Massachusetts, warning that annexation might lead to disunion. Temporarily forsaking nationalism and broad construction, he denied that the Constitution had given the Federal Government the power to acquire new territory. During succeeding weeks he and others published occasional articles in the same vein, and by March the opposition was in full cry. The *National Intelligencer*, the Boston *Atlas*, the New York *Evening Post*, and other Northern newspapers denounced the "mad project" of annexing a "pauper republic" as irrational, preposterous, and "manifestly against the provisions of the Constitution." Some laughed at Walker's fears of aggression from a British-dominated Texas and his suggestion that slavery could be gradually abolished by migrations across the Rio Grande. If his forecasts materialized, they asked, would we eventually be called on to annex Mexico and South America too?[5]

The *Madisonian* and a group of Calhoun's supporting newspapers led the defense, and a number of newspapers took various intermediate positions, striving for a measure of objectivity.[6] By the latter part of March the annexationists decided that, however

4. Robert J. Walker, *Letter of Mr. Walker, of Mississippi, Relative to the Reannexation of Texas in Reply to the Call of the People of Carroll County, Kentucky, to Communicate His Views on That Subject, passim.* Reprinted in Frederick Merk, *Fruits of Propaganda in the Tyler Administration*, pp. 221–52. The quotation appears on p. 19 (239). For a convenient summary of the pamphlet, somewhat longer than the above and emphasizing different arguments, see Justin H. Smith, *The Annexation of Texas*, pp. 140–44. Frederick Merk finds a kind of "safety valve" thesis in some of Walker's predictions that the annexation of Texas would relieve the pressure of slavery to expand. Frederick Merk, "A Safety Valve Thesis and Texan Annexation," reprinted in *Fruits of Propaganda*, pp. 95–120.

5. Webster's speech is summarized in Smith, *Annexation of Texas*, p. 139. For a summary of press opinions, includ-

ing the above quotations from the *National Intelligencer* and the *Atlas*, see Smith, pp. 180–84. Smith believes that Mexico may have been subsidizing the *National Intelligencer*. For other reactions, see New York *Evening Post*, March 16, 1844; March 18, p. 2; and James Patrick Shenton, *Robert John Walker, a Politician from Jackson to Lincoln*, pp. 38–39.

6. Smith, *Annexation of Texas*, pp. 184–88. After several anticipatory hints the *Madisonian* formally began its campaign to support the treaty on March 18, nearly a month before it was signed. Thereafter, until the Senate had defeated the treaty, hardly a day went by without a *Madisonian* editorial. A good indication that strong annexationist sentiment existed in the North was a letter from Lewis Cass, a born trimmer, to E. A. Hannegan, Detroit, May 10, 1844, which repeated Walker's warnings about Britain. Unidentified clipping, Walker Papers, No. 52.

powerful Walker's arguments, they needed more authoritative backing. Someone recalled the fiercely annexationist, Anglophobe letter which Andrew Jackson had written to a cohort a year earlier and which Thomas Gilmer had saved. Thomas Ritchie, editor of the Richmond *Enquirer*, took it, changed the date, cleaned up the old man's erratic spelling, and published it as a newly issued pronouncement from on high.[7]

Probably the ablest reply to Walker and Jackson was a series of letters by Theodore Sedgwick, Jr., published in the New York *Evening Post* and later in pamphlet form. He intensified Webster's argument that annexation would be unconstitutional. More to the point, he warned that annexation would probably lead to a difficult, dangerous war with Mexico, "commencing with a breach of treaty, waged for the maintenance of territory unjustly acquired, having for its avowed result the extension of slavery, accompanied with ruinous expense and destruction to commerce"—and carried on by a nation that had spent "six or seven years, and . . . forty millions of dollars in order to drive a handful of Indians from our own territory." Sedgwick conceded that Americans had reason to be jealous of England, which was apparently "urged on by an insatiable lust of dominion." But twenty years earlier, when the United States was much weaker, he added, England had listened to the Monroe Doctrine with respect. Now the British desired only peace with the United States, and they had done nothing effective to undermine slavery in Texas or make Texas a satellite of the Empire. Sedgwick also took issue with nearly all of Walker's points about slavery, Texan resources, and border trade, but his most effective passages were those which placed the Texas question in the larger framework of American relations with Mexico and Britain.[8]

By April, extremists on both sides were threatening secession if Texas were annexed or rejected. Clearly, the first duty of the Tyler administration was to mollify both groups before completing the treaty and sending it to the Senate. Instead, Calhoun produced one of the most incomprehensible documents of his enigmatic, cross-grained career. When he entered the State Department in March, he found on his desk a dispatch, dated December 26, from

7. Paul, *Rift in the Democracy*, pp. 82–83, 109–10. For the two versions of the letter, see Andrew Jackson, *The Correspondence of Andrew Jackson*, ed. John Spencer Bassett, VI, 201–2; and Washington *Madisonian*, March 21, 1844.

8. [Theodore Sedgwick, Jr.], *Thoughts on the Proposed Annexation of Texas*, pp. 22, 25–26, *et passim*. For a somewhat less favorable estimate of Sedgwick's pamphlet, see Smith, *Annexation of Texas*, pp. 189–91.

Aberdeen to the new British minister at Washington, Richard Pakenham, who had just been transferred from the British legation in Mexico City (see Chapter 8). In this dispatch Aberdeen assured the United States that, while Britain favored independence for Texas and would be happy to see the Texan government abolish slavery, she would not intervene there improperly to bring about abolition or in any way to dominate that government. This statement was a more official and explicit declaration of British abolitionist policy than the State Department had yet received. Still, it contained no really new information, and it was quite proper in form and pacific in tone. Furthermore, before his death Upshur had heard and had accepted the British assurances.[9]

Calhoun could have merely acknowledged receipt of the dispatch, but he chose instead to regard the note as an affront to the United States and to the proslavery South. British influence in Texas, he wrote Pakenham, would threaten the United States on "the weakest and most vulnerable portion of our frontier." Annexation, long desired by the Texans, was the only alternative. Then he went on to summarize the credo of the Southern racist: that the Negro was inherently inferior and that slavery "in reality, a political institution, [was] essential to the peace, safety, and prosperity" of the South.[10]

How can one explain the writing of such a letter, certain to inflame the already uneasy North, less than a week before the annexation treaty was to go to the Senate? Possibly Calhoun's basic motivation was Anglophobia. During the preceding summer Duff Green's warnings from London had greatly alarmed him, and since he entered the State Department wild rumors had been circulating about British intrigue in Cuba to foment slave revolts—the worst nightmare of the Southerner.[11] Several days before Calhoun wrote the letter Pakenham had told him that Britain could never view the American annexation of Texas with indifference and reserved full liberty of action in the matter. Calhoun had listened calmly and then proposed an exchange of notes in order to put the views of the two governments on record. Pakenham, suspicious of the

9. Earl of Aberdeen to Richard Pakenham, December 26, 1843, No. 9; Pakenham to Aberdeen, February 27, 1844, No. 5, GB, FO 115/83, ff. 182–86; 5/404, ff. 11–14.

10. John C. Calhoun to Pakenham, April 18, 1844, Manning, *IAA*, VII, 18–22. Pakenham then repeated the gist of Aberdeen's instructions and tried to withdraw without an argument, but Calhoun pursued him with another note, repeating some of his earlier views. Pakenham to Calhoun, April 19; Calhoun to Pakenham, April 27, ibid., pp. 22–25, 256–58.

11. Sioussat, "Calhoun," in Samuel F. Bemis, ed., *American Secretaries of State and Their Diplomacy*, V, 140–41.

proposal, asked Calhoun to send his views to London by way of American Minister Everett, but nevertheless Calhoun wrote his note. His principal biographer suggests that he never intended it to be published, but four days later, when the Senate called for all correspondence on the treaty, he included the note with the other documents. On April 27 it appeared in the newspapers.[12]

Assuming that Calhoun intended his communication for the American people as well as for Minister Pakenham, why did he use it to lecture on the value of slavery instead of developing the conventional Anglophobe arguments, which would have won support from all sections of the country? Possibly, he wished to solidify Southern support in the Senate for the treaty; possibly, he sought to create a Democratic bloc to reject Van Buren and nominate a Southern candidate at the convention or even to advance his own candidacy in 1844 or 1848.[13] If he aimed at any of these goals, he grievously underestimated the vigor of Northern abolitionism and the electoral strength of the free states. His old enemy Thomas Hart Benton believed that he looked toward the disunion then seething in South Carolina and thought only to give secessionists a good excuse to act by making sure that the treaty would fail.[14] If so, Calhoun was disloyal to his chief, his party, and his country. Whatever his reasons, he acted recklessly but with characteristic self-righteousness. By his action he ensured that the Texas question would dominate all others for the following year.

*   *   *   *

During the latter half of April the other principal American political leaders took positions on the Texas question from which retreat would be difficult. On April 22, ten days after signing the annexation treaty, Tyler sent it to the Senate for approval, accom-

---

12. Pakenham to Aberdeen, April 14, 1844, No. 22, GB, FO 5/404, ff. 157–76. Senator Benjamin Tappan of Ohio, a supporter of Van Buren, was responsible for the leak. Charles M. Wiltse, *John C. Calhoun, Sectionalist, 1840–1850*, pp. 169–71.

13. Smith, *Annexation of Texas*, pp. 201–19. Jackson's henchman, Francis P. Blair, argued that Calhoun was trying to split the Democratic party, after reading Van Buren's letter on Texas. Francis P. Blair to Andrew Jackson, May 2, 1844, Blair Family Papers, box 1, LC. Calhoun had probably not seen Van Buren's anti-Texas letter when he wrote his own, but Charles Sellers suggests that, instead, he was stimulated by a *pro*-Texas editorial of Blair in the Washington *Union*, which made him fear that Blair and Van Buren would capture the issue. Wiltse, *Calhoun, Sectionalist*, p. 176. Charles Grier Sellers, *James K. Polk, Continentalist: 1843–1846*, pp. 58–60.

14. Thomas Hart Benton, *Thirty Years View: or a History of the Working of the American Government for Thirty Years, from 1820 to 1850*, II, 589–90.

panied by a dignified and closely reasoned message that ably set forth the case for peaceful annexation of territory. Texas would be valuable to all sections of the country; its people were Americans; it had established its independence beyond all doubt, so Mexico could not reasonably object. The United States needed Texas to prevent encirclement by European powers: "The question is one purely American."[15]

Five days later, two of the principal Washington newspapers carried letters from Clay and Van Buren, opposing Tyler's treaty. Each man had acted after long thought and careful consultation with his advisers. Each declared that annexation was inexpedient as long as Mexico opposed it, but it might be feasible in the future. Clay's letter was shorter and more direct than Van Buren's. It probably represented his mistaken belief that the South was apathetic on the subject and that the most pressing need was to reassure Northern Whigs. Van Buren's letter was the product of much urging from Democratic leaders that he speak out on Texas. In it he doubtless hoped to restrain the ardent annexationism of Jackson and the Southern wing without alienating them altogether.[16]

During the following month three party conventions gathered at Baltimore to choose candidates and to decide how to deal with the Texas question. The Whigs nominated Clay by acclamation, soberly endorsed a protective tariff, and utterly ignored Texas and Oregon, in which the mass of people were more interested. Tyler's followers called a special convention at which they nominated him as an irregular candidate and loudly approved his annexation treaty. Finally, the Democrats, with Jackson's blessing, repudiated Van Buren. At the outset, annexationists and Van Buren's enemies pushed through a rule requiring a two-thirds vote for nomination; then they deadlocked the convention. After days of maneuvering, the exhausted delegates agreed on a less known man with Jackson's friendship, a clever political organization, and the air of vigor and victory—James K. Polk. The party platform combined action and caution: "reannexation" of Texas to please the South; "reoccupa-

15. James D. Richardson, ed., *A Compilation of the Messages and Papers of the Presidents, 1789–1897*, IV, 307–13. Tyler explained that he held up the treaty for ten days in order to give Calhoun time to write his reply to Pakenham and to allow a new senator, presumably a supporter, to take his seat. John Tyler to Jackson, April 18, 1844, Jackson, *Correspondence*, VI, 279.

16. For the original published texts of the letters, see Washington *National Intelligencer*, April 27, 1844; and Washington *Globe*, April 27. Smith, *Annexation of Texas*, pp. 239–45. Paul, *Rift in the Democracy*, pp. 114–24. Sellers, *Polk, Continentalist*, pp. 60–66. Oscar Doane Lambert, *Presidential Politics in the United States, 1841–1844*, pp. 129–34.

tion" of Oregon to placate the North; and an evasive tariff plank to unify farmers, merchants, and industrialists.[17]

Despite the calming influence of Clay and Van Buren, the partisan excitement aroused by the conventions and the victory of expansionism in the Democratic party whipped public opinion on the Texas question into an even greater frenzy as summer approached. In South Carolina, moderates pleaded for the reasoned solutions of statesmanship, but on May 15 a mass meeting at Charleston proclaimed that the defeat of the treaty would be "the denial of a vital right" to the South. Southern extremists called for "Texas or Disunion," and James H. Hammond declared of the Texas issue: "If the Union is to break there could not be a better pretext."[18] Much of Southern annexationism, however, was untainted by thoughts of secession. Andrew Jackson, half dead but still strong in his hatred of Calhoun, sent forth letter after letter urging the ratification of the treaty as a measure to benefit the whole nation, and many public men followed his lead.[19]

Nor was the North united against the addition of more slaveholding territory. At the end of March a Cincinnati constituent wrote to Senator William Allen that the whole area favored annexation "and will go the question with a perfect rush." The influence of the Walker and Jackson letters weighed heavily on this group, for most of them based their support on fear of European intrigue in the West. Some urged Walker to play down the slavery question and instead to push through approval of the treaty as the prelude to a campaign for Oregon against "our natural and avowed enemy."[20]

But the loudest objections in the North came from opponents of slavery and annexation. When the treaty went to the Senate, wrote John Quincy Adams in his diary, "with it went the freedom

---

17. Lambert, *Presidential Politics*, Chap. 6. Paul, *Rift in the Democracy*, Chaps. 5, 6. Sellers, *Polk, Continentalist*, Chap. 3. The terms *reoccupation* and *reannexation* were indirect jibes at the treaties of 1818 and 1819 with Britain and Spain, respectively, which were said to have surrendered American rights to Oregon and Texas. The Oregon plank was stronger and the Texas plank weaker than public sentiment at the time would seem to have warranted. Ibid., pp. 99–100.

18. Smith, *Annexation of Texas*, pp. 192, 204–8. *NNR*, 66 (April 27, May 25, 1844), 132–33, 199–201. James H. Ham-

mond to Calhoun, Silver Bluff, May 10, 1844, John C. Calhoun, *Correspondence of John C. Calhoun*, ed. J. Franklin Jameson, pp. 953–55.

19. Smith, *Annexation of Texas*, pp. 207, 252. Jackson, *Correspondence*, VI, 289–91.

20. William Parry to William Allen, Cincinnati, March 29, 1844, William Allen Papers, IV, LC. A. Hamilton to Walker, New York, April 30; Charles Drake to Walker, Ulster County, New York, April 24, Walker Papers, Nos. 070, 074. Both collections contain annexationist letters of all descriptions dating from this period.

of the human race." On April 24 Albert Gallatin presided over a mass meeting of three thousand persons in New York City. The meeting was disrupted briefly at its opening by a gang of ruffians calling "Hurrah for Texas!" and shouting sarcastic remarks about Wall Street and British gold, but it overrode the interruptions and passed resolutions declaring that annexation would be unconstitutional and would risk dishonorable war to add worthless territory and more slaves to the country.[21] Other Northerners, however, took Van Buren's view that Texas might be desirable in the future, provided the American government could obtain Mexico's consent to annexation. Abbott Lawrence and a group of moderates prevented the organization of a mass meeting in Boston like that in New York, fearing that it would fall into the control of "violent and mischievous agitators."[22]

Meanwhile, the Senate was trying to reflect on the annexation treaty in a Washington tense with emotion and politics. Apparently everyone was trying to influence the Senators. Tyler sent over to the Capitol a series of messages and correspondence purporting to prove British intrigue in Texas, but opponents of annexation ridiculed his evidence and denounced the treaty as the shameful product of land speculation and hypocrisy.[23] Jacksonians produced yet another call to arms, just received from the Hermitage. Followers of Clay and Van Buren took up their leaders' moderate positions. Calhoun's letter to Pakenham made at least as many enemies as friends for the treaty, while his overture to Mexico for consent to annexation (to be discussed later) confounded even his staunchest supporters.[24] Lobbyists, newspaper editors, and petitioners all added their voices, and at the outer edge of the melee stood Richard Pakenham and Alphonse Pageot, the British and French ministers, buttonholing opponents of annexation and urging them to defeat the treaty before the Atlantic packets could bring European newspapers with their expected criticism of American land-grabbing and slavery.[25]

From the outset neither Pakenham nor Charles Elliot thought

21. John Quincy Adams, *Diary*, XII, 13, as quoted in Smith, *Annexation of Texas*, p. 221. Philip Hone, *Diary of Philip Hone, 1828–1851*, ed. Allan Nevins, II, 692. New York *Evening Post*, April 25, 1844.

22. Abbott Lawrence to Crittenden, Boston, April 11, 1844, Crittenden Papers, ff. 1693–94.

23. Richardson, *Papers of the Presidents*, IV, 318–23. Smith, *Annexation of Texas*, pp. 224–26. Paul, *Rift in the Democracy*, pp. 119–21.

24. Smith, *Annexation of Texas*, pp. 259, 263–64.

25. Alphonse Pageot to François Guizot, April 27, June 13, 1844, Nos. 47, 56, France, MAE, CP, États-Unis, C, ff. 100–110, 211–14.

that the treaty had much chance of approval, and by the middle of May many Americans agreed.[26] Nevertheless, the debate continued for the rest of the month, in order that everyone might be heard and the various positions clearly established for the coming presidential campaign. One of the central figures was Thomas Hart Benton of Missouri, a Western leader of Jacksonian force and roughness but now linked to Van Buren. By nature an expansionist, Benton felt obliged to oppose the present annexation of Texas lest it bring war with Mexico; also, he detested Calhoun. For three days Benton held forth in the Senate, strutting about and tossing his great mane, as he referred now and then for additional fuel to a desk piled high with notes.[27] He developed the familiar arguments that Tyler risked or even intended an unconstitutional war with Mexico and ridiculed the *"raw-head and bloody-bones"* of British piracy that annexationists were shaking before the country. Spencer Jarnagin, a Tennessee Whig, supported Benton with all the more vigor because he too seemed an apostate from Jacksonian expansionism; and William Archer of Virginia, chairman of the foreign relations committee and special friend of Pakenham and Pageot, closed the debate with another warning against war and adverse world opinion.

Answering the principal argument of dishonorable war, Robert J. Walker repeated most of the inducements which he had already developed in his famous letter, and he taunted his opponents as cowards and enemies of progress. George McDuffie of South Carolina, a bosom friend of Calhoun, abandoned strict construction to defend the constitutionality of the treaty and predictably demanded national protection for slavery against British-inspired abolitionism. Near the end of the debate James Buchanan of Pennsylvania again applied the arguments of Walker's letter against Benton's oratory. Perhaps the usually cautious Buchanan was emboldened as some said by the hope that Tyler would appoint him to a vacancy on the Supreme Court. Certainly he offended many Northerners by his speech, in which he denounced Mexico's efforts to put down the Texan revolution of 1836 as "an act of unjust and wanton power" and greedy Britain, "imperious and arrogant . . . which never fails to make one extorted concession

---

26. Pakenham to Aberdeen, April 28, May 13, 1844, Nos. 36, 45, GB, FO 5/404, ff. 233–45; 5/405, ff. 87–91. Charles Elliot to Jones, Galveston, March 22, Anson Jones, *Memoranda and Official Correspondence Relating to the Repub-* *lic of Texas, Its History and Annexation*, pp. 329–30.

27. Paul, *Rift in the Democracy*, p. 135, US, 28C, 1S, *CG*, Appendix, pp. 474–86, 497–99, 568–76.

the foundation of demanding another."[28] As it turned out, "Old Buck's" next berth was the State Department, not the Supreme Court, and these sentiments did little to enhance the success of his diplomacy.

On June 8, weeks after defeat was obvious, the Senate rejected the treaty by a vote of 35 to 16. Many Northern states voted solidly against it; two Northern and four Southern states voted solidly for it; only one Whig and one New Englander supported it.[29] Undoubtedly, the opposition to a dishonorable war with Mexico and to the expansion of slaveholding territory were decisive factors in the unexpectedly severe defeat, but many other considerations weighed upon the Senators—personal dislike of Tyler, loyalty to Clay and his platform, and repugnance toward land speculation, to name a few. Calhoun was utterly deflated and for a time thought of resigning from the Cabinet. He had good reason to be discouraged, for about three weeks later the Senate also rejected a reciprocity treaty with the *Zollverein*, thereby indicating how low it valued his other goal, tariff reform.[30]

Although Calhoun talked of resigning and other Southern hotheads organized for disunion, Tyler pursued a plan which he had begun to develop weeks earlier. On June 11, with the full knowledge of the Texan envoys, he sent the rejected treaty and accompanying documents to the House of Representatives, suggesting that, while he had preferred a treaty, he would cooperate with any form of annexation which Congress desired, as long as it was constitutional. Before the session ended there was only time to introduce a few token bills, but Tyler's action, together with the election campaign now getting under way, made clear that the Texas question was far from dead.[31]

*   *   *   *

While Calhoun licked his wounds and Whig and Democratic politicians maneuvered for choice positions in the presidential

28. US, 28C, 1S, *CG*, Appendix, pp. 451–52, 529–33, 548–57, 588–90, 682–89, 693–96, 720–27, *et passim*. The Senate debate is summarized, with lengthy paraphrases of the principal speeches, in Smith, *Annexation of Texas*, Chap. 13. Buchanan's speech appears in James Buchanan, *The Works of James Buchanan*, ed. John Bassett Moore, VI, 5–44. The quoted phrases appear on pp. 28 and 32.

29. US, 28C, 1S, *CG*, p. 652. Smith *Annexation of Texas*, p. 273.

30. Lyon G. Tyler, *The Letters and Times of the Tylers*, II, 331. On the *Zollverein* treaty, see New York *Evening Post*, June 27, 1844, p. 2.

31. Richardson, *Papers of the Presidents*, IV, 323–27. Van Zandt and Henderson to Jones, June 10, 1844, No. 121 [122], Garrison, *DCRT*, II, 284–85. Smith, *Annexation of Texas*, pp. 281–88.

campaign, the shock waves generated by Tyler's annexation treaty spread out in ever-widening circles toward Mexico and Europe. Apparently, many political leaders in those areas had never expected Texas to agree to annexation. Confronted with the sudden realization of the American expansionist threat, they hastily began to improvise defenses, and even after the defeat of the treaty, the momentum of their planning carried well into the summer.

An initial obstacle to any defensive plans was the general repugnance which most foreigners and foreign governments felt by now toward the corrupt, decaying dictatorship of Santa Anna. His Excellency spent the first part of 1844 on his provincial estate, leaving the cares of government to Acting President Valentín Canalizo. The latter's appeals for funds with which to fight Texas were ignored by a Congress that knew all too well how the government had squandered the latest appropriation. In June, after months of cockfighting and loafing and accompanied by his new young wife, Santa Anna entered Mexico City in a triumphal procession, his coach drawn by Indians dressed as Aztecs. In the course of a long fiesta he dedicated a heroic gilded bronze statue of himself with outstretched hand pointed north toward the Texas he promised to reconquer. Some cynics remarked that it also pointed toward the mint.[32]

With his return, Santa Anna and his henchmen resumed their exploitation of foreigners. In 1843 Congress had passed a new tariff bill that prohibited the import of many useful articles which Mexico had no prospect of producing and had placed heavy restrictions on the participation of foreigners in the retail trade, which they largely dominated. In these familiar circumstances, foreign diplomats in Mexico City resumed their tedious arguments with the government.[33] During the winter the bondholders added their voice to the clamor when it became known that Lizardi and Company, the Mexican financial agent in London, had high-handedly issued new bonds on its own initiative and without the

32. Hubert H. Bancroft, *History of Mexico*, V, Chap. 11. Niceto de Zamacois, *Historia de Méjico desde sus tiempos más remotas hasta nuestros días*, XII, 329–30. Alleye de Cyprey to Guizot, June 18, 1844, No. 255, France, MAE, CP, Mexique, XXVII, ff. 154–56. Vicente Riva Palacio, *México a través de los siglos*, IV, 517, 518.

33. Jaime Delgado, *España y México en el siglo XIX*, II, 256–61. For Spanish

correspondence on these subjects, see *Rdh-m*, III, 6–8, 25–26, 36–38, 47–49, *et passim*. For British correspondence, see GB, FO 50/173, ff. 86–88, 133–35, 153–56, 176–79; 50/174, ff. 23–27, 44–46, 105–8, *et passim*. For French correspondence, see France, MAE, CP, Mexique, XXVI, ff. 46–50, 62–63, 74–78, 105–13, 160, 163–65, 168–79, 196–97, 220–21, *et passim*.

slightest authority, thereby diluting the value of securities British creditors already held.[34]

Foreigners were especially alarmed at the drastic measures Santa Anna now adopted toward Texas and Yucatán. On June 13 an order appeared in the government newspaper to the effect that any Mexicans (including, of course, Texans) found within one league of the left bank of the Rio Grande would be shot as traitors. In the same month Santa Anna's troops captured an ill-managed filibuster expedition from New Orleans, bound for Yucatán. The authorities promptly shot all the prisoners, including several French, Spaniards, and Americans. Then they beheaded the leader, Francisco Sentmanat, boiled his head in oil, and displayed it in a glass jar to discourage imitators.[35]

Europeans reacted to these developments in characteristic fashion. When British merchants, mineowners, and bondholders filled the Foreign Office mail with complaints, Aberdeen provided the new British minister, Charles Bankhead, with stern notes of warning to be read to Foreign Minister Bocanegra, but he carefully avoided anything like an ultimatum.[36] The French legation in Mexico City prepared an exhaustive list of "Griefs de la France contre le Mexique," while newspapers in France denounced Mexi-

34. Lester G. Engelson, "Proposals for Colonization of California by England in Connection with the Mexican Debt to British Bondholders, 1837–1846," *California Historical Society Quarterly*, 18 (June 1939), pp. 137–38. Leland Hamilton Jenks, *The Migration of British Capital to 1875*, pp. 112–13. Lizardi paid Santa Anna a bribe of 50,000 pesos, and it was widely known in Mexico City just how this had been divided up among the cabinet. Cyprey to Guizot, January 2, 1844, No. 211, France, MAE, CP, Mexique, XXVI, ff. 4–7. Percy W. Doyle to Aberdeen, January 29, 1844, Aberdeen Papers, BM, AM, vol. 43126, ff. 17–19. This was the second time in less than two years that bonds had been issued illegally. See Chap. 3, note 57.

35. GB, FO 50/175, *passim*. France, MAE, CP, Mexique, XXVIII, *passim*. Pedro Pascual Oliver to Primer Secretario de Estado, April 30, 1844, No. 389, *Rdh-m*, III, 51–52. Benjamin E. Green to Calhoun, July 13, 27, Nos. 12, 14, US, DS, D, Mexico, XII. E. Porter to Green, Frontera de Tabasco, July 20, Manning, *IAA*, VII, 639–40. Auguste Génin, *Les*

français au Mexique du XVIe siècle à nos jours, pp. 206–7. George Lockhart Rives, *The United States and Mexico, 1821–1848*, I, 655–57. Dennis E. Berge, "Mexican Response to United States Expansionism, 1841–1848," Ph.D. diss., University of California (Berkeley), 1965, pp. 112–15.

36. Aberdeen to Doyle, November 1843, No. 30; Aberdeen to Charles Bankhead, December 26, 1843, May 31, 1844, Nos. 5, 6, 13, GB, FO 50/160, ff. 125–31; 167–73, 177–82; 50/172, ff. 25–27, *et passim*. Bankhead had earlier been legation secretary at Washington under Sir Charles Vaughan and had served as chargé for considerable periods in the 1830s. He even played a role in ending the Franco-American debt crisis. Beckles Willson, *Friendly Relations, a Narrative of Britain's Ministers and Ambassadors to America (1791–1930)*, pp. 138–45. Thus, from 1844 to 1847 Britain's representatives in Washington and Mexico City were quite familiar with the backgrounds in both countries.

cans as barbarians and demanded extraterritorial provisions for European residents, as in Turkey or China. Guizot, however, who had learned patience from the British, shrugged his shoulders and advised firm perseverance, well-argued claims, and vigilance for the proper moment to achieve a settlement.[37] The Spanish minister, Pascual de Oliver, knew that his country was too weak to act alone, but he believed that, in order to survive, Mexico must have a European-supported monarchy.[38]

During the spring of 1844 exasperation toward Santa Anna gradually yielded to anxiety over American ambitions in Texas as a determinant of British policy. In January and early February Aberdeen consulted with Guizot about joint action in the Texas question, but he then decided to await further developments. At the same time, the British foreign minister sent Charles Bankhead to take over the legation in Mexico City from Chargé Percy W. Doyle and to relieve thereby the strained relations that had resulted from the flag incident of the preceding autumn. On February 29 Bankhead had a long interview with Foreign Minister Bocanegra, to whom he read the instructions about Texas which Aberdeen had sent to Pakenham in December. Bankhead expressed his country's confidence that Mexico and Texas could work out a satisfactory relationship, but he added that Britain would not compel Mexico to recognize Texan independence.[39]

Aberdeen was to regret this friendly gesture, for it stiffened Mexico's attitude toward Texas and aroused new hope of material aid from London. Shortly after this interview Santa Anna told American Minister Waddy Thompson, about to depart for Washington, that Bankhead had assured him of British intervention if the United States tried to annex Texas.[40] Santa Anna's minister in Washington, Almonte, may have unintentionally encouraged this expectation by remarking in a dispatch that Britain surely owed Mexico some support in reparation for her intrigues in Texas. But

37. Memorandum, "Griefs de la France contre le Mexique," France, MAE, CP, Mexique, XXVIII, ff. 87–123; Guizot to Cyprey, February 27, 1844, No. 42, XXVI, f. 104. Le constitutionnel, January 6, p. 1. Le journal des débats, March 16, p. 1.

38. Oliver to Primer Secretario de Estado, January 24, 1844, No. 347, Rdh-m, III, 13–16.

39. Ephraim Douglass Adams, British Interests and Activities in Texas, 1838–

1846, pp. 166–67. Cyprey to Guizot, March 16, 1844, No. 226, France, MAE, CP, Mexique, XXVI, ff. 140–48. Bankhead to Aberdeen, March 31, No. 9, GB, FO 50/173, ff. 64–67.

40. Thompson replied that the United States would welcome an opportunity to prove that it would not permit European interference in North America. Waddy Thompson to Upshur, March 25, 1844, Manning, IAA, VIII, 581–82.

Almonte, who was carefully reporting every new development in the annexation question, was too realistic to rely on effective aid from the British. He advised his government to play for time and meanwhile to send out agents who could arrange for privateers in Europe and foment uprisings in the United States.[41]

Just before Calhoun signed the annexation treaty he called in Almonte, intending to continue the efforts at conciliation which Upshur had begun almost two months earlier, for he realized that opponents of the treaty had a strong argument in their fear of a dishonorable war with Mexico. Calhoun asked Almonte's opinion on the acceptability of an offer of money to Mexico in compensation for Texas. Almonte avoided a direct reply but indicated that his government would probably not be offended at the offer, especially if at the same time the United States, Britain, and France would guarantee the permanence of the resulting boundary. After the signature of the treaty Calhoun again raised the question of monetary compensation. When Almonte replied that now Mexican dignity had been insulted, Calhoun justified the treaty by citing Americans' fear of British plotting so close to the nation's border and offered to send a special envoy to explain the matter to the Mexican government.[42]

In encouraging Calhoun to hope for a negotiated settlement, Almonte had been trying to gain time and to score a legal point by bringing Calhoun implicitly to acknowledge Mexican sovereignty over Texas. After the treaty was signed, the Mexican minister agitated against it in editorials and conversations with congressmen, assuring everyone that Mexico would fight. He sent off a special report to Mexico City, claiming to have virtually convinced the American public that the United States could not annex Texas without first indemnifying Mexico and predicting that the treaty would be defeated for this reason. Even Calhoun, he felt, believed that Mexican approval of the United States action was necessary, although the President stubbornly disagreed. Almonte also encouraged Santa Anna to expect that, in case of war, Mexico might count on the aid of two and a half million rebellious slaves and

41. Juan N. Almonte to Ministerio de Relaciones, March 4, 15, 16, 20, 29, 1844, Nos. 7, 8, 9, 10, 12, US, LC, /86, /96. Throughout the annexation crisis the Mexican government was also receiving accurate information on American opinion from its consul at New Orleans, Francisco de Arrangoiz, based largely on a survey of the American press and some information from unidentified correspondents. US, LC, /96.

42. Almonte to Ministerio de Relaciones, April 9, 1844, No. 14, US, LC, /96; same, April 18, No. 17, Barker transcripts, vol. 571, pp. 162–64.

many freed Negroes, wild Indians, and abolitionists and that the Northeastern states might even secede from the Union.[43] Emboldened by these fancies, Santa Anna and Bocanegra reaffirmed that under no circumstances would Mexico consent to dismemberment. If the United States Senate approved the annexation treaty, Almonte must deliver a vigorous protest and close the legation.[44]

Although Pakenham, who knew the Mexican temperament well, warned Calhoun not to expect negotiations, the American secretary instructed his chargé d'affaires at Mexico City, Benjamin E. Green, to assure Bocanegra that the United States bore no ill will toward Mexico and that British intrigue had forced him to sign the annexation treaty in self defense.[45] He sent these instructions by a special messenger, Colonel Gilbert Thompson, who was also empowered to negotiate on his own initiative if he saw an opportunity. In mid-May Thompson visited Santa Anna at his estate and explained to him that British political and commercial rivalry had compelled the United States to sign a treaty of annexation without consulting Mexico. He offered an indemnity and probably also hinted at the purchase of other territory. Santa Anna's replies were not encouraging.[46]

Colonel Thompson's arrival in Mexico City on May 22 created a great sensation, especially since it coincided with news that the Americans were massing troops east of the Sabine River. Thompson's presence may have been largely responsible for Santa Anna's arranging a triumphal entry into the capital several weeks later. In any case, after conferring with the messenger, Green sent a relatively mild note to Bocanegra, setting forth Calhoun's expla-

43. Almonte to Ministerio de Relaciones, March 20, 29, April 30, 1844, Nos. 10, 12, 24; Memorandum of instructions to José M. González de la Vega (the special envoy), April 11/14, US, LC, /86, /96. González de la Vega to Ministerio de Relaciones, New Orleans, April 25, and enclosure, Barker transcripts, vol. 571, pp. 128–33. At the same time the Mexican consul in New York was also urging his government to prepare for a long war as the only way of teaching the Americans a lesson. He favored a Fabian defensive strategy and also one of arming Indians and Negroes in the United States. Juan de la Granja to Antonio López de Santa Anna, May 7, reprinted in New York Herald, October 16, 1847, p. 2.

44. Mexico, Ministerio de Relaciones

to Almonte, May 10, 30, 1844, Nos. 9, 56, US, LC, /96. Bocanegra also proclaimed this determination in a circular letter of May 29 to other Mexican agents abroad. US, LC, /98.

45. Pakenham to Aberdeen, April 14, 1844, No. 22, GB, FO 5/404, ff. 165–67. Calhoun to Green, April 19, No. 1, Manning, *IAA*, VIII, 149–51.

46. Since Thompson seems to have conducted all his business orally, the principal record of his negotiations is a rather dubious account by Santa Anna. One version of this account was published in the Mexican press; another, perhaps more accurate, is in the Mexican archives. Smith, *Annexation of Texas*, pp. 288–93. Carlos Bosch García, *Material para la historia diplomática de México*, pp. 422–23.

nations about the British as cause for American policy in Texas and his desire to settle all unresolved questions "on the most liberal and satisfactory terms." Bocanegra promptly showed this note to Bankhead, told him that Mexico would reject all proposals for negotiation, and asked him pointblank, "In the resolution she has taken, will Mexico stand *alone?*" Cryptically, Bankhead presumed that Britain would not withdraw her sympathy. This was enough for Bocanegra, who immediately sent a stinging reply to Green, blaming American aid to Texas for the strained relations and repeating his warning of the preceding August that annexation would mean war. A few days later Colonel Thompson left for home with these unpleasant tidings, and for the next two months Green and Bocanegra exchanged notes that covered every aspect of the Texas question without coming to any agreement.[47]

In the short run, Santa Anna seemed master of the situation. After his personal mouthpiece, *El censor de Veracruz*, had published several editorials defying the United States, the nationalist press threatened war to the death and commented devastatingly on each new chapter of the Green–Bocanegra correspondence. The dictator called on Congress for thirty thousand soldiers and four million pesos, and late in June he told Bankhead that he was determined to reconquer Texas. At the same time, however, he hinted that he might recognize Texas instead, if American agitation for expansion ceased, and he also put out more feelers for British aid. Bankhead assured him that Britain in no way supported the annexationists.[48] With an unrealistic hope of British support, Santa Anna was now using the possibility of a negotiated settlement to feint with both Britain and the United States, but his grandiloquent public attitude had aroused such expectations

---

47. During Colonel Thompson's visit Bankhead heard that he and Green had orally offered Bocanegra $7 million for a settlement, from which $2 million was to be deducted for American claims. Bankhead to Aberdeen, May 30, June 28, 1844, Nos. 34, separate (confidential), 41, GB, FO 50/173, ff. 86–91, 93–97, 139–44. Green to José María Bocanegra, May 23, No. 5; Bocanegra to Green, May 30, No. 7, Manning, *IAA*, VIII, 586–91. For the rest of the Green–Bocanegra correspondence, see ibid., pp. 592–637, *passim*. See also memoranda by Bocanegra of conversations with Green and with Bankhead, US, LC, /339. Bocanegra repeated his earlier unyielding instructions to Almonte. Ministerio de Relaciones to Almonte, May 30, No. 56, US, LC, /96.

48. "Mégico y los Estados-Unidos," reprinted in *El censor de Veracruz*, June 26, 1844, US, DS, CD, Veracruz, V. Green to Calhoun, June 15, No. 7, Manning, *IAA*, VIII, 613–15. Bankhead to Aberdeen, June 29, No. 44, GB, FO 50/173, ff. 299–304. The uncertainty about Santa Anna's intentions appears also in the dispatches of the American consul at Veracruz. F. M. Dimond to Calhoun, May 31, June 3, 18, 12, Nos. 221, 222, 224, 226. US, DS, CD, Veracruz, V.

that it would be almost impossible for him to retreat without sparking a revolution. Worse, at the end of April he had stopped the regular quarterly payment on the American debt, thereby giving the United States legitimate grounds for complaint.[49]

*   *   *   *

In Britain and France public opinion and governments responded more slowly to the signature of the annexation treaty. Since American journalists reported only casual rumors about negotiations during January and February, European newspapers failed to indicate any immediate danger in the Texas question, and one Liverpool paper even suggested that annexation might be beneficial to British interests by removing a cause of friction with the United States.[50] But when the news of the annexation treaty burst upon Europe in the middle of May, it called forth loud protests: questions in Parliament, denials of information by the government, and sneers and scolding by the press at the "base and paltry passions" of "the Republican RICHELIEUS," "Mr. Tyler and his profligate Cabinet." "We have had many monsters in our days—monster concerts, monster meetings . . .," cried the *Times*, "and this is the monster BRIBE— . . . slavery and lands for the South and a market for the North—aggrandizement for the whole Union." The French government organ, *Le journal des débats*, called the American diplomatic correspondence "an audacious apologia of the very principle of slavery." But it labeled the treaty only an electioneering maneuver and no concern of France, even though it might lead to war with Mexico.[51]

While the British and French governments possessed somewhat fuller and more accurate advance information about the Texas question than the general public, there was no reason for them to act before the arrival of solid news about the treaty in mid-May. During February Aberdeen and Guizot had authorized their ministers in Washington to warn the American government

49. According to Green, the Mexican government expected to use the annexation treaty as an excuse for repudiating the whole Mexican debt to the United States. Clayton Charles Kohl, *Claims As a Cause of the Mexican War*, p. 55. However, Santa Anna opposed the suspension, at least on paper, in order not to give the United States a pretext for war. Santa Anna to Bocanegra, May 15, 1844, Barker transcripts, vol. 571, p. 141.

50. London *Times*, March 15, 1844, p. 5. Liverpool *Mercury*, no date, quoted in *NNR*, 66 (May 11), 161.

51. *NNR*, 66 (June 8, 22, 1844), pp. 225, 257. London *Times*, May 15, p. 6; May 18, p. 5; June 10, p. 4. *Le journal des débats*, May 20, p. 1.

against annexation, but Guizot's dispatch was two months en route, and when it reached Washington, the two ministers agreed that any action by them would simply aid the annexationists in the Senate. On learning belatedly of the joint instruction, Elliot hurried from New Orleans to the Texan capital to inform Houston, but he could not prevent the signature of the treaty. Neither Bankhead nor the French minister, Alleye de Cyprey, had any suggestions to make from Mexico City about Texan policy, but De Cyprey had become so disgusted with Santa Anna that in two different dispatches he proposed a military intervention to overturn his government and set up another.[52]

By the end of May, when news arrived from Washington suggesting that the Senate would probably reject the annexation treaty, Aberdeen had decided on a means of preventing its revival—joint Anglo–French effort to guarantee Texan independence and boundaries and to bring about recognition by Mexico. The preservation of the Republic of Texas was not the only goal, for to Aberdeen it seemed at least as important to strengthen the Anglo–French *entente* by joint action in a neutral area. In the spring of 1844 Anglo–French relations rested on dangerously shaky foundations. A ceremonial visit by Queen Victoria to France during the preceding autumn had created much superficial friendliness, but during the winter and spring the British government became increasingly anxious over the growth of the French navy. Although the French fleet was not yet large enough to challenge Britain directly at any point, it was fast being converted from sail to steam. In May one of Louis Philippe's sons, the Prince de Joinville, caused a great stir with an article advocating a "crash program" of naval construction and a race with Britain.[53]

During the same period French colonial ambitions in North Africa and the Pacific again chafed the British. After suppressing a rebellion in Algeria, French border troops repeatedly raided

52. Pakenham to Aberdeen, March 28, April 14, May 13, 1844, Nos. 16, 22, 45, GB, FO 5/404, ff. 100–109, 157–76; 5/405, ff. 87–91. Elliot to Aberdeen, April 7 and enclosures. Ephraim Douglass Adams, ed., *British Diplomatic Correspondence Concerning the Republic of Texas, 1838–1846*, pp. 304–15. Pageot to Guizot, March 28, April 13, 27, May 28, June 13, Nos. 44, 46, 47, 52, 56, France, MAE, CP, États-unis, C, ff. 62–82, 100–110, 140–47, 211–14. Alphonse de Saligny to Guizot, New Orleans, March 19, No. 9, ibid., Texas,

VII, ff. 61–65. Cyprey to Guizot, March 18, May 21, Nos. 228, 248, ibid., Mexique, XXVI, ff. 166–67, 291–96.
53. John S. Galbraith, "France As a Factor in the Oregon Negotiations," *Pacific Northwest Quarterly*, 44 (April 1953), 70. Wilbur Devereux Jones, *Lord Aberdeen and the Americas*, pp. 31, 37. C. J. Bartlett, *Great Britain and Sea Power, 1815–1853*, pp. 158–60. London *Times*, June 13, 1844, p. 5. Everett to Calhoun, June 17, No. 147, US, DS, D, Britain, LII.

Morocco, arousing fears that France intended to expand her African possessions. In the Pacific during November the French Admiral Abel du Petit-Thouars had formally annexed Tahiti and reopened that troublesome question. In February France disavowed Du Petit-Thouars' action, but throughout the spring clashes on the island between the French representatives and the British missionary-consul George Pritchard kept the problem before the two nations. There were good reasons for Aberdeen and Guizot to seek areas of agreement.[54]

Aberdeen's decision coincided precisely with the Democratic party's convention in the United States and the treaty debate. On May 29 he launched his plan of joint Anglo–French action in a long conversation with the Mexican minister, Tomás Murphy. Aberdeen told Murphy that if Mexico would recognize Texan independence, Britain would oppose annexation by the United States and would invite France to join her in guaranteeing not only the independence of Texas but even the boundary of Mexico. Bearing in mind American public opinion, Aberdeen explicitly disavowed any desire to force the abolition of slavery in Texas. Murphy of course had no authority to commit the Mexican government to recognition, and when he wondered aloud about reactions in the United States, Aberdeen remarked emphatically that "it would matter little to England whether the American Government should be willing to drop this question or not, and that, should it be necessary, she would go to the last extremity in support of her opposition to annexation." However, he made clear that such "extremity" of action carried two absolute prerequisites—recognition by Mexico and cooperation by France.[55]

The next step was to sound the French government on the matter. Two days after he had talked with Murphy, Aberdeen instructed Lord Cowley, the British ambassador to France, to lay before Guizot the joint guarantee he planned and also to suggest that the British and French ministers in Mexico should personally urge recognition on Santa Anna. On June 1 the British foreign

54. Jones, *Aberdeen and the Americas*, pp. 37–38. Jean Ingram Brookes, *International Rivalry in the Pacific Islands, 1800–1875*, pp. 138–43. *Cambridge History of British Foreign Policy*, II, 184–85. For comments, see London *Times*, January 25, 1844, p. 4; February 28, p. 5; and Everett to Upshur, March 2, No. 93, US, DS, D, Britain, LII.

55. GB, FO 50/180, ff. 23–25. Murphy's memorandum of the conversation, which he submitted for Aberdeen's approval, is quoted at length in Adams, *British Interests*, pp. 168–69. Although written in French, the most important phrases, especially those pertaining to French cooperation, were carefully quoted in English. Murphy gave the date of the interview as May 28.

secretary approached the third party to the transaction, Ashbel Smith, the Texan minister to Britain, and told him of the proposal, at the same time inquiring why the Texans and Houston seemed so favorable to annexation. Lacking instructions, Smith tried to explain the attitude of his government and added that in his opinion "a solid, permanent peace" with Mexico might prevent annexation.[56]

Two days following the interview with Smith, Aberdeen sent a description of his proposal to Bankhead in Mexico City, instructing him to prepare the Mexican government for it unobtrusively. On the same day he wrote to Pakenham in Washington. Although Aberdeen had already commented at length in an earlier dispatch about the exaggerations and misunderstandings contained in Calhoun's note of April 18, he went over the same ground again. While the British government deplored slavery, it recognized the obstacles in the way of abolition. For that reason Britain was determined not to offend American attitudes in this particular. By this involved explanation Aberdeen may have been trying not only to reassure the Tyler administration but also to divert its attention from the real purpose of the maneuver, which was to prevent the American annexation of Texas.[57] If so, he was attempting the impossible.

Having set out his lines, Aberdeen now had to await a reply from France. During the first week of June his ambassador, Lord Cowley, discussed the British proposal first with Guizot and then with Louis Philippe. Both approved of the general idea, but Guizot suggested that the joint declaration be extended to cover foreign grievances against Mexico, and the King quickly diverted the conversation to his current complaints against the Czar, who, he thought, was snubbing him. When the formal French reply reached London, it concealed lukewarm enthusiasm under a polite statement that the guarantee ought to be more specific rather than committing Britain and France unreservedly to "the fights and lacerations to which the new States of America may give birth."[58]

Approximately a week after receiving this reply Aberdeen

56. Adams, *British Interests*, pp. 170–71. Aberdeen to Lord Cowley, May 31, 1844, No. 162, GB, FO 27/690. Ashbel Smith to Jones, June 2, No. 55, Garrison, *DCRT*, III, 1485–88. The quoted phrase is on p. 1486.

57. Aberdeen to Bankhead, June 3, 1844, No. 16, GB, FO 50/172, ff. 33–36.

Aberdeen to Pakenham, June 3, No. 25, GB, FO 115/85, ff. 205–9. Adams, *British Interests*, pp. 172–74.

58. Cowley to Aberdeen, June 3, 10, 14, Nos. 283, 290, private and confidential, GB, FO 519/56. Guizot to Comte de Ste. Aulaire, June 14, No. 44, France, MAE, CP, Mexique, XXVII, ff. 23–24.

called in Smith, told him that Britain and France were entirely agreed about the annexation question, and proposed a "Diplomatic Act," a more formal convention with both Texas and Mexico which would ensure peace and guarantee both boundaries and Texan independence. This plan differed from the earlier proposal to Murphy in that Mexico would now be compelled to take part. The United States might participate also, if it chose, but Aberdeen did not expect this. In any case, the Diplomatic Act would give Britain and France the right of intervention to determine and prevent violations of the Act, including the annexation of Texas by the United States. The idea of submitting North American affairs to European settlement took Smith aback, and he advised the Texan government to go slow. However, he admitted that Aberdeen had spoken in the most friendly manner, and he believed that Britain would probably not put any pressure on Mexico without some cooperation from Texas.[59]

Before the text of the Diplomatic Act could possibly have made the long journey to Texas, Aberdeen learned that the American Senate had rejected the annexation treaty, and he also received other advice from Pakenham in Washington that considerably changed his views. During the Senate debates on the treaty both Pakenham and the French minister, Pageot, had kept in constant touch with Senator Archer and other opponents of annexation and had become fully aware of the intense American nationalism and suspicion of Europe on which the Texas question rested. Both men warned their governments not to do anything that would heighten these emotions. In particular, Pakenham's dispatch of June 27 declared flatly that the defeat of the treaty was not the end of the question, that Britain and France had everything to gain from Clay's victory in the election, and that if Aberdeen tried to carry out the Diplomatic Act, the United States would undoubtedly annex Texas at once. Pakenham's frank words obviously shook Aberdeen, who still had much to learn about American public opinion. At once he told Cowley in Paris to suggest

---

59. Ashbel Smith to Anson Jones, London, June 24, 1844, No. 57, Garrison, *DCRT*, III, 1153–56. Historians have naturally wondered whether Aberdeen would really have gone to war with the United States in a showdown. Justin Smith, E. G. Adams, and more recently Wilbur D. Jones have all found that Aberdeen was willing to go to war but did not expect that it would be nec-essary. Smith and Adams seem puzzled as to his reasons, since the Anglo-American stake in peace was overwhelming. Jones believes that the explanation lies in Aberdeen's great desire for cooperation with France. Smith, *Annexation of Texas*, pp. 390–94. Adams, *British Interests*, pp. 172, 232. Jones, *Aberdeen and the Americas*, pp. 34–37.

that all plans concerning the Diplomatic Act be deferred until after the American election. Guizot of course agreed, and the two foreign ministries sent out new instructions to their diplomats in Texas and Mexico.[60]

Even if Aberdeen had decided to push ahead with his Diplomatic Act during the summer, it is unlikely that France would have followed him very far, for several factors dampened Guizot's enthusiasm. One was the list of perennial French grievances against Mexico. More important was a campaign during May and June by newspapers of the liberal French opposition, which denounced the government for pulling Britain's chestnuts out of the fire and thus endangering the traditional Franco–American friendship. The opposition suspected even British humanitarianism, for, as one newspaper put it, "there is a speculation underneath, which profanes the work and disfigures the system," and another called abolitionism "a moral sign on the shop door."[61]

Another important dissuading factor was a pronounced increase in official Anglo–French tension at the end of the summer. In Tahiti French officials had peremptorily arrested a troublesome British consul. Britain protested, and the French government reluctantly agreed to pay an indemnity for his arrest. In North Africa, after a brilliant victory over the Moroccans in August, French forces withdrew to Algeria, seemingly at the British behest. Both actions aroused conservative nationalists against Guizot. During August and September the press in both Britain and France published sensational articles about Channel defenses, the comparative strength of the two home fleets, and a possible invasion of England. Under these circumstances Peel refused to trust the conciliatory statements of Louis Philippe and Guizot. Instead, he increased his support of the preparedness campaign being urged by the Duke of Wellington and other militarists. Seeing his pacific policy crumbling, Aberdeen did his utmost to restrain Peel. Finally, the prime minister agreed not to authorize construction of new warships lest this complicate relations with France. However, British resentment and suspicion continued through the autumn.[62]

60. Pakenham to Aberdeen, June 13, 27, 1844, Nos. 61, 76, GB, FO 5/406, ff. 95–98, 225–34. Pageot entirely agreed. Pageot to Guizot, June 27, No. 60, France, MAE, CP, États-unis, C, ff. 220–27. Aberdeen to Cowley, July 18, No. 202, quoted in Adams, *British Interests*, pp. 181–82. Cowley to Aberdeen, July 22, No. 371, GB, FO 519/56.

61. Smith, *Annexation of Texas*, p. 398. *Le correspondant*, 6 (June 1844), 508–10. *Le constitutionnel*, May 26, 1844, p. 2.

62. *Cambridge History of British Foreign Policy*, II, 184–85. A. B. Cunningham, "Peel, Aberdeen, and the *Entente Cordiale*," *Bulletin of the Institute of Historical Research*, 30 (November

The Tyler administration used every means at its disposal to take advantage of this Anglo–French friction. Late in June a new American minister, William R. King, had arrived in Paris, somewhat weakened by the effects of a rough crossing. When he presented his credentials to Louis Philippe, his knees shook and he had difficulty struggling through his presentation speech. After he survived that ordeal, King pulled himself together, and in later conversations with Louis Philippe and Guizot he explained the United States desire to annex Texas on grounds of security from British intrigue. He disavowed any hostile intent toward France.[63]

On receiving reports from King about the polite French statements of friendship, Calhoun furnished him with one of his characteristic dispatch-lectures, intended as much for Congress and the American people as for the French government. In it the secretary inferred with pleasure that France had rejected joint action with Britain in the Texas question, and he tried to stimulate French Anglophobia with a long exposition of British ambitions for commercial monopoly.[64] When the dispatch was later published and came to Aberdeen's attention, it caused an explosion. For the time being, however, Calhoun's message seemed to serve its purpose, for in mid-September King wrote privately to Tyler that although Guizot still leaned toward Britain, French public opinion was so touchy that Louis Philippe would not dare grant Britain anything but her most clear-cut rights. "In this state of things," King added, "we have nothing to fear from any union of action between these governments."[65]

*   *   *   *

1957), pp. 200–204. Bartlett, *Britain and Sea Power*, pp. 160–66. Sir Robert Peel to Aberdeen, August 12, 21, 1844, Aberdeen Papers, BM, AM, vol. 43063, ff. 303–10, 324–31. Aberdeen to Peel, August 22, Peel Papers, BM, AM, vol. 40454, ff. 229–30. Peel to Earl of Haddington, September 7, Peel Papers, BM, AM, vol. 40457, ff. 263–64. If war had come, Aberdeen and Guizot were determined to resign at once. Jones, *Aberdeen and the Americas*, p. 38.

63. William R. King to James Buchanan, Paris, July 1, 1844, James Buchanan Papers, I, ff. 121–26, LC. King to Calhoun, July 13, 31, Nos. 1, 2, Manning, *IAA*, VI, 535–40. There is some evidence that Calhoun received

intimations of French intentions indirectly from Mme. Alphonse Pageot, wife of the French minister and daughter of Major William B. Lewis, long an intimate of Andrew Jackson. Wiltse, *Calhoun, Sectionalist*, p. 201.

64. Calhoun to King, August 12, 1844, No. 4, Manning, *IAA*, VI, 441–49. King's original remark about Louis Philippe's statement was only: "He finally assured me, or gave me, at least, distinctly to understand, that in any event, no steps would be taken by his government, in the slightest degree hostile, or which would give to the United States, just cause of complaint." Ibid., p. 536.

65. King to Tyler, September 13, 1844, Tyler, *Letters and Times*, II, 328–29.

Long after Aberdeen and Guizot had decided to postpone joint intervention, the government leaders of Texas and Mexico continued reacting to the Anglo–French proposal, partly because of slow communications and partly because they misunderstood how much Aberdeen's proposal involved. When news arrived in Texas around the end of June that the American Senate had rejected the annexation treaty, there was considerable grumbling, but for several reasons the European representatives, Charles Elliot and Alphonse de Saligny, were unable to use the general disappointment to their advantage. For one, Santa Anna chose this moment for a declaration that, because of the negotiations for annexation, Mexico would renew its war with Texas and would shoot all Texan prisoners as traitors. Actually, Mexico was in no position to launch an offensive, but the Texans could not be sure of this.

At the same time Tyler, Jackson, and other prominent Americans assured the Texans that the administration had other plans for annexation in reserve, and as concrete evidence of its interest the American government had stationed troops on the Louisiana border and warships along the Gulf coast. Also, within Texas, Houston seems to have lost interest in public affairs as the summer progressed; a presidential election was to be held in September, and he could not constitutionally stay in office. Finally, a severe epidemic of yellow fever reduced all political activity and chased both Elliot and Saligny away to New Orleans or the Atlantic coast until cooler weather.[66]

The key figure in the Texas question for the next nine or ten months was to be Anson Jones, a Massachusetts country doctor who had entered politics in Texas. He had served as secretary of state, and now won the presidential election with lukewarm support from his chief. Jones was less colorful and shrewd than Houston but hard-working, frank in manner, and apparently stable in personality, although several years later he committed suicide in despair over the collapse of his political career.[67] In his attitude

66. Tyler sought to conciliate Texas by appointing as chargé Tilghman A. Howard, a personal friend of Jackson and Houston, but Howard died in the yellow fever epidemic soon after his arrival. For a detailed analysis of the Texan situation and Howard's mission, see Smith, *Annexation of Texas*, pp. 356–68, and for contemporary Texan comments, see *NNR*, 66 (July 27, Au-

gust 31, 1844), 338, 441. Llerena Friend, *Sam Houston, the Great Designer*, pp. 140–43. Houston's lack of any fixed policy appears clearly in a letter of July 8 to Jones. Jones, *Memoranda*, pp. 371–72.

67. Herbert Gambrell, *Anson Jones, the Last President of Texas, passim.* Smith, *Annexation of Texas*, pp. 373–74.

toward the annexation question he imitated the weathervane policy of his predecessor. During the treaty negotiations of the preceding April he had given his professional opinion that "one or two doses of *English* calomel and *French* quinine will have to be administered" to stimulate American action "and the case will be pretty well out of danger." After the Senate's rejection of the treaty, however, he told British Consul Kennedy that Texas had been "shabbily used" and that Britain should take advantage of Texans' disillusionment. Elliot regarded him as an ally, and during the election campaign one of his opponent's strongest arguments against him was that he opposed annexation and preferred to make Texas a commercial satellite of Britain.[68]

Given this background, historians have never devised a satisfactory explanation of Jones' reaction to the Diplomatic Act. During the "lame duck" period after his election, while he and Houston were winding up the affairs of the old administration, he received a dispatch from Smith in London dated June 24 (nearly three months earlier), bearing the British proposal. According to Jones' account, he read the note to Houston, who was tense and shaking from ague and quinine, and the President instructed him to accept the offer. Convinced that this was the transient whim of a sick man, Jones argued with him, but Houston had little more to say and presently went off to attend an Indian powwow, leaving behind a written order to accept the proposal. Jones suspected a secret agreement between Houston and Elliot; he was unwilling to recognize any European power's rights of arbitration in American disputes. Consequently, he disobeyed Houston's order and recalled Smith from London, with instructions to discuss the Diplomatic Act no further with Aberdeen. When Houston returned, he allowed Jones' action to stand without a comment.[69]

Jones insisted, in his memoirs, that he had rejected the Diplomatic Act because it would either defeat annexation or lead to a war between Europe and America in which his presidential administration, soon to begin, would be swamped. Ashbel Smith, a

68. Jones' endorsement on a letter from William S. Murphy dated April 4, 1844, Jones, *Memoranda*, pp. 335–36. William Kennedy to Aberdeen, Galveston, July 30, Aberdeen Papers, BM, AM, vol. 43126, ff. 111–12. Gambrell, *Jones*, p. 351. See also a pro-European article by Jones, "The Future Policy of Texas," *National Vindicator* (Washington, Texas), no date. Clipping in

France, MAE, CP, Texas, VII, f. 283. Duff Green, who stopped at Galveston briefly en route to Mexico just after Jones' election, described the confused situation but interpreted the outcome as a victory for annexation. Duff Green to Calhoun, September 27, October 3, 1844, US, DS, SA, XIII.

69. Gambrell, *Jones*, pp. 357–60.

colleague but no special friend of Jones, suspected that he wanted to reserve for himself the final glory of annexation or of alliance with Britain. British Chargé Elliot reported an entirely different version of Jones' reaction to the proposal, saying that the Texan had urged him to obtain prompt action from the British and French governments.[70] Whatever impression Jones may have given him, his rejection of the Diplomatic Act made little difference, since Britain had abandoned the device by then.

In Mexico, Aberdeen's move toward Anglo–French cooperation did not further British policies any more effectively than it had in Texas. Minister Bankhead's friendly gestures to Santa Anna on his arrival at his post had encouraged the Mexican president to proclaim the reconquest of Texas and to request new subsidies from Congress. Repeatedly during the summer Minister Almonte and the Mexican consul at New Orleans advised Santa Anna to push ahead with plans for invading Texas without waiting for European aid. The Mexican minister to France even told Louis Philippe that Mexico would rather see the United States annex Texas than recognize its independence, because annexation would increase American power so greatly that Britain and France would be compelled to support Mexico.[71] Although dismayed at these signs of Mexican intransigence, the British and French representatives in Mexico City continued their Sisyphean task of persuading Santa Anna to recognize Texas.

Aberdeen did not inform Bankhead of the Diplomatic Act but sent him a memorandum proposing a simple Anglo–French guarantee of Mexico's boundaries in return for Mexico's recognition of Texas. When Bankhead read the memorandum to Santa Anna late in August, Santa Anna, willfully or not, missed its point altogether and remarked to an adviser, "The English Government say we must either conquer Texas or grant its independence—what will Congress say to that?" To Bankhead's dismay, he considered announcing the whole confidential proposal to Congress as an incentive to appropriations. The British minister managed to pre-

70. Jones, *Memoranda*, pp. 43–44, 54–59, *et passim*. Adams, *British Interests*, pp. 195–96. Ashbel Smith, *Reminiscences of the Texas Republic*, pp. 63–64. Written long afterward, these reminiscences show signs of faulty memory.

71. Almonte to Ministerio de Relaciones, New York, July 17, August 16, 1844, Nos. 88, 28, Barker transcripts, vol. 569, pp. 24, 94. Same, July 20, No. 91. Francisco de Arrangoiz to Ministerio de Relaciones, August 14, No. 83, US, LC, /97. Máximo Garro to Ministerio de Relaciones, Paris, July 4, quoted in Antonio de la Peña y Reyes, *Lord Aberdeen, Texas y California*, pp. xx–xxii. Santa Anna also broached to the Spanish minister a plan to divide up Texas and offer it for European colonization. Oliver to Primer Secretario de Estado, July 30, No. 434, *Rdh-m*, III, 79–80.

vent publication of the memorandum, but the prospect of Mexican recognition became dimmer than ever.[72]

While Santa Anna was reviving the war against Texas, he was also becoming involved in a serious quarrel with the United States, more bitter and conclusive than the earlier arguments of Bocanegra with Waddy Thompson and Benjamin E. Green. To fill the post left vacant by Thompson, Tyler appointed Wilson Shannon, a onetime governor of Ohio, apparently for no better reason than that he was splitting the Democratic party there, and the party leaders wanted him out of the state. Shannon was appointed minister to Mexico in April, but for personal reasons he did not leave for his post until three months later. He arrived in Mexico City on August 27 after a long, tiresome journey, out of sorts because bandits had robbed him in broad daylight although the authorities at Puebla had promised him full protection.[73]

Shortly before Shannon's arrival, Bocanegra, shrewdly guessing that rough days lay ahead, had resigned from the foreign ministry. In his place Santa Anna appointed Manuel Crescencio Rejón, an intelligent, articulate ultra-liberal who had lost his former admiration of the United States and taken up a friendly attitude toward the European powers. Convinced that the United States had designs on California as well as Texas, Rejón determined not to yield an inch on the Texas question. As he confronted the new American minister, he consulted Bankhead, and he kept him fully informed of developments.[74]

On October 12 Shannon received instructions from Calhoun, denouncing the "savage ferocity" of Mexican war against Texas in the severest terms available to a diplomat and directing Shannon to protest against this war "in strong language, accompanied by declarations, that the President cannot regard . . . [the war] with indifference, but as highly offensive to the United States." The bearer of these instructions was Duff Green, sent to Mexico

72. Bankhead to Aberdeen, August 29, No. 66, GB, FO 50/175, ff. 207–11. However, Bankhead continued to hope for Mexican recognition. Bankhead to Aberdeen, August 29, No. 73, GB, FO 50/175, ff. 251–55.

73. B. B. Taylor to [William Allen], Columbus, Ohio, March 11, 1844, Allen Papers, IV, LC. Wilson Shannon to Calhoun, August 28, US, DS, D, Mexico, XII.

74. Green to Calhoun, August 20, 1844, No. 17, US, DS, D, Mexico, XII.

Oliver to Primer Secretario de Estado, August 23, No. 446, Rdh-m, III, 84–85. Frank A. Knapp, Jr., "The Mexican Fear of Manifest Destiny in California," in Thomas E. Cotner and Carlos E. Castañeda, eds., Essays in Mexican History, p. 197. Adams, British Interests, p. 188. The British Foreign Office archives contain copies of the Shannon–Rejón correspondence written on stationery of the Ministerio de Relaciones Exteriores.

as confidential observer. With his flair for invective and for attributing the most sinister motives to foreigners, Green was the worst possible adviser for an amateur diplomat facing a suspicious Mexican nationalist. The resulting disastrous encounter has usually been blamed on the hapless Shannon, but it is actually one more example of the erratic judgment that affected Calhoun in all matters connected with the Texas question.[75]

As soon as he received his new instructions, Shannon opened battle with a note declaring in rash and insulting language that the United States would not permit Mexico's "barbarous" efforts to reconquer Texas or to force alliances that would prevent annexation, a policy cherished by the United States for twenty years. Rejón repeated what Bocanegra had often argued in preceding months about American aid to the Texan rebels, but this time he attributed this aid more directly to the American government. Shannon blew up at these "gross and palpable" misrepresentations and gave his own version of Texan history, complete with quotations from Andrew Jackson; Rejón answered with other statements of Jackson and John Quincy Adams. Shannon implied that Rejón was a liar; Rejón retorted that Shannon did not even know the history of his own country. Finally, Shannon made the mistake of declaring that until Rejón withdrew his offensive notes he would break relations with the Mexican government. Naturally, Rejón stood his ground, and Shannon had no course but to withdraw to his legation and await instructions. He had painted himself into a corner.[76]

* * * *

75. Calhoun to Wilson Shannon, September 10, 1844, No. 6, Manning, *IAA*, VIII, 155–61. Indeed, some of Calhoun's enemies suspected that he was deliberately trying to provoke Mexico into insults which could be publicized in the United States to support annexation. Smith, *Annexation of Texas*, p. 323n2. According to Merk, Calhoun instructed Green to sound out the Mexican government on the sale of all territory north of a line along the Nueces River and then along 36° or 37° to the Pacific, including San Francisco and perhaps Monterey. Frederick Merk, *The Monroe Doctrine and American Expansionism, 1843–1849*, p. 141. Merk cites only an incomplete reference in Polk's diary. From other evidence, Calhoun apparently gave this instruction earlier in

the year to Colonel Gilbert Thompson. James K. Polk, *The Diary of James K. Polk during His Presidency, 1845 to 1849*, ed. Milo Milton Quaife, I, 312. Pakenham to Aberdeen, May 13, No. 46, GB, FO 5/405, ff. 94–96. In any case, Green warned Calhoun that Britain was probably trying to get California from Mexico. Duff Green to Calhoun, October 9, US, DS, SA, XIII.

76. Shannon to Manuel Crescencio Rejón, October 14, November 4, 8, 1844; Rejón to Shannon, October 31, November 6, 21, Manning, *IAA*, VIII, 644–49, 654–75, 680–92. The same volume contains Shannon's reports to Calhoun. For a brief account of the controversy, see James Morton Callahan, *American Foreign Policy in Mexican Relations*, pp. 124–26.

Through the summer and autumn of 1844 international correspondence and calculations about Texas ran parallel to the American presidential campaign, which no policy maker in Mexico City, London, or Paris could neglect. At the beginning of the campaign there were four men who might affect the outcome: the two major candidates, Clay and Polk, and two splinter candidates, Tyler and James G. Birney of the young National Liberty party, made up primarily of abolitionists in the Northeast. Birney threatened to split the votes of the Whig party, Tyler those of the Democrats.

The Democrats moved first against the threat by persuading Tyler to withdraw from the race, with fulsome flattery from Jackson and hints that his followers would be received back into the party.[77] Economic issues had so divided the nation that, at Robert J. Walker's advice, Polk hedged on the tariff so as to carry the important state of Pennsylvania. Although he had a clear-cut record in support of low tariffs, Polk wrote an open letter to John K. Kane, a minor Philadelphia politician, declaring that he had always favored a tariff for revenue with "such moderate discriminating duties as would . . . at the same time afford reasonable incidental protection to our home industry." The Whigs, reading the free-trade statements of Democratic campaigners in the South, attacked Polk's "weasel" words with sarcastic jibes at "accidental" and "transcendental" protection. British free-trade societies aided the Whigs with rash pamphlets supporting the Democratic position, but Polk's minimal concession probably won him Pennsylvania.[78]

Clay was less fortunate than Polk in dealing with the Texas question. By adopting a general expansionist program, the Democrats had some prospect of allying the South and the Northwest and could resign themselves to losing New England and perhaps New York too. But Clay, with support in both South and North, had to straddle any issue that threatened to divide these two sections. Seeing the unexpected strength of annexationism in the

77. Paul, *Rift in the Democracy*, pp. 176–77. Eugene Irving McCormac, *James K. Polk, a Political Biography*, pp. 267–70. Sellers, *Polk, Continentalist*, pp. 133–37. Robert Seager, II, *and Tyler Too, a Biography of John and Julia Gardiner Tyler*, pp. 231–32.

78. Paul, *Rift in the Democracy*, pp. 174–75. McCormac, *Polk*, pp. 260–61. Polk's letter to Kane is reprinted in Lambert, *Presidential Politics*, p. 206. Unlike most other historians, Sellers defends the Kane letter as forthright and carefully clear. Sellers, *Polk, Continentalist*, pp. 116–23. For Whig speeches and other comments on the tariff issue, see *NNR*, 66 (July 20, 1844), 324–25; 67 (September 14, October 5, 12), 28–31, 77, 90–95.

South, he wrote four letters explaining that he was no abolitionist and would be happy to see Texas annexed honorably. The Democrats circulated these letters widely in the North; abolitionists recoiled in disgust; and finally, when it was too late to be effective, Clay resumed his original opposition to immediate annexation.[79]

For their part, Polk and his lieutenants were satisfied to talk about Texas in general terms, privately opposing any immediate action. While still a candidate, Tyler contemplated calling a special session of Congress to consider a joint resolution for annexation. Rumors of a Mexican attack and of joint intervention by Britain and France strengthened Calhoun's arguments for such a session. But when Polk got wind of the proposal, he objected strenuously, lest it hurt the Democrats' chances. Tyler agreed and, overruling Calhoun, contented himself with a mild warning to Mexico.[80]

Other national issues received less attention than Texas and the tariff but affected votes here and there. The Oregon question attracted little attention outside the West. In New York and Pennsylvania the Democrats tarred the Whigs with antiforeignism, and both parties enlisted the support of hurriedly naturalized immigrants. The Whig issues of internal improvements at national expense and national subsidies to the states ("distribution") played a smaller role in the campaign than was expected.[81]

Early in the summer Clay seemed to be running ahead in a close race, but his letters on Texas confused his supporters, and the more aggressive, shrewd propaganda of the Democrats gradually pulled them ahead. In the end Polk won, 170 to 105. Votes in all sections of the country were divided—Polk even won Maine and New Hampshire—and it would be impossible to attribute the

79. The most thorough analysis of the Texan issue in the campaign is Smith, *Annexation of Texas*, Chap. 15. See especially pp. 305–6*n*11, for a concise summary of arguments for and against annexation. A good sample of Whig arguments against annexation is a letter from Waddy Thompson, former minister to Mexico. *NNR*, 66 (July 13, 1844), 316–19. On Clay's explanatory letters, see Lambert, *Presidential Politics*, pp. 174–77; and George Rawlings Poage, *Henry Clay and the Whig Party*, Chaps. 9–10. James E. Winston, "Robert J. Walker, Annexationist," *The Texas Review*, 2 (April 1917), 302–3. But the Democrats also hedged on Texas. See, for example, the statement

of Silas Wright in New York *Evening Post*, September 19; and Sellers, *Polk, Continentalist*, pp. 111–12, 128–29, 150–51, 154–55.

80. Wiltse, *Calhoun, Sectionalist*, p. 184. Sellers, *Polk, Continentalist*, pp. 132–33. A special session would have provided Benton with a forum for his divisive anti-Texas oratory. For contrasting views on the foreign danger to Texas, see *NNR*, 67 (September 21, 1844), 36.

81. Lambert, *Presidential Politics*, pp. 180–81, 187–90. In Chap. 7 Lambert reviews all the issues of the campaign. See also Sellers, *Polk, Continentalist*, Chap. 4, *passim*.

result to any single issue. It was generally assumed that Clay's hedging on Texas allowed Birney to absorb enough of his strength to throw New York's 35 electoral votes to Polk. Some have argued, however, that a stand on Clay's original Texan letter would have lost him Delaware, Maryland, North Carolina, and Tennessee (totaling 35 electoral votes), which he won by narrow margins.[82]

At the time, however, the results of the election seemed to be a victory for expansionism in general and for some sort of honorable but immediate annexation of Texas.[83] Only gradually did the victorious Democrats realize that the slavery question was forcing its way to the center of American politics and that the Texas issue had split their party permanently and weakened the Jacksonian ideal. Much later, the shrewd Buchanan called Texas "the Grecian horse that entered our camp."[84]

Most foreign observers were disappointed in the outcome, for, correctly or not, they regarded Clay as more responsible, cautious, and experienced than Polk, and they took too many of the Democrats' wild campaign slogans at their face value. Almonte wrote home that Clay's election would bring hope of justice for Mexico, but if Polk won, the United States would surely annex Texas and Mexico must seriously consider war.[85] Europeans also unhappily interpreted the election as a mandate for annexation. Guizot thought it deplorable on all counts, although the French Minister Pageot tried to console him that because of party splits Polk might retain some freedom of action. *Le journal des débats* declared: "With Mr. Polk begins the reign of other men for whom the horizon is the [only] limit for America." However, the *Journal* expected Polk to prove a weak executive, unable to prevent divisive intrigue.[86] British opinion was split, for aristocrats and nationalists

82. Sellers, *Polk, Continentalist*, pp. 108–9, 157–61. Lambert, *Presidential Politics*, pp. 194–200. Tyler, *Letters and Times*, III, 125, note.

83. The unreliability of the vote even as an indication of general expansionism is suggested by testimony such as that of a disgruntled New Yorker who wrote afterwards to Anson Jones that four-fifths of the people in New York and New Jersey, probably three-fourths of Pennsylvania, nearly all of New England, and large majorities in the rest of the North had "a deep and abiding feeling" against annexation, and that if the Democrats had come out openly for it, they would have lost. Instead, "in all the farming towns they took the ground that Mr. Clay was as much for Texas as Mr. Polk." Lot Clark to Jones, Lockport, New York, March 11, 1845, Jones, *Memoranda*, pp. 438–40.

84. Buchanan to Frank Blair, November 27, 1849, quoted and discussed in Paul, *Rift in the Democracy*, pp. 181–83. See also Sellers, *Polk, Continentalist*, p. 170.

85. Almonte to Bocanegra, August 18, 1844, Barker transcripts, vol. 569, p. 89.

86. Cowley to Aberdeen, December 2, 1844, No. 568, GB, FO 519/58. Pageot to Guizot, October 29, November 13, Nos. 68, 69, France, MAE, CP, États-unis, C, ff. 269–81. *Le journal des débats*, December 8, p. 1.

opposed American expansion to the West and South, while liberals sympathized with the still-remembered ideals of Jackson's party, and manufacturers and merchants hoped for lower tariffs under Polk.[87]

Clearly, both Americans and Europeans would have to wait for the full significance of the election to reveal itself. The vote had been close, and the victorious candidate was virtually unknown, his complex personality buried beneath a heap of campaign slogans. Meanwhile, Tyler and Calhoun had three more months in which to solve the Texas question.

87. Pakenham to Aberdeen, November 13, 1844, No. 123, GB, FO 5/409, ff. 18–21. For British press reactions, see *NNR*, 67 (December 28, 1844, January 4, 1845), 257, 280–81.

7

Annexation Completed

Although the British and French governments postponed their intervention in the Texas question during the summer of 1844 to await the outcome of the United States presidential election, events in Mexico and Texas could not stand still. At the end of the year, a revolution in the former country and rising tension in the latter had changed the circumstances with which Tyler, Calhoun, Aberdeen, and Guizot would have to deal.

Events in Mexico were more dramatic than in Texas. By the latter half of 1844, Santa Anna had finally come to the end of his resources. On November 2 General Mariano Paredes y Arrillaga, commander of the largest body of troops in the north, issued a revolutionary manifesto (*pronunciamiento*) protesting the rapacious taxation and waste of Santa Anna's administration. Paredes was a brave, strutting little man with aristocratic, proclerical family connections and a proud, intolerant wife. Formerly devoted to the dictator's cause, he had grown discontented with his own lack of advancement. His popularity with the troops and his ties with the pro-Spanish, conservative element—formerly Santa Anna's chief basis of power—made his movement dangerous to the dictator.

As soon as he learned of Paredes' *pronunciamiento*, Santa Anna left his country estate near Veracruz to take command of the nearest loyal troops. Congress and the Supreme Court declared the executive actions unconstitutional. Mobs raged through the capital, tearing down Santa Anna's monuments and digging up his buried leg, which they dragged through the streets at the end of a rope. On December 6 the city's garrison mutinied and imprisoned Acting President Canalizo. By general agreement among men of responsibility and property, the president of the Council of State, General José Joaquín Herrera, was named president *ad interim*, mainly because he was in a position of authority and had the reputation of being honest.[1]

1. George Lockhart Rives, *The United States and Mexico, 1821–1848*, I, 667–73. Niceto de Zamacois, *Historia de* *Méjico desde sus tiempos más remotas hasta nuestros días*, XII, 337–63. Thomas Ewing Cotner, *The Military and*

When the revolution broke out, the foreign diplomats in Mexico City were divided in their attitude toward Santa Anna. The American minister and his adviser, Wilson Shannon and Duff Green, favored any change, since they suspected that British gold was keeping the dictator in power and that Santa Anna was scheming to cede California to Britain in return.[2] The French minister, Alleye de Cyprey, long irritated at Santa Anna's cavalier neglect of French grievances, used such insulting language about him in public that the Mexican government unofficially requested the minister's recall. Guizot supported him, however, convinced that Santa Anna was trying to play off France against Britain, but he urged Alleye to behave with prudence and moderation.[3]

The rumors of Anglo–Mexican intrigue were somewhat exaggerated, for the British had as many unsatisfied grievances against Mexico as the French. When Santa Anna suspended payment of debts in order to obtain money to put down Paredes' revolution, the British minister, Charles Bankhead, protested with such good effect that he was able to elicit promises of some tariff concessions. More important, in the midst of the revolutionary upheaval, Bankhead had a long conversation with Santa Anna in which he persuaded the dictator, for the first time, to agree that he would recognize Texas in return for an indemnity from the United States and a favorable boundary guaranteed by Britain and France. The terms were not precisely those which Aberdeen had outlined earlier in the year; soon afterward the British abandoned the guarantee. Nevertheless, Santa Anna's concessions were enough to make Bankhead prefer him to any other leader.[4] The news of this offer, arriving weeks later in London, helped to bring about the renewal of Anglo–French intervention.

Political Career of José Joaquín de Herrera, 1792–1854, pp. 105–7 et passim. On Paredes, see Guillermo Prieto, *Memorias de mis tiempos, 1840 a 1853*, pp. 178–79.

2. Duff Green to John C. Calhoun, Mexico City, October 28, November 12, 1844; Galveston, November 29, John C. Calhoun, *Correspondence of John C. Calhoun*, ed. J. Franklin Jameson, pp. 975–80, 991–95, 1000–1002. Wilson Shannon to Green, January 15, 1845, Green Papers, box 3, LC. Shannon to Calhoun, January 16, No. 8, Manning, *IAA*, VIII, 696–98.

3. Máximo Garro to François Guizot, October 22; Guizot to Comte de Ste.

Aulaire, October 26; Guizot to Cyprey, November 27, No. 49, France, MAE, CP, Mexique, XXIX, ff. 148–49, 180–81; XXX, ff. 45–47. Pascual de Oliver to Primer Secretario de Estado, November 24, No. 498, *Rdh-m*, III, 117. *Le constitutionnel*, October 13, p. 1.

4. In addition to the above terms, Santa Anna insisted on the Colorado River as boundary and British protection during the period of negotiation. Charles Bankhead to Earl of Aberdeen, November 29, 1844, No. 102, Ephraim Douglass Adams, ed., *British Diplomatic Correspondence Concerning the Republic of Texas, 1838–1846*, pp. 433–36.

But neither Bankhead's moral support nor Santa Anna's own ingenuity could save the dictator. After feinting with Paredes, Santa Anna marched against Herrera in Mexico City, but he did not trust his officers enough to attack, and he lacked the strength for a siege. Near the first of the year he turned against rebellious Puebla, but by now his supporters were melting away, and, resigning his office, he took a small guard and headed for the Gulf coast. In mid-January a group of Indians, recognizing him by his peg leg, captured him in a village not far from the borders of his estate. According to one story, in their hatred of the tyrant and their sardonic native humor, they proposed to boil him alive and present him to the local authorities as a human *tamale*, seasoned with chiles and wrapped in banana leaves. However, the parish priest rescued the captive, and the Indians sullenly agreed to surrender him to the authorities unharmed. After months as a prisoner in the fortress of Perote, Santa Anna was quietly allowed to seek exile in Havana, the focal point of Mexican trade with both the United States and Europe, where he could observe events and plot to his heart's content.[5]

After Santa Anna's flight Paredes also subsided, but with his army and his conservative, nationalist following, he remained a constant threat to any administration in power. Mostly by default, Herrera assumed the full presidential prerogative. He was a professional soldier, a good Catholic but moderately liberal in political views, serious, cautious, unobtrusive, and so honest and frugal that he pawned his own jewels to pay the expenses of his inauguration. He came to office with a headful of sensible reforms, intending to overhaul the army and the civil service, undertake public works, stimulate agriculture and trade, and refund the foreign debt. His foreign minister was Luis G. Cuevas, an able but irresolute man who had held the same post with some credit during the French intervention of 1838–1839. Both Herrera and Cuevas began to hint publicly that recognition of Texas was the only possible settlement of the problem which stood in the way of all domestic reform.[6]

Unfortunately, at the moment the federalists seemed about

5. Rives, *US and Mexico*, I, 674–78. Zamacois, *Historia de Méjico*, XII, 366–84. Wilfrid Hardy Callcott, *Santa Anna, the Story of an Enigma Who Once Was Mexico*, pp. 211–14.

6. Cotner, *Herrera*, pp. 9, 31, 59, 93–94, 120, Chap. 6, pp. 131–34, *et passim*.

José Bravo Ugarte, *Historia de México*, III, 196. C. Alan Hutchinson, "Valentín Gómez Farías and the Movement for the Return of General Santa Anna to Mexico in 1846," in Thomas E. Cotner and Carlos E. Castañeda, eds., *Essays in Mexican History*, pp. 173–74, 180–81.

to achieve some of their goals they split into two factions over the Texas question. Moderates (*moderados*) were willing to support Herrera in conciliating the United States, even at the sacrifice of the lost province, but archliberals (who took the name *puros* during the following year) declared that compromise would only arouse the Americans' appetite for California and New Mexico. They felt that if Mexico refused to negotiate and stood on her honor, the people would unite behind the government and might possibly fend off an American attack. As *moderados* and *puros* drew apart, *santanistas* began to intrigue in the hope of recovering power. Also, Bankhead and De Cyprey remained skeptical about any new government as long as foreign grievances went unremedied, and Shannon stayed in his legation, officially incommunicado.[7] A man of good will surrounded by enemies, Herrera was just as likely to raise false hopes abroad as the deceitful opportunist whom he had replaced.

* * * *

While the overthrow of Santa Anna brought hope of a more flexible Mexican policy toward Texas, that republic continued to hesitate between independence and annexation to the United States. During the late summer of 1844 President-elect Anson Jones had disobeyed Houston's order to accept the Anglo–French Diplomatic Act for intervention and mediation. Shortly before, Houston and Jones reminded the American chargé, Tilghman A. Howard, that Tyler had earlier promised Texas protection against attack by Mexico. With the election campaign at its hottest, Calhoun did not care to reply to Houston in writing, but he told the Texan chargé privately that the American government fully acknowledged its obligation and would keep troops near the Sabine and ships along the Gulf coast.[8]

Four days after giving this private assurance of support, Tyler

7. Bankhead to Aberdeen, January 29, March 1, 1845, Nos. 6, 13, 14, 17, GB, FO 50/184, ff. 37–38, 88–89, 102–5, 162–64. To some degree the *moderado-puro* split was foreshadowed in the 1820s, and it has even been traced to factionalism in the late colonial period. Vicente Fuentes Díaz, *La intervención norteamericana en Mexico (1847)*, pp. 118–25.

8. Anson Jones to Tilghman A. Howard, August 6, 1844; Howard to Calhoun, August 7, Manning, *IAA*, XII, 360–61, 364. Charles H. Raymond to Jones, Washington, September 12, No. 131, Garrison, *DCRT*, II, 310–12. Duff Green assured Jones unofficially that, even though unauthorized, he would instruct the American commander at Pensacola to send forces if needed. Green to Jones, September 30, Anson Jones, *Memoranda and Official Correspondence Relating to the Republic of Texas, Its History and Annexation*, pp. 385–86.

and Calhoun learned that Howard had died of yellow fever. Anxious not to leave Houston and Jones without official American advice, they at once prevailed upon Major Andrew Jackson Donelson to accept the important but dangerous post of American chargé as a patriotic duty. Donelson was Andrew Jackson's nephew, an experienced Democratic politician who had already declined to become Tyler's secretary of the treasury. More important, he was a friend of Sam Houston and James K. Polk. After winding up his personal affairs, Donelson arrived in Galveston on November 11, confident of completing his mission by January.[9] A little over two weeks later Duff Green arrived from Mexico City to serve as consul, well laden with dispatches and gossip. Green at once plunged into land speculation and soon proved more hindrance than help, but at least he never influenced Donelson as he had Shannon.[10]

On November 21 Donelson took up residence in the frontier capital of Texas, Washington-on-the-Brazos. His log cabin was adjacent to the one occupied by Houston, so he was able to engage the President frequently in close conversation. Donelson discovered that Houston was disgruntled over the question of American protection and was wavering between the influence of the United States and England. The American chargé cleverly repeated some of Jackson's statements about the value of annexation and hinted that the old man feared lest Houston fall prey to ambition and try to make his nation a rival to the United States. At this Houston quickly replied, "No—No—No. . . . Tell Genl. Jackson that his counsels influence my spirit—that his words are treasures" and more of the same. Donelson also met President-elect Jones and pronounced him "as frank and cordial as could have been expected." Following that interview, Donelson predicted that the election of Polk would gradually swing Texas toward the United States.[11]

This slow gravitation was just what the British chargé, Charles

9. Justin H. Smith, *The Annexation of Texas*, p. 368. Charles M. Wiltse, *John C. Calhoun, Sectionalist, 1840–1850*, pp. 203–4. John Tyler to Andrew Jackson, September 17, 1844, Andrew Jackson, *The Correspondence of Andrew Jackson*, ed. John Spencer Bassett, VI, 319–20. Andrew J. Donelson to Mrs. Elizabeth Donelson, New Orleans, November 7, Andrew J. Donelson Papers, IX, 1885, LC. Donelson to Calhoun, November 11, Manning, *IAA*, XII, 371–72.

10. William Kennedy to Aberdeen, December 5, 1844; Charles Elliot to Aberdeen, December 29, Adams, *British Correspondence*, pp. 379–82, 400–403.

11. Donelson to Mrs. Donelson, November 28, 1844, Donelson Papers, X, 1898–99. Donelson to Calhoun, November 23, 24, December 5, Nos. 2–4, Manning, *IAA*, XII, 373–81. Quoted phrases are on pp. 376, 379. Smith, *Annexation of Texas*, pp. 369–71.

Elliot, feared. In a memorandum written after Polk's election he declared that the pressure of Texan public opinion, reinforced by speculators in lands and securities, would carry annexation in Texas if it could be put through the American Congress. Elliot was then in the United States, where he had spent the summer, and he did not return to the Texan capital until December 20. On his return, Jones assured him that Texans would give up annexation if Mexico recognized their independence. Jones hoped that the British and French governments would use their influence to bring about recognition by Mexico and would conclude some sort of definite agreement with Texas.[12] In New Orleans the French chargé, Alphonse de Saligny, encouraged Jones' roving minister, G. W. Terrell, to believe that France would give such support.[13]

At this point public opinion in Texas was still wavering, for national pride and imperialistic ambitions contended with the obvious economic and social advantages of union with the United States. Houston still seemed undecided; one of Robert J. Walker's friends described his behavior at several "frolics": "When *sober*, he was for annexation; but when *drunk*, or in liquor, he would express himself strongly against the measure!"[14] Anson Jones gave assurances on both sides of the question and later explained his inconsistencies on the ground of the evenly divided opinion in the United States. Dealings with European representatives, he explained, might stimulate jealousy in the United States or, failing that, provide a second protection against Mexican wrath.[15] Government officials in general and many members of Congress were unenthusiastic or openly opposed to annexation. However, planters, merchants, and probably the majority of the general public favored joining the United States, especially after the election of Polk became known. Donelson effectively supported the annexationists by giving publicity to Shannon's quarrel with Rejón as evidence of what the United States would do to defend Texas.[16]

12. Memorandum of Elliot, Philadelphia, November 14, 1844, GB, FO 5/409, ff. 50–58. Elliot to Aberdeen, December 21, 28, Adams, *British Correspondence*, pp. 393–400.

13. G. W. Terrell to Jones, New Orleans, November 22, Jones, *Memoranda*, pp. 404–5.

14. John G. Tod to Robert J. Walker, Washington, Texas, December 18/23, 1844, Walker Papers, No. 121, LC.

15. Herbert Gambrell, *Anson Jones, the Last President of Texas*, pp. 393–403, *passim*. Although Gambrell appears to accept Jones' noncommittal policy at face value, the bulk of Jones' writings show him to have been either skeptical about annexation or opposed to it. For Jones' explanation of his actions, see his *Memoranda*, pp. 78–82.

16. Donelson to Calhoun, December 5, 17, 1844, Nos. 4, [8], Manning, *IAA*, XII, 378–81, 387–89. There was a group of undetermined size in Texas that feared European influence. *NNR*, 67 (February 1, 1845), 337.

In the last week of December Duff Green almost discredited the annexation movement through his far-flung expansionist business deals and his uncontrolled temper. When he arrived in Texas, he apparently brought with him certificates for Mexican public lands issued to bondholders under the 1837 conversion. On the basis of these he proposed to inaugurate a great colonization project that would extend south and west, perhaps as far as the Pacific—"with powers not unlike those of the East India Company," according to Elliot, "but with no definite legal controul [sic] left to the Executive Government." In letters to Calhoun, Green wrote greedily of annexing a large bloc of Mexican territory along with Texas and even of seizing and holding Veracruz.[17]

In order to get his colonizing company under way, Green needed charters from the Texan legislature, but he made the mistake of offering Jones stock in exchange for his support. When Jones refused, Green lost his head entirely and threatened to call a popular convention and start a revolution. Jones is reported to have shouted back that "no damn demagogue" should dictate to him or rule his course of action. At the end of the stormy scene Jones revoked Green's exequatur (consular certification) and ordered him to leave Texas. For a moment Elliot and Saligny rejoiced, but Green apologized after a fashion, and the crisis abated without permanent effect.[18]

By the end of the year both Elliot and Donelson were warning their governments that they must exert themselves at once if they meant to win Texas. Elliot felt that Houston and Jones underestimated the strength of annexationism among the people. As for Donelson, on December 26 he wrote privately to Calhoun that the "lame duck" American Congress must pass an acceptable annexation bill at once, to be carried out by either Tyler or Polk. "Let us get annexation on any terms we can," he urged.[19]

17. Adams, *British Correspondence*, pp. 379–403, *passim*. The passage quoted from Elliot appears in a letter of December 29, 1844, to Aberdeen, p. 402. A description of Green's project appears in a letter of H. McLeod, Washington, Texas, January 1845, Unidentified newspaper clipping, GB, FO 75/13, f. 43. Green to Calhoun, November 12, 29, December 8, 1844, Calhoun, *Correspondence*, pp. 991–95, 1003, 1006–7.

18. Tod to Walker, December 31, 1844, quoted in James Patrick Shenton, *Robert John Walker, a Politician from Jackson to Lincoln*, p. 36. Gambrell,

Jones, p. 381. Elliot to Richard Pakenham, December 30, GB, FO 5/424, ff. 25–29. See also Elliot to Aberdeen, January 2, 1845, Adams, *British Correspondence*, pp. 407–10.

19. Elliot to Pakenham, New Orleans, November 30, 1844, GB, FO 5/409, ff. 123–26. Elliot to Aberdeen, Galveston, December 10; Washington, Texas, December 21, Nos. 15, 17, Adams, *British Correspondence*, pp. 391–96. Donelson to Calhoun, New Orleans, December 26, Calhoun, *Correspondence*, pp. 1011–13.

*   *   *   *

Annexation on any terms was exactly what Tyler and Calhoun intended. In his annual message at the opening of Congress on December 3 the President denounced Mexico for threatening a hopeless "war of desolation" against Texas. Such a war would only touch off revolt in her other provinces; United States annexation of Texas would in fact benefit Mexico. Since the election of Polk proved that most Americans favored annexation, and since there was no reason to believe that Texans had changed their minds about it, he urged prompt action. With this message Tyler sent to Congress all pertinent correspondence of the summer and early autumn, including Calhoun's provocative note to King on Franco–Texan policy (see Chapter 5). On December 18 he gave Congress the whole Shannon–Rejón correspondence, together with a message attacking Mexico in even stronger terms for meddling in American domestic affairs through Rejón's remarks about the South and slavery. Even in this message, however, Tyler recommended no action stronger than annexation.[20]

By this time the election of Polk had produced a perceptible shift of moderate opinion toward immediate action. Such newspapers as the New York *Courier and Enquirer* and the Philadelphia *Pennsylvanian* now supported annexation; the editors of the latter announced that they had only now realized "the vitality of the Texas question," by which they probably meant the importance of Texan markets. However, many others—the Boston *Atlas*, the New York *Evening Post*, the Washington *National Intelligencer*, and the Richmond *Enquirer*, for example—remained firm. The New York *American* denounced Shannon's "wretched bungle." The *Evening Post* ridiculed the anxiety of annexationists who argued that it was "now or never," and when its editor read Calhoun's July note to King, he declared triumphantly: "Here we have got on firm ground at last. We have the contrivers of the measure . . . explaining to a friendly power and to the world the motives and objects of their plans. *Slavery cannot continue in this country unless it continue in Texas, and it cannot continue in Texas without annexation; therefore we annex Texas, that we may perpetuate slavery.*"[21]

20. James D. Richardson, ed., *A Compilation of the Messages and Papers of the Presidents, 1789–1897*, IV, 340–45, 353–56.

21. Smith, *Annexation of Texas*, pp. 323–24. New York *Evening Post*, December 11, 1844, p. 2. For summaries and clippings on American reactions to the Shannon-Rejón correspondence, see Juan N. Almonte to Ministerio de Relaciones, December 16, No. 172 and enclosures. The phrase quoted from the

Immediately after Polk's election Almonte had become so alarmed at the prospect of annexation that he advised his government to provoke a showdown at once with the Tyler administration. By the time he read the President's annual message, however, the Mexican minister had concluded that the immediate threats were largely bluff and resumed his counsel of patience and rearmament. Even after the second message and the beginning of the debates Pakenham doubted that an annexation bill would pass both houses of Congress.[22] Calhoun, though confident of success, feared an alliance of Van Buren Democrats and Whigs in New York. Such an alliance became less likely as the new session progressed, for European newspapers criticizing Tyler's messages and Donelson's dispatches about the precarious situation in Texas strengthened the annexationists' case.[23]

The debate on annexation began in the House of Representatives about a week after Tyler's annual message, with the introduction of a joint resolution that restated most terms of the rejected treaty. Members of the House criticized several provisions: the vagueness of Texan boundaries, the undefined status of slavery, the assumption of the Texan debt, and the right of Texas to immediate statehood. A number of other resolutions followed, each designed to answer one or more of these objections, until it seemed likely that a stalemate would result. At this point, influenced in part by Donelson's dispatches, the Democrats decided in caucus that they would admit all proposals to the floor and try to find one which would satisfy a majority. This maneuver produced a long series of speeches reviewing all the old arguments pro and con—Texan resources and strategic value, the constitutionality and wisdom of adding more territory to an already unwieldy nation, and of course the extension of slavery. On January 25, by a vote of 120 to 98 the House adopted a resolution originally introduced by Milton Brown, a Tennessee Whig, that would admit Texas as a state, postpone the boundary question for later settlement by the Federal government, and leave the Texans to handle the problems of their debt and public lands. The resolution also

New York *American* appeared in that paper on December 13, US, LC, /42.

22. Almonte to Ministerio de Relaciones, November 9, No. 135, US, LC, /57. Same, December 14, No. 163, Barker transcripts, vol. 569, pp. 92–93.

23. Calhoun to Thomas G. Clemson, December 27, 1844; Calhoun to R. M.

T. Hunter, December 29, Calhoun, *Correspondence*, pp. 634–37. Cave Johnson to James K. Polk, December 12, quoted in Eugene Irving McCormac, *James K. Polk, a Political Biography*, p. 312. Wiltse, *Calhoun, Sectionalist*, p. 209. Smith, *Annexation of Texas*, pp. 336–37.

provided that Texas might be split into several states, and at the last moment a clause was added to forbid slavery north of the Missouri Compromise line (36°30′).[24]

Meanwhile, the Senate had begun discussion on a resolution introduced by Calhoun's lieutenant, George McDuffie of South Carolina, that embodied most of the earlier treaty. The discussion quickly revived an ancient personal feud between Calhoun's bloc and Thomas Hart Benton, who was leaning toward annexation. He feared, however, that rash action might provoke war with Mexico, and he opposed the United States' assuming the inflated Texan debt. Benton now proposed the negotiation of a new treaty that would require Mexico's approval, limit the Texan debt, and divide Texas into two parts, one slave and the other free. Other proposals also appeared. To prevent a deadlock, the Senate agreed to await action by the House, but when the Senate Foreign Relations Committee finally reported on the House resolution, it merely recommended that the Senate reject the resolution and table the other proposals.

At this critical point in the campaign Calhoun was entirely out of the battle for several weeks, confined to his room with a serious bronchial infection. Perhaps this was just as well, for his absence gave Francis P. Blair, Robert J. Walker, and other annexationists in and out of Congress time to work on Benton, using Donelson's dispatches and Jackson's letters, which all urged prompt, united action. On February 5 the Missouri Senator introduced a revised bill that omitted any reference to consent by Mexico or terms of annexation and simply appropriated $100,000 for new negotiations with Texas. Blair approved the proposal in Jackson's name, but the *Madisonian* declared that the mountain had brought forth the same old mouse, only without its tail.[25] Calhounites accused Benton of going just far enough to placate annexationists in his own state without preventing a deadlock. After other proposals were presented, a long debate began in mid-February, which gave Senators ample opportunity to examine the merits of the House resolution and their own bills, review all the old arguments, add a few new ones, and exercise their in-

---

24. US, 28C, 2S, *CG*, pp. 26–27, 191–94, *et passim*. Smith gives a succinct account of the debate, summarizing the principal speeches and arguments. Smith, *Annexation of Texas*, pp. 327–34. The final vote in favor included 8 Whigs, 53 free-state Democrats, and 59 Democrats from slave states; 80 out of 133 Northerners voted against the measure (p. 333).

25. Cited in Smith, *Annexation of Texas*, p. 337.

genuity in parliamentary procedure. By the last week of February, compromise was in the air, but no one seemed to know the formula that would make it materialize.

The crucial action was a proposal by Walker to combine the measures of Benton and the House as alternatives. Benton's new negotiations were to take place if Texas rejected the ready-made terms of the House resolution. Walker's ingenious solution lulled the doubts of some strict constructionists who regarded a simple joint resolution as unconstitutional, but it aroused suspicion in many persons, including Calhoun and most of the Whigs, who seemed inclined for a time to talk the measure to death. However, in a solemn evening session on February 27, before a large crowd of spectators and in an atmosphere alive with suspense, the Senate passed the House resolution and the hybrid Walker amendment, 27 to 25. Three Whigs voted with the unified Democrats to produce the necessary majority, which was almost evenly divided between the free and slave states (thirteen and fourteen, respectively). On the next day, after a short but sharp debate, the House accepted the Walker amendment by a larger vote than its original measure had received, and on March 1 Tyler signed the joint resolution.[26]

Several factors besides those already mentioned probably influenced enough votes to affect the final outcome, especially in the Senate. One of these was the prospect of acquiring Oregon, which had long seemed to Western expansionists a fair exchange for Texas. During the session Senator David R. Atchison of Missouri introduced a bill establishing territorial government as far north as 54°40'. Some Westerners may have voted for annexation of Texas in the hope of reciprocal support for the Atchison bill, but the session closed without any decision on Oregon (see Chapter 8).[27]

The role of President-elect Polk during the last days of the Senate session became the subject of much controversy three years later when Senator Benjamin Tappan of Ohio, an opponent of annexation, declared that he had voted for the compromise resolution only after receiving assurance from Polk that he would submit Benton's proposition to the Texans and start fresh negotia-

26. US, 28C, 2S, CG, pp. 16–17, 19, 244, 359–63, 371. Smith, *Annexation of Texas*, pp. 334–37. Wiltse, *Calhoun, Sectionalist*, pp. 211–14. Chaplain W. Morrison, *Democratic Politics and Sectionalism: the Wilmot Proviso Controversy*, pp. 5–8. On the debate, see also Frederick Merk, *Slavery and the Annexation of Texas*, pp. 121–59.

27. Smith, *Annexation of Texas*, pp. 349–52.

tions, which, of course, would have caused considerable delay. Blair and Benton then declared that Polk had similarly deceived at least four other senators. Polk denied having discussed the alternative proposals or even having formed an opinion on them before the passage of the bill, and many historians have accepted his statement.[28]

Polk's explanation, however, was considerably less than the whole truth. Eager for the annexation of Texas, he may have devised the Walker compromise himself; certainly, he exerted strong pressure on Walker to introduce the measure. The President-elect at least encouraged Benton's bloc to believe that he would negotiate a new treaty after his inauguration, and he postponed final selection of his cabinet just long enough to induce representatives of various hopeful Democratic factions in the Senate to vote for the compromise.[29] One of the lucky contenders for office was Walker, who became secretary of the treasury.

Most supporters of the bill expected that Polk would be the one to carry it out, and Calhoun's lieutenant McDuffie apparently assured Benton's followers that Tyler would not have the audacity to meddle with it. Calhoun and the rest of the cabinet, however, feared that Benton might delay annexation with his new treaty and that Texas, offended, might accept some counterproposal from Britain or France. Playing on Tyler's vanity, they persuaded him to close his administration with a flourish by dispatching the joint resolution at once. As a matter of courtesy he asked Calhoun to consult Polk, who would not express an opinion. Then, on the last night of his administration, Tyler ordered Donelson to present the resolution to the Texan government. Polk could have reversed the action after his inauguration, and he did, indeed, instruct Donelson to defer action for a time, but after the new cabinet had approved Tyler's instructions, Polk allowed his secretary of state, James Buchanan, to confirm them. As a matter of fact, Polk probably welcomed Tyler's impetuous action as a release from his own commitment to the Benton clique.[30]

28. Tappan's testimony is considerably weakened by the fact that in the preceding year he had written that he considered Polk an honest man. Polk answered the accusation at length in a letter to George Bancroft, September 9, 1848. *Massachusetts Historical Society Proceedings*, 43 (1909–1910), 110–14. The whole problem is examined in detail in Smith, *Annexation of Texas*, pp. 348–50n34. See also McCormac, *Polk*,

pp. 315–17.

29. Charles Grier Sellers, *James K. Polk, Continentalist: 1843–1846*, pp. 205–8, 217.

30. Smith, *Annexation of Texas*, pp. 352–55. Sellers, *Polk, Continentalist*, pp. 215–17. Sellers concludes that Polk certainly practiced deception but may have convinced himself that he had not (pp. 219–20). For a statement by Tyler, dated November 27, 1848, see Lyon G.

The passage of the joint resolution furthered the drift of American public opinion toward annexation. Webster regretted that the Senate's treaty-approval powers had been bypassed, and he warned Walker that the precedent might be used in the future for legislative annexation of Canada.[31] However, the principal New England Whigs accepted the *fait accompli* and prepared to close ranks against Polk's expected tariff reforms. A few diehards such as John Quincy Adams grumbled that the annexation would provide Britain with an excuse to seize Cuba.[32]

Adams' fears were not realized, but the passage of the joint resolution brought about an immediate and complete rupture of relations with Mexico. Almonte had strict instructions to ask for his passports if the annexation measure became law, and although Pakenham advised him to wait, he hurried home to organize Mexican resistance. For more than two years Almonte had carefully reported the growth of annexationism in the United States and had lobbied strenuously against it. In his final dispatch he described the United States as badly divided over the Texas question and unable to wage offensive war. Since many Americans opposed hostilities, especially Northern merchants, he predicted that the incoming Polk administration would immediately dispatch a special envoy with attractive promises. Almonte personally favored war as the only guarantee of Mexico's prestige and security. Short of open war, he recommended a series of defiant measures that would improve Mexico's position for negotiations: the dispatching of troops toward Texas, New Mexico, and the Californias; clerical exhortations to the faithful for defense of homes and religion; and a press campaign to inspire the people and appeal for foreign support against the hypocritical aggression of a slave power.[33]

Tyler, *The Letters and Times of the Tylers*, II, 364–65. Calhoun to Donelson, March 3, 1845, No. 4; James Buchanan to Donelson, March 10, No. 5, Manning, *IAA*, XII, 83–88.

31. Memorandum of Robert J. Walker, Tyler, *Letters and Times*, III, 152–53.

32. David Donald, *Charles Sumner and the Coming of the Civil War*, pp. 136–37. Ángel Calderón de la Barca to Primer Secretario de Estado, Washington, March 5, 1845, No. 67, Spain, AHN, legajo 5868.

33. Almonte to Ministerio de Relaciones, March 9, 1845, No. 26, US, LC, /70. Almonte told Pakenham that he would urge the Mexican government to recognize Texan independence. Pakenham to Aberdeen, March 29, GB, FO 5/425, ff. 92–94. Smith, *Annexation of Texas*, p. 430. However, Almonte's dispatches and later attitudes show his opposition to recognition. At the same time, Mexican Consul Arrangoiz at New Orleans was reporting that annexation was inevitable and that Mexico must fight unless she wished to lose even more territory. He felt that Mexico could wage an effective war on American commerce with privateers—a sentiment many other Mexican officials shared. Francisco Arrangoiz to Ministerio de Relaciones, December [probably March] 13, March 28, 1845, Nos. 50, 56, US, LC, /97, Pt. II.

While guided by a certain honorable logic, Almonte's analysis of American capabilities and intentions, like his earlier predictions, was just inaccurate enough to push Mexican policy closer to disaster. In any case, the government could not have carried out all his recommendations for energetic action, but it welcomed his reassurance that the United States could not launch an invasion. The news that the American Congress had passed the joint resolution arrived in Mexico by fast ship on March 21 and completely surprised the Herrera government, which had been hinting at a policy of recognizing and conciliating an independent Texas. Foreign Minister Cuevas announced the bad news to Congress in a speech full of lamentations and threats, and he addressed a formal protest to the European diplomats. When Bankhead and Alleye de Cyprey pressed him for a concrete statement of the government's intentions, his reply was more reasonable than his public pronouncements, but to Bankhead's disgust, he timidly refused to publish it, lest the opposition use it against him.[34]

* * * *

Throughout the winter of 1844–1845 American and Mexican leaders scanned newspapers and diplomatic dispatches from Europe, hoping to learn what Britain and France intended to do about the Texas question. The attitude of the British press was clear enough—bitter suspicion and hostility toward American ambitions. Even before the election the London *Atlas* regretted that a major naval power did not control Texas so as to lay waste the American South if necessary to prevent annexation. British newspapers regarded Polk's victory as "the triumph of everything that was worst" in America, and they denounced Tyler's annual message as "a most feeble and ponderous piece of presidential ambition." The *Morning Chronicle* started the new year with a description of Brother Jonathan standing "with open mouth, ready to gulp down limb after limb whatever may be chopped off from Mexico," and the *Morning Post* declared that "some day the republican monster must be checked."[35]

34. Bankhead to Aberdeen, March 31, 1845, No. 31, GB, FO 50/184, ff. 229–36. Salvador Bermúdez de Castro to Primer Secretario de Estado, March 29, No. 13, *Rdh-m*, III, 144–50. Cuevas' circular protest, dated March 28, and the noncommittal replies of Bermúdez and Bankhead appear in US, LC, /64. (Alleye de Cyprey renewed the earlier French offer of good offices.) For Cuevas' protest to Shannon and ensuing correspondence, see Shannon to Buchanan, April 6, No. 10 with enclosures, Manning, *IAA*, VIII, 705–11.

35. London *Morning Chronicle*, January 2, 1845, p. 4. Others quoted in *NNR*, 67 (February 8), 356–57. Smith, *Annexation of Texas*, pp. 325–26. How-

Undoubtedly, American politicians viewed this ferocity with a cool eye, keeping in mind the excesses of their own press. In any case, diplomatic dispatches were more reassuring. In the late autumn the American minister to France, William R. King, wrote privately to Calhoun about Louis Philippe's state visit to England and added: "But all this billing and cooing of the Sovereigns cannot change . . . the deep rooted hostility which [their peoples] entertain towards each other." At the end of the year King urged Calhoun privately to press forward toward annexation, predicting that Britain would grudgingly accept a *fait accompli* and that Louis Philippe was too prudent to risk his dynasty by shocking the French people with an Anglo–French alliance in the Texas question.[36]

Beneath these observed actions and policies, the British and French governments were working at cross purposes during the last three or four months of 1844. For the duration of the American presidential campaign Aberdeen and Guizot had abandoned any idea of guaranteeing Texan independence or Mexican boundaries. On September 30 Aberdeen instructed Bankhead to warn Santa Anna that if he tried to reconquer Texas and got into trouble, Britain would not help him. Almost a month later the foreign secretary went further and told Bankhead that, since Mexico would not recognize Texas, the plan for joint action proposed earlier in the year was to be abandoned.[37]

At this time, however, Guizot proposed a different sort of Anglo–French joint action, not to protect Mexico against the United States but to compel her to cease arbitrary arrests and summary executions and to abolish the everlasting restraints on foreign trade. Mistrusting Bankhead, Guizot approached Aberdeen directly, only to discover that the British law officers held a low opinion of the French legal case against the Mexican government. On November 15 the French ambassador in London reported that Aberdeen had expressed disapproval of the Mexican government

ever, the London *Atlas* recognized that Britain would have taken the same attitude toward foreign intervention in Ireland as the United States in the Texas question. Ibid.

36. William R. King to Calhoun, [October or November 1844], December 28, Calhoun, *Correspondence*, pp. 986–90, 1013–15. King to Calhoun, October 6, November 15, December 31, Nos. 4, 6,

9, Manning, *IAA*, VI, 540–45. However, King mistrusted Guizot, who, he felt, was blindly devoted to Britain. Garro to Ministerio de Relaciones, December 18, 1844, No. 30, Barker transcripts, vol. 571, pp. 75–79.

37. Aberdeen to Bankhead, September 30, October 23, 1844, Nos. 30, 34, GB, FO 50/172, ff. 73–77, 87–90. Smith, *Annexation of Texas*, pp. 402–3.

but would not risk war on such grounds.[38] A little over two weeks later, on December 2, Guizot discussed Franco–Texan policy with British Ambassador Lord Cowley. Since Britain had the greater interest in the Texas question, France would not risk war; however, she would refuse to recognize the annexation of Texas by the United States.[39]

Confronted with France's position, Aberdeen was forced to limit his own commitments. He replied to Guizot that without French support he would not guarantee Texan independence or boundaries. Twice during November and December he called in Mexico's Minister Murphy and warned him that Britain could do nothing to help Mexico unless that country recognized Texas. He sent a similar statement to Bankhead and repeated to him that if Mexico wished closer relations with Britain she should take steps to safeguard the security of British residents. Finally, he sent to Elliot copies of his correspondence with Cowley, Pakenham, and Bankhead, with the statement that, while Britain still hoped for the independence of Texas and trusted the Texan government to hold the people in check, Elliot must be careful to avoid the appearance of working against American interests: "You should in no way Commit your Government to any line of active policy with regard to that Country [Texas]."[40]

Early in January Aberdeen received a number of dispatches from the New World bearing information that was mostly out of date by the time he received it. Nevertheless, it caused him to undertake a new initiative in the Texas question. A dispatch of November 29 from Bankhead reported that Santa Anna, hard pressed by revolution, had agreed to recognize Texan independence on terms much like those Aberdeen had offered earlier in the year. At about the same time, he learned from Elliot that President Anson Jones and his officials still hoped to negotiate a British guarantee of Texan independence and boundaries. Perhaps even before these pieces of welcome news arrived, he received

38. Guizot to Ste. Aulaire, October 26, 1844; Ste. Aulaire to Guizot, November 2, 15, France, MAE, CP, Mexique, XXIX, ff. 214–16, 273–75, 301. Guizot hoped to bring the Spanish government into the joint action too. Guizot to Comte Bresson, ibid., f. 271.

39. Lord Cowley to Aberdeen, December 2, 1844, No. 568, GB, FO 519/58.

40. Ste. Aulaire to Guizot, December 30, No. 117, France, MAE, CP, Mexique, XXX, ff. 111–12. Tomás Murphy to Ministerio de Relaciones, December 1, 1844, January 1, 1845, Antonio de la Peña y Reyes, ed., Lord Aberdeen, Texas y California, pp. 3–4, 5–12. Aberdeen to Bankhead, December 31, No. 49, GB, FO 50/172, ff. 128–37. Aberdeen to Elliot, December 31, No. 13, Adams, British Correspondence, pp. 404–7.

from Pakenham a copy of the note which Calhoun had sent to American Minister King in Paris during July, implying that the French government had disavowed any idea of a joint Anglo–French policy in Texas. In the same dispatch Pakenham indicated that the House of Representatives would probably pass a resolution for annexation and that momentum might carry the measure through the Senate as well.[41]

The effect of these dispatches was cumulative. Alarmed at the possibility of French double-dealing, Aberdeen immediately obtained from Guizot and Louis Philippe a statement that Calhoun had exaggerated whatever King might have reported of his conversations about Anglo–French policy.[42] Nevertheless, the publication of such a dispatch in the American press would encourage the annexationists by suggesting a split between Britain and France. Calhoun's note required a demonstration of unity. The dispatches from Bankhead and Elliot provided an opening for such a demonstration.

On January 7, the day after he received reassurance from France about Calhoun's letter, Aberdeen sent Guizot a proposal that the two governments instruct their agents in Texas to advise Jones against annexation. They might say that Britain and France would spare no means that could be used "becomingly" to bring about Mexican recognition and would help to guarantee Texan boundaries. Guizot promptly agreed. On January 15 Aberdeen informed Murphy of the two governments' plans, and on January 17 and 23 Guizot and Aberdeen drew up dispatches to their two agents, instructing them to tender good offices in the terms Aberdeen had suggested.[43] Guizot, however, cautiously held back his instructions for two weeks.

41. The dispatches from Bankhead and Elliot are cited in notes 4 and 12. Pakenham to Aberdeen, December 29, 1844, No. 138, GB, FO 5/409, ff. 137–43.

42. Louis Philippe flatly denied having spoken to King in the terms described by Calhoun. Cowley to Aberdeen, January 3, 6, 17, 1845, Nos. 3, 10, GB, FO 519/59. These assurances only got Guizot further into trouble, for when the London *Times* and *Le journal des débats*, publishing the correspondence, accused Calhoun and King of lying, the American minister demanded that Guizot formally disavow the statement in the *Journal*, threatening to suspend relations if he did not.

Finally, Guizot issued the desired statement, explaining that his imperfect command of English (which he actually spoke very well) had created the misunderstanding. King to Buchanan, January 27, James Buchanan Papers, box 63, HSP.

43. Aberdeen to Cowley, January 7, 1845, No. 3, GB, FO 27/718. Cowley to Aberdeen, January 11, 13, Nos. 12, 15, GB, FO 519/59. Murphy to Ministerio de Relaciones, January 18, No. 2, Peña y Reyes, *Aberdeen, Texas y California*, pp. 13–15. Guizot to Alphonse de Saligny, January 17/30, France, MAE, CP, Texas, VIII, 235–36. Aberdeen to Elliot, January 23, No. 1, Adams, *British Correspondence*, pp. 428–33. Ephraim Doug-

After Aberdeen had written to Elliot, he proposed to Guizot a further step. This was a three-way declaration that Britain and France would do all they could to restore peace and to obtain Mexican recognition of Texas independence. For its part, Texas would do everything possible to maintain that independence. Although not explicitly forbidding American annexation, such a joint declaration could have been interpreted in the United States only as a hostile act. Guizot was willing, but this time his government balked. After consulting the cabinet council, he replied to Aberdeen that, according to his information, President Jones' word was not to be relied on, since he was dickering with the United States, and that Santa Anna had such a weak hold on the Mexican presidency that his promises were worth little as well. Consequently, the French government preferred to wait for more news before proceeding further. Almost at once Guizot learned of Santa Anna's overthrow, so he amended his instructions to Saligny in Texas, specifying that only private, informal talks were to be held with the Texas officials. While Aberdeen did not know of this latest retreat, the French government's lack of enthusiasm was obvious; he made no further proposals during the next two months.[44]

An important reason for Guizot's reluctance to pursue joint intervention in Texas at this time was a sudden boiling up of opposition to his policies in America and Tahiti, which produced a cabinet crisis in January and February and almost forced him to resign. As American Minister King had been reporting to Calhoun for months, a considerable group of Anglophobes in the Chamber and the press were unwilling that America's friendship be sacrificed to the interests of the wily British. They argued that France had nothing to lose if the Americans overran Texas: "On the contrary, all her efforts . . . should tend to found . . . states capable of counterbalancing the power of England in time of peace, and of giving us aid to fight her in case of a rupture." They accused Bankhead of seeking to make a deal with Santa Anna to favor British above French merchants in Mexico and found in Calhoun's much-publicized dispatch to King clear evidence that

lass Adams, *British Interests and Activities in Texas, 1838–1846*, pp. 198–200.

44. Aberdeen to Cowley, January 24, 1845, No. 13, GB, FO 27/718. Cowley to Aberdeen, January 27, 31, Nos. 41, 46, GB, FO 519/59. Guizot to Saligny, January 17/30, France, MAE, CP, Tex-as, VIII, 235–36. See also the account of two conversations between Aberdeen and the Texan chargé, G. W. Terrell, one before and the other after he learned of Guizot's hesitation. Terrell to Ashbel Smith, January 21, 27, Nos. 1, 2, Garrison, *DCRT*, III, 1170–73, 1175–76.

Guizot was talking out of both sides of his mouth in an effort to serve his British friends without seeming to do so.[45] Even the semi-official *Journal des débats* predicted the speedy American annexation of Texas. Despite the opposition attack, Guizot managed to hold his post. But he explained to Cowley that he disapproved of the *Journal*'s stand and would continue to work with Britain against the American annexation of Texas.[46]

In mid-April after Guizot had settled himself firmly in power again, Aberdeen instructed Cowley to propose a more cautious Anglo–French joint declaration, that would offer disinterested mediation between Texas and Mexico but would not undertake to guarantee anything. This time, Britain offered nothing more than that familiar, harmless panacea, "moral influence." Guizot, his activities curtailed by illness, delayed his formal reply to this proposal, but eventually both he and the cabinet council approved it.[47] His action had little effect, for by this time events in Texas had raced ahead of Aberdeen's plans. There the two European agents, Elliot and Saligny, were stretching their earlier, outdated instructions and trying to stave off annexation in a final crisis.

*   *   *   *

For once, circumstances in Mexico City seemed to be working for the Europeans. Early in March Foreign Minister Cuevas delivered a long *Memoria* to Congress, ably summing up Mexico's plight and hinting at reconciliation with Texas. A few days later he told British Minister Bankhead that the Herrera government would support Santa Anna's proposal of the preceding November, which had offered recognition in return for an indemnity and a guaranteed boundary. Cuevas cautiously stipulated that the Texan government must take the initiative for negotiations in order to save face for Mexico. On March 20 Bankhead sent a special dispatch to Elliot conveying this information—just one day before the arrival in Mexico of news from the United States that Congress

45. *Le national*, January 2–3, 1845, p. 2; January 4, p. 2; January 10, pp. 2–3; January 27, p. 4; February 3, p. 1. *Le constitutionnel*, January 20, p. 2.

46. Cowley to Aberdeen, January 13, 1845, Aberdeen Papers, BM, AM, vol. 43130, ff. 176–79. Same, January 31, February 3, 7, 10, 18, Nos. 44, 54, 57, 75, GB, FO 519/59. A few weeks later, Louis Philippe himself urged recognition of Texas on the Mexican minister,

so as to establish a buffer against the Americans. The king carefully avoided any direct suggestion of a French guarantee. Garro to Ministerio de Relaciones, March 25, Rives, *US and Mexico*, II, 86–88.

47. Aberdeen to Cowley, April 15, 1845, No. 46, GB, FO 27/718. Cowley to Aberdeen, April 18, 21, 28, Nos. 169, 176, 184, GB, FO 519/60.

had resolved to annex Texas. This news caused a great upsurge of Yankeephobia, which alarmed Cuevas, but he could not recall Bankhead's dispatch.[48]

Meanwhile, during the first two and a half months of 1845, Donelson was waiting in New Orleans for action by the United States Congress and encouraging his Texan friends by mail. On February 1 he assured Polk that there was no immediate danger of adverse action in Texas, even if Congress should adjourn without approving the American terms, but six weeks later he wrote that the House resolution had antagonized the Texan government. He advised Polk to get the issue before the people of Texas as soon as possible, so its supporters could expose British intrigue and explain away the bill's deficiencies. Most of this time Elliot and Saligny were in Texas, anxiously trying to interpret the news dispatches from the United States as favorably as possible. Early in March Jones' new secretary of state, Ashbel Smith, pressed them for their governments' guarantee of Texan boundaries. Lacking specific instructions, they shifted the talk to an armistice and the chances of recognition by Mexico, but Smith was not satisfied.[49]

During the last ten days of March the two envoys in Texas received the joint instructions sent by Guizot and Aberdeen in January, directing them to tender good offices in the Texan–Mexican dispute. At the same time news arrived from the United States that the Senate had passed the joint resolution for annexation. Donelson, it was clear, would soon arrive in Texas with concrete proposals which might appeal so strongly to public opinion that Jones and Smith would be unable to resist them.

Being then at Galveston, Elliot and Saligny set out at once for Washington-on-the-Brazos, where they arrived on March 27 and held several conversations with Jones and Smith. The situation was critical, for annexationist sentiment was growing rapidly among the people, some of whom suspected the president's aversion to the idea. In conference with the foreign envoys, Jones agreed to delay convening the Texan Congress for ninety days, but he told them frankly that he could not hold out indefinitely against public opinion. At Elliot's suggestion the two envoys proposed that

48. Bankhead to Elliot, March 20, 1844, GB, FO 50/184, ff. 205–7. Bermúdez de Castro to Primer Secretario de Estado, March 29, No. 13, *Rdh-m*, III, 144–50.

49. Smith, *Annexation of Texas*, p. 432. Adams, *British Interests*, pp. 207–8. Donelson to Polk, New Orleans, February 1, March 18, 19, 1845, James K. Polk Papers, XL, XLIV, XLV, LC. Elliot to Aberdeen, March 6, No. 10, Adams, *British Correspondence*, pp. 453–58. Saligny to Guizot, March 13, No. 62, France, MAE, CP, Texas, IX, ff. 22–30.

Elliot carry to Mexico from the Texas government a special offer of terms for a peace treaty. The four men drew up a memorandum that provided for recognition by Mexico, a promise by Texas to reject annexation, and negotiation or arbitration of boundaries and other disputed matters. On March 30 Elliot and Saligny set out for Galveston and New Orleans—and not a moment too soon, for a few miles outside the Texan capital they encountered Donelson, who inquired eagerly about Houston and members of the government. The two envoys replied evasively, put on long faces about their own affairs, and hurried on.[50]

They had been quite right in their guess about Donelson's mission, for he carried instructions from Calhoun and Buchanan concerning terms of annexation. With him was Polk's own agent, Governor Archibald Yell of Arkansas, a strong annexationist with many friends in Texas. The two men had chartered a steamer in a vain effort to beat Elliot and Saligny to the capital, and they traveled in a cloud of publicity and rumors. On their arrival Donelson's suspicions were increased when he learned that Smith was about to go on leave and that the government opposed calling a special session of Congress to consider the American proposals. To the Americans' dismay, Houston found objections to the proffered terms. Donelson wrote to his wife in disgust that Houston's private secretary had also turned against annexation, even though promised a reward from the Polk administration for his support.[51]

While Donelson tried to determine what commitments Elliot and Saligny had elicited from the Texan government, the two envoys made their way to New Orleans. From there Saligny continued his trip in the United States to divert attention from Elliot, who slipped on board a British warship and headed for Veracruz, much encouraged by Bankhead's letter of March 20, which he received just before his departure.

In Mexico City circumstances were preparing a favorable reception for the British envoy. Alarmed and outraged at the American joint resolution for annexation, the Herrera government made

50. Adams, *British Interests*, pp. 208–11. Smith, *Annexation of Texas*, pp. 435–36. Elliot to Aberdeen, March 22, April 2/3, 1845, No. 14; Jones to Aberdeen, March 31, Adams, *British Correspondence*, pp. 460–72. Saligny to Guizot, April 1, No. 65, France, MAE, CP, Texas, IX, ff. 52–68. At the same time, Jones sent Ashbel Smith on a secret mission to Europe, probably to obtain support for Elliot's venture. Smith,

Annexation of Texas, p. 412n47.
51. Smith, *Annexation of Texas*, pp. 434–41. Donelson to Buchanan, Houston, March 28, 1845; Washington, Texas, April 1, 3, 12, No. 18, Manning, *IAA*, XII, 392–93, 397–402. Donelson to Mrs. Donelson, April 2, Donelson Papers, X, LC. Memucan Hunt to Walker, April 8, Walker Papers, No. 149, LC.

ready for immediate war with the United States. However, when Cuevas raised the question of European aid in a talk with the new Spanish minister, Salvador Bermúdez de Castro, the Spaniard calmly and realistically demonstrated to him that Britain and France could not afford war with the United States, that the Americans would not have undertaken annexation without being certain of this factor, and that Mexico had not the least chance of victory, fighting alone. The three principal European representatives, Bermúdez, Bankhead, and Alleye de Cyprey, consulted with each other on how best to persuade Cuevas to make overtures to Texas. Against their advice Cuevas sent a stiff protest to American Minister Shannon, but his gesture had little effect, since Buchanan had already decided to recall Shannon.[52]

Such was the state of affairs when Elliot landed at Veracruz on April 11 and hurried up to Mexico City, his enthusiasm only slightly dampened by the usual encounter with bandits en route. His arrival caused a sensation in the capital, and the three European ministers joined efforts to urge the Texan proposals on the Mexican government, playing up the Texan concessions as much as they dared. Unfortunately, Cuevas' habitual timidity was increased by public outbursts of Yankeephobia and by the sudden appearance of American warships off Veracruz with messages for the American legation. Confronted with Elliot's proposals, the Mexican foreign minister haggled over details; more than a week elapsed before he had prepared a formal proposal for his own Congress. After they had received Cuevas' proposal, the legislators wasted still more precious time with a long-winded committee report and debate, spiced by rumors of Britain's designs on Texas. Fortunately, the warlike spirit against the United States had begun to subside; Cuevas, bolstered by Bankhead and Bermúdez, held firm; and Congress finally authorized negotiations. On May 19 the Mexican government formally accepted the Texan proposals, including recognition, and four days later Elliot set out again for Texas.[53]

52. Adams, *British Interests*, p. 211. Bermúdez de Castro to Primer Secretario de Estado, March 29, 30, 1845, Nos. 13–15, *Rdh-m*, III, 144–54. Bankhead to Aberdeen, March 31, Nos. 31, 32, GB, FO 50/184, ff. 229–36, 252–53. Cyprey to Guizot, March 27, No. 305, France, MAE, CP, Mexique, XXXI, ff. 73–81. Buchanan to Shannon, March 29, No. 10, Manning, *IAA*, VIII, 166–67. An unsigned letter from an informant of the American legation in Mexico City, dated April 18, vividly describes Mexican suspicions of both the United States and Britain at the time of Elliot's arrival. US, DS, D, Mexico, XII.

53. Adams, *British Interests*, pp. 212–14. Bankhead to Aberdeen, April 29, May 20, 1845, Nos. 46–48, GB, FO 50/185, ff. 71–81, 89–99. Bermúdez de Castro to Primer Secretario de Estado,

While the Mexicans were deliberating, Donelson and Yell remained in Texas, seeking to counteract the influences which the European envoys had left behind. Another special agent from Polk, Charles A. Wickliffe, soon joined them. Yell and Wickliffe seem to have promised Jones large appropriations for Texas after annexation, so the new state could buy up Indian lands and even acquire Santa Fe from Mexico. Donelson made no public appearances, but the other two canvassed the settlements, speaking at the annexationist meetings that were breaking out everywhere.[54]

In early April Donelson visited Houston, whom he regarded (with some exaggeration) as the real power behind the Jones administration. By this time American newspapers were beginning to dangle before Houston the hope of the American presidential nomination in 1848 or 1852, and Donelson bore an exhortation from Andrew Jackson, but at first these inducements had little effect. The joint resolution had satisfied Houston's earlier stipulations concerning debts and lands, but he continued to quibble over details, and Donelson departed, pessimistic about Houston's support. Back in the Texan capital, however, Jones raised Donelson's spirits by remarking that although he did not regard the American terms as very liberal, he had decided to call Congress into session to consider them. Donelson praised Jones' high character, and when the congressional call went out on April 15, he wrote to his wife that the annexation question was settled as far as Texas was concerned.[55]

Donelson may not have realized that Jones had acted only under extreme pressure from public opinion; some annexationist groups were even threatening to lynch him. Privately, Jones still hoped that Elliot would return from Mexico with an acceptable

April 15, 27, 28, Nos. 23, 29, 35, *Rdh-m*, III, 154–55, 158–64. Smith, *Annexation of Texas*, pp. 425–27; and Justin H. Smith, "The Mexican Recognition of Texas," *American Historical Review*, 16 (October 1910), 50–51. The enabling decree was proclaimed on May 17. Dublán and Lozano, *LM*, V, 17.

54. Smith, *Annexation of Texas*, pp. 434–35. Sellers, *Polk, Continentalist*, p. 222. Wickliffe had been postmaster general in Tyler's cabinet. For his instructions and report, see C. T. Neu, "The Annexation of Texas," in *New Spain and the Anglo–American West, Historical Contributions Presented to Herbert Eugene Bolton*, II, 77–78, 82–86. Glenn W. Price, *Origins of the War with*

Mexico, pp. 105–7, 108–9. On the spread of annexationist fervor, see Smith to Jones, April 9, 1845, Jones, *Memoranda*, pp. 446–49.

55. Smith, *Annexation of Texas*, pp. 437–42. Donelson to Buchanan, April 12, 1845, No. 18, Manning, *IAA*, XII, 400–402. Same, April 29, No. 21, Neu, "Annexation of Texas," II, 79–82. Donelson to Mrs. Donelson, April 4, 16, Donelson Papers, X, LC. Donelson continued in this attitude and several weeks later wrote to Polk that neither Houston nor the Europeans could thwart the Texan people. Donelson to Polk, May 11, 14, Polk Papers, LXXXI, LC.

alternative to annexation that he could present to Congress. Realizing that Congress would be dominated by his enemies, however, on May 5 Jones issued another proclamation calling for a special convention to consider the matter, on the grounds that the Texan Constitution did not authorize any one branch of the government to undertake such a momentous step as annexation. Probably even then the president hoped desperately for a reversal of public opinion, which would enable him to dominate the convention, but it was noted that he called Congress to assemble on July 4—"an ominous day," Pakenham remarked when he learned of it.[56]

As for Houston, he now changed his mind again and set out for the United States to consult Jackson, who died just before Houston arrived at the Hermitage. While passing through New Orleans Houston remarked offhandedly in a speech that he "had coquetted a little with Great Britain and made the United States as jealous of that power as he possibly could." Obviously, he was trying to rationalize several years of contortions with an eye to his future in American politics, but the statement aroused more questions than it answered, and Houston spent several years trying to explain what he had meant.[57]

All that remained now was to confront Elliot and overwhelm the Mexican proposals. Apparently, Jones gave Donelson no more than vague hints of his negotiations with the British and French chargés, but during April and May the Americans gradually pieced together the story of Elliot's mission and learned of its success. When Elliot arrived at Galveston near the end of May, Polk's agent Wickliffe was on hand to observe his movements, and a day or so later Donelson arrived to find out the terms of his agreement with Mexico. While in Mexico, Elliot had learned of Jones' first proclamation to convene Congress, but he still hoped that Jones would veto any resolutions for annexation and that his proposed agreement would carry the day. When he landed at Galveston and learned of the second proclamation, calling a general convention, he told his friends angrily that Mexico would declare war on Texas if the agreement fell through.[58]

56. Smith, *Annexation of Texas*, pp. 442–45. Pakenham to Aberdeen, June 9, 1845, No. 61, GB, FO 5/426, f. 59.

57. Smith, *Annexation of Texas*, p. 443. Llerena Friend, *Sam Houston, the Great Designer*, pp. 155–56. Frederick Merk, *The Monroe Doctrine and American Expansionism, 1843–1849*, pp. 61–63.

58. The reports of both Wickliffe and

Donelson on Elliot's secret mission were so vividly colored that they must have strengthened Polk's Anglophobia. Charles A. Wickliffe to Buchanan, April 3 [June 1], 1845, C. T. Neu, "The Annexation of Texas," II, 88–89. Donelson to Buchanan, June 2, Manning, *IAA*, XII, 421–44. Elliot to Aberdeen, off Veracruz, May 23, Aberdeen Papers, BM, AM, vol. 43126, ff. 72–75.

Recovering his poise, Elliot went up to the Texan capital and delivered his dispatches to Jones. On June 4 the Texan president formally announced the agreement with Mexico and proclaimed the end of the war. Wickliffe reported that this third proclamation came "like a peal of Thunder in a clear sky," reviving fears of British intrigue and arousing both nationalists and annexationists. Elliot realized that his heroics were too late. Sick and discouraged, he concluded that his further presence in Texas would only hasten the end of an already dying cause. About three weeks after his return from Mexico he packed up the British legation's records and departed for the United States, sending off a series of despondent letters to Aberdeen and Bankhead.[59]

Perhaps the most perplexing question associated with the rivalry between Donelson and Elliot was that of military aid by the United States to protect Texas from a possible attack by Mexico. Houston had demanded guarantees on this score before allowing his agents to negotiate the abortive annexation treaty of 1844. At that time he did not make clear exactly how far west and south Texan territory extended, but by the spring of 1845 a strong demand for the Rio Grande as a boundary had appeared among Texan extremists. When Donelson first came to Texas in April he had discussed the boundary question without committing the United States, but after his return with Yell in May, the two men assured Jones that the American government would help Texas secure the land to the Rio Grande, including eastern New Mexico.[60]

Jones' call for a special convention aroused such concern over Mexican revenge that his acting secretary of state called on Donelson to provide protection and declared that his government would welcome the passage of American troops through Texas "to its western frontier." On May 24 Donelson replied briefly that troops already on the Sabine River and warships in the Gulf would help Texas if necessary.[61] When Elliot returned from Veracruz, learned

59. Adams, *British Interests*, pp. 217–18. Wickliffe to Buchanan, June 13, 1845, Manning, *IAA*, XII, 433–34. Elliot to Aberdeen, June 12, 15, July 3, Nos. 17–19; Elliot to Bankhead, June 11, July 3, Adams, *British Correspondence*, pp. 495–505, 511–16. Elliot to Jones, June 12, 13, Jones, *Memoranda*, pp. 468–71. Elliot returned to Texas for several months early in 1846 but played no role in public affairs.

60. William Campbell Binkley, *The Expansionist Movement in Texas, 1836–1850*, pp. 125–26. Donelson to Buchanan, April 12, 1845, No. 18, Manning, *IAA*, XII, 400–402. Donelson, however, continued to have doubts about the legality of the Texan claim and held out as long as he could against moving American troops into the disputed area. Sellers, *Polk, Continentalist*, pp. 222–23, 228–29.

61. Ebenezer Allen to Donelson, May 19, 1845; Donelson to Allen, May 24, Manning, *IAA*, XII, 410–11, 418.

of the proclamation, and angrily threatened war, Donelson took this threat seriously. Elliot, he expected, would secretly send word to General Mariano Arista commanding in northeast Mexico, to attack across the Rio Grande and start a war between Texas and Mexico, supported by Britain. Donelson suggested to Buchanan that the American government ought to select a commander for the American troops and station him where he could confer with Donelson about immediate action as soon as the Texan convention voted on the joint resolution.[62]

According to one account, the United States intentions were even more warlike than these preparations would indicate. During May a squadron of American ships anchored at Galveston under the command of Robert F. Stockton, an aggressive young commodore who enjoyed the favor of the new administration. Special Agent Wickliffe was on board Stockton's flagship. The commodore sent his private secretary and General Sidney Sherman, commander of the Texan militia, to Washington-on-the-Brazos so that they might ask Jones for authorization to raise several thousand militia. According to Jones, the two emissaries proposed to seize the Mexican port of Matamoros as a precautionary measure. They denied having any written instructions for this action but said that Polk, sure of annexation, "wished Texas to place herself in an attitude of active hostility towards Mexico, so that, when Texas was finally brought into the Union, *she might bring a war with her*." Jones' memoirs record that he smiled and replied scornfully: "So, gentlemen, the Commodore, on the part of the United States, wishes me to *manufacture a war* for them." They agreed that Jones had stated the situation correctly. Jones' account related that, since he was still awaiting Elliot's return from Mexico, he kept up a temporizing discussion for several days before rejecting the Americans' proposal.[63]

Some historians, observing Polk's deviousness on other occasions, have accepted Jones' story at face value and have declared that Polk was trying to precipitate a "war by the act of Mexico" fully a year before it actually came to pass.[64] Several considerations,

62. Donelson to Buchanan, June 2, 4, 1845, Nos. 26, 27, Manning, *IAA*, XII, pp. 422-26. Actually, Elliot urged Jones to send Arista a copy of the truce proclamation, so the Mexican commander would not lose his head and attack. "The Mexicans," Elliot added, "had better leave the initiative in hostile proceedings to the United States." El-

liot to Jones, June 12, 13, Jones, *Memoranda*, pp. 468-71.

63. Jones, *Memoranda*, pp. 46-54 *et passim*.

64. Richard R. Stenberg, "The Failure of Polk's Mexican War Intrigue of 1845," *Pacific Historical Review*, 4 (March 1935), 39-68. Price, *Origins of the War with Mexico*, pp. vii-x, Chaps.

however, cast doubt on Jones' testimony. For one, he wrote his account five years later in a mood of bitter disappointment after the people of Texas had rejected him for public office. For another, his statement of Polk's responsibility rests on hearsay evidence and is contradicted by other testimony. Although Polk had announced his belief that Britain intended to make Texas "a dependency of her own" and had declared that he would not permit Mexico to send an army across the Rio Grande, Buchanan had also instructed Donelson that the United States would "studiously refrain from all acts of hostility towards that Republic [Mexico] unless these should become absolutely necessary in self defence."[65] There are scattered bits of evidence, however, to suggest that Jones did not make up his story out of whole cloth. First, rumors of American-sponsored incursions into Mexico had circulated for a year or more through Texas and the American South. During the winter and spring of 1844–1845 Duff Green had talked of such a plan without acting.[66] Second, the excuse of an expected Mexican attack across the Rio Grande was ready at hand to rationalize an offensive, for during May and June both Sherman and Wickliffe, to say nothing of other Texans, were emphasizing the danger of invasion (possibly at British instigation) and the need for protection.[67]

Third, Stockton was reputed to be an impetuous nationalist, and his statements show that at the least he was prepared to interpret defensive action broadly. On May 21 he reported to the Navy Department: "War now exists and as any & every man here fights on his 'own hook,' the Texians [sic] ought therefore in my opinion to take possession and drive the Mexicans over the other side of

6–9, et passim. Justin Smith manages to discuss Jones' account without involving Polk. Smith, Annexation of Texas, pp. 446–48. So does Jones' principal biographer. Gambrell, Jones, pp. 400–401.

65. Polk to Donelson, May 6, June 15, 1845. St. George L. Sioussat, ed., "Letters of James J. Polk to Andrew J. Donelson, 1843–1848," Tennessee Historical Magazine, 3 (1919), pp. 64–69. Buchanan to Donelson, June 3, Manning, IAA, XII, 93–94. Bancroft's orders to Stockton were more detailed but were not inconsistent. For example: "You will in all things relating to Mexico pursue a conciliatory course, unless Mexico should itself commence hostilities." George Bancroft to Robert F. Stockton, April 22, June 2, 15, Neu, "Annexation of Texas," pp. 79, 88–89,

90–91. The quotation is from p. 89. See also Sellers, Polk, Continentalist, pp. 225–26n23. The Navy Department assigned Stockton to duty in the Gulf Squadron and informed its commander that he should send Stockton to carry out his mission (in Texas) if war with Mexico seemed no longer probable. J. Y. Mason (acting secretary) to David Conner, March 29, April 2, 1845, David Conner Papers, box 13, NYPL.

66. Sellers, Polk, Continentalist, p. 224 n21. James Gregorie to Calhoun, May 23, 1846, Calhoun, Correspondence, pp. 1083–85. Kennedy to Aberdeen, April 3, 1845, GB, FO 73/14, ff. 74–75.

67. Wickliffe to Polk, Galveston, June 3, 4, 1845, Polk Papers, LXXXIV, LC. Wickliffe to Buchanan, Galveston, April 3 [June 1], Neu, "Annexation of Texas," pp. 88–89.

the river before the meeting of Congress." [68] According to later dispatches, he persuaded Sherman to call out Texan troops for border defense and sent a message to President Jones that, since American troops could not cross the Texan border until the Congress or the convention had voted annexation, Jones should permit volunteers to march to the border for defensive purposes "to enable them to give to the U.S. quiet and undisturbed possession." Stockton declared that Jones had agreed to send men after a few days' delay, and he denounced him as a near-traitor for proclaiming the armistice with Mexico after Elliot's return. [69]

Neither Jones nor Stockton was a completely unbiased witness, and Stockton's account of their exchange may have been camouflage for his own activities. On May 27 the commodore wrote privately to Secretary of the Navy George Bancroft that three fourths of the Texans would oppose annexation if they did not expect that the United States would defend their claim to the Rio Grande boundary. He added that he proposed to "settle the matter without committing the U. States.—The Major Genl [Sherman] will call out three Thousand men & 'R. F. Stockton Esq.' will supply them in a private way with provisions & ammunition." [70]

A man of independent means, Stockton might have been able to outfit such an expedition, but his actions belied his words. Immediately after writing this letter, he set out with Wickliffe and several others on a reconnaissance trip along the coast to the Rio Grande, as he had been instructed, but Wickliffe became so seasick that they soon turned back to Galveston. When Jones issued his armistice proclamation, Stockton thought it a sellout to Mexico and complained that the Texans had not made sufficient preparation against a Mexican attack, preferring to rely on American aid. "Disgusted with Texian diplomacy," he dispersed his ships to their regular posts in the middle of June and returned to Philadelphia. [71]

68. Stockton to Bancroft, Galveston, May 21, 1845, US, DN, OL, file microcopy 148, roll 167, No. 100.

69. Stockton to Bancroft, May 22, 26, June 4, 12, 1845, US, DN, OL, file microcopy 148, roll 167, Nos. 102, 103, 106, 109. The quotation is in the dispatch of June 12.

70. Stockton to Bancroft, Galveston, May 27, 1845, George Bancroft Papers, MHS. Price regards this letter as full confirmation of Jones' statement, arguing that Stockton would never have written in this fashion without authorization from Polk. Price, *Origins of the War with Mexico*, pp. 122–23. This argument is not convincing, inasmuch as elsewhere he depicts Stockton as strong-minded and apt to take the initiative.

71. Wickliffe took along as intermediary an acquaintance of General Mariano Arista, Mexican commander at Matamoros, apparently hoping to discover the real intentions of the Mexicans. Wickliffe to Buchanan, May 20,

Last, a few contemporary reports suggest some fear that Stockton had an attack in mind. As soon as Elliot landed in Texas on his return from Mexico, he learned that Stockton was trying to persuade Jones to call out volunteers and occupy the disputed territory to the Rio Grande. Elliot added that Jones confirmed this report and declared that he would not be made a scapegoat for war: "The United States must take all the responsibility, and all the expence [sic] and all the labour of hostile movements upon Mexico."[72] At this time Donelson too seems to have become nervous about Stockton's intentions, for he cautioned the commodore against aggressive action.[73]

While Stockton may have plotted with Texan expansionists for an invasion of northern Mexico, there is no conclusive evidence that he did more than encourage the Texans to defend themselves against a Mexican crossing of the Rio Grande. If the commodore had aggressive intentions, it is certain that these did not receive the slightest support from Donelson. Although he had reported in early June that he thought war inevitable, Donelson adhered to his defensive instructions, and as late as June 30 he was scrupulously explaining to the Texan secretary of state that the Polk administration could not pay the expenses of Texan resistance to Mexican invasion without an Act of Congress.[74] If the American chargé is free from suspicion of intrigue, may the same be said for the President, or did Polk simply direct Stockton's actions by a different line of command, through the Navy Department? No instructions of this sort have ever come to light. Further examination of the question must await a discussion of Polk's character and early policies.

The last stages of annexation presented mainly problems of law and formality. When the Texan Congress met, Jones delivered a message promising to carry out the popular will, whatever it might be. At Donelson's suggestion the members unanimously passed two joint resolutions, one accepting the American proposals and approving the convention and the other rejecting the pro-

1845, Neu, "Annexation of Texas," pp. 82–86. Wickliffe to Polk, June 3, Polk Papers, LXXXIV, LC. Stockton to Bancroft, June 4, 12, US, DN, OL, file microcopy 148, roll 167, Nos. 106, 109. See also Price, Origins of the War with Mexico, pp. 129–30, 145–48.

72. Elliot to Bankhead, June 11, 1845, Adams, British Correspondence, pp. 501–2.

73. Donelson to Stockton, June 22, 1845, quoted in Price, Origins of the War with Mexico, p. 148. This letter did not reach Stockton before he left Texas.

74. Donelson to Allen, June 30, 1845, Manning, IAA, XII, 441–43. Price, Origins of the War with Mexico, pp. 120–21, 125–26, 139, 148.

posed treaty with Mexico. On July 4 the convention, almost entirely comprised of American-born Texans, accepted the terms of the United States government and began to draw up a state constitution. In October the various Texan communities accepted this constitution by voice vote without accurately recording the margin of victory.[75]

Despite the renewed anti-British scare that news of the Elliot mission aroused in the United States, opponents of annexation mounted a final struggle during the summer and autumn of 1845. Horace Greeley's New York *Tribune* and a few other newspapers continued to editorialize against it, and Charles Francis Adams, son of the redoubtable John Quincy, and several other New Englanders formed the Massachusetts State Texas Committee as a kind of splinter party to propagandize and to prepare petitions for Congress, which quickly tabled them. When a formal bill of annexation and admission of Texas to statehood appeared before Congress, both houses promptly passed it by large majorities, and in February 1846 President Jones delivered his valedictory address and turned over his powers to the new state government. To no one's surprise, one of the two senators from Texas was Sam Houston.[76]

*　*　*　*

In Mexico there was little that the Herrera government could do to influence the Texan question beyond its last-minute acceptance of Elliot's terms. Cuevas would certainly not have accepted them without the steady, united pressure of the British, French, and Spanish ministers. Indeed, at one point in the proceedings, criticism from the opposition became so strong that the foreign representatives intervened to prevent him from resigning his post.[77]

Unfortunately, the unity among the European agents in Mex-

---

75. Smith, *Annexation of Texas*, pp. 455–60.

76. Smith, *Annexation of Texas*, pp. 464–68. Kinley J. Brauer, *Cotton versus Conscience: Massachusetts Whig Politics and Southwestern Expansion, 1843–1848*, pp. 125–58. Polk believed that annexation was legally completed when the Texas convention accepted the American terms. Nevertheless, a Treasury circular dated July 29 declared that for tariff purposes Texas was still considered a foreign country. When a chargé d'affaires arrived in Washington from the Texas government early in September, Polk overruled Buchanan and refused to receive him, declaring that to do so would deny the American right to defend Texan frontiers. *The Diary of James K. Polk during His Presidency, 1845–1849*, ed. Milo Milton Quaife, I, 17–20. NNR, 68 (August 23, 1845), 390.

77. Bankhead to Aberdeen, May 20, 1845, No. 48, GB, FO 50/185, ff. 91–99.

ico City soon disappeared, not to be re-created before the Mexican War. In the middle of June occurred the much celebrated outrage of the Baño de las Delicias. This was an outlandishly-named livery stable where a Mexican crowd attacked the French minister, Baron Alleye de Cyprey. De Cyprey, a fiery-tempered, grasping, unpopular Creole, demanded an official apology and full reparations. When Cuevas hesitated, De Cyprey broke diplomatic relations and precipitated a major crisis. A few months later, upon meeting an outspoken newspaper critic in the lobby of the Opera, De Cyprey spat in his face, and the government hustled the French minister out of the city for his own safety. Naturally, Guizot had to support his impetuous diplomat, and soon France found herself impaled again on the dilemma of 1838–1839—she could not resume relations with Mexico without obtaining a settlement of all accumulated grievances or suffering a calamitous loss of face. Thus, for all practical purposes, France was eliminated from the Texan and Mexican questions for the rest of 1845 and 1846.[78]

Late in June, while the Mexican press and public were still buzzing over the incident at the Baño de las Delicias, news arrived in Mexico City that Jones had called a special convention to vote on annexation. Assuming that the convention would approve the measure, the Mexican government now had to determine whether it would carry out its oft-repeated threat to declare war against the United States. Counting up fully nineteen thousand troops within marching distance of the Texan border, the government was tempted by overconfidence to declare war. Bankhead and Bermúdez de Castro pointed out, however, that many of these troops were unreliable, that Yucatán, Chihuahua, Zacatecas, and other centers of federalism were awaiting any opportunity for open revolt, and that an American squadron in the Pacific would surely use a Mexican declaration of war as an excuse to seize California.[79] After a great show of military preparations and much debate the government contented itself with securing an authorization from

78. All diplomatic correspondence related to the incident is collected in Antonio de la Peña y Reyes, ed., El Barón Alleye de Cyprey y el Baño de las Delicias.

79. Bermúdez de Castro to Primer Secretario de Estado, June 27, July 29, 1845, Nos. 75, 90, Rdh-m, III, 188–91, 195–200. Bankhead to Aberdeen, June 29, No. 68, GB, FO 50/185, ff. 240–43. Carlos María de Bustamante, El nuevo Bernal Díaz ó sea Historia de la inva-sión de los Anglo–Americanos en México, I, 37–44. During May and June Consul Arrangoiz at New Orleans, Mexico's one remaining diplomat in the United States, reported fully on annexationist sentiment, urging his government to send more troops to the frontier and to establish a subsidized newspaper in New Orleans to defend Mexican rights. Arrangoiz to Ministerio de Relaciones, May 21, 29, 1845, Nos. 74, 79, US, LC, /76, /97, Pt. II.

Congress to contract a war loan. The summer of 1845 was indeed an unhappy one for the Mexican people. The United States had seized one of their provinces and seemed able to invade their country at will, while prospects of aid from Europe had nearly vanished.[80]

For a time during April and May the British government warmed toward cooperation with Mexico, for Polk had taken an unexpectedly bellicose stand on the Oregon question in his inaugural address (to be discussed in Chapter 9), and this attitude seemed to confirm the worst of Britain's expectations about his policies in general. When Aberdeen learned from Guizot that Elliot and Saligny had obtained a draft treaty from Jones, he told Mexican Minister Murphy that he hoped for prompt approval by the Mexican government, and he instructed Bankhead to lend all possible support. At the same time, he told Elliot that Britain and France would offer to mediate on the basis of Texan independence. Privately, both Aberdeen and Peel disapproved of the secret mission to Mexico as likely to discredit the British reputation for frank, open diplomacy. Also, the draft treaty was a long chance, given the state of public opinion in Texas.[81]

As soon as Mexico's hesitation became apparent, British enthusiasm began to cool, and both Aberdeen and the press prepared themselves for the inevitable annexation of Texas by the United States.[82] To be sure, Aberdeen disapproved of Elliot's departure from Texas just as Congress and the convention were about to settle the annexation question, but his attitude was that of the sportsman who plays a losing game to the last wicket. Some time during July, when Murphy came to him with word that his government had decided to treat with Texas (obeying a dispatch of April 29, which had just arrived), Aberdeen wryly summarized his opinion of Mexican policy: "Following the good old Spanish

80. Vicente Riva Palacio, *México a través de los siglos*, IV, 543–44. Dublán and Lozano, *LM*, V, 19–23, 36.

81. Adams, *British Interests*, pp. 219–21. Aberdeen to Peel, May 11, 1845, Peel Papers, BM, AM, vol. 40455, ff. 43–44. Peel to Aberdeen, May 12, Aberdeen Papers, BM, AM, vol. 43064, ff. 209–10. Aberdeen to Elliot, May 3, July 3, Nos. 6, 7, 10, Adams, *British Correspondence*, pp. 481–86, 508–10. Murphy to Ministerio de Relaciones, June 1, No. 7, Peña y Reyes, *Aberdeen, Texas y California*, pp. 27–29. Same, May 29, Carlos Bosch García, ed., *Material para*

la historia diplomática de México, p. 503.

82. The immediate reaction of the Palmerstonian Whigs to the American annexation bill was to attack Aberdeen for his weakness in relying on French aid and to predict that the North would compensate itself for the Southern acquisition of Texas by seizing Canada. London *Morning Chronicle*, March 27, 1845, p. 4. In succeeding weeks, however, Polk's inaugural address and the Oregon problem largely replaced Texas as a matter for concern.

customs which you have inherited, you do everything too late."[83]

At this time, the Mexican minister to France, Máximo Garro, who knew nothing as yet of Alleye de Cyprey's troubles in Mexico City, was pressing the French government persistently for intervention in the Texas question. On one occasion he even suggested a tripartite treaty between Britain, France, and Spain, thus foreshadowing the intervention of 1861. Finally, Guizot told him bluntly that neither France nor Britain "could *ever* offer a guarantee which, in certain cases, might oblige them to intervene with arms. No: *such a guarantee is impossible* . . . but the Mexican Government may count on the *moral influence* of France and England, on their good offices, their friendly advice, and their energetic representations to prevent the Texans from violating treaties."[84] Within a month the arrival of Alleye's dispatches about the Baño de las Delicias nullified even this weak support.

* * * *

The principal American historians who have analyzed the annexation of Texas agree that for all practical purposes the election of Polk settled the question and that the efforts of Britain, France, and Mexico to negotiate some sort of compromise were doomed to failure.[85] One may go even further. Given the ties of blood and business between Texans and Americans, the closeness of the Texan settlements to the market center of New Orleans, and their remoteness from a disorganized, unsympathetic Mexican government, one may well wonder why the Texas question persisted as long as it did, and why it involved the foreign offices of five countries in a tangle of communications and proposals. If the American motto of the time was "Go ahead," why did the Tyler administration hesitate, inspiring similar hesitation and indecision in the other interested governments?

The answer to these questions seems to lie in various conflicts of interest that affected each of the five countries, conflicts that had to be resolved before each government could be certain of its policy. In the United States a powerful, clamorous opposition

83. Adams, *British Interests*, p. 223. Murphy to Ministerio de Relaciones, July 1, No. 8, Peña y Reyes, *Aberdeen, Texas y California*, p. 34.

84. Garro to Ministerio de Relaciones, June 17, 18, 23, 1845, Nos. 14, 15, 16, Barker transcripts, vol. 571, pp. 100–108. The quotation is on p. 105.

85. See, for example, Adams, *British Interests*, pp. 231–33; and Rives, *US and Mexico*, I, 618–19. Justin Smith finds a little more danger in the British efforts, but his conclusions are, in essence, not much different. Smith, *Annexation of Texas*, pp. 468–69.

to annexation dominated much of Northern opinion and stimulated dynamic expansionism in the South because a part of that opposition challenged the Southern institution of slavery. In their eagerness to legislate annexation and to scotch the efforts of the abolitionists, some Southerners such as Duff Green and Calhoun went to extremes, irritated Northern antislavery men unnecessarily, and complicated Southern problems of later years. While there were many antiannexationist arguments besides hatred of slavery, it is safe to say that without John Quincy Adams and his abolitionist cohorts the United States would have annexed Texas earlier and more peaceably.

In Texas the initial desire for annexation after the Battle of San Jacinto yielded ground to newborn national pride, nourished by resentment at the criticism of antiannexationists in the United States and by hope for European trade and loans and for Mexican recognition. The cost and difficulties of national existence weakened this Texan pride, but as long as the merits of annexation remained in doubt east of the Sabine and north of the Ohio, Texans too would weigh the question. Sam Houston, an enigmatic character torn by conflicting motives, understood his people and reflected their feelings accurately. Anson Jones, while probably at heart opposed to annexation, imitated Houston's ambivalence.

Whatever the American resolution of the annexation question, Texas could not grow and prosper without Mexican recognition and a negotiated boundary agreement that would put an end to costly border wars. Here again a division of feeling prevented decisive action. Mexican patriots, forgetting or ignoring their own independence movement, looked on the Texan revolt as a crime and refused to admit that they could never reconquer their lost province. At the same time a small liberal minority, desiring widespread fundamental reform of Mexican government and society, favored recognizing a *fait accompli* in order to move on to more important matters. The opportunist Santa Anna invoked patriotism but treated the Texas question primarily as a source of continued power and appropriations from Congress, creating his own unique blend of enlightened self-interest. As a professional optimist, he was inclined to see in every European expression of sympathy the hope of material aid in carrying out the policy of reconquest which, he was sure, would be to his and Mexico's advantage.

The British government, to which Mexicans looked for inspiration and support, was even more divided in its approach to the Texas question. Against its exasperated fear of American expansion it balanced the trade and other Anglo–American ties that made war with the United States almost unthinkable. Britain hoped for trade with Texas and an assured supply of raw cotton there, but half-consciously she imperiled both by permitting Elliot and others to intrigue against Texan slavery. British merchants, mineowners, and bondholders had a heavy stake in Mexican prosperity and naturally wished that country to retain its territory, but at the same time their perennial grievances against the Mexican government—debt postponements, forced loans, and poor security conditions—exhausted their patience and led them to accept an independent Texas and eventually a Texas annexed to the United States.

Foreign Secretary Aberdeen had a special reason for wishing to encourage the independence of Texas—his desire to open a field of cooperative action with France in order to strengthen the precarious *entente* of the 1830s. In carrying out this cooperative policy he enjoyed qualified support from Guizot, his *alter ego* in the Quai d'Orsay, but he faced opposition from British nationalists, whose ideas had changed little since Waterloo; even Peel sometimes questioned his Francophile policy. In France Guizot was as eager to maintain the *entente* as Aberdeen, but he too had to deal with a nationalist opposition, and the government of Louis Philippe was neither as well established nor as experienced in dynastic and international politics as that which operated in the name of Victoria. Also, France had fewer interests to develop in Texas, a longer and firmer tradition of friendship with the United States, and less patience with Mexican shortcomings than Britain. In the last analysis, Britain would not risk war in the New World without a guarantee of French support, and Guizot could not give this guarantee.[86]

For six or seven years after 1836, while the annexation question was deadlocked in the United States, the only slim chance for the continued independence of Texas lay in Mexican recognition and European trade, loans, and political support. These conditions would have permitted the young republic, freed from the fear of border troubles, to grow strong; new ties with the Old World might have counteracted the pull of Washington and New Orleans. Mexico prejudiced this chance by withholding recognition

---

86. For a detailed analysis of French policy, see R. A. McLemore, "The Influence of French Diplomatic Policy on the Annexation of Texas," *Southwestern Historical Quarterly*, 43 (January 1940), 342–47.

until 1845 and Britain and France by their tardiness in establishing political relations and their reluctance to lend money. From 1843 to 1845, as the annexationist campaign of the Tyler administration developed, Aberdeen and Guizot made belated efforts to bring about recognition by Mexico and some sort of territorial guarantee for Texas. These efforts, however, only stimulated American annexationism by giving its supporters, such as Robert J. Walker, an excuse to sound an alarm against European aggression in the New World.

The Texas question was a truly international question; it involved Europe more intimately in the affairs of the Western Hemisphere than any other question since the enunciation of the Monroe Doctrine. While its solution has seemed inevitable to latter-day American observers, the participants did not reach this solution until they had reviewed most of the alternatives. Their familiarity with the alternatives and certain problems that remained unsolved after annexation—the Rio Grande boundary and Northern abolitionist resentment, to name two—ensured that the next stage of American territorial expansion would also involve complex international diplomacy. By the summer of 1845 the Texas question might be resolved, but as Polk, Buchanan, Cuevas, Aberdeen, and Guizot were well aware, the questions of California and Oregon remained.

8

The Push to the Pacific

During the last two years of the Tyler administration, while the American policy makers and public concentrated their attention on Texas, affairs on the Pacific coast of North America continued to develop toward a crisis. As Mexico's grip on California slackened and Anglo–American diplomats considered how to settle their rival claims in Oregon, new waves of American emigrants headed across the mountains toward the ocean. Their presence heightened political tensions in California and Oregon and caused the diplomatic problems of these two border regions to converge.

At the same time European colonial rivalries in the central Pacific kept alive the interest of the British and the French in these problems. During 1843 two unauthorized efforts at annexation focused world attention on the Pacific islands. Late in that year an aggressive French admiral, Abel Du Petit-Thouars, raised his country's flag over Tahiti, only to be disavowed by his government. For some time afterward, quarrels between local French and British representatives there disturbed the cooperative policies of Aberdeen and Guizot.[1]

The United States showed little concern over Tahiti, but it resented European efforts to dominate Hawaii. Earlier in 1843 a British admiral, Lord George Paulet, acting without instructions from London, prevailed on the Hawaiian king to cede his domain to Queen Victoria and proclaimed annexation. Aberdeen repudiated Lord George's acts before the United States or France could protest, and at the end of the year Britain and France signed an agreement recognizing Hawaiian independence. Nevertheless, the brief show of force in the Islands alarmed Tyler, who considered addressing a strong note to the British. He remarked: "We should lose no time in opening a negotiation relative [to] the Oregon."[2]

1. *Cambridge History of British Foreign Policy*, II, 183–85, 263–65. Jean Ingram Brookes, *International Rivalry in the Pacific Islands, 1800–1875*, pp. 138–43.
2. Ralph S. Kuykendall, *The Hawaiian Kingdom, 1778–1854: Foundation and Transformation*, pp. 199–202, Chap. 13, *passim*. Brookes, *International Rivalry*, pp. 131–34. For Aberdeen's prompt disclaimer, see Earl of Aberdeen to Henry S. Fox, June 3, 1843,

* * * *

Some British were interested in California too, since it dominated the east coast of the Pacific and seemed about to throw off Mexican rule. British consuls regularly sent home warnings of American ambitions to possess the region. Robert C. Wyllie, an Anglo–Mexican merchant who was prominent among the holders of Mexican bonds, set forth a plan for British colonization by which land warrants from the Mexican government would be exchanged for the deferred bonds issued after the refunding operation of 1837 (see Chapter 2). In October 1843 he made a formal proposal to Foreign Minister Bocanegra, but the Mexican government hesitated to proceed unless Wyllie could obtain enough authority from the British bondholders to bind them firmly to any agreement.[3]

Much more substantial than Wyllie's dreams were the cash profits of Thomas O. Larkin and other American merchants at Monterey and Los Angeles, as well as the exuberant publicity they sent back East. In May 1843 a California enthusiast, Lansford Hastings, led forty or fifty emigrants south from Oregon to Sutter's Fort; more than half of them survived the march and a skirmish with Indians. Two other groups, totaling over a hundred men, set out from Missouri that year, and after suffering great hardships as they experimented with new trails and shortcuts, they arrived in the San Joaquin and Sacramento valleys. To be sure, the bulk of the "Great Migration" of 1843 went to Oregon, but by 1844 a recognizable California Trail branched off from the better-known Oregon Trail in what is now southern Idaho. As 1845 began, it was clear that the next years would bring even more American settlers to California.[4]

Perhaps the most important influence for American expansion into California was the exploration by John Charles Frémont. An ambitious young Army lieutenant, he had recently married

---

No. 23, GB, FO 115/81, ff. 124–25; and Edward Everett to Abel P. Upshur, August 15, No. 50, US, DS, D, Britain, LI. John Tyler to Hugh S. Legaré, May 16, Lyon G. Tyler, *The Letters and Times of the Tylers*, III, 111–12.

3. Ephraim Douglass Adams, *British Interests and Activities in Texas, 1838–1846*, pp. 240–42. Lester G. Engelson, "Proposals for the Colonization of California by England in Connection with the Mexican Debt to British Bond-

holders, 1837–1846," *California Historical Society Quarterly*, 18 (June 1931), 142–44. Hubert H. Bancroft, *History of California*, IV, 382–83, 451–52. Robert Crichton Wyllie, *Mexico*, pp. 40–77 *et passim*. In 1844 Wyllie decided to go to Hawaii instead and abandoned the project.

4. John W. Caughey, *California*, pp. 256–58. Some predicted thousands of settlers for 1845 alone, but the actual total for that year did not exceed 250.

the daughter of Senator Benton, now the leader of Western expansionists. During 1842 Frémont led an exploring expedition into the area west of South Pass, in Wyoming. Realizing the geographical and propagandist value of Frémont's findings, Benton helped him to organize a second expedition, which set out from St. Louis in 1843 and explored large areas of the modern states of Utah, Nevada, and Oregon, before winter caught them just east of the Sierras and Lake Tahoe.

Even though snow choked the passes, Frémont impulsively decided to cross the Sierras into California. His men nearly perished from cold and hunger, but on March 8, 1844, they staggered into Sutter's Fort.[5] When they had recovered their strength and replenished their supplies, they proceeded into the Sacramento and San Joaquin valleys and the San Francisco Bay area. Early in August the party arrived back at St. Louis, and Frémont began to write a report on California that was to make both him and the province household words throughout the United States.[6]

While explorers, publicists, and emigrants reconnoitered California, the American government sought a way to purchase at least part of the province. During the negotiations for the Webster–Ashburton Treaty, Webster had inserted into the discussions a suggestion that the United States might accept the Columbia River as northern boundary in Oregon if Britain would help persuade Mexico to sell San Francisco to the United States (see Chapter 4). After the completion of the treaty Webster continued to show interest in this three-way exchange, for he mentioned it to the Mexican minister, Almonte, and outlined it in some detail to Everett at London. Apparently Webster hoped to pursue this project if he were sent to Britain as special envoy or as minister, but neither appointment materialized, and when he left the cabinet, the project lapsed. Both he and Tyler seem to have thought that this exchange, along with the annexation of Texas, would satisfy all sections of the country. Even if they were right—which is unlikely—no amount of British persuasion would have reconciled Mexico to the loss of Texas and San Francisco at the same time.[7]

5. Although Frémont was supposedly a peaceable cartographer, his group took along a bronze howitzer. When his superiors learned that he had taken artillery into foreign territory, they sent an order recalling him, but his wife received it first and held it long enough for him to get the expedition under way. The howitzer was of no use to the expedition and finally had to be abandoned. Allan Nevins, *Frémont, the World's Greatest Adventurer*, I, 142–46 *et passim*.

6. Allan Nevins, *Frémont, Pathmarker of the West*, Chaps. 10–14.

7. Robert G. Cleland, "The Early

As matters stood in 1843, the chronic irritation produced by the Texas question and Commodore Jones' outrageous seizure of Monterey made Mexicans especially aware of the American threat to California. All through the year reports from Almonte and from the Mexican consul at New Orleans about emigrant groups leaving for the Far West fretted the officials in Mexico City. On July 14 Santa Anna issued secret instructions to Micheltorena that he should not admit any more Americans into the province. The prohibition against foreign participation in retail trade with which the Mexican government aroused the whole diplomatic corps in Mexico City two months later was not aimed particularly at California, but it threatened both American and British interests there.[8]

During the autumn Santa Anna briefly showed signs of relaxing his defense of California. The reason for his change of attitude was the possibility of war with Britain, growing out of the flag incident in September (see Chapter 5). On October 3, while discussing with Waddy Thompson the possible results of a Mexican war with Britain, the American minister suggested that the British might seize California. "Oh," replied the Mexican disingenuously, "your Government will not permit that: will it?" A few days later, in a similar conversation, Santa Anna declared flatly, "If there is danger of that [British seizure] we will cede it to you." Thompson hoped for a repetition of the Louisiana Purchase, but in vain, for the Anglo–Mexican crisis was soon over and Santa Anna no longer needed friends to the north.[9] Instead, at the end of the year, Thompson learned of the order forbidding American settlement in California and protested sharply. To his gratification, the Mexican government withdrew the order, which it lacked the strength to enforce anyway, but the spell was broken, and the customary cloud of mutual suspicion gathered again about the California question.[10]

Sentiment for the Annexation of California: An Account of the Growth of American Interest in California, 1835–1846," *Southwestern Historical Quarterly*, 18 (July 1914), 32–34. Frederick Merk, *The Oregon Question, Essays in Anglo–American Diplomacy and Politics*, pp. 205–11, 214–15. Fox to Aberdeen, February 24, 1843, No. 20, GB, FO 5/392, ff. 107–12. Tyler to Daniel Webster, no date, Tyler, *Letters and Times*, II, 261.

8. Irving Berdine Richman, *Califor-*

nia under Spain and Mexico, 1535–1847, pp. 274–75. Instead of enforcing the retail trade order, Governor Micheltorena levied full tariffs on goods entering from other parts of Mexico in the coasting trade, so as to protect New England shippers. Bancroft, *California*, IV, 428–33.

9. Waddy Thompson to Upshur, October 3, 14, 1843, Manning, *IAA*, VIII, 563–64.

10. James Morton Callahan, *American Foreign Policy in Mexican Rela-*

This cloud remained unbroken for the rest of Tyler's term as President. Almonte kept up a drum-beat of warnings about American ambitions. Throughout the Mexican Congressional session of early 1844, while Santa Anna tried in vain to obtain funds for the Texan war, an able deputy from Upper California, Manuel Castañares, took every opportunity to introduce eulogies of the province's resources, exhortations against foreign penetration, and pleas for more supplies and troops, until he became such a nuisance that few other deputies would speak to him.[11] During this uncertain period, in Monterey Larkin was keeping a close watch over British activities. He suggested to Calhoun and Walker that the best way of offsetting British influence might be to revive Webster's three-way exchange for San Francisco and the Columbia River boundary.[12] For their part, the European diplomatic representatives at Monterey and Mazatlán sent home anxious reports about American emigration and land purchases.[13]

All of these anxieties had some foundation. While Calhoun devoted most of his attention to Texas, he was enough interested in California to authorize his special agent, Colonel Gilbert Thompson, to include it in his offer of purchase when he visited Santa Anna in May. At the same time, the British minister in Washington suggested to Aberdeen that Britain and France join in a guarantee of Mexico's sovereignty.[14] On September 5, James A. Forbes, the British vice consul at Monterey, reported that local native leaders were ready to revolt for independence from Mexico and had inquired about Britain's willingness to accept California as a protectorate.[15] The French minister in Mexico City and French consuls on the west coast similarly urged the government

tions, pp. 140–41. Thompson to Upshur, January 4, 1844, No. 38, US, DS, D, Mexico, XI.

11. Juan N. Almonte to Ministerio de Relaciones, July 16, 1844, No. 84, US, LC, /57. Bancroft, California, IV, 412–17. Eustace Barron to Aberdeen, Tepic, January 20, No. 2, GB, FO 50/179, ff. 23–26. For other such rumors in Mexico City, see Frank A. Knapp, Jr., "The Mexican Fear of Manifest Destiny in California," Essays in Mexican History, T.E. Cotner and C. E. Castañeda, eds., pp. 198–99.

12. Thomas O. Larkin to John C. Calhoun, June 20, 1844, No. 7; Larkin to Robert J. Walker, August 4, Thomas O. Larkin, The Larkin Papers, ed.

George P. Hammond, II, 140–41, 181–83. Larkin to Calhoun, August 18, No. 9, Manning, IAA, VIII, 638–39.

13. Barron to Aberdeen, Tepic, January 20, 1844, No. 2, GB, FO 50/179, ff. 23–26. Louis Gasquet to Guizot, no date, reprinted in Abraham P. Nasatir, ed., "The French Consulate in California, 1843–1856," California Historical Society Quarterly, 11 (September 1932), 214–18.

14. Richard Pakenham to Aberdeen, May 13, 1844, No. 46, GB, FO 5/405, ff. 94–96. Bancroft, California, IV, 450n17.

15. James A. Forbes to Barron, Monterey, September 5, 1844, GB, FO 50/179, ff. 85–98. See also Adams, British Interests, pp. 242–43.

of Louis Philippe to forestall the British and Americans and to take the initiative in regenerating Mexico, beginning at the north with California.[16]

Tyler and Calhoun, Aberdeen and Guizot, all had more important concerns, however—the American presidential campaign, Texas, Tahiti, and others. In particular, Aberdeen laid down a hands-off policy on December 31, 1844, in a reply to Forbes' dispatch. When the dispatch arrived at London, the foreign secretary was exasperated with the Mexican government for its refusal to recognize the independence of Texas. In his reply he pointed out that Mexico would probably soon lose control over California as well, and he declared that Britain could not encourage an independence movement or assume the proposed protectorate. But, he added, "Great Britain would view with much dissatisfaction the establishment of a protectoral power over California by any other foreign state."[17]

Even before Aberdeen wrote, the anticipated revolution in California had begun. Since 1842 the province had been under the relaxed rule of Micheltorena, who had tried to maintain a balance between natives and foreigners and to avoid offending anyone. In November 1844 the rivalry between north and south, resentment against his thieving troops, and the ambitions of a few local leaders culminated in a rebellion led by the former native rulers, Juan B. Alvarado and José Castro. After considerable maneuvering and an abortive truce, the opposing forces met at Cahuenga Pass on February 20 for a decisive battle, which consisted mainly of a long-range artillery duel without any casualties. Deserted by most of his supporters, Micheltorena agreed to resign and return to Mexico, and a coalition government of northerners and southerners was patched together with Pío Pico, a senior member of the Assembly, as governor.

Americans and other foreigners took both sides in the revolt. John A. Sutter supported Micheltorena almost until the end and lost much influence thereby, while some merchants and malcontents of the interior urged the rebels on, more for personal than for imperialistic reasons. Larkin had lent money to Micheltorena,

16. Cyprey to Guizot, May 21, 1844, No. 248, France, MAE, CP, Mexique, XXVI, ff. 291–96. Abraham P. Nasatir, *French Activities in California, an Archival Calendar-Guide*, pp. 21–22.

17. Aberdeen to Barron, December 31, 1844, No. 3, GB, FO 50/179, ff. 9–12. See also Aberdeen to Bankhead, December 31, No. 53, GB, FO 50/172, ff. 148–52. Both are extensively reprinted in Adams, *British Interests*, pp. 247–50.

but he remained strictly neutral during the conflict. Afterward, he took his losses philosophically and soon established good relations with the new regime.[18]

Although that regime acknowledged Mexican sovereignty, it assumed practical autonomy for California. As the winter of 1844–1845 ended, personal attitudes in the province were not yet polarized—foreigner against native or American against European. The stream of American immigrants seemed likely to grow, however, and the publicity spread by Larkin, Frémont, and others would surely whet interest and ambitions back East. When Polk took office, elected on an expansionist platform, the situation in California rested in an uneasy balance that no one expected to endure very long.

*   *   *   *

American views on Oregon were somewhat more developed than those on California, thanks to the earlier negotiations with Britain and repeated debates in Congress. At the beginning of 1843 that body discussed Senator Lewis F. Linn's bill to grant lands in Oregon, which seemed to violate the joint occupation agreement. The exaggerated pretensions of Western expansionists, together with the apparent acquiescence of the Tyler administration, offended many British observers—so much so that Almonte half expected war. Late in January he urged the Mexican government to take advantage of Anglo–American friction in disposing of the Texas question.[19]

Actually, Tyler, Calhoun, and the Southern bloc in Congress were far more interested in Texas than in Oregon, and Webster thought most of the disputed territory worthless. Linn's bill failed, whereupon the London *Times* wrote patronizingly: "American statesmen are far too shrewd to intend anything by such vapouring, though they find it convenient to exhibit it in order to win the next senatorial election. . . . A mob will always follow the man

18. Richman, *California under Spain and Mexico*, pp. 278–82. Bancroft, *California*, IV, 418–20, 476–79, 494–95, *et passim*. John A. Hawgood, ed., *First and Last Consul: Thomas Oliver Larkin and the Americanization of California*, p. 18. George D. Lyman, *John Marsh, Pioneer*, Chaps. 35–36. As elsewhere in the book, Lyman tends to exaggerate Marsh's role. For Sutter's activities, see Richard Dillon, *Fool's Gold. The Decline and Fall of Captain John Sutter of California*, pp. 148–97.

19. Almonte to Ministerio de Relaciones Exteriores, January 25, 1843, as cited in George Lockhart Rives, *The United States and Mexico, 1821–1848*, I, 586.

who makes the most clatter in the world, and so crow they must for their lives."[20]

During most of the year the Oregon question simmered without much public notice by either government. Occasionally some rude American speech or editorial brought a question in Parliament, to which Peel or Aberdeen made a conventional, soothing reply. On the Fourth of July Lewis Cass, a prominent Michigan Democrat who had been an Anglophobe minister to France, excoriated British ambitions of world conquest: "With professions of philanthropy . . . she is encircling the globe with her stations wherever she can best accomplish her scheme of aggrandizement." Cass said he preferred war over Oregon to another compromise such as that over Maine: "It is better to defend the first inch of territory than the last. . . . Let us have no red lines upon the map of Oregon."[21]

Before the next session of Congress, Linn died, but his Missouri colleague, Senator Thomas Hart Benton, stepped into his role. In March 1844 a resolution for abandonment of the joint occupation agreement precipitated the annual debate on Oregon. As it began, a worried Kentuckian warned Senator James Buchanan that any delay in asserting American sovereignty would give the British "time to fasten their clutches upon that country. . . . [They] will never give up that country *without a war of some kind*."[22] In the debate Buchanan upheld the American title to every foot of the disputed territory, as far north as 54°40′. This stand complicated his duties when, later, he served as secretary of state. The British press continued to brush aside expansionist oratory as "pure unredeemed bluster—mere empty rattling," confident that American emigrant statistics were exaggerated and that in any case the British Navy could keep the coastline under control.[23]

20. London *Times*, May 4, 1843. Daniel Webster, *The Private Correspondence of Daniel Webster*, ed. Fletcher Webster, II, 153–54, 179–80.

21. *NNR*, 64 (March 25, April 29, July 29, 1843), 49, 132, 345. The quotation appears on p. 345. See also *United States Magazine and Democratic Review*, 12 (April 1843), 339–59; and Richard S. Cramer, "British Magazines and the Oregon Question," *Pacific Historical Review*, 32 (November 1963), 371–72.

22. Robert B. McAfee to James Buchanan, Harrodsburg, Kentucky, March 29, 1844, Buchanan Papers, I, ff. 106–7, LC. Like Aberdeen and Pakenham—and later Polk—McAfee argued that every sign of friendship or concession would be interpreted as weakness and encourage continued resistance. See also Baltimore *American*, reprinted in *NNR*, 67 (February 8), 357–58.

23. London *Times*, February 20, 1844, p. 5. Cramer, "British Magazines," pp. 372–75.

In 1843 a writer in the *Edinburgh Review* predicted: "Oregon will never be colonized overland from the Eastern States."[24] Even as the article appeared, several hundred American emigrants were proving him wrong. The journey required them to pack their families and goods into wagons, round up their livestock, and toil along a 2,000-mile trail from Independence, Missouri, to the Willamette Valley—up the muddy, shallow Platte River, across South Pass, and down a long gradient following the Snake and Columbia rivers. Some portions of the trail involved a dangerous trip on rafts, interrupted by falls and portages. Proper equipment for the march might well require an outlay of over a thousand dollars, and many emigrants, with little idea of the trials awaiting them, tried to take along too many of the wrong things. Not surprisingly, the Oregon Trail was soon littered with discarded furniture, trunks full of useless finery, wrecked wagons, and the bones of oxen.[25]

During the summer of 1842 the first large party survived the trek—over a hundred persons and perhaps eighteen covered wagons. The following spring began the "Great Migration," in which about a thousand people and five thousand head of cattle set out from Independence; most of them arrived in Oregon by late November. They proved once for all that large-scale emigration was practicable, even through deserts and across mountains. Many more persons followed during subsequent years, and from 1841 to 1845 the American population of the territory rose from about 400 to over 5,000.[26]

Problems of land ownership and security soon required the organization of a permanent government for Oregon. Dr. John McLoughlin and the other Hudson's Bay officials did not attempt to stem the migration and, indeed, fed many a starving newcomer on his arrival, but it was a foregone conclusion that the American settlers would not submit to the Company's control. Missionaries

---

24. "Whoever ... are to be the future owners of Oregon, its people will come from Europe." *Edinburgh Review*, 78 (July 1843), 101.

25. Oscar Osburn Winther, *The Great Northwest: a History*, pp. 108–10. Dorothy O. Johansen and Charles M. Gates, *Empire of the Columbia. A History of the Pacific Northwest*, pp. 257–61. The Indians were so much impressed with the extent of the migration that they called the broad trail "the Great Medicine Road of the Whites." George W. Fuller, *A History of the Pacific North-*

west, p. 189. In 1845 an alternate, all-land route was traced, branching off from the California Trail in western Nevada, but it did not affect the settlement of the Oregon question. Winther, *Great Northwest*, pp. 110–12.

26. The missionary Marcus Whitman, who visited the East Coast late in 1842, is often given much credit for expediting the "Great Migration." Winther, *Great Northwest*, pp. 122–24. Johansen and Gates, *Empire of the Columbia*, pp. 216–17. Fuller, *History of the Pacific Northwest*, p. 190.

had raised the question of home rule even before 1840; Linn had vainly tried to legislate congressional authority; and each caravan of 1842 and 1843 chose its own leaders en route. In the spring of 1843 a committee in the Columbia Valley drew up a temporary constitution based on the laws governing the Iowa Territory and on the Northwest Ordinance of 1787; on July 5 this constitution was adopted at a mass meeting. The following year an elected legislature considerably modified this first constitution, placing strict limits on land grants and reluctantly authorizing taxation.

During 1844, 1,747,158 acres of land were reported to have been sold in Oregon, mostly in lots of 80 or 160 acres, indicating actual settlement.[27] By 1845 political parties had appeared, and even the Hudson's Bay Company was paying taxes to the new government. Gossip was beginning to circulate that the American settlers intended to drive all Canadians, Indians, and half-breeds north of the Columbia River. Whatever the truth of these rumors, Oregon south of the river was a political entity, on the American model, but no one could say yet whether it would join the United States like Texas or remain an independent Pacific republic.[28]

*   *   *   *

While American emigrants trudged westward and Congress denounced the British, Aberdeen became increasingly anxious to settle the Oregon question, left in the air by Webster and Ashburton. Unfortunately, he had little confidence in Minister Fox, and after the Whig attacks on the Ashburton treaty, he could not afford to send another special envoy to the United States. Tyler, Webster, and perhaps also Upshur might have been willing to concede the Columbia River boundary if Britain could help the United States obtain part of California, but American–Mexican arguments over Texas made this settlement unlikely. Tyler postponed giving Everett formal instructions on Oregon, for he hoped to negotiate in Washington. Apparently, Webster informed his minister privately of his views; at any rate, Everett discussed Oregon unofficially with Aberdeen from time to time during 1843.[29]

27. Winther, *Great Northwest*, pp. 129–37. Johansen and Gates, *Empire of the Columbia*, Chap. 12. Fuller, *History of the Pacific Northwest*, pp. 195–202. The figure on land sales was reported in the Albany *Argus*, no date, and reprinted in London *Times*, February 11, 1845, p. 6.

28. Winther, *Great Northwest*, pp.

135–36. F. W. Howay, W. N. Sage, and H. F. Angus, *British Columbia and the United States*, pp. 116–17. For the reaction of the Hudson's Bay Company, see Merk, *Oregon Question*, pp. 245–49.

29. Webster to Everett, March 20, 1843, quoted in C. T. Johnson, "Daniel Webster, Lord Ashburton, and Old Oregon," *Washington Historical Quar-*

Encouraged by these conversations, the foreign secretary decided to probe further for negotiations. He would have preferred to deal with Everett in London and hinted as much to the United States government, but he recognized that Tyler's suspicious nature and the sudden shifts of American politics made Washington a better site. In early October he decided to replace Fox with Richard Pakenham, then on leave from the Mexican legation. Pakenham was well connected in England and Ireland, the son of a famous admiral and the nephew of the general whom Andrew Jackson had defeated and killed at New Orleans. Then in his early forties, Pakenham was described as "a man of the world, a real Irishman from top to bottom; very frank and generous, and full of all the vivacity of his country; and, withal, a very skilful and practical diplomatist." Aberdeen thought well of him for his work in Mexico, and Everett was favorably impressed on meeting him.[30]

While Aberdeen was selecting Pakenham, Tyler and Upshur finally decided to send Everett full powers to open formal discussions on Oregon. These arrived in London at the beginning of November, several weeks before Pakenham's departure, together with an elaborate history of the question and a statement of the American legal position. After arguing the American case at length, Upshur declared that the United States would settle for the extension of the forty-ninth parallel to the Pacific, "together with the right of navigating the Columbia, upon equitable terms."[31]

When Everett told Aberdeen that he had been instructed to negotiate, the foreign secretary replied that, since he had already appointed Pakenham, he would go through with his decision to transfer the discussion to Washington. Nevertheless, he allowed Everett to set forth the American offer, and during the next month the two men went over the Oregon question in great detail. Aberdeen declared that Britain could not accept terms she had earlier refused, and he urged Everett to make some sort of concession. The American minister pointed out that world opinion would

terly, I (1906–1907), 214. Everett to Upshur, August 15, 17, 30, No. 50, Manning, *CR*, III, 822–25. See especially p. 823n1. On the plan to obtain California, see the sources cited in note 7 and Tyler, *Letters and Times*, II, 440–41.

30. New York *Herald*, February 15, 1844, quoted in London *Times*, March 11, p. 5. Merk, *Oregon Question*, p. 216. Aberdeen to Sir Robert Peel, December 9, 1843, Peel Papers, BM, AM, vol. 40454, ff. 40–41. Everett to Upshur,

November 14, Manning, *CR*, III, 829–31. Jones rather unreasonably faults Pakenham for having earlier overestimated Texan sentiment in favor of reunion with Mexico. Wilbur Devereux Jones, *Lord Aberdeen and the Americas*, pp. 22, 28. *Dictionary of National Biography*, XV, 85.

31. Upshur to Everett, October 9, 1843, No. 62, Manning, *CR*, III, 210–30. The quoted phrase is on p. 230.

probably regard an even division of the disputed territory at 49° as fair, and he finally suggested that Tyler might be willing to bend the boundary line so as to give Britain all of Vancouver Island and access to the Strait of Juan de Fuca.[32]

Everett clearly intended his arguments to affect the instructions Aberdeen was then drawing up for Pakenham. In this the American minister was successful. Aberdeen's official statement, dated December 28, stipulated the boundary along the Columbia River and offered the United States free ports on Puget Sound and Vancouver Island without any territorial cession. If the United States rejected this settlement, Pakenham was to propose arbitration or extension of the joint occupation agreement. In private conversation before the envoy's departure, however, Aberdeen told him that he should try to draw from the American government the formal offer of these terms: a boundary at 49°, leaving all Vancouver Island to Britain; free ports for British use between 49° and the Columbia River; and free navigation of the Columbia River for both parties. The cabinet had not approved these terms, Aberdeen admitted, but if the United States proposed them, he thought that he could obtain the ministers' consent.[33]

Aberdeen and Everett had come close to agreement on terms almost identical with those of the final treaty in 1846. Unfortunately, neither government was ready to accept such terms; a considerable gap remained between Peel and Tyler. To be sure, the American President later wrote that he had consistently favored a settlement at 49° after hope faded for a three-way exchange in-

32. Everett to Upshur, November 14, 30, December 2, 1843, No. 69, Manning, *CR*, III, 829–37, *passim*. Everett pointed out one reason why Aberdeen was reluctant to concede more than the negotiators of 1826—that they, like himself, belonged to a Tory administration. To Everett's surprise, Aberdeen seemed to know nothing about the British offer of an enclave on the Olympic Peninsula, made in 1826. Indeed, his undersecretary, Henry U. Addington, denied any memory of the offer. Since Addington had been one of the negotiators in 1826, his words naturally carried great weight. Merk has proved beyond question that Britain did offer the United States an enclave north of the Columbia River, which was declined, and that the British negotiators then tried to expunge the offer from the record, lest it weaken later British efforts to obtain

the Columbia River boundary. Addington's convenient memory lapse, therefore, would seem very close to an outright lie. Merk, *Oregon Question*, pp. 168–70, 195–202, *et passim*.

33. Merk, *Oregon Question*, pp. 216–17. For the official instructions, see Aberdeen to Pakenham, December 28, 1843, No. 10, GB, FO 115/83, ff. 187–95. Aberdeen noted the oral instructions in a private letter of the following March, and Pakenham's reply indicated that the letter had not changed the earlier instructions. Aberdeen to Pakenham, March 4, 1844; Pakenham to Aberdeen, March 28, Aberdeen Papers, BM, AM, vol. 43123, ff. 233–38. The earlier letter has been published, as edited by Robert C. Clark, in *Oregon Historical Quarterly*, 39 (March 1938), 74–76.

volving San Francisco. Still, his annual message of December 5, 1843, could only antagonize the British, for in it he briefly asserted the American right to 54°40′ and implied that Britain was blocking the Americans' honest efforts to settle the question.[34]

It would seem that Tyler had some idea of using the same tactics as those of Polk two years later—assuming a strong stand to impress Britain and to win votes in the Middle West. Regarding the first purpose, Everett agreed with the President, for after further discussion with Aberdeen in March he reported that, in his opinion, Aberdeen would accept a compromise boundary at 49° if the United States continued to bluster about 54°40′ for a while and then yielded all of Vancouver Island to save British "face." But, added Everett prophetically, "Care must be had, not to state our right up to 54°40 [sic] so strongly, as to put ourselves in the wrong in receding from it."[35] Polk would have done well to heed this advice.

On Pakenham's arrival in Washington, he formed a gloomy impression of prospects for settlement. When the congressional session of 1843–1844 closed without action, he concluded that most of the oratory was intended merely for electioneering. As the spring advanced, however, he saw some danger in Tyler's desperate efforts to retain the Presidency, which might induce him to go to war with Britain, if he thought that such action would gain him political capital.[36] Pakenham established friendly personal relations with American officials and took just enough initiative for further negotiations to disprove Tyler's complaint that the British were obstructing action. Late in February Upshur seemed ready to discuss the question, but he was killed before any talks began. In March and April Pakenham continued his amicable policy with Calhoun and was able to report that he expected negotiations to resume as soon as Congress adjourned. But Calhoun's predisposition to delay, his involvement with other matters, and in particular

---

34. Richardson, *Papers of the Presidents,* IV, 258. After leaving the Presidency, Tyler wrote: "I looked exclusively to an adjustment by the forty-ninth degree, and never dreamed for a moment of surrendering the free navigation of the Columbia." Tyler to R. Tyler, December 11, 1845, Tyler, *Letters and Times,* II, 440–41, 447–48. It is hard to reconcile the statement about navigation with the October 1843 instructions to Everett (note 31), except by suggesting that Tyler thought the navigation question unimportant and may have forgotten his dispatch of two years earlier.

35. Everett to Calhoun, April 1, 1844, No. 106, Manning, *CR,* III, 854–56.

36. Pakenham to Aberdeen, March 28, June 13, 1844, Aberdeen Papers, BM, AM, vol. 43123, ff. 235–41. The quotation appears in the letter of June 13.

his concern over British intrigue in Texas led him to postpone formal consideration of Oregon until late summer.[37]

During August and September 1844 Pakenham and Calhoun held six conferences on the Oregon question. Pakenham repeated the standing British offer of the Columbia River as boundary, with free ports on Puget Sound and other inlets south of 49°. Calhoun replied with the familiar American claim to the whole Columbia River watershed, saying that the Senate would undoubtedly reject any treaty that conceded a line south of 49°. When Pakenham asked Calhoun why he expected Britain to make all the concessions, the American replied that his government might possibly yield all of Vancouver Island, leaving the Strait of Juan de Fuca open to both nations. Pakenham suggested arbitration by a third power, but Calhoun pronounced this a last resort. The British minister recognized that the secretary had conceded more than any previous negotiator, and he praised Calhoun's fairness and good humor. Since Calhoun's proposals did not quite meet Aberdeen's instructions, however, Pakenham decided to refer the whole matter to London, pending the outcome of the elections. Thus, the conferences ended in deadlock.[38]

When he received Pakenham's reports, Aberdeen again told Peel that he was willing to compromise the boundary at 49°, provided that Britain kept all of Vancouver Island and secured free access to ports on Puget Sound and navigation rights on the Columbia River. The prime minister, however, annoyed at reports of American rearmament on the Great Lakes, opposed withdrawal from earlier offers in the face of American bluster and favored sending a warship to the Columbia River. He also declared that he preferred arbitration to direct concessions. This last statement suited Aberdeen for the time being, and he instructed Pakenham

37. Pakenham to Aberdeen, February 27, May 13, July 29, August 29, Nos. 6, 47, 88, 99, GB, FO 5/404, ff. 16–19; 5/405, ff. 98–101; 5/407, ff. 82–87, 209–14. Wilbur D. Jones and J. Chal. Vinson, "British Preparedness and the Oregon Settlement," *Pacific Historical Review*, 22 (1953), 356.

38. For official accounts of the conferences and the accompanying correspondence, see Manning, *CR*, III, 893–903. For Pakenham's official reports, see Pakenham to Aberdeen, August 29, September 12, 28, 1844, Nos. 99, 106, Separate and Confidential, GB, FO 5/407,

ff. 209–14; 5/408, ff. 74–81, 100–106. Pakenham was undoubtedly encouraged to hold out against Calhoun's terms by inquiries from two members of the Senate Foreign Relations Committee, the friendly Archer and Buchanan, "our constant enemy and reviler." Both asked why England would not consent to arbitration so as to avoid a serious misunderstanding. Pakenham to Aberdeen, August 29, Aberdeen Papers, BM, AM, vol. 43123, ff. 243–46. See also Charles M. Wiltse, *John C. Calhoun, Sectionalist, 1840–1850*, pp. 205–6.

to continue pressing for arbitration at his discretion. Neither Peel nor Aberdeen seemed to attach much material value to Oregon, and Aberdeen regretted that the press and public of both countries had so exaggerated this value as to complicate negotiations based on moderation or common sense.[39]

Indeed, the persistent gap between the claims of the two nations seemed largely due to intangible factors. Since neither side would agree to terms it had already rejected, diplomats needed to find a compromise formula that would enable nationalists in both countries to claim a victory. To complicate matters, neither side wanted to take the initiative in proposing terms, for fear of committing itself prematurely and losing vantage in the bargaining. As a result, private channels of communication eventually became more important than official dispatches, and before the disagreement ceased, the British and American governments were exchanging ideas on Oregon by means of unofficial conversations between friends, letters between business associates, and even—one sometimes suspects—mental telepathy.

*   *   *   *

During the presidential campaign of 1844 and the "lame duck" period that followed, Oregon continued to attract attention in Congress and the press, although much less than Texas. At the Democratic convention, the Ohio, Indiana, and other Midwestern delegations, with help from George Bancroft, inserted an Oregon plank into the party platform, asserting the "clear and unquestionable" American claim to 54°40′ as boundary.[40] Clay ignored the Oregon question, and even the Democrats used it very little and that primarily in the Old Northwest. Here Robert J. Walker cir-

---

39. Pakenham proposed to Aberdeen that Britain suggest joint occupation of only the disputed area between the Columbia River and 49°, but Aberdeen doubted that the United States would agree, and Peel felt that, if so, there was no point in making the offer. Aberdeen to Peel, September 25, October 17, 22, 1844; Peel to Aberdeen, September 28, October 19, Robert C. Clark, "Aberdeen and Peel on Oregon, 1844," *Oregon Historical Quarterly*, 34 (1933), 236–40. On the Great Lakes armaments question, see Lord Stanley to Peel, September 5; Peel to Stanley, September 7, Peel Papers, BM, AM, vol. 40468, ff. 209–13. The Americans denied that

their new warships violated the Rush–Bagot agreement of 1817, but the most thorough student of the subject rejects their arguments. Kenneth Bourne, *Britain and the Balance of Power in North America, 1815–1908*, pp. 125–28.

40. There is little real evidence of a formal bargain at the convention between supporters of Texas and Oregon. James C. N. Paul, *Rift in the Democracy*, pp. 147–48. Edwin A. Miles, "'Fifty-four Forty or Fight'—an American Political Legend," *Mississippi Valley Historical Review*, 44 (September 1957), 295. Richard W. Van Alstyne, *The Rising American Empire*, p. 110.

culated a letter declaring that "Great Britain openly claims our territory, and proposes to plant her flag upon our soil, on the coast of the Pacific, for more than five hundred miles . . . and if Mr. Clay is elected, . . . England will obtain all she desires of Texas and Oregon." Neither Walker nor anyone else used the slogan "Fifty-four Forty or Fight!" in the campaign—contrary to the legend perpetuated in many textbooks.[41]

After the election Tyler's annual message recommended a chain of forts along the Oregon Trail to protect emigrants. As soon as Congress had organized itself, David R. Atchison, the junior Senator from Missouri, introduced a bill not only providing for forts but also setting up full territorial government as far north as 54°40′ and authorizing the President to allot land in the whole disputed area. Nothing was said about the joint occupation treaty with Britain; presumably the American government would have the courtesy to abrogate it before undertaking Atchison's program.[42]

As soon as Atchison's bill appeared, Pakenham went to Calhoun and expressed concern for the still-pending negotiations on Oregon. In January 1845 he formally proposed arbitration of the whole question. Calhoun minimized the danger of congressional action and declined to approve arbitration. During the secretary's illness, however, the House took up a bill based on Atchison's proposal and, to Calhoun's chagrin, passed it by 140 to 59, an even larger majority than the resolution for annexation of Texas. At Calhoun's suggestion Tyler sent a brief, soothing message to the Senate, assuring the members that negotiations with Britain were proceeding satisfactorily. During the next weeks Texas claimed the Senate's full attention. Although a Westerner tried in vain to bring the Atchison bill to a vote in its last minutes, the session terminated without any action on the bill. Apparently, no formal bargain had existed between West and South, but one or two Westerners professed great bitterness when the bill concerning Texas passed and that on Oregon failed.[43]

41. Walker's letter was dated June 29, 1844. See a clipping in GB, FO 5/407, f. 80. Miles, " 'Fifty-four Forty or Fight,' " pp. 291–309. Hans Sperber, "Fifty-four Forty or Fight: Facts and Fictions," American Speech, 32 (February 1957), 5–11.

42. Richardson, Papers of the Presidents, IV, 337–38. Pakenham to Aberdeen, December 12, 29, 1844, Nos. 134, 140, GB, FO 5/409, ff. 113–18, 158–65. Early in the session the Cushing treaty with China, opening five ports to American trade, came up for discussion in the Senate and drew more active attention to the Pacific. The treaty was approved on January 16.

43. Pakenham to Aberdeen, January 29, February 26, March 4, 1845, Nos. 9, 20, 23, GB, FO 5/424, ff. 46–48, 135–37; 5/425, ff. 7–8. Richardson, Papers of the Presidents, IV, 361–62. Justin H. Smith, The Annexation of Texas, pp. 349–52.

The debate in Congress and the echoes in the press helped to clarify a basic difference of opinion regarding the extent of American ambitions in the Pacific Northwest. A great many Americans, especially those living in the Mississippi Valley, wished to snatch every disputed square mile from "the all powerful maw of Great Britain" and even to annex Texas and Mexico as well. Their cry was, "This whole continent must be ours; our destiny is to carry our laws and our institutions throughout its whole extent."[44]

Other expansionists, more interested in trade than in emigration, concentrated their ambitions on the harbors opening onto Puget Sound and the Strait of Juan de Fuca and proposed that the United States and Britain reach a compromise settlement. One of these commercial conciliators was William Sturgis of Boston, member of a firm with extensive interests in the Pacific and China trade and a friend of the Barings. In January 1845 Sturgis delivered a lecture in which he predicted an independent Oregon and advocated a boundary along the 49° line to tidewater and through the middle of the Strait to the ocean, ceding all of Vancouver Island to Britain.

Sturgis' suggestion was hardly startling, for Aberdeen and Everett had independently come to favor this line of boundary. The lecture was immediately published as a pamphlet, and Sturgis' friends circulated it widely in Britain and America.[45] Most merchants preferred a boundary compromise, but some had enough confidence in the force of emigration to believe that the United States could bind the new territory to itself and rule it. Still another group, of which Calhoun was the chief spokesman, upheld American interests in Oregon but wished to delay a final decision as long as possible.[46]

Accounts of the Congressional debate over the Atchison bill focused much British attention on Oregon. At first the London *Times* sneered at the bill as mere bluff, but its passage by the House caused shock. In the British cabinet the American debate

44. Columbus *Daily Ohio Statesman*, January 15, 1845. Clipping in Walker Papers, No. 057, LC. New York *Express Courier*, January 31, as quoted in Clagette Blake, *Charles Elliot, R.N., 1801–1875, a Servant of Britain Overseas*, p. 97. For other extreme expansionist views of this period, see letters in the William Allen Papers, V, VI.

45. William Sturgis, *The Oregon Question, passim*. Van Alstyne, *Rising American Empire*, pp. 111–12. Sturgis

did not commit himself on one ticklish question, the navigation of the Columbia River.

46. Asa Whitney, promoter of a transcontinental railroad to Oregon, warned that an independent Oregon might become "our most dangerous and successful rivals [*sic*] in the commerce of the world." Leaflet enclosed with Asa Whitney to James K. Polk, April 18, 1845, Polk Papers, LXIX, LC.

widened the split between Aberdeen and Wellington over defense measures, which had developed during the Anglo–French crisis of the preceding year. It also strengthened Peel's doubts about the good faith of Calhoun's negotiations and his dislike of seeming to yield to pressure. What could Britain do, he asked, to guard against "infraction or palpable evasion of the Treaty—or some act implying insult and defiance?" He questioned Aberdeen's confidence that British settlers in the disputed area were more numerous than Americans, and he again proposed to increase British forces in Oregon.[47]

The foreign secretary applied to the Hudson's Bay Company for information and, in response, received a copy of a report by Sir George Simpson—some of its information over a year old. Aberdeen had no objection to the precautionary measures proposed by Peel, indeed, he suggested that, if the American Senate passed the Atchison bill, the flagship of the Pacific Squadron should visit the Oregon coast. Nevertheless, he opposed war preparations at home, which might arouse popular hysteria. At the beginning of March he assured Wellington that the United States Senate would probably defeat the bill and that the British settlers in Oregon were strong enough to hold all the territory north of the Columbia River.[48]

While he tried to placate the rest of the cabinet, Aberdeen discussed with Everett the possibility of having the whole question arbitrated. Despite Everett's objections to arbitration, Aberdeen instructed Pakenham to propose it again in Washington if the Senate failed to pass the Atchison bill. Everett wrote to Calhoun that he doubted whether either side would retreat beyond 49° and suggested that Britain might accept this line if given all of Vancouver Island. Aberdeen did not seem to object to the extension of United States law to cover American settlers south of the Columbia, but he warned Everett that any effort by the United States to obtain exclusive possession of Oregon would compel Brit-

47. London *Times*, January 10, 1845, p. 4. Peel to Aberdeen, February 23, Aberdeen Papers, BM, AM, vol. 43064, ff. 178–81. Reprinted in Jones, *Aberdeen and the Americas*, pp. 57–58. At the end of December Aberdeen had fully set forth his pacific policy respecting France. Wellington answered it somewhat ineffectually a few days later. Aberdeen to Peel, December 31, 1844, Aberdeen Papers, BM, AM, vol. 43064. Duke of Wellington to Peel, January

7, 1845, Peel Papers, BM, AM, vol. 40461, ff. 11–12.

48. Joseph Schafer, ed., "Documents Relative to Warre and Vavasour's Military Reconnoissance in Oregon, 1845–6," *Oregon Historical Quarterly*, 10 (March 1909), 3–5. Aberdeen to Wellington, March 2, 1845, Peel Papers, BM, AM, vol. 40455, ff. 3–6. Bourne, *Britain and the Balance of Power*, pp. 132–33.

ain to resist by military force. On March 1 the *Times*, which occasionally spoke for the Foreign Office, advocated arbitration, pronounced the Atchison bill a "flagrant encroachment," and called for defensive measures if it became law.[49]

The Oregon question, like that of California, rested in delicate balance as the Tyler administration came to a close, but the power of an alarmed Britain posed a greater threat to the United States than the fulminations of a chaotic Mexico. In both coastal provinces the influx of migrating Americans was certain to increase expansionist pressures during 1845, but the number of emigrants was much greater in Oregon than in California, and they had created their own political organization in the Willamette Valley. The terms of a reasonable boundary compromise had already taken shape in the minds of Aberdeen, Everett, and a few others, but nationalism, politics, and concern for protocol kept them from expression. Thus, Tyler bequeathed to his successor not only one crisis fully developed in Texas but another rapidly maturing in Oregon.

49. Everett to Calhoun, February 28, March 1, 1845, No. 269, Letterbooks, LI, 276–91, Everett Papers, MHS. Aberdeen to Pakenham, March 3, No. 8, GB, FO 115/88, ff. 63–65. London *Times*, March 1, as quoted in *NNR*, 68 (March 22), 33.

III

Oregon and the Rio Grande Boundary
1845-1846

9

Polk Takes the Initiative

Long before the success of United States policy in Texas was widely apparent, the new administration in Washington had begun to plan for expansion toward the Pacific. For Texas, Polk had in general followed a line of action that Tyler and others had laid out for him, but for Oregon he proclaimed a dynamic new policy in his inaugural address. Later, after an unexpectedly vehement blast of criticism from England, he withdrew slightly from his original stand, but when the British minister, blundering, seemed to close the door to further discussion, Polk gladly returned to his position of defiance. The result was a far more serious crisis in Anglo–American relations than any caused by the annexation of Texas.

Meanwhile, Polk kept a cautious eye on California and the Rio Grande, posting ships and troops to stations from which they might launch an immediate attack if Mexico should be so rash as to declare war. This done, he let Buchanan and his diplomats explore the possibilities of a negotiated peace with Mexico. As the summer of 1845 passed on into fall, he maintained pressure on both Britain and Mexico, outwardly serene and confident that both countries would give way and yield him what he wanted.

* * * *

What was the nature of the man who had taken the country's foreign policy in such a firm grasp? James Knox Polk was the son of a Presbyterian farmer in North Carolina. After moving to Tennessee, he became a lawyer and maneuvered himself upward through frontier politics to the United States House of Representatives. From 1835 to 1839 he was its Speaker; then he served a term as governor of Tennessee. Along the way he became a protégé of Andrew Jackson and, with a mixture of calculation and conviction, hitched his career to Jacksonian Democracy. As the Texas question emerged to national concern in the late 1830s, he quite naturally became an expansionist, but he was never a party to any "slaveholders' conspiracy" such as the abolitionists imagined.

When the Democratic convention nominated him for the Presidency, few voters knew him well, and Clay's Whigs hooted (to their later embarrassment): "Who is James K. Polk?" During the campaign even his own followers privately regarded him as "a modest, hard-working little man," "scarcely one of extraordinary mediocrity," "a man of respectable talents," but not much more. In order to prevent a party split, he had to promise that he would serve only one term. As a result, Democratic leaders began to plan their tactics for the campaign of 1848 even before his inauguration.[1]

No man of pride could have faced these circumstances without being either steeled or broken; they produced in Polk a determination to curb his rebellious party and be absolute master of his administration. At the time of his inauguration he was only forty-nine—a short, thin, angular man whose long, graying hair was brushed back from an unsmiling face with high cheekbones, restless, gray eyes, thin lips, and set jaw. He had few intellectual interests, little personal charm, and almost no sense of humor, although he had taught himself to enliven political speeches with sly innuendo to divert his frontier audiences.

As a good Jacksonian, he brought to the White House a conviction that the President, the only true representative of national interests, must dominate the government and be the very symbol of the common man. More than any other Jacksonian, Polk understood and accepted the hard, grinding work which this responsibility entailed and almost literally drove himself to an early grave. American politicians commonly took long vacations from the summer heat and the year-round strains of the capital, but for one period of thirteen months Polk never traveled more than three or four miles from Washington. He mastered the routine and details of every executive department, delegated power with great reluctance, and called for frequent and full accountings.

Such a man obviously had great will power and courage—or "guts," in the language of Bernard De Voto. The classic illustration of his determination is the oft-cited statement by his secretary of the navy, George Bancroft, to the effect that soon after inauguration the new President told him that the "four great measures" of his administration were to be reduction of the tariff, establishment of an independent treasury, settlement of the Oregon ques-

1. Frederick Merk, *The Oregon Question, Essays in Anglo–American Diplomacy and Politics*, pp. 365–66. Charles Grier Sellers, *James K. Polk, Continentalist: 1843–1846*, pp. 113–14, 163–65. The phrases quoted appear on p. 163.

tion, and acquisition of California. Since Polk achieved all four goals, his statement to Bancroft took on qualities of heroic prophecy, although Bancroft did not see fit to reveal it until years later, when he was an old man.[2] In the twentieth century, when dominant presidents became the general rule rather than the uncomfortable exception, Polk's record of accomplishments and his strong leadership gave his reputation new luster, by that time much needed.

While Polk's contemporaries and his biographers have given him full credit for determination, they have also recognized a certain indirection or deviousness in his methods. Gideon Welles thought it "sly cunning . . . duplicity . . . secretiveness"; and Allan Nevins has called Polk "cute" in the Yankee sense but "by his lights . . . eminently truthful and upright."[3] Literally truthful he may have been, but he kept his own counsel, let others guess (often wrongly) at his intentions, and ignored or privately resented the later recriminations. Beginning in August 1845, he kept a diary of his discussions and reactions. One cannot be sure that he was completely frank even with himself, but Polk's record brings the historian closer to the arcanum of presidential decision than is his usual lot.

What was Polk's attitude toward foreign policy? As a Westerner, long associated with domestic party politics and the Anglophobe Jackson, he could not have been expected to show a cosmopolitan spirit or much informed interest in international affairs. To be sure, he learned the routine business of the State Department so thoroughly that on one occasion he bet Buchanan

---

2. Bancroft wrote this account to James Schouler in February 1887, even adding the detail that Polk struck his thigh forcibly as he spoke. Bancroft gave much the same account to John Charles Frémont in a memorandum of September 2/3, 1886, this time limiting his specification to the conquest of California. In the latter case he stated that he had consulted his records, but he did not specify when he had written them. James Schouler, History of the United States of America under the Constitution, IV, 498. John Charles Frémont, "The Conquest of California," Century Magazine, 41 (April 1891), 923–24. Bernard De Voto, The Year of Decision, 1846, p. 7. On Polk's conception of the Presidency, see Charles A. McCoy, Polk and the Presidency,

Chap. 3.

3. Gideon Welles, "Review of Political History, " in Gideon Welles Papers, Articles, IX, LC. Quoted in Richard R. Stenberg, "President Polk and California: Additional Documents," Pacific Historical Review, 10 (June 1941), 219. James K. Polk, Polk, the Diary of a President, ed. Allan Nevins, p. xvi. For good short characterizations, see ibid., pp. xv–xix. See also Charles Grier Sellers, James K. Polk, Jacksonian: 1795–1843, pp. 278, 355–56, et passim; Eugene Irving McCormac, James K. Polk, a Political Biography, pp. 1–4, 7–9, 69, 139–40, et passim. No study is complete without frequent reference to The Diary of James K. Polk during His Presidency, 1845 to 1849, ed. Milo M. Quaife, 4 vols.

several bottles of champagne that he had made a mistake in drawing up a diplomatic document and won the bet (although he declined the champagne).

Like Theodore Roosevelt, Polk held in amused contempt
such diplomatic forms as the pompous announcements of royal
births. Unlike Roosevelt, however, he could not bypass the restricted official channels through friendly private discussions, for
he usually viewed foreign representatives with suspicion and treated them with stiff propriety.[4] One doubts, indeed, whether Polk
ever really appreciated the complex operation of international
give-and-take behind the forms, for he seemed to view foreign
relations as a matter of calculated bluff and bluster in which un-
flinching perseverance would eventually win the day. On the few
occasions when he agreed to compromise, as in the case of Oregon,
he acted slowly, reluctantly, and with an air of self-righteousness.
Also, he tried to spread the responsibility as broadly as possible.

Polk dominated a fairly able cabinet of professional politicians whose background and personalities occasionally influenced
the framing of foreign policy. Secretary of State James Buchanan
resembled his master in many ways: his Scottish Presbyterian fore-
bears, his childhood on a small farm, and the long, ambition-
driven push upwards through state politics. Buchanan was older
and more sophisticated and ingratiating than Polk; he reminded
one observer of a well-dressed, courteous British aristocrat.[5] Buchanan had once been a Federalist and was less devoted than Polk
to Jackson, nationalism, and the common man, but he controlled
a powerful Democratic organization in Pennsylvania, which had
contributed heavily to Polk's election. Coming from an industrial
state, he favored high tariffs but in this matter was willing to yield
to his chief without much struggle.

While both men were ambitious, persistent, and calculating,
Buchanan was irresolute on most large issues, since he lacked confidence in his own judgment or was unwilling to expose himself
to unpopularity. Where Polk gave the impression of being a master planner, his fingers on every issue, Buchanan often resembled
a finicky, cautious old maid. Characteristically, he stirred up more

---

4. Polk, *Diary*, II, 215–16, 285; III,
97–99. McCoy, *Polk and the Presidency*,
pp. 72–73.

5. Again, Allan Nevins has written
the most penetrating characterizations.
See his introduction to *Polk, Diary of
a President*, p. xxi; and *The Emergence*

of Lincoln, I, 61–64. The most recent
biography is Philip Shriver Klein, *President James Buchanan, A Biography*.
For opposition comment on the whole
cabinet, see *NNR*, 68 (March 15, 1845),
22.

trouble for Polk over patronage than over foreign policy and agonized for weeks over whether to leave the cabinet for the Supreme Court. At the outset, when Polk asked him, along with the other cabinet members, to forswear presidential ambitions while in office, Buchanan carefully hedged his reply.[6]

Until mid-1847 the secretary of state adhered rather closely to his promise, and although he sometimes disagreed with Polk over foreign policy, the opposition was undoubtedly good for Polk. In the Senate Buchanan had often attacked Britain and had taken a strong line on Oregon. Nevertheless, as Pakenham shrewdly predicted, he became more moderate, once he had assumed the executive responsibilities of the State Department. The British minister mistrusted his honesty and sincerity but found him always courteous, good-humored, and obliging. Considering the likely alternatives for the post, Pakenham hoped that Buchanan would remain in office.[7] Behind the scenes during much of the Oregon crisis the secretary worried over the possibility of war with Britain and did what he could to soften Polk's defiance and to open the way for compromise. Where California was concerned, however, he remained an expansionist most of the time.

Other members of the cabinet played smaller roles in the era of expansion. Secretary of the Treasury Robert J. Walker was a bustling, excitable little man, full of courage and a sense of melodrama, a hard-hitting Southern editorialist and a land speculator who caused abolitionists and sound-money men unjustifiable anxiety. Although he had done more than any other person to popularize the annexation of Texas, he turned away from expansionism for the time being and devoted himself to lowering the tariff, thereby winning many friends in Britain. After the war with Mexico began, he usually took the expansionist side in cabinet discussions.[8] The functions of Secretary of War William L. Marcy, self-educated, blunt, and humorous, became more important as war approached. The war required the expansion and renovation

6. For the text of Buchanan's acceptance, see George Ticknor Curtis, *Life of James Buchanan, Fifteenth President of the United States*, I, 547–49. Polk *Diary*, I, 98, 190, 201-2, *et passim*. Buchanan commonly called on Polk every day to report State Department business. Ibid., p. 83. Klein, *Buchanan*, pp. 169–70. Polk himself once described Buchanan as "an old maid." Polk, *Diary*, IV, 355.

7. Richard Pakenham to Earl of Aberdeen, March 29, May 13, 29, 1845; August 13, 1846, Nos. 33, 53, 54, 60, GB, FO 5/425, ff. 64–66; 5/426, ff. 9–15, 19–23, 45–48; 5/450, ff. 124–28.

8. Nevins, *Emergence of Lincoln*, I, 69–70, 144–45. On Walker's work for Polk in the campaign of 1844, see James C. N. Paul, *Rift in the Democracy*, pp. 174–77; and Sellers, *Polk, Continentalist*, pp. 117–20, 133–34, 136–38, 150–51.

of an inadequate army, but except in drafting orders to the generals he had relatively little to do with foreign policy.[9] Attorney General John Y. Mason and Postmaster General Cave Johnson confined their attention almost entirely to domestic matters.

Lowest in cabinet rank but by no means least in influence was Secretary of the Navy George Bancroft, a cultivated Bostonian and at the same time an enthusiastic Jacksonian, who had hoped for a diplomatic post and, indeed, eventually received the London legation. Bancroft's importance in foreign affairs sprang from two seemingly opposite factors. He led the cabinet in his early, open enthusiasm for the annexation of California. At the same time, through New England business friends close to the house of Baring, he kept open a portion of what had been the Whigs' broad channel to conciliatory British business opinion. More than anyone else in Polk's administration, Bancroft typified Americans' ambivalence toward Britain, for he had also published three volumes of what was to be his *magnum opus*, an ardently democratic, nationalistic history of the United States. In these volumes Britain was both praised as "the star of constitutional liberty" and damned for her "grasping avidity." Thus, when he entered the cabinet, Bancroft seemed well suited to deal with all the twists and turns of Anglo–American policy.[10]

The only congressional leaders of the time who deserve mention here were John C. Calhoun of South Carolina and Thomas Hart Benton of Missouri. As Senator, Calhoun was no less self-righteous than he had been as secretary of state, but after Texas had been annexed, he largely abandoned the militant expansionism with which he had stiffened the Tyler administration and took a moderate stand with respect to Oregon and Mexican territory.

Benton was a supporter and personal friend of Polk who gave him advice from time to time during 1845 and ever increasingly during 1846. He also exerted considerable influence over Buchanan, for the secretary, who did not read Spanish, distrusted the

9. Allan Nevins, *Ordeal of the Union*, II, 12, 50–51. Ivan Debenham Spencer, *The Victor and the Spoils, a Life of William L. Marcy, passim*. Polk appointed Marcy only after much backing and filling. The appointment widened a party split in New York. Sellers, *Polk, Continentalist*, Chap. 5.

10. Russel B. Nye, *George Bancroft: Brahmin Rebel, passim*. Allan Nevins, *Frémont, the World's Greatest Adventurer*, I, 235–36. Richard W. Van Al-
styne, *The Rising American Empire*, pp. 111–14. Watt Stewart, "George Bancroft," in William T. Hutchinson, ed., *The Marcus W. Jernegan Essays in American Historiography*, pp. 1–24. The first three volumes of Bancroft's *History of the United States from the Discovery of the American Continent* were published in 1834, 1837, and 1840. The phrases quoted appear in III, 12, 400, of that edition.

official translator of the State Department and brought many Mexican communications to Benton's home for translation and discussion.[11] During the first half of the Mexican War, Benton was often Polk's chief consultant on military matters, and if Congress had approved, the President would have appointed him lieutenant general in charge of all operations (see Chapter 13). Benton's influence was usually expansionist, for although he favored compromising the Oregon settlement at 49°, he led the congressional demand for California and eventually called for all-out war with Mexico and a dictated peace.

Because of the impending crises with Mexico and Britain, the American ministers to these countries were to be only a little less important than cabinet members in the development of policy. Polk did not send a new envoy to Mexico City at once, since Mexico had broken relations completely by the withdrawal of Minister Almonte, and he would not risk a rebuff. He felt some need to replace Edward Everett at London, however, for Everett was a Whig, a friend of Webster, and, even worse, a protectionist. At first the President tried to induce Calhoun to accept the post, doubtless hoping to get him out of the country without offending him. After considering the appointment for some time, Calhoun declined, since Polk would not promise him full support in negotiating treaties over Oregon, commerce, and fugitive slaves.[12] By this time British reactions to Polk's inaugural address seemed to require conciliation, and the President considered sending Martin Van Buren as a kind of good-will offering to Britain. Van Buren, however, also refused.[13]

After two other false starts, in mid-June Polk finally settled on Louis McLane, who had served Jackson as minister to Britain, secretary of state, and secretary of the treasury. Even though only fifth choice, McLane was admirably suited for the assignment, having prestige, a home in Baltimore—neither North nor South—previous knowledge of Whitehall and Westminster, and many business connections as president of the Baltimore and Ohio Railroad. Perhaps his only serious handicap was that he considered

---

11. The wife of the State Department's translator, Robert Greenhow, was in British pay and leaked confidential documents to the British legation. Allan Nevins, *Frémont, Pathmarker of the West*, p. 199. The standard biography of Benton is William Nisbet Chambers, *Old Bullion Benton, Senator from the New West*.

12. Charles M. Wiltse, *John C. Calhoun, Sectionalist, 1840–1850*, pp. 218, 220, 520n22. Sellers, *Polk, Continentalist*, p. 199.

13. M. A. de Wolfe Howe, *The Life and Letters of George Bancroft*, I, 267–73. Sellers, *Polk, Continentalist*, pp. 284–92.

Buchanan a political rival and never fully trusted him. Pakenham thought McLane's appointment satisfactory evidence that Polk wished to negotiate in a fair and friendly spirit.[14]

*   *   *   *

Although Polk had been in office for only three months, such evidence was important to the British government, for the Oregon question had assumed a new and alarming aspect. This tension was due in great part to Polk's statements in his inaugural address, delivered in a rainstorm "to a large assemblage of umbrellas" before the Capitol[15]—and carefully read by many other interested persons in America and Europe.

Since Polk had won the Presidency on a platform that included the "reoccupation" of all Oregon, and since expansionist Democrats had played up this theme in debates on the Atchison bill, everyone expected him to make some pronouncement on the subject. Polk was mainly concerned, in his first official statement, to establish his version of Jacksonian Democracy, so he devoted most of his speech to domestic issues. If he had wished to be truly diplomatic about Oregon, he might have dismissed the subject with a brief reference to pending negotiations; indeed, Calhoun tried to persuade him toward some such conciliatory attitude. But Polk had already determined that only a statement of defiant stance would impress Britain. In an early draft of the address he declared that the American title was "clear and ought to be indisputable—it should be asserted by all Constitutional means." He then invoked the noncolonization principle of the Monroe Doctrine in defense of his position, proclaiming: "Should any European power attempt to plant or maintain a colony on any portion of the territory claimed and owned by the United States . . . it is due to our interests, our safety and the national honour,—that it should be vigorously resisted." Finally, he called on Congress to extend United States law over the whole area.[16]

As Polk rewrote and polished his address, he toned down his language on Oregon, perhaps influenced by Calhoun and other

14. Pakenham to Aberdeen, June 28, 1845, No. 69, GB, FO 5/426, ff. 104–5. There was considerable argument in the American press over McLane's business associations and some criticism of his "unfavorable" West Indian commercial treaty of 1830. NNR, 68 (June 21, 1845), 243–45; (July 12), 290.

15. John Quincy Adams, Memoirs of John Quincy Adams, ed. Charles Francis Adams, XII, 179.

16. Two early drafts of Polk's inaugural address are in the Polk Papers, Series 5, box 2, LC. The passages on Oregon appear on ff. 6486K–L and [6543]. On Calhoun's efforts, see Sellers, Polk, Continentalist, p. 243.

conciliators. He deleted the passage on the Monroe Doctrine (which reappeared, somewhat altered, in his annual message to Congress nine months later) and introduced assurances that the United States did not intend to violate existing agreements. In its final form the passage on Oregon still sounded a defiant note, but Polk placed it inconspicuously near the end after ringing a number of peals and changes on Texas and other issues:

> Our title to the country of the Oregon is "clear and unquestionable," and already are our people preparing to perfect that title by occupying it with their wives and children. . . . The world beholds the peaceful triumphs of the industry of our emigrants. To us belongs the duty of protecting them adequately wherever they may be upon our soil. The jurisdiction of our laws and the benefits of our republican institutions should be extended over them in the distant regions which they have selected for their homes. The increasing facilities of intercourse will easily bring the States, of which the formation in that part of our territory can not be long delayed, within the sphere of our federative Union. In the meantime every obligation imposed by treaty or conventional stipulations should be sacredly respected.[17]

The careful reader might have observed that Polk had quoted the provocative phrase "clear and unquestionable" from the Democratic platform of 1844, but that—unlike the platform—he did not specify all of Oregon. In extending legal jurisdiction over Americans in the disputed area, he was only following the precedent set by Britain and the Hudson's Bay Company, and he had balanced his reference to the formation of state governments with a statement about the sanctity of treaties. The paragraph aroused little comment in American newspapers. The Anglophobe *Niles' Register* did not even mention it, but the moderate New York *Evening Post* remarked that Polk had expressed himself "strongly, and, we think, justly." James Gordon Bennett, the arch-expansionist editor of the New York *Herald*, wrote approvingly to Polk and promised his support.[18]

17. James D. Richardson, ed., *A Compilation of the Messages and Papers of the Presidents, 1789–1897*, IV, 381. There is no evidence that Buchanan encouraged Polk to moderate his language, although such an action would have been consistent with his later attitude. About three weeks before the inauguration Van Buren wrote to Polk, predicting that foreign affairs would primarily occupy his attention. He admitted that the time had come for action in Texas and Oregon but urged great caution. Martin Van Buren to Polk, February 10, 1845, Polk Papers, LXX, LC.

18. New York *Evening Post*, March 5, 1845, p. 1. James Gordon Bennett to Polk, March 10, Polk Papers, LXXIII, LC. *Niles' Register* published no comments except two reprints from the Charleston *Mercury*, grumbling about passages on domestic affairs and the tariff. *NNR*, 68 (March 15), 21.

Unfortunately, Polk's language was still too brusque for self-respecting Britons to accept calmly, especially as the congressional debate over the Atchison bill had already made the British government and public extremely sensitive about Oregon. The London correspondent of the New York *Commercial Advertiser* regarded the address as "unusual, inconsiderate, and in bad taste," especially while negotiations were still pending. The *Times*, a specialist in Yankee-baiting, outdid itself: "Ill regulated, overbearing, and aggressive . . . [Polk's] pretensions amount, if acted upon, to the clearest *causa belli* which has ever yet arisen between Great Britain and the American Union." But, it added with a sneer, "the same democratic folly which makes them [the Americans] arrogant in the cabinet, makes them habitually feeble in . . . the field." It expressed amazement that even the Americans would challenge Britain while facing a "contemptible and indecisive" war with Mexico. Another British editor remarked grimly: "There are certain animals that may be led, but won't be driven—[John] Bull is one of them." [19]

At first, Lord Palmerston's *Morning Chronicle* pronounced the address "pious without cant, frank without rudeness . . . a PRESIDENT'S speech of which a red-hot American patriot may be proud, and which a prudent American could not call too hazardous. . . . We fear to find him [Polk] a formidable and unscrupulous enemy," it concluded. In a few days the *Chronicle* turned to its customary argument that the weakness of Aberdeen and Ashburton had encouraged American insolence. At the same time a smaller group of business-minded moderates, represented by the *Economist*, recognized that Polk was really talking to Americans about American problems and regretted only his discourteous language about foreign nations. To them the most important parts of the address were those dealing with the state debts and the tariff. [20]

Naturally, the Whig leaders in Parliament instantly called on the government for its reactions. Aberdeen applied to Everett for the origin of Polk's quoted phrase "clear and unquestionable,"

19. New York *Commercial Advertiser*, April 23, 1845. Clipping in GB, FO 5/425, ff. 154–55. London *Times*, April 5, and *Wilmer & Smith's Times*, April 5, as quoted in *NNR*, 68 (April 26), 114–15. The London *Times* later declared that, while the annexation of Texas would not justify war with the United States, the American occupation of Oregon would, since it violated a specific British claim. However, it assessed the danger of attack as remote. London *Times*, April 10, p. 4.

20. London *Morning Chronicle*, March 28, 1845, p. 4; April 2, p. 4; April 9, p. 5. London *Economist*, n.d., quoted in New York *Evening Post*, April 24, p. 2.

but the American minister, being a Whig and not much interested in politics, missed the reference to the Democratic platform and could not enlighten him. With no knowledge of how seriously Polk had intended his statement, Peel and Aberdeen had somehow to placate extremists in Parliament while holding open the door for further negotiations. In the House of Lords Aberdeen took the position that Polk's address was not official, since Congress was not in session. The foreign secretary reaffirmed his determination to preserve the peace and declared that such words as "pusillanimous, cowardly, mean, dastardly, truckling, and base," which enemies (chiefly Palmerston) had hurled at him, would not shake that determination as long as it was consistent with national honor.[21]

This level of debate was harmless enough, but Peel took a stronger attitude in Commons. Polk's statement antagonized him completely, for he already suspected American bluster and doubted the good faith of Calhoun and other conciliators. Furthermore, he resented the Whigs' hints about another "capitulation." So he made a firm reply that worked up to a climax almost as forceful as Polk's own demands:

> I feel it my imperative duty, on the part of the British Government, to state in language the most temperate, but, at the same time, the most decided, that we consider we have rights respecting this territory of Oregon which are clear and unquestionable. We trust still to arrive at an amicable adjustment—we desire to effect an amicable adjustment of our claim; but having exhausted every effort to effect that settlement, if our rights shall be invaded, we are resolved—and we are prepared—to maintain them.

According to one observer, this statement brought forth more general and hearty cheers from both sides of the House than he had ever heard before.[22]

21. *Hansard Parliamentary Debates*, 3d series, LXXIX, cols. 115–23. Everett did not learn the meaning of "clear and unquestionable" until he returned to the United States. He informed Aberdeen as an afterthought when he wrote to congratulate him on the final settlement. Everett to Aberdeen, July 30, 1846, Aberdeen Papers, BM, AM, vol. 43123, f. 447.

22. *Hansard Parliamentary Debates*, 3d series, LXXIX, cols. 178–201. Like Peel, Aberdeen made a point of declaring Britain's rights "clear and un- questionable." New York *Commercial Advertiser*, April 23, 1845. Clipping in GB, FO 5/425, ff. 154–55. The radical Joseph Hume, normally opposed to armaments, told an American friend that in his anger he would have voted to double the Navy estimates. Charles A. Davis to Polk, London, July 18, Polk Papers, LXXXVIII, LC. Sellers disagrees with this view of Peel, believing that Polk was realistic in defying him with a strong stand. Sellers, *Polk, Continentalist*, p. 244.

The reactions of Peel and the *Times* made a strong impression on the American press, which now more than compensated for its early apathy toward Polk's statement. Thomas Ritchie, editor of the newly founded administration newspaper, the Washington *Union*, appealed to the Whigs not to make Oregon a party issue and warned Pakenham not to assume that Whig pacifists spoke for the administration. A good many editors took pleasure in answering Britain insult for insult, but most of them seemed to believe that the diplomats could settle the question to mutual satisfaction and that Britain would not think such a distant and valueless territory worth waging a war. Many suggested that Britain dared not fight and that the American forces, which had driven British shipping off the seas in 1812 and 1813, would now be even more devastating. "Why should we fear a conflict with Great Britain?" asked the Louisville *Daily Democrat*:

> We are fully her equals in national energy and courage—her superior in military resources, and . . . the disparity [in naval armament] is not so great as the press have alleged. . . . England is at any rate a mere *tenant at will* upon this continent. . . . The Canadas are ripe for rebellion, and the single states of Ohio and New York could . . . reduce them to subjection in six weeks, and put at defiance any force which England could bring against them.[23]

By and large, the press of the East and South took a more conciliatory position than that of the West. Echoing Calhoun, the New York *Evening Post* advised: "Let Oregon remain, as it is, for the next fifty years. When it is ripe it must drop where it is destined to fall." The New York *Evening Express* went further; it predicted that North and South "will hardly suffer a few hare-brained madmen of the west to plunge the country into a war." British newspapers, anxiously awaiting the American reaction, seized upon the sectional differences and probably overemphasized the conciliatory spirit of the coastal cities. The *Times* reminded the Americans of the expense of defending a remote, hostile territory and linked American aggressiveness in Oregon with the presumptuous annexation of Texas: "They are, in fact, parts of the same project of aggrandizement, and results of that system of policy first avowed by Mr. Monroe, which claims for the United States a territorial monopoly of the continent to which they belong."[24]

23. Washington *Union*, May 2, 1845, p. 7. Louisville *Daily Democrat*, n.d., quoted in New York *Evening Post*, May 16, p. 4. For other press opinion, see, ibid., April 25, p. 3; April 28, p. 2; May 16, p. 4; and *NNR*, 68 (May 10), 151–52.
24. New York *Evening Post*, May 6, 1845, p. 3. New York *Evening Express*, April 24, as reprinted in London *Times*,

The British reaction and the American counterreaction increased and complicated the pressures on the Polk administration, which had apparently not expected the transatlantic explosion.[25] Calhoun thought the inaugural statement "a profound blunder" and continued to advise "masterly inactivity," but James Kirk Paulding, who had been Van Buren's secretary of the navy, warned Bancroft that a crisis was rapidly approaching which would determine British or American hegemony in the New World. Paulding was confident that "a feeble or pusillanimous policy on the part of the United States" would simply delay an inevitable transfer.[26] Andrew Jackson, only a month away from death, scribbled a final exhortation, urging Polk to hold firm and blast the British again in his annual message: "To prevent war with England a bold and undaunted front must be exposed. England with all her Boast dare not go to war." Polk soothed the old man's anxieties, agreed that Peel was probably trying to test American nerve, and declared that he had no fear of war: "The negotiation will probably be re-opened very soon." [27]

* * * *

This temperate reaction was just what Pakenham had hoped for, and in the first weeks after the inaugural address he made every effort to establish friendly contacts with the new administration. During March he had two conversations with Buchanan, who awkwardly tried to explain away his anti-British speeches in the Senate and expressed profusely his desire for Anglo–American understanding. When Pakenham, as instructed, unofficially suggested that the Oregon question be arbitrated, Buchanan answered indirectly by saying that he still hoped for a negotiated settlement.

A few days later, influential Senator William S. Archer of

May 15, p. 8. See also London *Times*, May 9, p. 4; May 10, p. 6; May 24, p. 4. The passage quoted appears in the *Times*, July 7, p. 4. The High Tory *Colonial Magazine* argued that "a war with America . . . cannot but be productive of good," since it would destroy both American commerce and Southern slavery. Quoted in *NNR*, 68 (June 7), 218.

25. According to a later account by Thomas Hart Benton, Buchanan consulted him in early April and seemed to expect some further proposition from Britain which, of course, the public reaction made impossible. Thomas Hart Benton, *Thirty Years View*, II, 661.

26. John C. Calhoun, *Correspondence of John C. Calhoun*, ed. J. Franklin Jameson, pp. 653–54, 656–57, 659–64, 669–71. James Kirk Paulding to George Bancroft, June 14, 1845, Bancroft Papers, MHS. Paulding to Van Buren, May 8, Martin Van Buren Papers, series 2, roll 30, LC.

27. Andrew Jackson to Polk, May 2, 1845; Polk to Jackson, May 12, Andrew Jackson, *The Correspondence of Andrew Jackson*, ed. John Spencer Bassett, VI, 404–6.

Virginia, usually an Anglophile, reported to Pakenham a statement of Polk that, rather than break with Britain, he would consent to arbitration. When packets arrived bearing the menacing speeches and editorials from Britain, Pakenham noted with satisfaction the conciliatory statements of several influential Eastern papers and again pressed arbitration on Buchanan. At the end of April he wrote privately to Aberdeen that the ministerial speeches in Parliament had made Polk look foolish and that he was now afraid to go forward and ashamed to retreat. The British minister added that it might help Polk to accept arbitration if some European power would recommend it, and that in the long run (he commented, condescendingly) the rebuke would be good for the President.[28] He was later to revise this judgment.

But Aberdeen took a more serious view of Polk's speech in his dispatches to Pakenham than he had in Parliament. At first he declared that if the Americans rejected arbitration without making a counterproposal, Britain must consider the negotiations ended and must expect the abrogation of the joint occupation treaty and possibly some incident leading to war. He instructed Pakenham to "hold a temperate, but firm, language to the members of the Government, and to all those with whom you may converse. We are still ready to adhere to the principle of an equitable compromise; but we are perfectly determined to concede nothing to force or menace; and are fully prepared to maintain our rights."[29]

During the next two weeks the Foreign Office learned from Pakenham of his inconclusive talks with Buchanan, and on April 18 Aberdeen sent further instructions in case Buchanan should resume the discussion Calhoun had dropped in the preceding autumn. If so, Pakenham might add to the earlier British offer (the Columbia River as boundary) a proposal that all ports south of 49° be made free to both nations. If this proposal were rejected, Pakenham would have no alternative but to suggest arbitration

---

28. Pakenham to Aberdeen, March 29, April 28, 1845, Nos. 40, 49, GB, FO 5/425, ff. 102-5, 142-46; same, April 28, Private, Aberdeen Papers, BM, AM, vol. 43123, ff. 253-57. Aberdeen did make a gesture in this direction by unofficially suggesting the possibility of mediation by the French government, but the idea came to nothing. François Guizot to Comte de Ste. Aulaire, May 19, ibid., vol. 43133, ff. 135-37. That Pakenham was correct in believing the administration's attitude on Oregon to be conciliatory is confirmed by a report of James Hamilton to Calhoun on May 5 about recent talks with Polk, Buchanan, and Walker. Quoted in Sellers, *Polk, Continentalist*, p. 245n60.

29. Aberdeen to Pakenham, April 6, 1845, No. 21, GB, FO 115/88, ff. 153-55. This official dispatch was a reworking of a private note dated April 2. Aberdeen Papers, BM, AM, vol. 43123, ff. 249-50.

again.[30] A private letter of the same day considerably softened the abruptness of the official dispatch, however, and gave the British minister more room in which to maneuver:

If Mr. Buchanan should propose an extension of the 49th Parallel to the sea as the line of boundary, leaving us in possession of the whole of Vancouver's Island & the free entrance into the Straits of Juan de Fuca; although I would put forward in answer, our proposal described in my dispatch this day, I should not like to regard his proposal as perfectly inadmissible. It is possible that by some modifications it might be accepted, although I do not think it at all likely, & of course you will give no encouragement to the notion, but recur to arbitration in the event of our terms being rejected. At the same time, you might send Mr. Buchanan's proposal, if made, for the consideration of H. M. Govt.

I think it should be clearly understood that the navigation of the Columbia should be common to both Parties, & the Ports within the Straits of Juan de Fuca, & South of Lat. 49, should be free Ports, by whomsoever they might be occupied.[31]

These terms were the same that Aberdeen had instructed Pakenham in December 1843 to extract, if possible, from the Tyler administration. If he stated them more cautiously now than earlier, the change probably reflected the increased opposition of militarists in the British cabinet. At any rate, Aberdeen's note created an opening which skillful diplomats might enlarge and strongly hinted that at all costs they must keep up the negotiations. Unfortunately, the hint was lost on Pakenham.

Aberdeen's subtle directions were indeed realistic, for in the spring of 1845 both the United States and Britain had good reasons to work for a negotiated settlement of the Oregon question. At the moment when mailbags full of angry British editorials and letters were arriving in New York, the annexation of Texas hung in the balance, for no one knew yet whether the mercurial Houston and his compatriots would respond to Donelson or to Elliot, or whether Mexico could muster forces for an immediate invasion across the Rio Grande and the Nueces. In Britain, Peel had finally decided to stake the future of his government on tariff reform, and on February 14 he had brought in a budget abolishing all export duties and import duties on 430 items, including raw cotton. After a hot fight it was adopted. The campaign statements of the

30. Aberdeen to Pakenham, April 18, 1845, No. 22, GB, FO 115/88, ff. 157–59.

31. Aberdeen to Pakenham, April 18, 1845, Aberdeen Papers, BM, AM, vol. 43123, ff. 249–50.

American Democratic party (except in the Northeast), the nomination of the tariff reformer Walker to the Treasury Department, and the rising American opposition to the "black tariff" of 1842 gave Peel reason to hope for reciprocal concessions. His party, already divided by the debate on the budget, was subjected to further strain in March and April by a totally unrelated squabble in Parliament over government aid to Roman Catholic education.[32]

Even more important to the Peel administration was the fear that war with the United States might rupture the *entente cordiale* and drive France into the American arms. To be sure, *Le journal des débats* and other organs of the Guizot ministry loyally joined the *Times* in denouncing Polk's inaugural address, and even the opposition press commented sourly on American actions in Texas. Concerning Oregon, however, the French opposition sided completely with Polk, assured him that the British were only bluffing with their talk of war, and predicted that France too would gain if Britain made any concessions to the United States.[33]

Peel more than Aberdeen feared the involvement of France in Anglo–American hostilities, and the Duke of Wellington predicted the reappearance of an Armed Neutrality in Europe like that of the American Revolutionary period to prevent Britain from blockading the American coast.[34] Wellington and Sir Charles Napier warned of a direct French attack across the Channel, and Napier declared that, with the British Navy only partly converted from sail to steam, hardly a ship could be relied on to intercept the newest French units. Not everyone in the cabinet respected Sir Charles' "croaking," as one of them put it, but the possibility of a Franco–American coalition caused a few British writers to

---

32. Élie Halévy, *The Age of Peel and Cobden, a History of the English People, 1841–1852*, pp. 80, 85–86. James Patrick Shenton, *Robert John Walker, a Politician from Jackson to Lincoln*, pp. 77–78. American protectionists were scornful about the British concessions, especially since Peel retained preferential duties on British colonial sugar. See *NNR*, 68 (March 29, 1845), 52, 64; (April 5), 65; (May 17), 163; (July 19), 312–13; (August 2), 348–51; *et passim*. For the opposing side, see New York *Evening Post*, January 10, p. 4; February 26, p. 1; May 12, p. 2. Later, *Niles' Register* stated that Peel had whipped up British nationalist sentiment about Oregon to tide his government over a Parliamentary crisis. *NNR*, 69 (January 24, 1846), 322–23.

33. *NNR*, 68 (June 7, 1845), 210. *Le journal des débats*, July 9, pp. 1–2. *Le national*, April 17, p. 2. *La presse*, April 18, p. 1.

34. A long, gloomy memorandum by Wellington, dated April 8, 1845, is quoted in Kenneth Bourne, *Britain and the Balance of Power in North America, 1815–1908*, pp. 136–37. Although Wellington commanded much respect in the country at large, Peel and the rest of the cabinet now considered many of his fears exaggerated and sometimes tried to withhold from him documents that might arouse them. Ibid., pp. 137, 139. See also C. J. Bartlett, *Great Britain and Sea Power, 1815–1853*, pp. 168–70.

treat even the feeble United States Navy with more respect than usual.[35]

Under these circumstances Peel and Aberdeen began to work behind the scenes, the one to improve British chances of victory in a war with France and America, the other to prevent such a war. The Admiralty began to build up the Channel defenses and continued to maintain watchful patrols along the Oregon coast. These were now under the supervision of Sir George Seymour, the new commander of the Pacific Squadron, who had been selected for the post during the preceding autumn especially for his prudence in political situations. Seymour, who had to watch the French in Tahiti and Hawaii as well, maneuvered his eight or nine ships with great skill and discretion. The cabinet had other, personal contacts with the squadron, for Aberdeen's brother, Captain John Gordon, commanded the eighty-gun frigate *America*, which visited the Oregon coast during the summer, and one of the marines stationed on this ship was Lieutenant William Peel, son of the prime minister.[36]

The Oregon question also became entwined with the defense of Canada, which had greatly worried the Colonial Office for nearly two years. Although the Americans were constructing iron war steamers on the Great Lakes, the Canadians were apathetic and refused adequate contributions to their own protection. During the fall and winter of 1844–1845 the cabinet had occasionally considered adding fortifications north of the border and to that end ordered a complete survey of defenses in the St. Lawrence Valley.[37]

Sir George Simpson of the Hudson's Bay Company, who happened to be in England when the text of Polk's inaugural address arrived, took advantage of the resulting sensation to urge his own views on the cabinet, asking for more troops and warships and a battery to command the mouth of the Columbia River. Aberdeen

35. John S. Galbraith, "France As a Factor in the Oregon Negotiations," *Pacific Northwest Quarterly*, 44 (April 1953), pp. 69–71. Merk, *Oregon Question*, pp. 352–54. "Memorandum for Lord Haddington in consequence of the Note of Sir Chs. Napier to Sir Robt. Peel," June 9, 1845, Peel Papers, BM, AM, vol. 40458, ff. 57–64. (Haddington was then First Lord of the Admiralty.) On the American Navy, see London *Morning Chronicle*, n.d., quoted in *NNR*, 68 (August 30), 403–4. London *Times*, April 14, p. 6. *NNR*, 68 (May 3, August 16), 130, 384.

36. Earl of Haddington to Peel, February 26, 1844; Peel to Haddington, June 25, July 2, 5, August 5, 11, September 15, 1845, Peel Papers, BM, AM, vol. 40457, ff. 96–97; vol. 40458, ff. 92–93, 100–102, 122–23, 148–49, 159, 191–92. Barry M. Gough, "H.M.S. *America* on the North Pacific Coast," *Oregon Historical Quarterly*, 70 (December 1969), 296. The movements of Seymour's squadron are carefully recorded in his journal. GB, A 50/213.

37. Bourne, *Britain and the Balance of Power*, pp. 125–31.

felt that Simpson exaggerated the danger, but the cabinet authorized Sir George to spend a thousand pounds on defense measures. He crossed the Atlantic in April, and although Pakenham told him in Washington that most Americans wanted to settle the question peacefully, Sir George induced the governor general of Canada to dispatch two army officers on a secret reconnaissance mission to Oregon. Meanwhile, Simpson ordered McLoughlin to use more speed in moving the Company's headquarters out of Fort Vancouver.[38]

While Peel and Simpson looked to Britain's defenses in the Northwest, Aberdeen set out to convince the British public that Oregon was not worth fighting for. Realizing that the officials of the Hudson's Bay Company had lost almost all interest in the area south of Puget Sound, he also recognized the reasonable American need for an outlet on the Sound. Consequently, he joined forces with the free traders and the Baring clique and asked the Whig economist, Nassau Senior, to argue the cause of conciliation. An article over Senior's name but mostly written by American Minister Everett appeared in the London *Examiner* on April 26, declaring Oregon to be useful only "as a hunting ground, which enables the Hudson Bay Company to keep up its monopoly against the English people. . . . The only real point in dispute, therefore, is a point of honor."[39] The favorable reception of this article, especially in the United States, led Senior to publish another in the *Edinburgh Review* for July. Here he argued that each week of interruption in Anglo–American confidence cost businessmen twenty times the value of the disputed territory. After all, he pointed out, many British manufacturing companies employed more persons and capital than the whole Hudson's Bay enterprise.[40]

During May indications of relaxation in British policy began to reach the White House, where Polk and Buchanan were con-

---

38. Joseph Schafer, ed., "Documents Relative to Warre and Vavasour's Military Reconnoissance in Oregon, 1845–6," *Oregon Historical Quarterly*, 10 (March 1909), pp. 5–7. E. E. Rich, *The History of the Hudson's Bay Company, 1670–1870*, II, 723–26. Bourne, *Britain and the Balance of Power*, pp. 134–35. Charles P. Stacey, *Canada and the British Army, 1846–1871*, pp. 20–21.

39. London *Examiner*, April 25, 1845, pp. 269–70. Merk, *Oregon Question*, pp. 287–91.

40. *Edinburgh Review*, 82 (July 1845), 123–37. Merk, *Oregon Question*, pp.

291–96. The *Times* deplored this evidence of Whig disunity on Oregon, arguing that, whatever its intrinsic value, British honor and Pacific commerce justified a strong stand. London *Times*, July 19, p. 4. The *Morning Chronicle* took the same position. London *Morning Chronicle*, July 14, p. 4. The conciliatory effect of Senior's article in the United States was somewhat negated by a simultaneous blast against America in the *Foreign Quarterly*. *United States Magazine and Democratic Review*, 17 (November), 323–31.

sidering how to deal with Pakenham. By now they had fully reviewed Pakenham's negotiations—a procedure Polk should have undertaken before he composed his inaugural statement. On May 12 Buchanan informed the British minister that Polk would definitely reject arbitration. Under pressure from Pakenham, the secretary of state agreed to prepare a proposal as the basis of direct discussion; at the same time he inquired nervously about rumors that Britain had begun to fortify Vancouver Island. On May 21 Buchanan received a dispatch from Everett, belatedly urging arbitration and hinting that if the United States agreed to arbitrate, the British government would doubtless cooperate in finding an arbitrator who would extend the 49° line.[41] Meanwhile, Joshua Bates had informed his Boston friend, William Sturgis, that Aberdeen was amenable to the idea of a boundary along this line if it would give Britain the whole valley of the Fraser River (as it did). On May 25 Sturgis, hoping to play the role of mediator, forwarded the information to Bancroft. Three days later, Buchanan informed Pakenham that he had begun to draft a proposal.[42]

Probably because Polk wanted to select a new minister to Britain and give him time to reach his post, Buchanan did not present any proposal to Pakenham for over six weeks. There is reason to suppose that, even though McLane was Polk's fifth choice for the post, he was selected deliberately for negotiation and compromise, since he was known to oppose fifty-four-forty. According to a close associate, McLane declared to Polk that he deplored the extremism of the preceding Congress and favored a boundary at 49° and even arbitration if necessary.[43] Whether Polk wholly approved of these sentiments, he went ahead with the appointment, and McLane's later correspondence shows that he was supposed to be at his post in London when the American terms arrived so as to discuss them with Aberdeen and, if possible, work out a settlement on the order of that which Everett and Sturgis had

41. Pakenham to Aberdeen, May 13, 1845, Nos. 53, 54, GB, FO 5/426, ff. 9–15, 19–23. Edward Everett to James Buchanan, April 28, No. 307, Manning, CR, III, 955–62. In a later confidential note Everett suggested that rumors of British armament were largely false. Ibid., pp. 962–63. See also Sellers, Polk, Continentalist, pp. 244–45. At the same time, Ashburton was urging that both countries work to create an independent nation on the Oregon coast. Bancroft to Polk, April 27, "Polk corre-

spondence," III, 255, Bancroft Papers, NYPL.

42. William Sturgis to Bancroft, May 25, 1845; Bancroft to Sturgis, June 2; Sturgis to [Joshua Bates], June 16, Bancroft Papers, MHS. Pakenham to Aberdeen, May 29, No. 60, GB, FO 5/426, ff. 45–48.

43. John P. Kennedy to Robert C. Winthrop, June 27, 1845, Robert Winthrop Papers, MHS, as quoted in Merk, Oregon Question, pp. 342–43n13.

suggested. Thus it is apparent that, in the early summer of 1845, both Aberdeen and Polk were prepared to compromise. This interpretation would mean that Buchanan's terms were not a final American concession, as Polk later insisted, but merely a bargaining counter.[44]

If bargaining was what Polk and Buchanan intended, their plans went sadly awry because of their own awkwardness in diplomacy and Pakenham's lack of perception. Both in Buchanan's note of July 12 to the British minister and in a simultaneous dispatch to McLane he emphasized that Polk was making an offer only from a feeling of moral obligation, since Tyler and Calhoun had not responded to the latest British request for terms. He then proposed a boundary along 49° to the Pacific, bisecting Vancouver Island but granting Britain free ports south of that line. The dispatch to McLane indicated that the American government might concede the whole island to Britain, if required, but that Polk was determined not to grant the free navigation of the Columbia River under any circumstances. These terms were certain to be unacceptable to the British, and Buchanan unfortunately discouraged a counteroffer by Britain, since his note to Pakenham restated the American claim to all of Oregon, based on the shaky Spanish title and the incomplete American explorations.[45]

By trying to present the compromise as a gracious American concession rather than a joint abandonment of unreasonable claims, Polk and Buchanan risked a haughty British refusal. Pakenham did not even refer the American proposal to London. Outraged by Buchanan's legal case, he prepared a long refutation, dated July 29. At the end of this note, carried away by his own momentum, he rejected the compromise offer out of hand, on the ground that it was less than Albert Gallatin had offered in 1826.[46] In so doing, Pakenham violated the spirit of Aberdeen's instructions, especially those contained in the important private letter of April 18, and showed himself insensitive to the division of opinion in England.

---

44. This interpretation rests largely on McLane's testimony, principally in later letters to his son. Sellers, *Polk, Continentalist*, pp. 248–50, especially p. 249n67.

45. Buchanan to Pakenham, July 12, 1845; Buchanan to Louis McLane, July 12, No. 2, Manning, *CR*, III, 273–88. The note was presented to Pakenham at a formal "seventh conference" con-cerning Oregon, on July 16, ibid., p. 966. Polk thus preserved the appearance of continuity with Calhoun's six earlier conferences.

46. Pakenham to Buchanan, July 29, 1845, Manning, *CR*, III, 967–75. Pakenham to Aberdeen, September 13, October 29, Nos. 95, 114, GB, FO 5/428, ff. 18–28; 5/429, ff. 55–67.

Just as Buchanan had offended Pakenham, the British minister's reply now offended Polk, who had not been enthusiastic about the offer in the first place and had certainly been led to expect a more favorable reaction. Apparently, he decided at once to withdraw the original offer altogether, but he delayed action for several weeks because of disturbing news—in early August the cabinet received a rumor that Mexico was preparing to launch an attack across the Rio Grande.[47] While skeptical about the rumor, Buchanan advised Polk to postpone a reply to Pakenham and avoid stating the extreme American claim in language that might impel Britain into an alliance with Mexico. Buchanan's advice was reinforced by a private letter from McLane, delivered to Polk on August 19. According to McLane, the British government wished to compromise at 49°—provided that it might retain all of Vancouver Island—but was forced to move slowly because of opposition from the Hudson's Bay Company.[48]

McLane's letter might have indicated a fairly clear way to the settlement reached almost a year later; however, the angry President refused to believe the report, obviously assuming that Pakenham had acted on instructions to trick him.[49] For several days he and Buchanan and probably also other cabinet members exchanged views on Oregon and Mexico. On August 26, even before the threat of a Mexican attack had died down, Polk impatiently laid before the cabinet his earlier determination to withdraw the compromise offer concerning Oregon. Buchanan now agreed reluctantly, but he tried to insert a statement that the United States would discuss any further British proposition. Polk objected that Aberdeen would probably then suggest a line south of 49°, which he could not even consider, and the declaration of withdrawal, dated August 30, remained blunt and curt.[50]

47. The best evidence of Polk's early reaction is a letter of John Y. Mason (acting secretary of state in Buchanan's absence) to McLane, August 12, 1845, Polk Papers, LXXXIX, LC. See also Polk to Buchanan, August 7, Buchanan Papers, box 62, HSP. Sellers, *Polk, Continentalist*, p. 251.

48. Buchanan to Polk, August 11, 1845, Polk Papers, LXXXIX, LC. McLane to [Polk], August 4, David Hunter Miller, ed., *Treaties and Other International Acts of the United States of America*, V, 35–36.

49. Sellers, *Polk, Continentalist*, p. 251. Polk may also have been influenced by a letter he received at this time from his friend Robert Armstrong, American consul at Liverpool, reporting rumors that Britain had a mortgage on California. Robert Armstrong to Polk, August 4, 1845, Polk Papers, LXXXIX, LC.

50. Polk, *Diary*, I, 1–8. Buchanan feared that war would follow and that the American people would not support hostilities for the territory north of 49°. Polk later (November 29, 1845) declared that, had he agreed to a compromise at 49°, the people might well have overturned his administration, so that "as we came in on Texas the

On the same day, the President wrote to Sam Houston that he saw no hope of a treaty unless the Senate should approve terms in advance of signature and that he would "occupy strong and high ground on this question" in his annual message. Bancroft told Sturgis that the basic trouble lay in British jealousy of American advances in both Texas and Oregon, where the British Navy was powerless to halt the settlers: "They could enter a harbor, but how could they occupy it?"[51]

Probably the most deeply disappointed at the impasse was McLane, who had arrived in London at the beginning of August, somewhat weakened by seasickness but ready to negotiate on the basis of Buchanan's proposal to Pakenham. He hoped to return home in time to avoid winter storms on the ocean. On his arrival he found that Aberdeen had gone to the Continent with the Queen on a good-will visit, but McLane soon wrote privately to Buchanan that the Foreign Office had received the terms of Buchanan's offer and had forwarded them to Aberdeen. (At this time the American minister did not know of Pakenham's rejection.) While awaiting Aberdeen's return, McLane talked to other influential persons who happened to be in London. One of these was Joshua Bates of Baring Brothers, who told him of Nassau Senior's conciliatory article in *Edinburgh Review*, inspired by Bates and approved by Aberdeen. Thus McLane became aware not only of the foreign secretary's disposition to compromise the boundary at 49° (a settlement he too favored) but also of the private channel of communication and influence between the British government and Sturgis and Everett.[52]

Before long, however, the American minister was also commenting on an unexpectedly violent current of Yankeephobia in the British press and wondering whether the conciliators had not given Britain an exaggerated impression of American weakness

---

probability was we would have gone out on Oregon." Ibid., p. 107. One beneficial effect of Polk's quarrel with Buchanan was that it determined him to keep a diary of cabinet discussions and other events. Ibid., II, 100–101. For the text of the American withdrawal, see Buchanan to Pakenham, August 30, 1845, Manning, *CR*, III, 288–308. The rest of the note was certainly not curt, for Buchanan restated the American case at even greater length than he had earlier.

51. Polk to Sam Houston, August 30, 1845, Polk Papers, XCI, LC. Bancroft

to Sturgis, August 25, Howe, *Life and Letters of Bancroft*, I, 279–80. Sellers points out that Aaron V. Brown may have put the idea of prior Senate approval into Polk's head and suggests that Polk intended compromise even at this point, but he offers little supporting evidence. Sellers, *Polk, Continentalist*, pp. 253–54.

52. McLane to [Polk], August 4, 1845, Miller, *Treaties and Other International Acts*, V, 35–36. McLane to Buchanan, August 4, 22, September 18, Buchanan Papers, HSP.

and pacifism. If some of his friends in the government also seemed cool, the reason was doubtless that during the summer British policy in North America had suffered a series of setbacks. In June and July it had become increasingly obvious that the United States had a firm grasp on Texas. At the end of July the Colonial Office had received a long report from the governor general of Canada declaring that enormous expenditures and an elaborate offensive plan would be needed to secure the loyalty of the inhabitants.[53] Soon after this a preliminary dispatch arrived from the two army officers whom Simpson had sent on reconnaissance into the interior and who now described a "cordon" of American posts that threatened communications between Canada and Oregon. When Peel saw their dispatch, he decided not to authorize any further expenditure in that area until the officers reported from the West Coast, their ultimate destination.

The news from Canada revived the earlier argument within the cabinet over rearmament. When Aberdeen returned from France, he was so much depressed by the news—and doubtless also by Buchanan's proposal for Oregon—that he momentarily dropped his opposition to warlike preparations in Canada and gloomily admitted that there was real danger in that quarter, whether or not it originated in Oregon.[54] Peel was on the horns of a dilemma —should he leave some part of the widespread empire exposed to grave danger in case of war or, by trying to protect all of it, inflate the national debt? For the moment the colonial secretary, Lord Stanley, met the problem by drawing up an elaborate program of defense measures that were both less expensive and less provocative to the United States than those the governor general had recommended. In mid-September these proposals went out to Canada.[55]

53. Louis McLane to Robert McLane, August 22, 1845, Louis McLane Papers, University of Delaware (microfilm). Louis McLane to Buchanan, August 22, September 3, Buchanan Papers, HSP. The governor general of Canada, Sir Charles (later Baron) Metcalfe, called for two defensive armies of 25,000 each and between 50,000 and 100,000 men to undertake a massive invasion of the United States. Bourne, *Britain and the Balance of Power*, pp. 140–44. Wilbur Devereux Jones and J. Chal. Vinson, "British Preparedness and the Oregon Settlement," *Pacific Historical Review*, 22 (1953), 357–59.

54. Aberdeen to Peel, August 29, 1845,

Peel Papers, BM, AM, vol. 40455, ff. 116–21. Peel to Aberdeen, August 19, Aberdeen Papers, BM, AM, vol. 43064, ff. 264–67. Bourne, *Britain and the Balance of Power*, pp. 144, 149–50. While Aberdeen knew of Pakenham's rejection, he had not learned that Polk had withdrawn his terms.

55. Bourne, *Britain and the Balance of Power*, pp. 145–48. Lord Stanley to Aberdeen, August 18, 1845, Aberdeen Papers, BM, AM, vol. 43072, ff. 137–38. Stanley to Peel, September 1 (enclosing memorandum), 5, 12, Peel Papers, BM, AM, vol. 40468, ff. 353–56, 359–60, 366–70. Peel's statement is quoted in Galbraith, "France As a Factor," pp. 71–72.

Under these circumstances it is doubtful that, even if Mc-Lane had followed his original plan of action, he could have brought the British to terms as he hoped, in time to avoid a winter crossing of the Atlantic. But he was prevented from initiating the plan, for, late in August, a letter from Attorney General Mason gave him his first intimation that Polk intended to withdraw his offer. Surprised and distressed, McLane wrote a private letter to Buchanan on September 3, deploring the impasse and expressing fear that if Britain then offered to arbitrate the Oregon question and the United States refused, Polk would have sacrificed the support of world opinion. More significantly, he added that Calhoun's conciliation had led the British government to expect arbitration, and he described the Yankeephobia voiced in the press. He concluded: "We must fight, & cannot hope to live down their jealousy, their envy, their hostility and their affected contumely & scorn: but when we come to fight, let it be a fight in earnest, & let the world see that we fight in a good & just cause."[56]

McLane soon moderated his view of British enmity, but his letter could only have stiffened Polk's backbone and thus complicated the work of conciliation. Also, as McLane brooded over the administration's abrupt shift in policy, he decided that Polk and Buchanan were trying to undercut his prestige. For the remainder of his stay in England he filled letters to his son Robert with complaints and strong language about the administration.[57]

Aberdeen did not learn until the beginning of October that Buchanan had withdrawn his terms for Oregon. When Pakenham's delayed report finally arrived in London, it produced an exchange of dismal notes between the foreign secretary and the prime minister. Peel did not approve of Polk's offer at all, but Aberdeen had hoped that the American terms might be made acceptable through negotiation. Should negotiation fail, he had expected that Pakenham would maneuver Buchanan into assuming responsibility for breaking off the discussions. Instead, the Americans were now in a position to call on Britain for an initiative that might cause loss of face and bargaining counters. Aberdeen was powerless except to reprove Pakenham for overlooking his plain hint that the negotiations should be kept open

56. McLane to Buchanan, September 3, 1845, Buchanan Papers, HSP. Two weeks later an official dispatch described British rearmament, suggesting that it might be directed at either France or the United States. McLane to Buchanan, September 18, No. 5, Manning, *CR*, III, 978–80.

57. Louis McLane to Robert McLane, September 16, October 10, November 2, 18, 1845, McLane Papers.

as long as possible and to urge his vigilance for any opportunity to start them up again without prejudicing Britain's position.[58]

Pakenham too was extremely distressed at the unexpected effects of his blunder. He tried to defend himself by arguing that Buchanan's proposal had met none of Aberdeen's requirements and that, misled by Everett's advice, the Americans had expected Britain to agree to any terms. At one point in his explanations he pointed out that American policy toward Oregon would probably depend on the outcome of the quarrel with Mexico. If the Americans met trouble in their Mexican relations, they would probably temporize in Oregon; but if they got their way in Mexico, Britain would find them hard to deal with.[59]

*   *   *   *

The origin of the breach in American–Mexican relations during the summer of 1845 was the recent successful annexation of Texas and especially the obligation which the United States thereby assumed to defend the Texan frontier along the Rio Grande. Anson Jones, the last president of Texas, may have exaggerated when he declared that American agents proposed in Polk's name to "manufacture" a war with Mexico (see Chapter 7), but it is certainly true that the administration press struck warlike poses. Early in May, for example, the Washington *Union* heaped scorn on "Mexican gasconading about her pretended rights and pretended wrongs" and denounced her "insolence, stupidity and folly, very little favorable to the cultivation of liberal and conciliatory dispositions on our part. . . . If she now persists in carrying into effect her absurd threats of war, . . . she will exhaust what remains of disposition on our part to deal generously with her."[60]

58. Peel to Aberdeen, October 2, 3, 1845; Aberdeen to Peel, October 3, Aberdeen Papers, BM, AM, vol. 43065, ff. 1–9. Aberdeen to Pakenham, October 3, November 28, Nos. 64, 72, GB, FO 115/89, ff. 109–10, 213–21. Same, October 3, Aberdeen Papers, BM, AM, vol. 43123, ff. 261–62. After hearing Pakenham's explanations, however, both men softened and expressed concern over his distress. Peel to Aberdeen, November 22, BM, AM, vol. 43065, ff. 110–11. Aberdeen to Pakenham, December 3, BM, AM, vol. 43123, ff. 272–73.

59. Pakenham to Aberdeen, September 28, October 29, 1845; separate and confidential, Nos. 114, 115, GB, FO 5/428, ff. 187–92; 5/429, ff. 55–67, 69–74. Same, October 28, December 29, Aberdeen Papers, BM, AM, vol. 43123, ff. 264–70, 274–75. In the last-cited letter Pakenham reported that to his embarrassment Buchanan had offered to have McLane intercede in London to prevent his expected recall. "If you knew what it was to be pitied by such a man as Mr. Buchanan," he added, "you would understand that I could not but take the thing a little to heart."

60. Washington *Union*, May 9, 1845, p. 30.

This combination of defiance and patronizing self-righteousness, the hallmark of Polk's Mexican policy, was probably calculated to force Mexico into negotiations; instead, it added to the humiliation and fury of her war party.

At the same time, in May and June Polk was privately authorizing actions that might well lead to war. In April his chargé d'affaires in Texas, Andrew J. Donelson, had given Houston a general assurance of protection, and during the following weeks he encouraged the Texan government to make an official request for troops. As soon as Donelson reported signs of receptivity among the Texans, Buchanan replied that three thousand American troops would be moved to the border at once. The President, he explained, would "consider it to be both his right and his duty" to defend Texas "against the attacks of any foreign Power" after she had accepted the joint resolution, for she would then have assumed some characteristics of an American state.[61] At the same time, Polk's other agents, Charles A. Wickliffe and Commodore Robert F. Stockton, were promising security from Mexican attack, and Stockton was cruising along the Gulf Coast near Galveston as visible evidence of watchfulness.[62]

In this proffered protection the President always included the disputed territory between the Nueces and the Rio Grande. On June 15 he wrote to Donelson: "Of course I would maintain the Texan title to the extent which she claims it to be & not permit an invading army to occupy a foot of the soil East of the Rio Grande." Having made so firm a commitment to defend Texas, Polk naturally took alarm at reports from Stockton, Wickliffe, and finally from Donelson himself, warning that a Mexican invasion was likely.[63] On the same day that he wrote to Donelson,

61. Buchanan to Andrew J. Donelson, May 23, 1845, No. 7; Donelson to Buchanan, April 12, May 6, No. 18, Manning, *IAA*, XII, 92–93, 400–402, 408–9. Buchanan declared that the position of Texas would be similar to that of a Western territory just before Congress passed the enabling act to convert it into a state—a most dubious analogy. See also William Campbell Binkley, *The Expansionist Movement in Texas, 1836–1850*, pp. 125–26. Sellers, *Polk, Continentalist*, pp. 226–30.

62. Charles A. Wickliffe to Buchanan, May 20, 1845, Manning, *IAA*, XII, 412–15. Wickliffe even suggested the possibility of fighting southwest of the Rio Grande.

63. Polk to Donelson, June 15, 1845; copy in transcribed Polk correspondence, III, 288–90, Bancroft Papers, NYPL. The published version reads, "the Mexican title." St. George L. Sioussat, ed., "Letters of James J. Polk to Andrew J. Donelson, 1843–1848," *Tennessee Historical Magazine*, 3 (1919), p. 68. This is clearly not what Polk meant. On the same day, Buchanan sent a more cautious official dispatch promising protection in general terms but urging the Texans to delay action until their special convention had voted for annexation. Buchanan to Donelson, June 15, No. 9, Manning, *IAA*, XII, 94–97. On the background of these actions and in particular Donelson's reluctance

Polk ordered American troops across the border into Texas and strengthened the naval squadron in the Gulf.

The United States had kept a special "corps of observation" ready for over a year at Fort Jesup, just east of the Sabine River, under the command of General Zachary Taylor. Taylor was a tough, experienced frontier fighter, ill trained in orthodox tactics and rather contemptuous of military ceremony, an attitude that made him popular among his men. Since he was skeptical of the official reason for stationing his force near the border—to guard against Indian attacks—he was probably not surprised to receive an order dated June 15 that directed him to cross the Sabine. He was to encamp along "the [south] western frontier of Texas . . . on or near the Rio Grande del Norte, such a site as will consist with the health of the troops, and will be best adapted to repel invasion, and to protect what, in the event of annexation, will be our [south] western border."[64]

Some historians, suspicious of Polk's motives at every turn, have criticized the vague language of these instructions as a safeguard for the President; by their wording Taylor might be made the scapegoat for the war that would result if Mexico should attack his forces.[65] Considering how little officials in Washington knew about the geography of the area, however, it would seem only good sense for them to have allowed maximum discretion to the field commander. In mid-July Taylor encamped his troops on the south bank of the Nueces River at Corpus Christi—low, marshy ground where they were miserable in heat and cold alike. Although the site was wretchedly uncomfortable for the men, from a political point of view the position was well chosen, for it lay barely within the disputed territory and on the frontier

to claim territory beyond the Nueces see Sellers, *Polk, Continentalist,* pp. 228–29. Frederick Merk refutes at great length Polk's claim to the Rio Grande boundary. Merk, *Monroe Doctrine and Expansionism,* Chap. 6, *passim.* However questionable the title, the fact remains that in every reference to the subject Polk definitely assumed that this was the rightful boundary.

64. Justin H. Smith, *The War with Mexico,* I, 140–41. Brainerd Dyer, *Zachary Taylor,* pp. 144–53. William L. Marcy to Zachary Taylor, May 28, 1845. Bancroft (acting secretary of war) to Taylor, June 15, US, 30C, 1S, HED 60, pp. 79–82. Bancroft to Robert F. Stockton, June 15. Two weeks later Stockton

was allowed to return to the Atlantic coast, and the responsibility for defending Texas was transferred to the Gulf Squadron. Bancroft to David E. Conner, July 11, C. T. Neu, "The Annexation of Texas," *New Spain and the Anglo-American West,* II, 90–91, 93, 94–95. Bancroft ordered Conner not to interfere with Mexican troops already occupying points on the Rio Grande. If Mexico declared war, however, he was to dislodge these troops, occupy Tampico, and, if he had sufficient force, seize Ulua.

65. Richard R. Stenberg, "The Failure of Polk's Mexican War Intrigue of 1845," *Pacific Historical Review,* 4 (March 1935), 65–66.

of effective Texan settlement. The War Department approved Taylor's selection but warned him not to attack any Mexican forces in the disputed area. On July 30, however, it ordered him to "approach as near the boundary line, the Rio Grande, as prudence will dictate." Taylor stayed where he was; by autumn, with reinforcements sent by the Department, he had nearly four thousand men under his command.[66]

Whether the ill-equipped troops were intended as an army of conquest, they certainly did not act like one. After several weeks of summer heat in a Texan swamp, nearly a fifth of the men were on the sick list, and under Taylor's informal discipline the troops became totally disorganized. Nor were their officers any more aggressive. Before leaving Fort Jesup, Taylor had repeatedly denounced the annexation of Texas, and one of his subordinates, Lieutenant Colonel Ethan Allen Hitchcock, declared that to claim the Rio Grande as boundary was "impudent arrogance and domineering presumption."[67] In mid-August, when a false rumor spread that Mexico had declared war, Taylor ordered his officers to "make every preparation for holding Corpus Christi to the last extremity"; a few days later, however, he refused a request from Jones that a few men be sent to defend the outlying settlement of San Antonio. Faced by an enemy, he could not spare them, Taylor explained, but he would train Texan troops if they would enlist in the United States Army.[68] Despite this caution Jones continued to think of Taylor as an *agent provocateur*, and the Whig press at home denounced the move to Corpus Christi as "a taunting aggression, calculated to arouse into activity resentments which otherwise might have remained inert, though smouldering."[69]

There was not much likelihood that Mexican resentment would remain inert, for although the immediate burst of fury

66. Dyer, *Taylor*, Chap. 8. Marcy to Taylor, July 8, 30, August 23, 1845, US, 30C, 1S, HED 60, pp. 82–86.

67. Smith, *War with Mexico*, I, 143–44. Holman Hamilton, *Zachary Taylor, Soldier of the Republic*, pp. 163–68. Ethan Allen Hitchcock, *Fifty Years in Camp and Field*, ed. W. A. Croffut, p. 198.

68. W. W. G. Bliss to Ethan Allen Hitchcock, August 14, 1845, Ethan Allen Hitchcock Papers, LC. Taylor to Adjutant General, August 19; Taylor to Anson Jones, August 16, US, 30C, 1S,

HED 60, pp. 100–102.

69. Jones' account, written later, is too quixotic to be thoroughly convincing. At different points one finds him demanding protection against Mexico and pooh-poohing the Mexican threat. Anson Jones, *Memoranda and Official Correspondence Relating to the Republic of Texas, Its History and Annexation*, pp. 68, 105, 457–58. For the Whig denunciation, see "Will There Be War with Mexico?" *American Review*, 2 (September 1845), 222.

over President Tyler's joint resolution to annex Texas had spent itself by mid-April, resentment continued to flare up occasionally in the capital and the states. President Herrera called a special session of Congress for July 16, but on the preceding day news arrived that the Texan Congress had adopted an annexation law, and the fury broke out once more. Politicians made rash threats, and Foreign Minister Cuevas presented a long series of denunciations against American bad faith.[70] A declaration of war seemed inevitable.

At that point a few wise heads, possibly inspired by British Minister Bankhead, suggested that until American troops actually entered Texas, such a declaration would violate the Mexican–Texan armistice, repudiate the Elliot treaty, and contravene the Mexican–American treaty of 1831. *El siglo XIX*, a moderate liberal newspaper, reminded Congress that it would cost at least five million pesos a year to keep enough troops in the field and asked, where would this money come from? There were twelve or thirteen thousand soldiers in the northern provinces, but these were poorly equipped and were commanded by incompetent officers and generals of dubious loyalty. The navy contained two new steamers and three new gunboats at Veracruz, but the other ships were junk, and all of them, old and new alike, lacked trained crews and even adequate rigging.[71] As for European aid, the government was still at outs with France over the Baño de las Delicias incident, and quarrels were brewing with Britain and Spain. Liberals wanted no dealings with Europe, for in the opinion of Valentín Gómez Farías, England presented almost as great a threat to Mexico's sovereignty as the United States.[72]

Considering these dismal circumstances, and probably also hoping that the Anglo–American quarrel over Oregon would intensify, the ministers decided to wait a little longer. The Council of Government (Consejo de Gobierno) issued a report which

70. Niceto de Zamacois, *Historia de Méjico*, XII, 392–93. Vicente Riva Palacio, *México a través de los siglos*, IV, 542–43. William S. Parrott to Buchanan, June 10, 17, 24, 29, July 5, 12, 15, 19, 22, 1845; John Black to Buchanan, June 10, 21, July 3, 19, Nos. 337–39, 341, Manning, *IAA*, VIII, 724–35, 737–40.

71. *El siglo XIX*, quoted in *NNR*, 68 (July 19, 26, 1845), 306, 324. For budget figures see Wilfrid Hardy Callcott, *Church and State in Mexico, 1822–1857*, pp. 160–61. A thorough summary of the desperate situation in the summer of 1845 is contained in Salvador Bermúdez de Castro to Primer Secretario de Estado, July 29, No. 90, *Rdh-m*, III, 195–200. See also London *Times*, September 9, p. 6.

72. Valentín Gómez Farías to Francisco Vital Fernández, June 4, 1845; typed copy in Valentín Gómez Farías Papers, No. 1194, University of Texas Libraries.

merely proposed that Mexico declare war as soon as annexation became a fact. The minister of finance presented a loan project which would bring $15 million into the Treasury to pay military expenses, but every congressman realized that this plan would require a bond issue of $50 million. According to the *Times* correspondent, when the minister proposed to mortgage the remaining fragment of Mexican customs receipts, the people treated the suggestion as a joke.[73] Nevertheless, Cuevas put on a bold face in his dispatches to Minister Tomás Murphy in London and told him to inform Aberdeen that Mexico would fight to defend her honor.[74] About two weeks later, the Mexican states elected Herrera *de jure* president, and he reshuffled his cabinet. In the ministry of foreign affairs, Cuevas gave way to Manuel de la Peña y Peña, an able lawyer and a moderate liberal whose attitude toward the United States was cautious but conciliatory.[75]

Although news from Mexico during the summer of 1845 was disjointed and often contradictory, the Polk administration had some idea of the situation there. Buchanan had recalled Tyler's hapless minister, Wilson Shannon, who suffered the final indignity of being robbed again on his way to Veracruz.[76] The American consul general in Mexico City, John Black, remained at his post, and in the spring Polk had sent a confidential agent, William S. Parrott, to investigate the possibility of renewing diplomatic relations. Parrott was not a happy choice, since he held an inflated personal claim against the Mexican government.[77] His reports,

73. Parrott to Buchanan, July 22, 26, 30, August 5, 1845; Black to Buchanan, July 24, No. 343, Manning, *IAA*, VIII, 739–45. Report of the Consejo de Gobierno, July 19, US, LC, /67. London *Times*, September 9, p. 6. For the text of the loan authorization as finally passed, see Dublán and Lozano, *LM*, V, 36. The cabinet's information on the Oregon question came chiefly from dispatches written by Almonte before his departure from Washington, by Consul Arrangoiz at New Orleans, and by Minister Murphy in London. Juan N. Almonte to Ministerio de Relaciones, February 4, No. 9; Francisco de Arrangoiz to Ministerio de Relaciones, May 12, 13, Nos. 71, 72, US, LC, /149. Tomás Murphy to Ministerio de Relaciones, May 1, No. 6, Antonio de la Peña y Reyes, *Lord Aberdeen, Texas y California*, pp. 24–26.

74. Luis G. Cuevas to Murphy, July 30, No. 6, Peña y Reyes, *Aberdeen, Tex-*

as y California, pp. 31–32. See also Cuevas to Máximo Garro, July 30, Nos. 15, 16, Barker transcripts, vol. 571, pp. 96–98.

75. Thomas Ewing Cotner, *The Military and Political Career of José Joaquín de Herrera, 1792–1854*, p. 137. Riva Palacio, *México a través de los siglos*, IV, 543–44.

76. *NNR*, 68 (June 14, July 12, 1845), 225, 299.

77. Parrott was a dentist and later a merchant. Historians disagree as to whether Polk knew of his claim. Sellers suggests that the appointment was connected with Polk's determination to use claims for leverage against Mexico, but he has little evidence to show for this. Callahan, *Mexican Relations*, pp. 119, 146–47. McCormac, *Polk*, p. 383. Sellers, *Polk, Continentalist*, pp. 232–34. Waddy Thompson had reported at length and unfavorably on Parrott's claim. Manning, *IAA*, VIII, 524–25. The fullest

which required about a month to reach Washington, gave a reasonably accurate picture of anti-Americanism in Mexico City and the principal actions of the Mexican Congress. While they made clear the internal weakness of Mexico, Parrott and Black could repeat only hearsay about the troops in the north. The faintly remaining possibility of European aid caused a certain amount of uneasiness in the American press during the last stages of Texan annexation. By the end of July some newspapers in New Orleans were reporting rumors that Mexico would send thirty thousand soldiers to the border.[78]

Through the first half of the summer, however, the Polk administration did not expect war, and at the end of July Polk wrote to a friend that Taylor's troops and a squadron in the Gulf would probably prevent any rash acts by Mexico.[79] Nevertheless, a few days later, Baron Gerolt, the Prussian minister at Washington, threw the cabinet into confusion by telling Bancroft that, according to a confidential informant whom he would not identify, General Mariano Arista, then moving into northeastern Mexico, intended to cross the Rio Grande. Other troops in the north were to join him and would presumably overwhelm Taylor's small force.[80]

Buchanan was skeptical about Gerolt's information and suspected that if Herrera had sent troops north, he had done so to forestall an uprising that might interfere with his election as president.[81] However, Polk reacted vigorously to defend what he re-

account of Parrott's claim and career is Ethel Sadie Farabee, "The Career of William Stuart Parrott, Business Man and Diplomat in Mexico," M. A. thesis, University of Texas, 1944. For Buchanan's original instructions to Parrott, dated March 28, 1845, see Manning, *IAA*, VIII, 164–66.

78. Before mid-September Buchanan received over twenty dispatches from Parrott and Black, the last ones dated August 23 and 26. These are reprinted (not always *in toto*) in Manning, *IAA*, VIII, pp. 712–47. The most revealing account of Mexican financial weakness, written on July 12 by Parrott, did not arrive in Washington until September 1. Ibid., p. 737. The August war scare occurred during a gap of about six weeks when almost nothing of importance arrived from either Parrott or Black. For evidences of American uneasiness, see *NNR*, 68 (March 15, June

14, August 23, 1845), 17–18, 225–26, 388. Arrangoiz to Ministerio de Relaciones, July 24, Carlos Bosch García, *Material para la historia diplomática*, p. 518.

79. Polk to A. O. P. Nicholson, July 28, 1845, Polk Papers, NYHS. Bancroft to Henry Wikoff, May 12, Howe, *Life and Letters of Bancroft*, I, 288. Marcy to P. M. Wetmore, July 6, Marcy Papers, ff. 34478–79, LC. McCormac, *Polk*, pp. 376–78.

80. McCormac, *Polk*, pp. 378–80. Polk to Buchanan, August 7, 1845; Bancroft to Buchanan, August 7, James Buchanan, *The Works of James Buchanan*, ed. John Bassett Moore, VI, 223–25.

81. Buchanan to Polk, August 11, 1845, Polk Papers, LXXXIX, LC. Bancroft too became skeptical about Gerolt's information. Bancroft to Buchanan, undated note ("Wednesday Eve."), Buchanan Papers, box 62, HSP.

garded as "virtually a part of our country," recalling Buchanan from vacation and sending all available reinforcements and new instructions to Taylor. If Mexico put "a considerable force" across the Rio Grande, Secretary of War Marcy told the general, "such a movement must be regarded as an invasion of the United States and the commencement of hostilities," and Taylor must make every effort to protect Texas. Later instructions added that even an attempt to cross the river would be considered a hostile act. If Mexico thus provoked war, Taylor might cross the river and attack Matamoros, but "only . . . under circumstances presenting a fair prospect of success." At the same time, Bancroft sent secret orders to Commodore David Conner of the Gulf Squadron. In case of a declared war or a substantial Mexican attack across the Rio Grande, Conner was to blockade the Gulf Coast and even attack Ulua—but, again, only if success seemed highly probable.[82]

While these communications show how far afield Polk's mind was ranging, they bore only contingent instructions. As Polk explained in a letter of August 23 to Vice President George M. Dallas: "Our orders to our troops are to act strictly on the defensive and let the first hostile movement be made by the Mexican army." He told Dallas that he had been advised to call a special session of Congress but was inclined to believe that he had sufficient means at hand to conduct a defensive war until the regular session in December.[83] When Gerolt's rumor reached the cabinet, the Washington *Union* had been supporting the occupation of Corpus Christi against the Whigs' criticisms. On August 23 the *Union* shifted to the more general question in an editorial "Peace or War with Mexico?", and from then until August 29 daily editorials suggested the uncertainty of Mexican policy and the imminence of war.[84]

At the end of the month the crisis subsided, for dispatches arrived from Parrott indicating the dilemma faced by the Mexican Congress and a growing desire for negotiation. Letters from Ban-

82. Marcy to Taylor, August 23, 30, 1845, US, 30C, 1S, HED 60, pp. 84–86, 88–89. Bancroft to Conner, August 30, David Conner Papers, box 13, NYPL. Conner to Bancroft, September 3, 11, US, DN, LCS, File microcopy 89, roll 84, Nos. 108, 112. Sellers, *Polk, Continentalist*, p. 260.

83. Polk to George M. Dallas, August 23, 1845, Polk correspondence, III, 338–42. Bancroft Papers, NYPL. Same, August 28, Polk Papers, XCI, LC. J. Y.

Mason to McLane, August 12, Polk correspondence, III, 336–37, Bancroft Papers, NYPL. Polk also sent an agent to New York to investigate rumors that privateers were being fitted out there for Mexico. The report was negative. George Plitt to Polk, New York, August 28, Polk Papers, XCI, LC.

84. For sample editorials, see Washington *Union*, August 7, 8, 23, 1845, pp. 331, 334–35, 383.

croft's commercial friends confirmed the dispatches.[85] By August 30 Polk believed that the danger of war was declining and that his prompt dispatch of reinforcements to the border would prevent a Mexican attack.[86] Accordingly, on that day he sent Pakenham his withdrawal of the Oregon offer.

Polk's actions toward Britain and Mexico considerably reduced his choice of policies in both areas. By closing the door to negotiations over Oregon, he threw the initiative back upon Britain and made a stalemate inevitable. By declaring that the Rio Grande represented the line between peace and war with Mexico, he left the final choice to the Mexicans and, in effect, dared them to act. Both decisions proved difficult to reverse.

*   *   *   *

During 1845 the Americans' growing interest in California was an important subsurface factor in determining their attitude toward Mexico. It will be recalled that, in December 1844 a group of native Californians, aided by some Americans, had overthrown Governor Micheltorena and set up their own virtually autonomous government. News of these events did not reach the East Coast and England for nearly six months, but even without it American and British newspapers occasionally circulated rumors about rival ambitions in the West. The Americans, declared the London *Times*, "conquer provinces as the cuckoo steals a nest; . . . at no very distant period they will have made themselves masters of all such parts of the North American continent as are not defended by the forces and resolution of Great Britain." [87]

American newspapers quoted such statements as evidence

85. See especially Parrott to Buchanan, July 12, 1845, US, DS, D, Mexico, XII. Same, July 26, Manning, *IAA*, VIII, 741–43. (These dispatches were received on September 1 and August 25, respectively. The first is only partly reprinted in Manning, *IAA*.) William Kemble to Bancroft, August 29, September 3, Bancroft Papers, MHS. Kemble's contact was Peter Hargous, member of an American firm that had long been active in Mexican trade. See also a letter from a friend of Bancroft stationed on one of the American warships off Veracruz. John O. Bradford to Bancroft, August 17, ibid. Sellers attaches some significance to the fact that Parrott's dispatch of July 26 also recommended war for the purpose of acquiring Pacific territory. Sellers, *Polk, Continentalist*, pp. 262–63.

86. Polk to Sam Houston, August 30, Polk Papers, XCI, LC. However, as late as August 28 Polk was still concerned over the likelihood of a Mexican attack on Texas, which Taylor would have to repel. Polk to Dallas, August 28, ibid.

87. London *Times*, April 21, 1845, as quoted in *NNR*, 68 (May 31), 205. See also Norman A. Graebner, *Empire on the Pacific: a Study in American Continental Expansion*, p. 82, although the author does not clearly distinguish between British attitudes at this time and later in the year.

that Britain, having lost the game in Texas, would redouble her efforts to save California. Early in the spring a rumor spread through the press that, before his fall from power, Santa Anna had contracted with British Minister Bankhead to sell the province to Britain and thus discharge Mexico's debt to the British bondholders. Anti-imperialists ridiculed the report and dismissed talk of California as a foolish invitation to "disunion, anarchy, bloodshed and confusion," but some agitation appeared even among the Whigs for the acquisition of California as indemnity for American claims against Mexico.[88]

Although the rumor was not true, it contained enough substance to justify some alarm. During the spring the British consul in Mexico City, Ewen C. Mackintosh, and an Irish missionary, Father Eugene McNamara, worked out apparently separate plans to develop California under generous grants of lands and powers. McNamara proposed to introduce ten thousand Irish colonists as a buffer against American expansion. Both men presented their plans to the Mexican government, which postponed action, and although Bankhead reported on them approvingly to Aberdeen, the British government did nothing to encourage them. Indeed, when the rumor about the sale of California produced a question in Parliament, both Peel and Palmerston denied that their administrations had made any such agreement.[89] Britain opposed American aims in California as in Texas, but the remoteness of the province and lack of confidence in the Mexican government were to form insuperable obstacles to action.

Most historians assume that at his inauguration Polk had already matured a plan for acquiring California, arguing principally on the basis of Bancroft's much later anecdote about his "four great measures." There is little other direct evidence that in

88. Ángel Calderón de la Barca to Primer Secretario de Estado, Washington, March 5, 1845, No. 67, Legajo 5868, Spain, AHN. New York *Evening Post*, February 26, p. 1. New York *Journal of Commerce*, February 20, p. 2; March 5, p. 2. New Orleans *Tropic*, n.d., as quoted in *NNR*, 68 (May 17), 162. Graebner, *Empire on the Pacific*, p. 84.

89. Lester G. Engelson, "Proposals for the Colonization of California by England in Connection with the Mexican Debt to British Bondholders, 1837–1846," *California Historical Society Quarterly*, 18 (June 1939), 144. Hubert

H. Bancroft, *History of California*, V, 215–16. Charles Bankhead to Aberdeen, May 30, July 30, Nos. 51, 74, GB, FO 50/185, ff. 132–40; 50/186, ff. 18–22, 28–30. A full description of the plan was later discovered in the Mexican ministry of foreign affairs when the Americans occupied Mexico City. McNamara intended to found his first three colonies at San Francisco, Monterey, and Santa Barbara. Eugene McNamara to Cuevas, May 17, Nicholas P. Trist Papers, XXV, ff. 60447–50, LC. *Hansard Parliamentary Debates*, 3d series, LXXVIII, 430–32.

April and May he had any more than a general desire for annexation. Naturally, he said nothing of California in his inaugural address or in his initial instructions to Parrott, for Texas, Oregon, and the resumption of diplomatic relations with Mexico were more immediately important.

The only real indication of the administration's interest in California at this time was the decision of the War Department to send John Charles Frémont, the well-publicized explorer, on a third expedition across the Rockies into the Great Basin and possibly into California—in other words, into Mexican territory. The real organizers of the expedition were Bancroft and Senator Thomas Hart Benton, Frémont's father-in-law. Buchanan probably knew most of the details through his friendship with Benton, but apparently Marcy did not. Frémont later declared that the planners realized the possibility of war and that the administration had privately instructed him "if needed, to foil England by carrying the war now imminent with Mexico into the territory of California." Vagueness and controversy were to envelop Frémont throughout this expedition, and his statements in his latter-day reminiscences do not prove that at this time Polk intended any more than peaceful negotiations for the purchase of California.[90]

At the end of May, however, the news of the Californians' revolt against Micheltorena had an electrifying effect on press, public, and the Polk administration. Expansionist editors, led by James Gordon Bennett of the New York *Herald*, Moses Y. Beach of the New York *Sun*, and Thomas Ritchie of the Washington *Union*, burst out in new warnings against British seizure of the province. On June 2, for example, the *Union* came out strongly for peace with Mexico but warned that, peace or war, Northerners and Southerners alike were ready to cry "Westward, ho!": "The road to California will be open to us. Who will stay the march of our western people?"[91] Later in the month, at about the time Polk

90. On the validity of Bancroft's later statement about Polk's aims, see note 2 of this chapter. On the organization of Frémont's expedition and his instructions, see Nevins, *Frémont, Pathmarker*, pp. 202–4. For indications that at this time the Polk administration was probably confident of persuading Mexico to sell California, see Graebner, *Empire on the Pacific*, pp. 111–12; and Van Alstyne, *Rising American Empire*, pp. 139–40.

91. Washington *Union*, June 2, 1845,

p. 111; May 29, June 6, 16, pp. 99, 127, 159. Graebner, *Empire on the Pacific*, pp. 84–86; and Frederick Merk, *Manifest Destiny and Mission in American History, a Reinterpretation*, pp. 81–82. The State Department received first official news of the revolt on May 28. Thomas O. Larkin to Secretary of State, March 24, No. 20, Manning, *IAA*, VIII, 702–3. Concerning California, like Oregon, a segment of the American press urged moderation, and on July 15 the New York *Courier and Enquirer* reordered Taylor to move his troops into Texas, he sent another dispatch to Commodore John D. Sloat, commander of the Pacific Squadron, which, like that of Britain, cruised along the whole west coast of the American continents and into the Pacific as far as Hawaii. In this dispatch Polk declared that if Sloat learned beyond doubt of the outbreak of war with Mexico, he should seize San Francisco at once and blockade as many other California ports as possible.[92]

Without knowing explicitly of Polk's action, the British and French ministers in Washington could guess what might happen. In mid-June Pakenham predicted that war would bring the annexation of California, which he thought would be more generally popular among the American people than the annexation of Texas, since California would not provoke sectional rivalry. French Minister Alphonse Pageot, who exchanged information informally with Pakenham, urged his government not to lag behind Britain in forestalling the "presumptuous heedlessness" of the United States with stern warnings. During the summer of 1845 the new British commander in the Pacific, Admiral Seymour, also anticipated an American effort to seize California, and he instructed Captain John Gordon of H.M.S. *America* to visit the north Pacific coast and to aid the California natives if they should rebel for independence. But he was not to use force unless attacked.[93]

Unaware of the storm clouds gathering around them, the Californians resumed their easy-going life after the momentary excitement of the December revolt. Almost imperceptibly, however, the tension increased, as more ships called at Monterey and the other ports, and as new bands of Americans arrived from the East, to be hospitably received by the tolerant native government.[94] Somewhat prematurely, the diplomatic agents of Britain and France expected a crisis at almost any moment.[95]

So did the American merchant-consul, Thomas O. Larkin,

vived Webster's three-cornered proposal of 1842 for the purchase of San Francisco. Reprinted in London *Times*, August 2, p. 8.

92. Bancroft to John D. Sloat, June 24, 1845, US, 30C, 1S, HED 60, p. 231.

93. Pakenham to Aberdeen, June 12, 1845, No. 67, GB, FO 5/405, ff. 88–92. Alphonse Pageot to François Guizot, June 12, July 15, Nos. 89, 91, quoted in Abraham P. Nasatir, *French Activities in California, an Archival Calendar-Guide*, pp. 74–75. Gough, "H.M.S. *America* on the North Pacific Coast," pp. 298–300.

94. Bancroft, *California*, IV, 524–25, 571, 587–88, 604–7.

95. James A. Forbes to Eustace Barron, March 10, 1845, GB, FO 5/426, ff. 96–98. Barron to Captain John Gordon, June 3, GB, A 1/5562. Consul Guéroult to Minister, Mazatlán, August 13. Quoted in Nasatir, *French Activities*, pp. 182–83.

but he was not wholly confident of inevitable American destiny. He agreed with the European consuls that Mexican authority had virtually disappeared from California, but he accepted as genuine the rumor that Santa Anna had tried to sell the province to Britain, and he assumed that the British would help Mexico to reassert her authority. He was especially suspicious of Hudson's Bay Company officials who, he believed, were financing a Mexican expedition to reconquer California. Accordingly, he used every means to encourage popular support for the autonomous local government and to denounce British influence, for, as he said, "I consider that Peal [sic] and Aberdeen hold more power over the whole world than the united strength of any three or four kings or Empires."[96]

Larkin was wrong about the Hudson's Bay Company, for by 1845 it had almost entirely lost interest in California.[97] Furthermore, with or without British aid Mexico stood no chance of reconquering her province. In the early summer the government announced that it would send six hundred soldiers from Mexico City to Acapulco, there to embark for California, and at considerable expense it assembled transports at Acapulco. During the autumn some of the troops actually set out from the capital, accompanied by so many brass bands that the opposition press accused the government of intending to capture California, like Jericho, with trumpets. By the end of the year the expedition had collapsed. A revolution broke out along the line of march, and the would-be conquerors of California went over to the rebels, bag and baggage.[98]

* * * *

During much of 1845 a considerable part of the American press professed to believe that Britain and France—especially the former—were waiting eagerly to seize California if the Americans lowered their guard and that the two European powers were hoping in the meantime for a crippling war between the United States and Mexico. As the New York *Evening Post* put it in April: "One democracy set to fight another would cause John Bull to rub his hands with glee."[99]

96. Larkin to Dr. John Marsh, Monterey, July 8, August 19, 1845, John A. Hawgood, ed., *First and Last Consul: Thomas Larkin and the Americanization of California*, pp. 24–26, 32–33. The sentence quoted is on p. 33.
97. John S. Galbraith, "A Note on the British Fur Trade in California, 1821–1846," *Pacific Historical Review*, 24 (August 1955), 253–60.
98. Bancroft, *California*, IV, 524–29.
99. New York *Evening Post*, April 30, 1845, p. 1.

European reaction to events in the New World was more complicated than these highly colored fears represented. In December 1844 Aberdeen had drawn up a flat statement of British policy regarding California. Britain would stand aloof as long as Mexico claimed sovereignty or if California sought independence, but she "would view with much dissatisfaction [that is, might intervene to prevent] the establishment of a protectoral power over California by any other foreign state."[100] During the first nine months of 1845 Aberdeen held to this policy. Toward Mexico his attitude was no closer to American suspicions. To be sure, he had done everything in his power to prevent the annexation of Texas by bringing peace between Texas and Mexico. As hope of success faded, however, on May 31 he informed Bankhead in Mexico City that, should the United States annex Texas, Britain and France would "consider themselves entirely absolved from all further interference in the affairs of Mexico with reference to the United States."[101] His actions concerning Oregon seem to have been motivated by concern for British honor and legal rights and a respect for British public opinion rather than by a sense of genuine British interest in the disputed area. On the whole, it would be fair to say that, once the Texas question was settled, Aberdeen accepted the situation in North America and preferred that it be unchanged.

In France, meanwhile, the political situation in the Western Hemisphere became a point of contention between the administration of François Guizot and the liberal opposition. As fellow Latins the French suffered some pangs to see the Mexicans menaced by the Anglo–Saxon horde, but the liberal Mexican José M. L. Mora wrote home from Paris that the French despaired of Mexican leadership, stability, and honesty and looked on the government's threats as the impotent ravings of a nation uninstructed in diplomacy.[102] Opposition newspapers resented Guizot's efforts to cooperate with Britain in solving the Texas question, partly because they felt that Britain had coldly ignored their just complaints against Mexico and partly because they rejoiced to see proud, deceitful Albion suffer defeat.[103] Their repeated accusations that Britain was arming Mexico against the United States were wholly wrong, but since these were sometimes reprinted in

100. Aberdeen to Barron, December 31, 1844, GB, FO 50/179, ff. 9–12. Reprinted in Ephraim Douglass Adams, *British Interests and Activities in Texas, 1838–1846*, p. 248.

101. Aberdeen to Bankhead, May 31, 1845, No. 18, GB, FO 50/183, ff. 50–52.

102. *La presse*, March 3, 1845, p. 1. José M. L. Mora to Gómez Farías, Paris, May 20, Gómez Farías Papers, No. 1182.

103. *Le national*, March 18, 1845, pp. 1–2; April 17, p. 2; April 18, p. 1; May 11, p. 1; May 18, p. 2.

the United States, they helped to increase Anglo–American tension.

The pricking of the opposition press irritated the French government, which doubtless felt that France had real and valuable interests to develop on the Pacific coast. As a result, the government press further played into the hands of American nationalists by publicizing European concern for California. During the preceding year the government had published an extensive travel account by Eugène Duflot de Mofras, extolling the resources of California, and in February 1845 a review of the book in *Le journal des débats* bemoaned France's loss of Canada and asked rhetorically if England and the United States proposed to shut her out of the Golden West too. A few months later the *Journal*, reporting the news of Andrew Jackson's death, took the opportunity to deplore American expansionism again and predicted that, as the United States conquered all of North and Central America, it might split into sections and slavery be thereby perpetuated: "What a pedestal for the memory of a man!"[104]

Americans might take these journalistic effusions lightly, but they could no more ignore an official statement by Guizot than Britain could ignore Polk's inaugural address. In July an opposition leader in the Chamber of Deputies charged the government formally with having joined England in an effort to prevent the annexation of Texas. Guizot denied this, declaring that Texas had the right, as a sovereign state, to renounce her independence without interference from other parties, but that if Texas had preferred independence, France would have welcomed this decision. He went on:

[France's interest in the New World] is that the independent states remain independent, that the equilibrium of forces between the great masses which divide America continue, that no one of them become exclusively predominant. In America, as in Europe, by reason of our political and commercial interests we need independence, an equilibrium of the several states. This is the essential idea which ought to determine the policy of France in America. . . . She is not called upon to compromise herself, to bind herself regarding difficulties of the future; but it behooves her to protect by the authority of her name the independence of states and the maintenance of an equilibrium of the great political forces in America.[105]

104. *Le journal des débats*, February 26, 1845, p. 3; June 30, pp. 1–2; July 15, pp. 1–2.
105. This version is Frederick Merk's translation of the official report that appeared in *Le Moniteur*, June 11, 1845. Merk, *Monroe Doctrine and American Expansionism*, pp. 50–51.

Guizot spoke frankly but with moderation. Inasmuch as France had broken relations with Mexico over the Baño de las Delicias incident, kept few warships in American waters, and maintained only a small vice consulate in California, her threat might have seemed ridiculous. Nevertheless, as American newspapers reported his speech, they began to translate his carefully chosen words *"équilibre des forces"* as "balance of power," a phrase that had come to symbolize the treacherous dealings of decadent monarchies. To this expression they overreacted, just as Britain had overreacted to Polk's inaugural statement on Oregon. The outcry in the United States against the balance of power drew once again from the French opposition the charge that Guizot had sacrificed to his British masters "an old and useful alliance" with the United States.[106]

For the rest of the summer the European press speculated on the likelihood of a war between the United States and Mexico. Although some of the French opposition continued to accuse Britain of inciting Mexico to fight, the quasi-official organs in both countries opposed war, mainly because it would give the United States an excuse to seize California, which Mexico could not possibly defend. A few were pessimistic about the Americans' chances of success if they actually invaded Mexico, but no one had a good word to say for the Mexicans. Their valor, sneered the *Times*, "continues to decrepitate in proclamations." Both the *Times* and *Le journal des débats* advised Mexico to forget Texas and deplored her warlike posturings as electioneering devices, typical weaknesses of democratic government.[107]

---

106. Compare, for example, the version of Guizot's remarks appearing in *NNR*, 68 (July 5, 1845), 273. The French minister in Washington reported fully and complacently on the American outburst. Pageot to Guizot, July 15, No. 91, France, MAE, CP, Etats-unis, CI, ff. 109–13. See also the summary of American press opinion in *NNR*, 68 (July 12), 289. *Le constitutionnel*, July 18, p. 2. Merk, *Monroe Doctrine and American Expansionism*, pp. 51–60.

107. *Le constitutionnel*, August 14, 1845, p. 1. *La presse*, August 14, pp. 1–2; August 15, p. 1; September 3, p. 1; September 4, p. 1; September 12, p. 1; September 13, pp. 1–2. *Le journal des débats*, September 20, p. 1; September 24, p. 1. *NNR*, 69 (September 6), 16.

London *Times*, September 1, p. 4. Charles Elliot was especially pessimistic about the ability of the American forces to attack. Charles Elliot to Bankhead, New Orleans, July 3. Elliot to Aberdeen, New York, August 31. He thought that the real danger to Mexican territory was through migration. Elliot to Aberdeen, Galveston, June 15, No. 18, Ephraim Douglass Adams, ed., *British Diplomatic Correspondence Concerning the Republic of Texas, 1838–1846*, pp. 513–15, 543–47. Despite much doubt in Europe that there would be war, insurance premiums at Lloyd's on ships to America rose sharply, because of the fear that Mexico would commission privateers. *NNR*, 69 (September 27), 49.

*   *   *   *

Historians have found the first six months of the Polk administration a difficult period to interpret. Why should a new President, however self-confident and ambitious, go out of his way to create trouble simultaneously with two foreign countries—with Mexico by stationing troops in disputed territory and with Britain by withdrawing a compromise offer before Aberdeen and Peel could consider it? As already indicated, some historians answer the first part of the question by arguing that Polk was trying to provoke a Mexican attack on the United States, anticipating his successful maneuver of April 1846. According to this argument, Commodore Stockton was acting under official instructions in proposing to President Jones that Texas "manufacture" a war with Mexico and bring it with her into the Union. When this plan failed, declares one historian, Polk ordered Taylor beyond the Nueces in vague language that would enable him to shift the responsibility to the general if necessary, only to find that the cautious Taylor would not advance beyond Corpus Christi without explicit instructions to do so.[108]

This interpretation is open to serious criticism. It is reasonable to suspect that Stockton may have plotted aggressive action with Texan expansionists during his brief visit of May and June 1845, although many details of his intrigue remain sketchy. However, the idea that Polk directed or authorized his actions rests on surmise. When Bancroft became aware of Stockton's activities, he cautioned him to "avoid every act that can admit of being construed as inconsistent with our friendly relations [with Mexico]." On June 15 Buchanan emphatically warned Donelson that the Texans should not try to occupy the disputed territory until their convention (called for July 4) had formally approved annexation. In the meantime, as Bancroft told Stockton, the Texans "should be *encouraged* to repel" an invasion by Mexico.[109]

108. Stenberg, "Failure of Polk's Intrigue," pp. 39–68, *passim*; "Polk and Frémont, 1845–1846," *Pacific Historical Review*, 7 (1938), 211–27, *passim*. Glenn W. Price, *Origins of the War with Mexico: the Polk-Stockton Intrigue*, pp. vii–x, 9–13, 47–48, *et passim*.

109. Bancroft to Stockton, April 22, June 2, 15, 1845, Neu, "Annexation of Texas," II, 79, 88–91. Italics in original. Buchanan to Donelson, June 15,

No. 9, Manning, *IAA*, XII, 94–97. Sellers, *Polk, Continentalist*, pp. 225–26. In case an invading force should try to prevent or disrupt the Texan convention, Bancroft instructed Stockton to "regard such an attempt as an aggression on the United States, and . . . act accordingly, after consulting Mr. Donaldson [*sic*]." Neu, "Annexation of Texas," II, 91. On May 20 Polk's agent in Texas, Charles A. Wickliffe, did in-

Further evidence reinforces the conviction that Polk was not trying to provoke a Mexican attack during the spring of 1845. Buchanan solemnly assured the departing Mexican minister, Juan N. Almonte, and his own confidential agent in Mexico, William S. Parrott, that although the annexation of Texas was beyond question, the United States wished to reestablish diplomatic relations with Mexico and settle differences.[110] Polk confirmed this view in a letter to his friend Senator William H. Haywood of North Carolina:

> Care has been taken—that all our military and naval movements shall be strictly defensive.—We will not be the aggressor upon Mexico;—but if her army shall cross the Del Norte and invade Texas, we will if we can drive her army—to her own territory. Less than this—in good faith to Texas, I think this government could not have done. We invite Texas to unite her destinies with our own. She has accepted the invitation, upon the terms proposed, . . . and if because she has done so, she is invaded by the Mexican Army—surely we are bound to give her our aid in her own defence.[111]

These are not the words of a man who would rather fight than negotiate. Instead, Polk's every action in foreign affairs, beginning with his inaugural address, indicates that he preferred to take a bold stance at the outset in order to negotiate from a position of strength, real or apparent. This being the case, it was logical for him to send Parrott to inquire about the possibilities of negotiation and, hearing rumors of Mexican attack, to occupy at least part of the territory he intended to gain. From March through July all evidence from Polk and his cabinet suggests that no one expected Mexico to attack. Gerolt's confidential information caused a brief flurry of genuine surprise and hasty preparations that were entirely defensive. Instead of ordering Taylor to advance, Marcy instructed him to wait until the Mexicans crossed the Rio Grande. As for Taylor, instead of cautiously resisting involvement, by September he was telling his officers that if new orders did not come soon, he would advance without them.[112]

---

deed suggest to Buchanan that at Polk's recommendation the Texan Congress would readily direct troops to "expel all Foreign power west of the Rio Grande." But Wickliffe made the suggestion with reserve and clearly lacked prior instructions on that point. Ibid., pp. 85–86.

110. Buchanan to Almonte, March 10, 1845; Buchanan to Parrott, March 28, Manning, *IAA*, VIII, 163–66.

111. Polk to William H. Haywood, August 9, 1845, Polk Papers, LXXXIX, LC.

112. When Hitchcock warned Taylor that Polk might hold him responsible, the general replied that he would accept responsibility and that if told to use his discretion, he would leave for the Rio Grande at once without orders. Hitchcock, *Fifty Years*, pp. 200, 202–3. When Taylor suggested an advance in

The object of the intrigue that "plot historians" have posited was, of course, California. Without knowing of the revolt against Micheltorena, Polk sent Frémont on an exploring expedition which had some aspects of military reconnaissance, but this action, too, was consistent with his policy of negotiating from a strongly established position. The news of the revolt, coming as it did after rumors of a Mexican attack along the Rio Grande, simply added one more preparation for a possible war—the orders to Sloat.

Perhaps the strongest objection to the plot thesis is Polk's handling of the Oregon question. If the President intended to provoke a Mexican attack and war, why should he not temporize with Britain, continue negotiations, use them to pacify Western sentiment for the time being, and postpone a decision until the war with Mexico was over? By the same token, if he wished to protect California for future American expansion, why not encourage a compromise settlement over Oregon and insulate San Francisco from the nefarious influence of the Hudson's Bay Company with a belt of United States territory from 42° to 49°?

Two conclusions would seem inescapable. First, Polk did not want or seriously expect war with Mexico during the first five months of his administration, and even after he learned of Gerolt's rumor, he continued an essentially defensive policy. Second, he was improvising much of his policy as events developed.[113] When he entered the White House, Western politics seemed to require a strong statement on Oregon, and the ticklish state of negotiations with Texas seemed to require a gesture of conciliation toward Mexico. A few weeks later, the barrage of angry editorials from Britain and private indications of conciliation in the British cabinet made it advisable to resume the Oregon negotiations at the point where Calhoun had left them. At the same time, news from Mexico and California impelled Polk to assume a strong although essentially defensive stand and to prepare for a possible attack.

By early July the fury in Britain over Polk's inaugural address had died away and with it the immediate pressure for compromise. At this point two European darts stung the sensitive, nationalistic President—Pakenham's haughty rejection of his reluctantly proffered terms for an Oregon settlement and Guizot's statement about an "equilibrium of forces" in the Western Hemisphere. Polk at

---

a dispatch of October 4 to the adjutant general, he used much milder language, US, 30C, 1S, HED 60, pp. 107–9.

113. Merk suggests that during 1845 Polk pursued "a conscious policy of alternating pressures" against Mexico and Britain. Merk, *Manifest Destiny and Mission,* p. 66.

once decided to break off negotiations with Pakenham and to resume the bold stance of his inaugural; as soon as Baron Gerolt's rumor about Mexican attack began to fade, he directed Buchanan to draw up a blunt note in response to Pakenham's action. Guizot's statement turned Polk's mind again to the invocation of the Monroe Doctrine that he had deleted from his inaugural address, but he chose to hold his fire for a few more months—until his annual message to Congress in December.

At a cabinet meeting on August 26, after Polk had impressed his decision to withdraw the terms proffered for Oregon, he summed up his intentions in characteristic terms: "We should do our duty towards both Mexico and Great Brittain [sic] and firmly maintain our rights, & leave the rest to God and the country."[114] Whatever God might think of Polk's bold, improvised policy, it was certain that the country would not come to any agreement on it. The President's inaugural address and the rupture of negotiations with Britain encouraged Western expansionists to expect fifty-four-forty,[115] while Taylor's advance to Corpus Christi led the Texans to expect the Rio Grande and perhaps more. Any sort of compromise was likely to strike extremists as betrayal. Meanwhile, Calhoun's faction and many others inveighed against war, especially with Britain. By September 1845 Polk, the master strategist of domestic party politics, was releasing forces that might tear his party and the country asunder if he could not appease them with satisfactory negotiations.[116]

114. Polk, *Diary*, I, 4–5.

115. Early in August a mass meeting of two or three thousand persons, one of the largest ever held in southern Illinois, passed by acclamation resolutions in favor of fifty-four-forty and no compromise. John Law to Polk, Vincennes, Indiana, August 11, 1845, Polk Papers, LXXXIX, LC.

116. Sellers comes to a different conclusion regarding the rupture of negotiations, believing that Polk's withdrawal was necessary to "jog Peel and the British Cabinet out of their firmly rooted position on the Columbia River." Sellers, *Polk, Continentalist*, p. 258.

10

Polk Tightens the Screws

At the beginning of September 1845 every actor in the complex international drama seemed to pause briefly, as if waiting to see what the others would do. Recovering from his alarm at Baron Gerolt's rumors of Mexican attack, Polk had renewed his defensive orders to General Zachary Taylor and Commodore David E. Conner, instructing them respectively to cross the Rio Grande and to blockade the Gulf Coast, but only if the Mexicans moved first.[1] Polk thought that the mere show of force would prevent the Mexicans from attacking. The Virginia Whig, William S. Archer, who had consistently opposed the annexation of Texas lest it bring war with Mexico, agreed with Polk and approved the orders.[2] During the same week, Taylor in Corpus Christi was sending a confidential agent across the Rio Grande to reconnoiter the situation in Matamoros. Both the agent and the American consul there felt that war was unlikely and that if it did come, the northern tier of Mexican states would probably secede. It was rumored, however, that three thousand men were marching on Matamoros from the south, and American newspapers expressed concern for Taylor's safety.[3]

Rumors of troop movements in the north were as ominous to the Herrera government in Mexico City as to Taylor and his army, for in early September General Mariano Paredes y Arrillaga at San Luis Potosí controlled the northern forces, and no one knew whether he would decide to march north against the Americans

1. William L. Marcy to Zachary Taylor, August 23, 30, 1845, US, 30C, 1S, HED 60, pp. 84–86, 88–89. George Bancroft to David Conner, August 30, Conner Papers, box 13. Conner to Bancroft, September 3, 11, US, DN, LCS, file microcopy 89, roll 84, Nos. 108–12.

2. James K. Polk, *The Diary of James K. Polk during His Presidency, 1845 to 1849*, ed. Milo M. Quaife, I, 8–10, 13. James K. Polk to Robert Armstrong, September 13, 1845, Polk Papers, XCII, LC. Some newspapers that had resisted the annexation of Texas to the end, such as the Albany *Argus* and the New York *Evening Post* (both followers of

Van Buren), were now supporting decisive action against Mexico, while the Charleston *Mercury*, a former leader of the pro-Texan bloc, was moving toward pacifism. See a press survey in Washington *National Intelligencer*, September 4, p. 3; September 5, p. 3.

3. Taylor to Adjutant General, September 6, 1845, US, 30C, 1S, HED 60, pp. 105–6. On anxiety concerning Taylor, see *NNR*, 69 (September 13), 19–20. However, later issues collected reassurances that war was unlikely. Ibid. (September 20, October 4), pp. 33–35, 73–74.

or south against his own government. President Herrera was in no position to resist an uprising, for only the moderate liberals supported his conciliatory policy. A large faction of radicals (*puros*), for which Valentín Gómez Farías was the chief spokesman, suspected him of disloyalty and called for last-ditch resistance to American encroachments. The American consul in Mexico City, John Black, expected a military junta to seize power at any moment, but Polk's agent there, William S. Parrott, thought that the time had come to renew negotiations, for Mexico had neither the money nor the spirit for war. The much-vaunted military appropriations bill, he wrote, "*sleeps* in the Chamber of Deputies, where it will not soon be disturbed. . . . The Government and press have boasted so much, that they have to taper off gradually; consequently appearances of *fight* must be kept up for a *while*; but . . . an *amicable arrangement*, is in the mouth of every one who speaks on the subject."[4]

Anglo–American relations, though more amicable, also provided some grounds for concern. Polk and Buchanan had withdrawn their offer of terms in the Oregon question, and they felt that the Senate would probably reject any proposition Britain was likely to advance.[5] Pakenham had not yet informed the Foreign Office of this new, unwelcome development, so each government was waiting for the other's move. In London the cabinet was conducting a full discussion about the security of Canada, without much likelihood that it would spend any great sum thereon. During September the Admiralty sent an officer, who posed as a tourist in the United States, to examine American defenses along the Great Lakes.[6]

---

4. Parrott to Buchanan, August 26, September 2, 4, 1845; John Black to Buchanan, September 2, Manning, *IAA*, VIII, 746–50. The quotation appears on p. 748 (italics in original). As no military junta appeared, Black filled his correspondence during September with assurances that the Herrera government had no intention of declaring war against the United States. See, for example, Black to John Beldin (in Durango), September 20, US, DS, PR, Consulate, Mexico City, Letterbook IV, 137–38. The American consul at Veracruz had also "come to the conclusion, that all is talk and no cider." Enclosed with Conner to Bancroft, September 10, No. 23, US, DN, LSC, roll 84. See also F. M. Dimond to Buchanan, Sep-

tember 1, 9, Nos. 260, 261, US, DS, CD, Veracruz, V; and Dimond to J. McCluny, September 8, Conner Papers, box 2. The warship *Princeton* spent five days at Veracruz, September 10–15. On her return to Pensacola, one of her officers wrote a similar account of Mexican conditions. James S. Biddle to Conner, September 20, ibid., box 1.

5. Buchanan to Louis McLane, September 13, 1845, Polk Papers, XCII, LC.

6. Despite pressure from the Hudson's Bay Company and from militarists in the British government, the armament of Canada never kept pace with defense measures at home during the winter of 1845–1846. Kenneth Bourne, *Britain and the Balance of Power in*

In the Pacific Admiral Seymour rotated the ships of his little squadron between coastal ports and islands while trying to anticipate American actions in California. Near the end of August H.M.S. *America* arrived at the mouth of the Columbia River. Captain Gordon, Aberdeen's brother, reconnoitered the coastal area, but his attitude could scarcely have encouraged officials of the Hudson's Bay Company. "He does not think the country worth five straws," one of them wrote later, "and is surprised that [the] Government should take any trouble about it. He . . . told me plainly that we could not expect to hold the entire country." Like Seymour, Gordon suspected that the Americans were encouraging settlement in order to seize California.[7]

*   *   *   *

Fragmentary news from Mexico might indicate that the weak, exhausted Herrera administration hoped to negotiate its way out of trouble, but how could a proud government take the initiative, especially under the watchful eyes of its nationalist opposition? British Minister Charles Bankhead suggested asking Pakenham in Washington to intervene unofficially.[8] Because of Polk's attitude toward Britain at the time, however, such a move would probably have done more harm than good.

Fortunately, this indirection proved unnecessary, for in mid-September the State Department received a dispatch from Parrott, stating his firm belief that an American envoy "possessing suitable qualifications for this Court, might with comparative ease, settle, *over a breakfast*, the most important national question" and that he would be "hailed with joy," although the government could not act directly, because of the opposition.[9] On September 16 Polk and the cabinet discussed this dispatch, along with others from

North America, 1815–1908, pp. 145–49, 153–67. C. J. Bartlett, *Great Britain and Sea Power, 1815–1853*, p. 175. Sir H. Pelly to Earl of Aberdeen, December 1, 1845, Aberdeen Papers, BM, AM, vol. 43245, ff. 119–20.

7. Admiral Sir George Seymour, Journal, GB, A 50/213, f. 144v. Barry M. Gough, "H.M.S. *America* on the North Pacific Coast," *Oregon Historical Quarterly*, 70 (December 1969), 300–304. E. E. Rich, *The History of the Hudson's Bay Company, 1670–1870*, II, 727. See also Gordon's report to the Admiralty, October 19, Leslie M. Scott, "Report of

Lieutenant Peel on Oregon in 1845–46," *Oregon Historical Quarterly*, 29 (March 1928), 66–71.

8. Charles Bankhead to Richard Pakenham, October 16, 1845, GB, FO 5/429, ff. 100–102. Bankhead to Aberdeen, September 29, No. 94, GB, FO 50/186, ff. 209–17. Penciled question marks in the margin of this dispatch suggest that someone in the Foreign Office may have felt that Bankhead went too far.

9. Parrott to Buchanan, August 26, 1845, Manning, *IAA*, VIII, 746–47 Same, August 29, US, DS, D, Mexico, XII.

the American consuls at Mexico City and Veracruz which seemed to confirm Parrott's views. They decided to send a minister with instructions to negotiate a boundary agreement. He was to offer as much as $40 million if Mexico would accept a line along the Rio Grande and south of New Mexico and Upper California. The mission would necessarily remain a profound secret, of course, for if the British and French ministers at Washington learned of it, Polk feared that their governments would take immediate steps to frustrate it.[10]

For this delicate and important task Polk and the cabinet made a reasonably good choice—John Slidell, a rising Louisiana politician with fluency in Spanish and a reputation for prudence and excellent manners. Tall and impressive looking, with a dome-like brow, a square chin, and crafty eyes, Slidell later became a leading Southern nationalist and a close political ally of Buchanan, whom he helped to the Presidency. Polk had considered him for the mission as early as April or May. When Slidell was officially informed of his appointment in September, he told Buchanan that he had never expected war with Mexico and regarded that government's pronouncements as rodomontade, but he also doubted that Herrera would dare negotiate.[11] Apparently Polk's idea was to send Slidell off at once, but after the cabinet had agreed on his appointment, Buchanan produced some New Orleans newspapers that reported warlike threats from the Mexican government. On the next day the cabinet agreed to inform Slidell privately of his selection and reconnoiter further the practicality of the mission.

Accordingly, Buchanan instructed Consul Black in Mexico City to find out from the Mexican government whether it would receive "an Envoy from the United States entrusted with full power to adjust all the questions in dispute between the two Governments." In the curt self-righteousness characteristic of Polk, Buchanan added that, according to etiquette, Mexico, having broken relations, should make the first steps to renew them but that the United States, eager for peace, would "waive all ceremony

10. Polk, *Diary*, I, 33–35.
11. George Lockhart Rives, *The United States and Mexico, 1821–1848*, II, 67. Allan Nevins, *Ordeal of the Union*, II, 353. Nevins, *The Emergence of Lincoln*, I, 78. John Slidell to Buchanan, April 21, May, September 25, 1845, Buchanan Papers, box 24, HSP. George Ticknor Curtis, *Life of James Buchanan, Fifteenth President of the United States*, I, 591–92. Slidell reminded Bankhead's wife of an English country squire; she said that there was nothing American in his manner. Mrs. M. H. Bankhead to Sir Charles R. Vaughan, December 29, Sir Charles R. Vaughan Papers, file C, All Souls College, Oxford.

and take the initiative."[12] These instructions did not arrive in Mexico City until early October.

The Herrera government was now beset from all sides. The French minister, at outs with the government over the Baño de las Delicias incident, received his passports and left the country. Editorials and articles in British newspapers sent to Mexico destroyed any remaining hope of foreign aid in the recovery of Texas. The official Mexican journal blustered about Texas and national honor, to be sure, but at the Independence Day celebrations on September 16 it was noticed that Herrera's address contained no reference to the lost province. On the domestic scene, banditry and violence spread across the country, and amid rumors of civil war Paredes petitioned the government for more funds.[13]

Such was the situation in Mexico on October 10 when Black received Buchanan's instructions. He had a confidential interview the following day with Foreign Minister Manuel de la Peña y Peña, who immediately reported the gist of the conference to Bankhead. Encouraged by the British minister, Herrera and Peña agreed to receive "the commissioner of the United States, who may come to this Capital, with full powers from his Government, to settle the present dispute, in a peaceful reasonable and honourable manner." The government of Mexico hoped that the commissioner would have proper dignity and prudence and that his proposals would be discreet and moderate. Indirectly, the Mexicans informed Bankhead that among past American ministers they would be happy to receive Waddy Thompson but not Joel Poinsett or Anthony Butler. Peña told Black that Parrott and Commodore Conner of the Gulf Squadron would be equally unacceptable. He also demanded that the United States remove its squadron from Veracruz before the envoy arrived. Black sent home the correspondence and reported the courteous nature of his reception, but he commented indignantly that the Mexicans' promise of secrecy was not worth much, since they had informed Bankhead about the American proposal.[14] While Black waited for further

12. Polk, *Diary*, I, 35–36. Polk to Slidell, September 17, 1845, Polk Papers, XCII, LC. Buchanan to Black, September 17, 1845, Manning, *IAA*, VIII, 167–69.

13. Parrott to Buchanan, September 4, 6, 13, 18, 25, 29, October 4, 11, 1845; Black to Buchanan, October 9, No. 349, Manning, *IAA*, VIII, 750–60. Each one

reported to Buchanan his lack of confidence in the other, apparently fearing that Buchanan might appoint the other special envoy. Parrott to Buchanan, October 11; Black to Buchanan, October 18, ibid., pp. 760–61, 766–67.

14. Black to Manuel de la Peña y Peña, October 13; Peña y Peña to Black, October 15; Black to Buchanan,

instructions from Washington, he used his authority to order the American warships out of Veracruz, as a sign of good faith.

To all appearances the United States and Mexico had reopened the diplomatic channels with remarkable ease, but a semantic misunderstanding remained to clog the flow of negotiations. Peña's note had specified that Mexico would receive a "commissioner [*comisionado*] . . . to settle the present dispute," which evidently meant the annexation of Texas. Polk and the cabinet intended to send "a Minister"—by which it was soon clear they meant a regular minister plenipotentiary—to settle all questions outstanding between the nations and to purchase California if possible.

Since the Mexican government eventually based its refusal to receive Slidell on his erroneous title and credentials, it is important to examine how the misunderstanding came about. Parrott's dispatch of August 26 had mentioned "an Envoy"—a more general term—as did Bankhead in his report to Pakenham of his private discussions with Peña. Both Bankhead and Peña seemed to attach more importance to the identity of the American diplomat than to his title, and the Mexican reference to previous American ministers blurs the later distinction. Bankhead even explained away the "rather dictatorial style" of Peña's message as mere formality.[15] However, Benjamin E. Green, formerly secretary to the legation in Mexico City but then in Washington, seems to have warned the State Department that no Mexican administration, having once broken relations, would dare lose face by receiving a regular minister plenipotentiary without some concession or gesture of apology from the United States. Historians have cast doubt on Green's testimony, since he did not mention his warning until much later, but it is worth noting that in May 1846 Joel Poinsett wrote to Van

October 17, 18, 28, Nos. 350, 351, 352, Manning, *IAA*, VIII, 761–68. Black to Dimond, October 18, US, DS, PR, Consulate, Mexico City, Letterbook IV, 156–58. Bankhead to Pakenham, October 16; Peña y Peña to Bankhead, October 15; Bankhead to Aberdeen, October 30, No. 104, GB, FO 5/429, ff. 100–105, 111–14; 50/187, ff. 94–98.

15. Bankhead apparently misunderstood the Mexicans, for Peña y Peña carefully specified a *comisionado* in his letter to the British minister. Peña y Peña to Bankhead, October 15, 1845, GB, FO 5/429, ff. 113–14. Black too felt that much of the punctilio in Peña's

note was intended to assuage public opinion. As late as November 12 he wrote to a correspondent in Chiapas that American affairs looked quite favorable: "This Government has consented to receive an Envoy from the United States empowered to adjust all differences between the two countries and we may expect a Minister here from the United States by the first of January. . . ." Black to Dimond, October 18; Black to James C. A. McKinney, November 12, US, DS, PR, Consulate, Mexico City, Letterbook IV, 156–58; 174.

Buren that he had given someone in the Polk administration identical advice.[16]

A fine point, perhaps, but the Latin Americans were extremely punctilious, and Mexican sensitivities were already heightened. Polk's newspaper, the Washington *Union*, gave further evidence of the thinking within the administration in an editorial that ridiculed Mexico's "braggadocio threats" and then suggested that if she did not negotiate, Congress would probably declare war and "call all the military powers of the people to rally under the eagles of the republic."[17] One may fairly conclude that Polk had some idea of the semantic distinction involved in Slidell's appointment and that he was prepared to brush it aside and take a strong stand, as usual.

*   *   *   *

During the first half of October, while Polk and Buchanan were awaiting a reply from Black concerning the Mexican government's willingness to negotiate, ominous news arrived from California, which greatly increased the tension within the American cabinet and called for immediate action. Throughout the year the expansionist press had published occasional warnings against European intrigue at Monterey or San Francisco and called on the government to assist "the star of empire" on its westward march. Although interested in acquiring California, Polk outwardly ignored these urgings. Even when he received news in late May of the local revolt against Governor Manuel Micheltorena, he contented himself with sending orders to Commodore John D. Sloat of the Pacific Squadron to seize the key ports of California if war should break out. These orders were counterparts of the contingent orders sent to Taylor and Conner.

16. Benjamin E. Green's statement was dated August 8, 1889, Lyon G. Tyler, *The Letters and Times of the Tylers*, III, 174–77. For comments on it, see Justin H. Smith, *The War with Mexico*, I, 436; and Eugene Irving McCormac, *James K. Polk, a Political Biography*, pp. 392–93. Joel Poinsett to Martin Van Buren, May 26, 1846, Van Buren Papers, series 2, roll 30. Poinsett gave no date for his warning. Weeks after Slidell's arrival Black wrote to the United States consul at Veracruz, agreeing that it would have been better to send out a commissioner and suspected that "some one pretended to know and

understand more about the matter than he really did." Black to Dimond, January 31, April 2, US, DS, PR, Consulate, Mexico City, Letterbook IV, 242, 320–21. This was largely second guessing, as Black's earlier dispatches had contributed to the confusion. For a modern Mexican comment on the question, see the appendix by Luis Cabrera to his translation of James K. Polk, *Diario del Presidente Polk (1845–1849)*, ed. Milo Milton Quaife, II, 94–96.

17. Washington *Union*, October 2, 1845, as quoted in McCormac, *Polk*, p. 266.

Constant repetition of expansionist warnings in the press would probably have continued to increase the government's tension in any case, but Polk necessarily gave even greater weight to evidence from the most trusted American agent in California, the merchant Thomas O. Larkin. After his appointment as consul in 1844, Larkin reported regularly on British activities, especially those of the Hudson's Bay Company. He exaggerated their significance and always emphasized the potential resources of the country and the weakness of the Mexican rule.

While Larkin had not supported the revolt against Micheltorena—indeed, the fallen governor owed him money—he used the disorders to strengthen his arguments for local autonomy and urged his friends to propagandize for the acquisition of California and against expansion in Oregon. "Bring forward the country in its best light," he wrote to one correspondent. "Write every [thing] you know respecting English agents or Consul . . . or the H. B. Co agents, smuggling in C[alifornia], aiding revolution, acting for or counteracting the supreme or local Gov't in any way." The recipient of this letter sent it to Senator Lewis Cass, who took care that it was widely reprinted.[18]

Larkin had long done more than his share of publicizing California. Since 1843 he had been sending occasional articles on life in California to the New York *Herald*, and during 1845 he shifted to the New York *Sun* and other expansionist Eastern papers. On July 10, two days after writing the quoted letter, he sent off an article to the New York *Journal of Commerce*. Here he repeated rumors that Mexico had sold California to Britain, hinted that the Hudson's Bay Company was encouraging Mexico to reconquer the province, and declared that if the local Californians were allowed to rule themselves, they could maintain peace and quiet. He described the riches of the area and the extent of American trade and settlement. Finally, as a long-range solution to the government of California, he revived Webster's old plan for a tripartite agreement between Mexico, Britain, and the United States by which the United States would cede to Britain all of Oregon north of the Columbia River on condition that Britain persuade Mexico to cede California to the United States. He explained: "The Oregon

18. Thomas O. Larkin to John Marsh, Monterey, July 8, 1845, John A. Hawgood, ed., *First and Last Consul: Thomas Oliver Larkin and the Americanization of California*, pp. 18, 25. For a summary account of Larkin's earlier suspicions of Britain and France, see Rayner Wickersham Kelsey, "The United States Consulate in California," *Annals of the Academy of Pacific Coast History*, 1 (1910), 206-9.

will never be a benefit to the United States if England owns San Francisco."[19]

On the same day, Larkin drew up a more precise statement about British activities in an official dispatch to the State Department. Although he had informed Buchanan less than six weeks earlier that the province was at peace, he now declared that he had positive information of an expedition fitting out at Acapulco to reimpose Mexican rule, led by a European-educated general and financed in part by the Hudson's Bay Company. "There is no doubt in this Country, but the Troops now expected here in September are sent on by the instigation of the English Government under the plea, that the American settlers in California want to revolutionize the Country." Two British commercial houses in California, it was rumored, would pay the local expenses of the troops. Larkin pointed to the suspicious circumstance that Britain and France had recently established vice consulates in California, although there was no European commerce there except for that of the Hudson's Bay Company. The British vice consul was an agent of the Company, he added, and had presented to the new local government a bill for munitions that the Company had supplied to the rebels against Micheltorena.[20]

Buchanan received this alarming dispatch three months later, on October 11. Neither he nor Polk had any way of knowing that almost every statement in it was overdrawn. Actually, the Hudson's Bay Company had already decided to withdraw from California; the British vice consulate was a mere listening post, its dispatches virtually ignored in London; and the feared Mexican expedition of reconquest, totally unsupported by Britain, was about to collapse along the road to Acapulco (see Chapter 8). Polk and Buchanan knew Larkin to be a sensible Yankee, and his reports had hitherto been reliable.

Furthermore, his dispatch was partly confirmed by correspondence of early September from Parrott and Black in Mexico City, some of which arrived on the same day as the message from California. These reported a proposal from California for federal status in which the British legation seemed much interested, more rumors of a revolt by Paredes, and indications that Britain might

19. Thomas O. Larkin, *The Larkin Papers*, ed. George P. Hammond, IV, x–xii. Larkin to James Gordon Bennett, February 10, 1843; n.d., ibid., II, 6–9; Larkin to Moses Yale Beach, May 28, 31, September 30, 1845, ibid., III, 201–3, 215–20, 370.

20. Larkin to Buchanan, July 10, 1845, No. 25, Manning, *IAA*, VIII, 735–36. For contrast, see his No. 22 of June 6, ibid., pp. 721–22.

still support Mexico in the Texas question.[21] Several days after the arrival of Larkin's dispatch Marcy received a private letter from a New York friend with connections in California. These correspondents reported that the American and European inhabitants there were planning an agreement with Britain whereby California would be recognized as independent of Mexico, provided that she promise never to join the United States. Marcy's correspondent concluded: "If I was President I would order one of our Ships of War to go and take Monteray [sic] and all California & keep it as pay for what Mexico owes us. . . . [It is] in much danger of slipping from us and going to England."[22]

Larkin's report and the other, evidently confirmatory evidence must have deeply shocked Polk and his cabinet and influenced their policies for the following six weeks. Unfortunately, the trail of their reactions is obscure enough to permit a great historiographical quarrel that will probably never be settled to everyone's satisfaction. Polk wrote nothing at all in his diary about Larkin's dispatch. Between October 11 and 14 the cabinet discussed several other matters; on October 15 "nothing of interest occurred," as on the 16th; and on October 17 Polk shut himself up all day, worked on a draft of his annual message, and saw only cabinet members and a few other officials on apparently unrelated matters. During that period the only private evidence of agitation is a letter of October 14 from Buchanan to McLane, summarizing Larkin's dispatch. The secretary commented that the nation would burst into flames if the British seized California, that Larkin's news complicated the Oregon question, and that in his annual message Polk would advise ending joint occupation, as provided in the treaty.[23]

Although Polk and his advisers thus seem to have received the alarming rumors about California quietly, they reacted strongly by drawing up new instructions to Taylor, Larkin, and Sloat, which the various departments dispatched on October 16 and 17.

21. Parrott to Buchanan, September 2, 4, 1845; Black to Buchanan, September 2, No. 347, Manning, *IAA*, VIII, 748–50.

22. Aaron Leggett to Marcy, New York, October 16, 1845, reprinted in *California Historical Society Quarterly*, 11 (March 1932), 33–34. Leggett's principal authority was General C. W. Sandford. Both Leggett and Sandford had claims against Mexico. Leggett repeated from ex-Minister Wilson Shannon the well-worn rumor of a British mortgage on California. Some of his information may be traceable to Larkin, for in the letter he referred to an article of that same day in the New York *Journal of Commerce*.

23. Polk, *Diary*, I, 54–61. Buchanan to McLane, October 14, 1845, Polk Papers, LCIV, LC. See also John A. Hussey, "The Origin of the Gillespie Mission," *California Historical Society Quarterly*, 19 (March 1940), 55.

The message to Taylor directed him to approach the Rio Grande "as near . . . as circumstances will permit; having reference to reasonable security" and supplies, in order to check any Mexican or Indian attack. Details were left entirely to his discretion. The War Department wished him to report on local conditions in preparation for possible future orders to march to the Rio Grande or for opening hostilities.[24] As before, the orders were ostensibly defensive but subject to easy misinterpretation by suspicious Mexicans.

Simultaneously, Bancroft directed Commodore Robert F. Stockton, commanding the frigate *Congress*, to proceed secretly and as quickly as possible to California by way of Cape Horn and Hawaii with special dispatches for Sloat and Larkin. He was then to join Sloat's squadron. An ambitious expansionist, Stockton had already played a major role in the protection which Polk had afforded Texas six months earlier when annexation hung in the balance (see Chapter 7). The instructions he carried to Sloat directed that officer to conciliate the natives of California and to keep his forces ready to carry out any future orders from the Department in case of war. Bancroft also repeated his August instructions to Sloat regarding a reconnaissance mission to Oregon.[25]

A somewhat longer dispatch to Larkin appointed him confidential agent to report on events in California, the government of the province, its resources, and the attitude of its people toward the United States. Buchanan urged him to "exert the greatest vigilance in discovering and defeating any attempt, which may be made by foreign governments to acquire a control over that country." He assured Larkin that the United States would not interfere in any hostilities between California and Mexico but would "render her all the kind offices in our power, as a sister Republic" and would resist transfer to Britain or, indeed, any colonization by "foreign monarchies" in North America. Such transfer of government would deny to the natives "the blessings of liberty," injure American interests, and sow the seeds of war between Britain and the United States. While the Polk administration would use no influence to attract California into the Union, Buchanan added blandly, its inhabitants "would be received as brethren, whenever this can be done without affording Mexico just cause of complaint." He advised the Californians to "let events take their course" unless Britain or France tried to annex the province.

24. US, 30C, 1S, HED 60, pp. 89–90.
25. Rives, *US and Mexico*, II, 166, 168. For a biographical sketch of Stockton, see Price, *Origins of the War with Mexico*, Chap. IV.

"This they ought to resist by all the means in their power, as ruinous to their best interests and destructive of their freedom and independence."[26]

Bancroft later admitted that he and Polk did not expect open conflict with any European power over California, but since the presence of European warships in any Californian ports might be inconvenient, it was important to keep American forces on the West Coast under orders "in the event of war by Mexico to take instant possession of San Francisco and as many other places in California" as possible, before any European forces could act.[27] For this reason they decided to send duplicate instructions to Sloat and Larkin by special messenger across the continent. They chose as messenger Archibald H. Gillespie, a young marine lieutenant, apparently for no better reasons than that he was available and spoke Spanish.

Between Gillespie's selection and his departure his mission grew considerably more complicated. Originally, he was to carry a duplicate of the orders to Sloat in cipher and memorize the dispatch to Larkin, who had no cipher. On October 24 Polk discussed the circumstances of California with Senator Thomas Hart Benton, who happened to mention the expedition of his son-in-law, John Charles Frémont, at that time on the way into eastern California. Polk decided to have Gillespie seek out Frémont and repeat to him the instructions for Larkin. On October 30 Polk talked privately with the lieutenant, and about this time Benton produced a packet of family letters for Frémont, which Gillespie added to his pouch. Bancroft's business friends in Boston prepared papers to disguise Gillespie as a merchant, so that he could cross Mexico from Veracruz to the Pacific coast, rather than take the time-consuming route through the Rockies to the north. Considering the urgency of the mission, it required a surprisingly long time to organize; Gillespie did not leave for Veracruz until November 16.[28]

A young lieutenant disguised as a merchant, making his way across hostile territory to a half-unknown destination with one message in cipher, another memorized, and possibly oral instructions as well—nothing could be more fascinating to historian or

26. Buchanan to Larkin, October 17, 1845, Manning, *IAA*, VIII, 169–71.

27. Memorandum of George Bancroft, Newport, Rhode Island, September 2/3, 1886, quoted in John Charles Frémont, "The Conquest of California," *Century Magazine*, 41 (April 1891), 923–24.

28. Hussey, "Origin of the Gillespie Mission," pp. 48–53. Werner H. Marti, *Messenger of Destiny, the California Adventures, 1846–1847, of Archibald Gillespie, U.S. Marine Corps*, p. 7 *et passim*.

novelist. Did Gillespie have any private orders for Frémont from Polk, Buchanan, Benton, or from all of them? What did the "family letters" contain? Why did Gillespie need to communicate with Frémont at all? During the next years these questions emerged, as Frémont played an equivocal role in the annexation of California (see Chapter 12). They became burning public issues when he returned East to face court-martial for his irregularities and later to run for the Presidency. Eventually, the questions became entangled with the competition between his admirers and those of Larkin to give their heroes principal credit for the annexation of California.

Historians revived the debate over Frémont's orders during the 1870s and 1880s. When one of them flatly accused the explorer of lying, the aged Bancroft came to his defense with the statement that he had informed Frémont of Polk's plan for taking California. "The truth is," added the old man complacently, "no officer of the Government had anything to do with California but the Secretary of the Navy so long as I was in the Cabinet."[29] For years thereafter it was generally assumed that Frémont had received some kind of secret instructions through Gillespie—"not categorical orders to incite an American revolt, but such encouraging discretionary orders to do discreetly what they could to secure or 'save' California as would be apt to serve the same end."[30]

29. Bancroft memorandum, September 2/3, 1886, as quoted in Frémont, "Conquest of California," p. 924. See also Allan Nevins, *Frémont, the World's Greatest Adventurer*, I, 279–80. The controversy seems to have been started by John S. Hittell in his *History of the City of San Francisco*, pp. 100–106. The man who accused Frémont of lying— "unmistakably, unmitigatedly, hopelessly"—was Josiah Royce, in a letter to Henry L. Oak, August 8, 1885, cited by Robert Glass Cleland in his introduction to Royce's *California from the Conquest in 1846 to the Second Vigilance Committee in San Francisco, a Study in American Character*, p. xix. Another who upheld Larkin and attacked Frémont was Hubert Howe Bancroft in his *History of California*, IV, 706–7. For general accounts of the controversy, see Cleland's introduction, cited above, pp. xvii–xx; and Frederick Merk, *The Monroe Doctrine and American Expansionism, 1843–1849*, pp. 124–30.

30. Richard R. Stenberg, "Polk and Frémont, 1845–1846," *Pacific Historical Review*, 7 (1938), 211–27. The quotation appears on p. 222. Stenberg suggests that Polk kept information about the mission from Buchanan, that Gillespie and Frémont deliberately overplayed the significance of the instructions to Larkin to divert attention from secret orders, and that Polk inserted into his diary a brief, uninformative reference to his conversation with Gillespie in order to mislead future readers. Another writer develops much the same thesis, using principally California sources. Ernest A. Wiltsee, *The Truth about Frémont: an Inquiry*, pp. 29–30 et passim. Both Stenberg and Wiltsee make much use of inference from incomplete, circumstantial evidence, in the same way that Stenberg and Price set forth the Polk-Stockton "plot" concerning Texas in the spring of 1845 (see Chapters 7, 9). Nevins' first biography of Frémont plays up the roles of Benton and his daughter Jessie Benton Frémont in encouraging the explorer. Nevins, *Frémont, Adventurer*, I, 273–86.

It is almost impossible to document "discretionary orders" of this sort, since discretion forbids a written record. Some historians have wondered why Polk instructed Larkin and Sloat to conciliate the Californians, while ordering Frémont to incite the American settlers to revolt, and why he should have kept Sloat, his naval commander, in the dark as to Frémont's mission. The answer to these questions may be simply that Frémont overreacted to his instructions. Gillespie seems to have carried away from his interview with Polk the impression that he should persuade the Californians to declare their independence voluntarily and to petition for annexation.[31] Probably no one will ever know exactly what he said to Frémont. The explorer had been fully aware of Benton's expansionist views before he started his expedition, and he would not have needed much urging from anyone, for he was accustomed to taking the bit in his teeth.

What we do know from the written instructions to Larkin and Sloat is that Polk, with a mixture of initiative and caution, was trying to place the American cause in a strong position for several contingencies: continued nominal Mexican rule, a local revolt for independence, or outright war. He might well have regarded discretionary instructions to Frémont as an additional safeguard in case of war or British occupation. Why should he have relied thus on an explorer of little military experience and known impulsiveness? Situated months away from the expected events, Polk was forced to use whatever agents happened to be on the spot.

*　　*　　*　　*

For his direct negotiations with Mexico, however, Polk had carefully chosen his representative, John Slidell. While Gillespie

---

Other works, including Nevins' second biography, are more noncommittal about the responsibility of both Benton and Polk. Cardinal Goodwin, *John Charles Frémont, an Explanation of His Career*, pp. 96–99. Nevins, *Frémont, Pathmarker of the West*, pp. 237–41.

31. Archibald H. Gillespie to George Bancroft, Mexico City, January 16, 1846, *California Historical Society Quarterly*, 18 (September 1939), 222–28. Benton partly confirmed this view in an account published just after Frémont's defeat in the presidential election of 1856: "The verbal communications were that Mr. Frémont should watch and counteract any foreign scheme on California, and conciliate the good will of the inhabitants towards the United States." Thomas Hart Benton, *Thirty Years View*, II, 689. A modern writer denies the existence of any secret instructions at all. He says that Bancroft wrote his 1886 statement "in order to help Frémont out of a bad situation" and deliberately confused different sets of instructions in order to imply more than he cared to assert. George Tays, "Frémont Had No Secret Instructions," *Pacific Historical Review*, 9 (June 1940), 157–72. Other accounts agree in censuring Frémont to varying degrees for acting without governmental authorization. Hussey, "Origin of the Gillespie Mission," pp. 51–53. Hawgood, *First and Last Consul*, p. xxxviii. Marti, *Messenger of Destiny*, pp. 37–49, especially p. 41.

was completing his preparations for departure, news from Mexico seemed to indicate that the time had come for Slidell to approach Herrera's government directly. On November 6 the cabinet received two letters from New Orleans reporting that General Mariano Arista, commander of Mexican troops on the Rio Grande, favored settling the quarrel by negotiation and would not cross the river if Taylor agreed not to commit aggression.[32] On the following day Polk received Consul Black's dispatch of October 17, reporting that the Mexicans were willing to "settle the present dispute" with an American commissioner. Three days later William S. Parrott, the former private agent newly returned from Mexico, confirmed Black's report and expressed the opinion that Mexico would sell California and New Mexico. During this same week Bancroft also learned from Commodore Conner that the Mexican furor over Texas was subsiding and that Herrera's regime was gaining stability. "The presence of our army on the frontier and the concentration of the naval force before this place, begin to have their effect," Conner concluded. "All parties are becoming sensible of the danger of rushing into a war, without preparation and without resources."[33]

Confident that his policy of taking a strong stand was on the verge of success, Polk and his cabinet drew up Slidell's instructions, evidently without disagreement. On November 10, after talking to Parrott, Polk appointed him secretary of legation, although the Mexican foreign minister had explicitly declared his dislike for the agent. Later in the day the President signed the instructions and a private letter to Slidell and sent them off on a warship to Pensacola, there to be picked up by the envoy.[34]

The new mission to Mexico, began the instructions, was mainly designed to counteract foreign influence in Mexico against the United States and to restore peaceful relations. They continued with a paragraph on resistance to European sovereigns—a gloss

32. Undated memorandum in Buchanan's handwriting, Buchanan Papers, box 10, HSP. The letters came from Isaac D. Marks of New Orleans, who was apparently trying to set himself up as intermediary between Arista and Taylor. Marks then appeared in Washington to volunteer for Slidell's post. After Slidell had been in Mexico six weeks, Buchanan received another proposal from New Orleans for direct dealings with Arista through the American consul at Matamoros or some other special agent. J. W. Zacharia to Bu-

chanan, New Orleans, January 16, 1846, ibid., box 63. Polk did not follow this advice, but it certainly encouraged him to expect secessionism in northeast Mexico.

33. Polk, *Diary*, I, 91–93. Peña y Peña to Black, October 15, 1845; Black to Buchanan, October 17, No. 350, Manning, *IAA*, VIII, 763. Conner to Bancroft, October 20, No. 28, US, DN, LCS, file microcopy 89, roll 84.

34. Polk, *Diary*, I, 91–94. Stenberg, and California," p. 217.

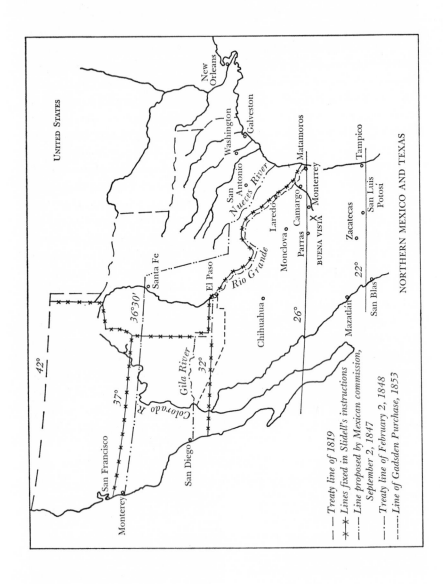

UNITED STATES

New Orleans

Washington

Galveston

San Antonio

Nueces River

Santa Fe

El Paso

Rio Grande

Chihuahua

36°30'

Gila River

42°

37°

32°

Colorado R.

San Francisco

Monterey

San Diego

Matamoros

Tampico

Laredo

Monclova

Parras   Camargo   Monterey

BUENA VISTA

Zacatecas

San Luis Potosi

22°

26°

Mazatlán

San Blas

— — Treaty line of 1819
—✗— Lines fixed in Slidell's instructions
— · · — Line proposed by Mexican commission,
        September 2, 1847
— · — Treaty line of February 2, 1848
— — — Line of Gadsden Purchase, 1853

NORTHERN MEXICO AND TEXAS

on the Monroe Doctrine without explicit mention—then launched into a long recital of American claims on Mexico. These, the instructions stated, had been fixed at $2,026,139.68 by the joint commission of 1840–1842, but Mexico had stopped paying interest on that sum after April 1843, and the commission had not had time to pass on other claims, which amounted to $3,336,837.05 (see Chapter 2).

Since Mexico was no better able to pay interest or principal in 1845 than in 1843, Polk proposed to liquidate the claims as a part of general boundary adjustments. Texas had won her independence fairly at San Jacinto, "one of the most decisive and memorable victories recorded in history." Polk did not bother to defend the Texan annexation to the United States (the one subject Mexico wanted to discuss) but briefly and emphatically asserted the Texan–American claim to the Rio Grande boundary on the south. He admitted that the claim did not include the upper Rio Grande Valley or Santa Fe but argued that the cession of all New Mexico would remove a trouble spot and a source of Indian raids too remote for Mexico to control.

As for California, Polk instructed Slidell to determine if Mexico had any idea of ceding it to Britain or France, an action which the United States "would vigorously interpose to prevent." At the end he authorized the minister to offer settlement of all debts and $5 million for Mexico's recognition of the Rio Grande as boundary and cession of New Mexico. He agreed to raise the money payment to $20 million for the addition of northern California including San Francisco and to $25 million for both San Francisco and Monterey.[35]

In a private letter to Slidell, accompanying his formal instructions, Polk emphasized his desire to annex New Mexico and California and urged that Slidell obtain an agreement if possible before the adjournment of the American Congress in March. Polk added ominously: "If unfortunately, you shall fail to effect a satisfactory adjustment of the pending differences between the two countries, (which I will not anticipate) we must take redress for the wrongs and injuries we have suffered into our own hands, and I will call on Congress to provide the proper remedies." On November 19 Buchanan paraphrased this last sentence in another official instruction to Slidell. Apparently Polk regarded these "proper remedies" as an unlikely last resort, for about a week later he wrote

35. Buchanan to Slidell, November 10, 1845, No. 1, Manning, *IAA*, VIII, 172–82.

flatly to his brother: "There will be no war with Mexico. Preliminary steps have already been taken—with the assent of Mexico—for resuming diplomatic relations between the two countries."[36]

The interpretation of these various official and private communications has caused almost as many differences among historians as the definition of *comisionado*. In general those writers who concede that Polk made an honest error in appointing a full minister plenipotentiary also accept his expressed desire for peace as bona fide and at least imply that he was more anxious to keep California out of British hands than to purchase it at once for the United States. A smaller, more skeptical group declare that the Slidell mission was mere camouflage for aggression, that Polk's wishes for peace and offers to purchase California were hypocrisy, and that from the beginning he intended the mission to fail, so that he might justify the declaration of war.[37]

It is more reasonable to believe that Polk was still improvising an aggressive policy as he went along. Plausible evidence indicates that as early as the beginning of October he understood Mexican intentions for the mission—an *ad hoc* envoy to discuss an offer of indemnity to Mexico for the loss of Texas—and that he was prepared to take a firm stand. Ever suspicious of Britain and France, he was convinced that European representatives in Mexico would do their best to prevent territorial cessions. Dispatches from Black and Larkin and his exchanges with Pakenham on Oregon had confirmed his fears of British machinations on the Pacific coast. Considering Polk's lively Anglophobia and his growing contempt for Mexican weakness and corruption, what was more natural than that he should continue his tactics of bluff, seizing the benefit of every doubt and boldly declaring as fact what he could not prove? Would Mexico receive Slidell? Well and good. Would she reject

---

36. Polk to Slidell, November 10, 1845, Letterbook, 1845–1846, pp. 125–31, Polk Papers, LC. Reprinted in Richard R. Stenberg, "President Polk and California: Additional Documents," *Pacific Historical Review*, 10 (June 1941), 217–18. Buchanan to Slidell, November 19, No. 3, Manning, *IAA*, VIII, 182–84. Polk to William H. Polk, November 27, Letterbook, 1845–1846, pp. 153–59, Polk Papers, LC.

37. The most outspoken in favor of Polk is, of course, Smith, *War with Mexico*, I, 94–95, 436. Others, who imply more than they actually say, are Rives, *US and Mexico*, II, 67–69; J.

Fred Rippy, *The United States and Mexico*, pp. 10–11; and James Morton Callahan, *American Foreign Policy in Mexican Relations*, pp. 151–52. A modern Latin writer takes much the same view on the basis of the same American documents: Carlos Bosch García, *Historia de las relaciones entre México y los Estados Unidos, 1819–1848*, pp. 103, 204–6. A somewhat harsher version of this interpretation is Richard W. Van Alstyne, *The Rising American Empire*, p. 141. The most explicit critics of Polk are Hubert H. Bancroft, *History of Mexico*, V, 340–42; and Stenberg, "Polk and California," p. 218.

him? Then would be the time to determine the next step. Meanwhile, let the British guess at his intentions.

The element of improvisation in Polk's policy toward Mexico became even more apparent during the following month. Early in December the State Department received another dispatch from Larkin, dated September 29, in which he toned down his warning of a punitive force en route from Acapulco and described the disunity of the native population. "The people hardly care what Flag is exchanged for their own," he added. Somewhat relieved that California was in no immediate danger of alienation by the British, Polk told Buchanan to instruct Slidell that if he could not purchase California, he must not sacrifice the restoration of good relations to "the pursuit of what is unattainable." In a private letter he took further precautions against a breakdown of negotiations on California by authorizing Slidell to go beyond the original maximum offer for its purchase.[38]

*   *   *   *

During the autumn of 1845, as the Polk administration tried to resume relations with Mexico and reacted in alarm to apparent British designs on California, it also had to determine what if anything should be done about the Oregon question. As the American press and public realized that negotiations had collapsed, rumors of an approaching crisis began to circulate. Insurance rates on British shipping in the western Atlantic were said to be rising. Although the British cabinet could not agree on an adequate program to defend Canada against attack by the United States, the Chicago *Democrat* reported tremulously that a British warship and two regiments of Highland Dragoons had been seen on the upper Great Lakes, as well as several thousand British-supplied Indians massing in the Manitoulin Islands.[39]

38. Larkin to Buchanan, September 29, 1845; Buchanan to Slidell, December 17, No. 4, Manning, *IAA*, VIII, 184–85, 755–56. Polk to Slidell, December 17, Letterbook, 1845–1846, pp. 198–201, Polk Papers, LC. Sellers comes to much the same conclusion about the instructions to Slidell—that Polk was aware of semantic distinctions and "did not shrink from war to accomplish his purpose." However, Sellers believes that by November Polk's plan of absorbing California through the activities of Larkin, Stockton, Gillespie, and Frémont reduced his desire to purchase the province. This change in purpose is not apparent from Polk's language in the instructions of November 10 and 19, which were written after he had drawn up his plans for California. Charles Grier Sellers, *James K. Polk, Continentalist: 1843–1846*, pp. 331–38 and especially p. 336. Sellers does not cite Polk's private letter of December 17, in which he tentatively agreed to raise the purchase price.

39. *NNR*, 69 (September 27, 1845), 49. Chicago *Democrat*, n.d., quoted in London *Times*, August 29, p. 5.

As always, British and European problems of this period were far more intricate than the few surface manifestations would indicate to the American public. One complicating factor, at first noticed only by the business sector in the United States, was a food crisis in Britain. Early in the summer, rain and cold weather in England had raised wheat prices, encouraged farmers of the Midwestern states, and helped to reduce British clamor over Polk's inaugural address (see Chapter 8). During July and August, England enjoyed more sun, but in the first week of September the fine weather broke, and heavy rains ruined a considerable part of the harvest. Meanwhile in Ireland a potato blight that had been gradually spreading for several years destroyed nearly half the crop, creating an unusual market for cereals.[40] Wheat prices at Danzig and Odessa were reported higher than in years, and it seemed likely that the St. Lawrence River would freeze before Britain could obtain much relief from Canada. At the end of September American wheat prices were still lower than those of Europe, but as each packet brought more news of rain and bad harvests, speculation in grain began and further disturbed an already unsettled financial market in both countries.[41]

Since the sliding scale of the corn laws operated automatically to hinder British wheat imports in periods of high prices, it was natural that the food crisis should hasten the efforts of free traders in both the Peel and the Polk administrations. On September 9, just two weeks after Polk had determined to withdraw his offer of an Oregon settlement, he and the cabinet were considering how to bring about a friendly settlement of several minor Anglo–American tariff problems.[42] In the same week, Secretary of the Treasury Walker discussed the tariff with Pakenham. He predicted a majority for tariff reform in the next House of Representatives and expressed a wish for lower British grain duties. Protectionist sentiment in America was still very strong, however, and Pakenham remarked that the existing system of Imperial preference suited

40. Thomas P. Martin, "Free Trade and the Oregon Question," *Facts and Factors in Economic History: Articles by Former Students of Edwin Francis Gay*, pp. 485–86. *NNR*, 69 (October 11, 18, 1845), 81, 97–98.

41. *NNR*, 69 (October 11, 18, 1845), 96, 112. New York *Evening Post*, October 11, p. 1.

42. Polk, *Diary*, I, 21–22. One matter, the much-vexed rough rice question, concerned a discriminatory British duty

on that commodity, and another concerned a discriminatory American duty on articles shipped from beyond the Cape of Good Hope and Cape Horn. The rough rice question was settled later in the year. Wilbur Devereux Jones, *Lord Aberdeen and the Americas*, pp. 76–77. This settlement increased Southern support for a commercial agreement. Martin, "Free Trade," p. 488.

many American farmers, who could ship their grain to Canada for milling. Still, the British food crisis and the apparent economic liberalism of the Polk administration placed a heavy premium on Anglo–American peace. As early as October British newspapers were suggesting that a commercial treaty would be a fair trade for concessions in Oregon.[43]

Another international factor, less obvious to the American public than the British food crisis, was the tension in Anglo–French relations, always precarious despite the friendly inclinations of Aberdeen and Guizot. During the summer of 1845 Francophobes in the Peel government, such as the Duke of Wellington and Sir Charles Napier, had pressed for greater defense expenditures. To support their demands, they raised the specter of a Franco–American alliance and thus troubled the economy-minded Peel, who could not completely exorcise their fears (see Chapter 8). At the end of August Lord Cowley, the British ambassador to France, visited London and confirmed Wellington's fears with accounts of an anti-British clique led by Louis Philippe's sons, who would provoke war within six months if the King should die.[44]

In September Queen Victoria paid a ceremonial visit to Louis Philippe at the Chateau d'Eu, acting a pantomime of Anglo–French amity; Aberdeen and Guizot used the occasion for a private discussion of Tahiti and other problems troubling the two countries. Behind the scenes in London, however, the militarists in Peel's cabinet were pressing the prime minister for more defenses, and when Aberdeen returned from the royal tour, he felt his position to be so much undermined that on September 18 he offered to resign. Naturally, Peel did not dare risk the public scandal such a break would cause. He shifted his policy again toward friendship with France, but Aberdeen could appreciate the narrow margin of his momentary victory.[45]

43. Pakenham to Aberdeen, September 13, 1845, No. 93, GB, FO 5/428, ff. 7–12. *NNR*, 69 (November 1), 132.

44. John S. Galbraith, "France As a Factor in the Oregon Negotiations," *Pacific Northwest Quarterly*, 44 (April 1953), pp. 71–72. Sir Robert Peel to Aberdeen, September 1, 1845, Peel Papers, BM, AM, vol. 40455, ff. 128–30. Duke of Wellington to Peel, August 7; Memorandum by Wellington, September 10, BM, AM, vol. 40461, ff. 154–61, 205–16.

45. Galbraith, "France As a Factor," pp. 72–73. Frederick Merk, *The Oregon Question, Essays in Anglo–American Diplomacy and Politics*, pp. 355–56. Aberdeen to François Guizot, September 16, 1845, Aberdeen Papers, BM, AM, vol. 43134, ff. 155–57. Aberdeen to Peel, September 18, Peel Papers, BM, AM, vol. 40455, ff. 159–62. Peel to Aberdeen, September 20, Aberdeen Papers, BM, AM, vol. 43064, ff. 349–52. Sir James Graham to Peel, September 22, Peel Papers, BM, AM, vol. 40451, ff.

Under these circumstances the British foreign secretary reverted to his policy of Anglo–French cooperation in North America and took up a proposal of the Mexican minister, Tomás Murphy. In mid-September Murphy had received dispatches of July 30 from Mexico City, the product of Foreign Minister Cuevas' brief impulse of bravado at the summer session of the Mexican Congress (see Chapter 8). Cuevas wrote his envoy that Mexico was about to go to war with the United States over Texas, and he instructed him to inform Aberdeen and to ask for British cooperation in avoiding the further loss of territory. On his own initiative Murphy added a hint that some sort of colonization grant in California might be converted to a British protectorate in order to allow Britain to defend the province without losing her status as a neutral.

Aberdeen replied that Britain could not act without France. He put forth a private feeler to Guizot while he broached the subject to Peel, saying that the French had begun well enough although timidly in Texas. Perhaps a direct interest might make them bolder in California. He added, however, that he did not expect any effective French reaction and implied that his only motive in sounding Guizot was to revive French good will toward Britain.[46]

In France the government and the opposition were still arguing over the wisdom of supporting Britain in its anti-American policy. By now, however, some of the opposition press had recognized that Britain was not encouraging Mexico to defy the Americans and that it might not serve the best interests of France for the United States to expand to the Pacific, seizing California and perhaps Oregon as well.[47] *Le journal des débats* had no doubts: If the United States expanded to the Columbia and St. Lawrence rivers and to Panama, swallowing up the Mexican silver mines on the way, Europe might one day be squeezed "between Russian autocracy on the East and the democracy of the United States thus aggrandized on the West."[48]

294–96. Peel to Wellington, September 21; Wellington to Peel, September 22, BM, AM, vol. 40461, ff. 235–44.

46. Aberdeen to Peel, September 23, 25, 1845, BM, AM, vol. 40455, ff. 172–75, 180–81. Peel to Aberdeen, September 24, 26, Aberdeen Papers, BM, AM, vol. 43064, ff. 357–60, 364–68. Luis Cuevas to Tomás Murphy, July 30, Nos. 6,

7; Murphy to Ministerio de Relaciones Exteriores, October 1, No. 15, Antonio de la Peña y Reyes, *Lord Aberdeen, Texas y California*, pp. 31–33, 42–47.

47. *La presse*, September 4, 1845, p. 1; September 12, p. 1; September 13, pp. 1–2.

48. *Le journal des débats*, September 20, 1845, p. 1; September 24, p. 1.

On October 2 Guizot answered Aberdeen's exploratory inquiry by saying that France would act with England in America wherever possible, thereby abandoning her old policy of association with the United States. He had cooperated with the British government in Texas and might do so again in California if Aberdeen could give him an intelligible proposal of the British course. On receiving this word, however, Aberdeen told Peel that in his opinion neither Guizot nor Louis Philippe would risk war with the United States over California. He felt it wiser for Britain to continue urging patience upon Mexico. With this he dropped the subject.

During October Cowley and Guizot reported a more amicable feeling in France and added that Louis Philippe was in excellent health for a man of seventy-three. These reports did not reassure Peel, who predicted that the outbreak of hostilities between Britain and the United States would immediately arouse warmongers in France.[49] Aberdeen continued seeking ways to strengthen the *entente*. In late November he explored the possibility of mediating between France and Mexico, thus strengthening both countries by ending the ugly dispute over the incident at the Baño de las Delicias. Nothing came of this idea either.[50]

Thereafter, Aberdeen did not return to a cooperative Anglo–French policy in any part of North America. However, he was still considering how to prevent the United States from acquiring California. By the autumn of 1845 he knew of the private project which Consul Ewen C. Mackintosh had put forward in Mexico City several months earlier for a British loan to Mexico on the pledge of California as security. British holders of Mexican bonds supported this plan, for it offered them some hope of recovering their money or, if not money, then land on the Pacific coast under the terms of the 1837 debt conversion (see Chapter 2). In October and November Aberdeen discussed the plan with J. D. Powles, the chairman of the bondholders' committee. The foreign secretary

49. Guizot to Aberdeen, October 2, 1845, Aberdeen Papers, BM, AM, vol. 32134, ff. 160–63. Aberdeen to Peel, October 3, 7, 11, 16, 20, 21; Peel to Aberdeen, October 8, 17, BM, AM, vol. 43065, ff. 7–8, 17–18, 32–33, 38–39, 41–52, 59–60, 67–69. Wellington continued to press for more coastal defenses but made no mention of Oregon. Wellington to Peel, October 5, 15, 26, Peel Papers, BM, AM, vol. 40461, ff. 259–80, 291–94, 303–6. Jones, *Aberdeen and the Americas*, pp. 68–71.

50. Aberdeen to Peel, November 27, 1845; Peel to Aberdeen, November 27, Aberdeen Papers, BM, AM, vol. 43065, ff. 112–16. The Anglo–French mediation in the Plata continued for a while longer. Jones, *Aberdeen and the Americas*, Chap. 4.

informed Tomás Murphy, the Mexican minister, of these talks and suggested that a direct proposition from Mexico would make a difficult business easier, but Murphy had no instructions.[51] Before long the corn laws and the Oregon question were preoccupying the Peel administration, and by the time the Mexican government was ready to discuss an arrangement for California, Aberdeen had recognized that Mackintosh's idea was visionary.

* * * *

It is in the context of a developing food crisis and perplexing Anglo–French relations that the course of the Oregon negotiations must be traced during the three months after Polk and Buchanan withdrew their proffered terms. For most of September they let the question drift. With Polk's permission, Buchanan showed all correspondence on the subject to Senator Benton, who approved of the actions taken thus far. During the last week of the month Buchanan received a private letter from McLane in London, very pessimistic about the attitude of the British press toward Oregon and the United States. Buchanan remarked to Pakenham that the times seemed unfavorable for further negotiation. Pakenham asked him whether he did not fear extreme action by the next Congress if no progress had been made by December. He suggested arbitration, but Buchanan shook off this suggestion, in the belief that the administration could restrain Congress. Soon after this conference, the secretary of state left Washington on vacation for the first ten days of October.[52]

During this time McLane in London held three conversations on Oregon with Aberdeen, one as soon as the foreign secretary had returned from the Continent in mid-September and two after Aberdeen realized to his dismay that Polk had withdrawn the terms and broken off the dialogue. All three conversations were clearly designed to inform McLane that Britain wanted a peaceful

51. Lester G. Engelson, "Proposals for Colonization of California by England in Connection with the Mexican Debt to British Bondholders, 1837–1846," *California Historical Society Quarterly*, 18 (June 1939), 145–46. Bankhead to Aberdeen, July 30, 1845, No. 74, with enclosed memorandum, GB, FO 50/186, ff. 12–22, 28–30. J. D. Powles to Aberdeen, November 27, Aberdeen Papers, BM, AM, vol. 43245, ff. 115–16. Murphy to Ministerio de Relaciones Exteriores, November 1, December 1, Nos. 17, 19, Peña y Reyes, *Aberdeen, Texas y California*, pp. 49–54, 56–58.

52. Polk, *Diary*, I, 48, 53–56. Pakenham to Aberdeen, September 28, 1845, GB, FO 5/428, ff. 187–92. McLane to Buchanan, September 3, Buchanan Papers, box 62, HSP. This letter arrived in Washington on September 22.

settlement but would not openly yield any important concessions. On the first occasion (September 13) Aberdeen admitted that Pakenham's rejection was not an ultimatum "and that at a proper time they would be prepared to assent to greater concessions, and a more equitable partition." He, too, suggested arbitration, but McLane replied that the American people and government would accept this solution only as the "last expedient," especially since European royal families were so closely interrelated that it would be impossible to find an impartial umpire.

In the same dispatch McLane reported extensive naval armament in England and expressed his belief that this preparation might be intended either for war with the United States or for an effort to maintain the Orleans dynasty on the throne of France. (As already noted, it was intended primarily for defense against France.) McLane closed with words of cheer on Mexico. Few if any in England, he wrote, believed that the Mexicans would dare to attack the United States; the Mexican government could obtain no war loans in London; and if the British government took any part in such a conflict, it would probably use its influence for peace.[53]

McLane's first conversation with Aberdeen occurred during the British cabinet crisis over French policy, a few days before Aberdeen threatened to resign. On September 30 and October 1, when McLane and Aberdeen resumed the discussion, Aberdeen had just learned about the Americans' withdrawal of terms and was awaiting a reply from Guizot to his tentative proposal for a joint policy to protect California. He told McLane that if Pakenham had transmitted Buchanan's terms "as he was expected to have done," the British government might have proposed acceptable changes for an agreement. He hoped for some indication from the United States that the negotiations were still open, so that he might undo Pakenham's error. McLane seized this opportunity to remark that the American public would probably not permit further negotiation, since it was already outraged by British and

---

53. As an argument in favor of a speedy settlement, McLane pointed out that insurance rates on American ships had become prohibitive and that the British had begun to monopolize the carrying trade. McLane to Buchanan, September 18, 1845, No. 5, Manning, CR, III, 978–80; IAA, VII, 270–71. A private letter to Buchanan on the same date added little of importance. Buchanan Papers, box 62, HSP. McLane obtained much of his information on British rearmament from a Yankeephile Englishman in Devonport. John P. Drake to McLane, September 6, November 15, ibid.

French interference in Texas and by the unremitting abuse the British press hurled at America. At the last interview, after Aberdeen had had an opportunity to consult Peel, he declared that he would let Pakenham in Washington carry on informal conversations to learn how the official channels might be reopened.[54]

Probably these conversations and especially McLane's reminder about the American public reaction to Anglo–French activities in Texas explain why, a few days later, Aberdeen abruptly dropped his idea of similar joint action to save California from the Americans. McLane reported to Buchanan that Aberdeen seemed to have in mind terms he thought Polk might accept. The American minister was quite correct; for nearly a year Aberdeen had been willing to consider a settlement along the forty-ninth parallel, retaining for Britain all of Vancouver Island as well as the right to navigate the Columbia River and use free ports south of the border (see Chapter 6). About ten days after his conversations with McLane the foreign secretary wrote to Peel that such a settlement would give Britain every part of the area that was worth claiming. He added that the interests involved were unimportant and that he could settle the question with McLane in half an hour on its merits alone.[55]

Aberdeen and McLane had anticipated nearly all the terms of the final settlement, but eight months of suspense and misunderstanding remained between them and the signing of a treaty, for the final decisions lay with Peel and Polk, and neither man would yet reduce the quarrel to its basic merits. The first problem for the British was to reopen normal diplomatic negotiations by undoing Pakenham's blunder. On October 3, after Aberdeen's discussions with McLane, the foreign secretary instructed Pakenham to approach Buchanan openly and offer to withdraw the British rejection of the American offer. The secretary would surely take back his own note, Aberdeen added hopefully, and negotiations could then proceed as though nothing untoward had happened. But Pakenham must by no means let Buchanan assume that Britain intended to accept his terms; they were to serve only as a basis

---

54. McLane to Buchanan, October 3, 1845, No. 9, Manning, *CR*, III, 980–84. McLane to Buchanan, September [October] 3, Buchanan Papers, HSP.

55. Aberdeen to Peel, October 17, 1845, reprinted in David Hunter Miller, ed., *Treaties and Other International Acts of the United States of America*, V, 48. By a coincidence, at the same time McLane was writing to his son that in his opinion the question "could be settled in 48 hours upon terms that before I left the P[resident] . . . actually agreed to accept." Louis McLane to Robert McLane, October 18, McLane Papers. See also L. McLane to Buchanan, November 3, Buchanan Papers, box 62, HSP.

for discussion. If this gambit failed, Britain would then be in a good position to propose arbitration again.[56]

There was little immediate cause for hope. McLane's account of his first conversation with Aberdeen produced no effect in Washington, but his second dispatch called forth a full-scale cabinet discussion on October 21. Polk laid down his basic policy for the remainder of the dispute. Since Britain had broken off the discussion, he would not renew it unless Aberdeen formally proposed a set of terms. Buchanan objected that to stall the Oregon question at that point would lead to war. Polk replied that he had reluctantly made earlier concessions on Oregon and was well satisfied with the situation as it stood. He did not expect Britain to offer acceptable terms, and he would either reject them outright or submit them to the Senate. Buchanan asked if he might tell Pakenham that any British terms would be submitted to the Senate "for their previous advice" before the President acted; Polk refused. Buchanan suggested that the proper tactic was delay, to avoid a crisis which might lead to war and loss of the territory. Polk defiantly repeated that he was satisfied with matters as they stood and would "take bold and strong ground" in his annual message, invoking the Monroe Doctrine against further colonization in North America.[57]

By now Pakenham had received Aberdeen's instructions to reopen the discussion on Oregon. The only results of his efforts, however, were a futile round of diplomatic fencing with Polk and a display of conciliatory anxiety by Buchanan. After two long conversations in the State Department, Buchanan suggested that if Pakenham cared to draw up a written statement, he would submit it privately to Polk and let Pakenham see Polk's reply, so that he might then withdraw his original note or make it official. Pakenham's note offered no specific terms but engaged in a certain amount of sophistry to "prove" that he had not rejected Buchanan's earlier terms and would be glad to hear more on the subject of Oregon. On October 28 Buchanan brought this note before the cabinet and proposed to offer terms in reply, as a basis of discussion: a boundary at 49°, reserving all of Vancouver Island to the British, but not the free navigation of the Columbia River.

All of these terms except the last agreed with the views Aber-

56. Aberdeen to Pakenham, October 3, 1845, No. 64, GB, FO 115/89, ff. 109-10. Same, October 3, Aberdeen Papers, BM, AM, vol. 43123, ff. 261-62. Most of the details come from the private letter.

57. Polk, *Diary*, I, 62-65.

deen had expressed to Peel less than two weeks earlier, but Polk refused to take the initiative. After considering the question overnight, he drew up a curt reply, in which he declined to renew the United States offer or to make any others and left the British minister to take any steps he pleased. He then told Buchanan that Pakenham must make his note official before he could see the reply. Buchanan resisted at some length—he had already assured Pakenham that he could see Polk's note privately—but the President was firm. When the secretary next saw Pakenham and put the choice to him, the British minister hesitated but decided not to expose himself to any further embarrassment, for, as he explained to Aberdeen, he expected that the American terms would probably have made matters worse.[58]

It seems clear that Pakenham's feinting and hesitation raised Polk's suspicions of British good faith. While the exchange with the British minister was going on, Thomas Wren Ward questioned the President closely about his Oregon policy and the likelihood of war with Britain, but Polk replied so chillingly that the Baring agent apologized for his temerity. Naturally the President assumed that Ward was seeking information for Pakenham.[59] Polk doubtless found encouragement to stand firm in a letter from McLane which arrived at this time. The minister felt that Aberdeen was uneasy about affairs on the Continent and not at all eager for an open break with the United States. On October 29 Polk wrote to McLane that in his opinion the terms Pakenham had rejected were the utmost that the United States could offer; they were also, he recognized, less than Britain would then accept. Clearly, the impasse must continue unless Pakenham brought forward another proposition.[60]

Other entries in the President's diary at this time show the direction and the increasing rigidity of his thought. On October 24, for example, he recorded that he had discussed the Oregon

58. Two parallel, detailed accounts of this exchange exist, one by Polk and the other by Pakenham. They do not disagree in any important respects, but naturally they reflect opposite points of view and intentions. Polk, *Diary*, I, 66–67, 75–76, 77–83. Pakenham to Aberdeen, October 29, 1845, No. 115; with this dispatch Pakenham enclosed a copy of his private note to Buchanan, dated October 25. GB, FO 5/429, ff. 69–78. A letterpress copy of the undelivered reply to Pakenham, dated October 28, may be found in Buchanan Papers, box 1, HSP. For a briefer account, see Buchanan to McLane, October 28, James Buchanan, *The Works of James Buchanan*, ed. John Bassett Moore, VI, 285–86.

59. Polk, *Diary*, I, 73–75.

60. McLane to Buchanan, October 10, 1845, Polk Papers, XCIV, LC. Polk to McLane, October 29, reprinted in Miller, *Treaties and Other International Acts*, V, 42–43. See also Buchanan to McLane, November 5, No. 13, Manning, *CR*, III, 309–10.

question with Senator Benton—perhaps their first long conversation since Polk's inauguration, although Benton was well aware of the administration's policies through his friendship with Buchanan. Starting from the assumption that negotiation was impossible, the two agreed that Congress should give the proper year's notice for the abrogation of joint occupation, extend American laws and Indian policy to Oregon, and station troops along the emigration route to protect settlers. Polk mentioned that he contemplated invoking the noncolonization clause of the Monroe Doctrine in Oregon; Benton pointed out that the British had already explored and settled the Fraser Valley (in present-day British Columbia). When the conversation turned to California, however, the Senator had nothing to say against invoking the Doctrine there. He agreed that "no Foreign Power ought to be permitted to colonize California, any more than they would be to colonize Cuba."[61]

Although American opinions on Oregon were hardening, optimism for a peaceable outcome had not entirely disappeared. Early in November Buchanan hinted obscurely to Pakenham that the Oregon question was closer to settlement than it had been six months earlier, which caused the British minister to wonder if Polk intended to combine it with some arrangement for California.[62] Several weeks later Aberdeen, writing to soothe Pakenham's distress over his blunder, also declared that the two nations were nearer agreement than previously, for if Britain continued to press for arbitration, the American leaders must either allow it, reopen negotiations themselves, or appear so wholly in the wrong that the worst Anglophobes in the country would not support their policy.[63]

* * * *

By the end of October most American newspapers had taken their positions on the Oregon issue. In general, the Democratic press was much more expansionist than that of the Whigs, the West more insistent and belligerent than the Northeast or the South. There were exceptions, of course. The nerve center of what

61. Polk, *Diary*, I, 68–72.

62. Pakenham added that Buchanan might have made the statement only to be polite, without meaning anything by it. Pakenham also reported his concern at the troublemaker Stockton's being sent to the Pacific. Pakenham to Aberdeen, November 13, 1845 (two dispatches), No. 119, separate and confidential, GB, FO 5/429, ff. 90–91, 138–40.

63. Aberdeen to Pakenham, December 3, 1845, Aberdeen Papers, BM, AM, vol. 43123, ff. 272–73. Aberdeen's optimism is the more remarkable in that the Peel cabinet was about to resign when he wrote the letter.

came to be called the "manifest destiny" impulse was a little group of New York editors: John L. O'Sullivan of the *Morning News* and the *Democratic Review* (who seems to have coined the phrase), James Gordon Bennett of the *Herald*, Moses Y. Beach of the *Sun*, and Levi D. Slamm of the *Globe*. The expansionist George Bancroft had his voice in Boston (the *Bay State Democrat*), and other papers of similar views formed a network over New England and New York, with extensions farther South through the Baltimore *Sun* and Thomas Ritchie's Washington *Union*. Most of these editors, however, believed more strongly in preaching than in fighting, and as the Democratic newspapers of the Northwest raised an ever louder clamor for war if necessary to fix the line at 54°40', many Easterners admitted the possibility of compromise at 49°.[64]

Through September and October Ritchie's *Union* had said little about Oregon, but several conciliatory statements in moderate newspapers at the end of that time seem to have stung the old man to action. On November 6 the *Union* raised the temperature of the debate by several degrees when it proclaimed: "THE WHOLE OF OREGON OR NONE—*this* is the only alternative as an issue of *territorial right*." If the United States were to make any concession to Britain, the *Union* added, it should do so out of expediency, not from a pretended inferiority of our title.[65] In subsequent issues Ritchie made clear that he had not given up the idea of compromise at 49°,[66] but it was his initial trumpet call that people remembered. He had polarized the issue and supplied extremists with a warcry. Further, many of his readers assumed that he spoke for the administration.

The day after the *Union*'s blast, Webster answered indirectly in a speech at Faneuil Hall. He proposed a compromise line at 49° and predicted that the restless Oregon settlers would form a great independent nation of Anglo–Saxons on the shores of the

---

64. Frederick Merk, *Manifest Destiny and Mission in American History, a Reinterpretation*, pp. 35–41. Slamm, the least known of the editors mentioned, represented Walker's interests with the *Globe*.

65. Washington *Union*, November 6, 1845, p. 643. For conciliatory statements before this editorial, see New York *Journal of Commerce*, October 30, p. 2; October 31, p. 2; and Wash-

ington *National Intelligencer*, November 4, p. 3. Another reason for Ritchie's blast may have been the increasingly pessimistic British dispatches about the food crisis, which arrived in the United States at the end of October. Charles M. Wiltse, *John C. Calhoun, Sectionalist, 1840–1850*, p. 249.

66. Washington *Union*, November 11, 1845, p. 659.

Pacific. Some expansionists also opposed the *Union*, arguing that a war with England over Oregon would only provide her with an excuse to seize California too.[67] Most Democratic editors, however, took stands much closer to Ritchie, and rumors swept across the country for the rest of the month, heightened by a series of inflammatory editorials by John L. O'Sullivan. In one of these, for example, he declared it a "duty, not merely to ourselves but to humanity and human progress" to resist British expansion in the Northwest as firmly as in Cuba or South America. On December 13 *Niles' Register* began to print a weekly summary of the situation, asking ominously, "Is War Brewing? Are We Ready?"[68]

Questions of this sort so alarmed Anglophiles that they intensified their efforts toward conciliation. Edward Everett, who had remained on friendly terms with Aberdeen after leaving the London legation, approached Bancroft soon after the first *Union* editorial appeared and asked for Polk's permission to send a letter to the British foreign secretary, urging him to compromise. Both Polk and Bancroft disapproved of Everett's proposal, but during the next weeks Everett wrote to Aberdeen on his own initiative. He told Aberdeen and his other British friends that whether the *Union* editorial represented Polk's views, Calhoun's bloc would hold the balance of power in Congress and could prevent passage of any bills for taking possession of the whole territory or compel the acceptance of a reasonable British offer. He warned Aberdeen emphatically that neither Calhoun nor any other Americans would agree to concede more than a line along 49° and all of Vancouver Island.[69]

67. C. T. Johnson, "Daniel Webster and Old Oregon," *Washington Historical Quarterly*, 2 (1907–1908), 11. Pakenham to Aberdeen, November 13, 1845, No. 122, GB, FO 5/429, ff. 121–22. The text of Webster's speech appears in Washington *National Intelligencer*, November 11, p. 3. See also New York *Journal of Commerce*, November 8, p. 2; November 15, p. 2; and New York *Evening Post*, November 10, p. 2.

68. See summaries of press opinion in New York *Evening Post*, November 7, 1845, p. 3; November 11, p. 3; November 15, p. 1. Washington *Union*, November 8, 10, 11, 12, 14, 17, 18, pp. 651, 655, 659, 663, 670, 679, 682. O'Sullivan's editorials are quoted at length in Merk, *Monroe Doctrine and Expansion-*

ism, pp. 75–78. *NNR*, 69 (November 15, 22, December 13, 20), 166, 187–88, 225–26, 241. The portentous questions first appeared at the head of the summary on December 13.

69. Edward Everett to Bancroft, Boston, November 10, 17, 1845; Bancroft to Everett, November 14; Bancroft to McLane, December 12, Bancroft Papers, MHS. Everett to Aberdeen, November 15, December 10, Aberdeen Papers, BM, AM, vol. 43123, ff. 429–34. Everett to Lord Jeffery, December 15, Letterbooks, LXXVII, 182–88, Everett Papers. McLane had already written to warn Buchanan of Everett's correspondence. McLane to Buchanan, October 18, Polk Papers, LCIV, LC.

In Europe the *Union*'s call for "THE WHOLE OF ORE-GON OR NONE" exploded like a bombshell, filling the British and French press with shock waves and echoes through late November and most of December. Some reacted haughtily; for example, one British official declared the statement a vulgar bluff which "such Puppies of Statesmen" were impudent enough to try on Aberdeen. The principal London papers repeated this idea, and (in an odd metaphor) one called the *Union*'s declaration "a mere *brutum fulmen* destined only to feel the pulse of John Bull."[70] The *Journal des débats*, shocked at the talk of war between England and America, quoted Voltaire's remark about the insanity of two civilized nations' fighting over *"some arpents of snow"* in Canada, and a British journal lamented that sensible politicians such as Adams, Clay, and Webster "seem to disappear like other lost species of American life."[71]

The news of Webster's speech at Faneuil Hall had a mixed effect on British opinion. As evidence that moderate views existed in the United States, it calmed the press, encouraged the pacifists, and brought a rise in consols (funded government securities, the barometer of the Stock Exchange). As an indication that even enlightened Whigs insisted on a compromise at 49°, however, it dampened the spirits of British nationalists. Aberdeen's only reaction to dispatches from the United States was to instruct Pakenham to propose arbitration again.[72]

At this time McLane analyzed British attitudes in a long private report (which Polk did not receive until late in December). He pointed out that the *Times* and possibly also some cabinet members were indulging in the illusory expectation that Calhoun would support Webster's proposal for an independent Oregon. McLane hoped that the continental nations would not form an alliance to bring this about and thus restrict American expansion. For

70. G. W. Featherstonhaugh to Vaughan, December 4, 1845, Vaughan Papers, file C. (Featherstonhaugh had been a member of the northeastern boundary commission.) British press reaction appears in *NNR*, 69 (January 3, 1846), 280–81. Periodical articles for 1845 are summarized in Richard S. Cramer, "British Magazines and the Oregon Question," *Pacific Historical Review*, 32 (May 1963), 375–77.

71. *Le journal des débats*, December 1, 1845, clipping in GB, FO 27/729. See also a penetrating analysis of the

American situation in *Le constitutionnel*, December 5, p. 1. The American minister, William R. King, warned Buchanan that England might attack without warning and urged him to impress on Congress the need for preparations. However, King was still optimistic about a compromise settlement. William R. King to Buchanan, November 28, Buchanan Papers, box 62, HSP.

72. Aberdeen to Pakenham, November 28, 1845, No. 72, GB, FO 115/89, ff. 213–21.

Webster he had nothing but scorn. McLane felt that Polk would do much good by taking a strong stand on Oregon in his annual message, as long as he did not rule out further negotiations.[73]

* * * *

While Ritchie, Webster, and other editors and politicians discussed the steps to be taken, Polk and his cabinet were busy drawing up one of the most important public papers of the administration—the President's first annual message to Congress. True to his habits of careful deliberation and mastery of every detail, Polk began work more than two months beforehand, discussing the tariff section of the message as early as September 30. Through October and November he worked steadily, writing drafts, getting oral and written comments from the cabinet (many of which he rejected), polishing, copying, and drafting anew. To judge from his diary, the sections that provoked the longest and most frequent discussions were those dealing with the tariff and Oregon. As the day of delivery approached, Polk began to ask outsiders to read and comment on the document, with elaborate warnings of secrecy. On the evening of November 28, for example, he showed two copies of the manuscript to Vice President Dallas and to Thomas Ritchie, each man in a different room of the White House. As Polk later wrote in his diary with sly satisfaction, neither man knew that the other had seen the message.[74]

Polk's first annual message and the three which followed were the longest so far in American history; indeed, the messages of only two other nineteenth-century Presidents, James Buchanan and Grover Cleveland, were to exceed his in length.[75] Over half of the 1845 message dealt with matters of interest to Europe and Mexico. Polk began with a statement of pride at the annexation of Texas, "a bloodless achievement," nonimperialistic, "the deliberate homage of each people to the great principle of our federative

73. McLane to Polk, December 1, 1845, Polk Papers, LCVI, LC. See also L. McLane to R. McLane, December 1, 2, McLane Papers. Polk's friend Robert Armstrong, American consul at Liverpool, gave somewhat similar advice, pointing out that British military preparations were mainly defensive and not well designed for war with the United States. He suggested that they might be intended to employ the starving or to divert public attention. Rob-ert Armstrong to Polk, November 4, December 4, Polk Papers, XCV, XCVI, LC.

74. Polk, *Diary*, I, 48, 105–6, *et passim*. Sellers, *Polk, Continentalist*, pp. 326–30.

75. At that, only one of Buchanan's annual messages matched any of Polk's four. Polk's message appears in James D. Richardson, ed., *A Compilation of the Messages and Papers of the Presidents, 1789–1897*, IV, 385–416.

union." He deplored the efforts of European governments to prevent annexation by imposing a restrictive promise on Texas as the price of Mexican recognition and added complacently: "From this example European Governments may learn how vain diplomatic arts and intrigues must ever prove upon this continent against that system of self-government which seems natural to our soil, and which will ever resist foreign interference."[76]

Turning then to Mexico, he reported the withdrawal of the Mexican minister, thus breaking diplomatic relations with the United States, the threatening proclamations, and the troop movements ordered by the Mexican government. "As a precautionary measure" he had ordered a squadron of warships into the Gulf of Mexico and a military force to the western frontier of Texas, with orders to "commit no act of hostility against Mexico unless she declared war or was herself the aggressor by striking the first blow." By recognizing Texan independence, Mexico had waived her rights in that region, and Polk rejected the validity of any conditions or restrictions on that recognition. He then recounted the history of American claims against Mexico in much the same language he had used in Slidell's instructions, informed Congress of the special mission, and recommended that it withhold further action until news arrived from the envoy. Buchanan had objected briefly to some parts of this section and offered milder versions, which Polk rejected.[77]

Polk's discussion of Oregon, probably the most immediately important part of the message, began with a brief recital of earlier negotiations, leading up to the Calhoun-Pakenham meetings of August and September 1844 (see Chapter 6), the unsatisfactory terms offered by the British, and the resulting impasse. Polk declared that because of the prior negotiations he had felt an obligation to make a final offer to Britain, but he emphasized that he would never concede to any foreign country the right to navigate a river through the heart of American territory. Britain having rejected the offer, "the civilized world will see in these proceedings a spirit of liberal concession on the part of the United States, and this Government will be relieved of any responsibility which may follow the failure to settle the controversy."

Since all efforts at compromise had failed, what should Congress do to protect American citizens in Oregon? Polk urged

---

76. Passages quoted appear in Richardson, *Papers of the Presidents*, IV, 387–88.

77. Polk, *Diary*, I, 99–100. Phrases quoted appear in Richardson, *Papers of the Presidents*, IV, 388–89.

scrupulous respect for existing treaties and recommended that Congress first give the required year's notice for abrogation of the treaty of 1827, which had renewed joint occupation of the territory. He pointed out that Parliament had passed laws protecting fur traders, granting the Hudson's Bay Company exclusive trading rights with the Indians, and extending British legal jurisdiction within the disputed territory. Accordingly, he again recommended that Congress place American settlers in Oregon under American law, establish an Indian agency, and erect forts along the emigration route. Congress might also consider granting land to the settlers, but Polk was not sure that such action would be proper until the treaty lapsed. Once again he flatly rejected the British compromise terms and proclaimed defiantly: "Oregon is a part of the North American continent, to which, it is confidently affirmed, the title of the United States is the best now in existence." On the testimony of Polk's diary this section of the message owed much more to Benton than to Buchanan, for it closely followed Polk's conversation of October 24 with the Senator despite several later efforts by the Secretary of State to soften the language or to remove some of the most provocative statements.[78]

Immediately following the section on Oregon came what was in later years to be the best-known passage in Polk's message—his invocation of the Monroe Doctrine, the first important public reference to it since 1823. The passage has an interesting history. Polk had inserted into his inaugural address a short, blunt reference to the noncolonization principle applied to Oregon but decided later to omit it. After Guizot's "balance of power" speech during the summer, the President received occasional suggestions that he answer Guizot with Monroe and "stamp the impress of American statesmanship on the history of the world."[79] When he began to plan his message, he consulted Benton on how best to invoke the Monroe Doctrine, and Bancroft discussed the noncolonization principle with John Quincy Adams, its originator. Polk asked Buchanan and Bancroft to compose drafts on the Doctrine. They complied, Bancroft producing a "purple passage" on democracy and Buchanan a somewhat more sober statement of American interest in the New World.[80]

78. Polk, *Diary*, I, 69–72, 89, 99–100, 102. The sentence quoted appears in Richardson, *Papers of the Presidents*, IV, 397.

79. John McKean to Polk, New York, September 19, 1845, Polk Papers, XCIII,

LC.

80. These drafts are contained in "Messages and Speeches, 1845," series 5, box 2, Polk Papers, LC. Among other things Bancroft declared, "Our country can never extend its territory by

The final version used in Polk's message incorporated phrases from both Bancroft and Buchanan. The rapid growth of the United States, "the expansion of free principles, and our rising greatness as a nation," Polk stated, had attracted the European powers' attention and elicited the counterprinciple of a "balance of power" in the New World. This latter policy, arising from the jealousy of European nations, could not be applied to the American continent. Nations of the New World must be free to choose their own destinies, including entrance into the American Union. Polk quoted Monroe's message on noncolonization and declared that "no future European colony or dominion shall with our consent be planted or established on any part of the North American continent." His point of departure was undoubtedly Guizot's statement about Texas and the "balance of power." It is clear, however, that Polk had Oregon and California even more closely in mind, for the statement occurred immediately following his strong passage on Oregon, and it was his closest approach to mention of California. Most significant, he had discussed with Benton the application of the Monroe Doctrine to both of these areas.[81]

After invoking the Monroe Doctrine Polk dealt with several topics of lesser importance and then turned to the tariff. Briefly distinguishing between revenue and protective duties, he indicated that he was more interested in revenue, and that when "incidental protection" was afforded, "all the great interests of the country, including manufactures, agriculture, commerce, navigation, and the mechanic arts, should, as far as may be practicable, derive equal advantages" from it. He criticized the tariff of 1842 primarily for its inequity and recommended that Congress modify it by abolishing arbitrary minimum values, substituting *ad val-*

conquest; for the principles of our constitution preclude the possibility of governing a country against the will of its inhabitants. . . . We know of no possible extension of our territory but by consent; we have no cause but for joy at the prosperity of all other states throughout the world & more especially of those upon our borders. Disclaiming not only the desire but the authority to make an increase of our territory by conquest, we can as little favor the introduction among us of wars or negotiations for a balance of power, as for any other antiquated form of policy, which is destined to vanish before the better influences of the increasing in-

telligence of mankind." On the discussion with Benton and Adams, see Polk, *Diary*, I, 69–72; and John Quincy Adams, *Memoirs of John Quincy Adams*, XII, 218–19. The phrases quoted from the final version of the message appear in Richardson, *Papers of the Presidents*, IV, 398–99.

81. For discussions of this part of the message, see Dexter Perkins, *The Monroe Doctrine, 1826–1867*, pp. 85–101; and Merk, *Monroe Doctrine and Expansionism*, Chap. 1, pp. 60, 78–79, *et passim*. Neither writer seems to have observed Polk's inclusion of the Doctrine in an early draft of the inaugural address.

orem for specific duties and setting up "a system strictly within the revenue standard." [82] The rest of his message dealt mostly with internal questions such as a "constitutional treasury" banking system and preemption, and he closed with a benediction quoted from the recently fallen Jackson.

Two of the departmental reports that accompanied Polk's message are worth notice. Emulating his master, Walker had worked long hours during the autumn on the Treasury report, overriding, with Polk's support, Buchanan's strong protectionist scruples. Concerning the tariff, Walker's report filled in the details of Polk's recommendations, arguing that if the United States consulted its true interest, it would not wait for reciprocal trade agreements: "Let our commerce be as free as our political institutions, . . . and nation after nation will soon follow our example." The future of the United States depended on its farmers, who could soon "feed and clothe the world" if given a market for their surplus crops. Continued protection might force down wages and cause social upheaval, the Secretary hinted, but cheap lands would raise wages and obviate protection. His arguments were to serve tariff reformers as a model for many years. [83]

A somewhat less dramatic report was that of Marcy for the War Department. Although the whole Department was miserably understaffed and the Army consisted of only fourteen regiments, Marcy took a calm attitude toward current requirements. He asked for a few small appropriations to repair fortifications and recommended that the President be authorized to double the number of privates in each company if he thought it necessary. Only in case circumstances required "a force considerably larger than a permanent peace establishment" would he consider raising new regiments. Marcy's was certainly not a "crash program" of rearmament, but he explained to Benton in a private letter that these recommendations were intended only for a peacetime establishment; they would not be adequate in case of foreign attack. He felt that the President ought to be empowered to accept as many as fifty thousand volunteers and state troops for service of one year, and he indicated that his proposed expenditures for fortifications were merely a first installment. [84]

82. The quoted phrases appear in Richardson, *Papers of the Presidents*, IV, 404, 406.

83. US, 29C, 1S, SD 2, pp. 4–15. James Patrick Shenton, *Robert John Walker, a Politician from Jackson to Lincoln*, pp. 74–76. For a detailed analysis of Walker's report, see Edward Stanwood, *American Tariff Controversies in the Nineteenth Century*, II, 57–69.

84. US, 29C, 1S, SD 1, pp. 193–206. Marcy to Thomas H. Benton, Decem-

After Polk's message had been read to Congress, Democrats in Washington flocked to the White House to congratulate him, and soon letters began to arrive from the party faithful all over the country. Western expansionists were delighted with his firm statement about Oregon, and Southerners such as Calhoun's lieutenant, Senator George McDuffie, approved the tariff section.[85] A few Whigs—Senator Archer, for one—praised the passage on Oregon, but neither they nor Vice President Dallas liked the tariff recommendations, and the Pennsylvania delegation was "struck with despair." Nevertheless, Buchanan was well satisfied with the reaction among his many friends in Congress and anticipated no difficulty in obtaining the requested legislation.[86]

In the American press the message merely continued the debate over peace or war with Britain. The semiofficial Washington *Union* declared that "the American heart" would "throb with delight" at the reaffirmation of the noncolonization principle, but Horace Greeley sniffed that "all the gas . . . about 'the balance of power on this Continent' [was] the paltriest fishing for thoughtless huzzas, worthy rather of a candidate for constable than a President of the United States." Whig organs such as the *American Review* and the *National Intelligencer* accepted the Monroe Doctrine as a principle of national security and morality but opposed its use to camouflage American expansion. They called on the members of their party to "resist the lust for territorial aggrandizement, revived in our own day and among our own people from their Norman–Saxon ancestry."[87]

Niles' Register, often critical of Britain, generally approved the sections dealing with Texas and Mexico but declared of the passage on Oregon: "Our worst anticipations have been realized. Negotiation is abandoned.—Compromises have failed. . . . [But,] *if we are to fight,* . . . why then, we had better fight for all, . . . not only . . . 'all of Oregon,' but all of Canada and of Nova Scotia too. . . . The prize must be made something nearer worth fighting for."[88] Other papers agreed that the two countries had taken "very

ber 29, 1845, Polk Papers, XCVII, LC. Ivor Debenham Spencer, *The Victor and the Spoils, a Life of William L. Marcy*, pp. 141–42, 145. Few newspapers said much about Marcy's report, and those that did saw no great need for military preparations.

85. Polk, *Diary*, I, 109–12. Sellers, *Polk, Continentalist*, pp. 346–48. For a collection of letters on the message, see Polk Papers, XCVI, LC.

86. Polk, *Diary*, I, 110, 115–16. Shenton, *Walker*, p. 74. Buchanan to McLane, December 13, 1845, Buchanan, *Works*, VI, 342–43.

87. These newspapers are quoted and paraphrased at length in Merk, *Monroe Doctrine and Expansionism*, pp. 7–8, 79–81. See also Perkins, *Monroe Doctrine, 1826–1867*, pp. 101–3.

88. *NNR*, 69 (December 6, 1845), 209.

foolish positions" but expressed the hope that "the calm judgment, and mutual interests of two cognate peoples" would prevail.[89]

In December 1845 the chief obstacle to such an agreement was Polk's stubborn conviction that compromise at 49° was fundamentally wrong and that both Congress and the people would condemn him if he yielded to Britain. Privately criticizing Buchanan as "too timid and too fearful of War on the Oregon question," he proclaimed American rights and prepared once again to negotiate from an appearance of strength.[90] Three days after Polk sent his annual message to Congress, Bancroft dispatched new, secret instructions to Commodore Sloat off the Mexican coast at Mazatlán. Reassuring Sloat that the likelihood of war with Mexico was declining, he ordered him to move his squadron northward and to keep in constant touch with Larkin. Bancroft also sent him five hundred copies of Polk's annual message, which Sloat was to send by ship to Oregon for distribution among the settlers in the Willamette Valley, along with any rifles and other small arms that he could spare.[91]

From these measures, as well as from the terms of the annual message and the subsequent newspaper debate, it is clear that at the beginning of December Polk had brought the country to the verge of a crisis in foreign policy. On the Mexican front he had reinforced Taylor's troops at Corpus Christi and had dispatched Slidell to Mexico City with instructions to take Texan annexation for granted and push for the cession of New Mexico and California. On the Pacific front he had drawn in Sloat's little squadron, had reasserted the extreme American claim to Oregon, and had called on Congress to abrogate the treaty of joint occupation. While bringing pressure to bear on Mexico and Britain, he held out inducements for concession—money for the bankrupt bureaucrats in Mexico City, grain and markets for the distressed industrialists in London and Manchester. As Congress organized itself, not even Polk could know whether his aggressive gestures would thrust aside opposition at home and abroad, but if he had any doubts whatever, he did not reveal them, even to his diary.

89. Louisville *Journal* and New York *Courier*, n.d., quoted in *NNR*, 69 (December 20), p. 241.
90. Polk, *Diary*, I, 107. J. Polk to W. Polk, November 27, 1845, Letterbook, 1845–1846, pp. 51–55, Polk Papers, LC.
91. Bancroft to John D. Sloat, December 5, 1845, US, DN, LCS, I, 163, as quoted in Merk, *Manifest Destiny and Mission*, pp. 65–66.

11

The Oregon Debate

While the United States was reacting to Polk's annual message, Britain was undergoing a cabinet crisis brought on by the grain shortage and the potato famine in Ireland. Pressure for tariff reform was irresistible, but so many Tories opposed repeal of the corn laws that on December 5 Peel submitted his resignation. When Lord John Russell mustered his Whig forces, however, he found them split too on the question of returning the headstrong Palmerston to the Foreign Office. After two weeks of intraparty recriminations, which soon became public, Russell informed the Queen that he could not form a cabinet and, in Benjamin Disraeli's words, handed back the poisoned chalice to Peel. The Tories resumed office, uneasily aware that each step might be their last.[1]

The Oregon question was of little consequence in Peel's fall from power, but the "Whig abortion" and the Tories' return to Whitehall influenced Anglo–American relations in several ways. Peel sought to strengthen his cabinet by bringing to the Admiralty a strenuous militarist, the Earl of Ellenborough, who had just been recalled from India after waging vigorous war on the Sikhs. The new first lord expected hostilities with the United States and joined Wellington in calling for strong defensive measures. His powerful oratory in Parliament and his encouragement to Sir George Seymour of the Pacific Squadron raised new obstacles to Aberdeen's pacifism, even though Peel instructed Ellenborough to confer with the Foreign Office on every naval matter that might affect Anglo–American relations.[2]

In other respects the British political upheaval of December

1. For good, brief accounts of the cabinet crisis, see Blanche Cecil Woodham-Smith, *The Great Hunger, Ireland, 1845–9*, pp. 51–53; and Frederick Merk, *The Oregon Question, Essays in Anglo–American Diplomacy and Politics*, pp. 270–72. Donald Southgate, *"The Most English Minister . . .," the Policies and Politics of Palmerston*, pp. 177–78.

2. Albert H. Imlah, *Lord Ellenborough; a Biography of Edward Law, Earl of Ellenborough, Governor-General of India*, pp. 234–36 *et passim*. Earl of Aberdeen to Sir Robert Peel, December 29, 1845, Peel Papers, BM, AM, vol. 40455, ff. 292–93. Peel to Aberdeen, January 29, 1846, Aberdeen Papers, BM, AM, vol. 43065, ff. 141–43.

encouraged the forces of peace. In every European chancellery the possibility of Palmerston's return to power caused consternation. This alarm so impressed Russell that he exerted every effort to counteract it. On January 12, for example, he delivered a speech in Glasgow in which he eulogized the rewards of peace with the United States and stated flatly that "it would be disgraceful for two such nations to go to war."

More notably, the "Whig abortion" freed the hands of the Peel government in the matter of the corn laws, and it was soon obvious that the only real opposition to repeal lay in the agrarian right wing of the Tory party, which Peel now tried to conciliate. The prospects for restoration of good relations with the United States brightened, for the approach of repeal encouraged tariff reformers in the United States, especially in the South, which was lukewarm toward the campaign for fifty-four-forty.[3] Although Peel and Aberdeen would not admit any connection between their policies concerning trade and Oregon, liberals on both sides of the Atlantic took heart. As the *British Quarterly Review* put it in February:

> Let England repeal her corn-laws, and cease to interfere with the peaceful progress of the Anglo-Saxon race over the continent of North America, and the irritation and jealousy of the United States may mitigate and die away. In all else the democratic tendency is in our favour. It is the aristocracy, and not the democracy, it is the capitalists, and not the working millions of these great States, that are the patrons of restrictive tariffs. . . . Let us hope that a mere point of honour as to the ownership of the Oregon [*sic*], or the ultimate destinies of the Mexican Provinces, may not be suffered to exasperate and increase these feelings of hostility.[4]

* * * *

Two or three days after Peel and his cabinet returned to office, the text of Polk's annual message arrived in England, where it had been awaited with some apprehension. The *Examiner* found the message less dreadful than it might have been, and both the *Morning Chronicle* and the *Times* praised the section on the tariff.

3. Merk, *Oregon Question*, pp. 272–75.

4. *British Quarterly Review*, 3 (February 1846), 233. Peel thought that the admission of American maize would "go far to promote a settlement of Oregon." Peel to Lord Francis Egerton, January 6, Charles Stuart Parker, ed., *Sir Robert Peel, from His Private Papers*, III, 324.

"What Mr. Polk proposed to Congress, purely from a regard to American interests," declared the *Chronicle*, "is precisely that for which we should have stipulated, had we been negotiating for British interests."[5]

Yankeephobes, however, haughtily rejected Polk's interpretation of the Monroe Doctrine as "a convenient system of original and axiomatic claims." His "insane counsels" on Oregon impressed them as cheap politics, and they reminded their readers that an American "can hardly be judged by European standards of moderation, decency, and honor." They did not, at any rate, call for war. Impressed by the food crisis and the need for trade, the *Economist* suggested that if Britain should repeal the corn laws, Polk might agree to arbitration in Oregon. The *Morning Chronicle* put the same idea in less tactful language: "Your genuine Yankee will sell house and home, with all the family heirlooms to boot, without a sigh, if he can make a 'spec' by the transaction." A few days later the *Chronicle* added shrewdly: "There is certainly no want of adroitness in the tactics assumed by Mr. Polk. . . . While he threatens us with war, he bribes us to peace."[6]

With Polk's inaugural address in mind, no one in the British cabinet was much surprised at his annual message. When Aberdeen read it, he wrote to Peel that it was, if anything, more moderate than he had expected. He welcomed Polk's offensive references to France, for these would surely alienate French opinion from the United States.[7] At the same time, Aberdeen received at least two indirect evidences of conciliatory spirit from the United States government. A mutual friend, Dr. Henry Holland, repeated to him Bancroft's opinion that the Oregon question should have been settled in the preceding July and that Americans did not desire war any more strongly than the British.[8] Also, American Minister McLane came to him with an unofficial inquiry about Britain's

5. London *Examiner*, December 27, 1845, pp. 817–18. London *Morning Chronicle*, December 26, p. 4. London *Times*, December 24. For a convenient survey of early British press reactions, see New York *Evening Post*, January 24, 1846, p. 1.

6. London *Economist*, n.d., quoted in New York *Evening Post*, January 24, 1846. London *Morning Chronicle*, December 23, 1845, p. 4; December 27, p. 4.

7. Aberdeen to Peel, December 25, 1845, Aberdeen Papers, BM, AM, vol. 43065, ff. 127–28. Same, December 28,

29, Peel Papers, BM, AM, vol. 40455, ff. 290–93. Aberdeen was amazed that Polk had not mentioned the British arbitration proposal. Peel curtly advised silence and preparation. Peel to Aberdeen, December 26, ibid., ff. 282–83.

8. George Bancroft to Henry Holland, December 12, 1845; Holland to Bancroft, London, January 3, 1846, Bancroft Papers, MHS. Holland was a London medical doctor who was prominent in London society and well acquainted with many members of the cabinet.

"extensive warlike preparations"; he encouraged the British government to take the initiative in making a new proposal.[9]

Aberdeen reacted to these American feelers with a mixture of firmness and cordiality. To McLane he explained that the defense measures antedated the recent crisis over Oregon and had no direct reference to an Anglo–American rupture. They were, he emphasized, less extensive than rumored. He repeated his statement of hope for a fair compromise and mentioned that he had instructed Pakenham to offer arbitration. Aberdeen pointed out to Holland also that British public opinion might prevent successful negotiation, leaving arbitration as the only solution. In a letter to Edward Everett he was even more blunt: "The truth is that everything depends on the real disposition of the President, and of the people by whom he is directed, whether Ministers, or Mob." On its own merits the Oregon question might be settled in an hour. He concluded: "We are sincerely and anxiously desirous of a peaceful issue; and if you share this desire, we shall assuredly arrive at it. But if you desire war, as assuredly you will have it, for well as you know my love of peace, and my determination to preserve it, I shall be perfectly powerless in such a case."[10]

Even while warning the Americans that the British people might balk, Aberdeen took steps to modify public opinion. This time he turned to an independent Tory newspaper, the powerful *Times*, a notorious Yankee-baiter and often a critic of Peel and most of the cabinet. The young editor of the *Times*, John Delane, was an admirer of Aberdeen and occasionally used his paper as mouthpiece for the Foreign Office, which sometimes returned the favor with discreet tips. In December Aberdeen had given Delane the greatest "scoop" of all—advance notice of Peel's probable resignation. Now he apparently prevailed on the *Times* to support compromise in Oregon.[11]

9. James Buchanan to Louis McLane, December 13, 1845, No. 20; McLane to Buchanan, January 3, 1846, No. 30, Manning, *CR*, III, 312–13, 989–92.

10. McLane to Buchanan, January 3, 1846, No. 30, Manning, *CR*, III, 989–92. Holland to Bancroft, January 3, Bancroft Papers, MHS. Aberdeen to Edward Everett, January 3, Aberdeen Papers, BM, AM, vol. 43123, ff. 436–37. At about the same time, Peel commented in characteristically blunter fashion than Aberdeen: "We shall not reciprocate blustering with Polk, but shall quietly make an increase in Naval and Military and Ordnance Estimates." Peel to Lord Egerton, January 6, quoted in Wilbur Devereux Jones and J. Chal. Vinson, "British Preparedness and the Oregon Settlement," *Pacific Historical Review*, 22 (1953), 360.

11. Merk, *Oregon Question*, pp. 297–300, 303. Merk admits that Aberdeen never revealed in writing that he had inspired the *Times'* change of policy but regards as virtual proof his comment to Everett in a letter of January 3 that the editorial was "temperately written." Charles C. F. Greville believed that Aberdeen had leaked news

As late as December 30 and January 1 the *Times* was still demanding the Columbia River boundary and declaring that the covetous Americans "violate the whole system of the pacific economy of the world, and proclaim a direct hostility to all the principles of civilized nations." On the following day the wind changed. A brief statement praised the courteous tone of the correspondence between Buchanan and Pakenham on Oregon (published with the annual message) and declared that, since both countries' titles were obscure, "equality of holding is dictated by justice." On January 3 the conversion was complete, for a full-dress editorial called on Pakenham to renew the proposal made by Gallatin in 1826 and 1827: the forty-ninth parallel to the sea, reserving to Britain all of Vancouver Island, the use of the Strait of Juan de Fuca, and free navigation of the Columbia River. Such a compromise "would concede all that the most successful war could acquire—a sovereign but barren domain; . . . but it would retain for Englishmen that privilege to which they are justly entitled—the privilege of *sharing* in the traffic between North America and the English settlements in the Pacific." [12]

When Everett saw the *Times* editorial, he wrote to Aberdeen that its terms were all the United States had any right to expect, and he informed Bancroft and Webster at once that it was a semi-official representation of Aberdeen's views. [13] Nevertheless, Peel's cabinet remained divided. All through January the new first lord of the admiralty, Lord Ellenborough, urged warlike measures on the prime minister—stronger defenses in Canada, and the stationing of warships off Chesapeake Bay to encourage British-born

---

of the cabinet split to the *Times* in December at least partly for its effect on the United States, hoping that the prospects for repeal of the corn laws would encourage American moderation in Oregon. Charles C. F. Greville, *A Journal of the Reign of Queen Victoria from 1837 to 1852*, ed. Henry Reeve, II, 46–48.

12. London *Times*, December 30, 1845, p. 4; January 1, 1846, p. 4; January 2, p. 4; January 3, p. 4. Merk, *Oregon Question*, pp. 301–3. The *Times* later pointed out that Gallatin's line had actually run along 48½°, not 49°. London *Times*, February 26, p. 5. However, it did not propose the more southerly line.

13. Merk, *Oregon Question*, pp. 303–

4. However, Everett protested to Aberdeen at the latter's statement in his letter of January 3 to the effect that the outcome of peace or war depended on the United States government. Everett to Aberdeen, Boston, January 28, 1846, Aberdeen Papers, BM, AM, vol. 43123, ff. 438–41. Everett to Daniel Webster, February 2, Everett Papers, LXXVIII, 36–38. Webster later (February 26) wrote to Evelyn Denison deprecating Polk and the "foolish vaporing" of extremists on Oregon, urging a compromise settlement, and predicting the ultimate independence of the territory. Denison passed on a copy to Aberdeen with a covering letter, dated March 24. Letterbook, Aberdeen Papers, BM, AM, vol. 43290, ff. 8–9.

sailors to leave American service. Peel wisely vetoed the latter measure and postponed a decision about building warships on the Great Lakes.[14]

While maintaining a firm stance against the war party, he yielded to Aberdeen's request for more conciliatory language on Oregon in the Royal Speech to Parliament. This address, coming late in January, struck a balance between the two forces in the cabinet by declaring that Britain desired peace, while recommending continued increases in the naval and military estimates. Comments in both Houses referred temperately to the unfortunate dispute with the United States—a striking contrast to the angry, defiant remarks of the preceding spring.[15]

While Britain was moderating its reaction to Polk's annual message, observers on the Continent followed the Anglo–American discussions with keen interest. *Le journal des débats* declared the message reasonable in substance but deplored its demagogic tone; some of the French press called the message warlike or mere bluff. Guizot was somewhat chagrined that France had been treated with less respect than Britain, and he told the British chargé d'affaires that he proposed to abandon France's traditional friendship with America. Labeling the Monroe Doctrine strange and unacceptable, he declared that France would follow her own desires in maintaining "commercial, political, even territorial interests" in America. But when Minister King expressed alarm at these words, Guizot assured him that France did not intend hostile acts. The French opposition, led by Thiers, attacked Guizot's Texan policy again and repeated that American expansion would counterbalance British pretensions.[16]

14. Earl of Ellenborough to Peel, January 18, February 7, 1846, Earl of Ellenborough Papers, PRO 30/12/4/29, Britain, Public Record Office. Peel to Ellenborough, January 18, February 8, Peel Papers, BM, AM, vol. 40473, ff. 41–42, 53–54.
15. Aberdeen to Peel, January 19, 1846, BM, AM, vol. 40455, ff. 300–301. Peel to Aberdeen, January 29, Aberdeen Papers, BM, AM, vol. 43065, ff. 141–43. McLane to Buchanan, February 3, No. 34, Manning, *CR*, III, 995–1005. Sellers has considerably oversimplified these complex developments, in the belief that Polk's strong stand, aided by Peel's brief loss of power, caused the prime minister to shift to

Aberdeen's position on Oregon. He makes no mention of Ellenborough. Charles Grier Sellers, *James K. Polk, Continentalist, 1843–1846*, pp. 372–76.
16. For French press opinion on Polk's message, see *Le journal des débats*, December 26, 1845 (clipping in GB, FO 27/729); surveys in New York *Evening Post*, January 24, 1846, p. 1; and *NNR*, 69 (February 7), 366–67. On Guizot's views, see *Le journal des débats*, January 13, pp. 2–3. Henry Reeve to Aberdeen, Paris, December 26, 1845; January 14, 22, 24, 1846, Aberdeen Papers, BM, AM, vol. 43245, ff. 150–53, 207–10, 228–31, 233–36. For opposition views, see *Le journal des débats*, January 21, p. 3; *La presse*, January 13, p.

*   *   *   *

Polk's annual message and the opening of Congress started a new cycle of discussion on Oregon throughout the United States. In the cabinet the President's bold language worried Secretary of State Buchanan, who tried to draw him out further. Several days before the message went to Congress, Pakenham, conversing with Benton, had put out a feeler regarding a compromise boundary at 49°, Britain to retain Vancouver Island and free navigation of the Columbia River. Benton, who flatly opposed free navigation, probably told Buchanan of the exchange. Seeing an opportunity for compromise, at the first cabinet meeting after the President's delivery of the annual message the secretary pressed Polk to state whether he would submit such a proposal to the Senate for its advice. Polk would not commit himself.

Despite this lack of encouragement, a few days later Buchanan prepared a draft of instructions to McLane in which he stated that the President would feel "strongly inclined" to submit a compromise proposal to the Senate. On December 13 Polk rejected the passage and substituted the curt statement that he would submit a proposal if he thought it justifiable. To Buchanan's protests Polk merely replied that he intended to keep control of the subject in his own hands, "that we had the advantage of Great Brittain [sic], and that if anything more was done that Governm[en]t must move voluntarily and of its own accord, and without any intimation or assurance of what I would do." [17]

Meanwhile, Polk expected Congress to carry out the recommendations of the annual message firmly, quickly, and with a minimum of debate. For this purpose he relied especially on a bloc of Democrats from the Middle West who demanded all of Oregon to 54°40′, in the full confidence that Polk would support this demand with war if necessary. The best known of this group was the ponderous Lewis Cass of Michigan, perennial candidate for the Presidency. Among his followers were the hot-tempered Edward A. Hannegan of Indiana and David R. Atchison of Missouri, a rival of Benton. Another Westerner of some promise and even greater hopes was William Allen of Ohio, the new chairman of the foreign relations committee—a tall, gaunt man who rather resembled Andrew Jackson and whom Charles Sumner described as a

1; January 18, p. 1; and *Le national*, January 22, p. 1; February 3, p. 1.

17. James K. Polk, *The Diary of James K. Polk during His Presidency,* *1845 to 1849,* ed. Milo M. Quaife, I, 117–23. Philip Shriver Klein, *President James Buchanan, a Biography,* p. 181.

"tobacco chewing spitting loud voiced ferocious blackguard."
Allen could speak with biting sarcasm and florid eloquence but
had few ideas to offer except impulsive patriotism. At the beginning of the session he favored compromise and consulted with
Polk along that line, but eventually he joined the extremists.[18]

On the Oregon question the Western extremists in the Senate
faced a potentially powerful coalition, largely Eastern and Southern, consisting of the entire Whig minority and many Democrats,
who fervently hoped that their President would spare them the
choice between war and a party schism. The Whigs numbered
many effective leaders—William S. Archer of Virginia, the friend
of both Polk and Pakenham, John J. Crittenden of Kentucky,
Daniel Webster, and others. (Henry Clay was still in retirement.)
Among the moderate Democrats was one Westerner, Thomas Hart
Benton of Missouri, long Polk's friend but now partly alienated by
his demand for 54°40′. The real leadership of the moderate cause,
however, lay in the bony hands of John C. Calhoun, who had deliberately provoked sectional rivalry in his eagerness for the annexation of Texas but now spoke the language of compromise and
restraint. Urged by many friends, Calhoun decided at the last
moment to return to the Senate and use his prestige to prevent
war. Eventually he controlled a bloc of seven Democrats.

In a strictly party vote Polk had a majority of thirty to twenty-
four in the Senate, but since Calhoun and Benton both opposed a
strong stand on Oregon and also hated each other, the action for
which he called was not likely to be either quick or decisive. The
situation in the House was not much more encouraging. Here the
Democrats had a majority of over fifty; their moderates were
weaker and less vocal than in the Senate; and perhaps one third
of the Whigs were at least mildly expansionist. But the House
Whigs had the best leaders: Robert C. Winthrop of Massachusetts,
the radical Joshua R. Giddings of Ohio, and the cantankerous
maverick, John Quincy Adams. The Democratic leaders of the
future—Stephen A. Douglas, Jefferson Davis, Howell Cobb, and
others—were as yet too young and inexperienced to exert much
force.[19]

Between the delivery of the annual message and the Christmas
recess there was time for only a few preliminary exchanges. Cass

18. Reginald Charles McGrane, *William Allen: A Study in Western Democracy*, pp. 56, 76, 103–4, 374–76, *et
passim*. Sumner's remark is quoted in
Merk, *Oregon Question*, p. 376. On Allen's appointment as chairman of the
foreign relations committee, see ibid.,
pp. 374–76.

19. Sellers, *Polk, Continentalist*, pp.
310–24 and Chap. 9, *passim*.

opened the Oregon question with a resolution inquiring into the condition of the country's defenses, accompanying it with the first of many Western war whoops. The Senate approved the resolution unanimously, for although the Whigs earnestly opposed all talk of war, they did not care to risk the stigma of disloyalty. Meanwhile, several resolutions appeared in both houses for giving Britain notice to abrogate the Oregon treaty and for extending governmental and military protection to Oregon.[20] Across the country nationalists applauded the fifty-four-forty men, thus pushing Western Whigs toward the Cass bloc. An admirer wrote to William Allen: "If we can defeat the British in this we may be said to be free indeed . . . [but] if Oregon is an independent state and in league with England the whole of England's navy may be brought to batter down our Atlantic seaports."[21]

Near the end of December John L. O' Sullivan published the most famous editorial of the decade in the New York *Morning News*, incidentally adding the term *manifest destiny* to the American orator's vocabulary:

> Away, away with all these cobweb tissues of rights of discovery, exploration, settlement, continuity, etc. . . . Were the respective cases and arguments of the two parties, as to all these points of history and law, reversed—had England all ours, and we nothing but hers— our claim to Oregon would still be best and strongest. And that claim is by the right of our manifest destiny to overspread and to possess the whole of the continent which Providence has given us for the development of the great experiment of Liberty and federated self-government entrusted to us.[22]

On the other side, moderates such as the New York *Evening Post* reasoned quietly that war over Oregon was neither likely nor advisable. The *Post* deplored extreme attacks on the administration

20. Sellers, *Polk, Continentalist*, p. 362. US, 29C, 1S, *CG*, pp. 45–47, 54–60. *NNR*, 69 (December 13, 20, 27, 1845), 230, 245–46, 258. Richard Pakenham to Aberdeen, December 29, No. 137, GB, FO 5/430, ff. 155–60.

21. Charles Pletcher to William Allen, Washington, December 8, 1845, Allen Papers, IX. Sellers, *Polk, Continentalist*, p. 361. Some saw in war an excuse to repudiate the individual states' debts to British bondholders. R. L. King to John C. Calhoun, Racine, Wisconsin Territory, December 10, in Chauncey S. Boucher and Robert P. Brooks, eds., *Correspondence Addressed to John C. Calhoun, 1837–1849*, pp. 310–11.

22. New York *Morning News*, December 27, 1845, as quoted in Albert K. Weinberg, *Manifest Destiny, a Study of Nationalist Expansionism in American History*, p. 145. The phrase had already appeared in the July–August issue of the *Democratic Review*, which O'Sullivan also edited, but it was popularized by the December editorial. Julius W. Pratt, "John L. O'Sullivan and Manifest Destiny," *New York History*, 45 (1933), 222–24.

lest these increase the possibility of a break. Indeed, the stock market had fallen since the gathering of Congress, but Pakenham wrote home that the furor was a good sign, for if the dangers and discomforts of war could be brought home to the public, compromisers might have a chance to be heard.[23]

Just as Congress recessed for Christmas, Calhoun arrived in Washington, convinced that only he could save the country from a disastrous war and perhaps seeing a golden opportunity to organize a Southern bloc in the Democratic party. Two of his followers in Congress tried to persuade him to support the administration's policy of giving notice, lest Polk isolate and ruin him as a Southern leader. Calhoun refused their advice; instead, he persuaded them to organize a bipartisan peace coalition in the Senate that would follow his leadership against Western extremists. On December 22 he called at the White House and urged the President to restrain his supporters and to delay any action to abrogate the joint occupation treaty. Polk declined.[24]

The President had probably anticipated Calhoun's opposition, but he now had good reason to resent it for its effect on Britain. The day before Calhoun's call, he had received a private letter from McLane, dated December 1, reporting that British leaders and some New York merchants counted on Calhoun to resist fifty-four-forty and to insist on a compromise boundary or arbitration. McLane deplored the unpatriotic tone of the moderate American press, too much given to "undervaluing & depreciating the democratic spirit." He added: "I am entirely convinced that we will never have a fair chance abroad until we can have a proper tone & self respect at home."

In an official dispatch, sent simultaneously, McLane predicted that Pakenham would be instructed to propose arbitration. If the United States indicated that it preferred direct negotiation, Britain would then make a new proposal; if the Americans rejected arbitration outright, Britain would treat its offer as an ultimatum and "abide the result." McLane partly undid the effect of this warning in his private letter, which not only complained about Calhoun and the moderates but also remarked that, short of abso-

23. New York *Evening Post*, December 20, 1845, p. 1; December 22, p. 2; December 27, p. 1. The *Post*, however, wanted to be sure that Britain would compromise at 49° in order to give the United States the necessary ports. Pakenham to Aberdeen, December 29, No. 138, GB, FO 5/430, ff. 172–78.

24. Charles M. Wiltse, *John C. Calhoun, Sectionalist, 1840–1850*, pp. 251–52. Sellers, *Polk, Continentalist*, pp. 363–64, 371–72. Polk, *Diary*, I, 131–32.

lutely discouraging negotiations, he was "inclined to think that a bold and decisive tone . . . would not only do no harm but would prove ultimately beneficial."[25]

The problem, as is true so often in diplomacy, was to gauge the firmness of the language to be used toward Britain. When Polk presented McLane's communications to the cabinet, Buchanan urged the President to let him encourage Pakenham to reopen negotiations by telling him that any British proposal would be respectfully considered. He also advised Polk to tighten the national defenses. Polk readily accepted the latter suggestion and arranged for conferences with the congressional military and naval affairs committees to discuss increased appropriations. The resulting measures were introduced in Congress during January.

Regarding a new British proposal, both President and cabinet agreed that arbitration was not to be considered, if only because it would be impossible to find an impartial umpire. Although no one said so, they all doubtless realized that arbitrators, when confronted with a mass of contradictory evidence, had a tendency to split the difference. Such a decision might push the boundary south of 49°.[26]

After the cabinet had rejected arbitration, Polk yielded a little ground. He conceded that he might consult the Senate if the British offered a boundary at 49°, retaining all of Vancouver Island but granting the United States several free ports north of the line. He allowed Buchanan to take down an innocuous written statement for Pakenham that omitted specific terms and stated merely that Britain had no reason to suppose that her proposals would not be respectfully considered. A few days later, on December 27, Polk returned to the subject of his own accord and asked the cabinet if, indeed, they felt that a British proposal for a boundary at 49° should go to the Senate. After some discussion the members unanimously agreed that it should. Then they voted once more against arbitration.[27]

As luck would have it, on that same day Pakenham appeared at the State Department with the expected proposal for arbitration. In a friendly, detailed conversation with Buchanan, the

25. McLane to Polk, December 1, 1845, Polk Papers, XCVI, LC. McLane to Buchanan, December 1, No. 24, Manning, *CR*, III, 984–86.

26. Polk, *Diary*, I, 133–34. James O. McCabe, "Arbitration and the Oregon Compromise," *Canadian Historical Review*, 41 (December 1960), 308–27. Merk,

Oregon Question, Essay VII.

27. Polk, *Diary*, I, 134–36, 147. Buchanan kept the written statement in his records, and it was even printed in James Buchanan, *The Works of James Buchanan*, ed. John Bassett Moore, VI, 348.

British minister suggested that a foreign state should serve as arbitrator in order to circumvent the American prejudice against crowned heads. The proposal assumed that Britain had a right to part of the disputed territory and that the arbitrator's function would be only to draw a compromise line, but in Buchanan's account of the discussion he reported Pakenham as saying that "the British government would be glad to get clear of the question on almost any terms; that they did not care if the arbitrator should award the whole territory to us." This was not enough for Buchanan, who replied that, even if Polk were to agree, the Senate would probably reject an arbitration treaty.[28] Immediately, the secretary drew up a formal refusal, which Polk and the cabinet approved. As they closed the door again, they left a crack of light by quoting from the earlier withdrawal of August 30: The President, declared the note, "cherishes the hope that this long-pending controversy may yet be finally adjusted in such a manner as not to disturb the peace, or interrupt the harmony now so happily subsisting between the two nations."[29]

*   *   *   *

This warmed-over expression of pious optimism was not enough to bring forth a new set of terms from Britain. If Polk had been better acquainted with diplomatic procedures and language, he might have found a more effective way to invite renewed direct negotiation without explicitly abandoning the American claim to $54°40'$, but, as usual, he was wary of taking any action that might be interpreted as a sign of weakness.[30] Pakenham was inclined to blame some of the President's intransigence on Edward Everett, who, he thought, had given his friends in Washington the

28. Two detailed accounts of this conversation are preserved, one by Pakenham and the other by Buchanan. Pakenham to Aberdeen, December 29, 1845, No. 138, GB, FO 5/430, ff. 177–78; Buchanan, *Works*, VI, 350–53. The conversation also embraced American land grants and forts in Oregon, the rights of the Hudson's Bay Company, and the probable extent of a war. At one point Buchanan facetiously proposed the Pope as arbitrator, and for a moment Pakenham took him seriously.

29. Buchanan to Pakenham, January 3, 1846, Manning, *CR*, III, 314–15. Polk, *Diary*, I, 151. At the same time, Polk wrote privately to McLane that Britain must take the initiative with a proposal, that he would be inclined to submit such a proposal to the Senate, but that he would have to judge it on its merits. Polk to McLane, December 29, 1845, Letterbook, 1845–1846, pp. 216–24, Polk Papers, LC.

30. Sellers feels that Polk committed a blunder comparable to Pakenham's of the preceding August in not hinting more broadly that Britain should open a new cycle of negotiations with a compromise proposal. Sellers, *Polk, Continentalist*, pp. 377–78. Polk's action was at least consistent with his earlier actions, and he may have felt that, all in all, McLane's communications of early December canceled each other.

impression that Britain would consent to almost any terms to avoid war. The British minister was not deeply downcast at the American refusal, for he could observe clear signs that American anxiety over war was growing and that moderates were increasing their influence in the government. For example, Senators Archer and Benton told him that a group in Congress would support a compromise line at 49°, giving Britain Vancouver Island and temporary navigation rights on the Columbia River. A few days later Calhoun stated that he was confident of defeating any provocative measures in the Senate. William W. Corcoran, a prominent banker-lobbyist, added his assurances, which Pakenham suspected had come from someone in the cabinet.[31]

Although Aberdeen received all this information simultaneously, near the end of January, it is clear that he was more impressed by Polk's brusque language than by private indications of a cooperative spirit in Congress. Perhaps he agreed that, for the time being, the conciliators had overdone their assurances. In any case he decided to apply a little more pressure. Accordingly, on January 29 he called in McLane for a talk, still friendly and courteous but with more overtones of menace than in earlier conferences. The flat rejection of arbitration, said Aberdeen, made him doubt the sincerity of the Americans' repeated desire for a peaceful settlement. He declared that "if ever there existed a Minister of peace, . . . [he] was that man," but that he could no longer resist measures proposed by his cabinet colleagues for the defense of Canada. Consequently, he gave McLane to understand that the British government would soon send thirty sail of the line, along with steamers, other war vessels, and armament across the Atlantic. "From this conversation," Aberdeen wrote later to Pakenham, "Mr. McLane cannot doubt that the matter has become very serious, and that we are fully in earnest in preparing for an unfavourable result."[32]

31. Pakenham to Aberdeen, December 29, 1845, Aberdeen Papers, BM, AM, vol. 43123, ff. 274–75. Same, December 29, 31; January 2, 1846, Nos. 138, 140, and a private, confidential letter, GB, FO 5/430, ff. 172–78, 186–88. Corcoran was close to many in the administration and especially to Buchanan.

32. Aberdeen to Pakenham, February 3, 1846, Aberdeen Papers, BM, AM, vol. 43123, ff. 278–80. In this account of the conversation Aberdeen did not mention his reference to warships. The source for that part of the talk is McLane's account of it: "In the course of the conversation, I understood that these would consist, independent of military armaments, of the immediate equipment of thirty sail of the line, besides steamers and other vessels of war." McLane to Buchanan, February 3, No. 34, Manning, CR, III, 1003. See also McCabe, "Arbitration and the Oregon Question," p. 321.

But Mr. McLane was not so much impressed. As early as December he had felt that British public opinion would eventually compel the Peel government to compromise at 49°, with adjustments for Vancouver Island and temporary navigation of the Columbia River. Until the end of the year he had consistently reinforced Polk's policy of a bold front, and his conversations with Aberdeen on December 30 and 31, followed by the shift of the *Times,* apparently convinced him that the government had privately decided to accept these terms. On January 3 he reported the increases in British armaments without attaching much importance to them. He described the effect of the annual message on Britain as "highly gratifying" and praised "the able and perspicuous exposition of our title" contained in the documents that accompanied the message. Various personal letters which McLane wrote during the month contained similar sentiments: that compromise spirit was spreading in Britain and that judicious firmness would eventually enable him to elicit a compromise offer from the government, so long as Polk could prevent Western extremists from provoking British anger.[33]

Under the circumstances it is not surprising that McLane qualified Aberdeen's warning. In a long official dispatch of February 3 the American minister summarized nearly a month of developments. He devoted almost the first half of it to the debate in Parliament on the Royal Speech, quoting at length conciliatory statements about Anglo–American relations. Then he turned to his recent interview with Aberdeen and briefly described the foreign secretary's disappointment at Polk's rejection of arbitration. McLane felt that if the refusal had been less categorical, Aberdeen would have offered terms and that if Polk would authorize him to take the initiative he could quickly elicit such an offer "without any improper commitment of the President." He warned again that no British statesman would concede more than 49°, with a boundary adjustment for Vancouver Island and temporary navigation on the Columbia River for the Hudson's Bay Company.

33. McLane to Buchanan, December 1, 1845; January 3, 1846, Nos. 24, 30, Manning, *CR*, III, 984–86, 989–92. McLane to Polk, December 1, 1845; January 17, 1846, Polk Papers, XCVI, XCIX, LC. McLane to Bancroft, January 15, Bancroft Papers, MHS. McLane even wrote to Calhoun on January 3, encouraging his campaign in Congress for compromise, in the hope that this would keep Polk and the Westerners from becoming inflexible. Sellers criticizes this action as disloyal and attributes it to McLane's concern lest Buchanan jealously shut him out of the negotiations. Sellers, *Polk, Continentalist,* pp. 380–81. The letter was inconsistent with McLane's usual views on the Senate compromisers, and he probably regretted it later.

How seriously did McLane view British naval and military preparations at this time? In his account of the January 29 interview he mentioned the government's decision to send warships and other armaments to Canada and conceded that these would place Britain "in a situation to act and strike as promptly and signally as she could have been with her energies exclusively directed to that end." Peel's campaign for the repeal of the corn laws had convinced him, however, of the essentially peaceful intentions of the British. Summarizing the status of the corn law question, he pointed out that leaders of both parties supported repeal as a means of restoring friendly relations with the United States. He added: "They would adopt the proposed scheme to very little purpose, if, for the sake of a degree of latitude on the Pacific, they should destroy the commercial intercourse of Great Britain with all the Atlantic states."[34]

Undoubtedly McLane suspected that Aberdeen's warning to him and the dispatch of the ships to Canada were tactical moves to satisfy the militarists in the cabinet, to shock Polk out of his intransigence, and perhaps also to help him control Western extremism, if that was what restrained him from renewing direct negotiations. McLane's skeptical attitude toward the British threat is even more apparent in the private letter to Buchanan that he customarily sent with the official dispatch. Here he declared flatly that a slight modification in the Polk administration's original proposal would have made it acceptable to both Peel and the Whigs and that, on reflection, Aberdeen would realize that Polk had no choice but to reject arbitration. Unless the next steamer brought indications that Congress would go beyond the President's recommendations, McLane was sure that Britain would take the initiative and offer a compromise settlement based on the American offer (49°) with modifications (presumably concerning Vancouver Island and navigation of the Columbia River). He hoped that Polk would not reject such an offer, at least without consulting the Senate.[35]

Thus, at the end of January 1846 Anglo–American diplomacy over the Oregon question seemed to have reached an impasse. Each side had addressed the other in terms of calculated firmness. Neither side, it is clear, was wholly impressed by the other's firm-

34. McLane to Buchanan, February 3, 1846, No. 34, US, DS, D, Britain, LVI. Most of this dispatch is reprinted in Manning, *CR*, III, 995–1005, omitting, however, the section on the corn laws and the revealing statement quoted.

35. McLane to Buchanan, February 3, 1846, Buchanan Papers, box 63, HSP.

ness, because conciliators in both countries seemed to indicate that concessions were in order.

*   *   *   *

Meanwhile at the beginning of the month Congress was returning from its Christmas recess. Polk still hoped for prompt action on the measures for Oregon which he had proposed in his annual message, so as to improve his bargaining position with Britain. But already he had begun to prepare some of his supporters for the possibility of compromise. For example, on December 24 he called in Allen and read McLane's dispatches to him. Allen agreed that arbitration was out of the question and advised Polk to consult the Senate if Britain proposed a compromise line at 49°. Polk approved the advice. On the same day Senator Hopkins L. Turney of Tennessee warned him that a split was developing in his party, for Western extremists were "almost mad on the subject of Oregon," in their efforts to carry the administration with them. Asked how he would receive a British proposal for compromise, Polk replied to Turney more cautiously than he had spoken to Allen, merely indicating that he would feel inclined to take the advice of the Senate confidentially before acting on the British overture.[36]

As soon as the Senate reconvened, the Western bloc pushed forward to commit the administration firmly to 54–40. Calhoun managed to gain a little time by diverting some of the earlier Oregon resolutions to the foreign relations committee, but Hannegan quickly proposed new resolutions declaring that Oregon was American territory up to 54°40′ and that any concession by the administration would be unconstitutional and counter to the best American interests. Calhoun led the debate on these resolutions, pointing out their dangerous implications and their inconsistency with previous efforts to divide the territory. Then he introduced several resolutions of his own, reaffirming the constitutional formula for treaties and declaring that a negotiated compromise at 49° would fall well within the President's powers. Hannegan burst out with a few angry words; then Calhoun, Benton, and Archer

36. Polk, *Diary*, I, 139–42. The Allen Papers contain a memorandum from Polk's friend Senator William H. Haywood, Jr., of North Carolina, analyzing possible lines of action for the Senate and advocating what was probably Polk's greatest desire—that Congress pass a law directing (not advising) the President to give notice of abrogation. Haywood gave various precedents. The memorandum is undated but was apparently written on January 6, 1846. Allen Papers, X, 41893–95.

led a successful move to table both sets of resolutions.[37] This action left for the Senate's consideration a more restricted resolution by Allen, representing Polk, which simply proclaimed a year's notice to Britain for abrogating the joint occupation treaty.

During the skirmish, Calhoun told Pakenham that he was optimistic about keeping the Senate under control, but he had no success whatever in drawing Polk out to an open stand for compromise.[38] On January 4 one of Calhoun's cohorts, a South Carolina representative, warned Polk again of a party split and urged him not to insist on giving notice to terminate the treaty. Polk replied with as concise a statement of his policy as he had yet put forth: "I remarked to him that the only way to treat John Bull was to look him straight in the eye; that I considered a bold & firm course on our part the pacific one; that if Congress faultered [sic] or hesitated in their course, John Bull would immediately become arrogant and more grasping in his demands."[39]

A week later Calhoun called at the White House to renew the argument. Polk repeated much of his earlier statement and added that, to judge from McLane's latest reports (those of early December), Peel and Aberdeen did not want war, although they had advanced no new proposal for compromise. Under these circumstances he believed that giving notice was the most promising way to preserve peace. Frustrated, Calhoun returned to the Capitol, gathered his forces, and obtained a postponement of debate until February 10, so that the Senators could turn to other business, pending further news from Britain.[40]

While they waited, the subject of Oregon arose from time to time, either explicitly or by indirection. On January 14, ostensibly to carry out Polk's recommendation concerning the Monroe Doctrine, Allen introduced a resolution declaring to the world "that any effort of the Powers of Europe to intermeddle in the social organization [the slavery system] or political arrangements of the Independent nations of America . . . would justify the prompt resistance of the United States." Moderates squelched this resolu-

37. Wiltse, *Calhoun, Sectionalist*, pp. 252–53. Edwin A. Miles, " 'Fifty-four Forty or Fight'—an American Political Legend," *Mississippi Valley Historical Review*, 44 (September 1957), 303.

38. Pakenham to Aberdeen, January 2, 1846, No. 1, GB, FO 5/446, ff. 1–2.

39. Polk, *Diary*, I, 153–56. In his correspondence Polk sometimes used telling phrases more than once. The meta-

phor of looking John Bull in the eye appeared several times in one form or another. See, for example, Polk to Gideon J. Pillow, February 4, 1846, Letterbook, 1845–1846, pp. 320–25, Polk Papers, LC.

40. Polk, *Diary*, I, 159–62. Wiltse, *Calhoun, Sectionalist*, p. 254. Sellers, *Polk, Continentalist*, pp. 366–69.

tion by a narrow vote, 28 to 23.[41] Crittenden then introduced another resolution to let the President act on his own initiative concerning the Northwest boundary. By this move he hoped to throw on Polk the responsibility for any resulting war. The resolution was accepted for later discussion. Pakenham welcomed this move, in the expectation that the resulting publicity would demonstrate Britain's reasonableness to the whole country. At this point the minister felt that the moderates' campaign had nearly succeeded, and that the Senate would have to choose between a gentle statement of notice and no action at all.[42]

Meanwhile, the initiative had passed to the House of Representatives, where the administration's forces were strong enough to prevent the peace bloc's move for postponement. Whig and Democratic resolutions were introduced, the one for further negotiation or arbitration, the other for giving notice. Robert C. Winthrop deprecated empty "schoolboy" talk about honor and war over "a vast and vacant territory" and pointed out that, since British as well as American honor was at stake, neither side should be asked to accept less than the other had previously offered. By this statement, Winthrop meant that the United States should yield the navigation of the Columbia River in some form. Two days later, Joshua R. Giddings turned his wrath upon "the weak, helpless, slaveholding South," which, having secured Texas with the support of Northern votes, "now require the party to face about—to stop short, and leave the power of the nation in their hands." He demanded annexation of the Canadas, Nova Scotia, and New Brunswick to provide six new free states.[43]

John Quincy Adams brought to the House debate its most dramatic moment. Utterly ignoring the fact that as President he had supported a compromise settlement, he upheld the United States title to all Oregon, on Biblical grounds. When challenged to substantiate this amazing claim, he had the clerk read several chapters of Genesis, culminating in God's command to man: "Be fruitful and multiply, and replenish the earth, and subdue it."

41. Frederick Merk, *The Monroe Doctrine and American Expansionism, 1843–1849*, pp. 95–97. US, 29C, 1S, *CG*, pp. 197–98.

42. Pakenham to Aberdeen, January 15, 1846, No. 5, GB, FO 5/446, ff. 27–29. Webster thought at this point that there would be no war, but he also felt that Polk was overconfident and that success would depend on Britain's desire for peace. Daniel Webster to

Fletcher Webster, January 14, Daniel Webster, *The Letters of Daniel Webster*, ed. C. H. Van Tyne, p. 306. D. Webster to David Sears, January 17; D. Webster to Franklin Haven, February 2, Daniel Webster, *The Private Correspondence of Daniel Webster*, ed. Fletcher Webster, II, 215–17.

43. US, 29C, 1S, *CG*, pp. 86, 132–34, 138–40.

Then he launched into a defense of effective occupation and the American destiny to "make a great nation" in Oregon "instead of hunting grounds, for the buffaloes, braves, and savages of the desert."[44] Like Calhoun, he argued from inevitable American emigration, but unlike him he reached an activist conclusion, not "masterly inactivity." Ironically too, Adams' doctrine of effective occupation was a restatement of the argument which Britain had used during the seventeenth century to defend its settlements in North America and the West Indies against Spanish claims.

While the House argued and the Senate marked time, more indications of willingness to compromise arrived from Britain, but no clear-cut initiative. On January 16 Pakenham again proposed arbitration, this time in a two-step procedure—judgment on the exclusive claim, presumably followed by the drawing of a compromise line. Polk had no intention of considering arbitration, but, hoping for further word from Britain, he waited over two weeks before submitting Pakenham's note to the cabinet. Eventually, he replied with a brief refusal on February 4.[45] In the meantime news bulletins and communications from McLane reported the "Whig abortion," the conciliatory editorial of January 3 in the *Times*, and Aberdeen's soothing statements at the turn of the year about British defense measures. On January 24 the President proposed to the cabinet a formula similar to those suggested by the press during preceding months. Under this arrangement the United States would agree to a reciprocity treaty for lower tariffs and would pay Britain "a round sum" with which to compensate the Hudson's Bay Company for the cession of all Oregon.[46]

A few days later, Polk and Buchanan drew up new instructions in reply to McLane's communications through January 3. An official dispatch of January 29 informed the American minister that Pakenham's second proposal for arbitration would be

44. US, 29C, 1S, *CG*, pp. 340–42. John Quincy Adams, *Memoirs of John Quincy Adams*, ed. Charles Francis Adams, XII, 243–44. Moderates commented that Adams was simply parading the arguments of all great annexationists "from Sesostris to Gen. Houston" and reminded him that the British also had claims arising from effective occupation. Baltimore *American*, n.d., reprinted in *NNR*, 70 (March 14, 1846), 31. For Pakenham's comments on the debate in Congress, see Pakenham to Aberdeen, January 5, 13, Nos. 2, 4, GB, FO 5/446, ff. 3–4, 21–23.

45. Pakenham to Buchanan, January 16, 1846; Buchanan to Pakenham, February 4, Manning, *CR*, III, 318–20, 993–95. Polk, *Diary*, I, 207–9.

46. Polk, *Diary*, I, 191–92. Sellers attributes this proposal to Polk's alarm at McLane's dispatch of January 3 (No. 30) concerning British military preparations. Sellers, *Polk, Continentalist*, pp. 381–82. But the cabinet meeting to which he refers took place on January 24, whereas the dispatch was not received until January 26. Polk, *Diary*, I, 193. Manning, *CR*, III, 989.

rejected and that further suggestions of that sort would only complicate the problem. However, they authorized him to tell Aberdeen "cautiously and informally" that, although Polk had taken a stand for all of Oregon, he would submit any compromise proposal to the Senate for "previous advice"—that is, before taking any action. They emphasized: "The President will accept nothing less than the whole territory, unless the Senate shall otherwise determine."

In a private letter Polk explained—perhaps too elaborately—why he was thus passing the responsibility to Congress. McLane's reports had indicated that Peel, on returning to power, would probably propose a compromise settlement at 49°, which would cede Vancouver Island to Britain along with permanent navigation rights on the Columbia River. In his annual message, Polk continued, he had rejected such a settlement, and the people supported him, so the Senate must now take the responsibility for accepting it. He added that McLane might informally explore the possibility of a "package" proposal that would involve a reciprocity treaty, but he had little hope that this idea would yield results.[47]

Thus on exactly the same day, January 29, Aberdeen in London warned McLane that Britain would send ships to Canada, and Polk and Buchanan in Washington completed instructions containing a carefully veiled hint of compromise. It was about three weeks before either side learned of the new developments. Polk may have made his slight concession in response to what McLane had written earlier about British defense measures, although the minister's report really added little to the President's knowledge. Direct information on this point is lacking, for problems of patronage virtually crowded Oregon out of his diary during the last half of January.

In any case, the news of British rearmament pricked the Senate to act on Polk's earlier requests for increased defense appropriations, and the chairman of the naval affairs committee reported out a suitable bill. The debate on this bill and the concurrent debate on Oregon in the House of Representatives led to a request (moved by Webster) that the President send Congress all pertinent correspondence with McLane and Pakenham. After considerable discussion in the cabinet Polk decided to submit the

47. Buchanan to McLane, January 29, 1846, No. 22, Manning, *CR*, III, 316–18. Polk to McLane, January 28, Letterbook, 1845–1846, pp. 286–89, Polk Papers, LC. Julius W. Pratt, "James Knox Polk and John Bull," *Canadian Historical Review*, 24 (December 1943), 342–43.

correspondence with Pakenham on arbitration, and Buchanan persuaded him to add McLane's dispatches describing British rearmament. Bancroft also privately supported the bill for more naval appropriations and at Polk's request sent the Senate a confidential memorandum about American defenses on the Great Lakes.[48]

By this time the rising temperature of public opinion and the debate in the House had convinced Calhoun that some sort of bill for giving notice to Britain on joint occupation would surely pass. News of the "Whig abortion" and a private letter from McLane that described British sentiment for peace and tariff reform encouraged him to hope for an eventual compromise offer, and he sensibly determined to muffle the sounds of Western extremism as much as possible, lest British opinion take offense and shy away. Whigs in the House aided him with attacks on Polk's warmongering as soon as they learned that arbitration had been refused. As a result, when the resolution for giving notice approached a vote in the House, Calhoun's supporters managed to soften it by inserting an amendment explaining that it was not intended to interfere with negotiations for amicable settlement of the Oregon dispute. On February 9, after a great deal of confusion, the House of Representatives passed the resolution in this mild form by a margin of three to one.[49] The moderates had won an important victory in the Oregon debate.

When the Senate resumed its discussion on the following day, however, Calhoun faced more formidable opposition. Hannegan introduced new resolutions declaring that all Oregon was American territory, which neither President nor Congress could legally cede away. This time Allen—hitherto a supporter of Polk's firm-

---

48. Pakenham welcomed the publication of the correspondence, as it would demonstrate British reasonableness. Pakenham to Aberdeen, January 29, 1846, Nos. 9, 11, GB, FO 5/446, ff. 44–49, 71–75. In the cabinet discussion Walker opposed sending in any of the correspondence. Polk, *Diary*, I, 209–10, 212. The correspondence submitted to Congress consisted of Buchanan's instructions of December 13 to McLane, McLane's long dispatch of January 3, Pakenham's notes of December 27, January 6, and January 16, and Buchanan's replies of January 3 and February 4. US, 29C, 1S, *CG*, pp. 332–35. A few passages were omitted from Mc-

Lane's dispatch of January 3, but the omissions probably did not affect the over-all impression created by the dispatch—mixed indications of rearmament and conciliation. Bancroft memorandum, February 16, Bancroft Papers, MHS.

49. Wiltse, *Calhoun, Sectionalist*, pp. 254–57. Sellers, *Polk, Continentalist*, pp. 386–87. Pakenham to Aberdeen, January 29, 1846, No. 8, GB, FO 5/446, ff. 39–40. Calhoun to Thomas G. Clemson, January 29, John C. Calhoun, *Correspondence of John C. Calhoun*, ed. J. Franklin Jameson, pp. 679–81. On the private letter from McLane, dated January 3, see note 33.

ness, looking toward compromise—took a stand with his fellow Westerners. On February 10 and 11, doubtless in response to a barrage of letters from expansionists, he delivered a dramatic speech of impassioned demagoguery, calling on Europe to stop interfering in American affairs through claims, terrorism, and "diplomatic duplicity." Lest Oregon become another Maine, he challenged the government to tell the truth to the American people:

> Tell them that arrogant England—their hereditary enemy, the enemy of all free governments—is seeking to snatch it from them, to fence us out from the Pacific Ocean. . . . Tell them these things, and ask, if they are ready thus to surrender this vast territory, from the mere dread of invasion by a rabble of armed paupers, threatened to be sent by a bankrupt government, whose whole power of the sword and the dungeon is required to stifle the cries of famine at home, or to protect its own life, against the uplifted hands of starving millions.[50]

Hannegan followed with more of the same. When one of Calhoun's bloc, Walter T. Colquitt of Georgia, answered in moderate language, Hannegan interrupted him with jibes about the "Punic faith" of the South, which had promised to support Oregon in return for Texas. The Senate prepared for a long debate. A majority now admitted that the United States must end joint occupation of Oregon. The real issue was whether the notice of abrogation should be an invitation to negotiate, as the House had proposed, or a shout of defiance, as Allen and his allies wished. Polk's original request for a bare, noncommittal statement of notice was almost lost in the shuffle. It was necessary that the Senate also decide whether the United States should extend its full sovereignty over Oregon at once or should await Britain's reactions to the other resolution.[51]

*   *   *   *

As members of Congress thundered and schemed, their wrangling both reflected and increased the confusion that prevailed among the people. A sampling of American press and public

---

50. US, 29C, 1S, CG, Appendix, pp. 834–42. The quoted passage appears on pp. 841–42. See also McGrane, *Allen*, pp. 109–11.

51. US, 29C, 1S, CG, pp. 360–64, 370– 74, 378–82. Pakenham to Aberdeen, February 14, 26, 1846, Nos. 15, 19, separate and confidential, GB, FO 5/446, ff. 107–9, 157–59, 177–80. Wiltse, *Calhoun, Sectionalist*, pp. 257–58.

opinion during the winter of 1846 is enough to show the wide divergence of views on Oregon and on the possibility of war with Britain.

By January and February a new slogan, "Fifty-Four Forty or Fight," had stamped its irresistible alliteration on the public mind.[52] The principal themes of extremist argument sprang from both the natural expansionist pride of the people and the more artificial fury of the Democratic press. One theme was defiance of England, the traditional enemy. "Don't let England have one inch of our soil," wrote a patriot, who then volunteered to march on Oregon, the "Italy of America," rather than let Britain "contaminate [it] with her foul and grasping hand." "Let us have war [rather] than the permanent establishment of the British on the Pacific," wrote another. "Let Britain domineer over Afghanistan & butcher myriads of Chines [sic] opium eaters," but let her stay away from America. "We see by the conduct of England and France in meddling with the affairs of the Argentine Republic what they would do, if they dared to do it, with the United States and Mexico."[53]

The second theme was that of manifest destiny—that divine favoritism which to John L. O'Sullivan was America's "true title" to the territory. A "speech in sonnets" published by the *Democratic Review* proclaimed this theme with full orchestration:

> We cannot help the matter if we would;
> The race must have expansion—we must grow
> Though every forward footstep be withstood,
> And every inch of ground presents its foe!
> We have, thank Heaven! a most prolific brood;
> Look at the census, if you aim to know—. . . .
> We must obey our destiny and blood,
> Though Europe show her bill and strike her blow!

A New Yorker declared that even war was desirable to spread "the Egis of Republicanism" and revolutionize Europe. Any timidity now, warned another, would flood America with "oceans of blood

52. Miles, "Fifty-Four Forty or Fight," p. 305. Wags spelled the slogan "Phifty-phour Phorty or Phight," and the cabalistic initials *P.P.P.P.* began to appear here and there.
53. H. H. Thompson to Allen, Allegheny City, Pennsylvania, February 16, 1846; R. Hill Jarvis to Allen, New York, March 9; William H. Cook to Allen, Hillsville, Virginia, February 19; John Somers to Allen, Chillicothe, Ohio, January 30, Allen Papers, X, XI. On European intervention in South America, see also an article by Caleb Cushing in *United States Magazine and Democratic Review*, 18 (March 1846), 163–84.

... if indeed it does not destroy the last hope of Philanthropy in the ultimate freedom of man." The conflict between "true" and legal titles raised no doubts for O'Sullivan and his followers.[54] Even some Whigs declared, with John Quincy Adams, that "the earth is given to man . . . not to build wigwams, but to build houses and cities. . . . The question is, whether the British right of hunting there shall stand in the way of civilization."[55]

A third theme was suspicion of "the ungrateful South"—suspicion so deep that in some letters from Northerners one wonders whether "Fifty-four Forty or Fight" was directed at Britain or at the plantation aristocracy. The Southerners, complained one man, "have now got Texas and they are much inclined to give Oregon the cold shoulder." Some called the moderates in Congress "old grannies"; others accused them of traitorous collusion with Pakenham.[56] Predictably, Calhoun received the heaviest fire. Some citizens thought him up to his old nullifying tricks, for his actions suggested that he wanted to be first man in South Carolina rather than second man in Washington. One Ohioan predicted ominously: "If the Southern Members cause the defeat of any part of Oregon I believe *Political* Abolitionism will greatly increase by it, and it will *sour* the *Stomachs* of a great number at the North and West against the South and their slave policy."[57]

From the nature of their position the moderates were somewhat less positive and explicit than the extremists. A great many of them—possibly a majority—believed firmly in acquiring territory as long as this could be done without war. A logical corollary of this argument was to disparage northern Oregon beyond 49° and to declare that the whole Columbia Valley and the shores of Puget Sound would amply satisfy the needs of American emigrants and

54. Ibid. (February 1846), pp. 92–93. Samuel J. Mickles to Allen, Syracuse, New York, January 7, 1846, Allen Papers, X. See also James Parker to Allen, Somerset, Ohio, March 19; Jarvis to Allen, March 9, ibid., X, XI. Weinberg, *Manifest Destiny*, pp. 144–52.

55. *American Review*, 3 (February 1846), 127. One predicted that possession of Oregon would produce an enormous trade with China, make the United States master of the Pacific, and result in a population of 76 million by 1876. [Illegible signature] to Allen, New York, March 12, Allen Papers, XI.

56. Thornton Grimsley to Allen, St. Louis, February 7, 1846, Allen Papers, XI. H. C. Whitman to Allen, January 31, ibid., as quoted in McGrane, *Allen*, p. 107. Washington *Times*, n.d., paraphrased in *NNR*, 70 (March 14), 17.

57. R. H. Wendover to Polk, Lexington, Massachusetts, March 24, 1846, Polk Papers, CI, LC. Richard Purcell to Allen, Lebanon, Ohio, February 9; M. A. Goodfellow to Allen, Wooster, Ohio, February 1; the quotation is from Joseph Kithcart to Allen, Mount Pleasant, Ohio, January 14, Allen Papers, X, XI.

traders. Many moderates were confident that negotiation would secure these areas for the United States.[58] Former President Tyler continued to advocate that the United States exchange Puget Sound for British aid in obtaining San Francisco, and a number of expansionist newspapers followed his thinking. As a correspondent of the New York *Herald* put it: "We must surrender a slice of Oregon, if we would secure a slice of California." But many opposed such a trade.[59] Others declared that obtaining California would probably mean war with Mexico and expressed the hope that Polk would keep his hands free for such a fight: "One war is a dose at a time."[60]

A prominent motif in moderate writing was the inglorious but realistic argument that Britain would beat the United States in any imaginable war. The only two steam frigates the United States owned would be forced to hide in port, leaving the British Navy free to lay waste the whole Atlantic coast. While the United States struggled to build ships, Britain would drive Americans out of Far Eastern and Latin American markets. An Anglo–American war would probably lead to British occupation of California; it might cost the United States Texas as well.[61]

Since Britain had rights in Oregon as well as the United States, many Whigs believed that it was their duty to encourage compromise. But the movement for lower tariffs in Britain and in the United States sometimes threatened to split the Whigs and, indeed, all moderates. At one point the Washington *Union* tried to divorce the two issues, denying that Walker's tariff proposals had any relation to the Oregon question. A group of newspapers had already spread the rumor, however, that Pakenham was offering to compromise the Oregon boundary at 49° in return for tariff

58. James Manney to Willie P. Mangum, Beauford, North Carolina, February 2, 1846, Willie P. Mangum, *The Papers of Willie Person Mangum*, ed. Henry T. Shanks, IV, 381–83. New York *Evening Post*, February 4, p. 1. Sellers, *Polk, Continentalist*, pp. 357, 386. Some writers, of course, disparaged the value of all Oregon. *North American Review*, 62 (1846), 229.

59. John Tyler to R. Tyler, December 23, 1845, Lyon G. Tyler, *The Letters and Times of the Tylers*, II, 448–49. New York *Herald*, February 3, 1846, p. 3. Norman A. Graebner, "Maritime Factors in the Oregon Compromise," *Pacific Historical Review*, 20 (1951), 340

et passim. New York *Evening Post*, February 10, 1846, p. 3; February 11, p. 1.

60. New York *Herald*, February 5, 1846, p. 2.

61. New York *Journal of Commerce*, n.d., reprinted in *NNR*, 69 (February 7, 1846), 354–55. New York *Courier and Enquirer*, n.d., reprinted ibid. (January 17), 306. See also ibid. (January 31), 350–51. Joel R. Poinsett to William B. Lewis, January 5, Andrew Jackson–William B. Lewis Correspondence, IV, no. 307, NYPL. [Illegible signature] to Allen, Baltimore, February 11, Allen Papers, XI. New York *Herald*, February 3, p. 3.

reform and even had a packet ship ready to carry the welcome news to England.[62] The protectionist *Niles' Register*, while opposing war, scoffed at such rumors. In return, the New York *Evening Post* castigated protectionists as hypocrites and accused some Whigs of being more willing to fight for profits than for Oregon.[63]

No simple, clear-cut recital of motives and arguments can give an accurate picture of the public clamor over Oregon during the winter of 1846. The New York *Herald* sneered at the debate in Congress: "Sublimity and farce—eloquence and twaddle—sense and folly—wit and stupidity—selfishness and patriotism—are all blended together in admirable disorder."[64] The division was neither entirely partisan nor entirely sectional.[65] *Niles' Register* aptly described the national contention as "a melee between crowds armed with shelalah [sic]."[66]

*　　*　　*　　*

If public opinion in the United States was a puzzle to Americans, small wonder that the British did not know what to make of it. Late in January, Duff Green wrote to a friend on the British Board of Trade, blaming the war crisis on misinformation and overattention to local affairs. On the one hand, he said, Britain expected that, should hostilities break out, a grand alliance of Mexicans, Negroes, and Indians would revolutionize the West and South, burn the cities, and foment disunion, while the British Navy attacked the Atlantic and Gulf coasts. On the other hand, Green added, many Americans were confident that an Anglo–American war would throttle the British cotton industry, stimulate Ireland to rebel, and forge a grand alliance between the United States, France, and Russia. Eventually, they were sure, a starving population would compel the British government to sue for peace.[67]

62. *American Review*, 3 (February 1846), 128. The *Union's* denial of a deal with Britain is reprinted in *NNR*, 70 (March 7), 1. For earlier rumors, see *NNR*, 69 (February 14), 370; and New York *Herald*, January 17, p. 2.

63. *NNR*, 69 (February 28, 1846), 404. New York *Evening Post*, March 3, p. 3.

64. New York *Herald*, January 9, 1846, p. 2; January 13, p. 2.

65. Sellers, *Polk, Continentalist*, pp. 370–72. John Hope Franklin, "The Southern Expansionists of 1846," *Journal of Southern History*, 25 (1959), 323–28.

66. *NNR*, 70 (March 7, 1846), 4–5. The editor referred specifically to a hot argument over arbitration by the Washington *Union* and the Washington *National Intelligencer*.

67. Duff Green to J. MacGregor, Annapolis, January 26, 1846, Green Papers, box 3, LC. An example of the British extremism he described was a proposal made to Aberdeen that Britain invade the lower Mississippi Val-

Green exaggerated, and he ignored the growing undertow of conciliation that pushed strongly against the tide of xenophobia, creating unpredictable eddies and crosscurrents. Henry Wheaton, visiting London, found a more conciliatory spirit there than he had expected: "There is a sincere desire for peace with us," he wrote, "and no exagerrated [sic] notion of the value of the Country [Oregon] to them; but a strong determination not to yield to threats, and a strong feeling of their tremendous power of annoying us." [68] Lord Ashburton went even further and wrote to Webster that he would be glad if the two countries could obliterate the real cause of the everlasting boundary squabbles—British rule over Canada. "As long as we are neighbors on the great Continent which you begin to think should wholly belong to you," he declared, "we shall never really be friends, and I have long wished we could find a decent Excuse to let the work of Annexation be completed." [69]

Throughout the winter the tone of the British press continued to fluctuate between defiance and conciliation. For a time in February a journalistic tempest in a teapot raged in London over a shocking discovery—a British mapmaker had produced a globe that supported the American claim to all of Oregon. As this scandal faded, a mail packet arrived with American newspapers that expressed relief at the moderation with which the British received Polk's annual message—the echo of an echo. The *Morning Chronicle* reported reactions in New York City with the pleased comment: "Never was there a better illustration afforded than this of the pacific tendencies of commerce." Considering also the lack of American military preparations, the *Chronicle* minimized the importance of Western extremism, and the *Times* trusted that Americans had laughed down Cass' proposals to seize Oregon by force. Underestimating the developing split in Con-

---

ley, using a regiment of Haitian troops to arouse the Southern slaves, who would then be freed and moved to the British West Indies. D. Turnbull to Aberdeen, Jamaica, January 7, February 7, Aberdeen Papers, BM, AM, vol. 43245, ff. 190–93, 263–66.

68. Henry Wheaton to Calhoun, London, February 10, 1846, Calhoun, *Correspondence*, pp. 1071–73. McLane had asked Wheaton, who was then United States minister to Prussia, to come to London and help him in the negotiations.

69. Viscount Ashburton to Webster, London, January 1846, Webster, *Letters*, pp. 308–9. Ashburton, like Webster, opposed free trade. Soon after writing this letter William Sturgis proposed that he and Ashburton be appointed to arbitrate the Oregon question. William Sturgis to Bancroft, February 8, 16, Bancroft Papers, MHS.

gress, the British press and public passed February in uncertainty and perhaps a little boredom, for Parliament was entangled in an endless debate on the corn laws, and business was dull.[70]

In the first week of March, however, the British finally realized that Western extremism amounted to more than background rumblings. First came the diplomatic correspondence which Polk had released to Congress almost a month before, revealing that the Americans had categorically rejected arbitration. This information caused a sudden drop in consols and the general money market.[71] Then followed the news that the House of Representatives had passed the bill to give notice of the end of joint occupation. This brought a grim tightening of lips and determined editorials exhorting the government to stand firm against American opportunism. The *Times* declared that now the peace of the world rested on Polk, "a man actuated by the most deplorable motives" and likely to snatch at the increased powers which war would give him and the Democrats. The *Examiner* accused the President of using Western extremists to provoke hostilities or British capitulation, since he could not obtain a clear majority for war by more direct means. The *Times* saved a little venom for John Quincy Adams and his Biblical quotations: "A democracy intoxicated with what it mistakes for religion is the most formidable apparition which can startle the world."[72]

Naturally the burst of British patriotism weakened the attractions of Anglo–American tariff reform, which during February had seemed to offer a promising opening for negotiations. News that Robert J. Walker's low tariff bill had been introduced into Congress, arriving in the midst of the March windstorms, drew only a few approving remarks.[73] As yet, however, the British press made little effort to associate the Oregon question with American expansion into Mexico, except for an occasional reminder that the rest of the world must necessarily be interested in "a direct menace and a systematic aggression, planned by a Government and backed by a people." In March the *Times* warned the Polk ad-

70. *NNR*, 70 (March 14, 21, 1846), 18, 48. London *Morning Chronicle*, February 16, p. 5; February 17, p. 6. London *Times*, February 18, p. 5.

71. *NNR*, 70 (March 21, 1846), 48. London *Sun*, March 3, as quoted in New York *Evening Post*, March 20, p. 3.

72. London *Times*, March 5, 1846, p. 4; March 11, p. 5. London *Examiner*, March 7, p. 146. London *Morning Chronicle*, March 5, p. 4; March 7, p. 5. *NNR*, 70 (April 4), 65.

73. London *Morning Chronicle*, March 17, 1846, pp. 4–6. For general comments on the relationship between corn laws and Oregon, see also *NNR*, 70 (March 14, April 4), 17, 66; and *Le journal des débats*, February 28, p. 1.

ministration that Mexico would follow (or perhaps even precede) Britain into war with the United States.[74]

The Peel cabinet took note of the journalistic furor during March but did not materially alter its actions in the Oregon question. Aberdeen had received Polk's annual message with confidence in an eventual compromise and had pursued a threefold policy through the early winter, restraining Wellington and Ellenborough in the cabinet, disparaging the value of Oregon in the press, and warning the United States through McLane not to press him too far. Soon after his interview of January 29 with McLane made that warning explicit, two separate developments strengthened his hand and reassured him that his policy was sound.

The first of these developments was vitally important—the conversion of Lord John Russell. Early in January Russell had publicly deplored a war crisis over Oregon. On January 23, during the debate following the Royal Speech, he denounced Pakenham's blunder of the preceding summer—a gesture that did Peel and Aberdeen no harm. At about this time Russell received a letter from Edward Everett, written in late December, which urged him to support the Peel administration in a compromise boundary along 49°—Britain retaining Vancouver Island—since this settlement would satisfy both British honor and American desires for first-class Pacific seaports. When Russell showed the note to Palmerston, the latter's reply (dated February 2) was scornful, but Lord John decided to act on Everett's suggestion. Soon afterward, he privately promised Aberdeen his support in bringing Parliament to yield the Columbia River and to accept a compromise boundary.[75]

Less than a week after Russell's promise, on February 9 or 10, a messenger arrived in London from Oregon with news about the prospects there that further encouraged Aberdeen's pacifism. This man was Lieutenant William Peel, son of the prime minister, formerly stationed on a warship in the Pacific Squadron. He had left the Northwest Coast during the preceding October and carried his messages home by way of Honolulu and Mexico City, the usual

---

74. London *Times*, February 11, 1846, p. 5; March 11, p. 5.

75. Merk, *Oregon Question*, pp. 258–61. Merk reprints Everett's letter of December 28 to Aberdeen *in toto* and much of Palmerston's commentary on it. For Russell's remarks on Pakenham, see Manning, *CR*, III, 999–1000. It is not clear whether these remarks were

delivered before or after Russell received Everett's letter. McLane of course noted Russell's public statements on Oregon and undoubtedly suspected that he had a special understanding with Aberdeen. However, Russell's conversion was not positively known to Polk until after the Oregon settlement was completed.

circuitous route. Peel's dispatch bag contained letters from Aberdeen's brother, Captain Gordon of H.M.S. *America*, and from John McLoughlin of the Hudson's Bay Company, and young Peel doubtless supplemented the letters with his own observations.

All these reports agreed as to the basic situation. American emigrants, strongly anti-British, were moving into the Columbia Valley in ever-increasing numbers, and they had appeared at the head of Puget Sound. Lieutenant Peel, Captain Gordon, and McLoughlin described the flourishing American settlements and the local governments the Americans had established with the acquiescence of the Hudson's Bay officials. The implications were clear—the Company and the British government had best cut their losses and do what they could to save Vancouver Island and access to the Strait of Juan de Fuca around its southern tip.[76]

The effect of these two developments on Aberdeen is not recorded in his writings, but it must have been considerable. Russell's promise effectively isolated Palmerston and silenced or neutralized any complaints of his about "capitulations" in Oregon. Lieutenant Peel's information encouraged Aberdeen to continue his campaign in the press, belittling Oregon as a possession, and advocating a compromise boundary. This time he furnished ideas and data to a prominent Tory politician, J. W. Croker, who published an unsigned review in the March issue of *Quarterly Review*. Here he advocated the 49° boundary and deprecated the fur trade of the Columbia Valley as "diminishing so rapidly that its loss will be inconsiderable."[77] Peel's reports probably also hastened the reconciliation of the Hudson's Bay Company to a negotiated settlement. By the beginning of March Aberdeen was

76. Peel's dispatches included letters of Captain J. Gordon, September 2, October 19, 22, 1845; John McLoughlin, July 19, August 30, September 15; and William Peel, September 27, 1845, January 2, 1846. They are all reprinted in Leslie M. Scott, "Report of Lieutenant Peel on Oregon in 1845–46," *Oregon Historical Quarterly*, 29 (March 1928), 51–76. Peel may also have presented the views of Lieutenants Warre and Vavasour, who had begun their survey of the Oregon coast before his departure. A full account of their opinions may be found in Joseph Schafer, ed., "Documents Relative to Warre and Vavasour's Military Reconnoisance in Oregon, 1845–6," *Oregon Historical Quarterly*, 10 (March 1909), 8–13. Their formal report was not submitted until later and probably did not affect the outcome of the Oregon crisis. See also Barry M. Gough, "H.M.S. *America* on the North Pacific Coast," *Oregon Historical Quarterly*, 70 (December 1969), 300–303; E. E. Rich, *The History of the Hudson's Bay Company, 1670–1870*, II, 725–28; and Charles H. Carey, *A General History of Oregon Prior to 1861*, I, 401–3; II, 457–58.

77. Merk, *Oregon Question*, pp. 304–7. *Quarterly Review*, 77 (March 1846), 563–610; the quoted phrase is on p. 599. About this time Aberdeen may also have arranged with the Whig leader, the Earl of Clarendon, for a conciliatory speech in Parliament. Merk, *Oregon Question*, pp. 220–23.

discussing terms with Sir John H. Pelly, a Company official—navigation of the Columbia River, remuneration for loss of trade south of 49°, and the value of the Company's assets in that area.[78]

The road to compromise was not yet entirely open in Britain, however, for Lord Ellenborough had not abandoned his ambitions for British naval expansion. On March 1, just as the press campaign against the United States was about to revive, the first lord of the admiralty wrote a letter to his chief, urging more enlistments and appropriations. Unless Britain crushed the United States in the opening weeks of an Anglo–American war, argued Ellenborough, she would have to withstand a cross-Channel attack from France. He lamented that while Britain was doing nothing, the Americans were preparing for war.[79]

More than two weeks later, in the midst of the journalistic furor over the House passage of the Oregon bill, Peel replied to Ellenborough that he did not feel justified in going beyond the estimates which Parliament had already made for military appropriations. The Opium War was ended in China; the danger of war with France had largely passed; yet within the last year Britain had increased her seamen by four thousand and her naval estimate by £540,000. He added ironically that it would really be better to go to war than to incur many of its evils by constantly increasing preparations. The country might go so far into debt during peacetime that if war actually came, its credit would be crippled. Clearly, Aberdeen had kept the prime minister aware of the antiwar bloc in the United States, for Peel declared that all news from across the Atlantic admitted the superiority of British naval armament. Polk must realize this fact, he added, and that knowledge would probably encourage a peaceful settlement.[80]

If the prime minister had reacted differently to Ellenborough's urging, the first lord could have carried out an aggressive policy on the Pacific coast through a fully cooperative agent, his squadron commander, Admiral Sir George Seymour. During the preceding summer Seymour had been anxious enough about Ore-

78. Sir John H. Pelly to Aberdeen, March 13, 1846, Aberdeen Papers, BM, AM, vol. 43245, ff. 322–25.

79. Ellenborough to Peel, March 1, 1846, Peel Papers, BM, AM, vol. 40473, ff. 76–79. The strongest American ship in the Pacific (then in the East Indies) was the 100-gun *Columbus*, but Ellenborough thought Seymour's flagship

Collingwood (80 guns) her equal and the other British ships superior to the American. Memorandum, ibid., f. 82.

80. Peel to Ellenborough, March 17, 1846, ibid., ff. 120–23. McLane to Buchanan, March 17/18, No. 36, Manning, *CR*, III, 1011–15. McLane to Buchanan, March 17, Buchanan Papers, box 63, HSP.

gon and California to send Captain John Gordon and H.M.S. *America* on reconnaissance to the north Pacific coast (see Chapter 9). Seymour learned of Polk's annual message and of Ellenborough's appointment to the Admiralty in the early spring of 1846, while he was stationed off the coast of Peru. At once he drew up a long memorandum on United States ship concentrations in the eastern Pacific and advised that Britain keep a ship or ships constantly off Oregon to protect British settlers. He also advocated convoys and patrols off South America to protect the valuable British trade around Cape Horn in case of war and to give the Latin American nations a wholesome respect for British power. Finally, he wanted to prepare for an attack on American trading and whaling ships in the Pacific—and all without neglecting British vigilance in Tahiti and elsewhere. These many activities would require reinforcements, and Seymour requested two more ships of the line and better repair facilities.[81]

Seymour's memorandum did not arrive in London until June 8, when the Oregon crisis was almost over. Nevertheless, knowing the general British policy regarding Oregon, he sent several ships to the Oregon coast and issued contingent orders to all his captains for immediate action in case of war with the United States.[82] While Seymour continued to suspect American intentions regarding California, he made no specific provision regarding that province, for, as he told Ellenborough, he had never received any statement of British policy concerning it. Nevertheless, his orders loaded and primed the British cannon and aimed it at the whole Pacific coast of North America.

Restrained by Aberdeen, by party weakness, and by concern for the budget, Peel would not order that cannon fired unless the United States provoked a war. By early February Aberdeen had done all he could to warn the Polk administration not to go to extremes. Now it remained to be seen whether that administration

---

81. Sir George Seymour to Admiralty, Payta, March 6, 1846, No. 19, GB, A 1/5568. Seymour to Ellenborough, March 7, Ellenborough Papers, PRO 30/12/4/20. Gough, "H.M.S. *America* on the Oregon Coast," pp. 306–8.

82. Seymour to Commander Gordon, *Cormorant*, March 6, 1846; Seymour to captains and commanders of the squadron, March 6, Seymour, Journal, ff. 201, 202, GB, A 50/213. A month later, Sey-

mour was still focusing his attention on Oregon. Guessing that Stockton and the *Congress* were proceeding there, he had sent north ships which could enter the Columbia River if necessary, but he gave their captains strict orders to take no action that might complicate a peaceful agreement. Seymour to H. A. T. Corry, April 7, No. 27, ibid., 1/5561.

and the United States Congress would renew direct negotiations or find the formula which would enable Britain to do so without a loss of honor.

* * * *

About the middle of February the Oregon question entered a period of climax in the United States. At that time the House had passed a compromise resolution of notice, and the Senate had begun what promised to be a long debate over its wording. On February 20 and 21 a new assortment of bulletins and dispatches arrived from London. These included the text of the conciliatory Royal Speech to Parliament, Peel's unequivocal demand for repeal of the corn laws, McLane's long, involved dispatch of February 3, and his letter of the same date to Buchanan. In these communications, as has been seen, the American minister reported on conciliatory statements in Parliament, described his interview of January 29 with Aberdeen, and qualified the latter's remarks about reinforcements to Canada with his own convictions that the British government intended peace and compromise.

The statement that thirty ships of the line and other war vessels would soon be en route to Canada impressed Polk and the cabinet more powerfully than the bulkier evidence of Britain's desire for conciliation—and certainly more than McLane intended.[83] On February 22, even though it was Sunday, Walker and Bancroft called at the White House to read the dispatch. On the next day, Polk discussed it with Bancroft and Buchanan, who advised him to let McLane tell Aberdeen explicitly that Polk would submit to the Senate a British proposal for a boundary at 49°, granting temporary rights of navigation on the Columbia River—a direct invitation of the sort which Polk had hitherto rejected. At the regular cabinet meeting on February 24 the President polled the members on Buchanan's plan. All agreed except Postmaster General Cave Johnson, who predicted that this move would encourage Aberdeen to ask for even more. Polk gave no opinion himself but accepted Buchanan's offer to draw up a compromise draft.

Later in the day Senator William H. Haywood, Jr., of North Carolina, a moderate and an old college friend of the President,

83. When the Foreign Office received a dispatch from Pakenham reporting this reaction, McLane showed Aberdeen the passage in his dispatch of February 3 that had alarmed Polk and Buchanan and remarked: "There is certainly nothing in it to warrant Mr. Buchanan's interpretation." McLane to Aberdeen, March 17, 1846, Aberdeen Papers, BM, AM, vol. 43123, ff. 451–53.

called at the White House with the news that Calhoun and his bloc planned to introduce a resolution into a secret session of the Senate, urging Polk to negotiate a compromise settlement. Calhoun and Webster were sure that they could muster the votes for passage, but, Haywood added, Calhoun's old enemy Benton opposed tying the President's hands in such a manner. This knowledge strengthened Polk.[84]

On the following day, February 25, a Whig caucus rejected the resolution on the grounds that it might let the President evade the responsibility for compromise. Anxious to get some news of the maneuver into the transatlantic mails, which were due to leave next day for England, Calhoun and his henchman Colquitt made their way through a snowstorm to the White House to seek Polk's approval. Armed with Haywood's information, the President objected that such a resolution would command too small a majority to impress anyone, but he assured Calhoun that if Britain proposed a compromise line along 49° or "with slight modifications," he would submit the proposal to the Senate for its opinion. To Calhoun's dismay, however, Polk flatly rejected the idea of granting Britain navigation rights on the Columbia River. Calhoun returned to the Capitol and gave up his resolution, while the debate continued over the major proposition of giving notice.[85]

Later in the same day the cabinet put the final touches on the new instructions to McLane, and Buchanan added the usual explanatory private letter, both dated February 26. In the official dispatch the secretary recited all the objections to arbitration and gave that proposal the *coup de grâce*. He protested that Britain's move to send warships to Canada would "set this country in a blaze" and hoped that the government would reconsider. Buchanan also denied, however, that his earlier rejection of arbitration had been intended to discourage direct negotiation. He now stated explicitly the terms Polk would be willing to submit to the Senate: the 49° boundary and the cession of Vancouver Island—without either the previously mentioned free ports on each side or perpetual British rights of navigation on the Columbia River. Regarding this last point he was positive and categorical.[86]

84. Polk, *Diary*, I, 242–47. Wiltse, *Calhoun, Sectionalist*, p. 259. Calhoun also consulted Pakenham, who approved of the maneuver and even advised him on tactics. Pakenham to Aberdeen, February 26, separate and confidential, GB, FO 5/446, ff. 177–80. Polk would have been furious at this, but apparently Haywood knew nothing about it.

85. Polk, *Diary*, I, 249–54, 255–56. Sellers, *Polk, Continentalist*, pp. 387–90.

86. Polk, *Diary*, I, 252–53. Buchanan to McLane, February 26, 1846, No. 23, Manning, *CR*, III, 320–26.

In his private letter Buchanan stated his opinion that the Senate would approve these terms as well as his fear that British insistence on navigation of the Columbia River would bring negotiations to a standstill. He urged McLane (and indirectly Britain) to act quickly, for Calhoun was losing his popularity and public opinion was more extreme than either Congress or the administration, as he predicted that the congressional elections of 1846 would show. "The truth is," he concluded, "that the discreet friends of peace clearly perceive that the question must be settled peaceably within the year, or war may be the consequence."[87] In keeping with this heightened concern, at the next cabinet meeting (February 28) Buchanan proposed a special message to Congress, calling for more defense measures. Polk commented in his diary on the secretary's "bolder and more detached" tone on Oregon and on his fear of war.[88]

Several historians regard this episode at the end of February as the turning point in the negotiations over Oregon. "Polk had carried his game of looking John Bull in the eye a trifle too far, and John Bull was looking back with menacing glance," says one, "Polk's eye wavered."[89] It is highly probable that the news of British warships' preparations to sail into the Atlantic alarmed the President to the extent of allowing McLane to suggest terms which he would regard as acceptable—a measure he should have taken much earlier. Nevertheless, the colorful language of a later day tends to oversimplify a complicated situation. Ironically, Polk interpreted the Aberdeen–McLane conversation as Aberdeen intended—in spite of McLane's efforts to soften the British warning. The minister's contradictory dispatch might well have puzzled the President and, indeed, did puzzle at least one member of his cabinet, Secretary of the Navy Bancroft. Also, it is probably significant that Polk's decision to give ground coincided with a new effort toward compromise by Calhoun's bloc in Congress—an effort the administration barely managed to repulse.[90]

87. Buchanan warned McLane that the British must not form their impression of American public opinion from what they read in newspapers, mostly conciliatory and published in coastal cities. Buchanan to McLane, February 26, 1846, Buchanan, *Works*, VI, 385–87.

88. Polk, *Diary*, I, 257–58.

89. Pratt, "Polk and John Bull," pp. 344–47; quotation is from p. 346. See also Jones and Vinson, "British Preparedness," pp. 361–62; and Klein, *Buchanan*, p. 182.

90. Bancroft to Sturgis, February 23, 1846, Bancroft Papers, MHS. Wiltse, *Calhoun, Sectionalist*, p. 259. It is interesting that the doughty expansionist John Quincy Adams thought the news from England "altogether pacific and conciliatory." He gloomily predicted a compromise settlement and a low tariff. Adams, *Memoirs*, XII, 247–48.

Whatever Polk's motivation, the instructions of February 26 to McLane were only a step toward a negotiated settlement. Polk continued to write about looking John Bull in the eye.[91] Perhaps more important, he persisted in withholding an important British *desideratum*, navigation of the Columbia River. On the British side, Aberdeen did not immediately respond to Polk's change of attitude, preferring to wait until the Senate acted on the resolution of notice.

More evidence of Polk's new disposition toward conciliation is to be found in the course of the Senate debate. In a two-day speech on March 4 and 5 Senator Haywood defended compromise at 49° and created a sensation among the extremists by stating that in his opinion the administration stood committed to accept such an offer. Haywood further affronted the extremists by suggesting that several of them were using Oregon to support their presidential ambitions; he refused to be swayed by "factious meetings got up by demagogues" to cow the Senate. Probably, like Allen and Hannegan before him, Haywood went a little too far. After the first day of his speech congressmen hurried to the White House for confirmation of Haywood's position, but they met only Polk's denial that he had authority to speak for the administration. It is difficult to believe that Haywood would have said anything without first consulting his old friend, and indeed Benton later wrote that there had been complete agreement between them.[92]

The Westerners concluded that, despite his earlier promises, Polk was preparing to desert their exposed position. As Haywood finished his speech, Hannegan exchanged several heated comments with him. Then Hannegan lost his temper and declared that if Polk supported Haywood's views, he had betrayed the Democratic platform and was therefore "an infamous man," speaking "words of falsehood and with the tongue of a serpent."[93] After a caucus, the Western extremists delegated Hannegan and Atchison to go to the White House and force Polk to declare himself. Forewarned, Polk put them off with a characteristic mixture of boldness and evasion. He regretted the display of Democratic disunity, he said; he would not declare his policy beyond the state-

---

91. James K. Polk to William H. Polk, March 27, 1846, Letterbooks, 1845–1846, pp. 378–83, Polk Papers, LC. See also J. Polk to A. O. P. Nicholson, April 2, Polk Papers, NYHS.

92. Thomas Hart Benton, *Thirty Years View*, II, 662–67. US, 29C, 1S, *CG*,

pp. 456, ff. Polk, *Diary*, I, 262–64. Pratt, "Polk and John Bull," pp. 347–48.

93. US, 29C, 1S, *CG*, pp. 458–60; Appendix, pp. 369–78. Benton, *Thirty Years View*, II, 663–66. Sellers, *Polk, Continentalist*, pp. 391–92.

ments in his earlier speeches; he was responsible only to God and to the country, which he felt approved his actions up to that point. Later, to Allen, Polk repeated with emphasis that no one had authority to speak for the President, but he refused to disavow Haywood's remarks.[94]

Attributing the whole fracas to Presidential fever, Polk maintained his inscrutability in public and urged prompt action on the measure. In private talks Polk encouraged the moderates. First, he repeated to Benton his most recent instructions to McLane— that if Britain proposed a boundary at 49°, retaining Vancouver Island and temporary rights of navigation on the Columbia River, he would submit the proposal to the Senate for its advice. Benton called to his attention a resolution of Crittenden, supported by Whig pacifists, which would authorize the President to give notice at his discretion. Although reluctant to take any advice from the opposition, Polk now asked Buchanan to discuss Crittenden's resolution with some of the Western Democrats and to try to work out wording that was agreeable to them.[95] The reason for these concessions may be found in the spectacle of party disunity that confronted the President. Probably another factor was the simultaneous cabinet discussion of dispatches from Slidell that Polk interpreted as a call for more decisive action in Mexico (see Chapter 12).

Haywood's speech and the violent reaction of the Western extremists increased the confusion in the American press.[96] At this juncture John C. Calhoun decided that the time had come for him to lead his people out of the wilderness, and he announced that he would address the Senate on March 16. Before packed galleries he delivered one of the ablest speeches of his career, explaining why he had decided to support a modified form of notice to Britain. At the beginning of the session, he declared, such a stalemate had existed between the United States and Britain that abrogation of the joint occupation treaty would have been practically the same as a declaration of war. Since that time, however, strong evidence suggested that public opinion in both countries, the British government, and a majority in the United States Senate had come to favor compromise. If the session closed without some action, Britain would take no initiative, and the Oregon question would be thrown into the maelstrom of the fall by-elections. Hence, he had decided to abandon his policy of "masterly inactivity" (which he

---

94. Polk, *Diary*, I, 270–80. Merk, *Oregon Question*, pp. 382–83.
95. Polk, *Diary*, I, 285–88.

96. For a cross section of American press opinion on Haywood's speech, see London *Times*, April 10, 1846, p. 5.

still preferred) and would support a resolution for giving notice somewhat similar to that passed by the House.[97]

With Calhoun's speech the Oregon debate passed the point of diminishing returns, but both cabinet and Senate continued to argue and to shift positions. Polk further puzzled press and public about his intentions with a special message on March 24, in which he called attention to British rearmament, repeated his earlier recommendations for defense measures, and at the same time declared that he did not consider a resolution of notice to be a warlike act. During the cabinet's discussion of this message, the hitherto cautious Buchanan joined Walker in a proposal to insert a paragraph that censured the Senate for its delay. As Buchanan revealingly complained, Cass was making too much political capital out of fifty-four-forty. The other members of the cabinet wisely suppressed the censure, and Polk lamented in his diary that aspirants to the Presidency made bad advisers.[98]

By this time sentiment for compromise was spreading in the Senate, as first Webster and then McDuffie announced that they would concede temporary navigation of the Columbia if necessary for a settlement. Benton then formally supported giving notice. It was clear that a resolution would pass and probable that it would encourage continued negotiations. The principal remaining issue was petty indeed—whether to direct the President to transmit the notice, as the House wished, or to leave him some discretion (and thus responsibility), as Crittenden and the Whigs proposed.

With the approach of a compromise settlement the tempers of Western extremists grew shorter. Teased by Benton, Hannegan indulged in another tantrum. When Crittenden's settlement of the final issue won a preliminary vote, Allen gave rein to his passions in a coarse diatribe against the Senate—"divided, faltering, paltering, manacled, hampered, with a frightful unwillingness to meet responsibility." Crittenden, wholly aware of who was trying to evade responsibility, administered a tongue-lashing to "this our Caesar" who presumed to lecture the Senate on its duties, simply because he held "the little petty office of chairman of the Committee on Foreign Relations."[99]

97. US, 29C, 1S, CG, pp. 502–6; Appendix, pp. 471–76. Useful summaries of the speech and reactions appear in Merk, Oregon Question, pp. 383–84; and Wiltse, Calhoun, Sectionalist, pp. 260–61.
98. James D. Richardson, ed., A Com-

pilation of the Messages and Papers of the Presidents, 1789–1897, IV, 426–28. Polk, Diary, I, 296–98. For a reaction to Polk's special message, see NNR, 70 (March 28, 1846), 49–50.
99. US, 29C, 1S, CG, pp. 581–83, 680–83; Appendix, pp. 422–30, 510–14. Sel-

It was all over but the voting. By a humiliating margin of 40 to 14 the Senate rejected Allen's version of notice in favor of the Crittenden resolution, slightly modified, which left final action to the President and advocated "that the attention of the Governments of both countries may be the more earnestly and immediately directed to renewed efforts for the amicable settlement of all their differences and disputes in respect to said territory." Polk remained unenthusiastic about the Crittenden resolution, but since he feared that a deadlock now might continue through the session, he put pressure on the House to conform. After several days of haggling, a conference committee approved the Senate draft, with minor changes. On April 23 both houses passed the Oregon resolution by large majorities.[100]

Long before these actions, Aberdeen had guessed the probable outcome of the debate and was awaiting it calmly. This attitude greatly distressed McLane, who feared that it indicated a waning desire to compromise. In mid-February the American minister received Buchanan's instructions of January 29, authorizing him to hint at terms which Polk would be willing to submit to the Senate but also asserting that Polk would insist on all of Oregon if the Senate would not take the responsibility of compromise. Aberdeen gave more weight to Polk's flat assertion than to his hint but remarked that, if the American government absolutely rejected arbitration, he would have to consider what proposal he could make through McLane.

This attitude did not greatly encourage the American minister, for in the same conversation, Aberdeen, clearly at the insistence of the Hudson's Bay Company, insisted that if the Columbia River were navigable, any agreement must specify free navigation for British subjects. McLane wrote home for further instructions and advised Polk to determine authoritatively whether the Columbia were navigable. At the same time McLane wrote a long letter to Calhoun, warning him that further debate would weaken the cause of peace by convincing the British of American disunion. If an immediate resolution of notice seemed impossible to obtain, he advised the Senate to reject arbitration once for all and declare that it would postpone further action for a year.[101]

lers, *Polk, Continentalist*, pp. 395–96. McGrane, *Allen*, pp. 117–19.

100. Merk, *Oregon Question*, pp. 387–88. Sellers, *Polk, Continentalist*, pp. 396–97.

101. McLane to Buchanan, March 3,

1846, No. 35, Manning, *CR*, III, 1006–11. Same, March 3, Buchanan Papers, box 63, HSP. McLane to Calhoun, March 3, Calhoun, *Correspondence*, pp. 1076–79.

On March 15 McLane received Buchanan's more conciliatory dispatch and letter of February 26, the products of the cabinet's debate over the British warships. The American minister was amazed that Polk should have considered the fleet as intended for an attack on the United States. He transmitted to Aberdeen Polk's long statement about terms that he would deem suitable to refer to the Senate, but since the foreign secretary still favored delay, McLane merely mentioned the terms informally in conversation. To Buchanan he repeated his earlier prediction that Britain would insist on navigation of the Columbia to some extent, and he deplored the loose talk in America about Oregon—especially that of the Whig conciliators, who, he feared, would lead the British officials to think that they might safely delay a settlement through the year.[102]

Thus, as the Oregon debate dragged to a close in the middle of April, the British sat by with maddening aplomb, watching the Senate's actions. If it should approve the mild House resolution, the Foreign Office would be able to reopen negotiations without losing face. This result was not at all what Polk had intended when he referred the question to Congress in December. He had hoped for a quick, vigorous declaration from a united government and people that would force the British to take a damaging initiative while he remained aloof. Instead, he had been obliged to drop hints about compromise—not enough to cause British action but more than enough to alienate Western Democratic leaders, thereby risking a party split. The debate had really proved that Americans were badly divided over Oregon and that the majority of them, including their President, did not want fifty-four-forty intensely enough to fight for it.

102. McLane to Buchanan, March 17, 1846, No. 36, Manning, *CR*, III, 1011–15. Same, March 17, Buchanan Papers, box 63, HSP. McLane warned Buchanan that the British could not be cowed into yielding anything they regarded as a point of honor and that navigation of the Columbia would probably fall into this category.

12

"War . . . by
the Act of Mexico"

While Congress wrangled over Oregon, the country's relations with Mexico were rapidly deteriorating. Polk gave Mexican affairs only occasional bursts of attention during the winter of 1845–1846, but these were enough to involve the country in risks of war fully as grave as those on the Anglo–American front. Just before Congress convened in December, an American envoy landed at Veracruz with hopes of purchasing California and resuming peaceful relations. When the debate on Oregon ended in April, the envoy had returned home, his mission a failure, and an American army, occupying disputed territory on the Rio Grande, was preparing to defend itself against a Mexican attack. There was at least one important difference between the threats of war with Britain and with Mexico. Debates in Congress and newspaper editorials had made every alert citizen reasonably familiar with the dangers and attractions of a British war. But the American people knew next to nothing about national prospects in a war with Mexico, and as spring came, they were only beginning to realize how close they stood to such a war.

*   *   *   *

After receiving assurances in early November that Mexico wanted to negotiate, Polk dispatched John Slidell with instructions to renew regular diplomatic relations—under the assumption that the annexation of Texas was a *fait accompli*—and to offer a sliding scale of payments for the Rio Grande boundary, California, and New Mexico. Polk feared interference with the mission from European diplomats in Mexico. But early in October Aberdeen had told his minister at Mexico City, Charles Bankhead, that he should encourage Mexico to stay on friendly terms with the United States and not to rely on British aid in case of war.[1]

Slidell left Pensacola on November 20 and arrived at Mexico

---

1. Earl of Aberdeen to Charles Bankhead, October 1, November 28, 1845, Nos. 34, 36, GB, FO 50/183, ff. 88–91, 98–100.

City on December 6 with Consul John Black, who had ridden out to Puebla to meet him and inform him of the situation. The auspices for successful diplomacy were certainly not encouraging. The mild, well-intentioned Herrera had come to power almost a year earlier with far-sighted plans for reform, but he had taken only half measures in dealing with the chronic Mexican problems. While the War Department soaked up the few drops of ready cash, *agiotistas* dominated the Treasury, eager to mortgage resources and property to their creditor-allies. The government tried the patience of well-wishing foreign merchants by postponing tariff reform and then publishing a new set of duties that offered little relief to anyone.[2]

After the impotent fulminations of the Mexican Congress over the annexation of Texas during the preceding summer had ceased, public resentment had begun to die down. In mid-November, however, the government received a report from General Mariano Arista in the northeast that American troops at Corpus Christi were marching on Matamoros.[3] By now, even the official newspapers admitted that American migration threatened Mexico's sovereignty in California, and the ignominious collapse of the highly advertised rescue expedition during the autumn made clear that Mexico might lose that province, whatever she did. In the face of these staggering problems Herrera's cabinet was divided. Some members recognized that no defense of any sort was possible without money, but the minister of war brushed aside financial worries and called for an all-out offensive against the United States. After all, he wrote, the American opposition consisted of nothing more than "some miserable colonists, a few hun-

2. London *Morning Chronicle*, November 12, 1845, p. 4. José Bravo Ugarte, *Historia de México*, III, 196. Carlos Pereyra, *Tejas, la primera dismembración de Méjico*, pp. 233–34. Niceto de Zamacois, *Historia de Méjico desde sus tiempos más remotas hasta nuestros días*, XII, 386–88. Vicente Riva Palacio, *México a través de los siglos*, IV, 542. On the tariff problem, see F. M. Dimond to James Buchanan, July 30, September 1, October 1, Nos. 251, 260, 265, US, DS, CD, Veracruz, V. Bankhead to Aberdeen, August 29, October 30, Nos. 83, 103, GB, FO 50/186, ff. 106–8; 50/187, ff. 13–18.

3. Juan Álvarez to Valentín Gómez Farías, November 11, 1845. Gómez Farías Papers, as quoted in Wilfrid Hardy Callcott, *Church and State in Mexico, 1822–1857*, pp. 140–41. Dimond to Buchanan, October 28, November 1, 8, 29, Nos. 270, 271, 275, 278, US, DS, CD, Veracruz, V. Arista must have learned about Polk's October dispatch instructing Taylor to advance (see Chapter 10), for the American troops were still at Corpus Christi. The foreign minister communicated the news to Consul Black, who at once informed the United States consul at Matamoros that an American envoy would soon arrive at Mexico City to begin negotiations. John Black to J. P. Schatzell, November 22, US, DS, PR, Consulate, Mexico City, Letterbook IV, 181–82.

dred adventurers, and a handful of speculators from New Orleans and New York."[4]

In stating this opinion the minister was responding to opposition newspapers of both extremes—conservatives and *puros* alike —which railed at the cowardly Americans and "that vile gang of hypocrites and philosophers" in the National Palace who were preparing to sell out to them. Under the scare headline "HORRIBLE BETRAYAL!" one paper denounced Parrott as "a shameful *cheat*, a *leper*." When Slidell landed at Veracruz, another paper greeted him with full details of his plan to purchase New Mexico and California and called on the people to rise up against the rascally government before they were overrun by Anglo–Saxons: "A few months more, and we shall have no country at all!"[5]

A strong government might have ignored some of this abuse, but Herrera and his cabinet also had to consider the troops in the north, supposedly intended for the invasion of Texas but ill paid and apt to revolt at any moment. Their commander, General Mariano Paredes y Arrillaga, was in San Luis Potosí, plotting rebellion with several factions. Even the *puro* leader Valentín Gómez Farías, a stout Yankee-hater, seems to have been treating with Paredes against Herrera.[6] Throughout the autumn, rumors of troop movements circulated in central Mexico, but even in early December Paredes was reluctant to act, for General Arista, commanding forces on the Rio Grande, refused to join him. Then Herrera precipitated a crisis by commanding Paredes to move

4. These opinions appear in memoranda of Pedro Fernández del Castillo (minister of finance) and Pedro María Anaya (minister of war), dated November 19 and December 2, 1845. They were directed to the minister of foreign relations (Manuel de la Peña y Peña) and written in answer to a request by President Herrera. Mexico, Secretaría de Relaciones Exteriores, US, LC, /70. Peña y Peña's defensive attitude is clearly shown in a dispatch to the Mexican minister to France, summarizing the situation. Peña y Peña to Máximo Garro, November 28, No. 27, Barker transcripts, vol. 571, pp. 116–18. On December 3 Castillo issued a circular letter to the state governors describing the desperate condition of the Treasury and appealing for a loan. In their replies most governors only described their own problems, but those of Oaxaca and San Luis Potosí offered $6,000 and $33,000, respectively. US, LC, /87. See also Carlos María de Bustamante, *El nuevo Bernal Díaz ó sea Historia de la invasión de los Anglo–Americanos en México*, I, 72.

5. These passages appear in *El amigo del pueblo*, November 1, 1845, pp. 227–28, and *La voz del pueblo*, December 3. Both of these newspapers were radical federalist organs of Mexico City. US, DS, CD, Veracruz, V; D, Mexico, XII. See also Frank A. Knapp, Jr., "The Mexican Fear of Manifest Destiny in California," in Thomas E. Cotner and Carlos E. Castañeda, eds., *Essays in Mexican History*, pp. 197–98, 201–5.

6. Gómez Farías to Mariano Paredes y Arrillaga, October 1845, Gómez Farías Papers, as cited in Callcott, *Church and State in Mexico*, pp. 138–39.

north and reinforce Arista against the rumored American invasion. Paredes refused, pleading a lack of supplies. Herrera ordered him to Mexico City on charges of insubordination, and on December 14 Paredes proclaimed a revolution.[7]

Under these circumstances Herrera and his officials had no desire whatever to negotiate with any American envoy. Consequently, when Black reported Slidell's arrival at Veracruz, Foreign Minister Manuel de la Peña y Peña responded with unhappy surprise and improvised objections to receiving him. The government had not expected Slidell until January; it was unprepared to negotiate; Parrott (appointed secretary to Slidell) was *persona non grata*. After Slidell had arrived in the capital and sent Black to the foreign ministry with his credentials, Peña gained time by submitting them to the Council of Government.[8]

The council and Peña developed several reasons, more or less plausible, for not receiving Slidell. Since he had left the United States before the United States Congress convened, there was no evidence that the Senate had confirmed his appointment. Slidell's credentials named him minister plenipotentiary, the title of the departed Shannon, whereas Mexico had agreed to receive only a commissioner. The credentials instructed Slidell to negotiate for the Rio Grande boundary and for the purchase of California and New Mexico—absolutely unthinkable to the Herrera government —whereas Mexico had agreed to discuss only the annexation of Texas.

Peña's note to the American legation laid greatest stress on the question of Slidell's title. Many historians assume that he was quibbling and that Polk had committed only a minor *faux pas* in naming Slidell minister plenipotentiary. This judgment is not quite fair to the Mexican government. The rupture of relations was valuable as a weapon of some force against the United States government, since it might diminish confidence among American businessmen and lead them to put pressure on Washington. If Mexico now received a regular minister plenipotentiary and re-

7. Riva Palacio, *México a través de los siglos*, IV, 545–46. Thomas Ewing Cotner, *The Military and Political Career of José Joaquín de Herrera, 1792–1854*, pp. 145–46. John Slidell to Buchanan, December 27, 1845, No. 4, Manning, *IAA*, VIII, 800–803. Dimond to Buchanan, November 29, No. 278, US, DS, CD, Veracruz, V. On clerical complicity in the revolt, see Vicente Fuentes Díaz, *La intervención norteamericana en México (1847)*, pp. 165–68.

8. Black to Slidell, December 15, 1845; Slidell to Buchanan, December 17, No. 3; Black to Buchanan, December 18, No. 355, Manning, *IAA*, VIII, 777–84. Slidell to Buchanan, December 18, 30, Buchanan Papers, box 24, HSP.

sumed diplomatic relations without obtaining any concessions in return, she would give up this weapon, lose face, and abandon hope of receiving any compensation for Texas.

Herrera, however, was not fundamentally opposed to any negotiations, for while Peña consulted the council, he drew up a long circular letter to the state governors, asking their advice and preparing them for the surrender of Texas. Realistically he pointed out that a war with the United States, however just, would be hopeless, for Mexico lacked sufficient resources and allies. Advertising the nation's weakness would encourage further American aggression. Texas held no real value to Mexico, for only population could create value; even if Mexico defeated the Americans, it could retain the conquered province only by turning it into an armed camp. Peña concluded his sensible analysis by citing past authorities to support the legality and honor of ceding territory in time of stress.[9]

It seems clear that the Mexican foreign minister did not intend to shut off negotiations permanently when he courteously asked Slidell to obtain new credentials for settlement of the questions that threatened to involve the two nations in hostilities. Slidell replied with a statement of American grievances and claims in order to demonstrate that the annexation of Texas had not been the only cause of broken relations, and he cited the correspondence of October and November in defense of his title. By that time Paredes' revolt had broken out, and Slidell carefully refrained from communicating privately with Mexicans of any faction.

To Buchanan, Slidell described Mexican government leaders as corrupt and ignorant. Whichever side won, he declared, the United States must insist on the retraction of Peña's note, for the Mexicans would attribute American peace overtures to timidity and increase their demands unless convinced by "hostile demonstrations" that the United States was determined to achieve its ends. To Polk he wrote privately that hope of aid from Britain was stimulating Mexican resistance. "A war would probably be

9. Peña y Peña to [Consejo de Gobierno], December 11, 1845, US, 30C, 1S, HED 60, pp. 58–61. Gabriel Valencia [for the Consejo de Gobierno] to Ministerio de Relaciones, December 16. México, Secretaría de Relaciones Exteriores, *Memoria, 1846*, Appendix, pp. 11–16. Peña y Peña to Governor of the Department of ——, December 11. Antonio de la Peña y Reyes, ed., *Algunos documentos sobre el tratado de Guadalupe y la situación de México durante la invasión americana*, pp. 3–26. See also a defense of his policies, which he wrote for his successor. Peña y Peña to Ministerio de Relaciones, February 3, US, LC, /101.

the best mode of settling our affairs with Mexico," he thought and then added: "But the failure of the negotiation will be very disagreeable and mortifying to me." [10]

* * * *

More than once Consul Black reported rumors that if Paredes overthrew the government, he would make way in turn for a Spanish prince to set up a monarchy in Mexico.[11] This harebrained scheme had developed from the growing friendship between the Spanish legation in Mexico City and local proclericals and wealthy reactionaries. Spain had not recognized Mexican independence until 1836 or sent over a minister until 1839. For the next five or six years this official, like other foreign diplomats, contended with problems of security, forced loans, tariffs, and claims while losing faith in the Mexicans' ability to govern themselves. In 1840, when the Mexican conservative José M. Gutiérrez de Estrada was forced to flee the country for publishing a promonarchist pamphlet, he went to Spain to seek support for his plans. From time to time the Spanish minister in Mexico sent home dispatches describing republicanism in Mexico as "an exotic plant," unsuitable to Mexican character or customs, and suggesting that if some outside influence could inspire the latent monarchism and bring order among the confused, bickering right-wing factions, the resulting government might steel Mexico to resist American aggression.[12]

The Spain of 1845 was a most unlikely sponsor for such a risky venture. Its nominal ruler was a fifteen-year-old girl, Isabella II; the country had not yet fully recovered from the Carlist Wars; and the government was weak and faction-ridden. Nevertheless, proponents of a Spanish monarchy in Mexico gained a hearing in the cabinet of General Ramón Narváez. Spain had no lack of candidates for a Mexican throne among the Queen's relatives. A cousin, Don Enrique, about twenty-two years old, was eventually settled on as the most likely prospect for a Mexican king.

10. Peña y Peña to Buchanan, December 20, 1845, US, 30C, 1S, HED 60, pp. 52–53. Slidell to Peña y Peña, December 20, 24; Peña y Peña to Slidell, December 20; Slidell to Buchanan, December 27, No. 4, Manning, *IAA*, VIII, 785–803. Slidell to Polk, December 29, Polk Papers, XCVII, LC.

11. Black to Buchanan, December 20,

30, 1845, Nos. 356, 358, Manning, *IAA*, VIII, 785, 806.

12. Jaime Delgado, *España y México, en el siglo* XIX, II, 138–39, 340–41. Pascual de Oliver to Primer Secretario de Estado, April 20, December 18, 1842, January 24, 1844, Nos. 85, 192, 347, *Rdh-m*, II, 35–37, 176–77; III, 13–16.

The spearhead of the movement was Salvador Bermúdez de Castro, an impulsive young intellectual with enthusiasm and energy but no previous diplomatic experience, who was posted to Mexico as minister in 1844, with oral instructions to foment a monarchist revolution. Two *leitmotivs* ran through his correspondence with the Spanish foreign office: his assurances that a monarchist movement would be easy to organize, and Madrid's warnings that under no circumstances should Spain's influence be evident. The movement must seem to be wholly spontaneous.[13]

The flabbiness and unpopularity of Herrera's regime gave Bermúdez his opportunity, and he found a willing partner in Lucas Alamán, the pro-European financial expert of the 1820s and 1830s (see Chapter 2), who had been out of the government for years. Working through Alamán, Bermúdez obtained the confidence of the ambitious Paredes at San Luis Potosí. To him and to a few other intriguers the Spanish minister promised money, medals, titles, and influence—whatever he thought would attract them most powerfully. By midsummer of 1845 Paredes had agreed to seize power at the proper moment, convene an assembly of right-wing notables, and invite Spain to provide a prince for Mexico.

In a dispatch of October 31 the Spanish government approved these plans. To assist the plotters, it agreed to send a warship or two inconspicuously to Havana and to place a fund in the Cuban Treasury for general expenses—eventually two million reales. As usual, the Spanish government moved slowly, and through the autumn and winter, while Paredes fidgeted in San Luis Potosí, Bermúdez de Castro and the Spanish foreign ministry discussed details in long dispatches, like two old men playing chess by mail. A full cycle of correspondence from Mexico City to Madrid and return usually required about four months.[14]

The lack of money increased Paredes' indecision, and even though Bermúdez collected three hundred thousand pesos from

13. The diplomatic correspondence of Bermúdez de Castro for this period is contained in two different archives in Madrid. His ordinary dispatches, unconnected with the monarchist plot, are in the regular files, legajo 1649, Biblioteca de Asuntos Exteriores. His correspondence and all other documents relating to the monarchist plot are gathered in legajo 5869, caja 1, Archivo Histórico Nacional. Many of these are summarized in a memoran-

dum of the foreign ministry, dated February 17, 1846, but containing many entries after that date. Citations will be made to this memorandum.

14. Salvador Bermúdez de Castro to Primer Ministerio de Estado, August 28, 1845, No. 109, Oficio to Bermúdez de Castro, October 31; Memorandum, February 17, 1846, AHN. While Bermúdez was waiting for Paredes' revolt, he was giving advice to Herrera's government about its reception of Slidell.

merchants in Mexico City, ostensibly for use against the Americans, the government sent only part of it to the army. At this moment, Herrera precipitated the revolution by ordering Paredes to reinforce Arista in the north. Paredes' Plan of San Luis Potosí, which Bermúdez and probably Alamán wrote for him, called only for the reestablishment of a strong, conservative, centralized republic, but covert monarchists could read his real intent between the lines. After some hesitation, Paredes marched to Mexico City; the bribed garrison in the capital revolted; Herrera resigned; and on January 2, 1846, Paredes entered the city in triumph.[15]

At once Bermúdez began to realize the problems he faced in directing the actions of his puppet. Before the entrance into Mexico City Paredes' advisers had persuaded him to liberalize the Plan of San Luis Potosí. He appointed a reasonably moderate cabinet, including as secretary of war the anti-American Juan N. Almonte and as foreign minister Joaquín M. Castillo y Lanzas, a distinguished jurist whom American Consul F. M. Dimond of Veracruz thought well disposed toward the United States. By the end of January Bermúdez was reporting to Madrid that the new President, on whom the whole monarchical plot rested, possessed only military talents: bravery, strict leadership, and energy. He lacked experience in dealing with either politicians or businessmen and was also vain, impetuous, and much too fond of liquor.[16]

Like a good soldier the new President attempted to rid the government of sycophants and to tighten up the administration, and he set an extraordinary example of frugality by refusing to live in the National Palace. Bermúdez and Alamán prevailed on him to issue a proclamation that would pave the way for monarchy by recognizing the power of Congress to choose any suitable form of government for Mexico. Then Alamán and his conservative cohorts rigged the electoral machinery to ensure a subservient Congress.[17] The press, only partly muffled, buzzed with guesses,

15. Riva Palacio, *México a través de los siglos*, IV, 553–54. Cotner, *Herrera*, pp. 147–50. C. Alan Hutchinson, "Gómez Farías and the Movement for the Return of General Santa Anna to Texas in 1846," in Thomas E. Cotner and Carlos E. Castañeda, eds., *Essays in Mexican History*, pp. 181–82. Bermúdez de Castro to Primer Ministerio de Estado, November 28, December 27/30, 1845; Memorandum, February 17, 1846, AHN.
16. Dimond to Buchanan, January 12, 1846, No. 309, US, DS, CD, Veracruz, V. Bermúdez de Castro to Primer

Ministerio de Estado, January 24, No. 184, BAE, legajo 1649. Same, January 29, No. 190; Memorandum, February 17, AHN. On Paredes, see also Guillermo Prieto, *Memorias de mis tiempos, 1840 a 1853*, pp. 178–79.
17. Dublán and Lozano, *LM*, V, 105–19. Bermúdez de Castro to Primer Ministerio de Estado, January 29, 1846, No. 190; Memorandum, February 17, AHN. Zamacois, *Historia de Méjico*, XII, 413–17. Riva Palacio, *México a través de los siglos*, IV, 552–57. For an unflattering picture of administrative confusion un-

especially after a new daily, *El tiempo*, began to bemoan the excesses of democracy. Subsidized with funds from the Cuban Treasury and written or edited largely by Alamán, *El tiempo* gradually moved toward an open declaration for monarchy as a means to restore the prosperity of colonial days and prevent further American aggression.[18]

The spreading reports of monarchist intrigue split Paredes' centralist backing and spread confusion among liberal federalists. Moderates who had supported Herrera and conciliation saw that the last chances of an agreement with the United States were flickering out. *Puros* approved Paredes' apparent hostility to the United States but would have nothing to do with either centralism or monarchy. Desperate for leadership, liberals began to think more kindly of the despised Santa Anna, who, for all his opposition to federalism, at least had the reputation of being an anti-Spanish patriot.[19]

In mid-February Almonte resigned from the cabinet to plot in his own behalf. Paredes replaced him in the war department with another ambitious general, the sharp-faced, scheming José María Tornel, a veteran of Santa Anna's last cabinet, whom Bankhead later pronounced "the evil genius of Mexico" for his raw opportunism and his senselessly aggressive policies against the United States.[20] Confronted by liberal opposition, Tornel seems to have prevailed on Paredes to issue a calming statement that he would maintain the present system of government until Congress could approve any change. At the same time *El tiempo* moderated its tone. Paredes and Bermúdez de Castro indirectly approached

der Paredes, see Manuel Rivera Cambas, *Los gobernantes de México*, II, 286–93, *passim*. Dimond to Buchanan, February 2, No. 317, US, DS, CD, Veracruz, V.

18. *El tiempo*, especially front-page editorials in the issues for January 25–30, 1846. The first issue to call openly for a monarchy was that of February 12, p. 1. Charles A. Hale, "The War with the United States and the Crisis in Mexican Thought," *The Americas*, 14 (1957–1958), 170–71. Bravo Ugarte, *Historia de México*, III, 197.

19. For the opposition, see especially *El republicano*, March 1, 1846, p. 1, and succeeding issues. See also *Memorial histórico*, January 22, as quoted in Bustamante, *Nuevo Bernal Díaz*, I, 111. For brief surveys of the Mexico City press, see Riva Palacio, *México a través de los siglos*, IV, 552; and Prieto, *Memorias, 1840 a 1853*, pp. 179–83. Hutchinson, "Gómez Farías and the Return of Santa Anna," pp. 182–83.

20. Bankhead to Viscount Palmerston, September 28, 1847, No. 87, GB, FO 50/211, ff. 242–44. See also Justin H. Smith, *The War with Mexico*, I, 25, 46. Almonte's resignation was variously reported as due to a petty quarrel with Paredes or his opposition to monarchism. Black to Buchanan, February 27, 1846, No. 362, US, DS, CD, Mexico City, IX. Bankhead to Aberdeen, February 27, No. 22, GB, FO 50/195, ff. 276–79. On Tornel's overconfidence, see Homer C. Chaney, "The Mexican–United States War, As Seen by Mexican Intellectuals, 1846–1956," Ph.D. diss., Stanford University, 1959, pp. 3, 12.

Bankhead for a discussion of the situation—the first cautious step toward requesting British aid—but the British minister, lacking instructions, declined to become involved. Throughout the monarchist intrigue he reported to the Foreign Office that, while most Mexicans had become disgusted with republicanism, few would give a moment's support to a Spanish prince.[21]

Slidell had a general idea of the unsettled political conditions and spent January and February waiting to see the outcome. At the end of December he informed Buchanan that he intended to retire to Jalapa, halfway to Veracruz, as a demonstration of American firmness, but because the roads were unusually thick with bandits, he waited three weeks before leaving the capital. During this period he wrote privately to the secretary of state that the government seemed to want him to stay in Mexico City. He thought also that he had a better chance of negotiation with Paredes than with Herrera, since the new President had more nerve. Just before Slidell finally departed for Jalapa, he hinted to the Paredes government through a confidante that he could relieve its financial embarrassments. He felt that, although near-bankruptcy might compel the Mexicans to start negotiations, they would stall as long as the United States seemed at all likely to fight Britain over Oregon. Copies of Polk's annual message had arrived in Mexico about January 10, and it had raised expectations of an Anglo–American war. In mid-February Slidell sent home copies of El tiempo and again mentioned his suspicions of a monarchist intrigue, which would reduce the prospects for the success of his mission, but he soon regained some of his optimism.[22]

Since a widespread conviction existed in the United States that Europe was united in a desire to save Mexico from American expansion, the reactions of the European governments and press to the accession of Paredes and the intrigues of Bermúdez de Castro are of interest. Tomás Murphy, who remained Mexican minister to Britain through the change of administrations, maintained his pressure on Aberdeen for loans and other aid, but the foreign secretary merely advised him wryly to exercise the Mexican penchant for going slow. Aberdeen added that, much though Britain

21. Bankhead to Aberdeen, February 27, March 10, 1846, Nos. 22, 23, 28, 32, 34, GB, FO 50/195, ff. 276–79, 281–82, 306–9; 50/196, ff. 15–17, 22–24.

22. Slidell to Buchanan, December 27, 29, 1845; January 10, 14, 1846; February 6, 17; March 1, Nos. 4–10, Manning, IAA, VIII, 800–813, 815–17. Same,

January 10, George Ticknor Curtis, Life of James Buchanan, Fifteenth President of the United States, I, 593–94. George Lockhart Rives, The United States and Mexico, II, 78. On the Oregon question, see Bankhead to Aberdeen, January 30, No. 14, GB, FO 50/195, ff. 185–87.

deplored the American threat to California, she could not act without France or until the Oregon crisis was resolved. The Mexican chargé in Paris also warned his government not to count on British or French aid.[23]

At the same time, urged by Bermúdez, the Spanish government was sounding out Paris and London on the subject of monarchical restoration in Mexico. Guizot advised Spain to take care but cautiously added that if the Mexican government and people freely declared themselves in favor of monarchy, it would seem logical to place a Spanish prince on the throne. French approval, however, would depend on British cooperation. For his part, Aberdeen told the Spanish ambassador that Britain would not disapprove of a constitutional monarchy, would welcome a Spanish prince, and would unite with France and Spain to stabilize the new throne as much as possible. Peel agreed. Both of them emphasized that the change must represent the free and spontaneous will of the Mexican people—an impossible requirement that reduced the gesture to nothing.[24]

Of course this *démarche* was confidential, but the European press soon got wind of the plot. Newspapers in Madrid unwisely made knowing references to the impending departure of Don Enrique to a foreign throne. The London *Times* reprinted some of these, and on January 15 it commented that the reconquest of Mexico would be easy and a Spanish prince popular in Mexico. A month later it declared that whatever Polk might say about the Monroe Doctrine, the Mexican people had a right to choose whatever form of government they wished. In France the press paid little attention to the question, remarking only that a Spanish prince would be objectionable and that, since the Anglo–American power struggle was intimately involved, the French govern-

23. Tomás Murphy to Ministerio de Relaciones, London, January 1, February 1, 1846, Nos. 2, 4, Antonio de la Peña y Reyes, *Lord Aberdeen, Texas y California*, pp. 60–64. Fernando Mangino to Ministerio de Relaciones, Paris, January 29, Barker transcripts, vol. 571, pp. 120–22. Sellers attributes Aberdeen's restraining remarks to Polk's aggressive stand on Oregon. Charles Grier Sellers, *James K. Polk, Continentalist, 1843–1846*, pp. 332–33. It is difficult to follow this reasoning.

24. Summaries of communications from the Spanish chargé in Paris and the Spanish ambassador in London, dated February 14 and March 20, 1846,

respectively, are contained in Memorandum, February 17, AHN. For an explanation of the discrepancy in dates, see note 13. The British chargé at Paris, Henry Reeve, took an active interest in the intrigue, seeing in it a chance to revive joint Anglo–French action against American expansion. Henry Reeve to Aberdeen, Paris, January 12, copy in letterbook, Aberdeen Papers, BM, AM, vol. 43288, ff. 47–51. For Aberdeen's tepid reaction, see also Aberdeen to Bankhead, February 28, April 30, July 16, Nos. 6, 14, 2, GB, FO 50/194, ff. 13–14, 29, 56–57. Aberdeen to James Morier, April 29, Aberdeen Papers, BM, AM, vol. 43246, ff. 66–67.

ment should stay out of the intrigue.[25] Bermúdez de Castro was displeased at the premature publicity thus given to his plans, but he tactfully blamed it on the American press and continued his efforts to cover his tracks.[26]

* * * *

Newspapers in the United States were so deeply absorbed in the Oregon question that they paid only occasional attention to Mexico during the winter of 1845–1846. When Slidell began his mission, many were confident of his success, provided that European powers did not encourage Mexico to resist his approaches. This optimism gradually disappeared during January and February, but moderates such as the New York *Evening Post* advised against a cheap display of valor at Mexican expense, especially as long as the Oregon crisis remained unresolved. Jingoists like the New York *Herald* called for action: "It is quite time for our government then to send a fleet to the Gulf of Mexico, and . . . for our army of occupation to pass the Rio Grande. There is no use to be trifling any longer with the Mexicans." Reports of monarchist intrigue (usually attributed to Britain as much as to Spain) aroused fears for the safety of California and caused editors to mention and endorse the Monroe Doctrine.[27]

The President had heard rumors about the monarchist plot as early as November 1845, and he apparently regarded Britain rather than Spain as the prime instigator, for his view of the British role in Texas, California, and Oregon predisposed him to believe that Peel and Aberdeen were capable of almost any trickery to restrain American expansion.[28] Undoubtedly his fear of monarchism reinforced his implied reference to the Monroe Doctrine in his original instructions to Slidell and his explicit invocation of the Doctrine in his annual message.

25. London *Times*, January 15, 1846, p. 4; February 12, p. 7. *Le national*, January 18, p. 1. *Le constitutionnel*, February 15, p. 2. See also Riva Palacio, *México a través de los siglos*, IV, 557–58.

26. Bermúdez de Castro to Leopoldo O'Donnell (captain general at Havana), January 27, February 26, 1846, AHN, legajo 5869, caja 1.

27. *NNR*, 69 (December 6, 20, 1845; January 24, 1846), 209, 244, 323. New York *Evening Post*, February 2, p. 2. New York *Herald*, February 3, p. 2;

February 8, p. 2; February 27, p. 2; February 28, pp. 2, 3. Quotation is in issue for February 3. Washington *Union*, February 17, p. 975. It was also rumored that Britain would receive Cuba for her part in the monarchist intrigue. Smith, *War with Mexico*, I, 135.

28. Polk's friend, Consul Robert Armstrong at Liverpool, wrote him in mid-October about British encouragement to Spain. Robert Armstrong to James K. Polk, Liverpool, October 19, 1845, Polk Papers, XCIV, LC.

During the first weeks of the new year Polk began to learn of Slidell's difficulties just as the Congressional debates over Oregon caught fire. On January 12 the State Department received dispatches from Slidell and Black, describing the discomfiture of the Mexican government at Slidell's premature arrival and the precarious political situation. In his dispatch Slidell declared that, according to the best information, Herrera and his government wanted to settle all differences with the United States but dared not take the responsibility.[29] Such a state of affairs could only encourage Polk to take a more forward position. The dispatches arrived at a moment when he was resisting Calhoun's suggestions for compromise on Oregon and proposing to look John Bull "straight in the eye." The Senate had postponed further debate on Oregon, and the House showed no signs of carrying talk into action. Polk was in a defiant mood and thought the status of the Oregon question offered no good reason for restraint in the Mexican theater of operations.

As a result, on January 13 Marcy sent to Taylor new orders that had probably been already prepared, at least in part, when the dispatches arrived from Mexico. All through the autumn Taylor had been waiting uncomfortably at Corpus Christi, idle and restless. In a long report on October 4 he had recommended that, to facilitate a boundary settlement, he be permitted to march to the Rio Grande and occupy strong positions at Point Isabel and Laredo. Now the administration gave him the orders he had requested. While he was authorized to occupy points opposite Matamoros and Mier and near Laredo, he must not try to navigate the river and must not treat Mexico as an enemy. The instructions added, however: "Should she assume that character by a declaration of war, or any open act of hostility towards us, you will not act merely on the defensive, if your relative means enable you to do otherwise."[30]

29. Slidell to Buchanan, December 17, 1845, No. 3, Manning, *IAA*, VIII, 780.

30. Zachary Taylor to Adjutant General, Corpus Christi, October 4, 1845; William L. Marcy to Taylor, January 13, 1846, US, 30C, 1S, HED 60, pp. 90–91, 107–9. In his diary Polk mentioned a cabinet discussion on January 13 of dispatches from Mexico (sent on December 17 and 18 by Slidell and Black) but not the orders to Taylor. James K. Polk, *The Diary of James K. Polk during His Presidency, 1845 to 1849,* ed.

Milo M. Quaife, I, 164. A modern Mexican writer attributes Polk's decision regarding Taylor's advance to knowledge that Paredes had led his troops south, away from the border. Luis G. Zorrilla, *Historia de la relaciones entre México y los Estados Unidos de América, 1800–1958,* I, 192. No evidence has been found to support this allegation. Furthermore, Polk had not received Slidell's No. 4 of December 27, announcing Paredes' revolt.

A few days later Polk and Buchanan drew up new instructions for Slidell in response to his reports that the Mexican government would probably rebuff him. These instructions coincided almost exactly with the American rejection of Pakenham's second proposal to arbitrate the Oregon question. On January 20 Buchanan wrote to Slidell, approving his conduct so far. If Mexico should "consummate the act of folly" by turning him away, he must arrange to "throw the whole odium of the failure of the negotiation upon the Mexican Government." [31]

Three days after sending this message Polk and Buchanan received a full account of Slidell's frustrating argument with Peña over credentials and of the Paredes revolution. On January 28 they replied to him in language bearing the unmistakable threat of war: "Should the Mexican Government, however, finally refuse to receive you, the cup of forbearance will then have been exhausted. Nothing can remain but to take the redress of the injuries to our citizens and the insults to our Government into our own hands." The instructions moderated this strong stand with the statement that "every honorable effort should be made before a final rupture," and they overruled Slidell's proposal to require the new government formally to retract Peña's note. [32] On the following day Polk explained privately to his brother that the anti-American tone in Paredes' revolutionary *pronunciamiento* "was probably to enable himself to obtain power, and not with the intention—to carry out his declamations." He described his order to Taylor as "a precautionary measure" but repeated the statement that if Slidell were ordered home, the American government would take its own measures of redress. [33]

<hr/>

31. Buchanan to Slidell, January 20, 1846, No. 5, Manning, *IAA*, VIII, 185–87. This statement has seemed to reinforce the belief of some critical historians that the Slidell mission was a sham, intended only to convince the world that Polk had used every means to avoid war. See, for example, Louis M. Sears, *John Slidell*, p. 61. The sentence is an exact quotation from Slidell's dispatch of December 17, 1845 (No. 3), which had just arrived in Washington. Manning, *IAA*, VIII, 782. Thus, Buchanan was doing no more than approve a casual suggestion of his envoy, made before Slidell could be at all certain of the Mexican actions.

32. Buchanan to Slidell, January 28, 1846, No. 6, Manning, *IAA*, VIII, 187–

89.

33. James K. Polk to William H. Polk, January 29, 1846, Letterbook, 1845–1846, pp. 301–10, Polk Papers, LC. A letter from Marcy confirms the attitude of the President and cabinet at this point: uncertainty as to future course and preparation to express indignation if Slidell should be finally rejected. Marcy to P. M. Wetmore, February 1, Marcy Papers, XI, LC. Contrast this with a statement in the *Union* justifying the order sending Taylor to the Rio Grande—written nearly three months later, when Slidell's rejection had become known: "War was threatened against everything American. We knew not when the blow might fall upon Texas, upon our citizens in Mexi-

Once again Polk had chosen to negotiate from a position of strength, staring the opponent straight in the eye and hoping he would blink first. McLane had recommended this tactic toward Britain; Slidell had suggested it as the only way to deal with Mexico; and in a few days Polk received additional advice on the subject. On February 13 and 16 Colonel Alexander J. Atocha called at the White House with a confidential message from Mexico's former president, Antonio López de Santa Anna, then an exile in Havana. Atocha was a naturalized Spanish-American, formerly of New Orleans, an audacious yet ingratiating adventurer with a long record of speculation in Mexican government contracts. Herrera had expelled him from Mexico as a *santanista,* and since then he had been pressing claims in Washington against the Mexican government.

Atocha told Polk that Santa Anna approved of Paredes' revolution, that he might soon return to power, and that he favored a boundary line up the Rio Grande and across the mountains to San Francisco, in return for $30 million. Atocha made clear that no Mexican regime could consent freely to such terms; the United States must save face for Mexico by pretending to apply force. Thus, he said, Santa Anna advised that Polk order Taylor to the Rio Grande, collect a naval force at Veracruz, and instruct Slidell to retire to a warship and demand payment of the money Mexico owed to American citizens. These threatening actions would provide Paredes with an excuse to yield. When the American offer of money became known, he would gain the support of the Church and the archbishop of Mexico, to whom the government owed half a million dollars. Finally, Atocha held out hope of a secessionist movement in the northeast, led by General Mariano Arista.[34]

Atocha's tale was an ingenious mixture of half-truths and plausible lies. Santa Anna might have sold territory to the United States if he had dared, but Atocha recommended exactly the wrong way to bring about negotiations with Mexico—insulting national honor by trying to dictate peace at the cannon's mouth. In fact, by suggesting that Slidell retire to a warship and demand the payment of claims, Atocha was encouraging him to repeat the very maneuver which the French minister, Baron de Deffaudis, had

co, our commerce in the seas—even upon our minister." Washington *Union,* April 18, p. 1183. This was an exaggerated description of the situation in April—still more of that in January.

34. Polk, *Diary,* I, 222–25, 227–30. On Atocha's background, see Bermúdez de Castro to Primer Secretario de Estado, March 10, 1847, No. 444, *Rdh-m,* IV, 46–49. *NNR,* 68 (July 19, 1845), 306–7.

executed in 1838 and which had precipitated a costly and nearly useless French intervention (see Chapter 2). Some of Atocha's other statements were also quite mistaken. The archbishop of Mexico was hand in glove with the Paredes administration, and although the government was certainly on the edge of bankruptcy, the Church and most other reactionary supporters of Paredes were determined to prevent any further encroachments by the United States.

Why should Santa Anna have put forth such an astonishing overture at this time? It is possible that he intended to use American money to buy his way into the Paredes administration, but the monarchist plot supplies a more credible explanation. He surely knew of the plot, for Havana was noisy with rumors, and he was intimate with the Spanish captain general. Santa Anna had no fixed prejudice against any form of government as long as he controlled it. A Mexican monarchy firmly supported by Europe, however, might indefinitely postpone his return to power, and even if he became prime minister, Spanish favorites of the new king might be expected to limit his actions. The border dispute offered a way of countering the monarchist threat, for an ultimatum from the United States would probably precipitate a crisis before Paredes, Bermúdez de Castro, and the Spanish government were prepared to cope with it. In such a crisis Santa Anna could resume his role as defender of the fatherland against either Europe or the United States—or even both at once.[35]

Polk could recognize a rascal when he saw one. He sent Atocha away without any intimation of his reactions but noted in his diary that he would not trust such a man, who, he thought, would betray any confidence if his interest required him to do so. Nevertheless, the idea of seeking a confrontation with Mexico appealed to him, since it confirmed his own views. On February 17, therefore, he proposed to the cabinet that Slidell should retire to a warship and deliver an ultimatum. Most of the cabinet approved, but Buchanan flatly opposed the plan. The secretary's opposition was partly personal, for he had recently been at outs with Polk over patronage, but he argued cogently that, with Slidell waiting on board a warship, the United States would be forced to make a quick choice between peace and war. If Slidell returned home instead, the United States would have more time to delib-

---

35. Hutchinson, "Gómez Farías and the Return of Santa Anna," pp. 183–84. Callcott, *Santa Anna*, pp. 227–31. Rob- ert B. Campbell to Buchanan, Havana, January 7, 1846, Manning, *IAA*, XI, 351.

erate, and Congress would probably be more cooperative. Meanwhile, a naval officer could present demands, and if Mexico proved compliant, Slidell could easily return.[36]

Two days later, Polk gave way temporarily and told Buchanan that he would wait a little longer for further news from Slidell. The President's willingness to delay probably resulted from both hope and caution. Slidell's messages had emphasized the financial weakness of the Mexican government and the likelihood of revolts in the provinces. Also, Bancroft had received news from one of his merchant friends that the Paredes government was disguising its real sentiments toward the United States, that its members wanted to avoid war, and that there was every prospect of an amicable settlement in a short time.[37] Undoubtedly Polk also took into consideration the more threatening appearance of the Oregon question, for on February 21 the State Department received McLane's dispatch of February 3, which precipitated a cabinet discussion of British military preparations and resulted in new instructions from Buchanan, unofficially suggesting terms of a compromise settlement.

* * * *

The Polk administration had only postponed a crisis in its relations with Mexico, for the President still believed firmly in the efficacy of a strong stand, and Buchanan had differed with him only as to the method of presenting American demands. While Polk paused, the Spanish minister to Mexico, Bermúdez de Castro, continued exhorting Paredes to hold firm, as he hoped for an Anglo–American war and anxiously expected ships and money from Cuba.[38] Both Paredes and his monarchist allies put on a bold front; *El tiempo*, for example, called the United States "a colossus with feet of clay," which owed its prosperity to trade with Britain rather than to republican institutions. The United States government was weak, its laws ignored, the writer charged; it had no

---

36. Polk, *Diary*, I, 233–36. Memorandum of Buchanan, February 17, 1846, Polk Papers, C, LC.

37. Polk, *Diary*, I, 238. Slidell to Buchanan, December 29, 1845; January 10, 14, 1846, Nos. 5–7; Black to Buchanan, December 30, 1845, No. 358, Manning, *IAA*, VIII, 804–10. A portion of Slidell's dispatch of January 14, not reprinted in Manning, may be found in US, DS, D, Mexico, XII. See also

W. Kemble to Bancroft, New York, February 3, 1846, Bancroft Papers, MHS. Kemble's information came from Louis E. Hargous, an American merchant in Mexico City.

38. Bermúdez de Castro to Primer Secretario de Estado, February 26, 1846, No. 202; Memorandum, February 17, AHN. Same, February 27, No. 203, BAE, legajo 1649.

nationality or public spirit because of the many immigrants among its people.[39]

At the end of February Slidell was still in Jalapa, awaiting a change of heart by the Mexican government. There he received a month-old dispatch from Buchanan (January 28), informing him that Taylor had been ordered to the Rio Grande and that he should make every honorable effort to bring the Paredes regime to negotiate quickly. On March 1 Slidell submitted to Foreign Minister Castillo y Lanzas a brief note which was just short of an ultimatum. In it he explained that Washington had approved all his actions; that if Herrera had remained in power, he would have requested his passports some time earlier; and that it was now time for Mexico to choose between peace and open rupture with the United States. He instructed Consul Black, who delivered the note, to indicate orally that he expected an answer within two weeks. Slidell apparently had some real hope of success at this point, for he informed Buchanan that all of Mexico's efforts to arrange new loans had collapsed. Also, monarchist rumors had diverted public attention from the American threat, and Almonte's resignation from the cabinet had removed an implacable Yankeephobe from the government.[40]

Slidell was too optimistic. His note somewhat daunted members of the Mexican government, but the Mexican sense of honor, reinforced by outside advice, held firm. Castillo y Lanzas submitted the note to the Council of Government, which replied that its earlier opinion was unchanged and that the menacing American troops and ships were proof of bad faith. (By this time the Mexican government knew of Taylor's impending move, and American squadrons had taken up stations at Veracruz and Mazatlán.) Bermúdez de Castro also advised Castillo y Lanzas that the Americans were seeking a pretext for war, and that he should refuse to receive Slidell in the hope of arbitration by friendly powers. Privately, Bermúdez reported to Madrid that the American commissioner's presence in Mexico at that moment jeopardized the whole monarchist plan.[41]

39. *El tiempo*, February 5, 1846, p. 1.

40. Buchanan to Slidell, January 28, 1846, No. 6; Slidell to Joaquín M. Castillo y Lanzas, March 1; Slidell to Buchanan, March 1, No. 10, Manning, *IAA*, VIII, 187–89, 814–17. On March 6 Slidell, who was still at Jalapa, scribbled off to Buchanan a rumor that Mexico had actually sent two commissioners to the United States to negoti-

ate. Ibid., p. 817.

41. Valencia to Ministerio de Relaciones, March 6, 1846, México, SRE, *Memoria, 1846*, Appendix, pp. 28–30. Bermúdez de Castro to Primer Ministerio de Estado, March 29, No. 218, *Rdh-m*, III, 266–69. Same, March 29, No. 220; Memorandum, February 17, AHN.

The Oregon question and Anglo–American relations also influenced the Mexicans' thinking. At the beginning of the year Minister Tomás Murphy in London had reported only that Aberdeen was advising Mexico to go slow in antagonizing the United States. In mid-March, perhaps while the Paredes government was considering Slidell's note, another dispatch arrived from Murphy, reporting that Aberdeen seemed very unwilling to see California pass into American hands. Murphy surmised that Britain would probably take active measures to prevent this if the Oregon question were settled and would certainly do so if there should be an Anglo–American war. While Mexican officials deliberated, newspapers in the capital reprinted American press reports about the Oregon debate, and on March 11 the government received a New Orleans newspaper containing the correspondence between Buchanan and Pakenham in which the United States government rejected both British proposals for arbitration.[42]

Under these circumstances, Paredes redoubled his efforts to reach an understanding with Bankhead; he was observed to visit the British minister's home five times in a single day. Paredes and Castillo y Lanzas asked Bankhead to communicate any instructions he received on Mexican–American relations and also on the monarchist intrigue; they also urged him to transmit to London their request for a protectorate of some sort. The British minister agreed to report the conversations to Aberdeen, but he would not commit his government beyond a general statement of good will toward Mexico. He recommended that they answer Slidell's note prudently; they should suggest some alternate arrangement about the official character of the American envoy in order to learn whether Slidell carried flexible instructions as well as to gain time. More than once during the next two weeks Bankhead urged Paredes not to provoke the Americans with aggressive action against Taylor in the hope that, as summer approached, sickness would weaken his troops.[43]

42. Murphy to Ministerio de Relaciones, January 1, February 1, 1846, Nos. 2, 4. The date of receipt is not given, but the Mexican government acknowledged the dispatch on March 23. Peña y Reyes, *Aberdeen, Texas y California*, pp. 60–61, 62–64. *El monitor republicano*, March 7, p. 4. Black to Slidell, March 12; Black to William S. Parrott, March 14, US, DS, PR, Letterbook IV, 292, 296–97. The New Orleans newspaper (dated February 21)

was undoubtedly printing the correspondence Polk had just sent to Congress (see Chap. 11, note 48).

43. Black to Slidell, March 10, 14, 1846, Manning, *IAA*, VIII, 829, 830. Bankhead to Aberdeen, March 7, 10, 30, Nos. 29, 31, 32, 36, 45, GB, FO 50/196, ff. 1–3, 9–13, 15–17, 28–35, 161–65. Bankhead also showed Castillo y Lanzas a long letter from Vice Consul James A. Forbes in California reporting Frémont's arrival and predicting that with-

But the Mexicans preferred to follow their impulses. Their reply to Slidell was delivered at the last minute after the Spanish minister had spent four hours with Castillo, smoothing it out and restraining its diffuse wanderings. The resultant note briefly informed the American envoy that he would not be received and proceeded to recite the history of the Texas question, attributing both the original revolution and the annexation to a calculated plot by the United States government. The American appointment of a minister plenipotentiary was an act "which the undersigned does not permit himself to qualify." Castillo ended with the statement that if war resulted from the rejection, it would be entirely the fault of the United States.[44]

Slidell's reply to the Mexican note was completely predictable. He defended the United States government against the accusation of a plot to seize Texas, citing Jackson's proclamation of neutrality during the revolt, Mexico's utter inability to reconquer Texas, and her recognition of that republic in 1845. If war came, he continued, the Mexican government could not shift the blame to the United States, for although the United States government had stationed "a few ships of war" and "a small military force" near Mexico, the Mexican government had openly declared its intention to fight and had rejected with insults the Americans' offer to negotiate.[45] He asked for his passports, and since these were slow to arrive, he waited for two weeks before sailing from Veracruz on March 31.

Slidell's last reports to Buchanan revealed an incomplete grasp of the Mexican situation. When he received Castillo's reply to his note of March 1, he could not be sure whether the government had rebuffed him from fear of the opposition or with confidence in European aid. While hitherto he had given little weight to rumors of a monarchist plot, he was coming to believe them. He suspected that British Minister Bankhead was its moving force and did not mention Bermúdez de Castro in connection with the plot. He expected the Paredes government to collapse at any moment, but he considered further negotiation useless, since the Mexicans regarded all friendly advances as a sign of either weak-

---

out prompt action Mexico would lose the province. Bankhead to Aberdeen, March 30, No. 43, James Alexander Forbes to Eustace Barron, San Francisco, January 26, 28, No. 2; Forbes to Agustín Olvera, January 28, GB, FO 50/196, ff. 134–53.

44. Bermúdez de Castro to Primer Secretario de Estado, March 29, 1846, No. 218, *Rdh-m*, III, 266–69. Castillo y Lanzas to Slidell, March 12, Manning, *IAA*, VIII, 818–23. The quoted phrase is on p. 821.

45. Slidell to Castillo y Lanzas, March 17, 1846, Manning, *IAA*, VIII, 824–28. The quoted phrases are on p. 827.

ness or treachery. While it was proper to place the United States in a strong moral position by exhausting all means of conciliation, he concluded: "We shall never be able to treat with her [Mexico] on fair terms, until she has been taught to respect us."

Just before sailing, Slidell received Buchanan's instructions of March 12, which generally approved his final request for reception and gave him full discretion about his departure but suggested that his early return to Washington might hamper the settlement of the Oregon question. Slidell replied that if he had received this information earlier, he could have procrastinated indefinitely with the Paredes government, but of course it was much too late now to turn back.[46]

Probably Slidell would have learned more about Mexican politics if he had remained in Mexico City instead of moving to Jalapa. However, the situation in March and April 1846 was obscure enough to confuse even an "old hand." Denounced by opposition newspapers for inaction against the American threat, Paredes finally sent long-promised reinforcements north under the command of General Pedro Ampudia. There was a lag in Ampudia's response to these orders, for he had to put down a mutiny among his troops before he could get them to move. Late in March a Veracruz newspaper revived republican fears of monarchy by publishing an account of mysterious funds that the Spanish minister, Bermúdez de Castro, had withdrawn from the Treasury at Havana. Once again Secretary of War Tornel persuaded the President to answer republican critics with a conciliatory manifesto. This document declared that the government was not promonarchist. Further, it did not intend either to recognize the American flag in Texas or to take aggressive action there. The manifesto was pompous and intentionally ambiguous, but its antimonarchist assurances so displeased Paredes' reactionary minister of finance that he resigned from the cabinet. These actions did little to quiet the republicans' fears, and the publication of the government's correspondence with Slidell stimulated Yankeephobia.[47]

46. Buchanan to Slidell, March 12, 1846, No. 7; Slidell to Buchanan, Jalapa, March 18; at sea, April 2, Nos. 11, 13, Manning, *IAA*, VIII, 189–92, 828–31, 837–39. The quoted sentence is on p. 831. Black, too, favored postponing further action at this point, for he was sure that Mexico would not declare war. Also, time was working for the United States in clarifying European policy and the monarchist intrigue.

Black to Dimond, April 4, US, DS, PR, Consulate, Mexico City, Letterbook IV, 322–23.

47. Bankhead to Aberdeen, March 10, 30, 1846, Nos. 33, 36 (with enclosure), 39, GB, FO 50/196, ff. 19–20, 28–35, 38–49, 106–8. Bermúdez de Castro to Primer Ministerio de Estado, March 29, No. 219, BAE, legajo 1649. Same, March 29, No. 220; Memorandum, February 17, AHN. Dimond to Buchanan, March

Another element of uncertainty was Juan N. Almonte, recently resigned as minister of war. He began at once to organize a movement against Paredes, who, becoming suspicious, sent him on a mission to France with instructions to seek renewal of diplomatic relations and aid in defending California. Not being ready to revolt, Almonte left Mexico City, but he booked passage only to Havana, where he joined Santa Anna in temporary exile. Almonte was probably responsible in part for an antimonarchist revolt that broke out in Veracruz just as he was passing through the city.[48] Government forces suppressed it quickly, but another erupted farther south in Oaxaca and smouldered there until Paredes was finally overthrown.

Surveying these confusing developments, the American consuls in Mexico City and Veracruz assured the State Department that a considerable number of federalists throughout the country looked to negotiations with the United States as the only salvation from monarchism and European domination.[49] Still, despite Santa Anna's overture to Polk, it was not likely that his return to the presidency at this point would have led at once to negotiations with the United States. Mexican liberal republicans might feel themselves to be between the devil and the deep—between a Bourbon monarch and American annexationists—but they were not yet ready to make a choice of evils. In the words of the leading antimonarchist newspaper: "The protection of the United States is the worst snare that can be set out for our nationality and independence."[50]

While Slidell was preparing to embark for home, Taylor and his little army arrived on the north bank of the Rio Grande near the site of present-day Brownsville, Texas, and took a threatening position deep in the disputed territory. Marcy's orders of January 13 had instructed him to move without delay, but when Taylor received them on February 3, he realized that he knew very little about the country across which he would have to march, so he

18, No. 324, US, DS, CD, Veracruz, V. Zamacois, *Historia de Méjico*, XII, 442–43. Dennis E. Berge, "Mexican Response to United States Expansionism, 1841–1848," Ph.D. diss., University of California (Berkeley), 1965, pp. 191–92.

48. Riva Palacio, *México a través de los siglos*, IV, 558. Bankhead to Aberdeen, March 30, 1846, No. 43, GB, FO 50/196, ff. 155–57. Dimond to Buchanan, March 31, April 1, 5, Nos. 326, 327, 329, US, DS, CD, Veracruz, V. [Ben H.

Wright] to Nicholas P. Trist, Havana, April 11, Trist Papers, XXI, ff. 59524–25, LC.

49. Black to Buchanan, March 19, 1846, No. 363, Manning, *IAA*, VIII, 832–33. Dimond to Buchanan, March 21, No. 325, US, DS, CD, Veracruz, V. See also Slidell to Buchanan, April 2, No. 13, Manning, *IAA*, VIII, 837–39.

50. *El republicano*, April 18, 1846, p. 4; April 20, p. 3. See also Berge, "Mexican Response," pp. 193–94.

spent weeks gathering information. After further preparation the troops finally got under way on March 8. Taylor had assured Mexicans visiting Corpus Christi that his march was not a warlike move and that he still expected peaceful negotiations. As he broke camp, he issued a pronouncement in English and Spanish that his troops would respect all civil and religious rights of the local inhabitants and would pay for all supplies "at the highest [market] prices."[51]

In New Orleans a rumor circulated to the effect that Taylor intended to occupy points all along the Rio Grande from Laredo to the Gulf of Mexico. But he wisely kept his four thousand men together—since he might have to face twice that many Mexicans—and struck directly through the disputed territory about two hundred miles toward the Mexican city of Matamoros, on the south bank of the Rio Grande just above its mouth. The troops marched across a strange, deserted prairie, fields of bluebonnets and other flowers giving way to sand, marshes, gullies, and twisted chaparral. A little over half way to Matamoros a small body of Mexicans came out to meet them and tried to frighten them away by taking up a position in an arroyo, which made them seem to be a much larger force. The Mexican commander had prudently forbidden an attack, and when the Americans came boldly on, the Mexicans galloped back toward the city. As he approached the Rio Grande, Taylor made a detour to the coast with part of his troops, established connections with his naval reinforcements, and left a detachment to set up a supply base at Point Isabel.[52]

On March 28 Taylor reached the Rio Grande opposite Matamoros and established a temporary camp. During the digression to Point Isabel a Mexican deputation had come out from the city with a formal protest by the district prefect that Taylor brushed aside. Once in camp, he sent his second-in-command to announce to the Mexican commander at Matamoros that the Americans' intentions were peaceful and to propose joint measures which would prevent violence along the border while the two governments negotiated. (Taylor did not know yet that Slidell had given up his mission.) Since the Mexicans persisted in regarding the American

51. Smith, *War with Mexico*, I, 145–46. Taylor to Adjutant General, Corpus Christi, February 26, 1846; Taylor, Order No. 30, March 8, US, 30C, 1S, HED 60, pp. 117–20.

52. Smith, *War with Mexico*, I, 146–48. Taylor to Adjutant General, en route to Rio Grande, March 18, 21, 25, 1846, US, 30C, 1S, HED 60, pp. 123–25. 129–30. For the report in New Orleans, see Alphonse de Saligny to François Guizot, Plaquemines, March 14, No. 93, France, MAE, CP, Texas, IX, ff. 233–35. Saligny had not returned to France from his post in Texas.

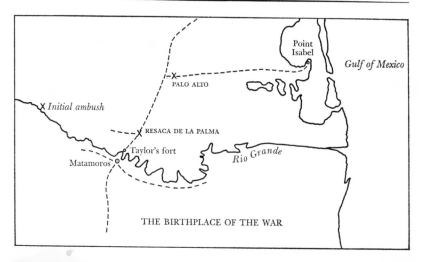

Point
Isabel

Gulf of Mexico

╳
PALO ALTO

╳ Initial ambush

╳ RESACA DE LA PALMA

Taylor's fort

Matamoros

Rio Grande

THE BIRTHPLACE OF THE WAR

incursion as an act of war, Taylor began to construct a fort with a battery of four eighteen-pounders. "These guns bear directly upon the public square of Matamoras [*sic*], and within good range for demolishing the town," he reported. Taylor had concluded that there were only about two thousand Mexican troops of poor quality in the city, and he felt that his precautions would effectively prevent a surprise attack.[53]

A few days later General Pedro Ampudia arrived in Matamoros with reinforcements. Ampudia ordered all American residents out of the city into the interior, and on April 12 he sent Taylor a peremptory letter, demanding that the Americans withdraw beyond the Nueces River within twenty-four hours and threatening military action if they refused. Taylor countered by asking his naval auxiliary offshore to blockade the mouth of the Rio Grande—an act justifiable only by a state of war, although he described it as "a simple defensive precaution." When the Mexicans protested, he repeated his offer of an armistice, pending negotiations. His offer was refused, and during the next two weeks the Americans finished their fort. Meanwhile, General Mariano Arista took command in Matamoros. Arista was an ambitious politician-soldier, stocky and boastful, with bushy red hair and beard, who had refused to support Paredes' revolutionary movement and was clearly playing his own game in the northeast.[54]

53. Smith, *War with Mexico*, I, 148. Taylor to Adjutant General, Point Isabel, March 25, 1846; opposite Matamoros, March 29, April 6; Minutes of interview between Generals W. J. Worth and R. D. de la Vega, March 28,

US, 30C, 1S, HED 60, pp. 129–38. The sentence quoted is on p. 133.

54. Taylor to Pedro de Ampudia, April 12, 1846. Taylor to Adjutant General, April 15, US, 30C, 1S, HED 60, pp. 138–40. Rives, *US and Mexico*, II,

Morale among the American troops was considerably higher than it had been at Corpus Christi, but at least one officer had his doubts about the wisdom of the venture. "We have not one particle of right to be here," wrote Colonel Ethan Hitchcock in his diary. "Our force is altogether too small for the accomplishment of its errand. It looks as if the government sent a small force on purpose to bring on a war, so as to have a pretext for taking California and as much of this country as it chooses." For decades Polk's political opponents, Northern abolitionists, and a few historians were to agree with Hitchcock.[55]

Whatever Polk's motives, there can be no doubt about the risks he and Taylor were incurring. On April 23 Taylor sent home a report about the "*quasi* war" in which he was engaged. His men had found the body of an American officer not far from camp, but he was willing to believe that the man had been killed by robbers. An outpost had clashed in the midst of a rainstorm with Mexican irregulars from across the river, suffering several casualties. When Arista assumed command he issued a proclamation appealing to European-born soldiers in Taylor's army to desert, and he informed Taylor that in his opinion war had begun and he intended to prosecute it. Taylor reinforced his patrols.[56]

On April 25 occurred the decisive act for which all had been waiting. Expecting a large force of Mexican regulars to cross the river, Taylor sent out a reconnaissance patrol of 63 men who marched upstream more than fifteen miles before dawn in search of the enemy. Coming on a large farm, surrounded by a stockade of chaparral, they stopped to investigate without bothering to post a sentinel, and while they were inside this trap, a force of several hundred Mexicans fell upon them. Their retreat cut off, some Americans broke through the stockade and fled in utter disorder, but during the fighting the captain in command and 15 others were killed or wounded. The Mexicans took the survivors as prisoners to Matamoros, where they were decently treated.

Taylor reported the skirmish to Washington on the following

140–41. For a characterization of Arista, see Joseph Milton Nance, *After San Jacinto, the Texas–Mexican Frontier, 1836–1841*, pp. 438–39n23. After the Mexican War he was elected President of Mexico in 1851 and served until overthrown in January, 1853.

55. Ethan Allen Hitchcock, *Fifty Years in Camp and Field*, ed. W. A. Croffut, p. 213.

56. Arista's predecessor, Ampudia, also had orders to attack as soon as possible, so the change of command probably made little difference. Smith, *War with Mexico*, I, 149. Taylor to Adjutant General, April 23, 1846, US, 30C, 1S, HED 60, pp. 142–44. Arista's proclamation, dated April 20, appears ibid., pp. 303–4.

day and remarked briefly, "Hostilities may now be considered as commenced." He also requested the governors of Texas and Louisiana to send him eight regiments of troops—about five thousand men.[57] To him the war presented only a military problem, which he proposed to solve as quickly and directly as possible. To the politicians in Washington, however, the war was not that simple, for it involved complications of diplomatic relations with Britain, domestic party and sectional rivalries, and volatile, unpredictable public opinion.

*   *   *   *

Long before Polk learned of the fighting on the Rio Grande, he and his cabinet had tried to regulate the disputes with Britain and Mexico so that they would not come to the boiling point at the same time. When he dispatched Slidell to Mexico and prepared his annual message to Congress, he may have intended first to bluff Britain into compromise on Oregon, aided by a strong resolution of notice from Congress, and then to apply the same technique to Mexico.[58]

Whether Polk had consciously drawn up a timetable of diplomatic crises, no one can doubt that throughout March and April he fretted over the long-drawn-out debate on Oregon.[59] On March 20 he and the cabinet eagerly examined British press reports, more than two weeks old, which described the reaction in London to the news that the House had passed the resolution of notice. The British newspapers expected war if the Senate passed the resolution and doubted that Polk was strong enough to restrain the extremists in his party. Consols fell more than one point.[60]

In the next instructions to McLane, dated March 28, Buchanan said little except that the President would receive any British proposals made through McLane but would not again transfer negotiations to Washington. A day later Bancroft also wrote to the American minister, describing the debate in Congress and giving his opinion that the Senate would overwhelmingly approve a rea-

57. Taylor to Adjutant General, April 26, 1846; W. T. Hardee letter from Matamoros, April 26, US, 30C, 1S, HED 60, pp. 140–41, 291–92.

58. Sellers, *Polk, Continentalist*, p. 405. If Polk did have such a timetable, it is strange that he did not instruct Slidell explicitly about stalling his negotiations before Buchanan's dispatch of March 12. See notes 46 and 62.

59. See, for example, Polk, *Diary*, I,

276, 289, 325, 345; and Polk to A. O. P. Nicholson, April 2, 1846, Polk Papers, NYHS.

60. Polk, *Diary*, I, 293–94. For samples of the sort of British comments he must have read, see London *Times*, March 5, 1846, p. 4; London *Morning Chronicle*, March 5, p. 4; London *Examiner*, March 7, p. 146; and a summary later reprinted in *NNR*, 70 (April 4), 65.

sonable British offer—which he interpreted to include temporary navigation rights on the Columbia River. As for Mexico, Bancroft listed the forces which the United States had massed on her border and coast but added that the prospects for a peaceable settlement in that quarter were better than at any previous time.[61]

Bancroft's statement reflected Polk's hopes and what the President wanted the British to believe. The remarks about Mexico considerably stretched the latest meager, stale information from Slidell, a dispatch of February 17 which indicated only that he had retired to Jalapa and was waiting for the Paredes administration to fall apart. On March 12 Buchanan had instructed Slidell to return to Mexico City and make a "strong but respectful" demand for reception and negotiations while letting it be known discreetly that the United States would gladly relieve Paredes' financial embarrassment in return for a favorable settlement. At the end he mentioned the Oregon question and suggested that Slidell remain in Mexico until it was settled.[62]

During the latter half of March Polk received further outdated dispatches from Mexico which reinforced his wishful belief that the Mexican government might be receptive to an offer of money.[63] Grasping at this hope, he suggested to the cabinet that the administration ask Congress for a special appropriation of perhaps a million dollars, so that if Slidell did manage to bring Paredes to the point of signing a treaty, he could offer him, as the final inducement to sign, enough ready cash to pay his army. Everyone but Buchanan approved of the idea, and Polk consulted Benton, Allen, and other senators, using as precedent Thomas Jefferson's request of 1806 for a similar secret service fund.[64] The

61. Buchanan to McLane, March 28, 1846, No. 26, Manning, *CR*, III, 326–27. Bancroft to McLane, March 29, Bancroft Papers, MHS.

62. Slidell to Buchanan, February 17, 1846, No. 9 (received March 9). Buchanan to Slidell, March 12, No. 7, Manning, *IAA*, VIII, 189–92, 813.

63. In his diary entry for March 28 Polk mentioned discussing with the cabinet hopeful dispatches from Slidell. Polk, *Diary*, I, 305–6. These must have been Slidell's No. 8 of February 6 (received on March 16) and No. 9 of February 17 (received on March 9), Manning, *IAA*, VIII, 811–13. Polk may also have been influenced by a dispatch from Consul Dimond at Veracruz, reporting an increase of pro-American

spirit, which was sent on February 20 and arrived in Washington on March 16. US, DS, CD, Veracruz, V. At about the same time Bancroft also heard indirectly from Louis and Peter Hargous, who felt that if Slidell talked less of California, he would obtain the Rio Grande boundary for one or two million dollars. R. R. Waldron to Bancroft, New York, March 6, Bancroft Papers, MHS.

64. Polk, *Diary*, I, 306–8. The precedent Polk cited was not a happy one. To be sure, Jefferson got his appropriation, which was intended for the purchase of Florida, but he split his party in the process and was never able to put the money to its intended use.

moment was scarcely propitious for asking favors of Congress, however, for tempers were frayed over the Oregon debate, and Western Democrats were sour with suspicions of Polk's treachery.

When Polk finally consulted Calhoun, the South Carolinian declared that he heartily approved of negotiations with Mexico, and the two men discussed desirable boundaries. The President said that he would prefer the Rio Grande and a line along 32° (near the present boundary) but would accept a line through New Mexico, farther north, if that boundary would include the whole coast of Upper California. Calhoun expressed grave doubts about putting a secret appropriation through Congress, and after further thought, on April 3 he indicated to the President that he would not support the measure.[65]

Later, during the war, Polk returned to the idea of a private fund to facilitate negotiations with Mexico. His discussion with Calhoun at this time proved purely academic, for on the evenings of April 6 and 7 the State Department received two bundles of mail from Slidell and Black: their dispatches from March 1 to 19 and Slidell's whole correspondence with Castillo y Lanzas, including the ultimatum, the Mexican rejection, and Slidell's request for his passports. Within little more than twenty-four hours the character of the Mexican situation had completely changed. Even before the second set of dispatches arrived, Polk raised the subject at the regular biweekly cabinet meeting, and all members agreed with him that if Slidell returned home empty-handed, the President should send to Congress a special message "recommending that Legislative measures be adopted, to take the remedy for the injuries and wrongs we had suffered into our own hands."[66]

Did this mean a formal declaration of war or merely congressional approval of further troop movements and other gestures? For the next three weeks Polk's diary contains only occasional cautious references to "strong measures" as he consulted with the cabinet and with other party leaders. On April 17 he wrote to Slidell in New Orleans, summoning him to Washington as soon as possible with his information on Mexican conditions and adding that he would delay action on Mexican matters until the envoy's arrival.[67]

65. Polk, *Diary*, I, 311–14, 315, 317. Calhoun described the line he had contemplated establishing while secretary of state: northwest from the Gulf of Mexico through the barren land between the Nueces and the Rio Grande, and west along 36° or 37° to the Pacific, giving the United States San Francisco and perhaps Monterey too. For such a line he said that the Tyler administration would have paid $10 million. Ibid., p. 312.

66. Polk, *Diary*, I, 319.

67. Polk to Slidell, April 17, 1846, Let-

There were other good reasons for delay. First, dispatches received during April from Consul Black in Mexico City, Consul Dimond in Veracruz, and Commodore Conner of the Gulf Squadron all mentioned strong opposition to Paredes' regime from federalist groups that were well disposed toward the United States. Black declared that the monarchist threat had come to a standstill; Dimond described the intrigues of Almonte and *santanistas* at Veracruz; and Conner offered the opinion that Mexico was too distracted and impoverished to commit any act of hostility toward the United States.[68]

A second reason for waiting was the state of the Oregon question. Several congressmen with whom Polk discussed the Mexican situation during April—Houston, Allen, and Calhoun—approved of the delay for this reason, and Calhoun in particular advised Polk to take no action toward Mexico before a settlement with Britain. In reply, Polk urged Calhoun to push the Senate debate toward conclusion, since it was clear that Britain would not act while it was still going on. The President added that, whatever the Senate did, he must submit the Mexican question to Congress before the close of the session.[69] Dispatches from McLane at this time confirmed Polk in his conviction that Peel and Aberdeen were waiting for the terms of the Senate resolution. Otherwise, McLane's dispatches were somewhat reassuring, for he repeated pacific declarations by Aberdeen and quoted a remark of Peel in Parliament which indicated that he still hoped to renew negotiations over Oregon.[70]

On April 23 Congress finally passed a compromise version of the resolution giving notice for the end of joint occupation. Dur-

---

terbook, 1845–1846, p. 442, Polk Papers, LC. Taking a hint from Buchanan's latest instructions, Slidell had announced that he would go directly to his home, rather than report first in Washington. Slidell to Buchanan, April 9. Curtis, *Buchanan*, I, 599. Same, April 15, Buchanan Papers, box 24, HSP.

68. Black to Buchanan, March 19, 1846, No. 363 (received April 27), Manning, *IAA*, VIII, 832–33. Dimond to Buchanan, April 1, 5, Nos. 327, 329 (received April 27), US, DS, CD, Veracruz, V. David E. Conner to Bancroft, March 19, April 9, Nos. 56, 59, US, DN, LSC, roll 85.

69. Polk, *Diary*, I, 327, 337–38. Two

days later, Polk made the same comment in a letter to a political henchman. Polk to Gideon J. Pillow, April 20, 1846, Letterbook, 1845–1846, Polk Papers, LC.

70. McLane to Buchanan, March 17, April 3, 1846, Nos. 36, 37, Manning, *CR*, III, 1011–15, 1017–21. However, in these and in private letters to Buchanan, McLane deplored the publicity given to his negotiations and declared that the evidence of American disunity would make it difficult to obtain substantial concessions from Britain. McLane to Buchanan, March 17, April 3, 10, Buchanan Papers, box 63, HSP.

ing the next week Buchanan and Polk sent messages to McLane, formally announcing that in a year the United States would consider the joint occupation treaty at an end. They also indicated that the next move was for the British government to make and suggested that if it intended to offer terms for an Oregon settlement, it should act before Congress adjourned.[71]

As soon as the cabinet had approved the Oregon notice (April 25), Polk reverted to the Mexican question. Conciliation having failed, he declared, "We must take redress for the injuries done us into our own hands." Having "forborne until forbearance was no longer either a virtue or patriotic . . . we must treat all nations, whether great or small, strong or weak, alike, and . . . take a bold and firm course toward Mexico." Asked for opinions, Buchanan agreed that a declaration of war was in order, and the other members of the cabinet a bit more reluctantly consented to discuss the text of a special message to Congress the following week.[72] At the next two cabinet meetings Polk continued to postpone discussion in the hope of receiving up-to-date reports from Taylor on the Rio Grande. The most recent dispatch, dated April 6, had stated that he was completing his fortifications and that the Mexicans refused to discuss his advance, regarding it as an act of war. Taylor had concluded: "They are only waiting . . . [Ampudia's] arrival with heavy reinforcements to attack us." [73]

By now, circumstances at home were crowding in on Polk, making clear that he could not delay a Mexican settlement much longer. The outcome of the Senate debate had done nothing to mend the split in public opinion over the Oregon question. On the one hand, moderates were more certain than they had been, earlier, that Oregon was not worth a war; that the war scare was bad for business; and that Britain was ready to compromise at 49° if the United States would make some concession on navigation of the Columbia River.[74] After Congress passed the resolution of notice, Benton, Vice President Dallas, and Calhoun's bloc tried

71. Buchanan to McLane, April 28, 1846, No. 27, Manning, *CR*, III, 329–30.

72. Polk to McLane, April 29, 1846, Letterbook, 1845–1846, pp. 462–66, Polk Papers, LC. Polk, *Diary*, I, 353–54.

73. Taylor to Adjutant General, April 6, 1846, US, 30C, 1S, HED 60, pp. 133–34. Polk, *Diary*, I, 363, 374, 379.

74. For samples of these moderate opinions, see *Merchants' Magazine*, 14

(May 1846), 435–39; and *NNR*, 70 (May 2, 9), 130, 131, 145. Many Southerners were resentful because the administration and Congress were devoting excessive attention to Western measures in general—Oregon and internal improvements—and ignoring the loyal Democrats of the South. Charleston *Mercury*, n.d., reprinted in *NNR*, 70 (May 16), 175.

to persuade Polk to accompany the resolutions with a statement inviting a settlement at 49°, but he held to his earlier position that Britain must take the initiative.[75]

On the other hand, sentiment for occupying all of Oregon was still strong throughout the country, and the mail of Western extremist Senators was full of praise for their "noble Stand."[76] Fortified by this support, the extremists continued to spread their suspicions that Polk intended to sell out at 49° and added that if he should, they saw no reason for a showdown with Mexico. As the Chicago *Democrat* put it: "Why should we not compromise our difficulties with Mexico as well as with Great Britain? The same doctrine that our Southern friends preach about surrendering Oregon to the 49th would apply to surrendering of all Texas to the Nueces. If it is wicked to go to war with England for disputed territory, it is not only wicked but cowardly to go to war with Mexico for the same reason."[77]

The persistent split in the Democratic congressional delegation threatened not only Polk's intended settlements with Britain and Mexico but also his whole domestic program. On April 14 a low-tariff bill prepared by Walker was finally brought out for discussion by the House, and for a time there seemed some likelihood that a coalition would form to push through Walker's bill and also a bill for an independent treasury, the main item in his financial program.[78] When a movement took shape to adjourn Congress until October, Polk told the speaker of the House that he would forbid the action and he expected the rank and file of his party to support him. One editorialist suggested scornfully that the President's only accomplishment might prove to have been the abolition of dancing in the White House.[79]

During the latter half of April a far less astute politician than Polk might have concluded that the best glue for mending a split party was patriotism. Earlier, he had hoped merely to bluff the

75. Polk, *Diary*, I, 324–25, 337–38, 348–49. Sellers, *Polk, Continentalist*, p. 397.

76. Reuben Beers to William Allen, Mt. Pleasant, Iowa, May 4, 1846; William Mims to Allen, Americus, Georgia, May 9; "Old Dominion" to Allen, New Orleans, May 19, Allen Papers, XIII, LC. The phrase is quoted from Mims' letter. Even such Whigs as Seward and Thurlow Weed encouraged the Democrats on Oregon. W. H. Seward, Thurlow Weed, and G. C. Bronson to Allen, Albany, April 18, ibid.

77. Chicago *Democrat*, n.d., as quoted in Don E. Fehrenbacher, *Chicago Giant: a Biography of "Long John" Wentworth*, p. 64.

78. Edward Stanwood, *American Tariff Controversies in the Nineteenth Century*, II, 70–71. *NNR*, 70 (March 14, 1846), 19. New York *Herald*, n.d., as reprinted in London *Times*, May 5, p. 7.

79. Polk, *Diary*, I, 368–71, 373–74. New York *Herald*, April 22, 1846, p. 3.

Mexican government into negotiating, using Taylor's army as a show of strength and formal war as a threat and a last resort. Now, however, he must force the issue and demand an immediate declaration of war, not only to maintain the strong front against Mexico but also to confound the opposition at home. The affront to Slidell might serve to justify such a declaration, but a Mexican attack on Taylor would be much more effective. Such an attack, however, would involve considerable risk, for if the American troops were defeated in a major battle, the administration might be in a worse position. Already newspapers were denouncing Polk because he had not provided Taylor with enough troops.[80]

For the time being the President and cabinet could do nothing but await news from the Rio Grande and Slidell's arrival in Washington. On May 6 Polk received a dispatch from Taylor reporting that Mexican reinforcements had arrived and that he had blockaded the river mouth. Buchanan too seems to have received word privately from friends who anticipated an attack.[81] On May 7 reassuring letters, written in mid-April, arrived from McLane in London. Aberdeen had gone out of his way to explain that "after the passage of the resolutions [*sic*] he could resume the negotiation with less embarrassment than he should feel before."[82] The near certainty that Britain would soon offer a compromise settlement and thus provide a basis for time-consuming talks undoubtedly strengthened Polk's determination to force a decision with Mexico.

No scenarist could have squeezed more suspense and irony out of the next four days' actions. On Friday morning, May 8, Buchanan came to the White House with Slidell, just arrived from New Orleans. The President and Slidell agreed that no alternative remained for the United States but to redress its own grievances against Mexico, and Polk added that "it was only a matter of time" before a suitable message would go to Congress.[83] On the next morning the cabinet held a full discussion of the Mexican question. All agreed that if the Mexicans attacked Tay-

80. New York *Herald*, April 23, 1846, p. 2; May 1, p. 3.

81. Polk, *Diary*, I, 380. Taylor, however, doubted that the Mexicans would attack. Taylor to Adjutant General, April 15, 1846, US, 30C, 1S, HED 60, pp. 138–39. Philip Shriver Klein, *President James Buchanan, a Biography*, pp. 186, 449, 474.

82. McLane to Buchanan, April 17/ 18, 1846, No. 41, Manning, *CR*, III, 1023–27. Same, April 18, Buchanan Papers, box 63, HSP. The quotation appears in Manning, p. 1026. In his private letter McLane expressed some fear that if the Senate delayed much longer, Aberdeen would yield the Foreign Office to Palmerston, thereby delaying a settlement.

83. Polk, *Diary*, I, 382.

lor, Polk should send a war message at once. Polk felt that the "excited and impatient" state of public opinion required immediate action, and he proposed that the cabinet help him draw up a war message at the next regular meeting the following Tuesday, attack or no attack. Everyone approved except Bancroft, who wanted to await action by the Mexicans. Buchanan then took his accustomed position on the fence, his vote remaining with Polk but his opinion leaning toward Bancroft. The cabinet finally agreed to take up on Tuesday a draft statement of grievances which Buchanan had prepared, and the meeting adjourned at about two o'clock in the afternoon.[84]

Four hours later the adjutant general called at the White House with Taylor's dispatch of April 26, which reported the Mexican attack on his reconnaissance party, trapped in the stockade of chaparral, and the resulting casualties. Polk at once called an evening meeting of the cabinet, which voted unanimously to send a war message to Congress on Monday. Buchanan and Marcy agreed to put their departmental clerks to work copying out the correspondence that must accompany the message. A few congressmen, catching wind of the news, appeared during the evening to approve the President's decision.

On Sunday morning everyone in Washington knew of the crisis, and Polk realized that at all costs he must have his message ready on Monday, to take full advantage of the public indignation. He and Bancroft worked on it part of the morning; then he attended church services with his wife, nephew, and niece. Afterward, Buchanan and Bancroft came to the White House to examine the draft. Bancroft stayed for dinner and worked with the President until the message was finished. Meanwhile, on their own initiative, two pro-administration members of the House military affairs committee called a meeting at which the committee drew up a bill appropriating $10 million to fight the war. (When these members came to inform Polk of their action, they hinted broadly that they would accept high-ranking commissions.) All evening a procession of cabinet members and congressmen filed in and out of Polk's office, consulting with him about the attack and his intentions. On Monday morning Polk revised the message and showed it to Cass and also to Benton, who read it with reservations. At noon Polk sent it to the Capitol.[85]

Polk's message laid great stress on the "liberal and honorable" terms, the "fair and equitable" principles which his government

84. Polk, *Diary*, I, 384–85.   85. Polk, *Diary*, I, 386–90.

had advanced in its relations with Mexico and on American grievances against Mexico. These included the long-unpaid claims
mentioned in his annual message, the Mexican government's unreasonable refusal to receive Slidell, and the military threat along
the Texas frontier. All grievances were bound up together: "The
redress of the wrongs of our citizens naturally and inseparably
blended itself with the question of boundary." Polk believed that
the Herrera government would have negotiated with Slidell, had
not an army clique first threatened and then overthrew that government. Since the revolution did not represent the people of
Mexico, it had changed the basis of government. Polk therefore
had felt justified in giving the new administration opportunity to
open negotiations, but Paredes too rejected Slidell "in terms that
may be considered as giving just grounds of offense to . . . the
United States." By so doing the Mexicans "violated their plighted
faith," for they had bound themselves to receive an American
envoy.

The principal purpose of the message was to brand the Mexicans as aggressors. Near the beginning Polk declared flatly: "After
a long-continued series of menaces [they] have at last invaded our
territory and shed the blood of our fellow-citizens on our own
soil." Later he elaborately justified Taylor's presence on the Rio
Grande. From its independence Texas had exercised jurisdiction
to that river, and the United States Congress, accepting that boundary, had set up the Nueces–Rio Grande strip as a revenue district.
The frontier was exposed; the Mexicans threatened invasion; the
United States had an obligation to protect Texas. Hence, he had
sent Taylor to the Rio Grande as a purely defensive move, with
instructions not to disturb the peaceful relations between the
United States and Mexico unless the Mexicans committed acts of
hostility. The President then briefly described the events of April
24 and 25. After further reference to the unpaid claims and to the
disruption of commerce, Polk drew together the strands of his
indictment in words the country was not soon to forget:

> The cup of forbearance had been exhausted even before the re-
> cent information from the frontier of the Del Norte. But now, after
> reiterated menaces, Mexico has passed the boundary of the United
> States, has invaded our territory and shed American blood upon
> the American soil. She has proclaimed that hostilities have com-
> menced, and that the two nations are now at war.
> As war exists, and, notwithstanding all our efforts to avoid it,
> exists by the act of Mexico herself, we are called upon by every con-

sideration of duty and patriotism to vindicate with decision the honor, the rights, and the interests of our country.

At the end of his message the President summoned Congress formally to "recognize the existence of the war" and to furnish appropriations and authority to raise a large volunteer force.[86]

A cynic might have felt that Polk's war message sounded as if it had indeed been written on Sunday, for it combined the self-righteous wrath of the Old Testament with the long-suffering patience of the New. It stated the American case to the observing world in the strongest possible manner. More than that, it epitomized Polk's whole policy toward Mexico since his inauguration, by assuming what was not yet proved, by thrusting forward to throw his adversary off balance, and by maintaining a show of reluctance and sweet reason to placate moderates and pacifists at home. Naturally, Polk did not mention California. For all the uninformed reader might have guessed, the Mexicans could have completely satisfied him at any time by paying several million dollars of claims or by yielding a few square miles of barren borderland.

When he sent the message to Congress Polk had some idea of the furor it would arouse, for after Benton read it, he remarked that he had never approved of sending Taylor to the Rio Grande and that, while he would vote men and money for defense, he would not support an "aggressive war on Mexico." [87] The general strategy of administration Democrats was to call for troops to defend national territory and honor, to emphasize patriotism and Mexican treachery, and to avoid letting the opposition examine too closely either the dispatches accompanying the war message or the question of how hostilities had begun. Even before the news of the attack on Taylor had arrived, they squelched a House resolution by Garrett Davis of Kentucky inquiring whether rumors of Mexican attack were true and whether this attack had occurred on Mexican or American soil.[88]

As soon as Polk's message had been read, the House voted to table the great sheaf of supporting documents but, after some argument, ordered them printed. Then a member of the committee on military affairs introduced the bill prepared over the weekend authorizing the President to resist foreign invasion by

86. James D. Richardson, ed., *A Compilation of the Messages and Papers of the Presidents, 1789–1897*, IV, 437–43. The *Union* went even further than Polk in eulogizing the "Christian virtues" of the United States. Washington *Union*, May 15, 1846, p. 51.
87. Polk, *Diary*, I, 390.
88. US, 29C, 1S, *CG*, p. 781.

calling up fifty thousand militia and volunteers for six months and one year, respectively, and appropriating $10 million. Jacob Brinkerhoff of Ohio struck the proper patriotic note by declaring that he did not care how or why the war had begun but only wanted to crush the enemy at once and obtain an honorable peace so as to avoid another "twopenny war" like the War of 1812. Accordingly, he inserted into the bill a preamble seconding Polk's view that war already existed by act of Mexico. Brinkerhoff's action caused some outcry and the proposal of softening amendments. After allowing a token debate, however, the controlling administration bloc pushed through the bill with the Brinkerhoff preamble by a vote of 174 to 14. The bitter-enders were a little group of abolitionist Whigs led by John Quincy Adams.[89]

In the Senate Calhoun's bloc and the Whigs were prepared to fight more than a rear-guard skirmish. After the reading of the message Calhoun rose to call for extra deliberation on so vital a matter as a declaration of war, and he opposed printing copies of the supporting documents, lest the country interpret this act as approval of the message. He then raised a distinction between purely defensive hostilities and war. Whigs and Democrats alike professed their eagerness to reinforce Taylor's beleaguered troops. As the Whig John M. Clayton of Delaware put it, "I go for the soldiers and the millions at once, to support the honor of the country and the army."

Benton took up Calhoun's distinction between defense measures, which lay within the Executive's power, and a declaration of war, which did not. He proposed to divide Polk's recommendations along this line, sending parts of the message to the committees on military affairs and foreign relations, respectively. Allen agreed, since this division would place the more controversial portion under his control. So did Calhoun, hoping to provide the necessary troops at once while debating the broader question of war with more deliberation. Clayton then attacked the proposed declaration of war. He suggested that by sending Taylor to the Rio Grande Polk had committed "acts which necessarily tended to provoke war . . . without consulting Congress" and added that a congressional censure seemed in order. Allen, Houston, and others sprang to Polk's defense, and Crittenden pulled together the Whig case with a thoughtful statement of his doubts. Mexicans had shed American blood, to be sure, but on whose soil and under what

89. US, 29C, 1S, *CG*, pp. 791–95. Probably the decisive vote was that by which Brinkerhoff's preamble was fastened to the original bill, 123 to 67.

circumstances? Apparently the Mexicans believed that the United States government had insulted them. Did not such uncertainty call for negotiation rather than a declaration of war?[90]

Opposition such as this from the Whigs and Calhoun was only to be expected. At all costs, however, Polk had to retain the loyalty of the rest of the Democratic senators. Fortunately, Cass lent his support—an important influence among the Oregon extremists— but the President also needed that of Benton, who had already declared that he did not believe in the claim of the Rio Grande as boundary. On Monday evening the Missourian called at the White House in his capacity as chairman of the committee on military affairs to ascertain how many troops and how much money the President thought he needed to defend the country. Polk parried the question with the reply that he could not answer it until he knew how much authority Congress would grant him—whether, in fact, the Senate would approve the House bill recognizing a state of war. Benton declared that the House had acted too fast, and although Buchanan and Marcy spent the better part of an hour trying to convince him that Mexico had already precipitated a war, Benton left the White House unsatisfied. Polk wrote in his diary: "All that can save the Bill in the Senate is the fear of the people by the few Democratic Senators who wish it defeated."[91]

The President undoubtedly shared his problem with other Democratic senators who visited him during the evening, for the Van Burenite John A. Dix of New York called in Frank Blair, the veteran henchman of Jackson, who told Benton early the next morning that he "was bound to stick to the War party or he was a ruined man." Benton yielded, summoned his committee for deliberation, and later at a Democratic caucus both he and Allen reported that their committees would support the House war bill.[92]

When the Senate convened at noon, the two committees reported the House bill for debate and precipitated the crisis which the opposition had hoped to postpone. Desperately Calhoun and the Whigs twisted and turned, trying to vote troops and money without creating a state of war or approving the Brinkerhoff

90. US, 29C, 1S, CG, pp. 782–87. At the end of the day's session Benton's Military Affairs Committee reported an earlier bill to raise the Army by six or seven thousand men by increasing the size of each company. Ibid., pp. 788–89. For an account of the debate on the war bill, see also Sellers, Polk, Conti-

nentalist, pp. 416–18.

91. Polk, Diary, I, 391–93. Frank B. Woodford, Lewis Cass, the Last Jeffersonian, pp. 239–40.

92. Sellers, Polk, Continentalist, p. 418. The quotation is taken from a letter of Montgomery Blair to S. P. Lee, May 13, 1846.

preamble and, by implication, Polk's whole program. Vice President Dallas and the administration majority blocked them at every point. Calhoun strove for a day's delay in which to consider the mass of accompanying documents; Allen demanded instant action; and the Chair ruled that in the confusion no one had objected to the second reading of the bill. Calhoun, Clayton, and others proposed to refer the question of war to Benton's military affairs committee; the Senate rejected their motion. Clayton moved to amend the preamble; the Chair ruled that other amendments had priority. Calhoun and various Whigs tried to distinguish between defensive action and war or to cast doubt on reports of unprovoked Mexican aggression; the administration bloc replied by wrapping themselves in the flag, denouncing Mexican atrocities, and calling for an end to American forbearance.

Eventually Crittenden conceded that he favored chasing the Mexican troops across the Rio Grande and so punishing them that they would never dare attack again. Someone asked the obvious question, What was the difference between such a campaign and outright war? As the distinctions of the pacifists became ever more fine-spun and unrealistic, the administration's supporters rejected one amendment after another by a narrow but steadfast majority of four or five. Finally, calm deliberation yielded to obscurantism and a fear of seeming disloyal. When Allen and his cohorts forced the war bill to a vote, it passed by a majority of 40 to 2, but Calhoun and two others sat silent while two Whigs grimly called out, "Ay, except the preamble."[93]

Even some administration senators, especially in the Van Buren bloc, rubbed their twisted arms and murmured against domination by the Executive. "I am too sick of the miserable concern here to write or say anything about it," Dix wrote a friend. He shared the suspicions of Blair, Allen, and Benton that Secretary Walker and his cronies had a financial share in the claims that figured so largely in Polk's message, but all four of them, he declared, were "determined . . . to support the President in his measures."[94] Outside of the Senate prominent Van Burenites wrote to

93. US, 29C, 1S, CG, pp. 795–804. The bill was referred to the House for approval of minor changes before it went to the President for his signature. For a discussion of the motives guiding various Senators, especially the Whigs, see Frederick Merk, *Manifest Destiny and Mission in American History, a Reinterpretation*, pp. 92–95.

94. Sellers, *Polk, Continentalist*, pp. 419–20. His sources are letters from John A. Dix to Azariah Flagg, May 15, 1846, and from E. B. Lee to S. P. Lee, May 17.

their patron denouncing Polk's mismanagement of negotiations with Britain and Mexico and his capricious handling of military appropriations.[95]

Insofar as public opinion can be measured, it is probable that the gamut of emotions in Congress, both open and private, fairly represented the diverse views of the American people. Like the members of Congress, the people as a whole were stunned by the sudden demand for war, but the administration bloc spoke for a large number of patriotic expansionists who demanded prompt, unquestioning support of the President and the endangered troops. On May 13, the day Polk signed the war bill, a mass meeting of twenty thousand in Philadelphia—the "largest town meeting ever assembled in our city," according to one observer—adopted supporting resolutions. Elsewhere, sentiment was a little slower to crystallize, but soon demonstrations, posters, and speeches spread through the Ohio Valley and the South, exhorting young men to enlist: "Ho, for the halls of the Montezumas!"[96]

Aside from unthinking impulses to patriotism and glory, enthusiasts for war seized at a variety of rationalizations, some improvised for the occasion, others reshaped from deeply felt prejudices. Idealism was sometimes uppermost: for example, Parke Godwin declared that "the question of extending *constitutional republican institutions* over this whole continent is one of the broadest, noblest and most important that was ever presented to any nation." Crude land hunger, however, motivated much of the war spirit: "While we are at it—all should be settled & when I say all, it means *Considerable*, California not excepted." Another incentive was contempt for Mexico, for the "execrable miscreant" Paredes and the "recreant, craven" Herrera: "Public opinion, rapidly, begins to demand that our vengeance upon Mexico should be most signal."[97]

Many warhawks merged the Mexican and British enemies, declaring that Britain was standing behind Mexico in her defiance or that a quick, crushing victory over Mexico would impress all of Europe and lead to a favorable settlement in Oregon.[98] Suspicious of Polk, the New York *Herald* received the war news with hysteri-

95. Churchill C. Cambreleng to Martin Van Buren, May 16, 1846; Henry D. Gilpin to Van Buren, May 24, Van Buren Papers, series 2, roll 30, LC.
96. Smith, *War with Mexico*, I, 194–95. Robert M. Lee to Robert J. Walker, May 13, 1846, Walker Papers, no. 252.
97. Parke Godwin to editors of *Harbinger*, as quoted in Sellers, *Polk, Continentalist*, p. 420. John P. Jones to Allen, Cincinnati, June 5, 1846; Edward Archbold to Allen, Woodsfield, June 8, Allen Papers, XIV, LC.
98. *NNR*, 70 (May 9, 1846), 160. S. Penn, Jr., to Marcy, St. Louis, May 19, Marcy Papers, XI, ff. 34610–11, LC.

cal editorials about the administration's vacillation and "imbecile counsels on the Rio Grande," but after Congress had acted, the *Herald* reflected that the war might "lay the foundation of a new age, a new destiny, affecting both this continent and the old continent of Europe."[99] A Southerner advised Robert J. Walker to disregard Britain's protests: "England will not relish our obtaining such good footing on the Pacific, and rest assured she will guard that English pond as the apple of her eye. She lectures us about Texas and will about Calafornia [sic] like a father who drinks and chews tobacco does his son—'These are bad practices my son but I have got in the habit and cannot help it. But *you must* not do as I do.'"[100]

Many Americans consented to the war with misgivings about its justice, necessity, or expediency. A widely reprinted article declared that Polk had grossly blundered in failing to perceive that the true secret of American greatness was peaceful growth, not fighting; Americans "could only become the strongest of people in time of peace, by exposing themselves to be the weakest in time of war."[101] Commercially oriented journals reflected uncertainty when they reported that business in New Orleans and on the Gulf coast had contracted sharply during the crisis. *Niles' Register* questioned whether Polk's strong-arm methods toward Congress did not distort the Constitution and asked if the armed forces were ready for a possible double war with Britain and Mexico.[102]

Whigs were especially uneasy, aware that opposition to the War of 1812 had dealt a death blow to the Federalist party and dismayed to see their arguments for a strong national government and President snatched up by a Democrat. Webster wrote hopefully to his son that Polk probably expected a short war and quick negotiations. Thomas Wren Ward told his Baring associate, Joshua Bates, that if Britain and France would intervene to prevent a war, all would come right, but he feared that they would let the Americans have a taste of fighting. He was surprised that Polk had apparently given up his policy of purchasing desired territory.[103]

99. New York *Herald*, May 9, 1846, p. 2; May 10, p. 2; May 11, p. 2; May 12, p. 2; May 13, p. 2. Quoted phrases are in the May 13 issue.

100. Felix Huston to Walker, Natchez, May 21, 1846, Walker Papers, no. 262.

101. Apparently this article first appeared in the New York *Courier des États Unis*, then was reprinted in the New York *Courier and Enquirer. NNR*,

70 (May 30, 1846), 195.

102. *NNR*, 70 (May 16, 1846), pp. 162–63. For commercial press opinion, see (May 23), p. 192.

103. Daniel Webster to Fletcher Webster, June 1, 1846, Daniel Webster, *The Letters of Daniel Webster*, ed. C. H. Van Tyne, pp. 329–30. Thomas Wren Ward to Joshua Bates, Boston, May 15, Ward Papers, MHS.

Even at this stage, violent opposition to the war was evident here and there. Both Whigs and Democrats, especially in the Northeast, warned that Polk had exploited national patriotism for a war of conquest to obtain more slave territory. Perhaps naturally, the most vocal resentment emerged first among members of Congress who had witnessed the administration's tactics at first hand. Polk had violated "every principle of international law and of moral justice," declared Joshua R. Giddings of Ohio. If the Mexicans should stoutly resist Taylor, added Luther Severance of Maine, "they are to be honored and applauded for doing so."[104] Calhoun was especially vehement, for he feared that the war might defeat American hopes in Oregon and perhaps bring intervention by Britain and France. To a relative he wrote: "Never was so momentous a measure adopted, with so much precipitancy; so little thought; or forced through by such objectionable means."[105]

Thus Polk obtained his war bill under pressure of deceptive public enthusiasm and coercive tactics that exploited partisan loyalty and Whig patriotism. Its passage did not put an end to discussion in Congress, for on the day the Senate approved it, a debate in the House on the annual appropriation for West Point slid into an argument over the Rio Grande boundary.[106] During the following weeks opposition to the war might burst into any sort of irrelevant congressional discussion. Polk had his war; now it was up to him to win his goals before mercurial public opinion turned against him.

104. Both men are quoted in Sellers, *Polk, Continentalist*, p. 421. Philip Hone, *Diary of Philip Hone*, ed. Allan Nevins, II, 763. Frederick Merk, "Dissent in the Mexican War," in Samuel Eliot Morison *et al.*, *Dissent in Three American Wars*, pp. 40–45.

105. John C. Calhoun to Thomas G. Clemson, May 12, 1846; Calhoun to Andrew Pickens Calhoun, May 14, John C. Calhoun, *Correspondence of John C. Calhoun*, ed. J. Franklin Jameson, pp. 689–91. While many approved Calhoun's stand against the war, his principal biographer feels that it cost him considerable support. Charles M. Wiltse, *John C. Calhoun, Sectionalist, 1840–1850*, p. 284.

106. US, 29C, 1S, *CG*, pp. 806–9, 812–17. In roll calls on a group of war measures during this session, 92.6% of Senate Democrats took prowar positions, while 7.4% (Calhoun and McDuffie) were antiwar. Of the Whigs 84.2% were antiwar and 15.8% moderate. No Whig was classified as prowar. In the House the positions on the same measures were as follows: Of the Democrats 45.2% were prowar, 52.6% moderate, and 2.2% antiwar; of the Whigs 23.1% were prowar, 16.9% moderate, and 60% antiwar. Southern congressmen were more militant than those of other sections. Joel H. Silbey, *The Shrine of Party: Congressional Voting Behavior, 1841–1852*, pp. 76–78.

IV

The Winning of the West
1846-1848

13

Oregon Compromised, California Occupied

The Mexican attack on Taylor's forces and the United States declaration of war began more than three months of uninterrupted success for the Polk administration. In every theater of action, from London to the Pacific coast, events swept the American cause forward toward its ambitious goals. Even while Polk was ramming his declaration of war through Congress, Taylor thrust back the advancing Mexicans and occupied the border town of Matamoros, south of the Rio Grande. At the same time, in mid-May, the Senate resolution of notice concerning Oregon stimulated the British government to reopen negotiations, which led within a month to a definitive treaty and solved the problem. By the time the treaty was signed, Parliament had decided to repeal the corn laws; news of this action gave the necessary push to congressional debate on the tariff, which produced a reform bill at the end of July and further strengthened the Anglo–American *rapprochement*. During the final negotiations over Oregon and the tariff debate, unbeknownst to the two governments, American armed forces along the California coast were cooperating with irregular groups of natives and emigrants to seize that province for the United States.

This succession of triumphs naturally reinforced Polk's already firm confidence in his own judgment. Perhaps, however, so much good fortune would turn out to be a curse in disguise, for he and the country had undertaken a more difficult and dangerous operation than anyone foresaw.

* * * *

The news of war alarmed and distressed the American who was perhaps best able to appreciate its significance—Joel Poinsett of South Carolina, the onetime minister to Mexico and also secretary of war, acquainted alike with the enemy and with the American fighting forces. "There exists at Washington an extraordinary degree of ignorance and presumption in relation to Mexico," he wrote to former President Van Buren. Poinsett had warned the Polk administration that the Mexicans would fight if Taylor moved to the Rio Grande. Oh no, he was told, they would not cross the Rio Grande unless war broke out between Britain and the United States. Poinsett foresaw possible disaster in attacking an almost inaccessible country defended by a people subject to anti-Protestant fanaticism. In any case, the blockade and the threat to European mining interests in Mexico would raise new difficulties with Britain and France, while the invasion would strengthen the monarchists in Mexico.[1]

Poinsett was certainly right about the administration's ignorance and optimism. After Slidell's return home most of Polk's formal information about affairs in Mexico City came from John Black, the experienced but not very forceful American consul, whom the Mexicans allowed to remain at his post until April 1847. His continued presence there undoubtedly encouraged the President to expect peace overtures from the Mexicans, as did Black's dispatches, which painted a picture of an unpopular military regime urged on toward monarchism by clerical and European influences and trying to divert criticism by engaging in a sham war against the United States. At the end of May Black wrote hopefully, "I think this Government would eagerly embrace, the first chance whereby they might have an amicable arrangement of all differences."[2]

Accordingly, Polk prepared for a short conflict which would convince the Mexicans that their soundest course was to sue for peace. His first major act was to offer command of all military operations to General Winfield Scott, the ranking officer in the regular Army and a hero of the War of 1812 whose reputation and long experience entitled him to the post. Polk felt little confidence

1. Joel Poinsett to Martin Van Buren, May 26, 1846, Van Buren Papers, series 2, roll 30, LC. Poinsett to Thomas Hart Benton, May 18, Joel Poinsett Papers, XVI, HSP. As secretary of war under Van Buren, Poinsett had done much to reorganize the Army.

2. John Black to James Buchanan, May 26, 1846, No. 374, Manning, *IAA*, VIII, 855. This dispatch was received in Washington on June 13, in the midst of Polk's preparations and discussions of war aims. Black is briefly described in M. S. Beach, "A Secret Mission to Mexico. Origin of the Treaty of Guadalupe Hidalgo," *Scribner's Monthly*, 18 (May 1879), 139. While he remained in Mexico City, Black gathered a little information of military value, apparently without any efforts at concealment, and sent it to the American forces. For his views of Mexican opinion on monarchy and the war, see Black to John Slidell, March 10, 14; Black to Buchanan, March 19, April 21, May 14, 21, 23, 26, June 13, Nos. 363, 366, 370, 372, 373, 374, 377, Manning, *IAA*, VIII, 829, 830, 832–33, 844–45, 851–55, 864. Same, April 25, 26, May 16, June 1, Nos. 367, 368, 371, 375, US, DS, CD, Mexico City, IX. See especially a letter of February 24 by an unidentified liberal leader in Guadalajara, enclosed with Black's dispatch No. 363 of March 19. These dispatches were received in Washington between the beginning of April and late July.

in Taylor, but he also thoroughly disliked Scott, who was a Whig of known presidential ambitions and a pompous egotist with a love of ceremony, a thin skin, and a propensity for ill-timed jibes and criticism. Indeed, on several occasions during the war Polk came near to cashiering his difficult general. It was fortunate for the country that he could not find any satisfactory substitute, for Scott proved to be the most capable American military commander between the Revolution and the Civil War.[3]

The next tasks of the President and the cabinet were to draw up a proclamation of war and a circular letter to American legations abroad—official justifications of hostilities to the country and the world. The proclamation caused little trouble, for Polk simply followed James Madison's model of 1812, varying the wording to indicate Mexico's responsibility for the war.[4] On May 13, Buchanan's draft of a circular letter, however, touched off one of the liveliest arguments yet experienced in the cabinet, for in it he disavowed explicitly any territorial ambitions beyond the Rio Grande boundary and declared that the United States had not gone to war to acquire either California or New Mexico. As Buchanan explained to his colleagues, he was afraid that Britain and France would side with Mexico if they knew that the United States intended to annex these territories. Naturally cautious, he kept in mind that the Oregon question was still unsettled and perhaps also that Pennsylvania and the Northeast were shot through with abolitionist, antiwar sentiment.

Astounded at the Secretary's embarrassing proposal, Polk declared that territory would probably be the only means with which Mexico could pay American claims and that he would fight all the Powers of Christendom to the last man before he would pledge himself not to acquire Mexican territory if he could do so honorably. "Neither as a citizen nor as President," he added, "would I permit or tolerate any intermeddling of any European Power on this Continent." Walker supported him excitedly; the other cabinet members joined in; and Polk wrote out a substitute draft. In its final form, the circular letter proclaimed: "We go to war with Mexico solely for the purpose of conquering an honorable and

3. Justin H. Smith, *The War with Mexico*, I, 196–98. The standard biography is Charles Winslow Elliott, *Winfield Scott, the Soldier and the Man*. Scott had a great many vigorous critics in his day, and even now admiration of him is not unanimous. See, for example, Edward S. Wallace, *General William Jenkins Worth, Monterey's Forgotten Hero*, pp. 192–93.

4. Manning, *IAA*, I, 33n1. Compare with the text of Madison's proclamation in James D. Richardson, ed., *A Compilation of the Messages and Papers of the Presidents, 1789–1897*, I, 512–13.

permanent peace. Whilst we intend to prosecute the war with vigor, both by land and by sea, we shall bear the olive branch in one hand and the sword in the other; and whenever she will accept the former, we shall sheath the latter." In the copy of the letter sent to McLane, Polk and Buchanan inserted the assurance that although the American Navy would blockade Mexican ports, it would allow British mail steamers to pass, as the French had done during the intervention of 1838–1839.[5]

On the same day Polk and Bancroft drew up orders for the commanders of the Gulf and the Pacific squadrons, which further clarified the administration's intentions. They ordered Commodore David E. Conner to blockade as much of the Gulf coast as his forces permitted, seize Tampico if he had the means to do so, keep in constant communication with Taylor's army, and encourage secessionism in the coastal states. Since Commodore John D. Sloat in the Pacific already carried contingent orders to seize San Francisco and blockade the coast in the event of war (sent on June 24, 1845), Bancroft merely told him to carry out these orders. A few days later, the secretary of the navy wrote again to emphasize the importance of holding San Francisco and instructed Sloat to seize Monterey, Mazatlán, and possibly Guaymas too, if he could.[6]

As the first orders went out to Conner and Sloat, Marcy also instructed Colonel Stephen W. Kearny, commanding a regiment of regulars at Fort Leavenworth on the Missouri frontier, to call on the state governor for additional troops and set out toward Santa Fe to protect traders. On the following evening, May 14, Polk summoned Marcy and Scott, and for over four hours the three men discussed the plan of campaign in northeastern Mexico and the forces they should send to Taylor. It was agreed that Scott should take over Taylor's command, "march a competent force into the Northern Provinces and seize and hold them until peace was made," while smaller detachments of two and four thousand men occupied Santa Fe and Chihuahua. The President, however, continued to distrust Scott as "rather scientific and visionary in his views." From his diary it is clear that neither Polk nor Marcy

5. James K. Polk, *The Diary of James K. Polk during His Presidency, 1845 to 1849*, ed. Milo M. Quaife, I, 396–99, 403. Manning, *IAA*, I, 33–34; VII, 27–28. James Buchanan, *The Works of James Buchanan*, ed. John Bassett Moore, VI, 485–86.

6. George Bancroft to David E. Conner, May 13, 1846; Bancroft to John D. Sloat, May 13, 15, US, 30C, 1S, HED 60, pp. 233–36. The contingent orders of June 24, 1845, are on p. 231. For the background to these orders, see Chapter 9.

appreciated the amount of preparation required for these campaigns.[7]

At the same meeting the high command decided to issue a call for twenty thousand volunteers out of the fifty thousand authorized by Congress, apportioning quotas among the states of the Ohio Valley and the South, which were closest to the theater of action and also the most enthusiastic supporters of the war. Later, Polk decided to appoint officers to these units from the civilian volunteers rather than promote and transfer regular Army officers.[8] Historians have widely condemned this decision to rely chiefly on units of short-term volunteers led by amateurs, arguing that in the burst of initial patriotism men would willingly have signed up for the duration of the war if given no choice and that fuller use of regular Army officers would have shortened training periods and reduced blunders and casualties. But Polk disliked professional armies, and he loudly proclaimed the merits of the "citizen soldiers." Also, his experience with political patronage had suggested that the prospect of local military appointments might help to keep Congress in line.[9]

The first two weeks of planning by the administration were enveloped in a fog of anxiety about the safety of Taylor's troops, exposed to attack by superior Mexican forces across the Rio Grande. New Orleans seethed with rumors of disaster, which correspondents duly reported to Polk and members of the cabinet. On May 10 Marcy wrote to a close friend that Taylor might be cut off from his supply base at Point Isabel, and that if he were, the people would surely blame the War Department, although the Department had left all tactical decisions to the general. Newspapers reported that the Mexicans had cut to pieces a small liaison detachment and that the Americans had fled in all directions. Two thousand Creek Indians were said to be in the field, supporting the Mexicans.[10]

7. Polk, *Diary*, I, 396, 443–44. Smith, *War with Mexico*, I, 286.

8. Polk, *Diary*, I, 400–401, 403–4, 407–8, 412.

9. Smith, *War with Mexico*, I, 190–95. Charles A. McCoy, *Polk and the Presidency*, pp. 119–20. Ivor Debenham Spencer, *The Victor and the Spoils, a Life of William L. Marcy*, pp. 151–53. Polk also consulted Roman Catholic bishops and arranged to send Spanish-speaking priests with the troops to assure the Mexican people that the United States would not interfere with their religion. Polk, *Diary*, I, 408–11.

10. A good picture of conditions and rumors in New Orleans is given in the correspondence of D. Hayden to Robert J. Walker, New Orleans, April 29, May 3, 4, 5, 10, 1846, Walker Papers, Nos. 239, 240, 242, 244, LC. James E. Saunders to James K. Polk, Mobile, May 5, Polk Papers, CIII, LC. Marcy to P. M. Wetmore, May 10, Marcy Papers, XI,

The truth was wholly different from the rumors, for during the climactic week when news of the original Mexican attack reached Washington, Taylor was winning the first two battles of the war and thereby putting his forces out of immediate danger. Truly, danger existed, for he had built his fort on a point of land formed by a curve in the Rio Grande, with a marsh at his rear. A road paralleled the river, and the Mexicans might have used it to surround him. On April 30, indeed, the main Mexican force began to cross the river below Matamoros, but very slowly, for they had few boats. Seeing a threat to his communications with Point Isabel, Taylor promptly led most of his men out of camp toward the supply base, leaving behind a small garrison and a battery to hold the fort. During the ensuing action a Mexican detachment surrounded and bombarded the fort, but Taylor seems to have been little concerned about it, and the garrison held out.[11]

Unable to intercept Taylor's withdrawal, Arista and over four thousand Mexican troops took up a position on the road to the coast and awaited his return. On May 3, after a forced march, the Americans reached Point Isabel, where a few days later recruits from New Orleans and about five hundred sailors and marines from Conner's Gulf Squadron joined them. Leaving most of these reinforcements to defend the supply base, Taylor set out again for the Rio Grande fort on May 7 with about twenty-two hundred men and over two hundred loaded wagons.

That afternoon he met the Mexican army, drawn up in a line across the road at Palo Alto ("Tall Timber")—an oddly named battle site, since it was actually a prairie of shoulder-high grass, with a few boggy pools and patches of chaparral protecting the Mexicans. The Americans advanced silently, evidently intending to force the center of the Mexican line, and teams of oxen hauled the artillery into position. Both sides began to fire their biggest guns, and the American superiority in ordnance—one of the deciding factors in the war—became immediately apparent, for the Mexican fire was too light and often fell short, but the Americans' shots opened huge gaps in the Mexican troops. Sometimes a single shot seemed to mow down a swath of riflemen. Eventually the grass caught fire, and a thick cloud of smoke covered both armies.

ff. 34606–7, LC. New York *Tribune*, May 18, as reprinted in London *Times*, June 9, p. 6. New York *Herald*, May 18, p. 2.

11. On May 3, after the Matamoros batteries had opened fire on the fort, the Americans cannonaded the city for five hours, doing much damage. F. L. Giffard (British vice consul) to Charles Bankhead, Matamoros, May 13, 1846, GB, FO 50/197, ff. 100–105.

Taylor did not exploit his advantage by ordering an infantry attack, and the Mexicans withdrew in good order under cover of night. The Americans did not realize their victory, and next morning they were surprised to find the enemy gone.

After retreating a few miles toward Matamoros, Arista took up a more formidable defense position behind a swampy *resaca* (former channel of the river), surrounded by dense chaparral through which the attackers would have to force their way. In the Battle of Resaca de la Palma Taylor launched a frontal attack along the main road, sending first dragoons and then, more properly, infantry to capture the Mexican guns while flanking parties made their way painfully through the chaparral. The Mexicans, shaken by the cannonading of the day before and by unfounded rumors that Arista was planning to sell out to the enemy, fought bravely, but once they had begun to give way, their morale collapsed, and their line crumbled. Arista himself barely escaped, leaving behind his baggage, his tent, his desk, and his papers, which included a government order that Taylor was to be sent to Mexico City as a prisoner. Once again the Americans could scarcely believe the extent of their triumph and did not harry the Mexicans as they fled pell-mell across the Rio Grande. Many of the officers arrived back in Matamoros well ahead of their troops.[12]

The battles led directly to the American occupation of Matamoros on May 18 and 19, for Arista realized that his officers' humiliation had undermined their loyalty, and he evacuated the city without further fighting. The victories by American regulars against odds of two to one enormously encouraged the whole Army, and Taylor's soldiers made a hero of him, describing how he had sat on his horse "Old Whitey," one leg over the pommel of the saddle, and had calmly issued orders in the midst of danger and confusion. ("Take those guns, and by God keep them!") Among his officers, however, doubts were increasing concerning his knowledge of strategy, for they saw how little he planned his moves or exploited his successes. He showed, said one, "perfect inability to make any use of the information" he received and

12. Smith, *War with Mexico*, I, Chap. 8. Robert Selph Henry, *The Story of the Mexican War*, Chap. 3. For Taylor's laconic account of the two battles, see Zachary Taylor to Adjutant General, May 9, 1846, Nos. 35, 36, US, 30C, 1S, HED 60, pp. 295–96. The second battle, Resaca de la Palma, is so named after a slough near the original American position, but in Mexico the engagement is usually called Resaca de Guerrero, after the Mexican position, where the fighting actually took place. For a description of the rout as it appeared from Matamoros, see Giffard to Bankhead, May 13, GB, FO 50/197, ff. 100–105. Giffard praised Taylor's magnanimous behavior to the defeated enemy.

seemed "*utterly, absurdly* incompetent to wield a large army."[13]

The American people, untrained in the niceties of military tactics, saw only the smashing victories and, after the weeks of anxiety, were well satisfied with Taylor's generalship. When the news arrived in Washington on May 23, Polk merely noted the bare facts in his diary, devoting much more space to his quarrels with Scott. Marcy heaved a sigh of relief; no one would accuse the War Department of issuing wrong instructions now. The press gloated that after these victories the Mexicans would confine themselves to guerrilla tactics. The residents of New Orleans could scarcely contain themselves for joy, and so many volunteers jammed the recruiting offices that the Army representatives began to reject a few. A friend of Walker assured him that he could have thirty thousand men by mid-June from the South alone. "For Heavens sake let the boys go ahead," he urged. "All they want is munitions of war, transportation, & subsistence."[14]

*   *   *   *

As the war was gathering momentum, the Oregon question entered its final phase. During the same week in May when Polk wrote his war message and Taylor won his first two battles, news arrived in London that the United States Senate had passed the resolution of notice. The British were fully prepared; for months their press had been weaving arabesques on the Senate debate and approving every expression of moderate opinion. There were some reservations: While recognizing the increasing likelihood of a settlement at 49°, the *Times* stood out for the British point of honor, demanding some compensation for yielding the Columbia River boundary.

British newspapers welcomed the end of the long debate, which they had found as tedious as the continuing proceedings in Parliament over the corn laws. Few had anything to say against the moderate wording of the notice—"extremely dignified and becoming," "mild and inoffensive, and indeed friendly towards Eng-

13. On the occupation of Matamoros, see Smith, *War with Mexico*, I, 177–79; and Henry, *Story of the Mexican War*, pp. 71–73. Taylor to Adjutant General, May 18, 1846, No. 40, US, 30C, 1S, HED 60, pp. 297–98. Taylor's quoted comment appears in Henry, *Story of the Mexican War*, p. 62. The officers' phrases quoted are in Smith, *War with Mexico*, I, 179.

14. Polk, *Diary*, I, 422, 425, 428–29. William L. Marcy to P. W. Wetmore, May 28, 1846, Marcy Papers, XI, ff. 34620–21, LC. New York *Evening Post*, May 25, p. 3. Aimé Rogers to Ministère des Affaires Étrangères, New Orleans, May 17, 1846, No. 43, France, MAE, CP, États Unis, CII, ff. 109–10. Hayden to Walker, May 17, Walker Papers, No. 258, LC.

land." Polk would probably take his time about abrogating the treaty. "We expect that the negotiations will outrun the notice." The *Morning Chronicle*, however, felt obliged to warn Peel and Aberdeen not to repeat the "capitulation" of 1842 and thus "supply every American demagogue with a new fact to prove that [Britain] . . . is *squeezable*—that there needs nothing but a vigorous application of the screw to force her down to any point of concession that may be desired."[15]

At the same time, the British commented gloomily or threateningly on the helpless condition of Mexico and on Taylor's ominous move to the Rio Grande: "Mexico, and not the Oregon [*sic*], is the end and aim of the United States." "The [disputed] ground is Mexican as much as Middlesex is English," wrote a correspondent to the *Times*. "What would Europe say if the French took a start and occupied the left bank of the Rhine?" The editors railed at the Americans' "stupid disbelief of danger, which they mistake for courage. . . . [Polk] has allowed [the United States] . . . to forfeit a character for discretion without gaining a character for strength." The *Times* predicted that Polk would declare war on Mexico, seize California, and then stall the Oregon question; it warned the British government to obtain a fair settlement as quickly as possible. The *Morning Chronicle* agreed that the Americans were after "the two C's," California and Canada. Their alarms about Britain's designs on San Francisco, it added, resembled the pickpocket's cries of "Stop thief!"[16]

The United States declaration of war and the news of business interruptions in New Orleans withered the British money market like a hard frost. United States 6 per cent bonds fell almost four points at once, and insurance companies inserted a war clause into all transatlantic contracts. For days the press inveighed against American "wanton aggression" and "republican cupidity," comparing Polk's sense of honor to Falstaff's and asserting smugly that even in Afghanistan Britain had never maintained that she was occupying British soil. The editors eagerly reprinted every rumor of disaster to Taylor's forces and predicted bankruptcy and social revolution as a result. Underneath the angry scorn, however, a strain of anxiety about the Oregon question was clearly discern-

---

15. London *Times*, April 18, 1846, p. 5; May 8, p. 4. London *Sun*, May 4, as quoted in *NNR*, 70 (May 30), 208. London *Morning Chronicle*, May 11, p. 4; May 15, as quoted in *NNR*, 70 (June 6), 210.

16. Letter of A. B. to London *Times*, May 10, 1846. *Times*, May 13, p. 7; May 14, pp. 4–5; May 15, p. 4. London *Morning Chronicle*, May 25, p. 4. See also London *Journal of Commerce*, May 16, p. 4.

ible, and some believed that the belated American military preparations were actually intended for a war with Britain.[17]

The battles of Palo Alto and Resaca de la Palma disappointed British hopes, but the national *sang froid* and love of a "good show"—and probably also the desire not to back a loser—asserted themselves at once. The *Times* declared that the "incontestable superiority" of the Americans deserved success and praised Taylor's dispatches for "succinct energy" and modesty—qualities, the newspaper noted, that were usually absent in American rhetoric. "The conduct of the Mexican army," it added, "demonstrates the utter inability of that Government to protect any portion of its domains from invasion: and it degrades the descendants of the Spanish Americans still lower in the rank of nations." Continental journals also disapproved of the war, but their reactions were naturally somewhat more detached than those in Britain.[18]

The British government reacted to the events of April and May with more calculation and restraint than the press, for it bore the responsibility of escaping from the Oregon dilemma without sacrificing British honor. As spring advanced, British leaders continued to hear privately from American moderates.[19] McLane and others reiterated that the Peel administration still wanted peaceful negotiation and that British preparations for war were not solely or perhaps even primarily directed at the United States. McLane added that it would be well, however, if the Senate ended its debate on Oregon soon, for there was danger that extremist Western pronouncements might stir up British nationalists again, and Peel and Aberdeen would do nothing while the debate was in progress.

---

17. London *Journal of Commerce*, May 30, 1846, pp. 4, 5. London *Morning Chronicle*, May 30, p. 4; June 2, p. 4. London *Times*, June 9, p. 6; June 11, p. 4. L. McLane to Buchanan, June 3, No. 54, Manning, *IAA*, VII, 276–78. On June 4 British holders of Mexican bonds met and accepted new terms recommended by their committee—90% of their holdings in new 5% stock. Holders of deferred bonds (see Chapter 2) were to receive 60% in the new stock. There was general resentment but a feeling that under the circumstances existing in Mexico no other arrangement was possible. London *Times*, June 5, p. 6.

18. London *Times*, June 15, 1846, pp. 4, 5. Nevertheless, the British press continued to condemn American aggres-

sion. Ibid., June 18, p. 4. London *Morning Chronicle*, June 18, p. 4. For a summary of Continental opinion, see Frederick Merk, *The Monroe Doctrine and American Expansionism, 1843–1849*, pp. 162–71.

19. For example, letters of Daniel Webster written in late February were shown by their recipients to Aberdeen at about the same time, a month later. Evelyn Denison to Aberdeen, March 24, 1846; Viscount Ashburton to Aberdeen, March 30; Aberdeen to Ashburton, April 2, Aberdeen Papers, BM, AM, vol. 43245, ff. 350–53, 366–67; vol. 43246, f. 1. Robert B. Rhett also wrote to Aberdeen in the same sense. Robert B. Rhett to Aberdeen, March 27; Aberdeen to Rhett, May 4, BM, AM, vol. 43245, ff. 362–63; vol. 43246, f. 79.

Above all, the Peel government might fall at any moment, an event that would bring the unpredictable Palmerston to the Foreign Office.[20] Aware of these circumstances, Polk too was now willing to negotiate for a boundary at 49°, but he attached two conditions: The British must make the first move, and he would not concede the perpetual free navigation of the Columbia River.[21]

The question of free navigation was the last vestige of the tangled claims and counterclaims that had exasperated Anglo–American diplomats for over two generations. By the spring of 1846 it was fairly clear that the river was not continuously navigable from the ocean to the point at which it crossed the forty-ninth parallel. At first McLane was inclined to believe that Britain might be satisfied with temporary navigation rights or might open the St. Lawrence River freely to the Americans in exchange. In his note of May 3, however, he predicted that Aberdeen would probably insist on permanent navigation rights, including the right to portage around the rapids in the main stream.[22] If they were asked to concede everything else south of 49°, Peel and Aberdeen would not give the Whigs and Palmerston an opening by yielding navigation rights, which Gallatin apparently recognized in 1826.

Polk told his cabinet privately that he was willing to allow navigation rights for a few years, but because he had opposed conceding these rights in his annual message and anticipated the wrath of the fifty-four-forty bloc at any compromise settlement, he was determined not to grant navigation rights forever. Fear of the political opposition was the principal reason for the final impasse. Polk must have ground his teeth when he read McLane's statement that, because of the long debate and indecision over Oregon, the British seemed confident that the Senate would yield perpetual navigation, even if the President did not.[23]

20. McLane to Buchanan, March 17, April 3, 17/18, 1846, Nos. 36, 37, 41, Manning, *CR*, III, 1011–15, 1017–21, 1023–27. McLane to Polk, April 30, Polk Papers, CII, LC. McLane to Buchanan, May 4, Buchanan Papers, box 63, HSP. McLane to Bancroft, May 4; Henry Holland to Bancroft, London, April 17; William Sturgis to Bancroft, Boston, April 22, Bancroft Papers, MHS.

21. Polk, *Diary*, I, 372–73, 376–77. See also Marcy to Wetmore, April 20, Marcy Papers, XI, ff. 34598–99, LC.

22. McLane to Buchanan, February 3, May 3, 1846, Nos. 34, 43, Manning, *CR*, III, 995–1005, 1028–33.

23. McLane to Polk, April 30, 1846, Polk Papers, CII, LC. Charles Grier Sellers, *James K. Polk, Continentalist, 1843–1846*, pp. 394–95, 405–6. Some weeks earlier, Pakenham had estimated that the Western extremists did not number more than a fourth or even a fifth of the Senate. Richard Pakenham to Aberdeen, March 29, No. 34, GB, FO 5/447, ff. 126–31. In his private letter to Polk, cited in note 20, McLane also reported that a known friend of Lewis Cass, supposedly a fifty-four-forty man, had indirectly approached Aberdeen to urge renewed negotiations. This was Nathaniel Niles, a minor

When Pakenham reported the Senate resolution of notice, he pronounced it proof of the Senate's desire to settle the dispute amicably, although he added that most senators had made up their minds as to the proper terms.[24] Aberdeen's hopes had been realized, for the resolution changed the situation materially. Its correct, dignified language might be taken to supersede the provocative threats of Polk's earlier speeches, and it gave Aberdeen hope of convincing the rest of the cabinet that Britain could make a new offer without losing face.

McLane called on Aberdeen as soon as the news of the Senate's action was publicly announced on May 7, although Buchanan's official statement of notice did not reach him until a week later. The American minister felt that a majority of the cabinet—perhaps including Peel—opposed taking the initiative even now and preferred only to invite a further offer from the United States. But Aberdeen was confident of winning them over, for he promised to send detailed new instructions to Pakenham by the next transatlantic steamer, due to leave on May 19.[25] The foreign secretary and the American minister continued their negotiations at intervals throughout the intervening period. (At the same time Polk was launching the war with Mexico, and Taylor was pushing forward to occupy Matamoros.) Uncertain of events in America,

---

American consular official who took it upon himself to tell Baron James Rothschild that the United States government was willing to concede navigation rights to the Hudson's Bay Company and other British traders for a long period. Rothschild informed Peel. Peel to Aberdeen, [April 25], enclosing [Nathaniel] Niles to Baron James Rothschild (copy), March 29, Aberdeen Papers, BM, AM, vol. 43065, ff. 170–71. McLane also mentioned that Robert Owen was in London on a mission of peace. The American minister concluded that if the Oregon question were amicably settled, this would forever refute the adage that too many cooks spoil the broth. McLane to Polk, April 30, Polk Papers, CII, LC. Louis McLane to Robert McLane, May 4, McLane Papers, University of Delaware Library.

24. Pakenham to Aberdeen, April 28, 1846, No. 49, GB, FO 5/448, ff. 219–22.

25. L. McLane to Polk, May 8, 1846, Polk Papers, CIII, LC. This letter was received on May 23, the same day as McLane's dispatch of May 3, cited in note 22. McLane had urged Aberdeen to make a conditional overture without waiting for the Senate vote. Aberdeen expected a conciliatory resolution that would allow such an overture, but he preferred to maintain British dignity, thinking it unlikely that Congress would adjourn without taking action. Aberdeen to Pakenham, May 4, Aberdeen Papers, BM, AM, vol. 43123, ff. 286–87. Thorough search of the Aberdeen and Peel Papers has revealed no information on the cabinet's debate over the instructions to Pakenham. Formal delivery of the official notice was briefly delayed by one of its provisions —that McLane deliver it directly to Queen Victoria. Since this was contrary to usual procedure, McLane and Aberdeen finally agreed that the notice should go to the Foreign Office. David Hunter Miller, ed., *Treaties and Other International Acts of the United States of America*, V, 90–95.

both Aberdeen and McLane seemed to realize that the moment for agreement was at hand, perhaps never to return.

Evidently without much difficulty they drew a boundary line, extending the existing one along the forty-ninth parallel to the coast and thence following the Haro and Juan de Fuca straits around the southern tip of Vancouver Island to the Pacific. McLane reluctantly agreed to recognize all British property rights south of the line, the United States receiving only unclaimed land as public domain. The Hudson's Bay Company, debarred by its charter from owning land, would retain its forts and trading rights unless it chose to dispose of them. All property rights would be subject entirely to American law; McLane believed that the agreement did not offer residents the option of remaining British subjects, as did the Jay Treaty of 1794.

Throughout the deliberations McLane tried to close the Columbia River to British navigation, while Aberdeen insisted that it be open and free to all British subjects north of the new border. At the last minute Aberdeen agreed to limit the privilege to the Hudson's Bay Company and its subsidiaries, which would enjoy it on the same basis as American citizens. McLane was deeply unhappy at having to make even this concession, for he believed that Polk would reject it out of hand. In his dispatch he explained that Aberdeen was motivated partly by pride and by concern for British interests, which were implicitly guaranteed by concessions. Also, the foreign secretary was convinced that Polk would not dare to reject the terms on his own volition and that the Senate would accept them. McLane added one note of optimism in private letters to both Polk and Calhoun: If the senators insisted on limiting the Company's navigation rights to a period of years, Aberdeen would probably accept that restriction. McLane warned them, above all, not to delay, for the repeal of the corn laws now seemed certain; once this was accomplished, Peel would resign, probably before the end of June.[26]

McLane's version of the compromise did not agree in all details with the instructions which Aberdeen drew up for Pakenham

26. McLane to Buchanan, May 18, 1846, No. 44, Manning, *CR*, III, 1033–40. L. McLane to Polk, May 18, 28, Polk Papers, CIII, LC. L. McLane to John C. Calhoun, May 18, John C. Calhoun, *Correspondence of John C. Calhoun*, ed. J. Franklin Jameson, pp. 1081–83. L. McLane to R. McLane, May 18, McLane Papers, University of Delaware Library. McLane told Polk that he had emphasized the British reliance on the Senate and had hinted at the acceptability of Senate revisions in his official dispatch so Polk might release it to the Senate and thus facilitate a modification of the British draft.

on the same day, to be sent on the steamer of May 19. Probably anticipating that the document would be published, the foreign secretary reviewed the whole controversy in such language as to make it appear that the deadlock was due to American stubbornness. According to him, the British government was now reopening negotiations after Congress' notice, as a gracious gesture to circumvent "considerations of diplomatick punctilio or etiquette." The statement of the boundary was as McLane had understood it, but Aberdeen specified that the land rights of the Hudson's Bay Company at Fort Vancouver and along the Columbia River must be confirmed. He also insisted that the river must be open to both the Company and all British subjects trading with it.

Writing to Pakenham, the British foreign secretary inserted a note of finality. McLane had explicitly stated that the instructions would not be an ultimatum, and Aberdeen kept within the letter of this distinction, but in a private communication he required Pakenham to refer home for judgment any major changes. (Such referral would amount to a rupture of negotiations, as a change of the British cabinet was probable.) Although it was most unlikely, he added, "some state of things may have arisen in the United States" making it undesirable to present the proposed terms. If Pakenham felt that Aberdeen would want them withheld, he was granted discretion to do so.[27]

External circumstances undoubtedly helped to determine the timing and the details of the British offer. The imminent fall of the British cabinet placed pressure on the Americans, who knew little of Russell's changed views on Oregon and could not count on his ability to keep Palmerston in line. This factor also concerned Peel and Aberdeen, who were reluctant to close their desks while the country was faced with a major diplomatic crisis of their creation. It is also clear that Aberdeen counted heavily on a pacific majority in the American Senate. which might adjourn until after the autumn elections. Then it would yield to another, probably less favorable to the terms of agreement.[28]

27. Aberdeen to Pakenham, May 18, 1846, Nos. 18, 19, GB, FO 115/91, ff. 142–50, 152–60. Same, May 18. Miller, *Treaties and Other International Acts,* V, 79–81.

28. On May 28 Pakenham reported that adjournment of Congress was unlikely before August, since it had to settle the tariff question and make provision for the war, but of course this prediction did not reach London until mid-June. Pakenham to Aberdeen, May 28, 1846, Aberdeen Papers, BM, AM, vol. 43123, pp. 294–95. At some time after the departure of the May 19 packet Aberdeen showed a draft of the British proposal to Lord Clarendon, his closest contact among the Whig leaders, and received his approval. Earl of Clarendon to Aberdeen, June 12, BM, AM, vol. 43246, f. 163.

How much effect did the Mexican War have on Aberdeen's negotiations with McLane? The answer seems to be—less than many historians have thought. By mid-May the British government was well aware of Slidell's failure, Taylor's march to the Rio Grande, and the likelihood of some military incident. As soon as news of the congressional resolution on Oregon reached London, Mexican Minister Murphy called on Aberdeen to sound him on the possibility of British naval aid for the defense of California. Aberdeen countered with the suggestion that Britain and France might offer mediation; he denied that an Anglo–American war over Oregon was likely. Murphy then warned his government that it must depend on its own resources.[29]

When the United States declaration of war became known in London, Aberdeen made no effort to change his instructions to Pakenham. For his part, Pakenham interpreted the foreign secretary's reference to "some state of things" in the United States to mean hostilities with Mexico, but he later told Aberdeen that he had regarded it as neither politic nor worthy of Britain to hold out for a better settlement in Oregon because of American difficulties with Mexico. Aberdeen approved his refusal to allow the Mexican War to influence his actions and declared flatly that, successful or not, it would have made no difference whatever in the British terms.[30]

Pakenham's self-righteousness and Aberdeen's approval of his course may have been partly due to the fact that they knew of Taylor's victories when they made their statements. Indeed, it is likely that the battles of Palo Alto and Resaca de la Palma had more effect on the promptness and calm of the Anglo–American settlement than did the outbreak of the war. When the British learned that hostilities had broken out, many of them expected defeats for the Americans, believing that the war had begun before Polk was ready for it. In mid-May a Mexican financial agent had arrived in London to raise money and buy arms. McLane suspected that he had a considerable credit at Baring Brothers and that public officials were encouraging him, although Aberdeen emphatically denied the last. A serious setback to American arms on

29. Tomás Murphy to Ministerio de Relaciones, June 1, 1846, No. 8, Antonio de la Peña y Reyes, *Lord Aberdeen, Texas y California,* pp. 69–72. Murphy had made much the same proposal to Aberdeen in March with much the same results. Murphy to Ministerio de Relaciones, April 1, No. 6, ibid., pp. 65–68.

30. Pakenham to Aberdeen, June 7, 1846, Aberdeen Papers, BM, AM, vol. 43123, ff. 296–301. Pakenham reasoned that delay would be impolitic because success in the Mexican War would make the United States more demanding in Oregon. June 30, ibid., ff. 308–9.

the Rio Grande might not immediately have changed Aberdeen's stand on the Oregon terms, but if it had enabled Mexican agents to borrow money and purchase arms, American protests and resulting friction might well have delayed indefinitely the settlement of the Oregon question.

McLane was not alarmed at the onset of war with Mexico, for as long as the American Army could avoid defeat, he was confident that the war would improve relations between Britain and the United States. Nevertheless, he warned Polk that he should not reject Aberdeen's terms outright unless he wanted to fight Britain as well as Mexico.[31]

* * * *

The British decision to offer terms via the steamer of May 19 hastened a settlement of the Oregon question but did not make it automatic, for Polk was disposed to examine the terms carefully before he acted. On May 3 he told Benton that he would never concede perpetual navigation of the Columbia River, and he rejected the Senator's suggestion that navigation downstream was not important enough to withhold. Instead, he pressed Benton and others to push through the Senate the bill for organizing territorial government in Oregon that he had recommended in his annual message.[32]

For the next two or three weeks Polk was too much occupied with the Mexican crisis to pay much attention to Oregon, but in the midst of the war measures Congress passed a bill providing for a special rifle regiment to protect the emigrant trail. The Senate also discussed a House bill for territorial government but took no action on it. During the latter debate Benton spoke for three days, reviewing the whole Oregon question and eulogizing commercial opportunities on the Columbia River, "the North Ameri-

31. L. McLane to Buchanan, May 18, 19, June 3, 18, 1846, Nos. 44, 50, 54, 55, Manning, *IAA*, VII, 273–78, 281–84. L. McLane to Polk, May 29; n.d., but probably late May, Polk Papers, CIII, CIV, LC. L. McLane to Buchanan, June 18, Buchanan Papers, box 63, HSP. See especially the undated letter in the Polk Papers. Sellers suggests that if Aberdeen and McLane had not agreed on terms by the steamer of May 19, a settlement might have been impossible and that "by this narrow margin was possibly averted a [disastrous] double war" for the United States. Sellers, *Polk, Continentalist*, pp. 409–10. Sellers may have gotten this idea from a similar opinion of Calhoun in a letter of July 2. Calhoun, *Correspondence*, pp. 698–99. The notion that war was so imminent seems overdrawn. It is unlikely that delay would have endangered a settlement unless Polk had flatly rejected Aberdeen's terms or Taylor had suffered a rout on the Rio Grande.

32. Polk, *Diary*, I, 376–79, 381–82.

can route to India." He favored limiting territorial government to the area south of 49°. After this debate Pakenham reported that he did not fear any hostile congressional measure on Oregon for the rest of the session.[33]

When Polk received McLane's letters and dispatches of April 30 and May 3, setting forth the complications involving the question of river navigation, the President recorded no reaction, apparently waiting for more concrete evidence of British intentions.[34] This arrived on June 3 in McLane's long dispatch of May 18, recounting his negotiations with Aberdeen, and it aroused Polk's instant disapproval. The President felt that if the British actually submitted such terms as McLane had outlined, he could not accept them himself, and he doubted whether he ought to submit them to the Senate. The alternatives seemed to be war or allowing the Senate to bind him to a settlement he opposed. On June 4 he consulted the cabinet, which in general favored submitting the terms to the Senate with an explanatory message, although Buchanan cautiously declined to commit himself without further reflection.[35]

Two days later (June 6) Pakenham came to the State Department with the formal British proposal of terms, presented them to Buchanan, and read him excerpts from Aberdeen's instructions. These seemed to impress Buchanan, and he briefly discussed the navigation of the Columbia with Pakenham. Then he took the proposals to the cabinet meeting, which was being held that day. When Polk and the others examined the British terms, the question at once arose whether the proposed navigation rights would end with the existing charter of the Hudson's Bay Company, due to expire in 1859. Walker and Marcy thought so; Buchanan thought not; the President was doubtful. When he asked the members for their opinions, Walker, Marcy, Bancroft, and Postmaster General Cave Johnson declared in turn that the British proposals should go to the Senate for previous advice.

This left Buchanan. When Polk finally turned to him, he parried the question by saying that his answer would depend on Polk's accompanying message to the Senate. "He said," wrote Polk, "the 54°40′ men were the true friends of the administration

33. Polk, *Diary*, I, 404. Pakenham to Aberdeen, May 28, 1846, No. 64, GB, FO 5/449, ff. 78–81. For Benton's speech, see *NNR*, 70 (June 6, 13, July 18), 220–23, 234–39, 314–19.

34. The dispatch of May 3 arrived on May 23, the same day as the news of Taylor's victories. Polk, *Diary*, I, 418–19. Probably the private letter of April 20 arrived at the same time.

35. Polk, *Diary*, I, 444–45, 447–48.

and he wished no backing out on the subject." The President, though furious, held his temper and cut short the impulsive Walker's outburst. Instead, Polk outlined a covering statement, in which he summarized the position taken in the annual message and undertook to reject the British proposal if a majority of the Senate disapproved or refused to pronounce judgment. When he asked Buchanan to prepare a draft along these lines, the secretary declined, saying merely that he would comment on a draft by the President.

Later, Buchanan again refused to help Polk beyond suggesting that some of McLane's dispatches ought not to be sent to the Senate with the message. He then added, "Well! when you have done your message I will then prepare such an one [sic] as I think ought to be sent in." At this Polk, understandably, lost his temper and scathingly accused Buchanan of refusing to do his job while planning to create a public quarrel with the President. Polk's anger took the secretary aback. He disclaimed any underhanded intentions, and they patched up a truce. Two days later (June 9) in cabinet meeting Buchanan objected to Polk's draft as too round-about and at long last offered one of his own. Polk and the rest of the cabinet, in their turn, found this version unacceptable. Finally, in order to keep peace in his official family, the President revised his own draft, deleting some of the passages Buchanan had criticized. For his part, Buchanan agreed to an open declaration that he approved the message. On the next morning the British terms, accompanied by the much-fretted message, went to the Senate.[36]

How can one explain Buchanan's shift? His sympathetic gestures toward fifty-four-forty and the expansionists apparently contradicted his earlier efforts for compromise as well as his recent proposal that the United States disavow a desire to seize California from Mexico. It seems clear that Buchanan's boldness was largely play-acting, for Pakenham reported home that the secretary was extremely eager to conclude a treaty before the Peel cabinet fell from power.[37] Polk thought that Buchanan was making a bid for the support of Western extremists in a future campaign for the Presidency. Without explicitly rejecting this motive, Buchanan's most recent biographer suggests that he suspected that Polk might unfairly place on him responsibility for what might be a most unpopular settlement, but that he withheld his opposition until the

36. Polk, *Diary*, I, 451–62.
37. Pakenham to Aberdeen, June 7,

13, 1846, Miller, *Treaties and Other International Acts*, V, 81.

last minute in order to be sure of avoiding war.[38] Since Polk had deceived the fifty-four-forty bloc into expecting his support, and Buchanan was talking out of both sides of his mouth to Pakenham and the cabinet, neither man added to his stature in this episode. If one considers Polk's responsibilities, the precarious international situation, and the need for domestic unity, it is difficult to feel much sympathy for Buchanan.

When Polk submitted the British terms to the Senate, most of his accompanying message was devoted to justifying the request for advice. On the real issues he said merely that he still held to the position taken in his annual message but would accept the British proposal and negotiate a treaty if the Senate favored this action by a two-thirds majority.[39] However noncommittal he might appear on the surface, he and his subordinates had taken measures to ensure a favorable vote. Before submitting the terms he showed his message to Cass, who approved it, and to Allen, who felt that Polk ought to reject the terms without consulting the Senate. According to Benton, he and the President estimated the reactions of all the senators in advance, decided that they could rely on Whig support, and calculated that a two-thirds majority was safe before Polk took the plunge. Also, McLane had already told Calhoun that Britain would probably agree if the Senate insisted on putting a time limit on the navigation rights and Polk sent to the Senate that part of McLane's dispatch of May 18 which hinted at this compliant attitude and demonstrated Britain's reliance on Senate opinion.[40]

As events showed, most of Polk's precautions proved unnecessary. Allen moved to refer the President's message and the British terms to the foreign relations committee, where, as its chairman, he could delay action for a time, but his maneuver failed. On June 11 Haywood introduced a resolution to accept the terms. An amendment was put forward to end the navigation rights of the Hudson's Bay Company in 1853, but it was voted down. Then the Senate adopted Haywood's resolution, 38 to 12.

Buchanan and Pakenham at once drew up a formal treaty based on the British draft, and Polk submitted it to the Senate

38. Polk, *Diary*, I, 456. Sellers, *Polk, Continentalist*, pp. 393–94. Philip Shriver Klein, *President James Buchanan, a Biography*, pp. 181–82. Buchanan was especially worried about Vice President Dallas' rivalry for party control in Pennsylvania.

39. Richardson, *Papers of the Presidents*, IV, 449–50.

40. Polk, *Diary*, I, 462–63. Thomas Hart Benton, *Thirty Years View*, II, 674–75. L. McLane to Calhoun, May 18, 1846, Calhoun, *Correspondence*, pp. 1081–83.

on June 15. Again, a few Western extremists tried delaying tactics, seeking to amend the treaty so as to force a recognition that the United States was abandoning a legitimate claim. In one of the most sensible speeches of the entire Oregon controversy Benton declared that British explorations had created a strong claim to much of the area between the Columbia River and 49°; that the navigation right was a slight concession to make, in view of the territory the United States would receive from the treaty; and that a prompt settlement was necessary to reassure American businessmen and to help bring Mexico to terms. The Senate agreed, for it overwhelmingly rejected all amendments and on June 18 approved the treaty by a vote of 41 to 14.[41]

Whether from conviction or policy, Polk refrained from any public rejoicing over the settlement of the Oregon question. Even to McLane he continued to insist that only Tyler's concessions had led him to consider the British terms. He conceded that he and the public were satisfied, and later he offered to appoint McLane as secretary of state if Buchanan resigned. While McLane was pleased at this mark of favor, he complained to Andrew J. Donelson that Polk had made no use of the slight margin for negotiation on the navigation rights which he had secured with so much trouble and added, "If I had known that the President was not *insuperably* opposed to concede the navigation of the Columbia, I might have succeeded four or five months ago."[42]

Polk was undoubtedly right in supposing that the majority of the country approved a compromise settlement of the Oregon boundary if compromise was necessary to avoid war. For example, the New York *Herald* called it a victory of Anglo–American commercial interests over "a few political demagogues." Always expansionist, the irrepressible *Herald* predicted that all Oregon and Canada too would eventually fall into the American lap. "We can now thrash Mexico into decency at our leisure," it added complacently.[43] Since Polk had carefully arranged to share with the Senate any blame for the settlement, he now had to share the praise also. The Baltimore *Patriot* gave the major credit to three men:

41. For a summary of the Senate actions, see *NNR*, 70 (August 15, 1846), 374–75. Benton's speech appears in the issue for August 29, pp. 408–10.

42. Polk to McLane, June 22, 1846, Letterbook, 1845–1846, pp. 542–55, Polk Papers, LC. McLane to Polk, July 17, August 2, ibid., CVI. McLane to Andrew J. Donelson, July 8, Donelson Papers, XI, ff. 2231–32, LC. Buchanan had been considering a seat on the Supreme Court again, but he decided to remain in the cabinet.

43. New York *Herald*, June 11, 1846, p. 2; June 12, p. 2; June 14, p. 2. Albert K. Weinberg, *Manifest Destiny, a Study of Nationalist Expansionism in American History*, pp. 152–53.

to Webster, for clearly warning the British not to insist on a line south of 49°; to Calhoun, for vigorously resisting the Western extremists; and to Benton, for supporting the compromise so firmly that he left Polk no alternative. All three were quite willing to accept the praise, especially Calhoun, who wrote modestly to an admirer, "I would have had an equal triumph on the Mexican question, now the Oregon is settled, had an opportunity been afforded to discuss it." [44]

It was not to be expected that Polk could entirely escape the wrath of Westerners to whom he had held out the lure of fifty-four-forty in his inaugural address and his annual message. But he had carefully prepared for retreat ahead of time. When Senator Sidney Breese of Illinois sought an explanation, the President was able to tell him that, as early as December, he and Allen had agreed that it would be proper to seek Senate approval of a British proposal for compromise. Some extremists such as Cass were shrewd enough to foresee the final settlement in time to retreat with the President, but the passionate Allen and Hannegan could not, and Allen actually resigned the chairmanship of the foreign relations committee in his anger. He hoped for popular vindication, but his senatorial career was near its end.[45] Nevertheless, the residual bitterness in the Northwest over the settlement combined with abolitionism to hamper Polk's conduct of the Mexican War.

The news that the American Senate had voted to approve the treaty arrived in London on the same day that the Peel cabinet was to announce its resignation in Parliament. When Peel summarized his ministry's achievements in a final speech to the Commons, over a fourth of his address concerned the settlement of the Oregon question. At the same time, Aberdeen made a brief statement in the House of Lords, gracefully referring to McLane's cooperation. When Pakenham in Washington attributed the American compliance to concern over the Mexican War, Aberdeen disagreed. McLane's remarks had convinced him, he said, that the decisive factor had been the impending return of the Whigs and the Americans' desire to settle the question before Peel left office.[46]

44. Baltimore *Patriot*, n.d., as quoted in *NNR*, 70 (June 27, 1846), 258. Calhoun to Thomas G. Clemson, June 11, Calhoun, *Correspondence*, p. 697. For a survey of Whig editorials approving the settlement, see Washington *National Intelligencer*, June 24, p. 3.

45. Polk, *Diary*, I, 475–77. Sellers,

Polk, Continentalist, pp. 412–14.

46. Aberdeen to Edward Everett, July 1, 1846, Aberdeen Papers, BM, AM, vol. 43123, ff. 445–46. *Hansard Parliamentary Debates*, 3d series, LXXXVII, 1037–55. Pakenham to Aberdeen, June 13; Aberdeen to Pakenham, June 30, Miller, *Treaties and Other Interna-*

Elsewhere in Britain reactions to the settlement were mixed. At first Sir James Douglas of the Hudson's Bay Company thought that the United States had received more land than it had any reason to expect. During the following year, however, Earl Grey warned the House of Lords that Britain might lose Vancouver Island as well unless she could promptly provide inhabitants, and some men on both sides of the border felt that the Americans could have had more territory if they had waited for settlers and railroads to occupy it.[47] The British press accepted the compromise with only a few murmurs. "A national lie on the part of America has won her the boundary that she has obtained," declared the *Morning Chronicle*, and the *Times* warned the United States not to expect in the future that Britain would "overlook or connive at the excesses of an aggressive and rapacious policy."[48]

Despite the widespread satisfaction with the Oregon treaty of 1846, it contained at least one flaw. British subjects north of the border never used their navigation rights on the Columbia River enough to cause friction between the countries, but the international boundary was so vaguely traced in the waters between Vancouver Island and the mainland that no one knew for certain who owned the San Juan Islands in the middle of the Strait. These remained a focus of minor troubles until, through arbitration, they were awarded to the United States in 1872.[49] All in all, the treaty of 1846 was enough of an American victory to offset the much-criticized settlement of the Maine boundary in 1842, for the

---

tional Acts, V, 81–82. For a longer reflection on the Oregon negotiations, see Pakenham to Aberdeen, August 13, ibid., pp. 89–90.

47. Sir James Douglas to Dr. W. F. Tolmie, November 4, 1846. However, he had changed his mind before he wrote another letter, dated April 19, 1847. Quoted in W. N. Sage, *Sir James Douglas and British Columbia*, p. 139 n1. Lord Grey's speech is quoted in Richard W. Van Alstyne, *The Rising American Empire*, p. 117. See also Leslie M. Scott, "Influence of American Settlement upon the Oregon Boundary Treaty of 1846," *Oregon Historical Quarterly*, 29 (March 1928), 3.

48. London *Morning Chronicle*, June 30, 1846, p. 4. London *Times*, June 30, p. 4; July 23, pp. 8–9. Shortly after his return home McLane delivered an ad-

dress in New York containing a declaration that his early efforts to obtain a compromise at 49° had represented the views of the United States government at the time of his appointment. This statement seemed to accuse Polk of taking two positions at once, and the opposition press pounced on it immediately. Polk got McLane to issue another statement explaining the first one, and the *Union* demonstrated at length that there was nothing inconsistent about the President's support for 54°40′ and his willingness to compromise at 49°. Polk, *Diary*, II, 136–37, 139. Washington *Union*, October 1, p. 518. See also Richard S. Cramer, "British Magazines and the Oregon Question," *Pacific Historical Review*, 32 (May 1963), 380–81.

49. James O. McCabe, *The San Juan Water Boundary Question*, *passim*.

United States had obtained a wedge of territory to which she had little real claim from exploration or effective settlement.

*　*　*　*

Another subject of Anglo–American concern was brought to rest at about the same time as the Oregon question. This was the problem of the tariff, which Britain settled in June by repealing the corn laws and the United States in July by passing a new, lower schedule of duties. The connection between the questions of the tariff and Oregon has furnished historians with considerable grist for argument.[50] Whatever one concludes in this matter, it is obvious that many persons in both countries *assumed* the two were connected. To be sure, a few newspapers in both countries declared that this was not necessarily true, but the very vehemence of their denials suggests that a groundswell of public opinion had appeared.

Through the winter and spring of 1846 rumors circulated that the two governments were arranging to settle both questions at once.[51] There is no clear evidence that the government of either country associated the two questions closely, although at one point in February Polk did consider proposing an omnibus settlement (see Chapter 10). Instead, he and Peel followed their own separate paths toward tariff reform, the Englishman always a little ahead of the American. In both countries the fight over the tariff crossed party lines. Just as, in the United States, Pennsylvania Democrats joined Massachusetts Whigs to defend the tariff of 1842, so, in Britain, protectionism recruited supporters from among Lord John Russell's Whigs and a large section of country aristocrats in Peel's own party.

The British movement for tariff reform was probably more complicated than the American, for it rested on such diverse foundations as doctrinaire liberalism, humanitarian concern for urban

50. Thomas P. Martin, "Free Trade and the Oregon Question, 1842–1846," in *Facts and Factors in Economic History: Articles by Former Students of Edwin Francis Gay*, pp. 489–91. Charles M. Wiltse, *John C. Calhoun, Sectionalist, 1840–1850*, pp. 524–25n20. Frederick Merk, *The Oregon Question, Essays in Anglo-American Diplomacy and Politics*, pp. 309–36.

51. *NNR*, 59 (February 14, 28, 1846), 370, 404; 70 (March 7, 14), 1, 17; (April 4), 66. Articles from the New York *Herald* and the New York *Courier and Enquirer* are reprinted in the London *Times*, January 24, p. 8; March 13, p. 5; and May 15, p. 5. See also ibid., March 23, p. 4. A British letter is reprinted in the New York *Evening Post*, January 26, p. 2. See also London *Morning Chronicle*, February 16, p. 5; February 17, p. 6.

labor, the desire of factory owners to save money on wages, and sympathy or fear arising from the effects of the potato famine in Ireland. While the Parliamentary debate centered in the virtual removal of duties on wheat, Peel supported a general lowering of tariffs, including those on manufactured goods, and he proposed to compensate British farmers for the loss of protection by reforms in local finance, taxes, and poor laws. Despite his provisions for the farmers, Tory landowners throughout Britain rose against their nominal leader, branded him a parvenu traitor, and maintained a bitter debate for weeks in Parliament. Peel's measures could not have succeeded without the firm support of the Whig leaders, especially Russell, who had no desire to face the tariff issue when he should come to power. In June, Peel succeeded in limiting grain duties to one shilling (effective after three years of progressive reduction) and obtained many of his other reforms, but at a heavy price. Four days after Parliament approved his program, he resigned his office—his party split and his career blighted.[52]

In the United States, tariff reformers followed Peel's campaign intently and cheered every success.[53] Some hotheads among the group feared that Polk intended to back down from his campaign promises and would offer them some sort of placebo. The truth was that he had to move slowly after the Oregon question took on a threatening aspect, especially since his advisers included several prominent protectionists such as Buchanan. Polk and Robert J. Walker, the principal tariff reformer of the administration, decided to base their campaign on the need to increase tariff revenue—an especially useful appeal after the outbreak of war. Their bill was soon introduced in the House, but as long as the Oregon question occupied that body's attention, the bill was kept in committee, carefully nursed by the administration and watched over by a bloc Calhoun had formed for tariff revision.[54]

The Oregon question, the pressure of war measures, and protectionist obstructionism prevented debate on the tariff bill until

52. Donald Grove Barnes, *A History of the British Corn Laws from 1660 to 1846*, Chaps. 11, 12. A useful short summary of the British campaign is Élie Halévy, *The Age of Peel and Cobden, a History of the English People, 1841–1852*, pp. 104–23. Peel never returned to power after his resignation; he died five years later from injuries suffered in a riding accident.

53. See, for example, Pakenham to Aberdeen, February 28, 1846, No. 18, GB, FO 5/446, ff. 131–32.

54. Sellers, *Polk, Continentalist*, pp. 451–53. Rhett to Calhoun, September 18, 1845; R. K. Crallé to Calhoun, September 23, Calhoun, *Correspondence*, pp. 1049–54. Klein, *Buchanan*, p. 172. On Calhoun, see Wiltse, *Calhoun, Sectionalist*, pp. 241–43.

June 15. In the House, the administration's supporters were able to compromise enough to wedge through a reform bill, 114 to 95. In the Senate the fight was even closer, and many Western expansionists and Eastern Whigs had to reverse the positions on Anglo–American relations which they had recently assumed during the Oregon debate. After much backstage maneuvering, enough Democrats joined the Whig bloc against reform to produce a tie vote. Vice President Dallas, at heart a protectionist, had already decided that his best prospects lay in supporting the administration. As a result, the Senate passed the bill by his casting vote, 28 to 27. On July 30 Polk signed it into law.[55]

The bill fixed most duties at 30 per cent ad valorem, with a few as high as 40 per cent or as low as 20. Calhoun and his followers were disappointed not to have recovered the standard rate of 20 per cent fixed by the compromise tariff of 1833, but they had obtained important concessions; under the tariff of 1842 duties on shirtings, for example, had stood at 95 per cent and on many iron products over 100.[56] Iron manufacturers were aghast, and protectionists joined free traders in denouncing the measure as a sellout to the other side. In Britain the new tariff was viewed as a step in the right direction—toward free trade.[57]

American protectionists grumbled that the repeal of the corn laws would not benefit the United States, which would receive "only the *crumbs* that will fall from the rich man's table" in exchange for abandoning its own protection. Before the end of the year, however, George Bancroft, the new United States minister to Britain, was reporting great increases in annual American agricultural shipments to Britain—£ 7,500,000 of wheat and flour, nearly £ 1,000,000 of provisions, and others—and predicting that Britain would import £ 16,500,000 more than the year before and export £ 6,000,000 less. Bancroft also remarked that he had received a warmly cordial reception and saw signs of Anglo–American friendship on every side.[58] For the United States, the new

55. Sellers, *Polk, Continentalist*, pp. 453–68. Edward Stanwood, *American Tariff Controversies in the Nineteenth Century*, II, 71–81. US, 29C, 1S, *CG*, pp. 1105, 1112–13.

56. Wiltse, *Calhoun, Sectionalist*, pp. 271–72.

57. New York *Journal of Commerce*, n.d., reprinted in London *Times*, July 31, 1846, p. 3. *NNR*, 71 (September 19), 45–46. *Anglo-American*, 7 (August 8), 382. Washington *National Intelligen-*

cer, July 30, p. 3; August 1, p. 3. For an especially succinct demonstration of the range of American objections, see letters to Calhoun from James Gadsden, Abbott Lawrence, and James Hamilton, Calhoun, *Correspondence*, pp. 1085–90.

58. Boston *Atlas*, n.d., reprinted in *NNR*, 70 (May 2, 1846), 133. Bancroft to Buchanan, November 3, 17, Nos. 1, 2, US, DS, D, Britain, LVII. Merk, *Oregon Question*, pp. 320–24. Stanwood,

tariff would probably provide more revenue for fighting the war with Mexico, but whether the commercial gains would be permanent, only time would tell. At least the tariff had reinforced the Oregon settlement in bringing the Anglo–American crisis to an end.

*   *   *   *

While the United States government ended the Oregon controversy with a compromise, it was also solving the problem of California by different tactics—a combination of intrigue and military force. To this end both the Oregon compromise and Taylor's victories contributed by reducing Britain's desire to defend California for Mexico. At the same time, the formal recognition of a state of war provided the United States with a legal basis for its own military action there.

In the spring of 1846 the nominal governor of California was Pío Pico, a fat, good-natured farmer who had been chosen by inhabitants of the Los Angeles area after the overthrow of Michel-torena but who enjoyed little support in the north. Here, other native leaders, such as José Castro, Juan B. Alvarado, and Mariano C. Vallejo, hoped for domination.[59] Throughout the province separatism was rife.

Only for a brief period, late in 1845, had Aberdeen seriously considered intervening in defense of California, and then mainly as a means of encouraging Anglo–French cooperation. But private individuals had proposed plans for colonizing California with British and European settlers—an Irish priest, Father Eugene McNamara, and the British merchant-consul in Mexico City, Ewen C. Mackintosh. Late in 1845 J. D. Powles, representing British holders of Mexican government bonds, expanded the Mackintosh plan into a company guaranteed by the British government, which would purchase fifty million acres of land in California, paying for most of it with the nearly worthless bonds of the Mexican foreign debt. Herrera looked with favor on McNamara's plan, Paredes on that of Mackintosh; but the British government would have nothing to do with either of them.[60]

American Tariff Controversies, II, 83–93.

59. Justin Smith emphasizes the split between Pico and the northerners along the lines of their sympathies for Britain and the United States, respec-

tively. Smith, *War with Mexico*, I, 328–29.

60. Lester G. Engelson, "Proposals for the Colonization of California by England in Connection with the Mexican Debt to British Bondholders, 1837–

Rumors of these futile proposals were quite enough to stimulate anxiety in the United States about British designs on California. In June 1845, after learning of the revolt against Micheltorena, Polk had sent Commodore John D. Sloat of the Pacific Squadron contingent instructions to seize the principal ports in the event of war with Mexico over the Texas question. In October, after receiving exaggerated warnings from Consul Thomas O. Larkin, Polk instructed both Larkin and Sloat to watch the British carefully and to propagandize among the inhabitants in favor of eventual American rule. The President sent out two copies of these instructions—one with Commodore Robert F. Stockton, commanding the frigate *Congress,* and the other overland with Archibald Gillespie, a young marine lieutenant. Gillespie was instructed to communicate also with John C. Frémont, then exploring in California. At the same time Polk instructed John Slidell to purchase California if Mexico would sell and to be on his guard against British intrigue. He was to communicate directly with Larkin if necessary (see Chapters 9, 10).

Throughout the winter and early spring of 1846 the Oregon question crowded California from the news. In January a young Whig journalist reviewed the evidence of British interest in California. European occupation of California, like that of Cuba, he declared, "is an event which [the United States] 'CANNOT PERMIT IN ANY CONTINGENCY WHATEVER.' "[61] Larkin and many other Americans on the Pacific Coast rather expected war over Oregon, and some alarmists predicted that either Admiral Seymour would then occupy all the ports of California or Mexico, emboldened by British aid, would appropriate all American property and "gorge themselves on our very vitals." As the emigrant season began, everyone expected new waves of restive American settlers—the publicist Lansford Hastings predicted fifteen or twenty thousand for California and Oregon during 1846. Although this prospect alarmed Pío Pico and the other California officials, they took no steps to close the borders or otherwise to regulate the flow.

In March Hastings told Larkin confidentially that the United States government had agreed to subsidize at least part of the year's emigration.[62] Whether there was any truth in his remark, Polk

1846," *California Historical Society Quarterly,* 18 (June 1939), 144–46. Hubert H. Bancroft, *History of California,* V, 215–23. Peña y Reyes, *Aberdeen,*

Texas y California, pp. 43–44, 51–53.
61. *American Review* (Whig), 3 (January 1846), 82–99; quotation on p. 98.
62. Larkin to Jacob P. Leese, Febru-

kept very quiet about California until the United States and Mexico were actually at war, although he never took his eyes off his goal for long during this period of waiting. His plan of obtaining a secret fund of $2 million from Congress, for example, was primarily motivated by the hope of making a quick agreement for the purchase of California.

As soon as Congress agreed to a declaration of war on Mexico, Polk took steps to seize California before Britain could intervene. Angrily rejecting Buchanan's suggestion of a public announcement abjuring territorial gains as a war aim, he reviewed with Bancroft the previous year's instructions to Sloat and Stockton. Polk also discussed with Marcy and Scott how they might best maneuver available troops so as to reinforce Taylor while immediately dispatching an expedition into the Southwest. Between May 13 and June 8 Bancroft sent Sloat three dispatches instructing him to blockade the Mexican Pacific coast, to occupy all important ports from Monterey to Mazatlán if possible, to conciliate the natives of California, and in the event of a movement for independence to encourage annexation in every way.

At the same time, Marcy sent out orders to Colonel Stephen W. Kearny, commanding an Army regiment in Missouri. Kearny was to march on Santa Fe, ostensibly to protect American traders along the Santa Fe trail. On June 3, after further discussions in the cabinet, Marcy ordered Kearny to press on into Upper California before winter, enlisting on the way any emigrants who might like to volunteer.[63]

There was never any question that Polk regarded permanent possession of California as the first goal of the Mexican War. He told the cabinet frankly on May 30 that he intended to take California, New Mexico, and perhaps other parts of northern Mexico in order to strengthen the American position in peace negotiations. Three weeks later, Bancroft wrote to a merchant friend in Boston that if Mexico made peace at once, the United States gov-

---

ary, 1846, quoted in Reuben L. Underhill, *From Cowhides to Golden Fleece*, p. 99. Lansford Warren Hastings to Larkin, New Helvetia, March 3; Faxon Dean Atherton to Larkin, Valparaiso, Chile, March 4; Larkin to Secretary of State, Monterey, March 6, Thomas O. Larkin, *The Larkin Papers*, ed. George P. Hammond, IV, 220–21, 224–26, 232–33. Hastings to John Marsh, March 26, John A. Hawgood, ed., *First and Last*

Consul: Thomas Oliver Larkin and the Americanization of California, pp. 51–53. Bancroft, *California*, V, 57.

63. Bancroft to Sloat, May 13, 15, June 8, 1846; Marcy to Stephen W. Kearny, June 3, US, 30C, 1S, HED 60, pp. 153–55, 233, 235–37. Polk, *Diary*, I, 438–40, 443–44. Dwight L. Clarke, *Stephen Watts Kearny, Soldier of the West, passim*.

ernment might be satisfied with a boundary at 35°, cutting the Pacific Coast somewhere just south of Monterey, but that a month's delay would cost her three more degrees, down to San Diego. The merchant, well acquainted with California through trade contacts, replied at once with full information about the province and urged that the United States demand the more southerly boundary at once. Soon Walker was telling the cabinet, with some support from Polk, that the United States should insist on 26° as the boundary line.[64] The administration decided to reinforce Kearny with a volunteer regiment that was being formed in New York and put into its orders a proviso that its members would be mustered out in California—obviously with the hope that the men would settle there and help to Americanize it.[65]

Although they could not have known the entire content of these discussions, the British government leaders were well aware of Polk's designs on California. Throughout the winter and spring Mexico's Minister Murphy had tactfully urged defense measures on Aberdeen, while Paredes somewhat more insistently besieged Bankhead, the British minister in Mexico City, with pleas for aid.[66] Occasional warnings from British consular officials at Mazatlán and Monterey drifted back to the Foreign Office, and when Pakenham reported Polk's war message, he too mentioned the Americans' intention to seize "the Californias."[67] As Aberdeen and McLane hammered out the terms of the Oregon compromise, they were opposed by part of the British cabinet, some of whose reluctance, it seems clear, arose from concern over the United States intent to appropriate California.

The most concerned of the cabinet members was the first lord of the Admiralty, the Earl of Ellenborough, who had warned Peel in March about American armament and had spent his first four months in office reviewing the British strategic position in the Pacific. On May 16, two days before Aberdeen completed his draft of compromise terms on Oregon, Ellenborough summarized his findings in a long memorandum to the foreign secretary. He pre-

64. Clarke, *Kearny*, pp. 437–38, 495–97. Samuel Hooper to Bancroft, Boston, June 19, 25, 1846; Bancroft to Hooper, June 22, Bancroft Papers, MHS.

65. Spencer, *Victor and Spoils*, pp. 154, 158–59. Marcy to J. D. Stevenson, September 11, 1846, US, 30C, 1S, HED 60, pp. 159–62.

66. Murphy to Ministerio de Rela-

ciones, February 1, April 1, June 1, 1846, Nos. 4, 6, 8, Peña y Reyes, *Aberdeen, Texas y California*, pp. 62–72. Bankhead to Aberdeen, January 30, March 10, 30, Nos. 14, 31, 45, GB, FO 50/195, ff. 185–87; 50/196, ff. 9–13, 161–65.

67. Pakenham to Aberdeen, May 13, 1846, No. 55, GB, FO 5/449, ff. 35–38.

ferred a single great base at Hawaii—"a Malta in the centre of the Pacific, that is the best thing"—but realized that diplomatic considerations (meaning French jealousy) rendered this plan impossible to realize. Failing the establishment of a central base, he declared that Britain must have at least two strong points, one west of Tahiti and the other in the eastern Pacific, to safeguard British interests in Mexico and Oregon. After rejecting the Galápagos Islands, Socorro, and the Revillagigedos, he moved closer to California and briefly considered Guadalupe and Ceros:

> Their position is excellent—but look at San Francisco itself on the Chart, you will see that it is not only the finest Harbour, but the most easily defended—really unattackable from the Land side, and therefore as good as an Island, while towards the Sea it has facilities of defence which are hardly to be found anywhere except at Malta and Corfu.
>
> When we are about it, let us at once obtain possession, if we can, of the Key of the N. W. Coast of America. We must look forward to what the obvious course of events is bringing in, the passing of European population to the N. W. Coast of N. America and to its ultimate consequences on the Trade of the Pacific and of China, and take our measures at once.[68]

This imperial vision momentarily dazzled even the cautious Peel, but Aberdeen brought the cabinet back to reality with the advice that only Anglo–American hostilities over Oregon would justify Britain in seizing San Francisco. If a British claim there had already existed, as in the Columbia Valley, that would be another matter, but to establish one now would be tantamount to a declaration of war. Furthermore, Aberdeen pointed out, Mexico could do nothing to exclude American settlers, who would probably soon overpower the British anyway. If the quarrel over Oregon should end in war, he favored reaching an agreement for the control of California. As long as there was hope of settling the Oregon question peaceably, he opposed any measure that would block such a settlement.[69]

After Aberdeen had sent Pakenham the proposal concerning Oregon, Ellenborough continued to press for armed action on the Pacific coast. He called Peel's attention to Polk's naval prepara-

---

68. Earl of Ellenborough to Aberdeen, May 16, 1846, Ellenborough Papers, PRO 30/12/34/7. Apparently another reason why Britain did not consider Hawaii further was that the Admiralty thought Pearl Harbor too shallow for a naval base. Kenneth Bourne, *Britain and the Balance of Power in North America, 1815–1908*, p. 122.

69. Arthur Hamilton-Gordon Stanmore, *The Earl of Aberdeen*, pp. 183–84.

tions for war with Mexico and warned that when their new ships and guns were no longer needed against Mexico, the Americans would turn them on Britain. Peel and Aberdeen replied that the government was already running a deficit of about half a million pounds sterling, so further rearmament was financially as well as politically unwise. Ellenborough grumbled that economy measures were imprudent, in view of the likelihood that Britain would eventually have to fight the combined navies of the United States and France. Early in June he received Admiral Seymour's appeal, dispatched three months earlier, in which Seymour requested reinforcements so he could more adequately watch the French in Tahiti and the Americans in Oregon and convoy British merchant ships around Cape Horn (see Chapter 11).[70] About the middle of the month the Foreign Office also received a dispatch from Bankhead, reporting that Paredes had finally offered to mortgage California to Britain as security for a war loan—and to prevent American occupation.[71]

None of this new information swayed the judgment of Aberdeen and Peel, now firmly committed to peace in the New World. By early June a settlement of the Oregon question seemed probable, as did repeal of the corn laws; soon the cabinet would be leaving office. On June 1, even before receiving Paredes' latest proposal, Aberdeen had instructed Bankhead that his earlier appeals were futile.[72] When Seymour's request for reinforcements came to Aberdeen, he replied to the Admiralty that there was no longer any likelihood of Britain's engaging in hostilities and that any additional protection which British interests in Mexico might need as a result of the Mexican War and the American blockade should be furnished by the ships already on station. Before acquiring territory, the government would need to weigh the matter seriously, especially its probable effect on other powers.[73]

Just as he was leaving office, Ellenborough put a period to the debate on British strategy in the Pacific by writing disconsolately to Seymour of the elaborate plans his "timorous Colleagues" had

70. Ellenborough to Peel, May 29, 31, 1846; Peel to Ellenborough, May 30, Peel Papers, BM, AM, vol. 40473, ff. 326–27, 334–35, 344–47. Sir George Seymour to Admiralty, Payta, Peru, March 6, No. 19; H. T. L. Corry to H. U. Addington, June 9, GB, A, 1/5568. Corry and Addington were undersecretaries at the Admiralty and the Foreign Office, respectively.

71. Bankhead to Aberdeen, May 30, 1846, No. 73, GB, FO 50/197, ff. 120–23.

72. Aberdeen to Bankhead, June 1, 1846, No. 15, GB, FO 50/194, ff. 32–37. A large part of this is reprinted in George Lockhart Rives, The United States and Mexico, 1821–1848, II, 162–63.

73. Addington to Corry, June 19, 1846, GB, A, 1/5568.

rejected: "I do not hesitate to call them so. I could not do with them what I considered essential to our Naval Security, & had the Government been in a less critical situation I would not have remained here as long as I have done, to bear every responsibility without adequate power."[74]

* * * *

No matter what policies the governments in Washington and London might adopt, distance and roundabout communications to the Pacific effectively placed full responsibility on the local American and British agents. At the beginning of May Paredes sent troops to Mazatlán for transportation up the coast to the threatened province, but, once in the port, the soldiers joined a federalist revolt going on there. During April and May the Mexican government repeatedly appealed to British Minister Bankhead for help in defending California, but Bankhead steadfastly refused to take any responsibility involving his government.[75] At the end of April he submitted detailed reports on the Mexican situation, and the legation's secretary, Percy W. Doyle, going home on leave, carried additional oral messages to the Foreign Office. About a month later, after news of Taylor's victories arrived in Mexico City, Paredes offered to mortgage the Californias as security for a British loan—a proposal reminiscent of the earlier McNamara and Murphy projects but substituting military occupation for more gradual colonization. Bankhead was favorably impressed by Paredes' proposal, but he would not depart from his former noncommittal position and agreed only to transmit the proposal to his government.[76] As has been stated, Aberdeen rejected it.

Consequently, in the spring of 1846 the political future of

74. Ellenborough to Seymour, June 28, 1846, Ellenborough Papers, PRO 30/12/4/20.

75. On April 6, for example, Minister of War Tornel asked Bankhead to order one or more British warships to escort a battalion of Mexican troops from Mazatlán to Monterey or at least to lend them the protection of the British flag. Bankhead declined, with the statement that, if Sloat tried to detain the transports, the British would be obliged to defend them, thus risking a war with the United States (which, of course, was exactly what Tornel want-

ed). Bankhead to Aberdeen, April 29, 1846, No. 51, GB, FO 50/196, ff. 191–93. On the troop revolt, see Luis G. Zorilla, *Historia de las relaciones entre México y los Estados Unidos de América, 1800–1958*, I, 181.

76. Bankhead to Aberdeen, April 29, May 30, 1846, Nos. 58, 72, 73, GB, FO 50/196, ff. 264–72; 50/197, ff. 106–16, 120–23. Bankhead described the proposal as "an indirect offer of sale, and it is the first time that any such offer has ever been hinted at from a responsible authority."

California lay entirely in the hands of the Mexicans and foreigners who lived along the Pacific coast. At that time the unknown factor in the American formula was John Charles Frémont, who had crossed the mountains with about fifteen of his exploring party and had arrived at Sutter's Fort in mid-December 1845. Frémont had left the rest of his party to straggle into eastern California without him. With a temporary pass from Sutter, who served as a local magistrate, Frémont made several trips as far west as San Francisco Bay, seeking horses and supplies and also establishing contact with Larkin. He assured Castro and Alvarado that he and his band, when reunited, would confine themselves to exploration, but he did not clearly indicate whether they would move southward toward the Colorado River or northward to find new trails to Oregon. Polite but wary, the officials made no objection.

In mid-February Frémont rejoined his sixty men near the San Joaquin River, but instead of taking them north or south he marched them back to the coast, not far from Monterey, crossing en route the most heavily settled area of California. This action, unauthorized and even now only partly explained by his biographers, aroused the suspicions of José Castro, the district prefect, who peremptorily ordered him to leave California at once or be arrested and forcibly expelled. Instead, the stubborn explorer moved his camp to Hawk's Peak in the nearby Gavilan Mountains, built a rough log fort, raised the American flag, and wrote to Larkin that he would defend it to the death.

Castro did not try to attack Frémont but published a proclamation declaring the party "a band of robbers" and calling on the people to rally behind him against the intruder. Larkin profoundly disliked the heroics on both sides but, considering that Frémont might be acting under orders, did no more than mildly advise him to move away from the settled area. "I never make to this Government an unreasonable request, therefore never expect a denial," he added, "and have for many years found them well disposed to me."[77] Impulsively, Frémont broke camp on the night of March 9—he had held the fort only three days—and led his men back to Sutter's Fort and then up the Sacramento River toward Oregon. He had accomplished nothing except to put the Mexican authorities on their guard.

At the end of the month Castro called a military junta at

77. Larkin to John Charles Frémont, Monterey, March 8, 1846, Larkin, *Papers*, IV, 239–41. More detailed accounts of this episode are in Allan Nevins, *Frémont, the World's Greatest Adventurer*, I, 254–68; and Bancroft, *California*, V, 2–23, 58–59.

Monterey to advise him on defense measures and to determine the regional attitude toward Governor Pico to the south. The junta recognized the Paredes regime in Mexico City—a slap at Pico, whose authority stemmed from Herrera—and reaffirmed its confidence in Castro. Somewhat dismayed at these signs of independence to the north, Pico and the provincial assembly called a general council to convene at Santa Barbara on June 15. Some American residents suspected that one item on the council's agenda was a British proposal for a protectorate.[78] The rumor was partly correct, for Pico wrote to British Vice Consul James A. Forbes at Monterey that the departmental assembly and other influential men intended to declare the independence of California and to solicit British protection. Forbes explained that he had no authority to promise any assistance but advised Pico that the only means for saving the province from the Americans was a declaration of unqualified independence. To his disappointment, the continued opposition from the north induced Pico to rescind the order for the Santa Barbara council.[79]

Other participants moving into position for the crisis were the American and British Pacific squadrons. In March most of Sloat's ships had been anchored at Mazatlán for a number of weeks. He had two frigates, his flagship, the *Savannah*, and the *Constitution*, which he had called from the Far East during the preceding year; he expected Stockton in a third frigate, the *Congress*, at any time. His squadron also included four corvettes and a schooner. At the beginning of the year Seymour's squadron was based as usual off the Peruvian coast, its units cruising hither and yon across the Pacific. Late in March he moved his flagship, the frigate *Collingwood*, and some of his squadron north to San Blas on the Mexican coast south of Mazatlán.

The British and American squadrons were roughly equal in total strength, but, since he had more interests to defend in the Pacific area, Seymour was unable to concentrate as many ships at one point as Sloat.[80] Seymour received somewhat more regular and

78. Bancroft, *California*, V, 36–37, 59–63, 67–71. Bancroft rejects the possibility of a protectorate but documents the existence of the rumor. See also Abel Stearns to Larkin, Los Angeles, June 12, 1846, Larkin, *Papers*, V, 18–20.

79. James A. Forbes to Alexander Forbes, July 9, 1846, extract in GB, FO 50/198, ff. 259–63.

80. K. Jack Bauer, *Surfboats and Horse Marines. U.S. Naval Operations in the Mexican War, 1846–48*, pp. 136, 138–40. On the transpacific voyage of the *Constitution*, see Ethan Estabrook to Larkin, Mazatlán, February 21, 1846, Larkin, *Papers*, IV, 206–8. A statement of British, French, and American naval strength in the Pacific at this time is enclosed with Corry to Addington, June 10, GB, A, 1/5568. The *Collingwood*,

up-to-date news from central Mexico than Sloat, who often felt completely isolated. On April 1, just before Seymour arrived off the Mexican coast, Sloat learned of Frémont's brush with Castro. He immediately sent Captain John B. Montgomery and the corvette *Portsmouth* to patrol at Monterey and later at San Francisco.[81]

At this point Lieutenant Archibald H. Gillespie arrived in California with his messages for Larkin and Frémont, drawn up by Polk and the cabinet six months earlier. He had reached Sloat's base at Mazatlán in February, but, since there seemed no need for haste, the commodore sent him in a sloop to California by way of Honolulu, a commonly used route. On April 17 Gillespie recited his memorized instructions to Larkin and soon thereafter went inland to look for Frémont.

Larkin was much pleased to receive his commission as confidential agent and instructions to encourage the peaceful absorption of California, a policy he thoroughly approved and had already begun to carry out. He sent Buchanan a brief analysis of the political situation, in which he emphasized the weakness and complacency of the native leaders; this time, he did not exaggerate the British threat. He also drew up encyclopedic descriptions of the resources and the principal residents of California for the State Department, and during subsequent weeks he continued to write letters on local conditions for various New York newspapers.[82]

Larkin also sent letters to his principal merchant friends along the coast, informing them about portions of Polk's instructions, about Slidell's rejection, and about the arrival of the *Portsmouth* at Monterey. He felt that the only alternatives open to residents of California were war for independence or better political terms

carrying 80 guns, was stronger than any single American ship. Seymour's forces were actually weaker than he realized, for in early March Gordon had sailed for England in the *America* to carry $2 million of British-owned Mexican silver, thus disobeying orders, but probably convinced that Oregon and California were lost anyway. Seymour did not learn of Gordon's disobedience until mid-August; he had supposed him to be at Honolulu. Barry M. Gough, "H.M.S. *America* on the North Pacific Coast," *Oregon Historical Quarterly*, 70 (December 1969), 304–9.

81. Sloat to Black, Mazatlán, April 1, 1846, US, DS, CD, Mexico City, IX. Bauer, *Surfboats and Horse Marines*, p. 180. Fred Blackburn Rogers, *Mont-*

gomery and the Portsmouth, p. 20. Bancroft, *California*, V, 199–200. Joseph T. Downey, *The Cruise of the Portsmouth, 1845–1847. A Sailor's View of the Naval Conquest of California*, ed. Howard Lamar, p. 237.

82. Werner H. Marti, *Messenger of Destiny: the California Adventures, 1846–1847, of Archibald Gillespie, U.S. Marine Corps*, pp. 25–27. Bauer, *Surfboats and Horse Marines*, pp. 142–43. Larkin to Buchanan, April 17, 1846, Nos. 41, 42, Manning, *IAA*, VIII, 841–44. Larkin's surveys of California are reprinted in Larkin, *Papers*, IV, 297–300, 303–16, 322–34. Larkin to Moses Yale Beach & Sons, April, May 19; Larkin to James Gordon Bennett, May 20, 30, ibid., pp. 355–56, 379–80, 382–84, 402–4.

from Mexico: "Should the former now be the case, I beleive [*sic*] that the stars [and stripes] would shine over California before the 4th of July!" Conceding that the change from Mexican to American rule might not improve the merchants' lot, he nevertheless warned them that they would be much worse off as a European colony, under "heavy tax and impositions." Furthermore, it was clear that Polk would not allow any violations of the Monroe Doctrine. Throughout May, Larkin kept up this correspondence, urging his friends to send him any evidence of British intrigue, predicting a flood of immigration, and looking forward to the arrival of Stockton and the *Congress*. "Knowing what we do of affairs here," Larkin asked, "what object can you suppose . . . [Stockton] had in leaving all and coming to the North Pacific[?]"[83]

The climactic month of May, which brought the declaration of war by the United States and the resumption of Anglo–American negotiations over Oregon, also started a rapid sequence of events that placed the Americans in control of California. For some time rumors of war between the United States and Mexico had disturbed Seymour and Sloat, waiting with their ships at San Blas and Mazatlán, respectively. During April Seymour received dispatches from Minister Bankhead in Mexico City describing the frustration of the Slidell mission, and on May 7 a dispatch arrived which contained a copy of Aberdeen's long instructions of December 31, 1844, outlining British policy in California. For the first time Seymour had positive evidence that, while Aberdeen forbade interference in a domestic revolution, he would oppose establishment of a foreign protectorate over the province.

The dispatch from the Foreign Office was well over a year old, but British policy had not changed substantially in the meantime. Seymour acted on it at once; he posted one of his ships, the corvette *Juno*, on a secret mission to protect British interests on the California coast. Her captain, P. Blake, was instructed to confer with the British vice consul at Monterey, obtain a list of British residents in the province, and examine possible landing places near San Francisco. In case California declared her independence, Blake was to use his influence to prevent an American protectorate. However, Seymour made no effort to concentrate his squadron, and his other ships proceeded on their various missions.[84]

83. Larkin to Leese, Stearns, and Jonathan Trumbull Warner, April 17, 1846; Larkin to Stearns, May 23, 24, Larkin, *Papers*, IV, 295–97, 389–93. Larkin to W. A. Leidesdorff, April 23,

27; Larkin to Stearns, May 1, Hawgood, *First and Last Consul*, pp. 55–58, 60–62.

84. Seymour to Corry, San Blas, June 13, 1846, No. 43, GB, A 1/5561. Bankhead to Seymour, March 11, April 22;

A few days later, on May 17, Sloat received credible but unofficial word that a large body of Mexicans had crossed the Rio Grande and had killed or captured an American patrol.[85] He sent the corvette *Cyane* to Monterey with a letter to Larkin, informing him that he intended to bring his entire squadron to Monterey; he hoped that Larkin would be prepared to advise him on further action. Puzzled by Sloat's cautious language, the American consul concluded that he should expect another courier from Washington, but the days passed and none arrived. Nor did Sloat, for he hesitated to sail before receiving official word that war had been declared, so he remained in Mazatlán for several weeks, closely watched by a British ship.[86]

At the same time that Seymour was drawing up his secret instructions for the *Juno*, on May 9, Gillespie reached Frémont and his party, encamped far to the north on the California–Oregon border. He delivered to the explorer a copy of Larkin's instructions, the family letters from Frémont's wife and his father-in-law, Senator Benton, and an oral summary of the political situation. The events that followed have given rise to as much historical argument as the still-uncertain instructions Frémont received from his government. Frémont and Gillespie hastened to Sutter's Fort and, reaching there at the end of May, encamped nearby in the midst of American settlers, many recently arrived. These men were eager for action, having heard rumors that the United States and Mexico were at war and that the local officials planned to set Indians upon them and clear them out.

Exactly what Frémont said and did remains obscure, but it was enough to touch off a revolt against the local authorities. Probably he let the settlers understand that he had the support of the United States government. On June 10 overt action began when a group of Americans seized a band of horses intended for Prefect Castro. The rebels then captured the town of Sonoma, took Mariano Vallejo and other natives prisoner, and proclaimed a California republic, symbolized by a flag decorated with the crude figure of a bear. The movement spread to the Bay area; Frémont,

Eustace Barron to Seymour, November 28, 1845, No. 10; Seymour to P. Blake, Mazatlán, May 10, 11; Seymour to James A. Forbes, May 10; Seymour to Captains Gordon, Henderson, May 11, Seymour, Journal, GB, A, 50/213, ff. 213v., 215v., 216v., 218–19.

85. Edwin A. Sherman, *The Life of the Late Rear Admiral John Drake Sloat of the United States Navy* [etc.], pp. 62–64.

86. Bancroft, *California*, V, 202–4. Bauer, *Surfboats and Horse Marines*, pp. 144–45. Sloat to Larkin, May 18, 1846, Larkin, *Papers*, IV, 378.

who had unofficially advised the rebel leaders from the beginning, took command; and Captain Montgomery, who had moved the *Portsmouth* to San Francisco, sent several officers to Frémont for liaison and counsel. Meanwhile, Castro and Pico reached an uneasy truce with each other and prepared to resist the Americans. By the end of June several minor skirmishes had occurred, with a few casualties, and much of northern California between San Francisco and Sacramento was in rebel hands.[87]

Admirers of Frémont and frontier initiative have argued that the Bear Flag revolt rescued California from the British until American regulars could use the war to justify a formal occupation, but it would be as easy to demonstrate that the revolt complicated the occupation by turning native residents against the unruly intruders.[88] One person who feared such a complication was Larkin, who had always been on agreeable terms with Vallejo and Castro. He was dismayed at news of the uprising, which destroyed his plans for peaceful absorption, and for a time he would not believe that Frémont and Gillespie were involved in it. Eventually, however, he shrugged his shoulders, accepted the situation, and wrote: "If they have started the big Ball to roll forever and thro & thro' C[alifornia], I can not stop it." While observing and reporting on California to the State Department, he kept his own affairs free of politics and let events take their course. When Governor Pico protested to him about his cool attitude, he disclaimed all responsibility for his countrymen, for, as he said, he had no troops at his command and no influence over the rebels.[89]

The decisive encounter in California occurred, not in the interior, but on the coast, where the ships and merchants of the United States and Britain were concentrated. It has been suggested

87. Bancroft, *California*, V, Chaps. 4–8. Nevins, *Frémont, Adventurer*, I, 289–317, *et passim*. Marti, *Messenger of Destiny*, pp. 35–37, Chap. 3. Ernest A. Wiltsee, who holds the thesis that Frémont was acting under specific, confidential (and as yet undiscovered) orders from Polk, believes that both Larkin and Montgomery were privy to the secret and that Montgomery was actually operating under Gillespie's instructions at this time. Ernest A. Wiltsee, *The Truth about Frémont: an Inquiry*, pp. 20–28, 32, *et passim*.

88. The case against Frémont and the Bear Flaggers is most emphatically developed in Bancroft, *California*, V, 96–100. For statements of the rival view, see Wiltsee, *Truth about Frémont*, pp. 39–46 *et passim*; and Marti, *Messenger of Destiny*, p. 317. A sample of local reactions to the Bear Flag movement is José de Amesti to Larkin, Corralitos, July 3, 1846, Larkin, *Papers*, V, 100. For John A. Sutter's role see Dillon, *Fool's Gold. The Decline and Fall of Captain John Sutter of California*, Chaps. 12–14.

89. Hawgood, *First and Last Consul*, pp. 71–72. Larkin to Leidesdorff, June 18, undated, July 1, 1846; Larkin to Stearns, June 22, ibid., pp. 73–77, 80–81. Larkin to Buchanan, June 24; Pío Pico to Larkin, [June]; Larkin to Pico, July 5, Larkin, *Papers*, V, 71–72, 81–82, 104–5.

that Commodore Sloat might have prevented the Bear Flag revolt if he had moved his whole squadron to Monterey and had seized the port as soon as he received word of American–Mexican hostilities.[90] This is unlikely, for even the *Cyane*, which he sent north at once, did not arrive at Monterey until June 19, when the revolt had already begun. Nevertheless, the commodore's excessive caution contrasts sharply with the actions of nearly all of Polk's other agents in the Mexican War crisis. On May 31 Sloat belatedly learned of the battles at Palo Alto and Resaca de la Palma and accepted the existence of a state of war; yet he delayed action for more than a week. On June 7 he received notice that the American Navy had blockaded Veracruz. Upon this evidence of war, he finally sailed for Monterey.

When Sloat arrived at Monterey on July 1 or 2, he found two other American warships already at anchor, not including the *Portsmouth*, which had moved up to San Francisco. The political situation was confused, for unconfirmed reports of the Bear Flag revolt mingled with the older rumors of British intrigue. Sloat had no desire to reenact Commodore Thomas Jones' embarrassingly premature occupation of 1842, so he welcomed Larkin's advice to wait a few days before acting. Apparently, Larkin hoped that the local native population, frightened by the Bear Flaggers, would request Sloat's protection, thus facilitating the now inevitable occupation of the province by the United States. The presence of Castro in the Bay area with about four hundred men, gathered to put down the rebellion, may also have led the consul to fear an armed clash.[91]

Reports that the Bear Flag movement was spreading probably did more than any other circumstance to precipitate the final action. On July 5 Sloat received word from Montgomery, aboard the *Portsmouth*, indicating that Frémont had openly joined the Bear Flaggers and suggesting that the Mexican officials might be planning a campaign of extermination against American settlers.[92] The commodore called a council of war, at which some of his officers hotly urged action. Tormented by indecision, Sloat is said to

90. Larkin, *Papers*, V, vii.

91. Larkin to United States Commissioner and United States Consul for the Sandwich Islands, July 4, 1846, Larkin, *Papers*, V, 100–102. By now Larkin felt that the great inflow of Americans would bring about occupation during the year. See also Bancroft, *California*, V, 224–27.

92. John Berrien Montgomery to Larkin, Yerba Buena, July 2, 1846, Larkin, *Papers*, V, 94–96. Although Seymour and others assumed that Montgomery was aiding the rebels, he did no more than supply a few munitions, since Sloat had ordered him to remain neutral. Downey, *Cruise of the Portsmouth*, p. 129n7, 8.

have told Larkin, "We must take the place! I shall be blamed for doing too much or too little—I prefer the latter." Larkin and Sloat drew up a proclamation to the Californians, declaring the province annexed to the United States as a consequence of the war and extending peaceable American authority over them. On July 7 a detachment of 250 marines landed, marched to the custom house, and raised the American flag, while the three warships fired a twenty-one-gun salute. A few days later, Montgomery performed a similar ceremony at the little settlement of Yerba Buena (San Francisco), witnessed by about thirty inhabitants and a few dogs.[93]

Meanwhile, what of Admiral Seymour and the British squadron? When the *Juno* sailed from San Blas in May to reconnoiter, she carried on board the Irish priest-colonizer, Eugene McNamara, who had obtained permission in Mexico City to submit his proposal for colonization to provincial authorities. Stopping for a time at Santa Barbara, he secured from Governor Pico and the assembly a grant of three thousand square leagues, dated July 5, 1846. With the *Juno* in port, Pico appealed to Captain Blake for aid in resisting the Bear Flag rebellion. In a report to Seymour, which the admiral did not receive until late August, Blake described the uprising with considerable distaste. He repeated the rumor that Frémont was leading it as part of a systematic American plan of aggression and accused him of "organizing disturbances purposely to engender hostilities with the Country."

When Blake arrived in Yerba Buena six days later, he was surprised to see the United States flag flying over the settlement. Montgomery greeted him courteously and handed him a copy of Sloat's proclamation—all of which merely confirmed Blake's belief that the Americans had acted on a preconcerted plan. McNamara showed his grant to Larkin and asked him his opinion of its validity. When the consul declared that it was not in accordance with Mexican law, being larger than the maximum permissible size, McNamara abandoned his project.[94]

For a long time following the American occupation it was

93. Bancroft, *California*, V, 227–31. Hawgood, *First and Last Consul*, pp. 84–85. Bauer, *Surfboats and Horse Marines*, pp. 150–57. Okah L. Jones, "The Pacific Squadron and the Conquest of California, 1846–1847," *Journal of the West*, 5 (April 1966), 192–95. Larkin to Stearns, July 8, 1846; Larkin to Buchanan, July 10, Larkin, *Papers*, V, 115–16, 125–27. Rogers, *Montgomery and the Portsmouth*, pp. 57–70.

94. Bancroft, *California*, V, 217–20. Larkin to Buchanan, Los Angeles, August 19, 1846, Larkin, *Papers*, V, 204. Blake to Seymour, off Cape Concepción, July 5; Sausalito-San Francisco, July 17, Nos. 6, 7, GB, A 1/5562. Ernest A. Wiltsee, "The British Vice Consul in California and the Events of 1846," *California Historical Society Quarterly*, 10 (June 1931), 114–15.

believed that, after Seymour discovered Sloat's departure from Mazatlán, he guessed that the American intended to occupy California and set out in the *Collingwood* to race him for the prize.[95] H. H. Bancroft has gone to great lengths to disprove this myth, and after his book was published in the 1880s, Seymour's flag lieutenant, who was also his nephew and completely in his confidence, declared flatly, "I know for certain that Sir George Seymour never had orders to hoist the English flag in California, or to assume the protectorate of that dependency of Mexico in 1846, or at any other time. Neither was there a race between him and Commodore Sloat as to who would reach Monterey first."[96]

In addition to this evidence, it is now clear that Seymour's purpose in moving north was to carry out Aberdeen's much earlier instructions of December 31, 1844, which he had recently received. In a note of June 13 to British Minister Bankhead, written almost a week after Sloat had sailed, Seymour reported that he had received news of the proposed convention at Santa Barbara and intended to visit Monterey, reconnoiter, and try to persuade the inhabitants that they should resist annexation to the United States. But, he added, he expected to find that the inhabitants had voluntarily yielded to the Americans or that the latter had seized the port as a result of the outbreak of war with Mexico.[97]

Seymour's later report to the Admiralty explained his passive role in a spirit of unhappy resignation at the turn of events. He recognized the anti-British bias of the Bear Flaggers but approved Blake's inaction after Pico's request for aid, since he had no authority to give protection. The admiral also analyzed the feelings of Larkin and peaceable Americans accurately and described Sloat's occupation as a spontaneous move under cover of war. Since there had been no general declaration of independence, Mexico retained nominal title to the province. Aberdeen's orders not to intervene in this case and the legality of the American seizure—given a state of war—convinced Seymour that he should remain neutral. All he did, therefore, was to inform the Americans that he

---

95. One of Sloat's midshipmen claimed to have heard from British officers that as the *Collingwood* approached Monterey on July 16, Seymour had the quartermaster peering through a telescope toward the shore. When the man saw the American flag, Seymour stamped his foot and exclaimed, "*Then, by God, I am too late!*" Sherman, *Life of Sloat*, p. 79.

96. Lord Alcester to Clements R. Markham, London, May 19, 1887. "Californiana," *Century Magazine*, 40 (September 1890), 792–97. Bancroft, *California*, V, 207–15. Alcester was the former Lieutenant Beauchamp Seymour.

97. Seymour to Bankhead, San Blas, June 13, 1846, GB, FO 50/197, ff. 306–8.

would recognize only provisional occupation—not permanent possession, as Sloat's proclamation had announced. In the admiral's opinion, the Bear Flaggers had aroused so much anti-Americanism and the distance to Washington was so great that California would probably become an independent state. Under these circumstances, British control would be impossible without large bodies of troops and loyal emigrants. Lacking these, he thought it preferable not to involve British honor or interests with the struggle for possession of California.[98]

After staying at Monterey only a week Seymour weighed anchor for Hawaii and took Father McNamara with him. His departure may have been earlier than he had intended. On the day before his arrival, the long-awaited *Congress*, with Commodore Robert F. Stockton aboard, had sailed into the harbor, considerably strengthening the American naval force. Stockton had come around the Horn to Valparaiso, and then, despite the urgency of his orders, he had made a detour to Hawaii, never approaching the Mexican coast. He took over command at once from Sloat, who returned to the East Coast for another assignment.

Stockton's impulsiveness soon became evident in an ill-advised proclamation to the Californians, probably inspired by Frémont and Gillespie. In this document Stockton declared that the Americans had seized Monterey and San Francisco in reprisal for Mexican outrages on the Rio Grande and against Frémont and that he intended to conquer the interior and crush "these boasting and abusive chiefs . . . who unless driven out, will with the aid of the hostile indians [*sic*], keep this beautiful country, in a constant state of revolution and blood." When Sloat read the proclamation, he denied that it was an accurate account of his actions, and it increased the resentment the Californians already felt toward the Bear Flaggers and Frémont.[99]

Larkin continued his efforts to facilitate the American occupation. He had loyally supported Sloat, writing letters in his behalf to his merchant friends in the south and advising the Bear Flaggers to lay down their arms for a time and give Sloat a chance to organize his administration. Larkin had apparently known

98. Seymour to Secretary of Admiralty, Honolulu, August 27, 1846; Seymour to Pico, Monterey, July 23 (copy), GB, A 1/5577. Seymour to Forbes, July 22, Wiltsee, "British Vice Consul in California," pp. 118–19. Between Seymour's July and August dispatches he

learned of Gordon's defection in the *America*. See note 80.

99. Bancroft, *California*, V, 229, 256–58. Bauer, *Surfboats and Horse Marines*, pp. 158–62. For the proclamation, see Larkin, *Papers*, V, 175–77.

nothing in advance about Stockton's proclamation, but he favored extending American control into the interior and urged his friends to persuade Pico and the other officials to declare the independence of California: "This and this only can save the country. If the principal Natives do not openly—freely[,] frankly—and without prejudice to foreigners or fear of Mexico[,] for whom they have no sympathy[,] now come forward and proform [sic] this great and nobel [sic] act ... then they are woefully blind to their own honour and interest." Californians, he wrote, should "forget M[exico] as Mexico has forgot C[alifornia]."[100]

At first, the extension of the American conquest went well. By mid-August Stockton, Frémont, and Gillespie, uniting forces, had entered Los Angeles, scattered the government of Pío Pico, and proclaimed American authority throughout the province. Unfortunately, Gillespie's tactless administration soon provoked a revolt at Los Angeles, and before Stockton could come to his rescue, he was forced to surrender the town and retire to the coast.

After this setback, desultory marching and fighting by Americans and natives continued through the autumn until the arrival of General S. W. Kearny and his regular troops in December. Although Kearny and Stockton did not cooperate well at first, they managed to resolve their differences sufficiently to recapture Los Angeles on January 10, 1847, while Frémont pacified the north. Three days later the native leaders submitted to American rule in the "Cahuenga Capitulation"—actually a liberal agreement, free of vindictiveness, under which the Californians surrendered their arms and promised to obey American laws and to refrain from enlisting in the Mexican army. With this agreement the conquest of California was complete.[101]

Since Europeans had long foreseen the United States expansion to the Pacific, this conquest did not cause any great surprise. British newspapers went through the motions of protest: One compared the American occupation to the Norman Conquest as a "marauding and unscrupulous invasion," while another objected

---

100. Larkin to William Brown Ide, July 7, 1846; Larkin to James Stokes and Charles Maria Weber, July 7; Larkin to Stearns, July 14, August [6?], 7; Larkin to Robert Field Stockton, July 24; Larkin to Buchanan, July 20, [29], Larkin, *Papers*, V, 110–11, 132–34, 159–61, 180–82, 184–87. The quoted statements appear on pp. 133–34, 185–86.

101. For a brief account of these events, see Robert Glass Cleland, *A History of California: the American Period*, Chap. 16. Bancroft (*California*, V, Chaps. 11–16) is longer, but some details have been revised. See also Marti, *Messenger of Destiny*, Chaps. 4–6. Frémont and Kearny later quarreled, and Frémont was dismissed from the Army, court-martialed for mutiny, convicted, and then pardoned.

that Mexico had no right to give up territory mortgaged to British creditors.[102] In the United States, expansionists, both North and South, rejoiced that now their country was in a position to dominate the Pacific and to control the wealth of the golden East, as nature intended. "Some people seem to have very tender consciences of late as to conquests, etc.," wrote one, referring to the British. "I should like to know if half the earth is not now owned by the rights of conquests."[103]

"The rights of conquest" did not justify the American occupation for persons such as General Taylor, who felt that no British acquisition in the East was more outrageous than the United States seizure of California.[104] Others wondered whether the new territory would be free or slave, or whether it was enough to compensate the American people for a corrupt administration and an unpopular war. In short, by the time news of the final agreement at Cahuenga reached the East Coast, the question of California had merged with the larger question of how to secure peace with Mexico—a peace much desired but still as remote as ever.

102. London *Times*, July 15, 1846, p. 5; September 28, p. 4. The quoted phrase appears in London *Morning Chronicle*, August 3, p. 4.
103. F. W. Pickens to Buchanan, Edgewood, South Carolina, July 5, 1846, George Ticknor Curtis, *Life of James Buchanan, Fifteenth President of the United States*, I, 608–10. New York *Herald*, n.d., and New York *Journal of*

Commerce, December 17, quoted in Norman A. Graebner, "Maritime Factors in the Oregon Compromise," *Pacific Historical Review*, 20 (1951), 340–41.
104. Taylor to R. C. Wood, Camargo, August 23, 1846, Zachary Taylor, *Letters of Zachary Taylor from the Battlefields of the Mexican War*, p. 49.

14

The Expansion of the War

Even more than Polk and the American people realized, the length of the war was to depend on the staying power of the Mexicans. Ironically, Mexico, thanks to its history of confusion, mismanagement, and humiliation, was better prepared psychologically for a stalemate than the United States.

When Taylor began his advance to the Rio Grande, the immediate reaction of the Mexicans was defiant. Hard pressed by the opposition's demands for action, President Paredes sent first General Pedro Ampudia and then General Mariano Arista to Matamoros with reinforcements and orders to attack. On learning that the Americans had started to build a fort and had blockaded the mouth of the Rio Grande, Paredes drew up a formal proclamation, dated April 23, which may be regarded as the Mexican counterpart of Polk's war message. In this proclamation Paredes summarized "the ancient injuries and the attacks" Mexico had suffered since 1836 and revealed that he had ordered the northern army to advance on the Americans:

> I solemnly announce that I do not decree war against the government of the United States of America, because it belongs to the august Congress of the nation, and not to the Executive, to decide definitely what reparation must be exacted for such injuries. But the defence of Mexican territory which the troops of the United States are invading is an urgent necessity, and my responsibility before the nation would be immense if I did not order the repulse of forces which are acting as enemies; and I have so ordered. From this day defensive war begins, and every point of our territory which may be invaded or attacked shall be defended by force.[1]

1. This translation of Paredes' proclamation appears in George Lockhart Rives, *The United States and Mexico*, II, 142. For the whole text, see a flyer in GB, FO 50/196, f. 241. On the opposition press, see Dennis E. Berge, "Mexican Response to United States Expansionism, 1841–1848," Ph.D. diss., U. of California (Berkeley), 1965, pp. 191–92. On the Mexican government's orders to attack, see Salvador Bermúdez de Castro to Primer Secretario de Estado, March 29, 1846, No. 218, *Rdh-m*, III, 266–69; and John Black to F. M. Dimond, April 28, US, DS, PR, Consulate, Mexico City, Letterbook IV, 344–46. Smith cites these orders as important evidence of Mexican aggressive intent toward the United States. Justin H. Smith, *The War with Mexico*, I, 149–50, 155. The Mexican Congress did not formally declare war until June 16,

Thus, like Polk, Paredes proclaimed a war of defense. The American consul at Mexico City, John Black, dismissed the declaration as "nothing but a piece of humbug, to call the attention of the people, off from their doings here, and . . . to impress them with the idea, that it is the intention of the Government to commence hostilities, when people who know them generally believe that they have no intention of any such thing."[2] Events were to prove him wrong, and to this day in Mexican histories the war bears the title "Guerra de la Defensa."

*   *   *   *

When the news arrived in Mexico City near the end of April that Arista's army had captured an American patrol and drawn first blood in the long-expected conflict, it was accompanied by vague rumors of a more sweeping victory, which briefly exhilarated patriots and optimists.[3] Many Mexicans continued to hope for an Anglo–American war over Oregon and loans or ships from Britain with which to protect California. Some Mexican army leaders assumed that their European training and long experiences in civil wars made them invincible and that the ill-disciplined American volunteers, many of them Catholic immigrants, would be prone to desert.

Others who knew more about the two armies were much less confident. To be sure, the tough Mexican foot soldier could fight or march for days, clothed in rags and eating beans and tortillas, but he suffered from two grievous deficiencies—capable officers and dependable firearms. As one wag put it, the Mexican army had "brigades of generals rather than generals of brigades." Some officers were academically trained in European theory, but too many of them were political appointees, and almost no one in the higher ranks approached the best American professionals in tactical skill.

---

when it passed a resolution of General José María Tornel. The resolution listed as causes of the war American aid to the Texas revolution of 1836, the annexation of Texas, Frémont's entry into California, Taylor's advance and victories, and the Gulf blockade. José María Roa Bárcena, *Recuerdos de la invasión norteamericana (1846–1848)*, ed. Antonio Castro Leal, I, 38–39.

2. Black to James Buchanan, April 25, 1846, No. 367, US, DS, CD, Mexico City, IX.

3. Smith, *War with Mexico*, I, 115–16, 155, 442n28. Black to Dimond, May 5, US, DS, PR, Consulate, Mexico City, Letterbook IV, 363–64. See also reprints from various Mexican newspapers in *El monitor republicano*, April 7, pp. 1, 2. Enough Americans deserted to form a separate unit in the Mexican army, but they played a minor role. Richard Blaine McCornack, "The San Patricio Deserters in the Mexican War," *The Americas*, 8 (October 1951), 131–42.

Nearly all the infantry carried old flintlock muskets, discards from the British army. Knowing little of military drill, soldiers commonly fired from the hip without careful aim, to avoid the recoil. The Mexican army had a few good light cannons, but most were old and markedly inferior to the American artillery. Since the gunners had little training, maneuvers were out of the question.[4]

For some time before the crisis a few farsighted Mexicans had been discussing how best to carry on a war with the United States, if worse came to worst. Some favored fortifying the passes of the Sierra Madre and forcing the invaders to remain in the fever-ridden lowlands. Others wanted to fight on open plains, where the Mexican cavalry would have room to maneuver. Still others urged against any pitched battles, preferring to rely on guerrillas to harass American troops on the march and cut supply lines. At least one officer advocated a massive invasion of the United States.[5]

Internal weaknesses, however, imperiled even defensive measures. As usual the government was on the edge of bankruptcy, so that at the beginning of May it imposed a forced loan on the clergy in the capital and suspended payments on debts, thereby risking the united wrath of European creditors. (Paredes was astonished at the protests.)[6] Just as threatening, in April federalist leaders revolted in southern and western Mexico, raising a hue and cry against rumors of monarchism.[7]

4. Smith, *War with Mexico*, I, 156–57. Hubert H. Bancroft, *History of Mexico*, V, 303–4n48. The quoted phrase appears on p. 304. José C. Valadés, *Breve historia de la guerra con los Estados Unidos*, pp. 91–93. Bermúdez de Castro to Primer Secretario de Estado, May 29, 1846, No. 237, *Rdh-m*, III, 271–75. Bankhead to Aberdeen, April 29, 1846, No. 56, GB, FO 50/196, ff. 233–39. One scholar, examining the Mexican navy, concludes that it might have been used effectively for raiding if the Mexican government had been willing to risk the ships. Robert L. Scheina, "The Forgotten Fleet: the Mexican Navy on the Eve of the War, 1845," *American Neptune*, 30 (January 1970), 46–55.

5. Ramón Alcaraz *et al.*, eds., *Apuntes para la historia de la guerra entre México y los Estados Unidos*, p. 385. Those who participated in writing the book are listed on p. vii. For an indication of who was responsible for each major section, see Guillermo Prieto,

Memorias de mis tiempos, 1840 a 1853, pp. 265–66. For the invasion plan, see *El monitor republicano*, March 9, 1846, pp. 1–4.

6. F. M. Dimond to Buchanan, May 7, 1846, No. 338, US, DS, CD, Veracruz, V. Bankhead to Aberdeen, May 5, 7, Nos. 63, 65. GB, FO 50/197, ff. 4–9, 20–23. Bermúdez de Castro to Primer Secretario de Estado, April 29, No. 250, Legajo 1649, Spain, BAE. The Mexican government was so desperate that in order to obtain an advance of funds from the British firm Manning and Mackintosh it turned over to the firm for sale the two new Mexican warships *Guadalupe* and *Moctezuma*, constructed in Britain during 1842. These had been rusting at anchor, as the government had no money to man or equip them. Bermúdez de Castro to Primer Secretario de Estado, April 21, No. 229, Legajo 1649, Spain, BAE.

7. Black to Buchanan, April 26, 1846, No. 368, US, DS, CD, Mexico City, IX.

In the midst of these troubles, reports of Arista's defeats at Palo Alto and Resaca de la Palma and his retreat from Matamoros filtered back into central Mexico, spreading consternation and thick gloom. Since the government could not bring itself to publish an official announcement, rumors declared that the entire Mexican army had surrendered.[8] At Bankhead's suggestion an unidentified cabinet member sent a merchant friend to tell Consul Black that the government would now receive Slidell or some other envoy to discuss more than the Texas question. (The official was much surprised to learn that Black had no instructions to cover this possibility.)[9] Paredes himself went to the British minister, Bankhead, with an offer to mortgage California for a British loan, but Bankhead remained noncommittal. Faced with the pressing need to organize and equip more troops, the President could do no more than obtain extraordinary financial powers from Congress and hope for aid of some sort from the two greatest concentrations of capital, the Church and foreign merchants.[10]

The defeats at Palo Alto and Resaca de la Palma also gave the *coup de grâce* to the Spanish monarchist plot. When hostilities with the United States began, both cabinet and country were divided about the immediate feasibility of a monarchy in general and a Spanish prince in particular. A great majority of politically conscious Mexicans favored more stable government, but outside the capital at least, most of them would oppose a Spaniard with every means in their power, as the smouldering revolt in the south demonstrated. Unfortunately for the monarchists, the archbishop of Mexico died just at this time, weakening their strong ecclesiastical prop. The Spanish minister, Bermúdez de Castro, reported to his government that he had prepared a military movement to seize strategic points at a signal from Paredes, but that the president insisted on waiting for a victory in the north.[11]

Dimond to Buchanan, April 25, No. 334, ibid., Veracruz, V. Bankhead to Aberdeen, May 30, No. 74, GB, FO 50/197, ff. 126–28. Bermúdez de Castro to Primer Secretario de Estado, April 28, No. 238, Spain, Memorandum, February 14, AHN.

8. Bankhead to Aberdeen, May 30, 1846, No. 71, GB, FO 50/197, ff. 94–98. Berge, "Mexican Reaction," pp. 198–200.

9. Black to Buchanan, May 21, 1846, No. 372, Manning, *IAA*, VIII, 852–53. Black to Dimond, May 23, 28, US, DS,

PR, Consulate, Mexico City, Letterbook IV, 393–97. Bankhead to Aberdeen, September 7, No. 129, GB, FO 50/199, ff. 48–49.

10. Bankhead to Aberdeen, May 30, 1846, Nos. 72, 73, GB, FO 50/197, ff. 106–16, 120–23. Bermúdez de Castro to Primer Secretario de Estado, June 28, No. 264, *Rdh-m*, III, 277–80. Dublán and Lozano, *LM*, V, 135–36. Niceto de Zamacois, *Historia de Méjico desde sus tiempos más remotas hasta nuestros días*, XII, 488–90.

11. Bankhead to Aberdeen, April 29,

When the catastrophic news arrived from the Rio Grande, the president, desperately maneuvering to retain power, decided to embrace republicanism in a speech to Congress. Paredes' speech effectively alienated the monarchist bloc without winning over the republicans, who refused to trust him. Somewhat peevishly Bermúdez de Castro at once stopped publishing *El tiempo*, and the rest of the monarchist newspaper chain disappeared. He wrote sadly to Madrid that the monarchist party controlled Congress and might continue to expand, if only some leader could organize it and the country.[12]

Bankhead agreed with Bermúdez that a constitutional monarchy was probably the only hope for Mexico, but he felt that Bermúdez, Alamán, and their allies had set back their cause for many years by trying to force the issue and thus reviving Mexican hatred of Spain. Because of Mexican militarism, a foreign prince would need supporting troops. It was questionable whether any European nation would furnish them or whether the Mexican people would long tolerate foreign soldiers of any nationality.[13] From time to time monarchism stirred feebly in Mexico, and an occasional intriguer sought an interview with officials in London or Paris, but nothing comparable to the organized movement of 1845–1846 appeared again for more than a decade after the Americans had left Mexico.[14]

As the monarchist star sank below the horizon, another, more brilliant, rose in the east—that of Santa Anna, who for nearly a year and a half had been enjoying a comfortable exile in Havana. The two principal forces which restored him to power were as oddly matched as one could imagine: the chauvinistic *puros*, led by Santa Anna's long-deserted ally of the 1830s, Valentín Gómez Farías, and that archenemy of all Mexican patriots, the United States government. The *puros* saw in the shopworn dictator a hedge against monarchism and the best hope of organizing re-

---

May 30, 1846, Nos. 57–60, 72, GB, FO 50/196, ff. 254–62, 264–72, 274–77, 278–80; 50/197, ff. 106–16. Bermúdez de Castro to Primer Secretario de Estado, June 27, No. 268, Legajo 5869, Caja 2, Spain, AHN. Carlos María de Bustamante, *El nuevo Bernal Díaz ó sea Historia de la invasión de la Anglo-Americanos en México*, II, 154.

12. At least he stayed within his budget, for he had 10,000 pesos left over from his expense fund. Bermúdez de Castro to Primer Secretario de Estado,

March 29, April 28, May 29, 1846, Nos. 220, 238, 253, Spain, Memorandum, February 14; June 27, No. 268, Legajo 5869, Caja 2, Spain, AHN.

13. Bankhead to Aberdeen, May 30, June 9, 29, Nos. 72, 77, 90, GB, FO 50/197, ff. 106–16, 144–47, 294–98. Alexander Forbes to Bankhead, Tepic, July 2, GB, FO 50/198, ff. 38–45.

14. For example, José María Gutiérrez de Estrada to Viscount Palmerston, Paris, October 18, 1846, GB, FO 50/204, ff. 71–76.

sistance against the United States; Polk saw a man who might accept reality and negotiate a favorable treaty. A third party interested in Santa Anna was Britain, probably because he seemed to offer the best chance for stability and peace. Accordingly, the British consul in Havana treated the Mexican exile with great solicitude.[15]

The key figure in the negotiations between Santa Anna and Gómez Farías was Manuel Crescencio Rejón, a longtime ally of Gómez Farías and an inveterate Yankeephobe. He had made his peace with Santa Anna and had served him as his last minister of foreign relations before his overthrow. Although he accompanied Santa Anna into exile, Rejón continued to correspond with the *puro* leader. While the moderate Herrera was in power, Gómez Farías preferred to work with his underground in Mexico, but the accession of Paredes and the increasing rumors of monarchy made him more receptive to suggestions from Havana. In March 1846 Santa Anna sent to his agents in Mexico plans for a concerted uprising, but these misfired because of rivalries among local leaders. Late in April he wrote directly to Gómez Farías that the time had come to merge their parties and to "bring about a true fusion between the people and the army."[16]

At this time, Santa Anna and the United States were drawing closer together. The American consul at Havana established courteous relations and even invited him to the annual Fourth of July celebration in 1845, an engagement Santa Anna prudently declined. In February 1846 Santa Anna sent Alexander J. Atocha to solicit aid from Polk, offering the dubious advice that a strong stand would be the surest way of obtaining concessions from Mexico (see Chapter 11).

15. Goury du Roslan to François Guizot, Havana, August 7, 1846, No. 17, France, MAE, CP, Mexique, XXXIV, ff. 153–56. There is some evidence that Santa Anna tried to offer his services to Paredes. Luis Nicolau D'Olwer, "Santa Anna y la invasión, vistos por Bermúdez de Castro," *Historia mexicana*, 4 (Julio-Septiembre 1954), 50.

16. Santa Anna to Valentín Gómez Farías, April 23, 1846; quoted in José Fuentes Mares, *Santa Anna, aurora y ocaso de un comediante*, pp. 235–36. At the same time, Gómez Farías wrote to Santa Anna. Their letters crossed in the mails, perhaps by design. See C. Alan Hutchinson, "Valentín Gómez Farías and the Movement for the Return of General Santa Anna to Texas in 1846," in Thomas E. Cotner and Carlos E. Castañeda, eds., *Essays in Mexican History*, pp. 175–87, for a full account of the negotiations. Wilfrid Hardy Callcott, *Santa Anna, the Story of an Enigma Who Once Was Mexico*, pp. 225–29. Most of Rejón's correspondence with Gómez Farías is reprinted in Manuel Crescencio Rejón, *Correspondencia inédita de Manuel Crescencio Rejón*, ed. Carlos A. Echanove Trujillo, pp. 62–80. For a biographical sketch of Rejón, see ibid., pp. 9–21. On the pronouncement and the planned uprising, see Black to Buchanan, April 26, 1846, No. 368, with enclosures, US, DS, CD, Mexico City, IX.

As soon as Congress passed the war bill, Polk proclaimed a blockade of the Mexican Gulf coast but privately instructed Commodore Conner to let Santa Anna through if he tried to return home. During the first month of the war Polk was said to have sent a private agent to see Santa Anna in Havana, and an American newspaper reported that cronies of the Mexican exile had arrived in the United States, probably to make contacts.[17] Whatever the extent of these early feelers, Polk left no reference to them in diary or correspondence, and they came to nothing. In the confused days after hostilities began, Paredes imprisoned several *santanistas* and even Gómez Farías for a time, so that Santa Anna decided to wait in Havana for a few weeks longer. He continued to release enticing remarks that might find their way to the United States.[18]

During June, Polk decided to send a mission to Santa Anna. Not trusting Atocha, he chose as his emissary a young Navy commander, Alexander Slidell Mackenzie, the nephew of John Slidell. According to his later statement, the President orally instructed Mackenzie to find out tactfully whether Santa Anna would negotiate peace with the United States, if restored to power in Mexico. The commander went to Havana and on July 6, 1846, conversed for three hours with Santa Anna. Not appreciating diplomatic niceties, Mackenzie exceeded his instructions by writing out a memorandum of Polk's views, which he presented to his host. In this memorandum he stated that the President wanted Santa Anna restored to power, that he would insist on the Rio Grande boundary and at least part of California, and that he would pay liberally for these cessions.

Nothing could have been more bland than the Mexican's response. To be sure, he insisted that the Nueces River was the true boundary of Texas, but he reaffirmed his belief in liberal, republican principles for Mexico, expressed admiration for American political leaders, and declared that if Mexico remained in chaos or turned to monarchy, he would go to Texas and become an American citizen! Meanwhile he favored an early peace without European mediation. He felt that if Taylor could advance to

17. George Bancroft to David E. Conner, May 13, 1846, US, 30C, 1S, HED 60, p. 774. Smith, *War with Mexico*, I, 479n37. Luis G. Zorrilla, *Historia de las relaciones entre México y los Estados Unidos de América, 1800–1958*, I, 196. New York *Herald*, September 2, p. 2.

Bermúdez de Castro to Primer Secretario de Estado, August 28, No. 318, *Rdh-m*, III, 286.

18. Hutchinson, "Gómez Farías and the Return of Santa Anna," p. 187. New Orleans *Picayune*, May 19, as paraphrased in *NNR*, 70 (June 6), 211.

Saltillo, defeat Paredes, and occupy San Luis Potosí, the Mexican people would surely revolt and recall Santa Anna. At the same time the American Navy could easily capture Tampico and Veracruz. He cautioned Mackenzie to keep this advice strictly confidential, since the Mexicans might misinterpret his "benevolent desires to free them from war," but when the commander suggested informing Taylor, Santa Anna reluctantly consented.[19]

Mackenzie left the great man's presence firmly believing in his good faith and immediately visited Taylor at his headquarters on the Rio Grande to transmit Santa Anna's advice. Although Mackenzie soon learned that Santa Anna had confided the conversation to the British consul, he continued to think that self-interest if nothing else would direct the Mexican's policies toward the United States. Months after Santa Anna had returned to Mexico, Mackenzie continued to insist that his inclinations were peaceful. When rumors of the encounter surfaced, Mexicans naturally suspected that their general had sold out to the United States. No one has ever found conclusive evidence of this, but Santa Anna's patriotism was then, as always, shaped to serve his own interests. The most that can be said for him on this occasion is that his advice was as harmful to the United States as to Mexico.[20]

During the weeks after Mackenzie's visit to Havana, circumstances in Mexico improved Santa Anna's prospects for returning to power. *Santanistas* and liberals tightened their uneasy coalition; the government released Gómez Farías from prison; and rebellion spread through the west. When Paredes again appealed to Bankhead for aid, the British minister suggested making inquiries about peace negotiations through United States Consul Black. Paredes and his cabinet hesitated, for they had originally gained power by denouncing the Herrera regime for just such negotiations.[21]

19. Eugene Irving McCormac, *James K. Polk, a Political Biography*, pp. 439–40. Alexander Slidell Mackenzie to Buchanan, Havana, June [July] 7, 1846, Polk Papers, CV, LC. This letter is printed in Jesse Reeves, *American Diplomacy under Tyler and Polk*, pp. 299–307. The American consul at Havana, Robert B. Campbell, took no part in the discussion.

20. George Gordon Meade, *The Life and Letters of George Gordon Meade, Major-General United States Army*, I, 115–16. Mackenzie to Buchanan, July 11, 1846, Polk Papers, CV, LC. Mackenzie to Nicholas P. Trist, November 25,

Trist Papers, XXII, ff. 59806–7. Zamacois, *Historia de Méjico*, XII, 505–7. Bancroft, *Mexico*, V, 301–2. D'Olwer, "Santa Anna y la invasión," pp. 54–55.

21. Vicente Riva Palacio, *México a través de los siglos*, IV, 566–69. Bancroft, *Mexico*, V, 297–98. Bankhead to Aberdeen, May 30, June 9, 29, July 30, 1846, Nos. 72–74, 76, 78, 88, 89, 92, 100, 104, 105, GB, FO 50/197, ff. 106–16, 120–23, 126–28, 138–39, 153, 276–78, 284–87, 314–17; 50/198, ff. 155–57, 187–90, 192–93. If Paredes did put out feelers to Black at this time, it is not apparent from Black's dispatches. Black to Buchanan, June 13, 27, July 4, 11,

Bankhead believed that if Paredes had continued in power, he would have managed to open negotiations with the United States, but now the president's time had come. At the beginning of August he started north to take command of the army, leaving his vice president to control the government in Mexico City, and this action touched off the culminating revolt in Veracruz and the capital. Army officers arrested Paredes en route, and General José Mariano Salas assumed power as provisional president. With the aid of Gómez Farías, Salas ordered a new Congress to convene and declared the federalist Constitution of 1824 once more in force. He also issued a proclamation bidding Santa Anna to return and lead the army to "victory or a glorious death . . . on the banks of the Bravo." It was soon clear that Salas was merely keeping the presidential chair warm for the exiled hero. (This solicitude, however, did not apply to the leftover proceeds from Paredes' clerical loan, which soon disappeared from the Treasury.) [22]

Santa Anna was only too glad to accept the invitation, and on August 8 he boarded a specially chartered British steamer with Juan N. Almonte, Rejón, and Atocha. Santa Anna later denied that Mackenzie had informed him of his *laisser-passer* through the blockade. The steamer broke down midway in the voyage, and while the crew were making repairs, an American warship approached, inspected the derelict and its distinguished passengers, and allowed them to proceed as soon as the repairs had been completed. They landed in Veracruz on August 16, to be received by Gómez Farías' three sons, a broken-down infantry regiment, and a few stragglers. Considering the sullen aspect of the people, Santa Anna prudently retreated to his private estate after issuing a grandiloquent proclamation to the nation he had come to save. [23]

16, Nos. 377–81, Manning, *IAA*, VIII, 864, 871–75.

22. Bankhead to Aberdeen, August 1, 4, September 7, 1846, Nos. 108, 110, 111, 129, GB, FO 50/198, ff. 203–5, 227–28, 229–34; 50/199, ff. 48–49. Zamacois, *Historia de Méjico*, XII, 490–504. Bancroft, *Mexico*, V, 298–301. Riva Palacio, *México a través de los siglos*, IV, 570–72. Bustamante, *Nuevo Bernal Díaz*, II, 195–98. Dublán and Lozano, *LM*, V, 146–56. Hutchinson, "Gómez Farías and the Return of Santa Anna," pp. 189–90.

23. Ibid. Callcott, *Santa Anna*, pp. 237–41. Berge, "Mexican Response," p. 221. *NNR*, 71 (September 26, 1846), 49. Conner to Bancroft, August 16, 25, Address of Santa Anna, Veracruz, August

16, US, 30C, 1S, HED 60, pp. 776–85. Bankhead to Aberdeen, August 29, No. 121, GB, FO 50/198, ff. 345–48. For Santa Anna's later denials, see Antonio López de Santa Anna, *Apelación al buen criterio de los nacionales y estrangeros. Informe que el Ecsmo. General de división, Benemérito de la patria D. Antonio López de Santa-Anna, dió por acuerdo de la Sección del gran jurado, sobre las acusaciones presentadas por el Sr. diputado Don Ramón Gamboa*, pp. 16–19. H. H. Bancroft accepts this version of Santa Anna's return. Bancroft, *Mexico*, V, 301–2. For a Mexican account completely favorable to Santa Anna, see Valadés, *Breve historia*, pp. 81–87.

In the meantime Polk had decided to approach the Mexican government directly without waiting for Mackenzie's mission to bear fruit. On July 23 the State Department received a dispatch from Consul Black, stating his opinion that the Mexican government would welcome a peace commission; if he should be wrong in his judgment, it would do the government and country good "to give them a little more drubing [*sic*], and the nearer it can be done to the Capital the better."[24] Four days later, after consulting Benton, Polk and Buchanan sent a note by way of Commodore Conner, inviting Paredes to negotiate either in Mexico City or in Washington. The note mentioned no terms but remarked significantly: "The past is already consigned to history; the future, under Providence, is within our own power."[25]

This cheerless bid for peace did not arrive in Mexico City until August 30. By that time Salas was in the presidential chair, and Gómez Farías (treasury) and Rejón (foreign relations) headed a cabinet of liberals and Yankeephobes. Following a meeting, held that night, Rejón replied briskly that the executive could not decide such a momentous question at his discretion but needed to submit it to Congress, which would not convene until December 6. Bankhead was disgusted with what he regarded as the senseless obstinacy of the government, but he consoled himself with the reflection that Santa Anna probably had reached a secret understanding with the Americans.[26]

Soon after this futile exchange Santa Anna began a slow progress toward Mexico City, during which his spirits were refreshed by increasing signs of popular approval. As he approached the capital, functionaries hastily brought out portraits of the hero that had been gathering dust in odd corners since his last overthrow, while carpenters knocked together triumphal arches. On the eve of Independence Day he paraded through the city in an open carriage with Gómez Farías, dressed in civilian clothes and holding a copy of the Constitution of 1824 prominently displayed. For the time being, Salas remained provisional president, while Santa Anna took command of the army and threw himself into the tasks of recruiting, organizing, and improvising supplies. Two weeks

24. Black to Buchanan, June 13, 1846, No. 377, Manning, *IAA*, VIII, 864.

25. Buchanan to the Minister of Foreign Affairs of Mexico, July 27, 1846, Manning, *IAA*, VIII, 193–94.

26. Manuel Crescencio Rejón to Bu-chanan, August 31, 1846, Manning, *IAA*, VIII, 885–86, Zamacois, *Historia de Méjico*, XII, 508–9. Bankhead to Aberdeen, September 7, No. 128, GB, FO 50/199, ff. 31–35.

after his triumphal entry, on September 28, he led three thousand men north toward San Luis Potosí.[27]

From the outside the Mexican political changes since the outbreak of war seemed to favor Polk's ambitions. The stubborn nationalist Paredes had been overthrown and his monarchist clique dispersed. To be sure, the presence of Gómez Farías and Rejón in the cabinet made immediate negotiations unlikely, but rumors had begun to circulate about dissension within the Salas administration. The continuance of the war depended largely on Santa Anna, who had earlier listened to American talk of negotiations but had now apparently decided that the popular temper required action against the foe. This decision did not surprise British Minister Pakenham in Washington, who, being well acquainted with Mexican leaders, had never expected them to accept Polk's proposal.[28] Still, as Santa Anna marched northward, no one could be sure—perhaps not even the general himself—whether his military heroics were bona fide or merely an opening drum roll leading into a peace overture.

*　　*　　*　　*

British newspapers, as has been seen, reported the news of the war with outbursts against American greed and treachery, arising from long-nursed resentment at the nation's growth and from accumulated grievances over state debts, boundary quarrels, and slavery. Although the British press might warn dramatically that United States control of Mexico boded ill for Europe, no one proposed a rush to Mexico's rescue. Even before Taylor's victories were known, many observers assumed that Mexico was doomed. Others, considering Mexico's formidable geography, guessed that Polk would give up the war as soon as he had occupied California and other border areas.[29] The real danger to be feared from British

27. Callcott, *Santa Anna*, pp. 241–43. José Fernando Ramírez, *Mexico during the War with the United States*, ed. Walter V. Scholes, trans. Elliott B. Scherr, pp. 77–78. Valadés, *Breve historia*, pp. 95–97.

28. Ramírez, *Mexico during the War*, pp. 80–81. Rejón, *Correspondencia*, pp. 83–84. Richard Pakenham to Palmerston, August 13, September 28, 1846, Nos. 107, 109, GB, FO 5/450, ff. 114–18, 196–203.

29. Louis McLane to James K. Polk,

[May 1846], Polk Papers, CIV, LC. McLane to Buchanan, June 3, No. 54, Manning, *IAA*, VII, 276–78. Justin H. Smith, "Great Britain and Our War of 1846–1848," *Massachusetts Historical Society Proceedings*, 47 (June 1914), 451–62. London *Examiner*, May 30, 1846, p. 338; June 13, p. 370. London *Spectator*, May 30, as paraphrased in Frederick Merk, *The Monroe Doctrine and American Expansionism, 1843–1849*, pp. 165–66.

resentment was not armed intervention but a public offer of mediation, which would greatly inflame the antiwar bloc in the United States and embarrass the Polk administration. Humanitarianism, concern for British investments in Mexico, or the fear that Mexico would commission a fleet of privateers and ruin Anglo–American trade—any or all of these factors might sway the British government. McLane pointed out the danger and urged Polk to enforce a tight blockade, so as to forestall legalistic complaints and end the war quickly.[30]

In its relations with Mexico Britain had no reason to feel much but exasperation. First Mexico had postponed its recognition of Texas too long to support any of the Anglo–French plans for encouraging Texan independence. Then the Mexicans had ignored repeated advice from the British to forget their past losses, stabilize their government, reform their finances, and prepare realistically for their own defense. After more than a year of tedious negotiations, British bondholders and the Mexican minister in London refunded the long-unpaid debt in an agreement of June 4, 1846, that was highly favorable to Mexico. A month earlier, however, Paredes had abruptly suspended all debt payments of any sort in an action that was widely believed to have emanated from his minister of hacienda (treasury), a notorious speculator in local short-term notes. As soon as Gómez Farías became minister of hacienda in Salas' government, he repudiated the debt agreement.[31]

Bankhead deplored these evidences of Mexican irresponsibility and tried valiantly to offset the influence of men whom he regarded as Paredes' iniquitous advisers, in particular Secretary of War Tornel. The British minister repeatedly discussed Mexican–American relations and monarchism with Paredes and forwarded the president's appeals to London. After Taylor's victories Bankhead outlined the desperate Mexican situation in a group of simultaneous dispatches and added, in a private letter of May 31 to Aberdeen, that nothing would save Mexico except a European-

30. McLane to Buchanan, June 3, 1846, No. 54, Manning, *IAA*, VII, 276–78.

31. Bankhead to Aberdeen, May 5, 20, 1846, Nos. 63, 70, GB, FO 50/197, ff. 4–9, 60–63. For the terms of the agreement, see Chap. 13, n.17. Later in the year the Salas government approved the agreement but then revoked it again. Santa Anna finally proclaimed its ratification on July 19, 1847, but by that time the war had made any payments impossible. Edgar Turlington, *Mexico and Her Foreign Creditors*, pp. 91–94. Jan Bazant, *Historia de la deuda exterior de México (1823–1946)*, pp. 63–68. Valadés, *Breve historia*, pp. 68–70. For samples of the outraged public reaction in Britain, see New York *Herald*, November 16, 1846, p. 1.

supported monarchy. But Aberdeen had already fixed his policy. Before Bankhead's communications had left Mexico, he was writing to him that Britain could not undertake a war in which she would bear the principal burden against an enemy with whom she had no quarrel of her own and in behalf of an ally who had ignored all previous advice: "Solely in consequence of their wilful contempt of that warning, [the Mexicans] have at last plunged headlong down the precipice from which the British Govt. spared no efforts to save them." [32]

Aberdeen was more responsive to petitions for mediation from Britons with economic interests in Mexico. One of these, dated June 2, came from J. D. Powles of the London bondholders. Powles predicted much injury to British trade and other enterprises as a result of a war unjustly forced on Mexico. A few days later Aberdeen called in McLane to discuss the American proclamation of blockade. To allay fears of British intervention he read the American minister his most recent instructions to Bankhead and then brought up the subject of mediation. According to a British memorandum, the foreign secretary asked McLane to convey a mediation offer to the President.

According to McLane, however, Aberdeen told him that Britain would undertake any plan to further peace but did not intend to propose mediation, presuming that the offer would be rejected. McLane indicated that this supposition was correct, since war had been forced on the United States. Buchanan approved his response to the unofficial British "communication . . . in relation to the subject of mediation." Later, the Polk administration decided to deny that Aberdeen's cautious advance was an offer of mediation. Whatever the semantic distinction, each side had made its point. For the time being, neither would act lest the other set up exorbitant conditions and improve its bargaining position. [33]

When Palmerston succeeded Aberdeen in the Foreign Office,

32. Bankhead to Aberdeen, May 31, 1846, Aberdeen Papers, BM, AM, vol. 43126, ff. 27–28; May 30, Nos. 71–74, GB, FO 50/197, ff. 94–98, 106–16, 120–23, 126–28; Aberdeen to Bankhead, June 1, 1846, No. 15, GB, FO 50/194, ff. 32–36. This dispatch is reprinted in George Lockhart Rives, *The United States and Mexico, 1821–1848*, II, 162–63.

33. J. D. Powles to Aberdeen, June 2, 1846, reprinted in *NNR*, 70 (June 27), 258–59. McLane to Buchanan, June 18,

No. 55; Buchanan to McLane, July 27, No. 44, Manning, *IAA*, VII, 28–29, 281–84. Memorandum in GB, FO 50/216, ff. 186–92v. Smith, *War with Mexico*, II, 301–2, 503–4n14. For a discussion of whether Aberdeen's overture constituted a real offer, see McLane to Buchanan, August 15, No. 69, Manning, *IAA*, VII, 284–87. Pakenham to Aberdeen, June 28, July 13, 29, Nos. 82, 93, 99, GB, FO 5/449, ff. 204–7; 5/450, ff. 44–46, 80–83.

McLane took care to draw him out on the subject of the war. Subsequently, he reported to Polk that he saw no signs of any disposition to aid Mexico but that Palmerston might make a fairly explicit offer of mediation. McLane pointed out to the foreign secretary that a vigorous attack on Mexico was the best way to peace, but Palmerston would not accept his view that the Mexican government was on the verge of collapse.[34] Powles also petitioned the new administration to negotiate an alliance treaty with France and Mexico and so guarantee the territorial integrity of Mexico, but Palmerston's refusal was clear and absolute: "That, he said, would involve greater exertions & responsibilities than this country [Britain] could be expected to encounter. We have just settled our Oregon question with the United States. We can hardly be expected to raise up another object of collision directly."

When Powles reported these dismal tidings to his friend Consul Ewen C. Mackintosh in Mexico City, he attributed the new cabinet's policy to an ingrained distaste for the fecklessness of Mexican institutions:

> They are fully alive to the extent of British interests involved in that country, but beyond the offer of mediation which has been made, they are at a loss to know how they can assist Mexico. . . . *Nobody has any confidence in her power to govern herself.* I believe that both the British & the French Governments are so disgusted with the arrogance, the dishonesty & the rapacity of the United States, that they wo[ul]d encounter some risk for the protection of Mexico if they felt that they could *depend upon Mexico herself.* . . . But they see nothing in Mexico but internal discord and at home they hear nothing of her but complaints from merchants & Bond holders. The Mexicans have little idea of how deeply they have injured their political position by their neglect of their public credit in Europe.

Powles added that Palmerston regarded Mexico's long-maintained refusal to recognize Texas as stubborn folly and the rejection of Slidell's mission on a point of form as frivolity in the face of serious danger.[35]

Since Palmerston held Mexico in such low regard, it is not surprising that he also turned down Paredes' offer to mortgage

34. McLane to Polk, August 2, 1846, Polk Papers, CV, LC. McLane to Buchanan, August 15, No. 69, Manning, *IAA*, VII, 284–87.

35. Powles to Ewen C. Mackintosh, London, August 24, 1846, Manning and Mackintosh Papers, University of Texas Libraries. Powles was surprised at what he called Polk's impulsive offer to negotiate. In the long run, he hoped for a European protectorate over Mexico.

California, with the explanation to Bankhead in a note of August 15 that even if such a policy were otherwise feasible, Mexico did not have military control of the province and could not guarantee its transfer. Palmerston's only action was to instruct Bankhead to propose mediation. The foreign secretary told Pakenham to make a similar proposal to Buchanan—in terms somewhat more explicit than Aberdeen had used, but privately and unofficially, in order to avoid an outburst of Anglomania in the expansionist sector of the American press.[36]

Both sides rejected Palmerston's offer. Polk learned of it on September 10, while he was still awaiting a reply to the peace proposal he had made to Mexico in August. Without giving Buchanan time to return from a holiday, he convened the cabinet and drew up a brief refusal, on the grounds that mediation would probably prolong the war.[37] According to Bermúdez de Castro, Santa Anna and Rejón would not consider the British offer because they regarded it as proceeding entirely from selfish anxiety to preserve British trade and investments, for which they felt that Palmerston was all too ready to sacrifice Mexico's honor and territory. Later in the year, when Bankhead, under instructions, renewed the offer in stronger terms, the Mexican government referred it to Congress, thus unwisely giving it full publicity.[38] These actions increased Palmerston's scorn for the Mexican government, and thereafter he usually answered its appeals for aid by reminding it of this refusal to listen to British reason.

The British public accepted Palmerston's realistic policy with only occasional murmuring. At the end of August, Tories in the House of Commons raised questions about the effect of American expansion on British interests in Mexico. Palmerston answered by expressing doubt that the United States could annex such a large and diverse area and by pointing out that the government at Washington had accompanied its war measures with a beneficial lower tariff. This was not enough for Benjamin Disraeli, who seized the occasion to eulogize British commercial and financial interests

36. Palmerston to Bankhead, August 15, 1846, No. 4, GB, FO 50/194, f. 60. Palmerston to Pakenham, August 18, No. 10, cited in Smith, *War with Mexico*, II, 301, 504n17.

37. James K. Polk, *The Diary of James K. Polk during His Presidency, 1845 to 1849*, ed. Milo M. Quaife, II, 129–33. Pakenham to Palmerston, September 13 (with enclosure), 28, Nos. 116, 119, GB, FO 5/450, ff. 174–77, 196–203.

38. Bermúdez de Castro to Primer Secretario de Estado, September 24, 27, 1846, Nos. 332, 343, cited in Smith, *War with Mexico*, II, 368n7. Palmerston to Bankhead, October 31, No. 13, GB, FO 50/194, ff. 80–82. For a summary of British mediation efforts, see a memorandum of May 29, 1847, GB, FO 50/216, ff. 186–93.

in Mexico; he proposed a British protectorate, using Greece as a model. But he got no support, and the discussion closed with ironic Tory congratulations to Palmerston for his peaceableness.[39] A day or two later the *Times* agreed with the administration that, while the Mexicans' "contemptible weakness" did not justify "the arrogant and unjust dealings of the United States towards them," the vague, unproved possibility of damage to British trade or investments furnished no grounds for action.[40] As time passed, the two principal British contributions to the Mexican War continued to be olive branches and brickbats—mediation feelers from the government and insults from the press.

The role of onlooker suited France even better. The French minister to the United States, Alphonse Pageot, advised his government that successful mediation was unlikely until the American people became so tired of a deadlocked war that they rose up in protest. *Le journal des débats*, deploring American ambitions, again recommended a monarchy for Mexico, and later in the year a rightist pamphlet urged united European intervention lest Taylor's army seize Mexico's mines and shut off Europe's supply of silver. Characteristically, the French government would not consider acting alone, especially with the unpredictable Palmerston in the British Foreign Office.[41]

* * * *

Thus, free from any immediate risk of European interference, Polk could fight his war. When Thomas Hart Benton wrote his memoirs several years later, he acutely summarized the President's initial strategy:

> It is impossible to conceive of an administration less warlike, or more intriguing, than that of Mr. Polk. They were men of peace, with objects to be accomplished by means of war; so that war was a necessity and an indispensability to their purpose; but they wanted no more of it than would answer their purposes. They wanted a small war, just large enough to require a treaty of peace, and not

39. *Hansard Parliamentary Debates*, 3d series, LXXXVIII, cols. 978–95.

40. London *Times*, August 26, 1846, p. 5. For an echo of these sentiments in the Canadian press, see Montreal *Herald*, September 23, reprinted in New York *Herald*, October 24, p. 1.

41. Alphonse Pageot to Ministère des Affaires Étrangères, August 30, 1846, No. 132, France, MAE, CP, États Unis,

CII, ff. 207–10. *Le journal des débats*, September 19, p. 1. Anonymous, *Le Mexique et l'Europe* [etc.], *passim*. The liberal opposition continued to support the United States as a counterpoise to Britain. *Le national*, June 30, 1846, p. 1. *La presse*, June 26, p. 1. *Le correspondent*, 15 (July), 144–45. See also Merk, *Monroe Doctrine and American Expansionism*, pp. 167–71.

large enough to make military reputations, dangerous for the presidency. Never were men at the head of a government less imbued with military spirit, or more addicted to intrigue.[42]

In his first discussions with Marcy and Scott, Polk declared that the United States must seize the northern provinces of Mexico and hold them until a peace treaty was signed, and he lost no time in sending armies into California, New Mexico, and Chihuahua. By the end of June the cabinet was discussing with some heat whether the United States should demand a boundary at 32° (the latitude of El Paso) or 26° (the latitude of the mouth of the Rio Grande, including most of Chihuahua, Sonora, and Lower California).[43] This policy of limited attack and occupation underlay the early orders to Taylor and Kearny, Mackenzie's mission to Santa Anna, and the unsuccessful peace feeler of July.

Polk's plan for a short, sharp war and a quick peace immediately encountered obstacles. Taylor's two initial victories profoundly discouraged the Mexicans but failed to stifle their national pride, and the presence of nationalists such as Gómez Farías and Rejón in Salas' government discouraged any consideration of peace. Also, Polk and Marcy, who shared his chief's over-all strategic outlook, soon discovered that fighting even a small war required careful planning, intensive training, and tortuous logistics.

The reluctantly chosen commander, General Winfield Scott, held a much more realistic view of the war, and, recognizing how narrow had been Taylor's escape from disaster, he was determined to minimize such risks in the future. Unfortunately, Scott did not fully appreciate the political necessities behind Polk's strategy and replied to his impatient calls for action with patronizing explanations of military needs. Although Marcy tried to mediate between his two prickly colleagues, their tempers rose. Finally, Scott wrote imprudently to the secretary that he had no intention of placing himself "in the most perilous of all positions:—*a fire upon my rear, from Washington, and the fire, in front, from the Mexicans.*" At this imputation of treachery, Polk and Marcy changed their plan

---

42. Thomas Hart Benton, *Thirty Years View*, II, 680. This view is confirmed by a letter of Polk to his younger brother in Europe, advising him not to come home and enlist: "In regard to the Mexican war, my impression . . . is, that it will be of short duration. I doubt that there will be much more fighting unless it be in a guerrilla warfare." He thought that Paredes might stake everything in a single battle. James K. Polk to William H. Polk, July 14, 1846, Polk Papers, letterbooks, series 4, roll 57, LC.

43. Polk, *Diary*, I, 400, 403–4, 437–40, 443–44, 472–75, 481, 495–97. Marcy, however, earlier favored a boundary at 34° or 36°. William L. Marcy to Prosper M. Wetmore, June 13, 1846, Marcy Papers, XI, ff. 34652–53.

to send Scott to the front and kept Taylor in his field command for the time being. Scott continued to organize the Army, but his pompous protestations made him a laughingstock and confused the prosecution of the war.[44]

Meanwhile, the need for a speedy settlement became more pressing, as public opposition to the war organized and spread. During the congressional debate on Polk's war message and for a time thereafter the opposition was handicapped by the difficulty of distinguishing between patriotic defense and unjustified aggression.[45] The distinction became clearer day by day, as the facts about Taylor's activities on the Rio Grande circulated and the proadministration press aided the pacifists with ill-timed exhortations to war. A day or two after learning of Taylor's victories, for example, the Washington *Union* proclaimed: "We mean to conduct war against Mexico with all the vigor in our power. . . . *We shall invade her territory; we shall seize her strongholds; we shall even* TAKE HER CAPITAL, *if there be no other means of bringing her to a sense of justice."*[46]

Statements like this, which certainly called for more fighting than Polk had planned at that time, raised a storm of criticism. Calhoun's Charleston *Mercury* opposed Polk's call for fifty thousand troops, predicting that Mexico would sue for peace after a few more defeats and warning against militarism and dictatorship: "Let us not cast away the precious jewel of our freedom, for the lust of plunder and the pride of conquest." The Whig Richmond *Times* was willing to seize Mexican mines and Pacific harbors but scornfully rejected further advances, asking, "Are we prepared to place on a perfect equality with us, in social and political position, the half-breeds and mongrels of Mexico? The idea is revolting; and yet nothing less is to be expected from this

44. McCormac, *Polk,* pp. 418–20. Ivor Debenham Spencer, *The Victor and the Spoils, a Life of William L. Marcy,* pp. 151–56. Charles Winslow Elliott, *Winfield Scott, the Soldier and the Man,* pp. 423–32. Polk, *Diary,* I, 415–21, 424–26, 428–29. For Marcy's optimistic view of the war, see his letter to Wetmore, June 13, 1846, Marcy Papers, XI, ff. 34652–53. Scott also talked to Pakenham in such a way as to inform him that he was ashamed of the war and opposed to acquiring Mexican territory. Pakenham to Palmerston, September 28, private and confidential, GB, FO 5/540, ff. 208–10.

45. For example, see Washington *National Intelligencer,* May 16, 1846, p. 3. As one Whig writer put it succinctly: "We toast the *men,* but not the cause." *American Review,* 4 (August), 179. The question of voting supplies for armies in the field particularly tried the consciences and the ingenuity of the opposition. Frederick Merk, "Dissent in the Mexican War," in Samuel E. Morison et al., *Dissent in Three American Wars,* pp. 45–47.

46. Washington *Union,* May 29, 1846, quoted in Washington *National Intelligencer,* May 30, p. 3.

mighty annexation." "The conquest to us is worthless," added the Philadelphia *North American*, also Whig. "No wealth, for Mexico is beggared—no power, for if subdued it would exhaust us to watch her—no honor, for she is not a warrior worthy of our steel."[47]

At its best, the antiwar bloc recalled to Americans some of the noblest qualities in their country's tradition. The Richmond *Daily Republican* appealed for mercy and generosity: "Let us, whilst we terminate the Oregon controversy amicably with a great nation, show that we scorn to trample on the waning power of a feeble adversary." The independent New York *Journal of Commerce* went further and advocated free trade with Mexico to make possible her "complete political, moral, and industrial regeneration" even while the war was going on, but of course many Whigs, being protectionists, could not accept this corollary.[48]

An outstanding advocate of lenience was Joel Poinsett, who was still regarded in Mexico as a spearhead of imperialism, although he had always opposed war. In a series of articles for *DeBow's Review* Poinsett found "something noble and chivalrous . . . which compels respect" in Mexico's "high resolve" to defend the line she regarded as the rightful boundary of Texas. Considering the Mexicans' unfortunate history, "nearer to the sixteenth than the nineteenth century," Americans should not revile them for their ignorance but should rejoice that at least some of them were liberal and wanted to imitate American institutions. Poinsett recalled his warm reception by Mexican federalists during the 1820s and urged the administration to conciliate them rather than to attack and alienate them forever. In urging conciliation he was probably overly optimistic, for many left-wing federalists—the *puros* under Gómez Farías—had already rejected any thought of negotiating with the United States. Poinsett was on stronger ground when he advised against placing any trust in Santa Anna.[49]

Before long, these scattered antiwar arguments had gained

---

47. Extensive reprints of opposition editorials, from which these quotations are taken, may be found in Washington *National Intelligencer*, June 12, 1846, p. 3; June 20; June 29, p. 3. Thomas Ritchie of the Washington *Union* had just read the Charleston *Mercury* out of the Democratic party. Charles M. Wiltse, *John C. Calhoun, Sectionalist, 1840–1850*, p. 263.

48. Richmond *Daily Republican*, n.d., reprinted in Washington *National Intelligencer*, June 20, 1846. New York *Journal of Commerce*, July 11, 1846, quoted and refuted in Washington *National Intelligencer*, July 15, p. 3.

49. Joel Poinsett, "The Mexican War," *DeBow's Review*, 2 (July 1846), 21–24. Poinsett, "The Republic of Mexico," ibid., pp. 27–42. Poinsett, "Mexico and the Mexicans," ibid. (September), pp. 164–77.

coherence and had permeated large sections of major interest groups in the States. Many leaders of business and trade, now becoming centered in New York City, opposed the war as they had opposed the annexation of Texas because they feared to stimulate abolitionism and thus weaken the profitable economic ties with the South. There the immediate effects of the attack on Taylor were disastrous: bank credit in New Orleans congealed, cotton sales down, freight rates rising, and no market in sight for Western produce. Soon the fear of Mexican privateers and even of war with Britain made an indefinite interruption of the cotton trade seem probable. In London the news more than counterbalanced the cheering effects expected from repeal of the corn laws. Later in the year four hundred New York merchants offered a petition denouncing the war. As long as it lasted, the leading commercial journals and reviews kept up a chorus against "this unhappy strife, and the uncertainty which . . . hangs like an incubus over the market, paralyzing enterprise and retarding the growth of commercial confidence."[50]

As in most wars, the attitude of American churches reflected the mixed feelings of the people as a whole and their confusion between mercy and righteous indignation. Roman Catholics, especially their press, differed as to the justice of the war, but most agreed that, once begun, it must be fought through to victory. Some Protestants shared these feelings; others were divided or took no stand. Anti-Catholic animus against Mexico was considerably less intense than might have been expected, thanks to the war fervor of American Catholics and to distraction by other issues. Opposition to the war centered in the Quakers, the Congregationalists, and the Unitarians.[51]

The pacifism of the Quakers surprised no one. That of the New England churches was mainly due to one issue, which grew steadily as the conflict continued until it had swallowed up all other issues and dominated the opposition to Polk and his war.

50. Philip Foner, *Business and Slavery; the New York Merchants and the Irrepressible Conflict*, pp. 14–19. *NNR*, 70 (May 23, June 20, 1846), 192, 241. New York *Courier and Enquirer*, May 30, as reprinted in London *Times*, June 15, p. 5. Gurston Goldin, "Business Sentiment and the Mexican War with Particular Emphasis on the New York Businessman," *New York History*, 33 (January 1952), 54–70. The quotation appears on pp. 62–64.

51. C. S. Ellsworth, "The American Churches and the Mexican War," *American Historical Review*, 45 (January 1940), 301–26. Ted C. Hinckley, "American Anti-Catholicism during the Mexican War," *Pacific Historical Review*, 31 (May 1962), 121–37.

This issue was hatred of slavery and fear that it would expand into any territory acquired from Mexico. Eventually, James Russell Lowell put the matter in a nutshell: "They jest want this Californy So's to lug new slave-states in." Not satisfied with Florida, the South coveted Texas; not satisfied with Texas, she now wanted northern Mexico; where would this overbearing spirit lead the nation? Despite Northern business interests in the South, abolitionism so strained the Whig party in Massachusetts that it split into two factions, sardonically labeled "Cotton" and "Conscience" Whigs.[52] In their frenzy, abolitionists ignored the powerful antiwar sentiment that pervaded the South and discounted Calhoun's efforts to prevent Congress from declaring war. The South Carolina Senator's past indiscretions now returned to haunt him, for abolitionists pointed to his defense of slavery in the famous letters to Pakenham and King (see Chapters 5, 6) as evidence of his real attitude toward annexing Mexican territory.

Thus, out of many ingredients—abolitionism, antimilitarism, concern for business, fear of presidential tyranny, contempt for Mexico, and a sense of *noblesse oblige*—critics of the war prepared their recipe for opposition. Soon their arguments began to affect observant politicians in Congress and the cabinet. For example, as early as July 7, when Buchanan and Walker argued over trying to push the boundary south of 32°, Polk attributed the former's reluctance to "contracted & sectional" views about acquiring southern territory.[53]

The most serious opposition in Congress during the waning session appeared in response to the President's proposal for a special appropriation of $2 million. This sum he suggested in order to purchase California and New Mexico at once if Mexico showed any disposition to relinquish the provinces. During April Polk had already discussed such a fund with several advisers, only to lay the idea aside for the time being. At the end of July, as soon as Congress had passed the tariff bill, the President again proposed the special appropriation to the cabinet and to congressional leaders of both parties and sent a confidential message to the Senate.

52. "The Biglow Papers," *The Complete Writings of James Russell Lowell*, X, 63. Originally published in 1848. Burdett Hart, *The Mexican War, A Discourse Delivered at the Congregational Church in Fair Haven, on the Annual Fast of 1847*, pp. 12, 15, *et passim*. See also Anonymous, *The Mexican War*. On the Massachusetts Whig party, see Thomas H. O'Connor, *Lords of the Loom: The Cotton Whigs and the Coming of the Civil War*, pp. 64–73.

53. Polk, *Diary*, II, 15–16.

Hoping to share responsibility, he asked for a supporting resolution which, he thought, would spur the House to initiate the necessary money bill.[54]

Many Whig senators approved the appropriation but insisted that Polk secure it through a direct request to the House. As in the manipulations over Oregon, Polk's tactics of evasion and camouflage infuriated the opposition. On August 8, two days before adjournment, a Democrat who served the administration introduced the Two Million Bill into the House, and it came up for debate in the evening session, a boisterous occasion at which several members were drunk and general confusion prevailed. A minor Democrat from northeastern Pennsylvania, David Wilmot, offered an amendment, which borrowed the phraseology of the Northwest Ordinance of 1787 to declare that slavery should be prohibited in any territory acquired from Mexico. A bloc consisting mostly of Whigs and Northern Democrats passed the amended bill. But a filibuster developed in the Senate, and on August 10 Congress adjourned without taking further action.[55]

The origins of the Wilmot Proviso have always puzzled historians. While abolitionism was obviously its main foundation, it gained some support from protectionists and other enemies of the administration. Polk believed that, without the Senate filibuster, the administration's men in both Houses could have worked out a compromise. Perhaps he was right, for abolitionists had not yet perfected their arguments against the "slaveholders' war," and John Quincy Adams himself announced that he would vote for the Two Million Bill with or without the Proviso.[56]

Polk's impatience over the "mischievous & foolish amendment" arose from an assumption that, with two million dollars at his instant disposal, he could have prevailed on Salas or Santa Anna to negotiate a peace of annexation.[57] Events of the succeeding months proved his assumption wrong. The real significance of the Wilmot Proviso was that it focused opposition to the war on a weak point in the expansionists' case and provided for Polk's enemies a parliamentary device with which to harass the adminis-

54. Polk, *Diary*, II, 56–60, 71–72. Even Benton felt that Polk should approach the House directly.

55. McCormac, *Polk*, p. 442. Polk, *Diary*, II, 72–75. NNR, 70 (August 15, 1846), 374.

56. Charles Buxton Going, *David Wilmot, Free-Soiler*, Chap. 9. More recent interpretations emphasize the role of party politics and sectionalism. Chaplain W. Morrison, *Democratic Politics and Sectionalism: The Wilmot Proviso Controversy*, Chap. 1. Eric Foner, "The Wilmot Proviso Revisited," *Journal of American History*, 56 (September 1969), 262–79.

57. Polk, *Diary*, II, 75, 77–78.

tration and obstruct its policies for the remainder of the war. The harassment and the retaliatory fury of Polk's Democrats widened the developing crack between North and South.

* * * *

"Mexico is an ugly enemy," wrote Daniel Webster to his son just before Congress adjourned. "She will not fight—& will not treat." [58] The last words were prophetic, for within six weeks Polk learned that his first peace overtures had been rejected. In the meantime Taylor advanced slowly, hoping to end the war with victory in the field. As soon as he had occupied Matamoros in mid-May he wrote to the War Department for further orders, indicating how little he knew about navigation on the Rio Grande or the location of Mexican troops.

During May and June, Marcy and Scott sent him somewhat conflicting orders. Marcy told him to move up the Rio Grande as far as Laredo, if this were practical, and to occupy Monterrey, the state capital of Nuevo León, thought to be healthier than the coastal plain. He asked Taylor's opinion as to whether the campaign should extend south to Mexico City or remain in the northern provinces. A few days later, Scott ordered Taylor to seize "the high road to the capital," but, should this advance be successful, he authorized the general to "conclude an armistice for a limited time, and refer the proposition to treat of peace to the government here." At the same time, Scott detached some of Taylor's forces under Brigadier General John E. Wool and sent them on a detour westward to occupy Chihuahua. [59]

A number of factors complicated Taylor's execution of these orders. The plan of limited warfare—advancing, striking, and waiting for the enemy to make peace before repeating the cycle—demanded exceptional flexibility and coordination. Unfortunately, communications usually required three or four weeks to travel between Washington and the Rio Grande, and this time lag increased as Taylor advanced into Mexican territory. Clearly, neither the War Department nor the general fully appreciated each other's difficulties; for example, they quarreled about a shortage of wagons, for which neither was responsible. One may well won-

58. Daniel Webster to Fletcher Webster, August 6, 1846, Daniel Webster, *The Letters of Daniel Webster*, p. 343.
59. Zachary Taylor to Adjutant General, Matamoros, May 21, 1846, No. 43;

Marcy to Taylor, May 28, 30, June 8; Polk to Taylor, May 30; Winfield Scott to Taylor, June 12; R. Jones to John E. Wool, June 11, US, 30C, 1S, HED 60, pp. 281–83, 300, 323–28.

der whether Taylor ever fully understood the subtleties of Polk's war plan. The confusion and stresses of the campaign, the flood of unruly volunteers and camp followers, and the hot, sticky climate eventually wore away some of his bluff patience. He became suspicious of the President to the point of resenting Polk's delays in congratulating him on his victories. Ambitious Whig friends suggested that a triumphant general would have a promising political future, and Taylor, at first cheerfully contemptuous, began to listen to their blandishments. As word of these political interests got back to Polk, his doubts about Taylor's military capability returned.[60]

In one respect Polk's hopes for peace came close to realization, for early in the summer of 1846 secessionism was strong in northeastern Mexico. The state government of Coahuila had refused to recognize Paredes' regime until coerced by national troops. In February a dissident officer, José M. J. Carvajal, had visited Taylor at Corpus Christi with news of a cabal to overthrow the local government and a proposal for American support and negotiation of differences. He urged Taylor not to advance farther south, arguing that the two people should not come into closer contact until Mexicans were better acquainted with American institutions. Polk and Marcy received Carvajal's proposals, but they continued with their original plans and instructed Taylor to take advantage of Mexican disaffection but not to supply arms for the rebels. The cabal was unable to act before the beginning of hostilities. On June 1, after Taylor had occupied Matamoros, a Spanish–English newspaper, *República de Rio Grande y Amigo del Pueblo*, began publication. It denounced Mexican abuses—especially tariffs—and "British insolence," and it urged the inhabitants to proclaim an independent republic and free trade with the United States. So many secessionists in all districts of Coahuila, Tamaulipas, and Nuevo León communicated with Taylor that the correspondent of the New York *Sun* wrote home: "A new Star is shining out amid the ragged clouds of war."[61]

60. Smith, *War with Mexico*, I, 204–9, 227. David Lavender, *Climax at Buena Vista, The American Campaigns in Northeastern Mexico, 1846–47*, pp. 86–92. For a good summary of historical views regarding Taylor's military reputation, see Edward J. Nichols, *Zach Taylor's Little Army*, pp. 263–69. On communications problems, see Elliott, *Scott*, p. 444n25.

61. Justin H. Smith, "La República de Río Grande," *American Historical Review*, 25 (July 1920), 664–67. The quotation from the New York *Sun* appears on p. 667. Vito Alessio Robles, *Coahuila y Texas, desde la consumación de la Independencia hasta el Tratado de paz de Guadalupe Hidalgo*, II, 325. A copy of the first issue of the bilingual newspaper is in GB, FO 50/197, f. 288.

The Republic of the Rio Grande died a-borning. Taylor had little confidence in the movement, and United States sentiment about secessionism in Mexico was at best mixed, for many Americans preferred to win a total victory over a united enemy. Too, Polk was never willing to guarantee independence to the secessionists. For their part, the Mexicans had second thoughts about religious and racial antagonism and the competition of American imports. As the summer progressed, Taylor's slow movements caused doubts of his strength, and when Salas proclaimed the federalist Constitution of 1824, he raised hope for local autonomy within the Mexican system.

Perhaps most important, the influx of American volunteers, profiteers, and roughnecks into Matamoros drove away the influential upper classes and confirmed the worst fears of Yankeephobes. Soon the streets were filled with drunks carrying bowie knives, rifles, and pistols, which they used at the slightest provocation. Foreseeing such disorders, on July 9 Polk and Marcy sent Taylor urgent instructions to encourage dissension within Mexico and to ensure that his troops dealt honorably and kindly with the people.[62] As the Americans moved southward, their organization and discipline improved, but Polk's exhortations to foment secessionism came too late to have any significant effect. Although secessionists in the northeast continued sporadic intrigue throughout the war, they provided only minor aid to the Americans.

Taylor believed that the best way to encourage a local revolution was to carry out his original orders and advance toward Monterrey. At the end of July, therefore, he began to move most of his troops painfully up the shallow Rio Grande, some on steamboats, others on foot through dusty thickets of brush and mesquite along the banks. Within a month he had established new headquarters at Camargo, an ill-chosen, sickly site. Stung by Democratic editorials about his slowness (which his friends obligingly sent after him), on September 1 Taylor fired off a tactless complaint to Washington "in justice to myself and the service," blaming his troubles on the inefficiency of the quartermaster corps.[63] Then he turned up the San Juan River, a tributary of the Rio Grande, and marched his men toward Monterrey.

62. Smith, "República de Río Grande," pp. 668–70. F. L. Giffard to Francis Giffard, Matamoros, June 9, 1846; F. L. Giffard to Bankhead, August 5, GB, FO 50/197, ff. 290–93; 50/198, ff. 297–300. Marcy to Taylor, July 9, 1846, US, 30C, 1S, HED 60, pp. 333–36.

63. Smith, War with Mexico, I, 209–12. Taylor to Marcy, August 1, 1846, US, 30C, 1S, HED 60, pp. 336–38. Taylor to Adjutant General, September 1, 1846, No. 83, ibid., pp. 557–58.

Arriving at the outskirts on September 19, they found it to be a well-built city, protected on the south by a river and on the west by hills, and with a Mexican army occupying strong fortresses at the eastern, northern, and western entrances. Driven back as he approached from the northeast, Taylor sent the able General William J. Worth with a strong force around the north edge of the city during the night to attack the western defenses. Although drenched by rain, Worth's men seized the defenses after hard fighting, while Taylor's main forces battered away on the northeast. For three days the Mexicans fought stubbornly, but they gradually retreated into the center of the city, until on September 24 their commander asked for terms. Next day they began to evacuate the city.

Taylor had won a substantial victory over perhaps ten thousand defenders with an army of not more than 6,500 half-sick men at the end of a long supply route. Although Monterrey's inhabitants were on the verge of panic, the Mexican forces obtained lenient terms—the right to withdraw beyond the mountains to the southwest without surrendering their arms or giving their parole and a truce of eight weeks during which Taylor promised not to advance farther.[64] When he was later criticized for his generosity, Taylor justified his terms with many arguments. He did not know the true state of the defenders' morale; his men had already suffered heavily and, he judged, faced days of fighting through narrow streets. Even without the truce the troops were in no condition to advance beyond Monterrey. The Mexican commander, General Ampudia, told him that Santa Anna was ready to sue for peace; Scott's instructions authorized a truce under such conditions.[65] Unfortunately, by the time Taylor's dispatches reached Washington, Polk had shifted to a more aggressive policy, so the

---

64. Smith, *War with Mexico*, I, Chaps. 11, 12. Robert Selph Henry, *The Story of the Mexican War*, Chap. 9. Lavender, *Climax at Buena Vista*, Chap. 6. Edward S. Wallace, *General William Jenkins Worth, Monterey's Forgotten Hero*, Chaps. 8, 9. Riva Palacio, *México a través de los siglos*, IV, 581–89. Alcaraz et al., *Apuntes para la historia de la guerra*, Chap. 3. The truce was made subject to later orders by either government. In order to distinguish the two cities, that in northern Mexico will be spelled *Monterrey*, the port in California *Monterey*.

65. Taylor to Adjutant General, September 25, November 28, 1846, Nos. 91, 107, US, 30C, 1S, HED 60, pp. 345–46, 359–60. Taylor to R. C. Wood, September 28, Zachary Taylor, *Letters of Zachary Taylor from the Battle-fields of the Mexican War*, p. 61. Taylor to John J. Crittenden, October 9, John J. Crittenden Papers, X, ff. 1877–79, LC. See also letters by Jefferson Davis and Worth defending the armistice, reprinted in J. F. H. Claiborne, *Life and Correspondence of John A. Quitman, Major-General, U.S.A., and Governor of the State of Mississippi*, I, 262–69. Smith, *War with Mexico*, I, 259–60, 501–6. Lavender, *Climax at Buena Vista*, pp. 119–20.

news of the victory and the truce served only to widen the breach between them.

While the administration, press, and public followed Taylor's advance closely, they paid only occasional attention to the astounding successes of American armies farther west, mainly because poor communications caused the dispatches to arrive irregularly. By January 1847 Frémont, Stockton, and Kearny completed the conquest of California. During Kearny's westward march in the middle of the preceding August, he had occupied Santa Fe without meeting any serious resistance, had declared New Mexico annexed to the United States, and had established civil government there.

While Kearny was advancing in California, Colonel Alexander W. Doniphan pushed south to El Paso and, early in 1847, set out for Chihuahua city. Near there, on February 28, he won the only important battle of the campaign, at the Sacramento River, and captured the city without further fighting. Late in 1846 another army, under General John E. Wool, who was operating without definite instructions, entered Monclova and Parras, to the west and northwest of Monterrey.[66] Doniphan and Wool rejoined Taylor without attempting to establish permanent occupation of their conquests, as had been done in New Mexico and California. However, their easy penetration of northern Mexico and the receptiveness of the inhabitants deeply discouraged Mexican leaders, since these successes revealed how feeble was their government's hold on the northern third of the country.

*   *   *   *

Thus, before the war was a year old, the United States Army not only occupied the territories which Polk regarded as his goals but also demonstrated that it might not be difficult to extend these goals considerably. The tempting vistas of lands waiting for conquest concealed incalculable risks, for the difficult topography and climate were too little known in the United States, and the ever-expanding war was placing greater and greater strains on American finances, unity, and morale. Nevertheless, through 1846 and on into 1847 the dauntless President pushed forward, secure in his assumption that a strong attack was the shortest road to peace.

The key to further expansion of the war was to be the capture of Tampico and Veracruz. Even before the outbreak of hostilities

---

66. Rives, *US and Mexico*, II, 208, 213–19, 289–91, 368–76. Smith, *War with Mexico*, I, Chaps. 13–15. Henry, *Story of the Mexican War*, Chap. 14. Alcaraz et al., *Apuntes para la historia de la guerra*, Chap. 9.

Polk and his advisers had lightly considered a possible attack on the latter city's guardian fortress of Ulua. Replying to Bancroft's inquiry in the autumn of 1845, Commodore Conner of the Gulf Squadron submitted a formidable list of the reinforcements which he would need for such an attack; he also mentioned that he had a reasonably accurate plan of the fortifications.[67]

After the war had begun, Marcy inquired of Taylor on June 8 about the feasibility of an attack overland as far as Mexico City. Having received no reply, he and Polk drew up a longer inquiry on July 9, mentioning an attack on both Gulf ports and especially Veracruz, which, they had heard, could be taken by a landing force that would by-pass Ulua. "From *Vera Cruz* to the city of Mexico," they added, "there is a fine road, upon which the diligences or stage coaches run daily." Polk attached great importance to this inquiry, which he wrote himself, but apparently he did not discuss the matter at any length with the cabinet and the subject disappeared from his diary for nearly two months. During the summer, however, officials continued to gather data, and rumors of an imminent attack on Veracruz began to appear in the press.[68]

It would be interesting to know all the sources of information about the Mexican Gulf Coast and interior on which Polk based his judgments. From Consul Black he received encouragement and a few maps and itineraries. The President left no record of his own reading, but as soon as war was declared, Marcy began to devour everything about Mexico that he could obtain. He could not have missed William H. Prescott's *History of the Conquest of Mexico*, published in 1843 and now being widely read; it undoubtedly conditioned the American people at large to expect or accept an invasion from the Gulf Coast.

Marcy was especially impressed with Frances Calderón de la Barca's detailed memoirs about her two years' residence in Mexico during the early 1840s. Señora Calderón had little to say about Tampico, which she visited for only a day, but at Veracruz she mentioned the "miserable conditions" of Ulua, which the French had taken in three days. She described with distaste the hot, humid city (in mid-December) and the rough road leading toward the capital, but she went into raptures about the beauty and richness of the interior and its balmy climate, "that of a July day in Eng-

67. Conner to Bancroft, September 3, 1845, US, DN, LCS, roll 84, no. 108.
68. Marcy to Taylor, July 9, 1846, US, 30C, 1S, HED 60, pp. 333–36. Polk, *Diary*, II, 16–17. Dimond to Conner,

August 17, David E. Conner Papers, box 10, NYPL. For an example of press rumors, see Washington *National Intelligencer*, July 18, p. 3.

land."[69] Neither Marcy nor Polk mentioned reading a more pertinent book, the official account of the French intervention during 1838 and 1839. The two authors of this book, both trained observers, fully described the Gulf storms and above all the yellow fever, which almost wrecked the French expedition—this in a season that the American consul at Veracruz characterized in his dispatches as more healthful than the average.[70]

As long as Polk and the cabinet hoped for prompt and favorable negotiations with Santa Anna, their plans to attack the Gulf ports remained tentative and academic. On September 1 the government learned that Commodore Sloat had seized the Pacific port of Monterey and declared California an American possession.[71] A few days later the New York *Herald* printed a rumor from Mexico to the effect that Santa Anna had agreed to preliminary peace terms that included agreement on the Rio Grande as boundary and the establishment of an American protectorate over California. But unwelcome tidings soon arrived: on September 10 the British offer of mediation, which Polk declined, and on September 19 a message from the Mexican government postponing consideration of negotiations until the meeting of Congress in December. The Mexican rejection of Polk's offer apparently shook his self-confidence, although after some days' reflection he wrote to his brother that Santa Anna was probably just procrastinating until he was more securely in power, lest he cause a revolution.[72]

The President's next reaction was characteristic—a series of bold moves to expand the broad front already presented to the Mexicans and to convince them that there was no alternative to negotiation. He and Marcy instructed Taylor and other generals in northern Mexico to seize necessary supplies from the local popu-

69. Spencer, *Victor and Spoils*, p. 153. Frances Calderón de la Barca, *Life in Mexico*, pp. 24–27, 35, 524–26, *et passim*. Page references are to the 1931 edition. Sra. Calderón was the Scottish-born wife of the first Spanish minister to Mexico.

70. On the blockading difficulties and health conditions, see P. Blanchard and A. Dauzats, *San Juan de Ulua, ou rélation de l'expédition française au Mexique sous les ordres de M. le contre-amiral Baudin*, pp. 51–52, 68–75, *et passim*. L. E. Hargous to John Forsyth, Veracruz, August 25, 1838, No. 98, US, DS, CD, Veracruz, III. In his dispatch of September 3, 1845 (see note 67), Conner stated that he had examined facts and circumstances concerning the French attack, but he did not specify the book of Blanchard and Dauzats.

71. Ironically, the news of Sloat's occupation reached the United States government by way of the British legations in Mexico City and Washington. Polk, *Diary*, II, 107–8.

72. New York *Herald*, September 11, 1846, p. 4; September 12, p. 2. Polk, *Diary*, II, 129–33, 144–45. Polk to Gideon Pillow, September 22; James K. Polk to William H. Polk, October 2, Letterbook, 1845–1846, pp. 743–51, 787–96, Polk Papers, LC. The New York *Herald* agreed with Polk. New York *Herald*, September 24, p. 2.

lation, but without paying for them as their original orders had specified. More important, Polk, Marcy, and John Y. Mason, the new secretary of the navy, drew up plans for the immediate occupation of Tampico by Commodore Conner's Gulf Squadron and for a supporting Army campaign in the interior of Tamaulipas. Partly alienated from Taylor by his complaints and the reports of his political interests, Polk entrusted the command of this new expedition to Major General Robert Patterson, a recent Democratic appointee with almost no military experience. Since Sloat had taken California, and news now arrived that Kearny had seized Santa Fe, the occupation of Tampico and its hinterland would establish a strong line all the way across northern Mexico.[73]

Just after deciding on this advance Polk received Taylor's announcement that he had captured Monterrey in northern Mexico and had granted the Mexicans an eight-week truce. The public rejoiced, but the President bit his lip and complained to his advisers that Taylor had let slip the complete victory that would have compelled negotiations and had stymied any immediate advance with his truce. Buchanan and others agreed that Ampudia and his army had been "bagged" but could now retreat thirty miles beyond a mountain pass and prepare to fight again. Polk would probably have recalled Taylor but for his general popularity and the lack of a good substitute. Instead, the President merely ordered him to end the truce and prepared him for the detachment of troops to serve in the Tamaulipas campaign. After a discussion of strategy in the cabinet on October 20, it was decided to keep Taylor at Monterrey and to recall Wool's forces from Chihuahua.[74]

The fall congressional election campaigns now added to the administration's concern over its war strategy. After the adjournment of Congress in August the Whig press had developed its arguments against the war, the Walker tariff, and other administration measures. When Mexico rejected the American peace overture, the Washington *Union* proclaimed Polk's policy of vigorously pushing the war to "bring its pressure home to the people of Mexico . . . [and] make them feel the evils of the war

73. Polk, *Diary*, II, 144–50, 154, 175–76, 179–80. Marcy to Taylor, September 22, 1846; Marcy to Robert Patterson, September 22, US, 30C, 1S, HED 60, pp. 341–45. Lavender, *Climax at Buena Vista*, pp. 123–24.

74. Scott to Crittenden, Washington, October 19, 1846, Crittenden Papers, X,

ff. 1884–85. Polk, *Diary*, II, 181–86, 198–200. Marcy to Taylor, October 13, 22, US, 30C, 1S, HED 60, pp. 355–57, 363–67. Lavender, *Climax at Buena Vista*, pp. 123–24. Taylor had earlier doubted the wisdom of extending the supply lines farther.

more strongly, in order that they may appeal to their own Government for peace." This pronouncement produced a new Whig outburst to the effect that Polk was trying to conceal his past blunders with a war against the Mexican people which would continue for years. The *Union* retorted with accusations of treason.[75] As soon as Polk's role in the return of Santa Anna to Mexico became known, it added fuel to the flames. Even Kearny's almost bloodless occupation of Santa Fe caused trouble, for on instructions he proclaimed it United States territory without any act of Congress and thereby horrified strict constructionists.[76]

The administration party's losses in the by-elections were possibly no greater than usual, but they included some dramatic upsets—the defeat of able Governor Silas Wright in New York and setbacks in Buchanan's Pennsylvania. These losses served to discredit the administration before the whole nation.[77]

*　　*　　*　　*

When the electioneering ended in October, Polk faced a choice between two broad plans of war strategy—each with its advocates, and almost impossible to combine in a compromise. One plan, essentially defensive, would minimize commitment and risk. This was to strengthen the existing line of troops and fortifications across northern Mexico, organize United States government in California and New Mexico, encourage inhabitants of the northern provinces to secede (without guaranteeing their independence), and wait until the Mexicans grew tired of war and Santa Anna concluded that it was safe to negotiate. Buchanan favored this plan as the more prudent and less expensive; so did Marcy and Taylor.[78] Its principal drawbacks were that it required pa-

---

75. Washington *Union*, October 2, 1846, reprinted in Washington *National Intelligencer*, October 5, p. 3. Philadelphia *North American*, n.d., reprinted in Washington *National Intelligencer*, October 21, p. 3. Washington *Union*, October 30, p. 618.

76. St. Louis *Republican*, n.d., reprinted in Washington *National Intelligencer*, October 6, 1846, p. 3. Ibid., October 24, p. 3.

77. Washington *National Intelligencer*, November 7, 1846, p. 3; November 10, p. 3. Morrison, *Democratic Politics*, pp. 21–26.

78. Buchanan to Bancroft, December

29, 1846, Bancroft Papers, MHS. Spencer, *Victor and Spoils*, p. 160. For a time before the capture of Monterrey, Taylor felt that it would be necessary to take Veracruz and Mexico City. Taylor to Adjutant General, Matamoros, July 2, No. 68, US, 30C, 1S, HED 60, p. 331. Taylor to Crittenden, Camargo, September 15, Monterrey, October 9, December 12, Crittenden Papers, X, ff. 1859–62, 1877–79. Others who favored this plan of action were Poinsett and Donelson. Poinsett advised a senator that the United States should decide what territory it intended to keep and simply tell Mexico. "She will bluster

tience of the American people and offered little glory with which to silence the opposition.

The other plan was to seize Ulua and Veracruz, march an army to Mexico City, and dictate peace in "the halls of the Montezumas." Benton, Slidell, and ultraexpansionists in general favored such strategy as more heroic, faster, and the surer way to a complete and definitive victory.[79] This aggressive plan was much the riskier of the two, for it required complicated military operations over difficult and little-known topography, careful health precautions against a deadly climate, and long supply lines of a sort the United States had never before attempted. On the one hand, a single defeat might undo the effect of all previous victories and encourage Santa Anna to hold out for years; on the other hand, continued victories might create momentum and demand for unthought-of annexations.

The only element the two plans had in common was the capture of Tampico, equally important as the eastern anchor of a defensive line and as base and dress rehearsal for the descent on Veracruz. Orders had gone out for the Tampico expedition late in September. The Mexicans had intercepted Marcy's earlier dispatch of September 2 to Taylor, announcing the likelihood of such an expedition, and they would undoubtedly have anticipated it in any case. Convinced that the port was impossible to defend, for lack of adequate approach roads across the mountains, Santa Anna ordered its evacuation, and on November 14 Conner took it without difficulty or glory. Indeed, his principal problem was to improvise a garrison, for Patterson had been unable to coordinate his movements with the naval squadron. The American occupation was uneventful and played only a minor part in the rest of the war, while Patterson's campaign in the interior of Tamaulipas was abandoned as the front moved south.[80]

Through the autumn of 1846 Polk and the cabinet continued to argue the merits of the rival plans. During this critical period

and protest, but never attack you. Her leaders have too much at stake to venture so far from the Capital." Joel Poinsett to A. P. Butler, December 12, Joel Poinsett Papers, XVI, HSP. Andrew J. Donelson to Buchanan, December 22, Buchanan Papers, box 64, HSP.

79. Benton, *Thirty Years View*, II, 693–94. John Slidell to Polk, New Orleans, November 4, 1846, Polk Papers, CIX, LC. Same, January 6, 1846 [1847], Buchanan Papers, box 24, HSP.

80. Alcaraz *et al.*, *Apuntes para la historia de la guerra*, Chap. 5. Smith, *War with Mexico*, I, 276–82. Rives, *US and Mexico*, II, 292–93. Lavender, *Climax at Buena Vista*, Chap. 7. By November, Polk and his advisers realized that mountain passes and poor roads would render Tampico virtually useless for attacking central Mexico. Marcy to Wetmore, November 1, 1846, Marcy Papers, XI.

dispatches were received from Black describing Santa Anna's return to Mexico City and his apparently earnest preparations to attack Taylor's army. But Black continued to report antiwar sentiment as well. Many federalists, he declared, being antimilitarist, "wish to see their army destroyed, and they have great hopes, that the American army will do this service for them."[81]

Further encouragement to an aggressive policy came from renewed information that an invading army could land south of Veracruz and take the city by siege without having to attack the guardian fortress of Ulua. Seeking verification, Polk summoned to Washington F. M. Dimond, recently American consul at the Mexican port, who had already discussed an attack on Veracruz with Bancroft during the summer. In mid-October Dimond met with the President, cabinet members, and Army and Navy officers to exhibit a rough plan of Veracruz, Ulua, and their defenses and to explain how the port might be captured without heavy loss of life.[82]

On October 22, five days after this demonstration, Polk suggested to Taylor that he should occupy a defensive line near Monterrey and that he would probably have to transfer some men to a contemplated expedition against Veracruz.[83] This last statement, however, did not mean that the cabinet had finally decided to invade central Mexico. On November 7, discussing the budget estimates for the annual message, Buchanan advocated providing only for an army of 15,000 Regulars and 10,000 more men, to be enlisted for the duration of the war, and dispensing with the unruly volunteers. He argued that 25,000 men were quite enough for a defensive strategy. The rest of the cabinet persuaded him to agree to a contingent provision for 10,000 more—35,000 in all—and left open the question of strategy.[84]

A day before this discussion, Senator Benton had returned to Washington for the approaching session of Congress. Polk was apparently awaiting his advice, for he called him at once to the White House, and the two exchanged many ideas during subsequent weeks. Benton declared that the "go-ahead" temperament

81. John Black to Buchanan, September 3, 17, 22, October 17, 1846, Nos. 388, 390, 391, 397, Manning, *IAA*, VIII, 886–90. Same, August 27, September 12, 24, 26, Nos. 387, 389, 392, 393, US, DS, CD, Mexico City, IX. Some passages are omitted by Manning but may be found in the manuscript dispatches. The quotation is found in the dispatch of September 12, No. 389.

82. Polk, *Diary*, II, 179–80, 195–97. Dimond to Conner, August 15, 1846, Conner Papers, box 10.

83. Polk, *Diary*, II, 198–200, 204–5. Marcy to Taylor, October 22, 1846, US, 30C, 1S, HED 60, pp. 363–67.

84. Polk, *Diary*, II, 219–21.

of the American people demanded an active campaign against Mexico City, while defensive tactics would play directly into the hands of the proscrastinating Mexicans. When the choice of a commander for such an expedition came into discussion, Polk and Benton agreed that Taylor lacked the abilities required for it. Benton opposed the appointment of Scott and of other officers and finally offered to undertake the assignment himself if Congress would create a lieutenant generalship, raising him over the heads of all others. Polk considered this astounding proposal, but he decided that Congress would not approve it and set it aside for a time. On November 11 Benton reluctantly consented to accompany the invading force in the lesser capacity of peace commissioner, provided that the force was large, "for then it [the position] would be important & there would be dignity in it."[85]

By this time Polk and Buchanan had received letters from Slidell in New Orleans, suggesting that Santa Anna was undoubtedly willing to negotiate, but was waiting until Mexican nationalism had abated. If the Mexican Congress did not authorize negotiations during December, Slidell felt that the United States must attack Mexico City or prepare to fight indefinitely. An interior invasion from Monterrey by way of San Luis Potosí would not be impossible, but in any case he advised the seizure of Veracruz. At a cabinet meeting on November 14 Buchanan conceded the wisdom of taking Veracruz but continued to oppose any further expansion of the war. In discussions about troops he held firm, but when Marcy yielded to Benton's arguments for calling up more volunteers, the rest of the cabinet agreed with him and approved enlistment of nine regiments.[86]

Three days later, Polk and the cabinet agreed that an expedition should be sent against Veracruz, leaving for further discussion the more elaborate project of an inland attack toward Mexico City. Polk, his secretaries, and Benton reviewed the list of available commanders and selected Scott; from Polk's account Benton's voice was decisive. Scott had long hoped for the assignment, and when the President informed him, he accepted, close to tears, professing

---

85. Polk, *Diary*, II, 219, 221–22, 225, 226–28, 231–32. The quotation appears on p. 231.

86. Slidell to Polk, New Orleans, November 4, 1846, Polk Papers, CIX, LC. Slidell to Buchanan, November 5, George Ticknor Curtis, *Life of James*

Buchanan, Fifteenth President of the United States, I, 601–2. Polk, *Diary*, II, 234–35. Benton, *Thirty Years View*, II, 693–94. According to Benton, Polk had to order Marcy to call up ten regiments, but Marcy managed to get the number reduced to nine.

eternal loyalty, and naively assuming that Polk had forgotten his suspicions. He offered to take with him any volunteer generals whom Polk designated, a concession he must have regretted as events progressed.[87]

Realizing the dangers of delay, Scott left Washington for New York the day after his appointment and, after sending a tactful dispatch to Taylor, sailed for New Orleans on November 30. Unfortunately, headwinds prolonged his trip to nearly three weeks, and on his arrival he discovered the press full of sensational rumors about his plans. When these reports reached Washington, Polk jumped to the conclusion that Scott in his vanity had allowed the information to leak out, and his dislike of the general returned to the surface of his thinking.[88]

Meanwhile, Polk and the cabinet were trying to determine the contents of the President's annual message. By November 20 Polk had completed a rough draft of the section on the war, in which he proposed that the United States establish a boundary line which would secure enough territory to pay for the war costs and that Congress formally provide government for this territory. He did not describe an exact line, nor did he rule out a more active campaign in central Mexico, although of course he omitted all mention of the now approved attack on Veracruz.[89]

When Benton saw the President's draft, he concluded that the administration had given up any active prosecution of the war, and he pressed Polk to delete the passages on a defensive line in northern Mexico and on the organization of government. Buchanan and Walker opposed Benton's arguments for attack, but all agreed that the recommendations should be omitted, since without Benton's support they could not possibly win approval in the Senate. After meditating over night, Buchanan added that to sub-

87. Polk's decision was confirmed by a bad-tempered dispatch from Taylor that led the President to call him "narrow-minded . . . partisan . . . wholly unqualified for the command he holds." Polk, *Diary*, II, 236–37, 240–50. The quotation appears on p. 250. Elliott, *Scott*, pp. 441–42. Spencer gives more weight to Marcy than to Benton in the choice of Scott. Spencer, *Victor and Spoils*, p. 160.

88. Elliott, *Scott*, pp. 443–45. Scott to Taylor, November 25, 1846, US, 30C, 1S, HED 60, pp. 373–74. Polk, *Diary*, II, 327–28.

89. The question of a possible annexation south of the Rio Grande came up at this time because Buchanan had received a communication from one Dr. Aelaria de Masa (Polk's spelling), allegedly a secessionist from Tamaulipas, who declared that the people there were ready to revolt if the United States would promise not to annex them. Polk, *Diary*, II, 246, 254–59. (Letters on northeastern secessionism from Hilario de Mesa, written in December 1847, appear in Nicholas P. Trist Papers, XXVII, ff. 60876–79, LC.)

mit the questions of boundaries and occupation to Congress would diminish the executive prerogative and unnecessarily arouse the abolitionists.[90]

In its final form, as sent to Congress on December 8, Polk's second annual message was somewhat longer than his first but less dramatic and more defensive. He repeated what he had said in the war message to justify the war but lessened its force with long accounts of the United States claims and the Texas question. The truncated passage on war plans was an anticlimax, for in it Polk only pledged vigorous, unrelaxed prosecution of the war with the goal of "an honorable peace, and . . . ample indemnity for the expenses of the war" and American claims. He explained the military government of occupied territory as "the right and duty of the conqueror" but said nothing of congressional authorization. He made public his request for an emergency appropriation of $2 million to purchase territory and estimated that if the war lasted into the middle of 1848, the government would need additional loans of $23 million, thereby almost doubling the national debt. In their reports to Congress Marcy and Mason recommended the addition of troops and the purchase of a few new steamers.[91]

If Polk hoped that his message would unify the country in support of the war, he was soon disappointed, for the opposition answered the message with extravagant attacks on the President's usurpation of power and his mad, insatiable land hunger.[92] Polk contributed to the partisan spirit of the session by presenting Benton's proposal to create the rank of lieutenant general. Whoever held this office would be expected to coordinate movements in the north, attack Mexico City, and negotiate for peace. Everyone knew that the President intended to appoint Benton so a Democrat

90. Polk, *Diary*, II, 258–63. Benton, *Thirty Years View*, II, 693–94. Benton probably exaggerated the passivity of Polk's plans. McCormac, *Polk*, p. 456. For Buchanan's views see an undated memorandum by him in the Polk Papers, series 5, box 3, LC. Buchanan doubted that the Constitution was intended to cover occupied but unincorporated territory and fell back on the rights of a conqueror under international law.

91. James D. Richardson, ed., *A Compilation of the Messages and Papers of the Presidents, 1789–1897*, IV, 471–506; the passages quoted appear on pp. 472 and 494. For a discussion of Polk's increased attention to the claims question, see Clayton Charles Kohl, *Claims As a Cause of the Mexican War*, pp. 69–70.

92. Smith, *War with Mexico*, II, 278–79. Washington *National Intelligencer*, December 9, 1846, p. 3; December 12, pp. 3–4; December 15, p. 3; December 17, p. 3. For opinions on the message and the war from various parts of the country, see the issues for November 28, p. 3; November 30, p. 3; December 1, p. 3; December 21, p. 3; January 29, 1847, p. 4; February 5, p. 3. See also David D. Barnard's criticism of the message as oratorical sleight of hand. *American Review*, 5 (January 1847), 1–15.

might have the glory of eventual victory, even though the Missouri Senator had never held a higher military position than colonel of militia or even witnessed a battle. The proposal was one of the most discreditable acts of Polk's whole career, for it amounted to direct betrayal of Scott, who needed all possible support in organizing the most ambitious military operation the United States had ever undertaken. It also revealed the alarming degree to which the President's personal dislikes and party concern could overpower his common sense. In one of the most important decisions of the session the Senate tabled the measure. Congress, however, also displayed a flair for partisanship by delaying passage of a bill for the enlistment of ten more regiments (raised from an earlier proposal of nine) for the duration of the war.[93]

The most heated controversy of the session arose over Polk's request for a contingent fund to purchase territory from Mexico, which had inspired the Wilmot Proviso during the previous session. Nothing daunted, he repeated the request in his annual message and soon afterward raised the figure from two to three million dollars. Wilmot opened the debate with a slashing attack on slavery, and speakers in both houses soon entangled this question with territorial expansion and military strategy. The debate reached its climax on February 11, when Senator Thomas A. Corwin of Ohio, ridiculing the South's desires for more territory, scandalized even abolitionists by approving Mexican self-defense: "If I were a Mexican I would tell you, 'Have you not room in your own country to bury your dead men? If you come into mine, we will greet you with bloody hands, and welcome you to hospitable graves.' "[94]

Four days after this outburst the House added Wilmot's amendment to the Three Million Bill and passed it, 115 to 105, with both parties badly split. The Senate then passed the bill without the Proviso, 32 to 21, and later in the House enough votes shifted for removal of the Proviso, 102 to 97, and acceptance of the Senate's bill. Polk had his money, but he had further solidified Northern opposition to the war and to slavery.

* * * *

93. McCormac, *Polk*, pp. 463–64. After the bill for the lieutenant generalship failed, Polk offered Benton the post of major general (below Scott and Taylor in seniority), but Benton declined it. Ibid., pp. 470–71. The issue was complicated by Benton's opposition to including Slidell in the peace commission. Polk, *Diary*, II, 268, 270,

273, 275–77, 282–83, 286, 293, 294, 301, 310, 334.
94. Going, *Wilmot*, Chaps. 12, 13. Morrison, *Democratic Politics*, pp. 29–37. For Corwin's speech, see US, 29C, 2S, *CG*, Appendix, p. 217. On the public reaction to the speech, see Smith, *War with Mexico*, II, 278.

The decision to attack Veracruz and the request for the special appropriation represented the two halves of Polk's Mexican policy, force and persuasion. For many weeks none of his closest associates knew which would be uppermost.[95] One fact was certain—he continued to hope for negotiations with Santa Anna. The Mexican general's evacuation of Tampico and his concentration of forces at San Luis Potosí suggested that he was pinning all his hopes on one last battle—perhaps intended only to save face—instead of dispersing his troops and resorting to guerrilla warfare, as many observers had expected.[96] If so, he might still listen to an offer from the United States.

As Polk hesitated between his alternatives, he badly needed more detailed and reliable information from Mexico. Through the autumn Consul Black's reports had offered inconclusive evidence: a popular demonstration in Mexico City to revile the American "army of *cowards*," then a few days of stunned defeatism after the fall of Monterrey, then a recovery of foolish confidence.[97] These reports and Slidell's speculative advice from New Orleans were not enough. Late in November Polk began to send out special agents to observe conditions in Mexico and report on chances for peace.[98]

The best known of these agents was Moses Y. Beach, publisher of the expansionist New York *Sun*, who had many contacts with American Catholics and Democratic politicians. Through his friend, the former Mexican minister Juan N. Almonte, he felt that he also had an *entrée* into Mexican political circles. According to a later story, hazy in many details, during the late summer of

95. At the end of December Buchanan was sure that Polk intended "a crushing movement" on Mexico City. Buchanan to Bancroft, December 29, 1846, Bancroft Papers, MHS. But four days later, Polk told the cabinet that the only goal was Veracruz and that further operations would be decided after its capture. Polk, *Diary*, II, 300–301.

96. This rumor appeared in the New Orleans *Delta*, December 24, 1846; clipping in Polk Papers, CX, LC.

97. Black to Buchanan, September 17, 22, October 17, November 28, 1846, Nos. 390, 391, 397, 400, Manning, *IAA*, VIII, 887–90. Same, September 24, 26, 28, October 3, 8, 29, November 17, Nos. 392–96, 398, 399, US, DS, CD, Mexico City, IX. The quotation appears in

the dispatch of October 29, No. 398. The archival collection also includes revealing excerpts omitted from the dispatches published in Manning. The last dispatches discouraged Polk. Polk, *Diary*, II, 294.

98. Scott sent former Consul F. M. Dimond to Havana to recruit two agents who would go into Mexico and report on conditions. Dimond and the American consul at Havana prepared one man for the assignment, but he could not obtain a Mexican visa. Then they selected a Frenchman (unidentified) and chartered a ship to take him to Mexico. Scott to Campbell, November 23, Marcy Papers, XII. Dimond to Conner, Havana, January 15, 1847, Conner Papers, box 10. Nothing further is known of this project.

1846 a small group of Mexican aristocrats and ecclesiastics drew up terms of a possible compromise peace, including cession of all territory north of 26°, in return for an indemnity of $3 million. Their presumed incentive was the fear that continued war would drive the Mexican government to confiscate Church and other property. This group was said to have communicated the plan to officers in Taylor's army, who transmitted it to Beach and to Bishop John J. Hughes of New York. When Beach reported these peace feelers to Polk and Buchanan, they determined to send him on a "business trip" to Mexico, so he might investigate the truth of the reports and probably also assure Mexican Catholics that the United States intended no religious persecution.[99]

Beach had such a talent for improvisation and such a mixture of public and private interests that it would be unwise to place much weight on his unsupported word. The brief official instructions from Buchanan, dated November 21, carefully avoided authorizing him to negotiate openly. Also, five months later, Polk wrote in his diary that Beach had undertaken only to persuade Almonte and other Mexican acquaintances in the direction of peace "but was not clothed with any Diplomatic powers." At that time Polk realized that Beach might exceed his instructions, for he added that it would be a "good joke" if Beach presented the country with a treaty. Available evidence, however, does not indicate that in November the President expected his secret agent to open negotiations. Whatever Polk's expectations, Beach gathered letters of introduction from Bishop Hughes and others to influential persons in Cuba and Mexico, and early in December he sailed with a family group from Charleston to Havana and Veracruz.[100] As matters developed, his diplomatic efforts were probably more hindrance than help to the United States government.

Soon after the new year began, hope appeared from another direction. On the evening of January 11 Buchanan received a visit

99. M. S. Beach, "A Secret Mission to Mexico. Origin of the Treaty of Guadalupe Hidalgo," *Scribner's Monthly Magazine*, 17 (December 1878), 299–300; 18 (May 1879), 136–37. According to this account, Beach had earlier received information about the Spanish monarchical plot in Mexico from Mirabeau B. Lamar, former president of Texas and an officer in Taylor's army, and had transmitted it to Polk. Lamar and William L. Cazneau learned of the peace proposal from friends in Mexico City and told Beach.

100. Frederick Merk, *Manifest Destiny and Mission in American History, a Reinterpretation*, pp. 131–33. Buchanan to Moses Y. Beach, November 21, 1846, Manning, *IAA*, VIII, 195–96. Polk, *Diary*, II, 476–77. Although Dimond was organizing a similar observation project in Havana when Beach arrived there (see note 98), he knew nothing about Beach's mission. Dimond to Conner, January [16], 1847, Conner Papers, box 10.

from Alexander J. Atocha, the same man who had approached the administration during the preceding February with advice and bids for support from Santa Anna (see Chapter 11). Atocha had just arrived from Mexico by way of Havana—an emissary, he told Buchanan, from Santa Anna, Almonte, and Rejón, who had sent him to talk of peace. Two days later he repeated his story to Benton and showed him letters from Santa Anna and Almonte, written in late November, which expressed a desire for an honorable settlement, as well as a series of earlier letters from several Mexican leaders to prove that he enjoyed their confidence. When Benton asked about concrete peace terms, Atocha replied that his principals would be willing to sell California to the United States for fifteen or twenty million dollars and accept the Rio Grande boundary, setting aside the strip between that river and the Nueces as neutral ground. He proposed that the United States cease hostilities, raise the blockade, and send commissioners to Havana to meet representatives from Mexico.[101]

During the following days both Benton and Buchanan talked to Atocha several times, but Polk did not meet him. All three accepted his good faith and thought his terms close enough to American goals to justify probing further. Buchanan informed him that the United States could not consider neutralizing the strip between the Nueces and the Rio Grande and that the territorial purchase must include New Mexico as well as California. Atocha apparently did not balk at these changes. Since Mexico had already rebuffed one overture by the United States, Polk was unwilling to resume the initiative officially, and he particularly refused to lift the blockade during early negotiations lest Mexico import arms and revive the fighting.

After further exchanges it was agreed that Atocha should take a sealed message to Mexico City as an unofficial overture; a draft was drawn up, which he approved. The message, addressed to the Mexican foreign minister, declared that the United States was willing to appoint one or more peace commissioners as soon as the Mexican government signified its intention to take similar action. The American commissioners would have full power to negotiate, would meet their Mexican counterparts at either Havana or Jalapa (in Mexico, inland from Veracruz), and would have discretionary power to suspend hostilities and raise the blockade as soon as the first meeting occurred. Carrying this message, Atocha

101. Polk, *Diary*, II, 323, 325–27, 331–33. [Benton to Buchanan], January 14, [1847]; "Friday" [January 15], Buchanan Papers, box 64.

left Washington for New Orleans about a week after his first talk with Buchanan. At New Orleans he boarded a Navy revenue cutter, which was to take him to Veracruz and wait for him until he was ready to return.[102]

Once again Polk's hopes were to be disappointed. During Atocha's visit to the United States the political situation in Mexico had considerably changed. When he arrived in Mexico City with Buchanan's note, the Yankeephobe Valentín Gómez Farías had become acting president, and Santa Anna was far away to the north, preparing to do battle with Taylor. As soon as Atocha had delivered the American note, Gómez Farías placed him in close confinement and sent to Congress another version of the American terms, which then appeared in the newspapers. According to this published version, the United States announced that at the proposed meeting of peace commissioners it would demand the cession of all northern Mexico to 26°, for which it would offer $28 million in cash and renunciation of unpaid claims. When peace had been established, the Americans would place ten thousand troops on the new border to prevent Indian raids and would form an alliance with Mexico to forestall European interference.[103]

How should one reasonably judge Atocha's mission, the reaction of the Polk administration, and the later distortion of the United States offer? The Mexican background will be discussed in the next chapter. No one has ever proved that Santa Anna was irrevocably opposed to negotiating with the United States. During November and early December rumors were circulating widely in both countries that he had an understanding with Polk and would soon come to terms.

Polk may be criticized for accepting Atocha at face value, for both Slidell and Pakenham thought him unreliable, with "neither brains nor honesty."[104] Still, the President and his cabinet must have felt that they had little to lose in putting out an unofficial feeler, and the conspiratorial aspects of Atocha's mission may have seemed appropriate to the suspicious Polk, especially given his generally low opinion of Mexicans. It is impossible to say whether the letters from Mexican leaders that Atocha carried were genuine.

102. Polk, *Diary*, II, 331–33, 335–38, 339, 341–42. Buchanan to Minister of Foreign Affairs of Mexico, January 18, 1847, Manning, *IAA*, VIII, 197–98.
103. Bankhead to Palmerston, March 2, 1847, No. 16 and enclosure, GB, FO 50/208, ff. 208–9, 211–13. Meade, *Life and Letters*, I, 185, 190.
104. Slidell to Buchanan, March 21, 1847, Buchanan Papers, box 24. Pakenham to Palmerston, March 29, No. 40, GB, FO 5/469, ff. 229–33. The quoted phrase is Slidell's.

In any case, the concessions to which he agreed were probably his own responsibility.[105]

There is no reason to believe that the drastic terms announced to the Mexican Congress and public originated with Polk and Buchanan. To be sure, the proposal for a boundary at 26° resembled that which Moses Y. Beach claimed to have received from the Mexican proclericals, and among Atocha's supporting letters were some from Beach's friend Almonte. Also, it is possible that Atocha talked with Beach in Havana while en route to the United States, for they were both in that city at the same time. But there is not the slightest evidence in Polk's diary or correspondence to suggest that he was considering such terms at this period or had ever discussed them with Beach, and it is well known that Buchanan consistently opposed a boundary south of the Rio Grande until later in the war. Even if he and Polk contemplated such annexations, it would obviously have been bad tactics to specify territorial demands before Mexico had agreed to negotiate and imprudent to offer a formal alliance in violation of American tradition.

The terms Gómez Farías announced to the Mexican Congress were intended not to conciliate but to anger. If they agreed with suggestions from Beach's proclerical associates, this similarity was probably a deliberate device of the acting president to discredit the defenders of Church rights. One may well doubt whether Santa Anna would have approved the American note as drawn up with Atocha's consent, but he had no opportunity to see it before Gómez Farías released his own version of it to the public. After nationalists had had time to denounce the outrageous cessions, his acting foreign minister drew up a reply to Buchanan's proposal for peace commissioners, stating that the Mexican government would not consider the proposal until the United States had raised the blockade and withdrawn its armies from Mexican soil. "All civilized Nations," he concluded, "have recognized the justice of the rights of this Republic . . . in opposing an invasion, the least justifiable of all those known to the history of civilized nations."[106]

---

105. Perhaps the most suspect of Atocha's letters was the one from Manuel Crescencio Rejón, who had given every impression of being a fervent Yankeephobe. A letter from him might have especially impressed Polk and Buchanan, for he had been foreign minister as recently as September and October 1846.

106. José María Ortiz Monasterio to Buchanan, February 22, 1847, Manning, *IAA*, VIII, 896–97. After a private conversation with a Mexican cabinet member, Black reported that Gómez Farías had sent Buchanan's dispatch north to Santa Anna without showing it to the cabinet. Black to Buchanan, February 24, No. 408, US, DS, CD, Mexico City, IX.

While Polk awaited Atocha's return, he pressed Congress for action on his war measures and postponed long-range strategic decisions. At the same time the Veracruz expedition lumbered southward. After strenuous and often badly coordinated efforts by the War and Navy Departments, troops of all descriptions were assembled along the Gulf coast. Scott spent January and part of February in southern Texas, supervising operations, and on February 15 he left for Tampico. After further delays and last-minute preparations he and his flotilla, carrying most of his thirteen thousand men, set sail on March 2 for Veracruz.[107]

Several hundred miles to the west, Taylor was also moving south with his reduced army of less than five thousand, scattered rather widely over Coahuila. Furious at his superiors, he ignored or distorted successive orders to remain where he was. Instead, at the beginning of February he began to reconnoiter to the south of Saltillo, a city beyond Monterrey which he had occupied without resistance soon after the end of the armistice. Taylor was well aware that Santa Anna and a much larger army held San Luis Potosí, more than two hundred miles to the south, but he assumed that the Mexicans had neither the strength nor the disposition to cross the intervening desert.[108]

Because of slow communications, in mid-March Polk knew little about his two armies. According to his latest information, one of them was dangerously extended over a difficult terrain, facing an enemy who might attack at any moment; the other was poised to invest a port of uncertain defensive capabilities just as the fever season was about to begin. At this point, on March 20, Atocha arrived in Washington with the blunt Mexican reply to Polk's peace feeler. As in the case of his Oregon proposal to Pakenham of July 1845, the President felt that he had gone to the very limit of conciliation to stimulate negotiation, in the confidence that the Mexican leaders truly desired peace. Once again he felt betrayed, and he reacted with a burst of anger. In his own words:

> I at once declared to the Cabinet that the preliminary conditions required were wholly inadmissible, and that no alternative was now left but the most energetic crushing movement of our arms upon Mexico. Mr. Buchanan expressed the opinion that our army should not attempt to march to the City of Mexico. I replied that I differed

107. Rives, *US and Mexico*, II, 376–80. Smith, *War with Mexico*, I, 354–56, 362–68; II, 17–18. Elliott, *Scott*, pp. 445–51. Spencer, *Victor and Spoils*, pp. 161–64. Polk, *Diary*, II, 388.

108. Rives, *US and Mexico*, II, 287–89, 301–7, 340–48. Smith, *War with Mexico*, I, 282–83, 356–62, 368–74. Lavender, *Climax at Buena Vista*, Chap. 8, pp. 166–67.

with him in opinion, & that I would not only march to the City of Mexico, but that I would pursue Santa Anna's army wherever it was, and capture or destroy it. I expressed the opinion that if I had a proper commander of the army, who would lay aside the technical rules of war to be found in books, . . . one who would go light & move rapidly, I had no doubt Santa Anna & his whole army could be destroyed or captured in a short time.[109]

Thus the die was cast; thus Polk committed himself to the invasion of central Mexico.

Mature reflection on the events of the preceding nine months, however, leads to the conclusion that his decision was neither so abrupt nor so dramatic as it must have seemed to the cabinet members on that March day. Since Polk had first mentioned the possibility of a second expedition, the effective alternatives open to him had been eroded by external forces or by his own actions: the truce after Monterrey, the decision to attack Veracruz, the capture of Tampico, the differences with Taylor, and always the growing opposition at home and the stubbornness of the Mexicans. If any single action by Polk made inevitable the invasion of central Mexico, it was the decision to attack Veracruz. As he understood by March, large numbers of troops could not safely occupy the port through the fever season, due to begin in April.[110] They must advance into the interior or retire from the port. No President as unpopular as Polk would have dared to announce a fruitless evacuation to the American people when the triumphal bunting had scarcely been taken down.

But even if Polk made the crucial decision to attack Veracruz as early as November, he need not be accused of hypocrisy through the ensuing winter. All available evidence suggests that he did not realize how narrowly he had bound himself. There were ample reasons for restraint: antiwar sentiment all over the United States, the devil's choice offered by the Wilmot Proviso debates, and the urgings of Buchanan. Perhaps the most potent reason for hesitation was Congress' exasperating refusal to create an office which Benton could accept, thus forcing Polk to entrust conduct of the invasion to a pedantic and insubordinate Whig. As long as conditions in Mexico offered some hope of a negotiated peace, logic and habit dictated the continuation of familiar policies—pressure and strong talk mixed with bluff. When the hope disappeared,

109. Polk, *Diary*, II, 431–33. 110. Polk, *Diary*, II, 416.

Polk could not have turned back, even if he had wanted to. Perhaps fortunately, the Mexican government's reply was so insulting that for once he could yield to his impulses and create drama out of necessity.

15

The Impasse at Mexico City

If the factionalism in the United States hampered Polk's war effort, that in Mexico threatened to reduce the country to anarchy. Concern for national honor had been strong enough to impel the Mexicans into a hopeless war but not to obliterate traditional political and social rivalries. With President Paredes overthrown and monarchism temporarily discredited, wealthy landowners, proclericals, and other right-wing conservatives went into eclipse, but as the liberal federalists followed Santa Anna back into power during the summer of 1846, their moderate and radical (*puro*) factions bickered and scuffled with each other. For the time being under the weak provisional president, José Mariano Salas, the *puro* leader Valentín Gómez Farías enjoyed precedence. Moderates and conservatives watched him suspiciously, remembering his abortive anticlerical reforms of 1833 and fearing—quite correctly—that he would use the war emergency to revive these reforms.[1]

Finance was the most immediate problem, for the Treasury was empty again, and Santa Anna needed extraordinary funds to equip his army for its northward march. In September the government persuaded the clergy in the capital to guarantee another loan by mortgaging $2 million worth of the Church's less desirable property, but the arrangements became so much entangled with *agiotistas* and bribery that the army received little money. Meanwhile, as Santa Anna made his way north, liberal newspapers began to hint broadly that, since he was fighting to maintain the Church against Protestant Americans, the clergy should offer him more concrete aid than prayers.[2]

1. Vicente Riva Palacio, *México a través de los siglos*, IV, 572–76. Niceto de Zamacois, *Historia de Méjico desde sus tiempos más remotas hasta nuestros días*, XII, 519–21. For contemporary descriptions, see José Fernando Ramírez, *Mexico during the War with the United States*, pp. 66–85, *passim*. Guillermo Prieto, *Memorias de mis tiempos, 1840 a 1853*, pp. 193–99. C. Alan Hutchinson, "Valentín Gómez Farías: A Biographical Study," Ph.D. diss., University of Texas, 1948, pp. 661–71. Vicente Fuentes Díaz, *Gómez Farías, padre de la reforma*, pp. 200–203, 213–15. Valentín Gómez Farías to José María Luis Mora, August 29, 1846, in Genaro García and Carlos Pereyra, eds., *Documentos inéditos ó muy raros para la historia de México*, VI, 58–61.

2. As Santa Anna left Mexico City, he stopped ostentatiously at the shrine

During October and November the Salas government decreed further contributions but had no way of enforcing them. There was some talk of squeezing foreigners, and when hints of this appeared in the official newspaper, the British and Spanish ministers, Bankhead and Bermúdez de Castro, protested strenuously to the foreign ministry. New rumors reported that Santa Anna was planning to sell out to the Americans.[3] As public morale went to pieces, rioting broke out in Mexico City. Since Santa Anna's departure had left the capital virtually defenseless, groups of aristocrats, businessmen, and laborers began to organize battalions of the national guard to keep the peace and preserve property. Unfortunately, the volunteers were organized along social and factional lines, so their presence did little to unify Mexico City behind the war effort.[4]

When Congress finally assembled on December 6, the industrious politicking of the *puros* gave them a small margin of control. Taking up the British offer of mediation, they relegated it to committee, where it remained despite Bankhead's efforts to get it out.[5] Of greater immediate interest to politicians and country was the emergency election by Congress of a president who would serve until conditions permitted nationwide voting. Despite the recent

of Guadalupe Hidalgo to pray for victory, giving the press an opening to draw obvious conclusions. Riva Palacio, *México, a través de los siglos*, IV, 590–92. Ramón Alcaraz et al., *Apuntes para la historia de la guerra entre México y los Estados-Unidos*, p. 68. Zamacois, *Historia de Méjico*, XII, 516–18. Hutchinson, "Gómez Farías," pp. 651–55, 666–67. John Black to James Buchanan, September 22, 1846, No. 391, Manning, *IAA*, VIII, 888–89. Same, September 24, No. 392, US, DS, CD, Mexico City, IX. On the clerical refusal to contribute to the war effort, see Vicente Fuentes Díaz, *La intervención norteamericana en México (1847)*, pp. 168–78.

3. Dublán and Lozano, *LM*, V, 172–75, 212–13, 244. (The first law is printed under the wrong title.) Charles Bankhead to Viscount Palmerston, September 29, October 30, November 29, 1846, Nos. 141, 153, 157, 172, GB, FO 50/199, ff. 262–64; 50/200, ff. 75–77, 155–63; 50/201, ff. 95–97. Salvador Bermúdez de Castro to Primer Secretario de Estado, October 26, Nos. 362, 364, Spain, BAE, legajo 1649. Same, November 28, *Rdh-m*, IV, 7–8. Riva Palacio, *México a través de los siglos*, IV, 398. Carlos María de Bustamante, *El nuevo Bernal Díaz ó sea Historia de la invasión de los Anglo-Americanos en México*, II, 212–13, 244.

4. Bustamante, *Nuevo Bernal Díaz*, II, 235–43. One result of the riots was that Rejón was maneuvered out of the Foreign Ministry. Manuel Crescencio Rejón, *Correspondencia inédita de Manuel Crescencio Rejón*, pp. 93, 97–99. On the volunteer battalions, see Riva Palacio, *México a través de los siglos*, IV, 592–93; and Zamacois, *Historia de Méjico*, XII, 533–35, 538. The best known volunteer groups were the aristocratic *polkos*, so called because they danced the newly introduced polka at their balls. Some historians call the ensuing uprising "the revolt of the *polkos*." See also Black to Buchanan, October 17, 1846, No. 397, US, DS, CD, Mexico City, IX.

5. Zamacois, *Historia de Méjico*, XII, 545–46. Bermúdez de Castro to Primer Secretario de Estado, February 25, 1847, No. 433, *Rdh-m*, IV, 38–39. Bankhead to Palmerston, January 29, No. 6, GB, FO 50/208, ff. 140–44.

slurs against Santa Anna's loyalty, he was chosen, although by a fairly narrow vote. The *puros* concentrated their efforts on the vice presidency, which would control the government as long as Santa Anna stayed with the army. After much excitement they managed to elect Gómez Farías, who took office immediately.[6] The situation of 1833 had repeated itself.

* * * *

The new acting president lost no time in dealing with the Church. Gómez Farías had always regarded its wealth as an obstacle to social reform; its opposition had largely helped to nullify all money-raising decrees. With Santa Anna's approval the *puros* introduced into Congress a bill for the outright expropriation of Church property, which could then be sold to meet war expenses. For three days and nights the bill was debated in a continuous, stormy session, until on January 10 the exhausted moderates and conservatives yielded. The law authorized the government to raise $15 million by mortgage or sale of Church property, but the moderates managed to exempt hospitals, schools, and other charitable institutions, as well as sacred vessels and other accessories of worship.[7]

As Bankhead reported to the Foreign Office, the expropriation law threatened not only the Church but also many rural landowners, great and small, who owed it long-standing debts they might now be required to pay on short notice. Bankhead felt that most persons would have agreed to a fairly administered confiscation of monastic property but that they opposed the more far-reaching measure because they feared that officials then in power would simply enrich themselves with the proceeds. The clergy of Mexico City protested the decree at once, of course, and demonstrations suddenly appeared in the streets, while the moderate press joined in attacks on Gómez Farías.[8]

6. Riva Palacio, *México a través de los siglos*, IV, 572–73, 757–76, 599–600. Dennis E. Berge, "Mexican Response to United States Expansionism, 1841–1848," Ph.D. diss., University of California (Berkeley), 1965, pp. 233–34. Hutchinson, "Gómez Farías," pp. 704–19. Bankhead to Palmerston, December 30, 1846, No. 180, GB, FO 50/201, ff. 192–96.

7. Dublán and Lozano, *LM*, V, 246–52. Hutchinson, "Gómez Farías," pp. 726–28, 733–41. Riva Palacio, *México*

a través de los siglos, IV, 601–4. The text of the law appears on pp. 603–4n1. Wilfrid Hardy Callcott, *Church and State in Mexico, 1822–1857*, pp. 182–83. "Letters of General Antonio López de Santa Anna Relating to the War between the United States and Mexico, 1846–1848," ed. Justin H. Smith, *Annual Report of the American Historical Association for the Year 1917*, pp. 357–431, *passim*.

8. Bankhead to Palmerston, January 29, 1847, No. 7, GB, FO 50/208, ff. 146–

As he had in 1833, Gómez Farías had tried to accomplish too much, too fast. The disorders slackened for a time, but he found it impossible to enforce his expropriation, since he lacked the firm support of colleagues and Congress. When Santa Anna learned of the upheaval, he wrote from San Luis Potosí to deplore such drastic means, hinting that it might be safer to despoil foreigners, especially Spaniards.[9] Gómez Farías called on Church officials to give an accounting of their property and investments, and when they refused, he seized a few local holdings outright. Meanwhile, churchmen released a flood of pamphlets and editorials, and all factions began to calculate their military strength. By mid-February Gómez Farías had brought Mexico City to the brink of civil war without obtaining the needed funds, for few persons would buy Church lands.[10]

The failure of the national government to supply Santa Anna with adequate resources compelled him to improvise. Arriving at San Luis Potosí early in October with his 3,000 men, he soon more than doubled this group with the remains of Ampudia's forces, in retreat from Monterrey. By drawing together other scattered forces and levies of recruits, chiefly from the center and west, he eventually gathered an army of approximately 20,000. The people of San Luis Potosí, fearing an imminent attack by Taylor, worked diligently to furnish supplies, and Santa Anna seized from the local mint a quantity of silver bars, most of which belonged to Spaniards. Unfortunately, no amount of money could supply artillery to equal that of the Americans, and as late as February many of his men lacked complete uniforms, stores of food, and more than rudimentary tactical training.[11]

54. Black to Buchanan, January 28, No. 405, US, DS, CD, Mexico City, IX. George Lockhart Rives, *The United States and Mexico, 1821–1848*, II, 316–18. Riva Palacio, *México a través de los siglos*, IV, 603–6. A few state governments also vigorously protested. Zamacois, *Historia de Méjico*, XII, 556, 563, 566.

9. Characteristically, in a private letter he again approved the expropriation law. Riva Palacio, *México a través de los siglos*, IV, 607.

10. Dublán and Lozano, *LM*, V, 255–56. Rives, *US and Mexico*, II, 319–21. Alcaraz et al., *Apuntes para la historia de la guerra*, pp. 124–27. Riva Palacio, *México a través de los siglos*, IV, 631. Zamacois, *Historia de Méjico*, XII, 563–

70. Callcott, *Church and State*, pp. 185–91. Hutchinson, "Gómez Farías," pp. 746–55. Bermúdez de Castro to Primer Secretario de Estado, February 28, 1847, No. 443, *Rdh-m*, IV, 45–46.

11. José María Roa Bárcena, *Recuerdos de la invasión norteamericana (1846–1848)*, I, 138–40. Alcaraz et al., *Apuntes para la historia de la guerra*, pp. 70–71, 73–75. Wilfrid Hardy Callcott, *Santa Anna, the Story of an Enigma Who Once Was Mexico*, pp. 244–45, 249. Vito Alessio Robles, *Coahuila y Texas*, II, 344–45, 348–49. Justin H. Smith, *The War with Mexico*, I, 377–80. Antonio López de Santa Anna, *Apelación al buen criterio*, pp. 20–23. Berge, "Mexican Response," pp. 223–24. When Santa Anna called for troops,

As Santa Anna gathered his forces at San Luis Potosí, it was widely rumored that he intended to draw Taylor's army deep into Mexico, choose a favorable battleground as winter ended, and destroy the Americans with one blow.[12] At the end of January, however, he decided to advance on Taylor at Saltillo himself, motivated by the attacks on his loyalty, the difficulty of holding his ragged forces on the defensive indefinitely, and perhaps also by reports that many of Taylor's troops had been transferred to Scott. Between January 27 and February 22 the Mexicans made their way across 240 miles of mostly deserted and rough country, stopping occasionally to rest, but constantly harassed by hunger, thirst, and a freakish combination of weather conditions ranging from dusty heat to snow, sleet, and bitterly cold north winds. By the time they arrived near the American army, they had lost several thousand men on the way and were exhausted but still able to put 17,500 men in the field.[13]

Early in February, Taylor had pushed some distance south of Saltillo with about 5,000 men. As soon as he learned of Santa Anna's approach he hastily retreated and took up a very strong position about five miles south of the city at the hacienda of Buena Vista, where the main road passed through a gap in the hills and deep ravines favored the defense.

Santa Anna fully recognized the dangers of attacking this latter-day Thermopylae, but he sent a cavalry detachment around to cut off retreat to Saltillo and proceeded to envelop the American left, which seemed to occupy the most vulnerable position. Fighting continued through February 22 and 23, with much heroism on both sides. At several points force of numbers and Taylor's inept moving of American units almost brought a decisive Mexican breakthrough, but the Americans finally managed to drive back the enemy threatening their left, while they held firm in the center. If Santa Anna had attacked again on the third day, making better use of his cavalry, he might still have routed the Americans,

---

some states threatened to rebel, especially Zacatecas, whose capital he had sacked in 1835.

12. Antonio López de Santa Anna to [Juan N. Almonte], September 25, October 3, 1846. (The latter is a paraphrase.) Smith, "Letters of Santa Anna," pp. 363–66, 368. Many thought that he stayed in San Luis Potosí mainly to be able to march on Mexico City in case of an uprising. Black to

Buchanan, November 17, No. 399, US, DS, CD, Mexico City, IX. Bankhead to Palmerston, November 29, No. 173, GB, FO 50/201, ff. 99–101.

13. Roa Bárcena, Recuerdos de la invasión, I, 140–44. Alcaraz et al., Apuntes para la historia de la guerra, pp. 91–98. Santa Anna, Apelación al buen criterio, pp. 23–24. Callcott, Santa Anna, pp. 249–51. Rives, US and Mexico, II, 338–40.

but, discouraged, he judged his men incapable of the effort and withdrew during the night to a nearby town. Next day Taylor sent three officers to propose a discussion of peace terms, but Santa Anna declared that he had no authority to negotiate.[14]

In a council of war Santa Anna and his generals decided to abandon the campaign and retreat to San Luis Potosí. The Americans, exhausted by the battle and perhaps impressed by their envoys' report of Santa Anna's strength, made no effort at pursuit. The Mexicans' return march was as destructive as another day's fighting, and when the army arrived at San Luis Potosí about March 12, it had lost half its original number through casualties and desertions.[15] Long before this Santa Anna had sent dispatches to Mexico City proclaiming a triumph. American reports were somewhat more cautious, but the Battle of Buena Vista, in reality a draw, has usually been regarded as an American victory, on the technical ground that the enemy left the field first. Strategically, it accomplished little, and Taylor's force played a minor role for the rest of the war. Politically, the battle was more significant, for the tales of glory and the casualty lists whetted both patriotism and war-weariness at home, widening the partisan split. Perhaps most important, it made Taylor an irresistible candidate for the Presidency.

While Santa Anna was retreating to San Luis Potosí, revolu-

14. The most detailed account of the preparations and the battle is David Lavender, *Climax at Buena Vista: the American Campaigns in Northeastern Mexico, 1846–47*, Chaps. 8–11. However, it is based entirely on American sources. Shorter accounts appear in Smith, *War with Mexico*, I, Chap. 20; and Rives, *US and Mexico*, II, Chap. 40. In Mexican accounts the action is usually called the Battle of La Angostura ("The Narrows") from the configuration of the battleground. Roa Bárcena, *Recuerdos de la invasión*, I, 144–55, Chaps. 9, 10. Riva Palacio, *México a través de los siglos*, IV, Chap. 16. The account of Taylor's peace mission appears in Alcaraz et al., *Apuntes para la historia de la guerra*, pp. 108–9.

15. Santa Anna's decision to retreat aroused a storm of criticism in Mexico. Alcaraz et al., *Apuntes para la historia de la guerra*, pp. 109–15. José Fuentes Mares, *Santa Anna, aurora y ocaso de un comediante*, pp. 252–53. At the time, Santa Anna cited the lack of food for his troops. Santa Anna to Ministerio de Guerra y Marina, February 26, 1847, Antonio de la Peña y Reyes, ed., *Algunos documentos sobre el tratado de Guadalupe y la situación de México durante la invasión norteamericana*, pp. 46–48. José C. Valadés, *Breve historia de la guerra con los Estados Unidos*, pp. 151, 156. In his memoirs, written in his old age, Santa Anna maintained that he retreated because news of the revolt in Mexico City had reached his camp "by word of mouth." He undoubtedly expected some sort of uprising, but the revolt did not actually begin until three days after the battle. Antonio López de Santa Anna, *The Eagle, the Autobiography of Santa Anna*, ed. Ann Fears Crawford, p. 93. For a summary of Mexican historiography on the battle and the retreat, see Homer C. Chaney, Jr., "The Mexican-United States War, As Seen by Mexican Intellectuals," Ph.D. diss., Stanford University, pp. 25–26, 70–72, 106–10, 149–51, 192–93.

tion broke out in Mexico City. For nearly two months conservatives, led by the clergy, and some moderate liberals had been gathering funds and plotting to overthrow the government. The immediate cause of the uprising was an order from Gómez Farías to a conservative battalion of the national guard, transferring it to Veracruz for defense against the expected American invasion. The battalion refused to march, declaring that the vice president was only trying to get anti-*puro* forces out of the capital, and during the night of February 26–27 its leaders drew up a *pronunciamiento*. At once the Mexico City garrison joined in, calling for the dismissal of president, vice president, and Congress. Later, the revolutionaries reduced their demands to the resignation of Gómez Farías alone.

This act of disunion in the midst of a desperate war was the joint work of the Church, which feared for its lands, of factionalists who detested Gómez Farías for personal and political reasons, and of volunteer guardsmen who had no desire to leave home and fight on the remote Gulf coast. Gómez Farías resisted stubbornly, aided by a remnant of the national guard and by troops hurriedly brought in from nearby towns. The popular support the rebels expected did not appear, and after some days of desultory street fighting the revolution in Mexico City settled into a stalemate during the first week of March.[16]

Such was the situation that confronted Santa Anna as he marched his bedraggled army back to San Luis Potosí. There he received appeals from both sides to restore order, and he set out for the capital at once with a regiment. Arriving at the outskirts

---

16. Most American accounts of these events rely heavily on Riva Palacio, *México a través de los siglos*, IV, Chap. 17, which gives the text of the principal *pronunciamientos*. This work in turn takes many details from Ramírez, *Mexico during the War with the United States*, pp. 103–17. Other eyewitness accounts are by a moderate, Guillermo Prieto, in his *Memorias, 1840 a 1853*, pp. 200–205; and by the Spanish minister, Bermúdez de Castro, in his dispatches to Primer Secretario de Estado, March 3, 31, Nos. 446, 459, 460, with enclosures, *Rdh-m*, IV, 53–67. See also Roa Bárcena, *Recuerdos de la invasión*, I, Chap. 12; Alcaraz *et al.*, *Apuntes para la historia de la guerra*, pp. 128–36; and Zamacois, *Historia de Méjico*, XII, 628–39. More specialized studies in English are Callcott, *Church and State*, pp. 188–91; and Hutchinson, "Gómez Farías," pp. 759–65. The long Mexican historiographical battle over the responsibility of the Church is summarized in Chaney, "Mexican-United States War As Seen by Intellectuals," pp. 193–94, 222–24. Among many liberal accounts, Alfonso Toro, *La Iglesia y el estado in México* [etc.], Chaps. 7, 8, may be cited as typical. On Church involvement, see José Bravo Ugarte, "La misión confidencial de Moses Y. Beach y el clero mexicano," *Abside*, 12 (1948), 476–96; and Michael P. Costeloe, "The Mexican Church and the Rebellion of the Polkos," *Hispanic American Historical Review*, 46 (May 1966), 170–78.

of Mexico City ten days later, he paused to take the oath of office as president. Then he prevailed on both factions to lay down their arms and, after some haggling with the clergy, agreed to nullify the obnoxious confiscation laws in return for a donation of $2 million in cash. Finally, he appointed a new cabinet of moderate liberals and called on Gómez Farías to resign. When he refused, Santa Anna got Congress to abolish the office of vice president and to elect an inconspicuous supporter, General Pedro María Anaya, as substitute president to keep order in his absence. Having alienated most liberals permanently, Santa Anna then turned himself to the principal business of the hour—organizing his demoralized forces into some sort of defense against the Americans.[17]

During the revolt, an American agent was working behind the scenes in Mexico City and, if we are to believe his own accounts, trying to coordinate the uprising and a movement for peace with the United States. This man was Moses Y. Beach, publisher of the New York *Sun*, whom Polk had sent to Mexico late in November to investigate pacifist feelers from proclerical friends there (see Chapter 13). Beach carried no official diplomatic credentials and did not even speak fluent Spanish. But he had many private contacts, unlimited energy, and tempting proposals for business ventures—a national development bank and a transit route across the Isthmus of Tehuantepec. Both would profit from peace or an American occupation.[18]

Near the middle of January, Beach landed at Veracruz with his daughter and the latter's companion, Mrs. Jane Montgomery Storms, a journalist and dilettante in political intrigue.[19] Suspicion seems to have preceded them, for during the next two weeks, as they made their way to Mexico City, local officials repeatedly called them in for questioning or searched their baggage. Once in the capital, Beach presented his banking and Tehuantepec projects to government officials and began talks with his procleri-

17. Rives, *US and Mexico*, II, 391-94. Riva Palacio, *México a través de los siglos*, IV, 637-42. Valadés, *Breve historia*, pp. 168-69. Berge, "Mexican Response," pp. 249-51. Bermúdez de Castro to Primer Secretario de Estado, March 31, 1847, No. 459, *Rdh-m*, IV, 56-60.

18. Moses Y. Beach to Gómez Farías, February 6, [1847]. Gómez Farías Papers, No. 2520a. Frederick Merk, *Manifest Destiny and Mission in American History, a Reinterpretation*, pp. 129-34, passim.

19. Mrs. Storms was in the direct line of American expansionist promoters, for she and her father, a minor New York politician, had been associated with Aaron Burr in a Texas colonizing venture, and she later married William L. Cazneau, who for twenty years promoted the American annexation of Santo Domingo. Edward S. Wallace, *Destiny and Glory*, Chap. 12.

cal friends, in the midst of their protests against the expropriation law of January 10. He used Consul Black primarily for liaison, to arrange interviews with influential Mexicans; Black made only a routine comment about Beach in his dispatches, although he must surely have known what was afoot.[20]

In carrying out the public part of his mission, Beach seems to have gone far beyond its original purpose, the preliminary confidential discussion of peace negotiations. He concentrated his efforts on the proclerical clique and later claimed to have agreed on provisional peace terms with them: a boundary line at 26°, the cession of a transit strip across Tehuantepec, assumption by the United States of all American claims against Mexico, and payment of an additional sum to Mexico (perhaps $3 million). Also, he seems to have assured the proclericals that the United States would help them to disband the Mexican army and guarantee the Mexican constitution and private property (that is, against Gómez Farías' reforms). At the outset Beach acted as though his mission was intended to prepare the way for some other peace commissioner such as Senator Benton, but by the time he left Mexico, he was convinced that any offers by Benton to Santa Anna would simply encourage him to fight on.[21]

It is unlikely that Beach had any contact with Alexander J. Atocha when that individual arrived on February 13, bearing Polk's offer to open negotiations. For one thing, Beach regarded Atocha as the tool of Santa Anna and the anticlericals. Also, with Mexico City threatened by revolution, Gómez Farías so feared the effect of a peace feeler that, after receiving Atocha's communications, he placed him in confinement outside the capital and released a false version of the American proposal. This version contained the principal provision of Beach's agreement with the proclericals—a boundary at 26°. In all likelihood Gómez Farías had learned of Beach's intrigues and was using this device to arouse nationalist sentiment and to link the Church with the

20. Beach to Buchanan, New York, June 4, 1847, Manning, *IAA*, VIII, 906–7. M. S. Beach, "A Secret Mission to Mexico. Origin of the Treaty of Guadalupe Hidalgo," *Scribner's Monthly*, 18 (May 1879), 138–39.

21. Manning, *IAA*, VIII, 906–7. M. S. Beach, "Origin of the Treaty," pp. 138–39. Articles signed "Montgomery" (Mrs. Storms) in New York *Sun*, April 19, 1847, p. 2; May 6, p. 2; May 7, p. 2. The onetime Mexican consul general at New York met Beach and his party on shipboard between Havana and Veracruz and accompanied them to Mexico City, helping them over obstacles. He wrote to a friend that Beach's presence showed such eagerness for peace on the part of the United States government as to encourage Mexicans to further resistance. Juan de la Granja to Juan N. Almonte, January 13; De la Granja to Juan P. García, July 28, Juan de la Granja, *Epistolario*, pp. 24–25, 125–27.

enemy. If so, Beach had been working at cross purposes with his own government and was hampering the very negotiations he had been instructed to encourage.[22]

Of course he never admitted his faults. Instead, Beach told Buchanan that he had dissuaded the bishops from sending money to Santa Anna's army and even claimed much credit for the revolt of February 27. He hinted that he had timed it to coincide with Scott's landing at Veracruz and that he had obtained $40,000 from the clergy at a critical moment to keep the revolt active. Meanwhile, he sent Mrs. Storms to Veracruz to establish connections with Scott. (The general was indignant that "a petticoat" had been entrusted with such a mission.) Unfortunately, Santa Anna's sudden appearance in Mexico City upset all of Beach's plans. In his naïveté he was apparently willing to try negotiation with Santa Anna, but Black, horrified, convinced him that he would be arrested as a spy. Beach and his daughter slipped out of the city undetected and made their way to the American forces at Tampico. By the end of April he was back in the United States.[23]

Beach's romantic blunderings led to much expansionist publicity in his New York *Sun*, especially concerning the route across Tehuantepec. Also, he probably encouraged some Mexican pro-clericals to regard the United States as a *deus ex machina* that would prevent the seizure of their lands. But patriotism and Yankeephobia were too strong for anyone to have launched peace negotiations at this point, even without the rumors of territorial demands. After the rebellion had ended, for example, the government newspaper declared bluntly: "The United States may triumph, but its prize, like that of the vulture, will lie in a lake of blood. Let the destruction be complete; let even our invaders be horrified by their victory."[24]

*   *   *   *

22. For more details on the Atocha mission, see Chap. 13. New York *Sun*, April 19, 1847, p. 2. Alexander J. Atocha to Oficial Mayor de Relaciones Exteriores, Tepeyahualco, February 18, US, LC, /167. Black to Buchanan, February 16; Beach to Buchanan, June 4, Manning, *IAA*, VIII, 895, 906–7. Bankhead to Palmerston, March 2, No. 16 and enclosure, GB, FO 50/208, ff. 208–9, 211–13. Bermúdez de Castro to Primer Secretario de Estado, March 1, April 1, Nos. 444, 463, *Rdh-m*, IV, 46–49, 71–72. Both Bankhead and Bermúdez de Castro were aware of the genuine, moderate American terms. Bermúdez felt that Gómez Farías should have agreed to negotiate in order to gain a breathing spell.

23. Beach to Buchanan, June 4, 1847, Manning, *IAA*, VIII, 906–7. M. S. Beach, "Origin of the Treaty," pp. 139–40. New York *Sun*, April 15, p. 2; May 3, p. 2; August 16, p. 2. Bravo Ugarte, "La misión confidencial de Moses Y. Beach," 476–80. Luis G. Zorrilla, *Historia de las relaciones entre México y los Estados Unidos de América, 1800–1958*, I, 200.

24. *El diario del gobierno*, April 3,

Without knowledge of these pronouncements, Polk had already decided to invade central Mexico. The first step was to be the capture of Veracruz. On March 5, while Santa Anna's army was still trudging back to San Luis Potosí and Mexicans were taking pot shots at each other in the streets of their capital, Scott's flotilla, carrying some 12,000 troops, joined Conner's blockading squadron, at anchor off Veracruz port and its island fortress, San Juan de Ulua.

After some delay Scott landed nearly all his forces a few miles south of the city, where they began digging trenches in the sand dunes. He realized that he must capture Veracruz immediately, before yellow fever descended on his soldiers and Polk's impatient wrath on himself. Yet, a frontal attack on Ulua might be costly, for the Mexicans were reported to have strengthened it since the French intervention of 1838–1839. Accordingly, he called on the Mexican garrison of three or four thousand to surrender, and when the commander declared that he would resist to the end, Scott ordered a bombardment. For nearly four days guns on land and on the ships kept up steady fire, mostly at Veracruz itself rather than at the fortress. A large part of the city was destroyed; terror seized the inhabitants; and on March 29 both Veracruz and Ulua surrendered.[25]

The American troops marched into the city amid a volley of outcries at Scott's inhumanity. Foreign consuls protested that they had tried in vain to evacuate their compatriots after the bombardment began, but in London Lord Palmerston censured his British representative for not acting as soon as the Americans landed. The foreign consuls, he wrote, should have taken for granted that the

1847, as quoted in Berge, "Mexican Response," p. 252. See also *El republicano*, February 24, reprinted in Washington *National Intelligencer* and other American papers. Black to Buchanan, January 28, No. 405, US, DS, CD, Mexico City, IX.

25. Rives, *US and Mexico*, II, 380–89. Smith, *War with Mexico*, II, Chap. 22. Douglas Southall Freeman, *R. E. Lee, a Biography*, I, 223–34. Commander David G. Farragut, U.S.N., who had happened to witness the French seizure of Ulua in 1838, believed that a direct naval attack on the fortress was completely practicable. As early as 1845 he drew up a plan for such an attack, but the plan was rejected. Charles Lee Lewis, *David Glasgow Farragut, Ad-*

miral in the Making, pp. 242–46. For Mexican accounts see Alcaraz *et al., Apuntes para la historia de la guerra*, Chap. 10. Roa Bárcena, *Recuerdos de la invasión*, I, Chaps. 14–16. For the British consul's account, see Francis Giffard to Palmerston, March 29, 1847, No. 8 and enclosure, GB, FO 50/214, ff. 47–53. The principal dispatches by Scott and his officers are collected in US, 30C, 1S, SED 1, pp. 216–55. K. Jack Bauer, *Surfboats and Horse Marines: U.S. Naval Operations in the Mexican War, 1846–48*, Chaps. 7–8. Samuel Eliot Morison, *"Old Bruin," Commodore Matthew Calbraith Perry, 1794–1858*, pp. 206–11. For other American naval actions in the Gulf of Mexico, see the Bauer and Morison works *passim*.

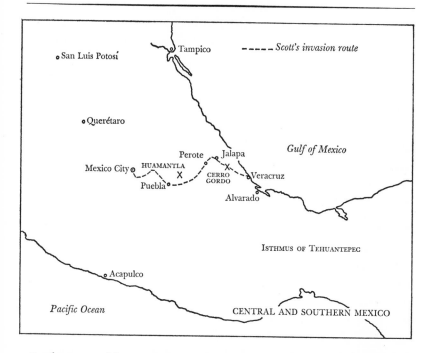

San Luis Potosí

Tampico

----- *Scott's invasion route*

Querétaro

Perote Jalapa *Gulf of Mexico*

Mexico City HUAMANTLA
X CERRO Veracruz
Puebla GORDO

Alvarado

ISTHMUS OF TEHUANTEPEC

Acapulco

Pacific Ocean

CENTRAL AND SOUTHERN MEXICO

attackers would use every practicable method to capture Vera-cruz.[26]

Having taken the city, Scott sent naval detachments to oc-cupy smaller ports on the Gulf coast, and he did what he could to restore order in Veracruz before moving inland. Rubble was cleared away, buildings repaired; the streets were thoroughly cleaned for the first time in years. To the inhabitants Scott issued a proclamation promising fair treatment, and he underlined it by severely punishing a few marauding soldiers. Realizing the value of clerical support, he treated Church property with special care; the general himself even carried a candle in a procession to the cathedral. As soon as the port was available for use, the Ameri-cans began to bring in a great supply of matériel—enough for an army of 150,000, reported the British consul. Within a few weeks Veracruz, like Matamoros and Tampico before it, was flooded with Yankee merchandise.[27]

26. Palmerston memorandum, June 1, 1847, GB, FO 50/214, f. 65. For the contemporary Mexican view of the matter, see Chaney, "Mexican-United States War, As Seen by Intellectuals," p. 31. One Mexican writer has defended Scott. Roa Bárcena, *Recuerdos de la invasión*, I, 300–303.

27. Rives, *US and Mexico*, II, 389–

90. Charles Winslow Elliott, *Winfield Scott, the Soldier and the Man*, pp. 460–62. Freeman, *Lee*, I, 235–36. Giffard to Palmerston, April 13, 1847, No. 12, GB, FO 50/214, ff. 74–77. New Orleans *Picayune*, April 23, reprinted in Wash-ington *National Intelligencer*, May 11, p. 3.

Although observers predicted that the Americans would need many weeks to organize a march inland, Scott was anxious to gain the foothills before the fever season; on April 8 his advance guard set out on the National Highway toward Jalapa, the first large town in the healthy zone. Six days earlier, Santa Anna had left Mexico City to join his own troops, which had already taken up an imposing defensive position near the village of Cerro Gordo, just east of Jalapa. Here the National Highway, roughly paralleling a small river, followed a narrow ravine that was dominated by several steep hills, especially El Telégrafo ("Cerro Gordo" or "Big Peak"). Many of the waiting Mexicans were sick or exhausted by a forced march of twelve hundred miles from Buena Vista, and the new recruits were overawed at tales of the Americans' invincibility.

As soon as the invaders made contact with Mexican outposts, their army encamped, while Scott hurried out from Veracruz to join his men. A careful reconnaissance disclosed the enemy's position—in the process Captain Robert E. Lee penetrated over densely wooded hills around the flank of the Mexican army. Roughly speaking, the situation was like Buena Vista in reverse, for the Mexican center was too strong for a direct assault from the highway. However, Santa Anna had ignored weak points on his left, relying for protection on the almost impenetrable hills and ravines. This time the forces were nearly equal, about eight or nine thousand men on each side.[28] The remainder of Scott's men were either on garrison duty in Veracruz or strung along the road.

The critical action of Cerro Gordo was an envelopment of the Mexican left by an American division (about equal to a modern regiment), which was required to move as quietly as possible over chasms so steep that, as Lieutenant U. S. Grant later wrote, the men had to lower and raise their artillery by ropes. Before Santa Anna fully realized what was happening, the Americans had occupied a lightly held hill that dominated the approach to El Telégrafo. At the climax of the battle one American unit stormed El Telégrafo, while another made its way behind the Mexican position to the highway, cutting off the main line of retreat. As the Mexicans saw their own guns turned on them, their whole left broke and fled, and soon the entire army was on the run into the hills and along the river valley. Santa Anna and his principal officers narrowly escaped capture, and the Americans seized great

28. Rives, *US and Mexico*, II, 394–96,   II, 41–47, 49–50.
398, 406–8. Smith, *War with Mexico*,

quantities of munitions and took over 3,000 prisoners—so many that Scott could not keep them confined; he released them on parole. A day later, on April 19, he and his troops entered Jalapa; other units soon occupied the barrier fortress of Perote after a short skirmish.[29]

Following Cerro Gordo, Scott might have been able to advance directly on Mexico City, but his supply lines were insecure, his men tired, and over 3,000 short-term volunteers ready to leave for home. Scott realized that he must avoid risking his army's precious prestige while pacifying the inhabitants, who vastly outnumbered the Americans. Accordingly, he issued another conciliatory proclamation, drawn up with the aid of local clerical advisers. Dated May 11, this document laid before the Mexicans the disgraceful impotence of their government, warned them against hopeless guerrilla warfare, and urged them to make common cause with the invaders against foreign monarchism. "Abandon at once those old colonial habits," he urged, "and learn to be truly free—truly republican. . . . *Remember that you are Americans*, and that your happiness is not to come from Europe." [30]

Unable to consider an advance into the central Valley of Mexico, Scott compromised on the capture of Puebla, a city of 80,000, the second largest in Mexico and a stronghold of pro-clericalism. Santa Anna, who had regathered a few thousand men from the debacle at Cerro Gordo, might have organized a resistance there, but he was unpopular with the inhabitants, and, being concerned about the firmness of the government in Mexico City, he fell back to the capital. On May 15 a division entered Puebla under the command of William J. Worth, one of Scott's best generals, who had earlier distinguished himself with Taylor at Monterrey. Worth made generous promises of civil and religious protection—some of them so extreme that Scott later had to modify them. The clergy welcomed the Americans, and the people, who had expected a crack army of giants, crowded around to stare at the ragged men, weary and ill, and to touch their battered rifles and guns wonderingly. The Poblanos "showed [the Americans]

29. Smith, *War with Mexico*, II, Chap. 23; and Rives, *US and Mexico*, II, 395–408. Grant's account of the enveloping action and its difficulties appears in *Personal Memoirs of U.S. Grant*, I, 132. See also Elliott, *Scott*, pp. 463–70. Dispatches by Scott and some of his officers appear in US, 30C, 1S, SED 1, pp. 255–302. For Lee's activities, see Freeman,

Lee, I, Chap. 15. For Mexican accounts, see Alcaraz *et al.*, *Apuntes para la historia de la guerra*, pp. 169–83; and Roa Bárcena, *Recuerdos de la invasión*, II, Chaps. 17, 18.

30. US, 30C, 1S, HED 60, pp. 968–74. Smith, *War with Mexico*, II, 61–67. Rives, *US and Mexico*, II, 409–14.

neither sympathy nor hatred," wrote the Spanish minister, Bermúdez de Castro. "They received them more like travelers than enemies."[31]

Scott and his troops remained in Puebla nearly three months. The basic reason for interrupting his campaign was that he had too few men to garrison the city, maintain the supply route to Veracruz, and mount an adequate attacking force. With short-term volunteers returning home by the hundreds and with over 3,000 of his men hospitalized, his effective forces had fallen below 10,000 by the end of June, despite the arrival of reinforcements from the States. In the city the people remained friendly, and food was never lacking; but the thin line of guards along the National Highway could not prevent a resurgence of guerrillas and bandits, and retaliation by the Americans against local inhabitants presaged a warfare of atrocities. The piles of stores mounted at Veracruz, while Scott eagerly awaited their arrival at Puebla. One train of 400 wagons and 1,200 loaded mules, for example, spent several weeks stalled in various defiles after losing half its convoy to the climate and the guerrillas. Meanwhile, in Veracruz as many as a hundred men sickened with yellow fever in a single day.[32]

Fortunately for Scott, the defeat at Cerro Gordo had profoundly discredited Santa Anna and so demoralized the Mexicans that at first no official undertook effective fortifications to defend Mexico City. Intrigue within the government kept the capital in constant ferment, while rumors of secession and revolution followed one another from the north and west.[33] As the summer of 1847 began, both Americans and Mexicans seemed paralyzed, and the war entered another phase of inaction and drift.

* * * *

In accordance with Polk's cyclical strategy of strike and wait, the time had now come for another peace overture. While Scott fought his way from Veracruz to Puebla, the President was mak-

31. Bermúdez de Castro to Primer Secretario de Estado, May 29, 1847, No. 498, *Rdh-m*, IV, 108. Smith, *War with Mexico*, II, 70–72. Alcaraz *et al.*, *Apuntes para la historia de la guerra*, Chap. 12. See also Santa Anna, *Apelación al buen criterio*, pp. 42–45.

32. Rives, *US and Mexico*, II, 411–14. Smith, *War with Mexico*, II, 73–74, 76–77. R. S. Ripley, *The War with Mexico*, II, 129–39. Giffard to Palmerston, May 15, 31, June 15, July 2, 1847, Nos. 17, 19,

20, 23, GB, FO 50/214, ff. 95–97, 104–6, 114–15, 120–21. Roa Bárcena, *Recuerdos de la invasión*, Chaps. 20, 21.

33. Smith, *War with Mexico*, II, 79–82. Riva Palacio, *México a través de los siglos*, IV, 655–60, 664–69. Ramírez, *Mexico during the War with the United States*, pp. 118–26. Bermúdez de Castro to Primer Secretario de Estado, April 29, May 29, June 29, 1847, Nos. 482, 498, 499, 517, *Rdh-m*, IV, 86–92, 107–14, 117–21.

ing appropriate preparations. His first action following the cabinet's decision of March 20 to send Scott inland, however, was a measure designed to exploit the American occupation for its duration. Polk issued an order raising the blockade on the Gulf ports, imposing a new tariff on foreign imports, and declaring that United States customs officials would collect the duties to help pay for the war. The cabinet had discussed the measure at intervals for several weeks. Remembering the hue and cry over Kearny's preemptive creation of territorial government in Santa Fe, Polk was careful to base his tariff decree on the military rights of a victor under international law rather than on the United States Constitution.[34]

The new tariff lowered most duties, in the hope of stimulating remunerative trade, but it aroused many complaints. Despite Polk's careful explanation, strict constructionists at home regarded it as executive piracy.[35] Foreign interests that held monopolistic grants in Mexico or public bonds payable out of Mexican customs receipts also cried "Stop, thief!" When some of them protested to the British Foreign Office, however, Palmerston mildly remarked that the United States had a right to set up any tariff it pleased, without regard to Mexican obligations. But the new decree had little immediate effect, for foreign ships avoided Veracruz, and six months later only one small cargo from Europe had been unloaded there.[36]

As soon as Polk learned that Scott had occupied Veracruz, he proposed to the cabinet that a peace commissioner be appointed to accompany the army inland and be ready to present a draft treaty to the Mexican government whenever it showed any willingness to negotiate. Had the Mexicans agreed to send commissioners to Havana, Polk would have appointed Buchanan to meet them, but as matters stood, the likelihood of a long wait and probably also concern about loss of face led him to seek another envoy.

Unwilling to offend any factions in Congress by selecting a prominent politician as peace commissioner, Polk readily agreed with Buchanan's suggestion that a temporary appointment go to a less conspicuous person, Nicholas P. Trist, the chief clerk and

34. James K. Polk, *The Diary of James K. Polk during His Presidency, 1845 to 1847*, ed. Milo M. Quaife, II, 416, 420, 422, 424–25, 431, 437–38, 440, 442–43, 446–47, 449–51, 454–55.

35. Cincinnati *Gazette*, n.d., reprinted in Washington *National Intelligencer*, May 5, 1847, p. 3.

36. Bermúdez de Castro to Primer Secretario de Estado, May 24, 1847, No. 486, *Rdh-m*, IV, 92–93. Ewen C. Mackintosh to Bankhead, April 29; Memorandum of Palmerston, June 21, GB, FO 50/209, ff. 150–53. James Patrick Shenton, *Robert John Walker, a Politician from Jackson to Lincoln*, p. 95.

de facto undersecretary of the State Department. The original understanding for the mission was that Trist would do no more than present a draft treaty; if the Mexicans wished to discuss its terms, the United States government would then appoint a full commissioner.[37] Characteristically, Polk urged extreme secrecy on both cabinet and Trist, lest the Whigs discover the maneuver and send agents to block negotiations. Polk was relentlessly determined to cow the Mexicans through a show of strength, for he wrote to his friend General Gideon J. Pillow: "If they still refuse to negotiate for peace, you may rely upon my fixed purpose to prosecute the War, with the utmost possible vigour."[38]

When Polk and the cabinet met on April 13 to draw up Trist's instructions, they made them as explicit as possible, in view of his low status. Apparently without much difficulty all agreed that the treaty draft should specify the Rio Grande boundary and the cession of New Mexico and both Californias. The addition of Lower California went beyond the terms considered in earlier cabinet discussions, but the instructions allowed Trist to abandon the demand for this territory, should he encounter solid opposition to its cession. Later dispatches, sent to him in July, repeated this discretionary provision and suggested that the line of 32° might be a more convenient boundary than the vague southern limits of New Mexico.[39] The boundary provisions represented a victory for the moderate expansionist Buchanan, inasmuch as Polk had leaned toward Walker's demand for a boundary at 26° (about the level of Matamoros) soon after the beginning of the war.[40] Walker obtained inclusion of an article granting the United States government and citizens free transit rights across the Isthmus of Tehuantepec, but Polk would not make it an express condition of peace. If Mexico agreed to adequate territorial cessions, the Ameri-

37. Buchanan favored Slidell if a commission of several men were to be sent, but Benton would not have him, and his presence might have offended the Mexicans unnecessarily. Smith, *War with Mexico*, II, 126. Polk, *Diary,* II, 263–64, 410, 412, 465–67.

38. James K. Polk to Gideon J. Pillow, April 15 [possibly 13 or 14], 1847, Letterbook, Series 4 (roll 58), pp. 357–66, Polk Papers, LC. Polk, *Diary,* II, 478–79.

39. The July dispatches also suggested that Trist try to draw the boundary to include Paso del Norte (modern El Paso) but made clear that, like Lower California, neither the 32° line

nor Paso del Norte was to be considered a *sine qua non*. From these dispatches it is plain that Polk expected Trist to obtain San Diego. Buchanan to Nicholas P. Trist, April 15, 1847, No. 1, Manning, *IAA,* VIII, 201–7. These pages also include the treaty draft. Same, July 13, 19, Nos. 3, 4, ibid., pp. 209–14.

40. Rives, *US and Mexico,* II, 426. Polk, *Diary,* I, 495–97. Buchanan's opposition to large annexations was based on his unwillingness to take in their "mongrel" inhabitants and his concern over the slavery question. Buchanan to James Shields, April 23, 1847, Letterpress, Buchanan Papers, box 1, HSP.

cans were willing to waive debts and claims that had existed at the beginning of the war, and the draft specified payment to Mexico of $15 million.

Buchanan wished to stop at this, but Polk insisted on adding to Trist's instructions complicated provisions that allowed him to offer maximum amounts from $20 million to $30 million for various territorial combinations. Also, the President declared that the cession of New Mexico and Upper California must be "a sine qua non of any Treaty." In arguing for higher payments and against insistence on the isthmian transit rights, Polk emphasized that the money involved was far less than the cost of another year of war, that the borderlands would be worth four times the proposed amounts, and that Tehuantepec was not an object of the war at its outbreak. Thus, he implicitly confirmed earlier indications that California and New Mexico had been goals of conquest from the beginning of hostilities, if not earlier.[41]

At first glance, Trist seemed to be a fairly good choice to negotiate a peace. His genteel background would satisfy the Mexicans' standards for emissaries, and he had irreproachable Democratic connections, having married Thomas Jefferson's granddaughter and served briefly as Andrew Jackson's private secretary. Other advantages were his legal training and a considerable knowledge of diplomatic procedure, gained from eight years as consul at Havana and two years as chief clerk of the State Department. He spoke Spanish fluently and, in Buchanan's words, was "perfectly familiar with the Spanish character." His moderate expansionist views harmonized with those of Buchanan, who may have proposed him for that reason. Trist's chief defects, as the secretary should have known, were personal pride, sensitive feelings, and outbursts of headstrong independence. Also, he was a compulsive letter-writer, long-winded and often tactless. In these respects he unfortunately matched General Scott, with whom he would necessarily cooperate closely. Scott, indeed, was as well qualified as Trist for the post of negotiator, but Polk naturally did not propose his name.[42]

41. Polk authorized Trist to offer as much as $25 million for New Mexico, Upper California, and the isthmian privileges, or for New Mexico and both Californias. He allowed Trist a little leeway in minor matters, such as the wording of a provision guaranteeing the rights of inhabitants in the ceded territory. The treaty draft specified that goods imported during the occupation must be exempt from taxation after the American withdrawal. Buchanan to Trist, April 15, 1847, No. 1, Manning, *IAA*, VIII, 201–7. The quoted phrase is on p. 206.

42. Polk, *Diary*, II, 467. Louis Martin Sears, "Nicholas P. Trist, a Diplomat with Ideals," *Mississippi Valley Historical Review*, 11 (June 1924), 85–92. See also Norman A. Graebner, "Party

An important circumstance favoring Trist's mission was the fact that the British government had resigned itself to an American victory over Mexico and would now exert every effort to further peace, preserve a reduced Mexican nationality, and restore prewar trade conditions. During the preceding autumn and winter the British press had recognized American victories grudgingly, minimized American gains wherever possible, and criticized Polk's handling of the United States Congress and the Mexican government. Polk's annual message struck the *Times* as incredible hypocrisy. "He has laid it on so thick as to form an inexpugnable edifice. His pyramid of mendacity is bombproof," it declared. But the *Examiner* was more realistic:

> If ever there was a ruling power, entitled to take a high tone in addressing those whom he ruled, it certainly is President Polk. He has been the greatest of American conquerors, the most successful of American diplomatists. He has half bullied, half wheedled England out of the Columbia River, has defeated the joint action of France and England in Texas, has occupied California, and threatens at this moment the capital of El Dorado, [San Luis] Potosi, with an American army. A little grandiloquence might have been permissible in such circumstances, and was even natural to an American. And yet on reading Mr. Polk's message, we find not a single trace of such an overweening sentiment.[43]

The United States minister, George Bancroft, also recognized the changing attitude, for he wrote in mid-January: "They do not love us; but they are compelled to respect us. . . . England sees that the Californias must be ours; and sees it with unmingled regret,

Politics and the Trist Mission," *Journal of Southern History*, 19 (May 1953), 140–42. While Trist was consul at Havana, he aroused much criticism from American sailors and shipowners for arbitrary treatment and failure to defend their interests. Although a congressional committee declined to take action against him, the weight of complaints against Trist suggests that he was lucky not to be censured. Robert Arthur Brent, "Nicholas Philip Trist, Biography of a Disobedient Diplomat," Ph. D. diss., University of Virginia, 1950, pp. 108–14. Another historian criticizes Trist's appointment because he favored only moderate annexations. Eugene Keith Chamberlin, "Nicholas P.

Trist and Baja California," *Pacific Historical Review*, 32 (February 1963), 57–58. See also the unfavorable view in Jack Northup, "Nicholas Trist's Mission into Mexico: a Reinterpretation," *Southwestern Historical Quarterly*, 71 (January 1968), 321–46.

43. London *Times*, November 9, 1846, p. 4; November 20, p. 4; December 31, p. 4; January 1, 1847. London *Morning Chronicle*, September 5, 1846, p. 4; October 28, p. 4; October 31, p. 4; December 3, p. 4; December 4, p. 4; December 31, p. 4. London *Examiner*, December 12, p. 785; January 2, 1847, p. 1. (The passage quoted appears in the January 2 issue.)

but remains 'neutral'." [44] He observed that capitalists were growing more favorable to an American loan. Palmerston was again at outs with France over the question of influence in Spain, but he lacked the united support of the British public. Russell, wrote Bancroft, was "resolved on friendship with the United States. . . . We can do without England better than England can do without us." The victories of Taylor and Scott in the late winter and spring added immeasurably to British respect. When the news of Veracruz arrived, aristocrats crowded around the American minister with congratulations. "You are the Lords of Mexico!" declared Viscount Ashburton. "How could you take the castle of Vera Cruz so soon?" asked Earl Grey. The occasion moved Palmerston to speak warmly about the immense superiority of the Anglo-Saxon race. [45]

Private British policy statements also recognized the American *faits accomplis*. Palmerston, as noted, accepted without hesitation Scott's bombardment of Veracruz and the occupation tariff. When Gutiérrez de Estrada approached him in an effort to revive the monarchist plot, Palmerston read his letters but did nothing. [46] Since Mexico and the United States had both rejected Britain's formal offers of mediation, Palmerston would not renew them, but he urged peace on the Mexican minister to Britain and consistently approved any efforts by his own agents in Mexico to furnish good offices between the belligerents. As he put it in a memorandum of June 1847:

> The great & signal Successes achieved by [the United States] . . . will of Course be found to have raised proportionably the Demands which the U.S. will in such negotiation make upon the Govt. of Mexico. Still it seems to H.M.'s Govt. that the sooner Mexico comes to an arrangement the less considerable will be the sacrifices which Mexico will have to make. . . .
>
> The Mexican Govt. will of Course endeavour to draw the British Govt. to give either in Fact or in appearance Some positive assistance to Mexico. But . . . it wd. not be consistent with the Interests of Gt. Br. to involve herself in a Rupture with the U.S., in aid of a

44. George Bancroft to Polk, January 19, 1847, M.A. deWolfe Howe, *The Life and Letters of George Bancroft*, II, 7–8.
45. Bancroft to Buchanan, January 4, 1847, No. 12, US, DS, Britain, LVII. Bancroft to Polk, November 3, 1846; January 4, 19, May 14, 1847; Bancroft to Buchanan, February 3, Howe, *Life*

and Letters of Bancroft, II, 2–4, 5–10, 17–19.
46. José María Gutiérrez de Estrada to Palmerston, Paris, October 18, November 9, 1846, unsigned memorandum enclosed with the latter; Palmerston to Gutiérrez de Estrada, November, GB, FO 50/204, ff. 71–86. Same, March 1, [1847], GB, FO 50/214, ff. 233–37, 239.

State like Mexico which can make no Effectual Efforts to defend itself, and which Gt. Br. could not undertake to defend without Efforts which would be wholly out of Proportion with the value to Gt. Br. of the object to be defended.[47]

*   *   *   *

Viewed from outside Mexico, therefore, the auspices for peace seemed favorable: the Mexicans badly beaten, the Americans receptive, the British complaisant. Trist almost ruined his mission at the start, however, through his unbridled egotism. His instructions and those which Marcy sent to Scott failed to make clear that he was not intended to supersede the general in any respect, and that the two must exchange all information and cooperate in their complicated task of conquering the country and negotiating a peace. By the time Trist landed at Veracruz, on May 6, he had developed delusions of grandeur. He immediately sent to Scott the ambiguous orders from Marcy and a sealed dispatch from Buchanan for the Mexican foreign minister, along with a curt covering letter of his own, directing Scott to transmit the dispatch to Mexico City.

Since Buchanan's message contained little more than a stiff refusal to withdraw troops before negotiating the peace and an announcement of Trist's presence, there was no reason for secrecy. Scott, now at Jalapa, was already suspicious of Polk's efforts to undercut his authority. Proud of his recent victory at Cerro Gordo and preoccupied with military affairs, he impatiently returned the dispatch to Trist with a blunt note. Trist journeyed to Jalapa, fuming, and on his arrival delivered to Scott thirty pages of denunciation—a "farrago of insolence, conceit and arrogance," according to the general, who compared Trist to "Danton, Marat, and St. Just—all in one." Trist wrote to his wife that he was determined to *"finish"* this *"imbecile."* He and Scott moved on to Puebla, refusing to have anything to do with each other, and both wrote long, highly imprudent letters of complaint to Washington.[48] The whole

47. Palmerston memorandum, June 21, 1847, commenting on a report by Bankhead of his cautious reply to a Mexican appeal for aid. GB, FO 50/209, ff. 172–75.

48. Elliott, *Scott*, pp. 475–86. Rives, *US and Mexico*, II, 427–32. McCormac, *James K. Polk, a Political Biography*, pp. 493–505. William L. Marcy to Winfield Scott, April 14, May 31, June 15,

July 12, 1847, US, 30C, 1S, HED 60, pp. 940–41, 960–63, 975–76, 998–1002. The principal correspondence between Trist and Scott appears ibid., pp. 813–25, 958–60, 996; and in Manning, *IAA*, VIII, 902–5n2. Buchanan to Minister of Foreign Affairs of Mexico, April 15, ibid., pp. 199–201. Trist's words are quoted—out of their original order—from Trist to Mrs. Nicholas P. Trist,

affair confirmed Polk in his opinion of Scott's disloyalty and raised serious doubts of Trist's competence. Convinced that they had missed "the golden moment for concluding a peace" after Cerro Gordo, the angry President momentarily considered recalling them both.[49]

As a result of the quarrel, Polk came to rely increasingly on information from General Gideon J. Pillow, his old political associate in Tennessee, whom he had placed in Scott's army. Polk's secretary told Pillow that he must use his own "cool good judgment" and advise Scott in such a manner as to convince the commander that the suggested ideas were really his own—an impossible assignment, for Pillow had little military ability. The divided lines of authority encouraged intrigue and led to a disreputable series of military trials and hearings after the war ended.[50]

The puerile quarrel between Trist and Scott occurred at a most unfortunate time, for the Americans needed to act with both subtlety and decision if they wished to take advantage of the extreme confusion within the Mexican government. In Mexico City the most apparent immediate reaction to Cerro Gordo was a fresh outburst of Yankeephobia. Nationalist newspapers, especially those on the liberal side, denounced Scott's Jalapa proclamation as hypocrisy and called his appeal against a European monarchy "a weak subterfuge," insisting that Paredes' movement had never had any chance of success.[51] Late in April Congress took out the old proposal for mediation by Britain, hacked it to pieces in a furious debate, and reburied it in committee. Unwilling to repudiate Santa Anna openly but suspicious of his loyalty, it also passed a law which authorized the government to take any action necessary for carrying on the war but declared that anyone who discussed negotiations with the United States would be deemed a traitor. A month later Congress somewhat obscured the validity of this law by readopting the federal Constitution of 1824, which

---

May 15, Trist Papers, XXIII, f. 60037, LC. Scott's words are quoted from Scott to Trist, May 29, Manning, *IAA*, VIII, 404-5.

49. Polk and the cabinet also considered sending Pierre Soulé or Jefferson Davis to advise Trist. Sending Soulé would have been like diluting kerosene with gasoline. Polk, *Diary*, III, 57-59, 62-63, 76-79, 85, 91. Buchanan wrote Trist a stiff official rebuke for the quarrel with Scott, but since they were personal friends, he added a gentler private letter saying

that Polk was "still . . . well disposed to do you justice." Buchanan to Trist, June 14, July 13, 1847, Nos. 2, 3, Manning, *IAA*, VIII, 208-13. Same, July 13, Trist Papers, XXIII, LC.

50. Polk to Pillow, April 15 [?], May 18, 1847; J. Knox Walker to Pillow, May 26, Letterbook, Series 4 (roll 58), pp. 357-66, 586-97, 669-74. Polk Papers, LC.

51. *Boletín de noticias*, April 27, 1847, p. 1; April 29, p. 1. *El monitor republicano*, April 24, pp. 2, 3; May 25, pp. 3-4.

placed the treaty-making power in the hands of the president. Nevertheless, the threat of punishment for treason remained a formidable obstacle to negotiation.[52]

Beneath this passionate nationalism, however, conflicting desires were producing complex currents and countercurrents, for the hopeless rout at Cerro Gordo had convinced some members of every political faction that Mexico had no alternative but to negotiate for peace. Many conservatives, both inside and outside the capital, feared that continuation of the war would bring new efforts to confiscate private property. In outlying states, especially to the north, liberal federalists still looked for American-sponsored secessionist movements. In Mexico City some moderate liberals hoped to buy peace and American withdrawal with territorial cessions. Perhaps the most interesting group was the *puros*, mostly concentrated in the capital. Frustrated by the overthrow of Gómez Farías and the collapse of his reform measures, but hostile to any territorial cessions, many of them repeatedly obstructed congressional actions by absenting themselves and preventing assembly of a quorum. Some *puros* were coming to favor negotiations, however, in the hope that they could induce liberal Americans to forgo annexations in favor of a temporary protectorate and help Mexico establish a democratic government, free from the domination of army and Church.[53]

Despite the congressional prohibition, individuals or groups were soon putting out secret, tentative feelers for peace discussions. During the April debates Foreign Minister Manuel Baranda, the strongest member of the cabinet, suggested to British Minister Bankhead that he sound out Scott for a truce, and when Bankhead properly refused such one-sided involvement, Baranda asked him to forward confidential peace proposals to the Americans. Bankhead consented, but for the moment the government went no further, and Baranda soon left the cabinet. There is some slight evidence that, at this time, a few moderates and *puros* in Congress were in roundabout communications with Scott, including perhaps even Manuel Crescencio Rejón.[54]

52. Riva Palacio, *México a través de los siglos*, IV, 655–56, 658, 664. Bancroft, *Mexico*, V, 525–26. Ramírez, *Mexico during the War with the United States*, pp. 118–44, *passim*. Dublán and Lozano, *LM*, V, 267–68, 275–79.

53. Riva Palacio, *México a través de los siglos*, IV, 664. Bustamante, *Nuevo Bernal Díaz*, II, 293–94. Bankhead to Palmerston, April 30, 1847, Nos. 42, 43,

45, GB, FO 50/209, ff. 126–34, 142–45, 162–64. Bermúdez de Castro to Primer Secretario de Estado, May 29, No. 498, *Rdh-m*, IV, 107–12. For an oversimplified view of the *puros*—that they all favored an American protectorate—see Fuentes Mares, *Santa Anna*, pp. 268, 282–91.

54. Bankhead to Palmerston, April 30, May 6, 29, 1847, Nos. 45–47, 54, GB,

All these projects were cut short in the middle of May by the news that Santa Anna, having retreated from Puebla, was approaching Mexico City with his troops. Gloomy over his reverses, he apparently considered resigning both the presidency and his military command. Instead, the Yankeephobe General José María Tornel convinced him that only a handful of people opposed him and that the national safety depended on his leadership. Santa Anna entered the city and set to work organizing its defenses, encouraged by Tornel and others who wanted the war to continue. The president told Bermúdez de Castro in a rambling monologue that he dared not undertake peace negotiations, since he was already under suspicion of dealing treasonably with the Americans.[55]

While Santa Anna hesitated between war and peace, Scott and Trist were taking up residence in Puebla, with only a vague idea of the situation in the capital. Aware of Britain's interest in mediation, Trist wrote to Bankhead on June 6, asking if he would transmit Buchanan's note to the Mexican foreign minister.[56] The British minister was quite willing but, being ill, sent his young attaché, Edward Thornton, through guerrilla-infested territory to Puebla with an oral reply. Arriving there on June 11, Thornton was astonished to find Trist and Scott refusing to speak to each other, so he conferred with each, separately. He told Trist of the strong sentiment for peace in Mexico City and advised Scott to remain in Puebla while feeling out the situation. Thornton observed that news of Polk's Three Million Act had raised noisy suspicions of bribery and added that it would be useful to have a sum of money ready for prompt payment to the Mexican government on the signature of a treaty. Trist denied that the appropriation was intended for bribes, but he admitted that Polk would be willing to pay Mexico for agreeing to the Rio Grande boundary and ceding Upper California.[57]

FO 50/209, ff. 162–64, 166–71, 190–91, 240–41. Bermúdez de Castro to Primer Secretario de Estado, May 29, No. 498, *Rdh-m*, IV, 110. Ramírez, *Mexico during the War with the United States*, pp. 126–33, 136–38, 144. Edward Thornton to H. U. Addington, June 29, GB, FO, 50/213, ff. 13–15.

55. Callcott, *Santa Anna*, pp. 263–64. Ramírez, *Mexico during the War with the United States*, pp. 145–46. Roa Bárcena, *Recuerdos de la invasión*, II, 164–71. Riva Palacio, *México a través de los siglos*, IV, 664–69. Bermúdez de Castro to Primer Secretario de Estado,

May 29, 1847, No. 499, *Rdh-m*, IV, 112–14. Prieto, *Memorias, 1840 a 1853*, pp. 207–19. Fuentes Mares, *Santa Anna*, pp. 269–70.

56. Trist knew so little about affairs in Mexico City that he was forced to rely on old newspapers that travelers might happen to bring to Puebla. Trist to Buchanan, June 3, 1847, No. 6, US, DS, D, Mexico, XIV. Same, June 13, No. 7; Trist to Bankhead, June 6, Manning, *IAA*, VIII, 908–14.

57. Trist to Bankhead, June 11, 1847, Manning, *IAA*, VIII, 910–11, note. Bankhead to Palmerston, June 26, No.

On Thornton's return to Mexico City, Bankhead presented Buchanan's note to a new foreign minister, Domingo Ibarra. For several weeks the government was unable to gather enough deputies for a discussion of peace negotiations, however, so Ibarra could send Trist only a brief acknowledgment.[58] During the last week of June, Thornton made a second trip to Puebla with this message, taking along British Consul Ewen C. Mackintosh, who was eager for peace and was in touch with high Mexican officials. A British merchant in Puebla, one Mr. Turnbull, also took part in the discussions. Turnbull assured Trist that Santa Anna was willing to negotiate but needed time and money to overcome the opposition of Congress. Much might be done if the Americans would abandon their plans to march on the capital, send $10,000 in cash at once to be distributed among Santa Anna's associates, and promise to pay $1 million on the conclusion of peace.[59]

At first Trist doubted that he could use United States funds for such obvious bribery, but he determined to make up his quarrel with Scott and to delay the advance on Mexico City, so as to consider what might be done. He made a courteous overture to the general; at this point he fell ill, and Scott's sympathy for the invalid completed the reconciliation. When Trist had recovered, he revealed to Scott his conversations with his British visitors, adding that their proposal was probably the only alternative to a long-drawn-out occupation of Mexico City. Scott agreed so readily as to suggest that he had already discussed the idea with the emissaries from the capital. He told Trist that he could easily supply the small

61; Thornton to Bankhead, June 14, GB, FO 50/210, ff. 1–27. Thornton to Addington, June 29, GB, FO 50/213, ff. 13–15.

58. Bankhead to Palmerston, June 29, 1847, Nos. 65, 67, GB, FO 50/210, ff. 106, 120–23. Domingo Ibarra to Buchanan, June 22, Manning, *IAA*, VIII, 914.

59. Neither Bankhead nor Thornton reported the second trip to Puebla. This account rests almost entirely on later narration by Pillow, to whom Trist apparently recounted all his action, as he had been instructed. Pillow to Marcy, January 18, 1848; undated statement by Pillow to court of inquiry; both are in US, DW, "Proceedings of a Court of Inquiry Held in Mexico and the U. S., under Confidential Instructions from the Secretary of War, 17th March 1848 in Regard to the Use of

Secret Service Money for the Purchase of a Peace," Office of the Judge Advocate General, General Courts Martial, 1812–1938, box FF-300, NA. An account of the Puebla discussions, using the court of inquiry proceedings but not the British Foreign Office archives, is Carlos E. Castañeda, "Relations of General Scott with Santa Anna," *Hispanic American Historical Review*, 29 (November 1949), 455–73. Pillow's account tallies with later correspondence between Scott and Trist and with the abundant reports on the conference of July 17, so it is probably reliable. See also fragmentary references to Thornton's presence in Puebla late in June. Trist to Scott, June 25, 1847; [Thornton] to L. Hargous, [July 3?]; memorandum by Scott, July 19; [Trist] to Thornton, July 3, Trist Papers, XXIV, ff. 60115–16, 60157–59.

down payment from his contingent fund and that he was also quite willing to pledge $1 million. "Such transactions have always been considered allowable in war," the general rationalized. "Also we cannot know that the money will silently go into other channels & that on the whole the US will not have to pay more than the acquisition is worth."[60]

Neither Scott nor Trist, however, wanted to undertake such a shady enterprise without sharing the responsibility. Therefore, Scott approached Pillow, knowing him to be a friend of Polk, and explained the plan. Scott argued that it would not be corrupt to bribe men who were so eager to sell their influence, and he cited as precedents American gifts to the Barbary rulers and to Indian chiefs. At first opposed to the plan, Pillow finally gave his approval, and on July 16 Scott sent off $10,000 to Mexico City with which to start the negotiations.[61]

Next evening the commander called a council of generals, including Pillow, and made a similar explanation, describing his payment hopefully as "bread thrown upon the waters." The generals all advised Scott to delay his advance until expected reinforcements arrived, but on the subject of the bribe most of them showed disgust or outright opposition. After the conference Pillow withdrew his approval, and either he or one of the others released details of the plan to the American press, where it later caused much trouble.[62] When Polk learned about it, he at once disapproved it strongly, but in view of his persistent efforts for the Three

60. Trist to Scott, June 25, July 16, 1847; [Thornton] to L. Hargous [July 3?]; [Trist] to Thornton, July 3, 15; Scott to Trist, July 17, Trist Papers, XXIV, ff. 60115–16, 60157–59, 60198–99, 60202–4, 60207–8. Louis Hargous' role here is not entirely clear. Probably he served as intermediary between Trist and Scott. During this period the two obtained a little information about the deadlock in Mexico City from intercepted Mexican letters. See also Elliott, *Scott,* pp. 490–91, 495–96.

61. Pillow to Marcy, January 18, 1848, US, DW, "Proceedings," box FF-300. Scott later submitted to Congress a statement concerning disbursement of his secret service funds. For July 16, 1847, there is an entry of $10,000. Other disbursements were smaller, usually under $500. In all, Scott paid out $42,470 from the funds, which had originally amounted to $30,000. US, 34C, 1S, SED 34, pp. 21–22, 24–26. Castañeda sug-

gests that, in all, Scott may have spent over $200,000 on the bribery project, but the evidence is inconclusive. Castañeda, "Relations of Scott with Santa Anna," pp. 471–73.

62. Pillow to Marcy, January 18, 1848. Statements at the court of inquiry by Generals David E. Twiggs, John Anthony Quitman, James Shields, and George Cadwalader. US, DW, "Proceedings," box FF-300. For published accounts by Quitman and by Colonel Ethan Allen Hitchcock (who attended the meeting as secretary), see J. F. H. Claiborne, *Life and Correspondence of John A. Quitman, Major-General, U.S.A., and Governor of the State of Mississippi,* I, 326–29; and Ethan Allen Hitchcock, *Fifty Years in Camp and Field,* ed. W. A. Croffut, pp. 266–68. The first account in the American press was published by the St. Louis *Republican* on November 22, 1847, and signed merely "Gomez." For a discus-

Million Act, one is tempted to suspect that what he principally disliked was the publicity.[63]

While Scott and Trist were trying to share their responsibility for the negotiations, Santa Anna in Mexico City was maneuvering with his legislature to the same end. Day after day Congress could do no business for lack of a quorum. In mid-July a congressional committee finally reminded the President that the Constitution of 1824 placed treaty-making in his hands. Soon afterward, the deputies began to disband.[64] Left to his own devices, Santa Anna sent word to Trist that he would now prefer to have the American army advance on the capital and frighten opponents of peace into submission. He also told Bermúdez de Castro that he intended to proclaim a dictatorship and make peace with the Americans as soon as they had attacked the defenders of Mexico City and had broken through their first line. He assured the Spaniard that he would give up California, since it could not be defended, but that the nation's honor would not let him concede the Rio Grande boundary.[65] Two days later, General Gabriel Valencia, a leader of the war faction, arrived in Mexico City with 4,000 men and boasted of their ability to defend the capital. Cautious again, Santa Anna impressed on the British representatives that Scott must advance on Mexico City to strengthen his hand.[66]

So far, Santa Anna was merely playing his familiar game of enticing the invader, in hopes of victory—improbable as that was—or at least absolution from responsibility. Just before Scott began his advance from Puebla, Santa Anna added one last refinement to his strategy. In a communication to the American general he asked that, if the Americans should carry the outer defenses of Mexico City, they would halt their attack and discuss peace terms. If Pillow's account is credible, Scott actually considered agreeing to Santa Anna's request but instead replied that, once the attack was under way, he might not be able to restrain his troops' im-

sion of its authorship see Castañeda, "Relations of Scott with Santa Anna," p. 458n6.

63. Polk, *Diary*, III, 245–46.

64. Rives, *US and Mexico*, II, 444–46. Berge, "Mexican Response," pp. 266–68. Trist to Buchanan, July 7, 1847, No. 8, unidentified letter, probably July 8; D. Garmendia to Juan G. Barrosa, July 13; M. Otero to José Joaquín Pesado, July 13. The last three letters were intercepted by the Americans. Trist Papers, XXIV, ff. 60166, 60169, 60176–79,

LC.

65. Pillow to Marcy, January 18, 1848, US, DW, "Proceedings," box FF-300. Bermúdez de Castro to Primer Secretario de Estado, July 27, 1847, No. 530, *Rdh-m*, IV, 124–27.

66. Bankhead to Palmerston, July 29, 1847, No. 75, GB, FO 50/210, ff. 178–80. [Thornton to Trist, July 29], Manning, *IAA*, VIII, 918, note. A copy in the Trist Papers identifies the writer. R. S. Ripley, *The War with Mexico*, I, 160.

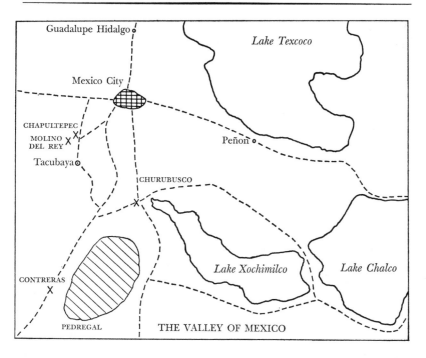

Guadalupe Hidalgo

Lake Texcoco

Mexico City

CHAPULTEPEC
MOLINO X X
DEL REY
Tacubaya

Peñon

CHURUBUSCO

CONTRERAS
X

Lake Xochimilco

Lake Chalco

PEDREGAL   THE VALLEY OF MEXICO

petuosity.[67] Thus, the last campaign of the war began with both sides partly committed to peace and neither general entirely sure whether the fighting would be merely a controlled demonstration or a real battle.

*   *   *   *

As the American troops made their way over the rim of the mountains and started down into the Valley of Mexico, Cortes and Prescott probably crossed Scott's mind. The defenses of Mexico City had changed somewhat, however, since the sixteenth century. A chain of lakes still dominated the eastern and southeastern approaches to the city, but these had shrunk, leaving marshes across which ran several key highways. Collecting most of his remaining

67. Pillow to Marcy, January 18, 1848, US, DW, "Proceedings," box FF-300. Apparently at this stage of the proceedings Trist was negotiating orally with an agent of Santa Anna in Puebla. No written communications have been found, so the account of this important step rests largely on the testimony of Pillow, who was strongly opposed. Later, however, Hitchcock confirmed Scott's reply in an open letter, which Rives believes was inspired by Scott. Rives, US and Mexico, II, 447. Several Mexican writers regard the whole maneuver as simply a device by Santa Anna to gain time for constructing Mexico City's defenses. Roa Bárcena, Recuerdos de la invasión, II, 159–62. Castañeda, "Relations of Scott with Santa Anna," pp. 468–69. Fuentes Mares, Santa Anna, pp. 272–77.

artillery, Santa Anna had massed about 20,000 men at Peñon along the principal eastern road, but after considerable reconnaissance Scott and his generals decided to advance around the edge of the southernmost lake to the two principal southern highways leading into the city. As they moved toward this position, Santa Anna shifted some of his men westward along interior lines to block the Americans' turning maneuver.[68]

The decisive actions were fought in and around the Pedregal, now a fashionable suburb south of Mexico City but at that time an almost impenetrable expanse of hardened, jagged lava. Two American divisions set out to construct a rough road across the waste but encountered an army under Valencia on the western edge. Pillow attacked prematurely, and the Americans were thrown back in disorder. That night, while the Mexican general celebrated his victory, Scott pushed reinforcements across the lava.

The following day, August 20, brought a shift of fortunes. Early in the morning the Americans launched a surprise counter-attack against Valencia, and when Santa Anna failed to come to his aid, routed him and won the Battle of Contreras. Later in the day Scott engaged another force under Santa Anna just north of the Pedregal at Churubusco. Worth's division had to deliver a frontal attack through the hotly defended town and against a bridgehead, a walled convent, and other buildings before the Americans could claim a second victory. Later, Scott was criticized for fighting the Battle of Churubusco, on the grounds that Valencia's defeat had cleared the highway to Tacubaya and the southwest corner of Mexico City. Probably the American commander lacked the necessary information for careful consideration of alternatives. He later argued that it would have been risky to bypass Santa Anna's army and leave it, undefeated, on his flank. In any case, the two victories maintained the Americans' reputation of invincibility and cleared all approaches to the capital.[69]

68. Rives, US and Mexico, II, 453–59. Freeman, Lee, I, 252–58. Santa Anna, Apelación al buen criterio, pp. 45–49. Alcaraz et al., Apuntes para la historia de la guerra, Chap. 16. Riva Palacio, México a través de los siglos, IV, 670–72.

69. Rives, US and Mexico, II, Chaps. 44, 45. Smith, War with Mexico, II, Chap. 26. Elliott, Scott, Chap. 36. Edward S. Wallace, General William Jenkins Worth, Monterey's Forgotten Hero, Chap. 13. Freeman, Lee, I, 259–72. (This account contains especially good maps.) Riva Palacio, México a través de los siglos, IV, 672–81. Roa Bárcena, Recuerdos de la invasión, II, Chaps. 23–25. Alcaraz et al., Apuntes para la historia de la guerra, Chaps. 17–19. Valadés, Breve historia, pp. 182–96. The Mexicans call the first engagement the Battle of Padierna. Scott's own report of the actions and the succeeding armistice is in US, 30C, 1S, SED 1, pp. 306–15.

Late in the afternoon of August 20 the remains of Santa Anna's army fell back, pell-mell, into Mexico City, but instead of pursuing the enemy Scott ordered his soldiers to halt the attack and find quarters for the night. In his report to Marcy he explained that he and Trist had received advice from "intelligent neutrals and some American residents" not to disperse the government and thus "excite a spirit of national desperation," but he did not mention his earlier dealings with Santa Anna. Indeed, he had exactly carried out the Mexican general's recommendations by breaking through the defenses but not entering the city. His decision to halt and regroup was probably sensible under any circumstances, for evening was approaching, and the men had already fought two battles that day. A headlong assault across the causeways and into the narrow streets might have led to ambush and rebuff or, if the troops had gotten out of hand, to looting and killing of civilians, which would have complicated peace negotiations.[70]

Soon after the fighting stopped, Thornton and Mackintosh rode out of the city to Scott's headquarters, ostensibly to provide for the safety of British residents but actually to make certain that Scott would not attack but would try to negotiate. Consul Mackintosh was doubtless largely responsible for this meeting. Apparently Scott's reply was inconclusive, for that night Santa Anna's foreign minister, General Ramón Pacheco, came to the British legation and asked Bankhead to persuade Scott not to sack the city. Bankhead, whose illness had reduced him almost solely to the role of observer, agreed only to transmit messages between the belligerents. Pacheco then handed him a reply to Buchanan's dispatch. It stated that the Mexican government would listen to Trist's proposals and open negotiations, "a treaty to be concluded within the period of a year thereafter." The last provision surprised Bankhead, but he added his own reassurances in two covering notes.[71]

On the next morning, the Mexican and British communications were transmitted to Scott, not by Thornton but by a Mexi-

70. Ibid., p. 314. Castañeda severely criticizes Scott for the decision, assuming that he was entirely taken in by Santa Anna's assurances. Castañeda, "Relations of Scott with Santa Anna," pp. 455–56, 469–70. Many American officers—for example, Pillow and Worth —also felt that Scott should have pushed on and taken the city. Pillow to Marcy, January 18, 1848, US, DW, "Proceedings," box FF-300. Raphael Semmes, *Service Afloat and Ashore during the Mexican War*, pp. 411–12. Scott

defended his decisions stoutly in his memoirs, and Justin Smith supports him. Winfield Scott, *Memoirs of Lieut.-General Scott, Ll. D*, II, 498–99. Smith, *War with Mexico*, II, 120–21.

71. Rives, *US and Mexico*, II, 494–98. Elliott, *Scott*, p. 521. Semmes, *Service Afloat and Ashore*, pp. 412–13. Bankhead to Palmerston, August 21, 1847, No. 76, GB, FO 50/211, ff. 1–4. Ramón Pacheco to Buchanan, August 20; Bankhead to Trist, August 20, 21, Manning, *IAA*, VIII, 921–22, 926n.

can general, Ignacio Mora y Villamil, who arrived at Scott's headquarters in an elaborate carriage. Mora carried neither credentials nor any written request for an armistice, but apparently his oral appeal was so strong that the American commander assumed the initiative and sent Santa Anna the formal proposal to end hostilities which should have come from the beaten foe. In this document he unfortunately referred to "this unnatural war," thereby giving Mexican propagandists a welcome opening. Santa Anna's minister of war returned an impudent reply, obviously designed for publication. In this he graciously accepted the American offer to terminate "this scandal" and sarcastically advised Scott to "take comfortable and well-equipped quarters . . . outside the range of the Mexican fortifications."[72]

Despite this show of scorn, Scott and Trist persisted with their policy of conciliation. When American and Mexican representatives met to draw up armistice terms, Scott abandoned his original intention of demanding to occupy the castle of Chapultepec as a visible symbol of American dominance. Instead, the final agreement, dated August 23, merely required both sides to stop fighting until further notice, exchange prisoners, and undertake no further military advances or fortifications. Scott would allow provisions to pass into the city, and Santa Anna would allow American agents to enter and buy supplies.

In a dispatch to Buchanan Trist explained that the terms were designed to protect Santa Anna from nationalist attacks, "as it is through him alone that any hope whatever of establishing peace presents itself." Since Congress had virtually disbanded in order to avoid responsibility for the peace, the Americans might find themselves "allies of the executive branch of the government." Trist hoped that it would be unnecessary to seize the capital and prolong the occupation, but even this possibility did not dismay him, for he thought that a firm occupation would require only 25,000 men and would have the support of "the best & most influential classes of society," including the clergy.[73]

Trist's reasoning was plausible, but he ignored the mercurial opportunism of Santa Anna. Without obtaining any material guar-

72. Rives, *US and Mexico*, II, 499. Elliott, *Scott*, pp. 522–24. Hitchcock, *Fifty Years*, pp. 279–80. Scott to Santa Anna, August 21, 1847; L. J. Alcorta to Scott, August 21, Manning, *IAA*, VIII, 922–23.

73. For the armistice terms, see US, 30C, 1S, SED 52, pp. 310–12. [Trist] to Buchanan, August 24, 1847, No. 13, Manning, *IAA*, VIII, 927–29. Semmes, *Service Afloat and Ashore*, pp. 419–20.

antees that the Mexicans would seriously negotiate, Scott had given him time to organize his forces for further defense. The easy terms and the American initiative for an armistice had created an impression of weakness and had tarnished the brilliance of the American victories. Three days after the agreement had been reached, Santa Anna allowed one of its provisions to be violated. A Mexican mob attacked the first American supply wagons to appear in the city, killing two teamsters, and although the government apologized, the American army obtained no supplies from the city during the armistice.[74]

Even before the mob action of August 26 Santa Anna and his cabinet had drawn up guidelines for peace discussions which reinforce the suspicion that he was only playing for time and seeking grist for propaganda. According to this memorandum, Mexico would recognize the independence of Texas, covering only the territory north of the Nueces River and only in return for an indemnity. Before negotiations on any other subject could take place, the Americans must evacuate all occupied territory and raise the blockade. The only further territorial change Santa Anna would consider was a trading post at San Francisco and a connecting road to Oregon. To secure these minimal concessions, the United States would be required to pay all costs of the war, cancel all Mexican debts, and confirm all Mexican land grants in Texas prior to 1836.[75] With the enemy at the gates of his capital Santa Anna was proposing to settle the war as though he had won it!

None of the first three men whom Santa Anna appointed to the peace commission wanted the position, but he finally persuaded former President José J. Herrera to serve and then added General Ignacio Mora y Villamil and two lawyers, Bernardo Couto and Miguel Atristain. Trist was pleased with the selection, since he thought these men fairly representative of the peace bloc.[76] He

74. Rives, *US and Mexico*, II, 506–8, 510–11. Smith, *War with Mexico*, II, 134–35, 394–95. At the time of the armistice the Americans had recent and fairly reliable information about the confusion in Mexico City, having just intercepted a group of private letters. Hitchcock, *Fifty Years*, pp. 285–86. Santa Anna's later view of the armistice—that he intended it as a breathing spell—appears in a letter to Manuel Crescencio Rejón, August 31, reprinted in Semmes, *Service Afloat and Ashore*, pp. 415–16.

75. Memorandum, August 24, 1847, US, 30C, 1S, SED 52, pp. 313–15.

76. Ibid., pp. 317–25. Mora y Villamil was one of Santa Anna's principal generals, an engineer and geographer. Couto had been a member of Herrera's cabinet and a leading moderate in Congress. He was probably the ablest of the group. Atristain, the least known, was said to have been placed on the commission at Mackintosh's instance. None of the group had much knowledge of diplomacy or of international law. Alcaraz *et al.*, *Apuntes para la*

later told Buchanan that through an unnamed contact he had access to the most private cabinet discussions, so he was aware of the sentiment there for negotiation. The Mexicans too had secret information, for they had intercepted one of Buchanan's July dispatches, censuring Trist for his quarrel with Scott and indicating that neither Lower California nor the 32° line was to be demanded as a *sine qua non*.[77]

At Trist's first meeting with the Mexican commissioners on August 27, he discovered that they were empowered only to receive his proposals. Accordingly, he gave them a copy of Buchanan's original draft treaty, which provided for the Rio Grande boundary, the cession of New Mexico and both Californias, and transit rights across Tehuantepec, leaving the amount of compensation to be determined. In his report to Buchanan he justified his use of these shock tactics on the grounds that they would save time. Learning that members of the Mexican government considered the American demands extortionate, he informed the cabinet confidentially of the highest price Polk had authorized him to offer (apparently $30 million). Trist also promised that he would enable the government to convert this sum to cash immediately at a premium and, either then or later, hinted that his informant might profit from this conversion.[78]

The formal instructions which the cabinet drew up for the Mexican commissioners retreated only slightly from the original impossible memorandum. The commissioners were to take high ground at the outset by demanding to know the Americans' motives for waging war and the basis of American territorial demands—negotiation or right of conquest. They might agree to recognize the annexation of Texas within the Nueces boundary, if the United States confirmed Mexican land grants there and canceled all Mexican debts and claims. The cession of New Mexico and the Californias and the Tehuantepec privileges were out of the question, but, if pressed, Mexico would agree to a trading post at San Francisco in return for a payment of $1 million every eight years. After the signature of the treaty the United States must immediately withdraw all military forces and pay all war damages,

historia de la guerra, pp. 267–70. Prieto, *Memorias, 1840 a 1853*, pp. 270–71. Trist to Buchanan, September 4, 1847, No. 15, Manning, *IAA*, VIII, 935. Bankhead to Palmerston, August 27, No. 77, GB, FO 50/211, ff. 6–9.

77. Trist to Buchanan, September 27, 1847 (postscript added September 28), No. 16, Manning, *IAA*, VIII, 956.

78. Trist to Buchanan, August 29, September 4, 1847, Nos. 14, 15, ibid., pp. 931–32, 935–36.

public and private. When they were informed of these terms, the Mexican commissioners declared that there was no point in proceeding and tried to resign, whereupon Santa Anna backed down a little more: They need only "approximate to [the terms] as much as may be possible."[79]

On September 1 and 2 Trist met the Mexican commissioners for the long-awaited discussion. He exerted himself to be flexible and persuasive, and in order to encourage direct speaking he agreed to treat all remarks as statements of individual opinion. As a result, the Mexicans unburdened themselves with great frankness, and apparently both sides worked seriously to find a practicable formula for peace.

Boundary issues occupied most of their attention. The Mexicans attached the greatest importance to the least valuable territory—the disputed strip between the Nueces and the Rio Grande—for it involved Mexican honor and the whole justification of the war. Indeed, one commissioner ran his finger over this territory on a map and remarked, "If we are to succeed in accomplishing a peace, herein does it lie," and at this the others nodded anxiously.

Scarcely less important to the commissioners was New Mexico, for its inhabitants had shown themselves unusually loyal to the nation, and its grazing industry furnished an important source of meat. Trist replied that, judging from the history of Louisiana and Florida, both inhabitants and herds would increase after annexation to the United States and that greater wealth would enable any loyalists to sell their holdings and move back to Mexico. This argument partly convinced the Mexicans, and one of them—probably Mora y Villamil—undertook to propose to Santa Anna the cession of at least the northern half of the territory.

Surprisingly, the Mexicans seem to have talked very little about Upper California. Trist readily abandoned his demand for Lower California, since his instructions allowed him to do so, and the Mexicans then declared that they must have the mouth of the Colorado River for a land communication with the peninsula. Here Trist also gave way, although Buchanan's instructions of July 13 and 19 had urged him to secure access to the Gulf of California. He yielded, in the conviction that the Mexicans were principally concerned with saving face, but he warned them of future friction over navigation in the lower river valley.

In the end, both sides summarized the discussion with a

79. US, 30C, 1S, SED 52, pp. 330–35.

memorandum specifying a boundary line from the Gulf of Mexico up the Nueces River; west and south to a point just north of Paso del Norte; thence due west and north around the south boundary of New Mexico; down the Gila and Colorado rivers to 33°; and along this latitude to the Pacific, just north of San Diego. Although only a little short of Polk's minimum demands, these terms would have represented a considerable propaganda victory for Mexico, since they did not give the Rio Grande boundary to the United States. Nevertheless, Trist declared that if the Mexican government would formally propose this boundary, he would take the responsibility of transmitting the proposal to Washington.

The discussion of other issues also shows the willingness of both sides to give and take. At first the Mexicans wished to insert a provision that the United States must abolish slavery in Texas, but Trist declared that Polk and the Senate would reject such a provision even if the territory were ten times as valuable and covered one foot deep with gold. Hearing this, the Mexicans yielded. At one point they demanded that the United States repair all damage to Mexican fortifications. Trist refused to promise these repairs, but he predicted that Scott would undoubtedly agree to return captured field artillery, for he had no desire to leave Mexico defenseless and, indeed, was determined to create a "healing peace." This phrase seemed to touch the Mexicans. Even more appealing to them was Trist's liberality with money. He had already practically promised that the United States would pay $30 million for less than its minimum territorial demand; now he also agreed that, immediately upon the signature of the treaty, the Americans would return all customs houses to Mexican control.[80]

Thus, Trist twisted or disobeyed his instructions at several points. He did so because he had Scott's firm support, because he felt that the members of the commission represented a significant bloc of Mexican opinion, because the issue of war and peace seemed evenly balanced within Santa Anna's government, and probably also because the terms conformed to his own idea of a

---

80. Trist's account of these important meetings is very jumbled. The summary here is reconstructed from various parts of his dispatch. Trist to Buchanan, September 4, 1847, No. 15, Manning, *IAA*, VIII, 933–40. Apparently the Mexican interpreter took only brief notes, for the published Mexican account is short and adds nothing of importance. US, 30C, 1S, SED 52, pp. 344–46. Roa Bárcena, *Recuerdos de la invasión*, II, 330–36. Semmes, *Service Afloat and Ashore*, pp. 422–23. The line of 33° would have given San Diego to Mexico, but apparently this point was not explicitly discussed, as it was in the negotiations of January 1848.

desirable, moderate peace. At the end of the discussions he returned to the American camp full of hope and good humor.[81]

His optimism was shattered the next day, for his informant in the government told him of a stormy cabinet argument, which lasted into the following day. As British Minister Bankhead later reported, when the Mexican commissioners presented the agreed terms and advised their acceptance, many of Santa Anna's cabinet fell in with them, but the foreign minister, General Pacheco, argued for continuation of the war. The chief opponent of peace was General Tornel, who had urged the original attack on Taylor across the Rio Grande and was probably responsible for the first instructions to the commission.[82]

In the end the warhawks carried Santa Anna with them. On September 5 the Mexican commissioners returned to Trist with the government's answer, and from the expressions on their faces he knew the answer before they spoke. Rejecting the terms agreed on by the negotiators, the government made a counteroffer: the Nueces boundary of Texas, no part of New Mexico, and California north of 37°, a line that would have given to the United States San Francisco and the Sacramento Valley but not Monterey. With the treaty draft was a brief note restating the Mexican views concerning the outbreak of the "unnatural" war and suggesting that Britain be asked to guarantee any treaty—a proposal neither Palmerston nor Polk could have accepted. Trist replied that, since the views of the two parties could not be reconciled, he must break off negotiations. He spoiled his otherwise dignified statement, however, with a long, rambling defense of the war and the American right of conquest.[83]

Was there ever any real chance of obtaining peace without an American occupation of Mexico City? At the risk of their reputations Scott and Trist had sent a bribe to Santa Anna and had granted him an armistice at a moment when it seemed that the Americans might enter the capital with slight opposition. Their

81. Hitchcock, *Fifty Years*, p. 291. Trist to Buchanan, December 6, 1847, No. 22, Manning, *IAA*, VIII, 984–1020.

82. Trist to Buchanan, September 27, 1848, No. 16, Manning, *IAA*, VIII, 953–54. Bankhead to Palmerston, September 28, No. 87, GB, FO 50/211, ff. 242–44. Pacheco's formal instructions to the commissioners laid greatest stress on the importance of retaining New Mexico and the Nueces boundary. Pacheco

to José J. Herrera *et al.*, September 5, enclosed with José María Luis Mora to Palmerston, November 1, GB, FO 50/215, f. 133. Alcaraz *et al.*, *Apuntes para la historia de la guerra*, pp. 278–79. Valadés, *Breve historia*, p. 207.

83. Trist to Buchanan, September 27, 1847, No. 16; Herrera *et al.* to Trist, September 6, with enclosure; Trist to Herrera *et al.*, September 7, Manning, *IAA*, VIII, 940–56.

critics declared then and later that the Mexican general had "humbugged" them with the help of the rascally British, who wanted only to protect their property from damage or confiscation.[84] At the same time, Alexander J. Atocha, observing from Veracruz, remained convinced that Santa Anna genuinely wished to negotiate but that Scott's forces were too small to enable him to do so with honor. Also, Gómez Farías and other Mexican xenophobes were certain that Santa Anna, Mackintosh, and the peace bloc were plotting to betray Mexico to the invader.[85]

Here, as in earlier instances, it is almost impossible to document Santa Anna's shifts of mind. On the one hand, Tornel, Pacheco, and others of his advisers wanted to continue fighting—whether for patriotism or for reasons of personal gain—and he faced rebellion by units outside the capital under Valencia or Paredes (newly returned from exile) if he showed signs of yielding to the enemy. Nationalists among both *puros* and moderates branded all negotiations illegal without the approval of Congress and accused Santa Anna of treason for agreeing to a truce on his own authority.[86] On the other hand, many influential persons of all political views were urging him to negotiate while he still held some power in the capital. British residents, official and private, and indeed nearly all foreigners were prominent among the peace bloc, hoping to minimize American demands, and they had maintained this position consistently throughout the war.[87]

In his dilemma Santa Anna had resisted his warlike advisers to the extent of appointing a conciliatory peace commission, and at least for a time he listened to their arguments. A dictatorship supported by American money was an alluring prospect for him, but only if he could hold power long enough to receive the money. For that reason Trist's desire to refer the revised boundary pro-

84. Semmes, *Service Afloat and Ashore*, pp. 412–27, *passim*. Wallace, *Worth*, pp. 157–59. Northup, "Trist's Mission to Mexico," pp. 331–36. Fuentes Mares, *Santa Anna*, pp. 281–82. See also the sources cited in note 70.

85. Atocha to Buchanan, September 4, 21, 1847, Buchanan Papers, box 66, HSP. Gómez Farías to Sra. Gómez Farías, Toluca, August 27; unsigned memorandum, September 4; Gómez Farías to Manuel González Cosío, Querétaro, September 19, Gómez Farías Papers, Nos. 2798, 2800, 2812.

86. Printed flyer containing a declaration of August 22, signed by Gómez Farías, Mariano Otero (a leading moderate), and others, Trist Papers, XXV, f. 60451, LC. Open letter of Otero to the governor of Jalisco, September 16, 1847, Peña y Reyes, *Algunos documentos sobre el tratado*, pp. 68–92. Berge, "Mexican Response," pp. 280–83.

87. The most explicit statement of this policy may be found in Bankhead to Palmerston, April 30, 1847, No. 46, with approving memorandum by Palmerston, June 21, GB, FO 50/209, ff. 166–75. Subsequent dispatches contain nothing inconsistent with this statement of aims.

posals to Washington may well have been the factor that finally turned Santa Anna against the negotiations. But even if he had reached an agreement with the United States, he probably would not have been content to rely on American promises, for he told the Spanish chargé d'affaires that he would not make peace until he could determine whether the European governments would guarantee the treaty.[88]

Whether Santa Anna's conciliatory gestures were genuine or sham, there is no doubt that he used the two-week armistice period to improve the defenses of Mexico City. Also, he spiced his formal dispatches to the Americans with slurs to please Mexican nationalists and possibly goad Scott to additional indiscretions. In the latter purpose Santa Anna was successful. When Scott declared the armistice at an end, he also accused the Mexicans of breaking the agreement by not letting the Americans purchase supplies within the city and by raising new fortifications.[89]

Scott's letter provided Santa Anna with another opportunity to obscure the peace issue with more serious accusations against the Americans and to pose as the savior of Mexico. Scott, he declared, had established a masked battery in Tacubaya, and his men had raided churches, sacked towns, and violated women. During the peace negotiations Santa Anna had restrained his wrath, hoping to end the "unnatural" conflict. He concluded that if Scott were determined to inflict "the horrors of war" on "the innocent and defenceless people" of Mexico City, "there will remain for me no other means of saving it than to repel force by force, with that energy and decision which my high obligations prescribe."[90]

The publication of this letter completed the discomfiture of Scott and Trist. Scott had fought his way to the enemy's capital over the most difficult terrain, scattering every force that enemy could muster against him. Trist had warped his instructions, risking censure from a suspicious master in Washington. Yet they had nothing to show for their efforts but an impasse—to all appearances as hopeless as before the landing at Veracruz.

88. Smith, *War with Mexico*, II, 135–38, 396–97. Rives, *US and Mexico*, II, 517–19. Ramón López to Primer Secretario de Estado, August 25, 28, 1847, Nos, 3, 5, Spain, BAE, legajo 1650. (Bermúdez de Castro had just departed for Europe on leave.)

89. Scott to Santa Anna, September 6, 1847, US, 30C, 1S, SED 52, p. 346.

90. Santa Anna to Scott, September 7, 1847, US, 30C, 1S, SED 52, pp. 346–48. The first two quoted phrases are reversed in order from the original.

16

Trist Signs a Treaty

"The American eagle has prevailed over the Mexican eagle: and now the former exults over his prize, which is, after all, a bunch of thorns and a serpent!"[1] While peace eluded Scott and Trist, the government and the people at home tried to adjust their ambitions to the succession of fruitless victories. The resulting argument over territorial goals deepened the divisions that had appeared in American public opinion as hostilities began.

During the first year of the war most territorial expansionists were content with the prospect of annexing Upper California and at least part of New Mexico. Occasionally an individual or a newspaper, especially in the Northwest, suggested going further and even incorporating all of Mexico, but as Congress fought over the Wilmot Proviso, such statements became less frequent.[2] Late in the spring of 1847, after the Battle of Cerro Gordo, a group of expansionist newspapers revived the idea, but during the summer, while Scott lay apparently idle in Puebla, news dispatches lost their excitement, so that the territorial question seemed less urgent.[3]

These wartime discussions of annexation did not produce any clear-cut sectional alignment and certainly did not justify the abolitionists' assertion that the whole war was a "slaveholders' conspiracy" to enrich Southern plantation owners and to enhance the South's position in national politics. Some sectionalist newspapers, to be sure, demanded Southern rights in the territory to be taken over. In February 1847, however, the champion of these rights, John C. Calhoun, delivered a notable speech in Congress opposing further conquests, and many other Southeastern leaders

1. Philadelphia *North American*, n.d., reprinted in Washington *National Intelligencer*, September 24, 1847, p. 3. The metaphor refers to the Mexican coat of arms.

2. John Douglas Pitts Fuller, *The Movement for the Acquisition of All Mexico, 1846–1848*, pp. 40–42, 47–48. Even before hostilities began, the New York *Herald* was predicting that, piece by piece, Mexico and the whole con-

tinent would follow California into the Union. New York *Herald*, May 2, 1846, p. 2.

3. Press opinion after Cerro Gordo is summarized and quoted in *NNR*, 72 (May 22, 1847), 184–85; and Washington *National Intelligencer*, May 13, p. 2. For other opinions, see ibid., May 8, p. 3; May 11, p. 3; May 17, p. 3; May 19, p. 3; and Washington *Union*, May 21, 22.

and editors were lukewarm toward expansion. The most annexationist area was the Ohio–Mississippi Valley from Illinois and Indiana to New Orleans and of course Texas, but evidences of scarcely less intense spirit were to be found in Pennsylvania, New York, and even New England.[4] Incomplete measurement of the votes in Congress during the period suggests that party loyalties tended to determine views on territorial expansion more effectively than sectionalism. These are not a sure guide, however, for both parties and especially the Democrats were divided on the subject.[5]

The most powerful argument in expansionist literature of 1847 was undoubtedly the unmeasured resources of central Mexico. A breathtaking vision of the New York *Sun* synthesized nearly all material advantages:

> God has not made a more magnificent land than Mexico. It is a paradise blessed with every variety of climate, every capacity of soil, and almost every species of fruit and flower on the face of the earth. . . . Behold the cotton, wheat, maize, indigo and cochineal fields [*sic*], a source of wealth inexhaustible. . . . Look down into those mines of [San Luis] Potosi, Zacatecas, and Durango. Look at the gold and silver glittering there in masses that wait for the pick of the saxon [*sic*]. . . . Cortez carried away ship loads of gold from the Aztec, and England is carrying ship loads from the Mexican, still thousands of mines groan with their golden burthen. Mexico is truly a magnificent country, over and under the soil bursting with everything the heart can desire.[6]

Others echoed these inaccurate but enchanting descriptions, with special attention to the wealth of the Mexican mines.

A reason for the increased interest in Mexico's resources was the appearance of several communications projects designed to cross the continental barrier and furnish easier access to California. One of these was a plan for a canal or a railroad across the Isthmus of Tehuantepec, in southern Mexico. Moses Y. Beach,

4. Fuller, *Acquisition of All Mexico*, Chap. 2, *passim*. On Calhoun's speech, see Charles M. Wiltse, *John C. Calhoun, Sectionalist, 1840–1850*, pp. 297–99.

5. Joel H. Silbey, *The Shrine of Party: Congressional Voting Behavior, 1841–1852*, Chap. 6, *passim*. Silbey's elaborate breakdowns of congressional voting cover a number of tallies relating to the war and to the extension of slavery but not to the question of territorial annexations specifically.

6. New York *Sun*, n.d., quoted in NNR, 73 (October 23, 1847), 113. Frederick Merk, *Manifest Destiny and Mission in American History, a Reinterpretation*, p. 113. See also New York *Sun*, May 20, p. 2; May 29, p. 2. Waddy Thompson felt that if Mexico were inhabited by Americans, her mineral production would increase fivefold and that "the mineral and agricultural exports alone would nearly equal all the exports of any other country of the world." Waddy Thompson, *Recollections of Mexico*, p. 204.

editor of the New York *Sun,* had tried to develop this project during his secret mission to Mexico early in 1847, and Trist was instructed to include transit rights across Tehuantepec in the peace treaty if possible. By that time the Mexican holder of the original concession had transferred his rights to the British consul at Mexico City, Ewen C. Mackintosh, representing London capitalists who were trying to obtain the backing of the British government. Secretary of the Treasury Walker, more interested in the isthmian project than the rest of the cabinet, still had hopes of rescuing the concession for American capital, and in April 1847 Vice President George M. Dallas published an enthusiastic article about the Tehuantepec route, which was widely reprinted. Beach kept the isthmian question in the public eye with articles in the *Sun* through summer and fall.[7]

By now, rival plans for transcontinental communications were being projected, which involved the Rocky Mountain area and parts of northwestern Mexico. Even before the war Asa T. Whitney and a few others, foreseeing the growth of Oregon and California, were trying to gain popular support for the construction of railroads from the upper Mississippi Valley to the Pacific. As soon as he learned of the Tehuantepec project, Whitney opposed it with arguments that navigation and climate would raise problems and that it would be impossible to operate and defend a canal in a politically unstable foreign country.[8] Further rivalry came from Southerners who wished to make Charleston, Memphis, or New Orleans the entrepôt for transcontinental trade. A regional convention at Memphis in November 1845 publicized the Southern plan, and one of its delegates, Colonel James Gadsden of South Carolina, proposed a railroad from Charleston to Monterey, California, or to Mazatlán, farther south.[9] In June 1847 *DeBow's Review* published enthusiastic descriptions of this route, citing as inducements the Mexican silver mines and the trade of the Far East—lures that were to attract railroad promoters to the Sierra Madre for more than half a century thereafter.[10]

---

7. Merk, *Manifest Destiny and Mission,* pp. 128–39. See also New York *Sun,* May 14, 1847, p. 2; New York *Herald,* April 3, p. 2; April 6, p. 2; April 12, p. 2.

8. Robert R. Russel, *Improvement of Communications with the Pacific Coast As an Issue in American Politics, 1783–1864,* pp. 11–16. Asa T. Whitney to Robert J. Walker, April 7, 1847, Letters, 1846–1848, p. 378, Walker Papers, LC.

9. Russel, *Improvement of Communications,* p. 13. Wiltse, *Calhoun, Sectionalist,* pp. 235–39. Merk, *Manifest Destiny and Mission,* p. 130.

10. Samuel A. Cartwright to Walker, November 29, 1845, Walker Papers, No. 209, LC. *DeBow's Review,* 3 (June 1847), 475–95.

Antiannexationists attacked these material inducements with profuse metaphors. The war itself, they said, which was "intended at first to fling around the Administration a halo of glory, is likely to hang around its neck like a mill-stone." The enticing Mexican lands were a "Trojan horse," "a bone of contention fraught with all the evils of Pandora's box."[11] Sometimes their arguments were no more consistent than their metaphors. In the first place, said some, Mexico's resources had been vastly exaggerated; they were not worth additional fighting. The money required would be far better spent cobwebbing the United States with railroads. Second, it would be impossible to assimilate completely an alien people who wanted to remain independent. Even if the upper classes were indeed willing to join the Union, as many argued, the mass of Indians, "bigoted, ignorant, idle, lawless, slavish, and yet free," would corrupt American politics and society, while a large standing army would lead to militarism and presidential dictatorship. Third, Europe would surely resist annexation. Fourth, if the Mexican fruit should become thoroughly ripe for Americans, it would fall of its own weight into their hands.[12]

Opponents of annexation particularly disagreed about its influence on the slavery question. Throughout the North was heard the *basso ostinato* of the abolitionists—that the increased territory would spread and perpetuate slavery in the United States. Not so, replied slaveholding antiannexationists, for the new territories would drain slaves from the border states, preparing them for abolition. Andrew J. Donelson, onetime agent of Texan annexation, warned that the land to the southwest of the Rio Grande was not suitable for slavery: "All that you take from Mexico lessens by so much the weight acquired in Texas by the slave holder."[13]

In their efforts to answer these contradictory arguments, the annexationists shifted ground as often as their opponents. The New York *Sun* raised the specter of a British protectorate: "England wants a cotton field, and thinks to get one when we abandon

11. Columbus (Georgia) *Enquirer*, n.d., reprinted in Washington *National Intelligencer*, December 1, 1846, p. 3. Richmond *Whig*, n.d., reprinted in *NNR*, 73 (September 18, 1847), 47. Columbus (Ohio) *State Journal*, reprinted in *NNR*, 72 (August 28), 408.
12. Expressions of these sentiments, often reprinted from other newspapers, appear in the Washington *National Intelligencer*, June 12, 1846, p. 3; February 5, 1847, p. 3; June 8, p. 2; October

21, p. 2; October 29, p. 2; October 30, p. 2; and November 4, p. 2. See also New York *Journal of Commerce*, n.d., reprinted in London *Times*, June 25, 1846, p. 8. A useful summary of the arguments appears in the New York *Journal of Commerce*, October 14, 1847, reprinted in Washington *National Intelligencer*, October 18, p. 3.
13. Andrew J. Donelson to Buchanan, May 15, 1847, Buchanan Papers, box 65, HSP.

Mexico." Realizing the damaging effect of the prejudice against slavery and backward races, some argued that the expansion of American sovereignty and institutions would actually bring freedom to Mexico. One man wrote to the Washington *Daily Union* that the war was "the religious execution of the country's glorious mission, under the direction of Divine Providence, to civilize and christianize, and raise up from anarchy and degradation a most ignorant, indolent, wicked and unhappy people."[14] One may well smile to see Beach alternate his panegyrics on Mexican resources with pious references to "the finger of Providence." In the mouths of reformers, however, the argument of regeneration was not sheer hypocrisy, and it matched the yearnings of some educated Mexicans, although many of these preferred to seek redemption under a European monarch.

A number of expansionist arguments were designed to counteract the paralyzing effect of the Wilmot Proviso. Some Northern newspapers agreed with Donelson that Mexican territory would not support slavery. A few abolitionists went further and advocated annexation, since it would add new free states.[15] Constitutionalists denied that Congress had the power to determine whether slavery should exist in annexed territory. Buchanan suggested that the acquired lands be partitioned by extending the Missouri Compromise line (36°30′) to the Pacific. When he published this proposal in August 1847, however, Northerners protested that it would give slaveholders perhaps four fifths of the eventual conquests.[16]

In the following month Vice President Dallas brought forth a more ingenious and flexible solution to the problem—let the people of each new territory determine whether they wanted slavery. If this were done, the known Mexican prejudice against the institution and the prevalence of Indian labor would assure abolition. Both Buchanan and Dallas were looking toward the Democratic nomination for the Presidency, which Lewis Cass eventually

14. New York *Sun*, May 17, 1847, p. 2; May 19, p. 2; May 21, p. 2 (quotation from May 17 issue). Washington *Daily Union*, October 14, quoted in Albert K. Weinberg, *Manifest Destiny, a Study of Nationalist Expansionism in American History*, p. 173. See other quotations on the same page.
15. Fuller, *Acquisition of All Mexico*, pp. 73–75. Merk, *Manifest Destiny and Mission*, pp. 168–71. *National Era*,

August 19, 1847, quoted in Weinberg, *Manifest Destiny*, p. 171.
16. Weinberg, *Manifest Destiny*, pp. 175–78. Chaplain W. Morrison, *Democratic Politics and Sectionalism: the Wilmot Proviso Controversy*, pp. 86–87. Polk knew of Buchanan's proposal and made no objection. James K. Polk, *The Diary of James K. Polk during His Presidency, 1845 to 1849*, ed. Milo M. Quaife, III, 142–43.

obtained, largely by appropriating Dallas' solution.[17] The positions of these presidential hopefuls indicated that the Wilmot Proviso was losing its force.[18]

Despite the efforts of antiannexationists there were signs by the fall of 1847 that a movement to incorporate large parts of northern and central Mexico or perhaps the whole country was beginning to gain strength. The continuing diplomatic impasse and the increasing cost of the war would be more likely to stimulate than to discourage this movement.

*   *   *   *

Aware that public opinion on territorial expansion was divided and apt to change, Polk avoided firm commitments so as to retain the widest possible freedom of action. Perhaps he had learned a lesson from his earlier assertion of the "clear and unquestionable" American title to Oregon. He had prevented Buchanan from announcing to the world in May 1846 that the United States was not fighting the war for annexations. In cabinet discussions during the following month Walker and Bancroft favored annexing California as far south as 32° or even 26°, the approximate latitude of the mouth of the Rio Grande. Buchanan disputed this proposal hotly, fearing that large annexations would stir up abolitionist sentiment in Pennsylvania and the North. Polk's reaction was characteristic: "I remarked that I preferred the 26° to any boundary North of it, but that if it was found that that boundary could not be obtained I was willing to take 32°, but that in any event we must obtain Upper California and New Mexico in any Treaty of Peace we would make."[19]

This continued to be the President's basic position for most of the next year. With much trouble he got Congress to appropriate $3 million as ready cash for the purchase of territory, and he

17. Fuller, *Acquisition of All Mexico*, pp. 75–76. Merk, *Manifest Destiny and Mission*, pp. 178–79. Morrison, *Democratic Politics*, pp. 87–92. Frank B. Woodford, *Lewis Cass, the Last Jeffersonian*, pp. 251–53.

18. Buchanan to George Bancroft, September 29, 1847, Bancroft Papers, MHS. Fuller, *Acquisition of All Mexico*, p. 78.

19. Polk, *Diary*, I, 396–99, 437–38, 495–97; II, 15–16. The quotation appears in I, 496–97. See also George Bancroft's correspondence, quoted in Richard W. Van Alstyne, *The Rising American Empire*, pp. 143–45. Marcy, who represented moderate opinion, favored a boundary at 34° or 36°. Ivor Debenham Spencer, *The Victor and the Spoils, a Life of William L. Marcy*, pp. 157–58. There seems to have been some confusion about geography in the cabinet's discussion, for Walker's 26° line was stated to include Tamaulipas, which lies mostly south of it.

also explored the possibility of annexing Coahuila and Tamaulipas through local secession. Nevertheless, at the beginning of January 1847, when the slavery question erupted in congressional debates, he retreated enough to write that the nation would acquire
no territory fit for slavery: "New Mexico and California is [*sic*] all
that can ever probably be acquired by Treaty, and indeed all that
I think it important to acquire."[20] The sliding scale of annexations
and payments set forth in Trist's instructions over three months
later followed Polk's flexible policy, and again the President took
a middle position between Buchanan, who wanted to offer less,
and Walker, who wanted to demand the Tehuantepec transit
rights as a *sine qua non*.[21]

Having dispatched Trist, Polk dropped the subject of annexations for several months. On July 19 he had Buchanan instruct
Trist to push the boundary line south from the Gila River to 32°,
if he could.[22] As Mexican resistance continued, Polk proposed that
the territorial demands be increased further and the purchase
price lowered. On September 7 Buchanan suggested limiting the
maximum price to $15 million (the same amount for which he had
originally argued) and extending the boundary along 31°30' or
31°. Walker and Attorney General Nathan Clifford then favored
adding Tamaulipas as far south as Tampico, and the familiar discussion broke out again, Polk cautiously approving the new demands. But Secretary of the Navy John Y. Mason pointed out that
if Trist had just negotiated a treaty, such revised instructions might
embarrass him seriously, so the cabinet decided to await further
news. As a final shot, Walker and Clifford declared that if the
Mexicans still refused to negotiate after the capture of Mexico
City, Trist should be recalled. Polk disagreed; it would be best,
he said, to keep an envoy there, as the Mexicans might change their
minds.[23]

Thus, during the disappointing campaign for peace outside
Mexico City, the President's expectations were rising. In mid-
September Polk received Trist's dispatch describing the armistice,
but his sole reaction was to hope that the Mexican government was
not merely playing for time.[24] On October 2 the mail from Vera-

---

20. Polk, *Diary*, II, 308. This impression is confirmed by a statement of
Buchanan: "The idea seems to have
been abandoned on all sides of acquiring territory beyond the Rio Grande
south of the Paso del Norte." Buchanan
to Bancroft, December 29, 1846, MHS.

21. Polk, *Diary*, II, 472–74. Buchanan
to Nicholas P. Trist, April 15, 1847, No.
1, Manning, *IAA*, VIII, 201–7.
22. Buchanan to Trist, July 19, 1847,
No. 4, Manning, *IAA*, VIII, 213–14.
23. Polk, *Diary*, III, 163–65.
24. Polk, *Diary*, III, 167, 170–72.

cruz brought a copy of a Mexican pamphlet that contained an account of Trist's negotiations with the Mexican commissioners and the text of the counterdraft proposed by the Mexican government. Not until more than three weeks later did the State Department receive Trist's own account of the negotiations, which confirmed that he had agreed to send home the Mexican proposal for greatly curtailed annexations.

Polk, however, had not waited for Trist's dispatch. When the pamphlet arrived, he was in bed with chills and fever, too ill to make important decisions, but two days later he had recovered enough to resolve on Trist's recall. When he consulted the cabinet, all agreed, and Buchanan sent off the necessary instructions on October 6. The Mexicans' counterdraft, he declared, proved that they had never seriously intended peace: "They must have known that the Government of the United States never would surrender either the territory between the Nueces and the Rio Grande or New Mexico or any portion of Upper California," and that it would not pay any reparations to Mexican citizens or allow double duties on goods imported into occupied ports. If Trist had signed a treaty by the time he received his recall, he might bring it with him, but otherwise he must immediately suspend negotiations and leave. Should the Mexicans decide later to reopen peace talks, they must make the first overtures through the American military commander, who would forward their communications to Washington.[25]

Thus, Polk initially based his decision to recall Trist on policy considerations—the need to maintain a strong stand toward the Mexicans. When the President received his envoy's account of the negotiations, however, his old suspicions of Trist and Scott returned. He directed Buchanan to send another recall notice to Trist (dated October 25), this time chastising him for letting the Mexicans think that the United States would consider giving up the valuable port of San Diego and the Nueces–Rio Grande territory, now part of a Texas Congressional district.[26]

With the earlier instructions to Trist, Polk also sent new orders to Scott (October 6). Since the Mexican people now seemed as responsible for the continuation of the war as the Mexican

25. Polk, *Diary*, III, 184–87. Buchanan to Trist, October 6, 1847, No. 5, Manning, *IAA*, VIII, 214–16. Charles A. Lofgren, "Force and Diplomacy, 1846–1848: the View from Washington," *Military Affairs*, 31 (Summer 1967), 63–64.

26. Buchanan to Trist, October 25,

1847, No. 6, Manning, *IAA*, VIII, 217–18. Same, October 24, 25, 27, Trist Papers, ff. 60581–82, 60615–18, 60621. Smith suggests that Pillow had led Polk to suspect Trist and Scott of deliberately playing into the hands of the Whigs. Justin H. Smith, *The War with Mexico*, II, 236, 464.

army, Marcy declared that "considerations of humanity" required that the Americans employ all measures of civilized warfare to make them agree to "fair and honorable terms." Scott was directed to stamp out guerrilla warfare "with the utmost allowable severity," sending guerrilla prisoners to the United States if necessary and punishing murder and robbery stringently. Scott must force the Mexican people generally to bear the main burden of sustaining the American troops—by which Polk and Marcy meant expropriation of supplies and perhaps levies of money. They announced that 3,000 additional troops were on the way to Mexico. With the augmented army Scott was to renew the attack on the Mexicans, scatter their forces, and prevent them from reassembling.[27]

The recall notice to Trist and Scott's new orders completed the impasse. Santa Anna would not or dared not consider ceding as much territory as the Americans' original minimum demand, and Polk was now inclined to regard that minimum as unacceptable. Still worse, both sides had formally claimed, as a point of honor, the virtually worthless tract between Corpus Christi and Matamoros—the birthplace of the war, now declared by each country to be an integral part of its domain. It remained to be seen whether further dispersal of the Mexican forces and seizure of Mexican property would make the government and people more amenable to the Americans' terms.

*　　*　　*　　*

Long before the new instructions could reach Mexico City, the situation there on which they were based had greatly changed. As soon as Scott decided to end the armistice, he began to organize an attack on the city. Following a rumor that there was an important gun foundry near the foot of Chapultepec, he ordered its capture, expecting no more than a minor skirmish. Instead, the move developed into the Battle of Molino de Rey (September 8), perhaps the bloodiest of the whole war. Although some of his advisers wanted to bypass Chapultepec, Scott then decided that he must invest the hill and the castle at its top before proceeding into the city. On September 13 a furious attack up the slope overcame a gallant but poorly organized Mexican defense and sent the remnants in a hasty retreat back into the city. Many of Scott's critics

---

27. William L. Marcy to Winfield　　Scott, October 6, 1847, US, 30C, 1S, **HED** 60, pp. 1006–9.

declared that these two battles were as unnecessary as Churubusco, and it does not seem now that they made the final assault on Mexico City any easier.[28]

This assault began as soon as Chapultepec was in American hands. The capital had few fortifications, but the American troops had to force their way along the approaching causeways and through two main gateways, suffering heavy casualties. Once in the city, they faced mostly street fighting, as in Monterrey. When the Americans had occupied about half of the city, Santa Anna and his troops evacuated it, along with most of the remaining congressmen and other national officials. On September 14 the municipal authorities surrendered the whole city and called on the people to stop fighting, whereupon Santa Anna denounced the president of the *ayuntamiento* (municipal council) for treason. The council president had surrendered mainly because Scott threatened severe reprisals if the resistance continued. Even so, during the next few days considerable brutality was committed by both sides, but property owners feared the Americans less than the *léperos* (rabble) and the convicts who escaped from the prisons after the guards had fled.[29]

With fewer than 6,000 men (his own estimate) Scott had captured the enemy's capital, but at a heavy cost, for the casualties suffered during August and September in the Valley of Mexico amounted to nearly one fourth of the men he had led out of Puebla.[30] The evacuation of Mexico City so discredited Santa Anna

28. George Lockhart Rives, *The United States and Mexico, 1821–1848,* II, Chap. 47. Smith, *War with Mexico,* II, Chap. 28. Charles Winslow Elliott, *Winfield Scott, the Soldier and the Man,* pp. 530–47. Douglas Southall Freeman, *R. E. Lee, a Biography,* I, 273–83. Vicente Riva Palacio, *México a través de los siglos,* IV, 685–95. José María Bárcena, *Recuerdos de la invasión norteamericana (1846–1848),* III, Chaps. 28, 29. Ramón Alcaraz et al., *Apuntes para la historia de la guerra entre México y los Estados-Unidos,* Chaps. 21, 22.

29. Rives, *US and Mexico,* II, 554–66. Smith, *War with Mexico,* II, 152–64. Elliott, *Scott,* pp. 547–52. Riva Palacio, *México a través de los siglos,* IV, 695–98. Roa Bárcena, *Recuerdos de la invasión,* III, Chap. 30. Alcaraz et al., *Apuntes para la historia de la guerra,*

Chaps. 23, 24. Charles Bankhead to Viscount Palmerston, September 28, 1847, No. 86, GB, FO 50/211, ff. 158–70. Robert S. Chamberlain, ed., "Letter of Antonio López de Santa Anna to Manuel Reyes Veramendi, President of the *Ayuntamiento* of Mexico City, Guadalupe, September 15, 1847," *Hispanic American Historical Review,* 24 (November 1944), 614–17. Dennis E. Berge, "A Mexican Dilemma: the Mexico City Ayuntamiento and the Question of Loyalty, 1846–1848," ibid., 50 (May 1970), 234–38. The *ayuntamiento* continued to exercise some governmental functions under Scott's authority. For over-all pictures of the American occupation, not very favorable to the invaders, see Alcaraz et al., *Apuntes para la historia de la guerra,* Chap. 27; and Smith, *War with Mexico,* II, Chap. 31.

30. Rives, *US and Mexico,* II, 564–65.

that he thought it best to resign the presidency. He retained command of the Mexican army, however, and in a final effort to recover his prestige he determined to attack the garrison Scott had left behind at Puebla. This detachment was now dangerously weak, consisting of fewer than 500 men, with nearly 2,000 in the hospital and the city populace showing signs of revolt.

Santa Anna laid siege to Puebla for about a week, and then, learning that American reinforcements were on the way from Veracruz, he set out to meet them. The result was an awkwardly managed skirmish at Huamantla (October 11), where the flight of the Mexicans destroyed the remaining scraps of Santa Anna's hopes. Ordered to appear before a military court of inquiry, he abandoned his command and headed for the Guatemalan border, but his escape was blocked by local opposition and he wandered around for several months. During the following spring he finally made his way into exile, first in Jamaica and then in Venezuela, where he again set up his listening post. This time, he was forced to wait five years before returning to power.[31]

When Santa Anna resigned the presidency, it devolved upon the presiding justice of the Supreme Court, Manuel de la Peña y Peña, a moderate who had served Herrera as foreign minister at the time of the Slidell mission. Then he had favorably considered a negotiated settlement; now he was firmly convinced of its necessity. Peña was fat, ceremonious, and full of dignity, a cautious, able lawyer and a proclerical who combined love of peace and respect for American power. Trist and Bankhead thought him timid, but he slowly took action. On September 27 he proclaimed himself president *ad interim* under the Constitution of 1824; next, he appointed another moderate pacifist, Luis de la Rosa, as foreign minister and temporary head of the cabinet; then he ordered Santa Anna relieved of his command. Finally, he went to Querétaro, a state capital about one hundred miles northwest of Mexico City, to organize his government and to wait for the scattered Congress to

For Scott's report on the campaign and the capture of Mexico City, dated September 18, 1847, see US, 30C, 1S, SED 1, pp. 375–95.

31. Rives, *US and Mexico*, II, 566–76. Smith, *War with Mexico*, II, 173–82. Riva Palacio, *México a través de los siglos*, IV, 697, 699–700. Roa Bárcena, *Recuerdos de la invasión*, III, 155–63, 180–82. For the charges against Santa Anna and his reply, see Genaro García

and Carlos Pereyra, eds., *Documentos inéditos ó muy raros para la historia de México*, XXIX, 201–335; and Antonio López de Santa Anna, *Apelación al buen criterio de los nacionales y estrangeros*, pp. 59–65. His later memoirs contain even more distortions and special pleading. Santa Anna, *The Eagle, the Autobiography of Santa Anna*, ed. Ann Fears Crawford, pp. 101–15 *et passim*.

convene. Peña's caution was probably justified, for only Congress could confirm his office and determine the validity of the April law that forbade peace negotiations.[32]

The new government was soon surrounded by splinter factions—*santanistas*, moderates, *puros*, and monarchists—who shaped their attitudes on war and peace to fit their own ideals and ambitions. Trist's informants in Querétaro reported to him that two rival peace groups had appeared there, one led by Foreign Minister De la Rosa and the other by Luis G. Cuevas, another moderate and ex-foreign minister. Irreconcilable *puros* still under Gómez Farías' influence refused to consider any sort of negotiations or to recognize Peña's government. Somewhere between Gómez Farías and De la Rosa was a group of moderates led by Mariano Otero, a brilliant young journalist–deputy. Otero had attacked Santa Anna's peace discussions after Churubusco, but he recognized that negotiations must be considered, if only the United States would offer honorable terms. Unfortunately, he defined these as limited to Texas, conceding at most the Rio Grande boundary— a wholly unrealistic position.[33]

The liberal press reflected the division of opinion. On one hand, the pacifist newspaper *El razonador* editorialized for peace in the name of "the interests of all concerned, common sense, philosophy, and all principles of expediency and justice." On the other, *El monitor republicano*, formerly a stalwart for continued war, evaded the issue for weeks, then supported Otero, and finally

32. Rives, *US and Mexico*, II, 584–88. Roa Bárcena, *Recuerdos de la invasión*, III, 234–37. Trist to Buchanan, October 1, 25, 1847, Nos. 17, 18; unsigned note, apparently by Trist, September 28, US, DS, D, Mexico, XIV. The October 1 dispatch, No. 17, and most of the October 25 dispatch, No. 18, are printed in Manning, *IAA*, VIII, 957–64. Edward Thornton to Palmerston, October 29, No. 6, GB, FO 50/212, ff. 71–76. For characterizations of Peña y Peña and De la Rosa, see Guillermo Prieto, *Memorias de mis tiempos, 1840 a 1853*, pp. 267–68; Thomas Ewing Cotner, *The Military and Political Career of José Joaquín de Herrera, 1792–1854*, p. 137; and Francisco Sosa, *Biografías de mexicanos distinguidos*, pp. 920–25. On conditions in Querétaro, see Prieto, *Memorias, 1840 a 1853*, pp. 260–62.

33. Rives, *US and Mexico*, II, 590–92.

Trist to Buchanan, October 25, 1847, No. 18, US, DS, D, Mexico, XIV. Valentín Gómez Farías to Manuel González Cosío, Querétaro, September 19; unsigned draft in Gómez Farías Papers, no. 2812. Gómez Farías *et al.* to President of Congress, Toluca, August 22; printed flyer in Trist Papers, XXV, f. 60451, LC. Otero's position regarding Texas was set forth in a public letter to the governor of Jalisco, written after the collapse of the negotiations. Reprinted in Antonio de la Peña y Reyes, ed., *Algunos documentos sobre el tratado de Guadalupe*, pp. 68–92. On Otero, see also Sosa, *Mexicanos distinguidos*, pp. 787–89. F. Jorge Gaxiola, *Mariano Otero (Creador del juicio de amparo)*, pp. 24–27, 55–56, 238–47, 261–79. "Estudio preliminar," in *Mariano Otero, Obras*, ed. Jesús Reyes Heroles, I, 9–190, and especially 83–86, 90–92.

returned resignedly to its first position, in fear that the Americans could not be trusted to abide by any treaty.[34]

At the same time, other factions muddied the immediate issue of negotiations. In Querétaro Juan N. Almonte was intriguing for the presidency, mostly with moderates, conservatives, and militarists who wanted to continue fighting. Also, just after the Americans had occupied Mexico City, former President Paredes, newly returned from exile, appeared in the capital to consult friends on the prospects of monarchism.[35] Most disturbing of all, Trist and the American army leaders observed a rising sentiment for an American protectorate over Mexico or even the permanent annexation of the whole country to the United States.

While it is impossible to sort out Mexican opinions like playing cards, it would appear that a protectorate appealed primarily to some moderates and to *puros* who had deserted Gómez Farías. Inheriting the liberal federalism of the 1820s, these persons hoped that the United States would free Mexico from Church and army and help her toward stability and progress. Another group, more pessimistic about native potentialities, wanted Mexico to join the Union outright. While this latter attitude was most common among foreign residents, it seemed to be spreading among the moderates, and even some of the higher clergy were willing to endure the distasteful American freedom of worship in order to protect Church property from the *puros*.[36]

34. *El razonador,* October 13, 1847, pp. 3–4; October 16, pp. 3–4; October 23, pp. 3–4; October 30, p. 4; November 6, pp. 3–4. The quoted phrase appeared on October 13. *El monitor republicano,* October 6, pp. 2–3; October 9, pp. 3–4; October 15, pp. 3–4; October 19, p. 3; October 29, p. 1; October 30, p. 1; October 31, p. 1; November 1, p. 1; November 2, p. 1; November 3, pp. 1–2.
35. Bankhead to Palmerston, September 28, 1847, No. 88, GB, FO 50/211, ff. 246–49.
36. Trist declared that 25,000 or 30,-000 men would suffice for indefinite occupation, but he recognized some dangers—for example, contamination by "the virus of spanish [*sic*] corruption." Trist to Buchanan, October 25, 1847, No. 18, Manning, *IAA,* VIII, 958–64. Hitchcock stated that the *puros* favored annexation. Ethan Allen Hitchcock, *Fifty Years in Camp and Field,* p. 309. This was certainly not true of Gómez Farías' faction. See, for example, a

manifesto of November 28, 1847, signed by Gómez Farías, Manuel Crescencio Rejón, and twenty others, denying the right of the government to alienate territory and calling for the continuation of the war. Peña y Reyes, *Documentos sobre el tratado,* pp. 93–106. Nevertheless, Fuentes Mares, citing Trist's dispatch, consistently refers to a single *puro* viewpoint favoring complete annexation to the United States. José Fuentes Mares, *Santa Anna, aurora y ocaso de un comediante,* pp. 287–89. Those *puros* who wanted American help, however, probably had in mind a program like that suggested in a long letter to Trist: military occupation, abolition of *fueros* (clerical and military immunities) and of internal customs duties, establishment of jury trial, freedom of religion, public works, and general stimulation of the economy. F. C. to [Trist], Mexico City, November 14, Trist Papers, XXVI, ff. 60666–71, LC. A group of *puros* who gained con-

Confronted by the divided opinions of Mexicans with whom they associated, Scott's officers could not agree on military and political strategies. Some favored occupying most of the country indefinitely; others urged a dignified retirement to northern Mexico, where the army could easily hold the territory which the United States wished to annex. Immediately after Cerro Gordo, General William J. Worth had sent Polk a memorandum proposing that the army organize puppet states in northern and eastern Mexico. These would be protected by frontier fortresses and American garrisons at Veracruz and Perote. In October, however, after the occupation of Mexico City, Worth decided that it would be unbecoming to evacuate central Mexico without a satisfactory peace. "That our race is finally destined to overrun the whole continent is too obvious to need proof." He conceded that the occupation of Mexico was a bit premature—perhaps by fifty years— "but what is half a century in the affairs of a nation like ours thoroughly imbued with the progressive spirit?" Worth proposed to divide Mexico into territories and to assign civil governors with competent military officers to advise them. He discounted American sectionalism and Mexican opposition with a shrug, saying that the dangers of disunion at home were negligible and the advantages to the Mexicans "too obvious to invite comment." [37]

General Persifor F. Smith came to quite different conclusions. A scholarly lawyer with considerable military experience gained in the Seminole wars, Smith feared that in Mexico the prevalent ignorance, clerical bigotry, poor communications, and superstitious anti-Americanism would hold up treaty negotiations indefinitely. The United States had proved its military prowess to the world, but protracted occupation of Mexico City would undermine the troops' morale, and petty defensive skirmishes would erode their prestige. Before the enemy could recover enough strength to counterattack, Scott should evacuate central Mexico, transport his whole army to the Rio Grande, and distribute his troops along a line running up the river and across the center of modern Chihuahua and Sonora to the Gulf of California.

Trist thought enough of Smith's plan to forward it to Wash-

---

trol of the Mexico City *ayuntamiento* in mid-December favored this program and also a loose political system in which Mexico City and the Federal District would be almost sovereign. Berge, "Mexican Dilemma," pp. 246–47.

37. William J. Worth, "Notes and Observations upon the War with Mexico, and Present Relations of the Belligerents," Perote, April 25, 1847, Polk Papers, CXV, LC. [Worth] to Marcy, October 30, Marcy Papers, XIV, LC.

ington. Personally, he feared that outright annexation might be the only alternative to a monarchy in Mexico, and he felt that the slightest sign of American intention to take over the country "would spread like fire over a sunburnt prarie [sic]." As he told Buchanan, he was carefully cautioning all Mexican groups not to commit themselves, since it was still uncertain which policy the United States government would adopt.[38]

While the British legation did not favor either a protectorate or complete annexation, it continued to aid Trist in his efforts to secure a treaty, and Consul Mackintosh served as the agent in Mexico City of De la Rosa's peace faction. At this point the Americans lost the counsel of the British minister, Charles Bankhead, whose illness had grown steadily worse. A semiparalyzed invalid, he departed on October 19, never to return. Late in November his attaché, Edward Thornton, moved the legation to Querétaro, and during the following month a chargé d'affaires arrived from London to replace Bankhead. This man was Percy W. Doyle, the legation secretary, who had served briefly as chargé during the flag incident of 1843 (see Chapter 5) and had been on leave in Europe for some time. Doyle was young, vigorous, and had many Mexican friends. Seeing the critical situation on his arrival, he stayed in Mexico City for the duration of the negotiations, so both the Americans and the Mexican government had access to British advice and a reliable channel of communication between Mexico City and Querétaro.[39]

In mid-October, as soon as Peña had set up his government, Trist sent a note to Foreign Minister De la Rosa, intimating that he would be willing to reopen negotiations.[40] De la Rosa promised

38. Unsigned, undated memorandum, identified on the docket as by Persifor F. Smith and enclosed with Trist to Buchanan, September 28, 1847, Marcy Papers, XIII, LC. Smith, *War with Mexico*, II, 377. Trist's covering letter mentioned that Smith had written out his views at Trist's request. For Trist's own views, see Trist to Buchanan, October 25, No. 18, Manning, *IAA*, VIII, 961–63. General Smith repeated his proposal with a few minor changes in a letter probably written about December 13. The name of his addressee is illegible. Franklin Pierce Papers, II, LC.

39. Trist to Buchanan, October 25, 1847, No. 18, Manning, *IAA*, VIII, 960.

Thornton to Palmerston, October 29, November 26, 1847, Nos. 1, 7, 8, 11; Percy W. Doyle to Palmerston, December 13, No. 3, GB, FO 50/212, ff. 1, 84–86, 89–90, 97–98, 204–9. Doyle remained in Mexico City partly at Peña's request. When Thornton learned in October that the Mexican government intended to ask him for Britain's good offices, he replied that, because of the Mexicans' earlier brusque rejection of British overtures, he could only refer such a request to London. In effect, however, he and Doyle supplied good offices to the negotiators throughout the period.

40. Trist to Luis de la Rosa, October 20, 1847, copy in Trist Papers, XXV, ff.

to appoint commissioners, but he delayed for several weeks until Congress convened. The *puros* who had boycotted the summer session now returned to their seats, hoping to force a continuation of the war. Soon after the session began, moderates and *puros* submitted proposals. For the moderates, Mariano Otero introduced a resolution requiring that peace negotiations be confined to the Texas question. For the *puros*, Gómez Farías and a few colleagues drew up an *exposición*, declaring that the nation had not yet exploited all its resources for resistance, and a resolution that the government should not listen to any peace proposals until American forces had evacuated all Mexican territory. The *puro* resolution came to a vote first and was tabled, 38 to 35. Then the *puros* turned against Otero's proposal, along with pacifists, who realized that limited negotiations would not bring peace. The improvised coalition voted it down, 46 to 29.[41]

For the remainder of the congressional session the administration's supporters managed to control the warhawks. In order to survey the national resources available for continuing the war, Peña had called an advisory conference of state governors, which met at Querétaro while Congress was debating. After hearing a gloomy report by the minister of war, the conference turned into an impromptu forum for pacifists. It took no formal action of any importance, except to issue a cryptic declaration that it would support the government in any constitutional measures. With this statement the governors may have intended to bypass the April law against negotiations.

Meanwhile, the moderate faction in Congress managed to elect General Pedro María Anaya president *ad interim* for a two-month period. Anaya, a former henchman of Santa Anna, appointed Peña y Peña as foreign minister and retained most of the old cabinet. He also appointed three peace commissioners: Bernardo

---

60564–65. Trist sent De la Rosa his note of September 7, written originally to the Mexican peace commissioners but not delivered to them after the rupture of the armistice. Manning, *IAA*, VIII, 945–53. He also composed another note for the same commissioners, again lecturing them unnecessarily on the causes of the war. Trist to J. Herrera *et al.*, October 28, ibid., pp. 964–68. Scott meanwhile aided the new government by enabling members of Congress still in Mexico City to reach

Querétaro. Berge, "Mexican Response," p. 291.

41. De la Rosa to Trist, October 31, 1847, Manning, *IAA*, VIII, 971. Rives, *US and Mexico*, II, 589–92. Berge, "Mexican Response," pp. 294–96. Gómez Farías' *exposición* and the *puro* resolution, along with the vote tallies, are published in Peña y Reyes, *Algunos documentos sobre el tratado*, pp. 93–106. On Otero's resolution, see Otero, *Obras*, I, 87; and Gaxiola, *Otero*, pp. 287–90.

Couto and Miguel Atristain of the group that had vainly negotiated in September, and a former foreign minister, Luis G. Cuevas.[42] With moderates in control of both executive and Congress, Mexico now seemed ready to negotiate.

In the midst of these preparations, on November 16, Trist received both of Buchanan's dispatches recalling him to Washington. For some weeks he had anticipated being replaced, and he was eager to rejoin his family. But Polk's decision to break off negotiations altogether, coming at a time when the peace party had finally gained control of the Mexican government, surprised and distressed him.[43] Nevertheless, his first impulse was to obey the instructions. He read them to Thornton, who was about to leave for Querétaro and who shared Trist's dismay.

As soon as the British attaché arrived in the provisional capital, he told Peña informally of the new development and, at Trist's suggestion, advised him to propose peace terms that Trist could carry back to Washington. Peña, however, insisted that the terms must come from the newly appointed peace commissioners, apparently fearing that to take any further initiative would weaken his position. He and Thornton wrote to Trist, urging him to stay in Mexico, on the grounds that his withdrawal would revitalize the war party and that by offering to renew relations he had committed himself to another round of negotiations.[44]

Trist was willing to give the Mexicans a little time in which to act, especially since it appeared that Scott could not immediately spare enough men to escort him to Veracruz. On November 27 he informed Buchanan that he would leave within ten days, but he also described the favorable outlook for peace, "the last chance for a treaty," and strongly advised him to appoint a new peace commission at once instead of trying to manage negotiations entirely from Washington.[45] Throughout the latter half of Novem-

42. Rives, *US and Mexico*, II, 592–94. Manuel de la Peña y Peña to Trist, November 22, 1847; Trist to Buchanan, November 27, December 20, Nos. 21, 23, Manning, *IAA*, VIII, 973–74, 980–84, 1021–24. On the governors' conference, see also Smith, *War with Mexico*, II, 464; Prieto, *Memorias, 1840 a 1853*, pp. 292–94; and Gaxiola, *Otero*, pp. 284–85.

43. Trist to Buchanan, October 31, 1847, No. 19, Manning, *IAA*, VIII, 969–70. Trist to Mrs. Trist, October 31, Trist Papers, XXVI, f. 60638. Buchanan continued to offer private reassurance. Buchanan to Trist, October 31, ibid., f.

60638.

44. Trist to Buchanan, October 31, 1847, No. 19; Peña to Trist, November 22; Trist to Peña, November 24, Manning, *IAA*, VIII, 969–70, 973–74, 980. Trist to Mrs. Trist, October 31; Thornton to Trist, November 22, Trist Papers, XXVI, ff. 60638, 60684–85. Thornton to Palmerston, November 26, No. 14, GB, FO 50/212, ff. 100–110. Peña to Bernardo Couto, November 24, as quoted in Roa Bárcena, *Recuerdos de la invasión*, III, 263–64.

45. Trist to Buchanan, November 27, 1847, No. 21, Manning, *IAA*, VIII, 980–

ber Scott, Thornton, prominent British merchants, and unnamed Mexicans bombarded Trist with arguments and pleas to disregard his instructions. Many predicted that if he failed to grasp the present opportunity to achieve peace, the fighting would resume, the Mexican government would fall apart, and the American army would face an endless occupation. Between December 2 and 4 Trist finally yielded and decided to remain in Mexico. Although he never made clear which factors shifted the balance, the decisive counsel may have come from his friend James L. Freaner, a correspondent of the New Orleans *Delta* who had proven to be both level-headed and reliable.[46]

Trist announced the reasons for his decision in a note to Thornton and in one of his longest dispatches to the State Department. He told the British attaché that he had proposed to the Mexican commissioners a boundary beyond which the United States could not recede—the Rio Grande from its mouth to El Paso and the line of 32° from thence to the Pacific. If the Mexicans would accept these terms, he would sign a treaty, in violation of his instructions, because he felt that the United States government desired peace and because he feared that the collapse of negotiations would extend the war indefinitely. Also, he was sure that no Mexican government would relinquish territory south of the line he described.[47]

In his dispatch to Buchanan, Trist repeated these points and emphasized the inconsistency between the Americans' professions of peace and a rupture of negotiations. He declared that many Mexicans favored outright annexation to the United States but that this could come about peacefully only through a straightforward American proclamation. He assumed that the United States government did not desire annexation of all Mexico, for it would probably destroy the American Union. Trist warned that con-

---

84. Trist to Thornton, November 24; Trist to Mrs. Trist, November 28, Trist Papers, XXVI, ff. 60707–8, 60743.

46. Elliott, *Scott*, pp. 559–60. Smith, *War with Mexico*, II, 238, 465. Thornton to Trist, November 22, 1847; Lionel Davidson to Thornton, November 23; William de Drusina to Thornton, November 24, Trist Papers, XXVI, ff. 60684–85, 60703–4, 60719. Davidson and Drusina were British merchants in Mexico City. Trist told his wife that he had made up his mind on December 4. Trist to Mrs. Trist, December 4, ibid., ff. 60751–52. However, he had

assured the Mexican commissioners on December 3 that he would negotiate a treaty. Couto to Peña, December 3, as quoted in Rives, *US and Mexico*, II, 597. On Freaner's influence, see A. H. Sevier and Nathan Clifford to Buchanan, Querétaro, March 15, 1848, US, 41C, 2S, SR 261, p. 9. Thomas J. Farnham, "Nicholas Trist & James Freaner and the Mission to Mexico," *Arizona and the West*, II (Autumn 1969), 247–60.

47. Trist to Thornton, December 4, 1847, Manning, *IAA*, VIII, 984–85n2. Thornton to Trist, December 11, Trist Papers, XXVI, ff. 60846–47.

tinued fighting or attempts to dismember Mexico would lead to anarchy and to guerrilla operations. He defended Scott's armistice after Churubusco and his negotiations with Santa Anna against recent attacks by the Washington *Union*, principal organ of the administration. Santa Anna, he admitted, was thoroughly unscrupulous but at that time would have done almost anything to save himself. Far from being the Mexican leader's dupes, Trist insisted that he and Scott had nearly succeeded in the negotiations and might still do so, if Polk approved the proposed boundary and allowed them to remain in Mexico.

Considering Polk's suspicious personality and the opinions he had already formed of Trist and Scott, one may doubt that any arguments would have reconciled him to his envoy's flagrant disobedience. Certainly Trist's dispatch could not do so. His reasoning was basically sound, but he drowned it in his usual ocean of rhetoric. At one point he remarked tactlessly: "Infallibility of judgment . . . is not among the attributes of a President of the United States, even when his sentences rest upon full & accurate knowledge of all the facts." Also, his attack on the *Union* hit close to the White House, and he chose to end his dispatch with thrusts at General Pillow, Polk's friend and political ally.[48] A few days later, Pillow, too, wrote to Polk, warning him that Trist was a trouble-maker and not to be trusted.[49]

*　　*　　*　　*

Trist's decision to continue negotiations could provide the Mexicans only a few weeks' respite, for after that time he might receive a presidential order for his arrest, and even sooner the arrival of reinforcements might remove Scott's excuse for remaining in Mexico City. Before it was known that Trist would stay, there had been indications that the Mexican government would accept Buchanan's draft treaty as a basis for negotiations.[50] Now,

48. Trist to Buchanan, December 6, 1847, No. 22, Manning, *IAA*, VIII, 984–1020. The sentence quoted appears on p. 1019.

49. Gideon J. Pillow to James K. Polk, December 12, 1847, Polk Papers, CXXI, LC. For a time during the summer Pillow and Trist had been close friends, and Pillow wrote with the outrage of one who felt himself betrayed. He was also bitter against Scott, who had ac-

cused him of writing an anonymous letter, signed "Leonidas" and much reprinted in the American press, criticizing Scott's handling of the army. See also Pillow to Polk, November 24, ibid.

50. General Mora y Villamil, one of the negotiators in the August round, reported this to Thornton. However, Thornton also told Trist that some officials regarded his threat to leave as a mere bluff. Thornton to Trist, Decem-

however, Anaya and Peña procrastinated. First they requested a formal armistice, which Scott refused, having learned his lesson. Then they explained that they could not instruct their peace commissioners until these were confirmed by Congress, whose members had again scattered to their homes.[51]

The Mexican leaders were naturally reluctant to sign an unpopular peace treaty and thereby risk overthrow by a revolution. Trist blamed the delay partly on the *puros'* conviction that a continued impasse would force the United States to abandon ideas of territorial annexation and to regenerate Mexico instead. He declared that the Whigs' attacks on the war, reprinted in the Mexican press, stimulated this hope, and he cited in particular a speech by Henry Clay denouncing annexationism. Later, when copies of Polk's annual message arrived, these hopeful reformers were able to twist one passage into a promise of an American protectorate until Mexico had achieved stability and prosperity. According to Trist, knowledge of this statement redoubled the energies of the *puros* against a treaty.[52] There is some evidence to suggest that he himself had seriously considered providing in the treaty for a temporary protectorate, in order to win the *puros'* support.[53]

Another reason for Mexican stalling was more apparent to Thornton than to Trist—the lingering hope that at the crucial moment Britain would intervene to moderate American demands or at least to guarantee the permanence of any settlement. At the end of 1846 Herrera had appointed a new minister to Britain,

---

ber 5, 1847, Trist Papers, XXVI, ff. 60836–37. Reinforcements of 5,000 men arrived in Mexico City on December 6, but Scott did not move to expand the occupation.

51. Roa Bárcena, *Recuerdos de la invasión*, III, 272–76. Thornton to Palmerston, December 11, 1847, No. 21, GB, FO 50/212, ff. 161–70.

52. Trist to Buchanan, December 20, 26, 29, 1847, Nos. 23–25, Manning, *IAA*, VIII, 1021–27, 1028–32. A great scandal was caused by a report that toasts had been drunk to total annexation at a banquet attended by members of the *ayuntamiento*. For days, leading *puros* denied that they had taken part. Hitchcock, *Fifty Years*, pp. 313–15. Roa Bárcena, *Recuerdos de la invasión*, III, 215–16. This episode long remained a bone of contention among Mexican historians. Homer C. Chaney, Jr., "The

Mexican-United States War, As Seen by Mexican Intellectuals, 1846–1956," Ph.D. diss., Stanford University, 1959, p. 155. For a convincing explanation of the incident and a revealing analysis of the power struggle in Mexico City's municipality, see Berge, "Mexican Dilemma," *passim*.

53. According to Roa Bárcena, Trist proposed to the Mexican commissioners that the United States guarantee the Mexican Constitution of 1824 and Gómez Farías' reforms of 1847 for eight years. Roa Bárcena, *Recuerdos de la invasión*, III, 277–78. Trist's papers contain draft articles, dated January 1, specifying a guarantee of the Constitution of 1824 for five years and "all needful assistance . . . to the said [Mexican] Government for its protection against intestine violence and usurpation." Trist Papers, XXVII, f. 61005.

José María Luis Mora, a *puro* expatriate and friend of Gómez Farías. Since then Mora, almost forgotten at home, had been vainly importuning Palmerston for aid. During November 1847, apparently on his own initiative, he proposed to sell California to Britain, in order to provide the British government with an excuse to intervene and save the rest of his country. For a moment Palmerston showed a flicker of interest, but he quickly realized the impracticality of such a transaction. He continued to instruct Doyle and Thornton that they should tender good offices without involving Britain in the terms of settlement.[54] Whether Anaya and Peña knew anything of Mora's overture, they awaited Doyle's arrival with hope of succor. One of Doyle's first actions, in mid-December, was to declare solemnly that he would advise both sides and transmit communications, but that the Mexican government must not expect either mediation or a guarantee of any sort.[55]

Doyle's statement removed one reason for delaying negotiations. At the same time Scott clarified the United States' intentions by announcing that he planned to occupy more of Mexico and that in all occupied areas taxes would be collected for the American army, dating from December 1, no matter whether they had already been paid to the Mexican government.[56] Soon afterward, Peña empowered his commissioners to begin negotiations. The first paragraph of his instructions, included apparently as a sop to the war party in Congress, required them to ask the United States to withdraw its troops at once and agree to submit all future disputes to arbitration. If this request failed, the commissioners might consent to a boundary running up the Rio Grande to El Paso, thence to the Gila River and along it to the Pacific coast just north of San Diego.

In return, the United States would be required to assume all Mexican debts and American claims against Mexico and to pay

54. José María Luis Mora to Palmerston, November 15, 17, 1847; Mora to Ministro de Relaciones Exteriores, November 30, December 30, Luis Chávez Orozco, ed., *La gestión diplomática del Doctor Mora*, pp. 28–48. Mora to Palmerston, December 17; Palmerston memorandum, December 25, GB, FO 50/215, ff. 164–67. Mora admitted to Palmerston that he had not communicated with his government on the subject. Palmerston to Thornton, December 28, No. 2, GB, FO 50/207, ff. 129–30.

55. Thornton to Palmerston, November 26, 1847, No. 14; Doyle to Palmerston, December 13, No. 3, GB, FO 50/212, ff. 100–110, 204–9.

56. Doyle to Palmerston, December 18, 1847, No. 6, GB, FO 50/212, ff. 216–17. M. R. Veramendi (governor of the Federal District) to Ministro de Relaciones Exteriores, December 14, US, LC, /349. Scott then tried to collect taxes, but failed. Thomas M. Davies, Jr., "Assessments during the Mexican War: an Exercise in Futility," *New Mexico Historical Review*, 41 (July 1966), 197–216.

an unspecified sum of money. Full provision must be made for inhabitants, property, and religion in the ceded territory as well as protection from Indian raids across the new border into Mexico. Also, the United States must abjure any future annexation of Mexican territory. Separate instructions, partly secret, required the commissioners to restrict the boundary to the Nueces River if possible, to demand $30 million in compensation, and to suggest payment in bonds of the British debt. In a private letter Peña told the commissioners not to break off negotiations for any cause without providing some channel for their resumption.[57]

The Mexican instructions were closer to Polk's minimum demands than any terms Santa Anna had ever considered seriously, and, as discussions began on January 2, 1848, Trist hoped for a speedy settlement. Nevertheless, a month of argument and suspense lay ahead of him. Mexico's moderate administration rested on shaky foundations, for at the news of treaty negotiations several states seemed ready to revolt, and the government had no funds with which to put troops in the field against them.[58] Also, less than a week after the discussions began, Anaya's term as president *ad interim* ended. The moderates had planned to elect José J. Herrera permanent president, but he was ill. Since Congress could not muster a quorum for a new election anyway, Peña, who was still presiding justice of the supreme court, resumed the presidential chair, with De la Rosa again as foreign minister. The arrival of more American reinforcements caused much speculation about Scott's intentions, especially at news of an uprising in San Luis Potosí. Scott considered marching against the rebels but decided that any show of force would further weaken Peña, and soon the rebellion died down.[59]

Against this shifting and uncertain background Trist and the three Mexican commissioners carried on their meetings in Mexico

57. For the principal instructions, see Peña y Reyes, *Algunos documentos sobre el tratado*, pp. 106–14. The additional instructions and the private letter are quoted and summarized in Roa Bárcena, *Recuerdos de la invasión*, III, 285. The instructions also specified details concerning the American evacuation of Mexico, the exchange of prisoners, and other military matters.

58. On December 31 Peña informed each state government of his administration's position on the peace question. During the next five weeks he received approving replies from Micho-

acán, Zacatecas, Jalisco, Durango, Colima, Chihuahua, and Sonora. He had already heard from the state of México. US, LC, /183.

59. Rives, *US and Mexico*, II, 604–6. Roa Bárcena, *Recuerdos de la invasión*, III, 301–2. Couto *et al.* to Trist, January 9, 1848; Peña to Couto *et al.*, January 11 (trans.), Trist Papers, XXVIII, ff. 61085–86, 61131. Trist to Buchanan, January 12, No. 26, Manning, *IAA*, VIII, 1032–34. Doyle to Palmerston, January 14, 19, Nos. 10, 12, GB, FO 50/ 219, ff. 72–79, 95–98.

City, weighing words and tracing lines on a map of northern Mexico that was only partly accurate but the best available.[60] Working from the bases of Buchanan's treaty draft and Peña's instructions, they converged toward agreement. Since neither Spanish nor English could be specified as the dominant language, they had to phrase the articles in both languages simultaneously, and the Mexican fondness for semantic subtleties sometimes extended the arguments to tedious length. To complicate matters for the historian, they kept no official transcript of the meetings, and Trist's report, prolix and rambling, leaves much to be desired.[61] Throughout the negotiations Trist was in constant touch with Doyle and Thornton; when he was pressed for time, they even helped him with translations.[62]

After Trist had disposed of the Mexicans' *pro forma* requests for arbitration and a guarantee by neutral powers, the most pressing and difficult task was to draw a new boundary. When Trist proposed the line of the Rio Grande and 32°, the Mexicans reluctantly agreed to the former. They also offered no objection to ceding the federal territories of New Mexico and Upper California, but they declared that the Constitution of 1824 expressly forbade the national government to alienate any part of a sovereign state. Since the states of Chihuahua and Sonora extended north of 32° and had protested against any transfer of their lands, the Mexican commissioners insisted that the boundary line follow the Gila River, as set forth in Buchanan's treaty draft, and also

60. The cartography of the peace negotiations was even more complicated than the negotiators realized at the time. The map they used was published by J. Disturnell of New York, and seven editions of it appeared in 1847, all differing in details. The copy Trist took with him to Mexico and the one preserved in the Mexican archives are of two different editions. And when Captain Robert E. Lee consulted with Trist on the location of San Diego, he used still another edition, published in 1846. For an exhaustive account of the problem see David Hunter Miller, ed., *Treaties and Other International Acts of the United States of America*, V, 340–70.

61. Trist left detailed memoranda of the first two days' discussions (January 2 and 3). Trist Papers, XXVII, ff. 61009–11. If he kept such records for all the meetings, the rest have been lost. The following account of the negotiations has been assembled from

three sources. Reporting to the State Department, Trist set forth the principal issues in nonchronological and often confusing form. Trist to Buchanan, January 25, 1847, No. 27, with two enclosed memoranda, Manning, *IAA*, VIII, 1034–59. Bernardo Couto, one of the Mexican commissioners, kept a detailed account of the sessions. Together with correspondence between the commissioners and Luis de la Rosa, it serves as the basis of a largely chronological account in Roa Bárcena, *Recuerdos de la invasión*, III, 285–301. Lastly, about halfway through the negotiations Doyle sent home a shorter account, as Trist had reported to him, along with a summary of Mexican peace proposals and Trist's reactions to each one. Doyle to Palmerston, January 14, No. 10, GB, FO 50/219, ff. 72–79, 83–87.

62. Undated notes and dockets in Trist Papers, XXVIII, ff. 61088–89, 61170–71.

tried to reserve the village of Paso del Norte (modern El Paso). Trist agreed to the line at the Gila but eventually held firm for El Paso.[63]

The most persistent boundary argument concerned the port of San Diego, which Trist had been instructed to secure. The Mexicans wished to retain control of the mouth of the Colorado River, so as to maintain a land connection between Sonora and Lower California. They proposed tracing a straight line to the Pacific north of San Diego, insisting that this was the traditional boundary between Upper and Lower California. Trist posed no objection to the land connection, and at one point, in the meeting of January 5, he conceded San Diego to Mexico. Two days later, however, he changed his mind and presented statements by Baron Alexander von Humboldt and others to prove that the port had long been included in Upper California. For days both sides ransacked old books and maps, seeking further information. Trist consulted several persons, including Scott's brilliant engineer and scout, Captain Robert E. Lee. On January 16 the commissioners wrote to De la Rosa that they could neither refute Trist's evidence nor budge his determination to keep San Diego. The line was finally drawn one league to the south of the port.[64]

Trist and the commissioners also argued at great length about the purchase price. The Mexicans insisted on $30 million; Trist had earlier mentioned $20 million; but now he was determined to

63. Trist to Buchanan, January 25, 1848, No. 27, Manning, *IAA*, VIII, 1049–51. Trist's account of discussions, January 2, 3, Trist Papers, XXVII, ff. 61009–11. Roa Bárcena, *Recuerdos de la invasión*, III, 286–87. Miller, *Treaties and Other International Acts*, V, 315–17. On January 5, when Trist momentarily yielded San Diego, he included El Paso in the concession but quickly reversed himself. The Mexicans had insisted that the village belonged to Chihuahua. As a matter of fact, a small part of Tamaulipas extended across the Rio Grande too, but the state authorities did not protest its transfer, and the negotiators apparently ignored the embarrassing fact.

64. Trist's memorandum to the State Department on the boundary between the two Californias is a triumph of obfuscation. Manning, *IAA*, VIII, 1044–49. In this paper he did not mention his brief concession. The Mexican account, which agrees with him on most

points, is much clearer. Roa Bárcena, *Recuerdos de la invasión*, III, 287–91. This is the chief authority for Trist's brief yielding on January 5. However, a fragmentary draft memorandum in his papers, dated January 4, explains why he made the concession—he was afraid to jeopardize the negotiations for a port that he believed to be of minor significance. He rationalized his judgment with the argument that Buchanan's instructions had included the cession of San Diego only because the secretary happened to be using a map that placed the territorial boundary to the south. Trist Papers, XXVIII, ff. 61025–29. The Trist Papers contain many notes indicating that not only the negotiators but also Doyle, Mackintosh, and General Persifor F. Smith were involved in the search for the correct boundary. Ibid., ff. 61040–79, *passim*. See also Miller, *Treaties and Other International Acts*, V, 317–18, 371.

pay no more than $15 million. Leaving the amount blank, the negotiators proceeded to a long discussion over the wording of the provision relating to American claims. Here Trist yielded slightly and, considering the duration of the war, raised the maximum amount allowable from $3 million, as provided in Buchanan's draft, to $3,250,000. When the conferees finally returned to the purchase price, the Mexicans unhappily accepted $15 million, of which $3 million was to be paid in cash, on ratification, and the remainder in four equal annual installments, bearing interest of 6 per cent.[65]

On January 13, while they were at odds over the boundary and the purchase price, Trist and the commissioners decided to pass on to other provisions. These were somewhat more easily arranged, although with a great deal of give and take. For example, the negotiators agreed that within a year from ratification residents in the ceded territory might elect to retain Mexican citizenship but in any case were free to remain in the territory and enjoy the appropriate rights conferred by the United States Constitution. After much argument Trist agreed to insert a provision honoring Mexican land grants in Texas and the ceded area. This was supposedly only a face-saving device, for the Mexicans assured him that their government had granted no lands since the beginning of the war, but neither Polk nor Congress would accept the provision.[66] Trist also agreed to a long article detailing the American responsibility to maintain order among Indians in the ceded territory, after the Mexican commissioners explained that this was necessary to induce the northern states to approve the treaty. Other subjects of discussion were an armistice after the signature of the treaty, procedure for liquidating the American occupation, and provisions for postwar commerce between the two countries.[67]

One article of Buchanan's draft treaty seems to have been left out of the discussion altogether—the grant of transit rights across the Isthmus of Tehuantepec. During 1847 the British merchant

65. Manning, *IAA*, VIII, 1051. Trist drew up a special memorandum on claims. Ibid., pp. 1052–56. He did not believe that, on adjudication, the total amount would reach $3 million. See also Smith, *War with Mexico*, II, 469–70.

66. Roa Bárcena, *Recuerdos de la invasión*, III, 293. In discussing the land grants Trist referred to the Florida treaty of 1819 as a precedent. Mann-ing, *IAA*, VIII, 1057–58. It is not clear whether he had in mind the embarrassment John Quincy Adams suffered after signing this treaty, on discovering that it validated several extensive last-minute grants by Spain in the ceded territory. Samuel F. Bemis, *John Quincy Adams and the Foundations of American Foreign Policy*, pp. 336–37.

67. Manning, *IAA*, VIII, 1058–59.

house of Manning and Mackintosh had acquired the concession that José de Garay had received in 1842 from the Mexican government. Consul Mackintosh, a prominent member of the house and the chief mover of the project, was apparently willing to sell the concession to the United States as a business deal, and Trist went so far as to draw up articles approving the transfer, which could be inserted into the peace treaty. As soon as Doyle arrived in Mexico, however, he insisted that Mackintosh give the British government an opportunity to sponsor the project, and he supported the Mexican commissioners in their refusal to discuss Trist's additional articles. Since Tehuantepec was not a *sine qua non* in Buchanan's instructions, and since Trist needed Doyle's aid in completing the negotiations, he dropped the isthmian question. A few months later the British government decided against the Mackintosh proposal, whereupon the consul sold his firm's interests to the American merchants Peter and Louis Hargous.[68]

Throughout the negotiations the Mexican commissioners made almost daily reports to Foreign Minister De la Rosa in Querétaro, and his replies considerably stiffened their resistance to Trist. As late as January 22 the foreign minister insisted on holding Trist to his brief consent to yield San Diego. On the next day, before receiving this communication, the commissioners implored De la Rosa to authorize immediate agreement on all outstanding questions before the arrival of new reinforcements compelled Scott to expand the occupation. Three days later, on receiving assurances that the lands of Sonora and Chihuahua had been preserved inviolate, De la Rosa finally accepted the boundary settlement.[69]

On January 26 he authorized the commissioners to sign the treaty, but he set up several unreasonable conditions, requiring the Americans to promise that they would withdraw from Mexico City at once, abandon all tax levies, turn over all revenues to the government, and immediately pay $300,000 or $400,000 on the purchase price. The last requirement was especially important to

68. Rives, *US and Mexico*, II, 606–7. Doyle to Palmerston, December 24, 1847, No. 7, GB, FO 50/212, ff. 220–22. Doyle enclosed the text of the additional articles that Trist had proposed to include in the treaty. Ibid., ff. 224–25. Palmerston felt that Parliament would never appropriate the large sum of money required to dig a canal and that it would be inadvisable to become involved with a grant from such an unreliable government as that of Mexico. Palmerston to Doyle, August 31, 1848, No. 38; G. R. Porter to Lord Eddisbury, August 12, GB, FO 50/218, ff. 77–79; 50/225, ff. 201–5.

69. Roa Bárcena, *Recuerdos de la invasión*, III, 292–93, 296–98.

Peña, for he anticipated revolts when the terms of the treaty were announced, and he had no money with which to suppress them.[70]

These demands must have seemed the last straw to Trist. As he had repeatedly told the commissioners, he was expecting at any time to receive peremptory orders from Polk that would undo all the accomplishments of the negotiations. Late in the evening of January 28 the American envoy called on Doyle to tell him that if he could not bring the commissioners to sign at once, the negotiations must cease. On the next morning Trist and Doyle approached the commissioners together. The Mexicans pleaded for more time, still hoping for unqualified authorization from their government. That afternoon a courier arrived from Querétaro, bearing a note of January 27 from De la Rosa in which the foreign minister abandoned most of his demands but continued to insist on an immediate cash payment. Trist would not agree to this requirement; after the fruitless financial deals with Santa Anna during the preceding summer, he had neither the authority nor the will to advance any money before the treaty was ratified.

Doyle and Trist then worked out a demonstration to impress the Mexican government. Trist drew up an official note to the commissioners in which he broke off negotiations, to cover his responsibility if a courier should arrive from Polk. At the same time Doyle informed them confidentially that Trist would withdraw the note and sign the treaty if by February 1 they could obtain from their government unqualified authority to sign it. Doyle also talked to Scott about his military plans and learned that he intended to march on Querétaro and disperse or seize the provisional government. At the request of the commissioners Doyle reported this conversation in a private note to De la Rosa. They also assured their government that the Americans would evacuate the capital promptly, without any express provision, once the treaty was signed. The commissioners added that they thought the demand for an immediate payment unbecoming.[71]

Confronted with the grim alternative of further fighting, Peña and De la Rosa yielded and authorized the commissioners

70. De la Rosa to Mexican commissioners, January 26, 1848. Quoted and summarized in Roa Bárcena, *Recuerdos de la invasión*, III, 297.

71. Roa Bárcena, *Recuerdos de la invasión*, III, 294–96. De la Rosa to Mexican commissioners, January 27, 1848, ibid., pp. 297–99. Rives, *US and Mexico*, II, 608–11. Doyle to Palmerston, February 1, No. 13; Doyle to Couto *et al.*, January 29; Doyle to De la Rosa, January 29, GB, FO 50/219, ff. 99–109, 112–14, 116–20. Trist to Scott, January 28; Trist to Couto *et al.*, January 29, Trist Papers, XXIX, ff. 61244–46, 61267–68. That Trist was bluffing in this maneuver is confirmed by a private note. Trist to Scott, January 28 (draft), ibid., ff. 61244–46.

to sign the treaty. The messenger who bore the dispatch covered the hundred miles to Mexico City in one day, arriving just within Trist's deadline. At the last moment the Mexican delegation insisted on signing the treaty outside the city, probably in order to avoid acting under the muzzles of American cannon. At 6:00 P.M. on February 2 the commissioners and Trist held the formal ceremony of signature at the little northern suburb of Guadalupe Hidalgo, near the site of the most famous religious shrine in Mexico. That evening Trist sent three copies to the United States with his friend, the journalist James L. Freaner.[72]

The Treaty of Guadalupe Hidalgo, which resulted from a blend of compromise, persuasion, and coercion, was in most respects a credit to all concerned. The ceded territory included Polk's major goals and at least as much as the United States could comfortably absorb at the time. The Americans could not have claimed Lower California by right of occupation, and the long, barren, exposed peninsula would have been a focus of trouble in the decade of filibustering expeditions that followed the war.[73] American devotees of states' rights could hardly object to Mexican scruples about lands belonging to the states of Chihuahua and Sonora. Despite these scruples, however, a later centralist government (again under Santa Anna) sliced a piece from the desired territory and ceded it to the United States in the Gadsden Treaty of 1853. The grant for communications across Tehuantepec was finally lodged in American hands, but the recipients were never able to carry out its terms.[74]

For the ceded territory Polk paid a price that both he and Buchanan had been willing to offer during most of the war. Of the other treaty provisions the only one which caused serious trouble was the requirement that the United States prevent Indian

72. Roa Bárcena, *Recuerdos de la invasión*, III, 299–301. Rives, *US and Mexico*, II, 611–13. Doyle to Palmerston, February 2, 1848, No. 14, GB, FO 50/219, ff. 122–24. Trist to Buchanan, February 2, No. 28, Manning, *IAA*, VIII, 1059–60. The text of the treaty as signed appears in US, 30C, 1S, SED 52, pp. 38–66.

73. During the war various American naval units maneuvered off the peninsula, blockaded it, and landed troops from time to time. Both Commodore Stockton and Commodore William B. Shubrick proclaimed American rule over Lower California, but at the beginning of 1848 the situation there had reached a stalemate. See Peter Gerhard, "Baja California in the Mexican War, 1846–1848," *Pacific Historical Review*, 14 (December 1945), 418–24; and Eugene K. Chamberlin, "Nicholas Trist and Baja California," ibid., 32 (February 1963), 49–63.

74. The later history of the Tehuantepec question is outlined in J. Fred Rippy, "Diplomacy of the United States and Mexico Regarding the Isthmus of Tehuantepec, 1848–1860," *Mississippi Valley Historical Review*, 6 (March 1920), 503–31. Paul Neff Garber, *The Gadsden Treaty, passim*.

raids across the border. This proved so difficult to fulfill that James Gadsden obtained Mexico's consent to cancel the provision in the treaty of 1853. Thus, all in all, the Treaty of Guadalupe Hidalgo created few problems, achieved the most important American war aims, and left a truncated but still viable Mexico.[75]

75. A recent account criticizes Trist sharply for disobeying his instructions. Jack Northup, "Nicholas Trist's Mission to Mexico: a Reinterpretation," *Southwestern Historical Quarterly*, 71 (January 1969), 321–46, and especially 344–45. Northup is justified in pointing out the gaps between instructions and treaty, but he fails to give due weight to statements of Buchanan allowing Trist wide discretion and to the exceedingly difficult circumstances in Mexico. Also, he has relied entirely on published sources.

17

The Apogee and
Decline of Expansionism

While Trist and his colleagues were trying to maneuver the Mexican government into accepting a treaty, a large part of the American public was blundering toward the conviction that the United States must annex all of Mexico. The news of Santa Anna's wholly unsatisfactory offer of early September, followed at once by the occupation of Mexico City, greatly stimulated the extremists, and they outdid themselves in gloating and crying for vengeance. As the New York *Globe* put it:

> The people of Mexico must be made to *feel this war*. . . . We must SEIZE HER MINES—*hold her towns*. . . . There is a spirit abroad which will not long be stayed—a spirit of progress, which will compel us, for the good of both nations and the world at large, TO DESTROY THE NATIONALITY *of that besotted people*. It would almost seem that they, like the Israelites of old, had brought upon themselves *the vengeance of the Almighty* and we ourselves had been *raised up to overthrow* AND UTTERLY DESTROY THEM *as a separate and distinct nation*.

The New York *Herald* carried the doctrine of constructive violence even further: "Like the Sabine virgins, she [Mexico] will soon learn to love her ravisher."[1]

The leadership of the all-Mexico movement and most of its members were Democrats. A few Whigs favored moderate territorial demands, but most of the Whig press followed the lead of the Washington *National Intelligencer* and the New York *Tribune* in opposing all annexation, except the port of San Francisco. The *Intelligencer* appealed to Polk not to pervert the originally announced purpose of the war—resistance to Mexican aggression—and went so far as to approve the Mexican proposal to neutralize the disputed Nueces–Rio Grande territory. It pointed out that Scott's victories had served only to unite the Mexican people and as evidence quoted a proclamation by the governor of Mexico state, an uncomfortable reminder of the American past: "Our

1. New York *Globe*, n.d., reprinted in Washington *National Intelligencer*, October 18, 1847, p. 3. New York *Her-* *ald*, October 8, p. 2. See also ibid., September 22, p. 2; October 1, p. 2; October 24, p. 2.

fathers died in order to give us independence, to free us from a foreign yoke. . . . Let us die rather than traffic away in a vile bargain what they purchased with their blood. Death is preferable to ignominy."[2]

The persistent flag-waving of the Democrats, however, embarrassed the Whigs and kept them on the defensive. Throughout the war the Democrats had played on their opponents' patriotism to force through war measures, and even now the *Intelligencer* had to approve sending reinforcements to Mexico. The fall elections settled nothing, for both parties could point to gains. After the elections the Whigs continued to attack annexations and to invoke the old American virtues, but they could not stem the expansionist tide. Instead, their opposition to annexation probably encouraged the Mexican government to delay negotiations, which angered the annexationists further and confirmed them in their demands.[3]

* * * *

While the all-Mexico movement gained strength, Polk was receiving widely varying advice from his generals in Mexico and from many others, both experts and amateurs. Some wanted him to extend the occupation of central Mexico, others to establish a defense line in the north.[4] Polk leaned in the direction of public opinion but took pains to preserve the greatest possible freedom of action. In mid-October, when the cabinet met to discuss the recall

2. Washington *National Intelligencer*, October 5, 1847, p. 3; October 9, p. 3; October 15, p. 3. The passage quoted is in the issue for October 9. For a summary of Whig arguments against annexation at this time, see *American Review*, 6 (October), 331–46. Naturally the division was not absolutely clear-cut. The pro-Taylor *National Whig* published flaming editorials for annexing all of Mexico, which were widely reprinted in the West. John Douglas Pitts Fuller, *The Movement for the Acquisition of All Mexico, 1846–1848*, p. 84. For an example of Democratic opposition to the movement, see *United States Magazine and Democratic Review*, 21 (August), 93–101.

3. Washington *National Intelligencer*, October 5, 1847, p. 3; October 1, p. 3. Two outstanding antiannexationist efforts after the elections were a speech by Henry Clay at Lexington, Kentucky, and an article by Albert Gallatin. Fuller, *Acquisition of All Mexico*, pp. 89–

91. George Rawlings Poage, *Henry Clay and the Whig Party*, pp. 165–66. *NNR*, 73 (November 20, 27, December 11, 1847), 190, 197–200, 235–39. Richard Mannix, "Albert Gallatin and the Movement for Peace with Mexico," *Social Studies*, 60 (December 1969), 310–18. For hostile reactions to the sentiments of Clay and Gallatin, see the issues of Washington *Union* for November 16–19, 24, 29, December 1, 3, 4, 6.

4. See sources cited in Chap. 16, notes 37 and 38. Captain J. G. Barnard to General Joseph G. Totten (chief engineer), October 11, 1847; memorandum by Totten, November 23, Marcy Papers, XIII, LC. Charles P. Fletcher to James K. Polk, October 9, Polk Papers, CXX, LC. Caleb Cushing to James Buchanan, October 31; James Gray to Buchanan, October 8; George L. Stevens to Buchanan, October 10; John Reynolds to Buchanan, November 20, Buchanan Papers, box 67, HSP.

of Trist, the President told its members that he favored pushing forward military operations and establishing stable provisional governments over all territory seized. He added that he would recommend to Congress the formal annexation of the Californias and New Mexico and the establishment of permanent territorial governments there. The cabinet unanimously approved; before he received news of the September negotiations or the occupation of Mexico City, Polk began to prepare a rough draft of his annual message, setting forth this policy.

But disagreement soon divided the cabinet and revealed that Polk's annexationism had limits. By early November Buchanan had admitted that he wished to be considered for the presidential nomination and was trimming his sails to the expansionist winds. In a meeting of November 9 the secretary told Polk "in an unsettled tone" that the President's message should either specify the Mexican territory that was to be held as an indemnity or announce that the United States would occupy all of Mexico and promise protection to its inhabitants. Buchanan was not yet ready to determine his own policy, but he implied that Mexico's cession should include the territory east of the Sierra Madre as well as the Californias and New Mexico and that the United States should withdraw its troops to that line. Polk restated his earlier proposition; Marcy sided with the President; and Walker, the most ardent annexationist of them all, warned Buchanan that if the United States government withdrew its troops from central Mexico without negotiating a satisfactory peace, the whole country would condemn it.[5]

Buchanan then proposed to insert into the message an explicit plan for a protectorate, with the comment, "What a glorious mission would this be for our Country! The war which Mexico has forced upon us would thus be converted into an enduring blessing to herself." The rest of the cabinet agreed with the general principle that the American army should help the Mexicans to establish a government that would negotiate peace. However, when Buchanan continued that if the protectorate failed to bring peace, "we must fulfil that destiny which Providence may have in store for both countries," Polk and most of the cabinet objected that this statement was too vague. Walker liked it, for he expected that

5. James K. Polk, *The Diary of James K. Polk during His Presidency, 1845 to 1849*, ed. Milo M. Quaife, III, 189–90, 192, 216–18. Although Polk was displeased at Buchanan's candidacy and would not give him any support, he did not invoke the renunciatory letter which he had required from Buchanan at the latter's appointment to the cabinet.

most people would interpret it to mean that the administration intended to take all of Mexico, but Polk refused to go so far and decided to retain his own draft of the paragraph.[6]

During the last days before its delivery Polk showed parts of the message to several Democratic politicians—Lewis Cass, Robert B. Rhett of South Carolina, Stephen A. Douglas, and others—and made a few changes of wording. After the message had gone to Congress, the President learned that Walker had inserted into his Treasury Report a passage looking to the occupation of all Mexico. He prevailed on the secretary to remove it, lest the country think that the administration was divided.[7]

It is not surprising that the resulting annual message left everyone somewhat puzzled as to American intentions in Mexico. After recounting American military successes, Polk justified territorial cessions on the grounds that Mexico had no other way of paying an indemnity and that neither Congress nor anyone else had expected to undertake a costly war for nothing: "The doctrine of no territory is the doctrine of no indemnity, and if sanctioned would be a public acknowledgment that our country was wrong and that the war declared by Congress with extraordinary unanimity [sic] was unjust." It would be particularly appropriate to annex the Californias and New Mexico, he went on, for the Mexican government was too weak to retain them anyway, and if the provinces tried to rule themselves, they would certainly fall to the control of some more powerful state. He also cited geographical propinquity and the months of peaceful American occupation as reasons why "they should never be surrendered to Mexico." Needless to say, he was careful not to mention the slavery issue.

Having set forth what he regarded as a minimal cession, Polk then briefly stated the policy agreed on in October: vigorous military action, occupation of seized territory, and establishment of temporary civil government in this territory. Withdrawal to a fixed line, he said, would merely encourage Mexico to continue guerrilla warfare indefinitely. He declared that he had never favored permanent conquest of all Mexico, but he conceded that chronic instability might require the United States to protect "the friends of peace in Mexico in the establishment and maintenance of a free republican government of their own choice," which would conclude an acceptable peace. If that policy failed, the

6. Polk, *Diary*, III, 226–27, 229–30. A draft of the passage which Buchanan proposed is in "Papers, Messages & Speeches, 1847," series 5, box 4, Polk Papers, LC.

7. Polk, *Diary*, III, 235–42.

United States would be forced to continue the occupation and settle the peace terms itself as its honor might demand.

To be sure, Polk had not declared that he would follow the dictates of "Providence" or manifest destiny or expansionist opinion, but he had left himself free to annex territory south of New Mexico and California if the Mexicans continued to fight. Also, he had warned the American people that they must face the possibility of a long occupation, and later in his message he hinted that this might well last through the fiscal year of 1848–1849.[8] Expansionists could take heart; pacifists would find no comfort in the President's words.

*   *   *   *

The American press reacted to the annual message by intensifying the arguments for and against annexation. The Philadelphia *Public Ledger* proposed to set up a legislature in Mexico City, "make General Scott Governor of the Whole . . . ; allow it three or four delegates in Congress; [and] open it to emigration from the United States and Europe. . . . Our Yankee young fellows and the pretty senoritas [Sabine women?] will do the rest of the annexation, and Mexico will soon be Anglo-Saxonized and prepared for the confederacy."[9] In Mexico some *puros* seized on Polk's implied promise of a protectorate and declared that a little more resistance to the invaders would end the danger of dismemberment. But the principal British and French newspapers interpreted the message to mean the annexation of all Mexico, and they wondered if the Americans realized what a large task they were assuming. The London *Examiner* remarked wryly, "They have now got a Catholic Ireland in Mexico."[10]

As Congress convened, its members reasonably represented the diverse national opinions, and they were eager to devote most of the session to the Mexican problem. The Democrats retained

8. James D. Richardson, ed., *A Compilation of the Messages and Papers of the Presidents, 1789–1897*, IV, 532–64. The sentences and phrases quoted appear on pp. 538, 542, 543, and 545. Polk also revealed that he had called up all of the 50,000 volunteers authorized by the act of May 13, 1846, and asked for authority to raise an additional force without specifying the number.

9. Philadelphia *Public Ledger*, December 11, 1847, as quoted in Frederick Merk, *Manifest Destiny and Mission in American History, a Reinterpretation*, pp. 125, 127. For criticism of the message, see Washington *National Intelligencer*, December 11, pp. 2–3; December 18, pp. 2–3; December 27, p. 2; *American Review*, 1 (new series, February 1848), 105–17; and *Christian Examiner*, 44 (January), 141.

10. London *Examiner*, January 8, 1848, p. 18. See also London *Times*, January 1, p. 4; and *Le journal des débats*, January 2–3, p. 3.

the Senate, but by a narrow margin the House had passed under the control of the Whigs, who set out to embarrass the administration by calling for the as yet unpublished correspondence relating to the Slidell mission and Polk's dealings with Santa Anna. A new member, Abraham Lincoln, made his first mark in national politics with his "spot resolution," calling on Polk to specify exactly where and on whose territory the war had begun.

In the Senate, Daniel S. Dickinson, a conservative Democrat from New York, sought to direct the debate toward a compromise settlement with resolutions favoring annexation in principle and the Dallas–Cass formula for "popular sovereignty" on the slavery issue. Calhoun replied with resolutions which declared that if the United States conquered all of Mexico, it could not hold so many populated areas in subjection as territories or admit them into the Union as states without twisting the American political system out of all recognition. In a full-dress speech before packed galleries he expanded on these dangers and formally disavowed Southern interest in Mexican territory.[11]

At the same time, during December and January, the election campaign of 1848 was getting under way. Aside from Calhoun, nearly all Democratic candidates for the presidential nomination favored annexing various parts of Mexico and at least temporarily directing that nation's affairs. In a public letter of December 17 Buchanan tried to wrest the support of Pennsylvania from Vice President Dallas by calling for a protectorate to "fulfil the destiny which Providence may have in store for both countries"—the phrase Polk had deleted from his annual message.[12] Cass, representing solidly expansionist Michigan, took over the formula of "popular sovereignty." General Franklin Pierce, fresh from Mexico, declared that the *puros* would support a program of regeneration. In contrast, many Whigs developed Calhoun's arguments against either annexation or a protectorate that might lead to annexation, whereupon the pro-Taylor *National Era* declared the annexation of Mexico to be "the deadliest blow that could be inflicted upon the system of slavery."[13]

By early February the movement to annex all Mexico had reached its greatest extent and intensity. Despite the force of abolitionism, it was probably stronger in the North than in the

---

11. Fuller, *Acquisition of All Mexico,* pp. 99–104, 131–34. Eugene Irving Mc-Cormac, *James K. Polk, a Political Biography,* p. 530. Charles M. Wiltse, *John C. Calhoun, Sectionalist, 1840–1850,* pp. 324–29. Polk, *Diary,* III, 287, 289–92.

12. Quoted in Merk, *Manifest Destiny and Mission,* pp. 119–20.

13. Fuller, *Acquisition of All Mexico,* pp. 106–8, 117–18.

South—certainly much stronger than in the Old South—but beyond that generalization historians do not agree on its geographical or political configuration.[14] The movement to annex all Mexico had not yet won over the cautious Polk, but through Buchanan and Walker it had reached deep into his councils. With or without his support it seemed likely to dominate the Democratic convention and make the impending presidential campaign a reprise of 1844, louder and more discordant. At that point, however, the hopes and plans of the ultraexpansionists suffered a rude setback, for on February 19 Trist's treaty arrived in Washington.

This treaty did not greatly surprise Polk or the cabinet, for Trist and Scott had been much on their minds during the past two months. Early in December newspaper reports and a letter from Pillow informed the President of the attempt to bribe Santa Anna during the preceding summer. Greatly shocked at this proposal, Polk had letters sent to Pillow, Trist, and Scott, asking for more information. Later in the month news arrived that Scott had ordered Generals Pillow and Worth court-martialed for insubordination. After some deliberation with the cabinet and congressional leaders, Polk decided to submit both these cases and the reports of bribery to a general court of inquiry. Then, exasperated at "Gen'l Scott's bad temper, dictatorial spirit, & extreme jealousy lest any other Gen'l Officer should acquire more fame in the army than himself," the President removed him from command and replaced him with General William O. Butler, an Ohio Democrat of modest military attainments.[15]

Polk had scarcely removed Scott when, on January 4, he learned that Trist had resumed negotiations, disobeying his recall notice. Eleven days later he received Trist's long, tactless dispatch of December 6. These communications increased Polk's fury; he

14. For example, Fuller believes that annexationist sentiment was strongest in the Northwest and emphasizes the support it received among some Whigs, while Merk finds the chief strength of the movement in the Northeast and believes that it was almost entirely confined to the Democratic party. Fuller, *Acquisition of All Mexico*, Chap. 3, *passim*, especially p. 115. Merk, *Manifest Destiny and Mission*, Chap. 6, *passim*, especially pp. 146, 155–56.

15. Polk, *Diary*, III, 245–46, 251–54, 261–63, 266–67, 269–76, 278–82. The statement quoted appears on p. 271. Polk's special concern for the reputation of his friend Pillow is obvious. Buchanan to Nicholas P. Trist, December 21, 1847, No. 7, Manning, *IAA*, VIII, 218–19. For both sides of the generals' quarrel, see Charles Winslow Elliott, *Winfield Scott, the Soldier and the Man*, Chaps. 41, 42; and Edward S. Wallace, *General William Jenkins Worth, Monterey's Forgotten Hero*, Chap. 15. At the inquiry Pillow gave extensive testimony on the bribery episode, and several other generals added their evidence, but Scott and Trist refused to testify in person, and the court finally dropped the matter.

wrote in his diary that Trist "has acted worse than any man in the public employ whom I have ever known."[16] He also informed Butler that Trist had no power to negotiate and should leave Mexico at once. It is significant, however, that Polk, Buchanan, and Walker hesitated to dispatch this letter, lest it prevent them from accepting a reasonable treaty if Trist should happen to have signed one before Butler's arrival. They finally silenced their doubts by assuring each other that if the terms conformed to Trist's original instructions, they might properly refer it to the Senate.[17]

Although President and cabinet were thus well prepared for the Treaty of Guadalupe Hidalgo, its arrival nevertheless precipitated a crisis. Polk called a special cabinet meeting for Sunday evening, February 20, at which the treaty was read aloud and informally discussed. The cabinet's first decision was to reject Article X, which validated Mexican land grants in Texas and the ceded territory. The President then proposed to submit the rest of the treaty to the Senate for consideration, since it conformed to Trist's original instructions. He reasoned cogently: if he rejected the treaty, the antiwar bloc in Congress would probably vote down measures to send more men and supplies, thus weakening the army in Mexico; if the army then retreated to a defensive line, this action would encourage the Mexicans to resist and might even imperil American possession of California. Anyway, Mexico would probably refuse to cede more territory.

Buchanan, however, was not convinced that the treaty should be accepted and pressed for a boundary along the Sierra Madre. The President confronted him: "Then you advise me not to send the Treaty to the Senate." "I do," replied the secretary. "Will you take the responsibility of its rejection?" "I will take all the responsibility which properly pertains to me as Secy. of State giving such advice." Polk was aware that Buchanan hoped for the Presidential nomination. In his view, the secretary expected that the cabinet would submit the treaty to the Senate anyway and hoped either

16. Polk, *Diary*, III, 282–83, 286, 300–301. Polk placed much of the blame on Scott, regarding Trist as the general's tool.

17. William L. Marcy to William O. Butler, January 26, 1848, US, 30C, 1S, SED 52, pp. 146–47. Polk, *Diary*, III, 310–14, 316–17. Soon afterward, Buchanan received a private letter from Alexander J. Atocha, offering to help bribe the Mexican Congress and intimating that he had the support of Scott and Trist. Atocha's approach raised Polk's suspicions of his agents. Ibid., p. 329. Alexander J. Atocha to Buchanan, January 12, Buchanan Papers, box 68, HSP.

to share the credit for an accepted treaty or to join the critics if the Senate rejected it.

The rest of the cabinet sat silent while Polk calmly reminded Buchanan that, at the beginning of the war, he had proposed to announce to the world a policy of no conquests. Yes, agreed Buchanan, "and you might have gone still further and added that I was opposed to the march of the army to . . . the City of Mexico, but the march was made—& the city taken after considerable loss of valuable lives & much money on our part, & I am not now willing to accept for indemnity what I would then have been very willing to take." He concluded with a comment that only the line of the Sierra Madre would give the United States adequate indemnity and security. Other members of the cabinet then expressed their views, only Walker supporting Buchanan, and the meeting adjourned. On the following day Polk and Secretary of the Navy Mason prepared a rough draft of the message to accompany the treaty, and on Tuesday Polk submitted it to the Senate.[18] The brief, noncommittal message explained the irregular conditions under which the treaty had been signed and recommended only the excision of Article X and of a secret provision allowing Mexico up to eight months for ratification, because of the unstable conditions in the country.[19]

A few conclusions may be drawn about Polk's decision to submit the treaty. His reactions to Trist's announcement that he would stay in Mexico and the fully developed arguments with which Polk confronted the cabinet only a day after he saw the treaty suggest that he had wholly or largely determined his course early in February. Undoubtedly, he had anticipated Buchanan's objections and had planned his answer to them.[20]

A number of historians have declared that Polk was chagrined at the terms of the treaty, because he had "determined to demand more territory than Upper California and New Mexico" and realized that if he now refused to submit Trist's handiwork to the Senate, his enemies would trap him with his earlier denials that he

18. Polk not only recorded the events of the cabinet meeting in his diary but asked his private secretary, J. Knox Walker, to write a verbatim eyewitness account, from which the quotations are taken. Polk, *Diary*, III, 346–51. Memorandum of J. Knox Walker, [February 22, 1848], Polk Papers, CXXIII, LC.

19. Richardson, *Papers of the Presi-*

dents, IV, 573–74.

20. In a private conversation on January 2 Polk and Buchanan had discussed annexations, Buchanan using almost the same language as in the later cabinet discussions and Polk maintaining a flexible position. Polk, *Diary*, III, 276–77.

was fighting a war of conquest.[21] To be sure, he was furiously resentful against Trist and Scott for actions which he interpreted as attempts to embarrass him, but when the treaty finally arrived, Polk quite properly wrote in his diary that he would judge it on its own merits rather than on those of its author.[22] It would be more consistent with the evidence of Polk's character and thinking to conclude that, as public expansionism increased, he was gradually modifying his own desires, but that he had not yet committed himself beyond Upper California and New Mexico. Above all, the willingness to share responsibility with a disobedient agent and especially with the Senate has the true ring of Polkish prudence.[23]

Within three days after its arrival in Washington the treaty had leaked into the press. On learning its terms, Mrs. Jane Storms, the companion of Moses Y. Beach on his peace reconnaissance a year before, wrote indignantly to Bancroft in Britain. "The volcanic force," she declared, "the onward, self relying, fearless, grasping, ambition of our republicans . . . the exaltation of conquest, the rage of acquisition" had become such a mania that the Senate would not dare to approve the treaty but would talk it to death.[24] Mrs. Storms was misled by wishful thinking, for the reaction over the country during the next week might better have been described as a collective sigh of relief. Some newspapers, indeed, approved the treaty terms outright, but more seem to have accepted them with distaste rather than continue the war: "Admit all [the treaty's] faults, and say if an aimless and endless foreign war is not far worse." "*We are glad to get out of the scrape even upon these terms.*" Some were more explicit on the benefits of peace: "The people do not so much care for the murder of Mexicans . . . ; but they do care for a pressure in the money market and a stagnation of business." [25]

A few expansionists stuck to their guns. Beach asked angrily

---

21. Fuller, *Acquisition of All Mexico*, pp. 142–48, *passim.* Smith, *War with Mexico*, II, 244–46. The phrase quoted is that of Fuller, p. 142. The only authority he cites (Polk, *Diary*, III, 276–77) does not justify such positive language.

22. Polk, *Diary*, III, 345. Polk did not see Trist's dispatches of December 29 and January 12 until after he had decided to submit the treaty. They so infuriated him that he at once issued orders for Trist to be taken to Veracruz as soon as possible. Ibid., pp. 357–58.

23. This analysis agrees generally with that of Merk, *Manifest Destiny and Mission*, pp. 184–88. Rives goes even further in suggesting that Polk may have secretly hoped for an acceptable treaty from Trist. George Lockhart Rives, *The United States and Mexico*, II, 625.

24. [Mrs. Jane Storms] to Bancroft, undated, Bancroft Papers, MHS.

25. For good surveys of these opinions, see Washington *National Intelligencer*, February 28, 1848, p. 3; March 3, p. 3; March 4, p. 3.

in the New York *Sun*, "Are we to give Mexico back to her military despots . . . ? Are all the passages to the Pacific Ocean to be handed over to England? . . . Is that all-important Isthmus to be formed into another Mosquito country, with Paredes its English-made sovereign?"[26] A more common expansionist objection was that it would be foolish to expect the treacherous Mexican government to carry out the terms of any treaty. The New York *Herald* professed to believe that Polk and Trist had only pretended to quarrel, so that the President might seem to be submitting the treaty against his will. Nevertheless, all available evidence indicates that the movement to annex most or all of Mexico collapsed rapidly after the announcement of the treaty terms.[27]

This decline did not guarantee, however, that the Senate would readily approve the treaty, for if extremists on both sides of the question combined—those who wanted more territory and those who wanted none at all—they might be able to muster more than the one-third vote needed to reject the settlement. Many senators looked beyond the treaty to the impending presidential campaign. Also, some held personal grudges against Polk. Benton, for example, was resentful over the impending court-martial of his son-in-law John Charles Frémont for mutinous behavior in California and had been moving out of the President's camp since the preceding autumn.[28] Western expansionists such as Edward Hannegan of Indiana might well remember Polk's "betrayal" in the settlement of the Oregon question almost a year earlier. Local interests throughout the country were still criticizing him because some months earlier he had vetoed "pork barrel" bills for river and harbor improvements and for spoliation claims. The President could not feel that even his cabinet was solidly behind him, for reports came to him that both Buchanan and Walker intended to work against the treaty.[29]

An ironic coincidence delayed action by the Senate and al-

26. New York *Sun*, March 2, 1848, reprinted in Washington *National Intelligencer*, March 10, p. 2. The *Intelligencer* declared that this was the only example of such sentiment which its editorial staff had found in the press.

27. The New York *Herald*'s suspicion was paraphrased in London *Times*, March 15, 1848, p. 4. Fuller, *Acquisition of All Mexico*, p. 149. On the collapse of the "all Mexico" movement see ibid., pp. 148–59.

28. Polk, *Diary*, III, 197–98, 228–30, 365–66.

29. Polk and Buchanan had an unfriendly exchange on a series of abusive articles appearing in the New York *Herald*. Polk, *Diary*, III, 353–56, 358–60. Walker's biographer declares that Polk let Walker remain in the cabinet only to avoid splitting the party but that Walker continued to lobby for the annexation of all Mexico. James Patrick Shenton, *Robert John Walker, a Politician from Jackson to Lincoln*, p. 104. On the "pork barrel" vetoes, see Charles Grier Sellers, *James K. Polk, Continentalist: 1843–1846*, pp. 472–75.

lowed time for public opinion to express itself. On February 21, the day before Polk proposed to submit the treaty, the uncompromising slavery-hater John Quincy Adams collapsed of a stroke at his desk in the House of Representatives. Two days later he died, and Congress adjourned for the remainder of the week.

When the Senate took up the Mexican treaty on February 28, it went into executive session at once and kept no record of the ensuing debate. One may form in microcosm some impression of the forces and issues involved, from the tribulations of the Foreign Relations Committee. The Senate had hardly reconvened when the committee chairman, Ambrose H. Sevier of Arkansas, came to Polk with the news that all the other members, including Webster, Benton, and Hannegan, favored sending a commission to Mexico to negotiate another treaty, since Trist was in fact an unauthorized agent after he learned of his recall. Polk professed to be surprised at the odd alliance, for he knew that Webster wanted none of Mexico and Hannegan all of it, but he blamed the phenomenon on the coming elections. When he reported the news to the cabinet, Walker became excited, fearing an anti-expansionist plot by Webster. To Polk's satisfaction both Walker and Buchanan set out to lobby against a new commission. In the end, the Foreign Relations Committee reported the treaty without any recommendation.[30]

For most of the next two weeks the floor debate continued in closed session. The Whigs tried to discredit the treaty with the issues of Trist's recall, slavery, and antiexpansionism, but their resolutions were tabled or defeated. For the Democrats Sam Houston introduced a resolution to require annexation of Lower California and most of northern Mexico to 22°, including Tampico and San Luis Potosí. Jefferson Davis proposed somewhat less extreme additions in another resolution. Only ten senators supported Davis, and Houston's resolution was never brought to a vote. Among the various amendments proposed, the only ones passed were designed to correct comparatively minor details. Article X on land grants and the secret article extending the time limit for ratification were removed, as Polk had suggested. The Senate amended Article IX by altering a promise of speedy statehood for the annexed territory and by changing the religious provisions to conform to the more general statement in the Louisiana treaty of 1803. It also tightened provisions for paying the installments of the purchase price.[31]

30. Polk, *Diary*, III, 363–66.   31. Fuller, *Acquisition of All Mexico*,

As the final vote approached, the basic question remained: Would the ends combine against the middle? Every day Polk conferred with senators. Through the first week they told him that approval was doubtful, but on the following Monday (March 6) the tide seemed to have turned, and on the next day Polk began to consider whom he should send to Mexico to exchange ratifications. Sure enough—on March 10 the Senate approved the treaty, 38 to 14, with four senators not voting. The action was neither clearly partisan nor clearly sectional. Of the opposing and abstaining senators ten were Whigs, eight Democrats; by sections, seven were Northerners, five Southerners, and six Westerners.[32]

*   *   *   *

Polk realized that the Senate's amendments might cause the Mexican government to repudiate the treaty. There was no time to be lost in obtaining the Mexicans' approval, for some senators wished to publish the speeches they had made during the executive session, and soon after the final vote the New York *Herald* printed some of the confidential correspondence relating to the Slidell and Trist missions. As soon as these documents reached Mexico, they would probably stir up the ultranationalists again.[33]

Consequently, the President determined to send a special envoy to Mexico with a full explanation of the Senate's changes. His first choice for the post was Louis McLane, the "trouble shooter" of the Oregon controversy, but McLane pleaded the excuse of his wife's illness. Polk then selected Senator Sevier, chairman of the Foreign Relations Committee, who accepted with some surprise. When Sevier suddenly fell ill, the President dispatched Attorney General Nathan Clifford as joint commissioner, to save time. In the commissioners' instructions and a long letter to the Mexican

---

pp. 153–54. Rives, *US and Mexico*, II, 633–36. The record of resolutions and votes appears in US, 30C, 1S, SED 52, pp. 3–37. David Hunter Miller, ed., *Treaties and Other International Acts of the United States of America*, V, 241–53. Concerning religion the original text went into great detail, specifying the "most ample guaranty" of freedom for clergy and "religious corporations or communities" and itemizing types of Church property to be respected by the American government. Ibid., pp. 241–42.

32. Polk, *Diary*, III, 367–77, *passim*. Fuller, *Acquisition of All Mexico*, pp.

155–56. Rives, *US and Mexico*, II, 636–37. If all abstaining senators had voted against the treaty, it would still have been approved. For a survey of press reactions to the Senate action, see Washington *National Intelligencer*, March 14, 1848, p. 3; March 22, p. 3; March 27, p. 3. See also Fuller, *Acquisition of All Mexico*, p. 157.

33. Polk, *Diary*, III, 376, 378, 385–86, 396–414. Polk was angry at the disclosure and suspected that Buchanan was responsible. A Senate committee interrogated a New York *Herald* reporter but learned nothing.

foreign minister, Buchanan made clear that the United States would not consider restoring Article X (concerning land grants) but that there might be some margin for adjustment in the provisions for paying installments of the purchase price.[34] Clifford left for Mexico at once, and Sevier recovered from his illness so quickly that both commissioners arrived within a week of each other in mid-April.

The situation that they faced in Mexico had not greatly changed since the signature of the treaty. The invading army had converted Mexico City into an American camp, while the Mexican government was still crowded into Querétaro. Communications with most other parts of Mexico had broken down, for roads and highways outside of the occupied zone were overrun with bandits, and states to the north and west were absorbed in their own problems. The secessionist movement in the northeast had taken on new life, but its supporters could not agree on establishing an independent government or petitioning for entrance into the American Union.[35]

In central Mexico many persons read the treaty with consternation, either resentful at the humiliating loss of territory or alarmed at the prospect of the Americans' departure. Talk of a European monarchy returned to the surface, as a desperate alternative to anarchy. Gómez Farías wrote sadly to his sons, "What a situation is ours! Some wish to give us a domestic tyrant, others . . . a foreign monarch, and [still] others . . . hope that we will accept an ignominious peace and disappear from the roster of nations. And the States see these dangers and do not act . . . to defend their true interests."[36]

Perhaps the most fantastic reaction to the treaty was a move-

34. Polk, *Diary*, III, pp. 372–73, 375, 378–83, 385, 386–87, 389–92. Louis McLane to Polk, March 7, 1848, Polk Papers, CXXIII, LC. Buchanan to Minister of Foreign Affairs of Mexico, March 18; Buchanan to Ambrose H. Sevier, March 18, No. 1; Buchanan to Nathan Clifford, March 18, No. 1, Manning, *IAA*, VIII, 221–33.

35. For descriptions of conditions in Mexico City, see Percy W. Doyle to Viscount Palmerston, February 13, 1848, No. 18, GB, FO 50/219, ff. 166–74. John A. Buchan to J. L. Colquhoun, Durango, October 11, 1847; Mexico City, April 13, 1848, GB, FO 50/217, ff. 150–53; 50/225, ff. 57–58. A *memoria* by Minister of War Pedro M. Anaya, May

8, surveying the condition of the army, also gives details about the general situation. Antonio de la Peña y Reyes, ed., *Algunos documentos sobre el tratado de Guadalupe*, pp. 51–65. On conditions in the northeast, see John J. O'Brien to Buchanan, Camargo, December 19, 1847, Buchanan Papers, box 67, HSP. See also Hilario de Mesa to Taylor, Matamoros, December 24, 30, Trist Papers, XXVII, ff. 60876–79.

36. Valentín Gómez Farías to Fermin, Casimiro, and Benito Gómez Farías, March 27, 1848, Gómez Farías Papers, No. 2940, University of Texas Libraries. *El monitor republicano*, January 31, p. 4.

ment by some reputable Mexicans who wanted Scott to resign his commission, make himself provisional president, and organize a professional army of American veterans. Backed by them, he might then either overhaul the government or lead Mexico into the American Union like Texas three years earlier. Scott's stern disciplinary measures, which had kept the unruly volunteers in some order, appealed to Mexican property owners, and he later declared that five of the wealthiest ones had offered him $1,250,000 as initial remuneration. His conciliatory treatment of the Church, adopted to facilitate the conquest, also undoubtedly won over some proclericals to his support. The idea of President Scott appealed to some Americans too, who foresaw an easy cession of California and New Mexico and perhaps further cessions through "masterly inactivity."[37]

But Scott retained his sense of proportion; furthermore, the office he coveted was the Presidency of the United States. On February 22, when the American guns boomed in honor of Washington's birthday, many Mexicans in the capital were sure that they signaled a *pronunciamiento*, but the days passed, and Scott rejected each offer as it came to him. The quarrels between Scott, Pillow, and Worth puzzled the Mexicans; they were astonished beyond measure when Scott's recall arrived and he made no move to defy it. Instead, he calmly prepared his written testimony for the court of inquiry and turned over the command to Butler. At the end of April, when the court had finished its hearings in Mexico, Scott departed, never to return.[38] Trist was more unruly, for, on receiving Polk's peremptory order to leave the country, he declared that he was now a private citizen and would stay in Mexico as long as he wanted to. Butler then arrested and deported him. Polk punished his disobedient envoy by peevishly refusing to pay his salary beyond mid-November, when the recall notice arrived in Mexico.[39]

One of the new commander's first duties was to agree upon an armistice with a new set of Mexican commissioners. These com-

37. See especially a long quotation from a letter of Scott to John M. Clayton, March 4, 1852, in Elliott, *Scott*, pp. 579–80. Winfield Scott, *Memoirs of Lieut.-General Scott, Ll.D.*, II, 581–82. Anonymous letter, apparently to Scott, Charleston, December 25, 1847, Trist Papers, XXVII, ff. 60882–85.

38. Doyle to Palmerston, March 14, 1848, No. 27, GB, FO 50/219, ff. 243–48. Elliott, *Scott*, pp. 584–86.

39. Trist's salary came from the President's secret service fund. Subsequent Presidents ignored his claim, but Congress awarded him $14,559.90 in April 1871. Shortly before that time President Grant also appointed him to a postmastership. Robert Arthur Brent, "Nicholas Philip Trist, Biography of a Disobedient Diplomat," Ph.D. diss., University of Virginia, 1950, pp. 222–24, 233–34, 246–48.

missioners were not prepared to negotiate until the end of February, and at that time they arrived with instructions to demand the evacuation of American troops from central Mexico at once, so that members of Congress might be freely elected to consider the peace treaty. Doyle persuaded the Mexicans to abandon this demand, and, once the two parties met, they were able to work out a procedure for temporary evacuation of each town at election time. In order to furnish the Mexican government with badly needed income, Butler agreed that it might resume collection of taxes, except for customs duties and a few others. The Mexican courts were to reopen, and the government might organize a small national guard in the Federal District. Both sides retained the right to suppress armed uprisings—a euphemistic way of saying that the Americans would support Peña y Peña's administration against any revolutions until the peace treaty had been safely ratified.[40]

The last provision was important, for at least one state, San Luis Potosí, withdrew its recognition of the central government as reprisal for signing the treaty, and two others, Jalisco and Oaxaca, attempted revolts, which were put down. Also, while the government took its time about holding elections and calling Congress together, Manuel Crescencio Rejón, Mariano Otero, and others agitated against ratification.[41] To answer them, Bernardo Couto of the peace commission prepared an *exposición* defending the treaty as a painful necessity but neither a national disgrace nor a permanent setback to Mexican development. "The negotiators," he remarked sensibly, "do no more than reduce to written forms the final result of the war." The territorial cessions were like an amputation performed to save the patient's life.[42]

The knowledge that the Americans would make an initial payment of $3 million as soon as the treaty was ratified strength-

40. Rives, *US and Mexico*, II, 645–47. Mariano Otero, *Obras*, I, 92–95. Doyle to Palmerston, March 14, 1848, Nos. 28, 29, GB, FO 50/219, ff. 249–56, 266–72. The text of the armistice appears in Dublán and Lozano, *LM*, V, 345–48.

41. Vito Alessio Robles, *Coahuila y Texas desde la consumación de la Independencia*, II, 395–96. Doyle to Palmerston, March 14, 1848, No. 29, GB, FO 50/219, ff. 266–72. Manuel Crescencio Rejón, *Correspondencia inédita de Rejón*, p. 20. José María Roa Bárcena, *Recuerdos de la invasión norteamericana (1846–1848)*, III, 312–14, 321–22. Rejón's argument is reprinted at length in Peña y Reyes, *Algunos documentos sobre el tratado de Guadalupe*, pp. 300–348.

42. "Exposición de motivos presentada por los Comisionados de México," March 1, 1848, ibid., pp. 139–68. The quoted sentence appears on p. 141. See also Roa Bárcena, *Recuerdos de la invasión*, III, 317n20.

ened Couto's case. So did the receipt of rather jumbled news from New Mexico, which seemed to indicate that the hitherto loyal inhabitants had voted to join the United States.[43] Nevertheless, a quorum of Congress did not appear at Querétaro until the beginning of May. Then followed six days of hot debate during which one deputy was borne into the Chamber on a sickbed so that he might deliver an impassioned speech against the treaty. Despite these heroic efforts the Chamber voted to approve it, 51 to 35, and on May 25 the Senate, less anti-American, followed suit, 33 to 4. When the American commissioners arrived in Querétaro later that day, the government celebrated the advent of peace with fireworks and brass bands, but some people threw stones at the commissioners' carriage.[44]

On May 30 ratifications were exchanged, and General Herrera, the moderate who had never wanted to fight the United States, was proclaimed the first postwar president. The American commissioners at once arranged to pay $3 million to his government, and Butler began to withdraw his troops. Despite delays, by mid-June the capital was evacuated, and at the end of July the last American troops left Tampico and Veracruz.[45] By that time Herrera's government had already suppressed one revolt.

Europe almost entirely ignored the Treaty of Guadalupe Hidalgo, for in February, before the news of its signature could arrive, the Revolution of 1848 broke out in Paris, and thereafter the tumult in France and central Europe monopolized attention. Gómez Farías had feared a renewal of monarchist plots, but in 1848 the idea of a prince for Mexico was further than ever from European minds. In London the Mexican minister, Mora, went to the Foreign Office with a request that Britain send the United States a pointed note expressing confidence that no future difference between the United States and Mexico, not even war, would disturb the new boundaries. Palmerston, his eyes fixed on the

---

43. Rives, *US and Mexico*, II, 648–49. Doyle to Palmerston, March 14, 1848, No. 29, GB, FO 50/219, ff. 266–72. Actually, the vote was cast by an assembly General Sterling Price had called into being for that purpose.

44. Rives, *US and Mexico*, II, 651–54. Roa Bárcena, *Recuerdos de la invasión*, III, 327–34. Henry A. Wise, *Los Gringos* [etc.], pp. 267–68. The remarks of Peña y Peña, De la Rosa, and Anaya are reprinted in Peña y Reyes, *Algunos*

documentos sobre el tratado, pp. 51–65, 168–92, 279–92. See also F. Jorge Gaxiola, *Mariano Otero (Creador del juicio del amparo)*, pp. 293–99; and Guillermo Prieto, *Memorias de mis tiempos, 1840 a 1853*, pp. 294–98.

45. Clifford caused some delay by not assuming enough responsibility for operations. As a result the Veracruz custom house remained in American hands beyond the date set for its transfer. Smith, *War with Mexico*, II, 475.

Continent, agreed to hope that the treaty would prevent further conflict, but that was all.[46] As in 1846, Mexico learned that she must defend herself without aid from Europe.

* * * *

Instead of ending with a flourish, Polk's diplomacy of annexation continued for several months, carried forward by its own momentum until it gradually ran down. After the signature of the peace treaty with Mexico, his government made ill-coordinated and wholly unsuccessful efforts to acquire two nearby territories, Yucatán and Cuba.

The peninsula of Yucatán, though poor in natural resources, attracted American expansionists because of its strategic position opposite Cuba and Florida, controlling one entrance to the Gulf of Mexico. Its leaders accorded only intermittent loyalty to Mexico City. A long-smouldering secessionist struggle during the early 1840s had made the Yucatecans for a time allies of the Republic of Texas and had helped to exhaust Santa Anna's slender resources before his overthrow in 1844. Early in 1846 the Yucatecans seceded again, and while Mexico was involved in fighting the United States, a bloody "war of castes" (actually races) between the Maya Indians and the white minority raged over the peninsula.

As the ultraexpansionist movement grew in the United States, some of its exponents included Yucatán in their agenda. "Make way for Yucatan!" proclaimed Moses Y. Beach, as he laid plans for a transit project across the nearby Isthmus of Tehuantepec. "The bravest, most generous and most liberal of the Mexican States . . . wishes to come into our Union! *She will bring with her the short route to the Pacific and Oregon*, which we need so much." In another article John L. O'Sullivan presented the peninsula's dry soil and limited rainfall in their best light and extolled the courteous, hospitable people, scions of "a populous and flourishing empire." [47] Expansionist interest in Yucatán lagged behind the spreading desire for other parts of Mexico, but by the spring of 1848 sensational newspaper accounts of the caste war and dis-

46. Gómez Farías to Manuel González Cosío, February 18, 1848, Gómez Farías Papers, No. 2903. Palmerston to José María Luis Mora, June 30, GB, FO 50/224, ff. 105–7.

47. New York *Sun*, March 11, 1846. New York *Morning News*, July 2. Both are quoted in Frederick Merk, *The Monroe Doctrine and American Expansionism, 1843–1849*, pp. 195–96. Except where noted, this summary of the Yucatán question is derived from Merk's longer account in Chap. 8.

cussion of transit routes had aroused in the American people a familiar mixture of sympathy and covetousness.

As long as the United States was engaged in fighting Mexico, the Polk government subordinated the question of Yucatán to the over-all needs of the war. In May 1847, after the occupation of Veracruz, the Navy seized El Carmen Island off the Yucatán coast and administered the customs office there. During the fall, the Yucatán government sent to Washington a special agent, Justo Sierra O'Reilly, with the request that the United States evacuate the port and allow free trade into Yucatán, since its government had proclaimed neutrality in the Mexican War. Buchanan merely agreed to loosen the restrictions on some trade.[48]

Several months later, Sierra returned to the State Department with a plea for American financial and military aid to end the caste war. Finally, on April 3, 1848, he brought to Buchanan a note from his government formally offering the United States "the dominion and sovereignty of this Peninsula" and stating that a similar offer was being made to the governments of Britain and Spain. In his covering note Sierra requested only munitions and armed intervention by American troops to pacify Yucatán, but he referred pointedly to the Monroe Doctrine.[49]

The Yucatecan gambit took Polk and his cabinet by surprise. The President declared that, rather than allow a foreign monarchy to annex Yucatán, "the U.S. should afford the aid & protection asked, but that this could only be done by the authority of Congress." After some discussion he referred the whole question to Congress without a formal recommendation. The United States, he said, could not accept sovereignty over the peninsula, but it could not tolerate European sovereignty there either, since this was contrary to Monroe's policy of 1823 and his own first annual message. Then he concluded rather anticlimactically that, should Congress advise action, the United States would probably have to confine itself to offshore naval patrols.[50]

Fortunately, the Mexicans had ratified the Treaty of Guada-

48. Justo Sierra O'Reilly to Buchanan, November 24, 1847; Buchanan to Sierra, December 24, Manning, *IAA*, VIII, 219–20, 974–80.

49. Sierra to Buchanan, February 15, 24, March 3, 7, April 3, 1848; Santiago Mendez to Buchanan, March 25, Manning, *IAA*, VIII, 1061–78.

50. Polk, *Diary*, III, 430–38. Richard-

son, *Papers of the Presidents*, IV, 581–83. The Buchanan and Polk drafts of the message are contained in Polk Papers, box 5 ("Messages and Speeches"), LC. Most differences were minor, but Buchanan's draft entirely omitted the passage indicating that the Yucatecans intended to offer annexation to Britain.

lupe Hidalgo by the time they learned of this message. It kindled new hope in American expansionists, aroused their opponents once more, and became inextricably entangled with party politics, for the nominating conventions would soon begin, and the expansionist Cass seemed to be the favorite of the Democratic party.

As soon as the President's message was read to the Senate, Hannegan of Indiana introduced a resolution prepared with Polk's aid and providing for a temporary occupation of Yucatán. He added a passionate denunciation of insidious British plots to dominate the Caribbean and the Gulf of Mexico. During the early days of May, Jefferson Davis, Sam Houston, Cass, and other senators repeated Hannegan's Anglophobe arguments and appealed to humanity and American ambitions. The Whig opposition punctured one expansionist argument after another. Why such sudden concern over savage Indians? How could even temporary occupation be reconciled with the Mexican treaty? What evidence had the administration ever produced to justify its alarums against Britain? "This cry of England's interference with the nations on this continent . . . has been dinged in our ears for the last six years," declared one senator. "[It] has done much for us in the way of acquiring foreign dominion." Finally, Calhoun hauled out his heavy artillery and systematically demolished Polk's arguments from the Monroe Doctrine and his notions that intervention would serve humanity or basic American interests.[51]

Leading newspapers repeated and amplified these opinions throughout the first half of May, while Justo Sierra fretted at the delay and privately encouraged expansionists in the press and in Congress. Realizing that aid without colonization would do Yucatán no lasting good, Sierra wanted to make occupation attractive to all interest groups, but the party entanglements reduced him to despair.[52] After several weeks the antiexpansionists, having shown their strength, offered a compromise settlement—military

51. Merk, *Monroe Doctrine and Expansionism*, pp. 209–19. The quoted passage, from a speech by Senator Jacob W. Miller of New Jersey, appears on p. 216. Calhoun spoke with special authority on the Monroe Doctrine, for he had been secretary of war in Monroe's cabinet during the discussion and promulgation of the Doctrine in 1823. See also Dexter Perkins, *The Monroe Doctrine, 1826–1867*, pp. 178–87.

52. Justo Sierra O'Reilly, *Diario de nuestro viaje a los Estados Unidos (La*

pretendida anexión de Yucatán), pp. 34–54, *passim*. The Washington *Union* was circumspect about Yucatán, confining itself mostly to reprints. In one issue it pointed out that there was no question of annexation but simply of preventing a European protectorate. Washington *Union*, May 3, 1848. Even Moses Y. Beach soft-pedaled annexation, admitting that Yucatán appealed to America to save, not to wed. New York *Sun*, May 4, p. 2; May 11, p. 2.

aid to Yucatán, but no occupation. Congress might have saved face for the expansionists by adopting such a measure, but the sudden news of a truce in the caste war allowed Hannegan to withdraw his bill altogether.

Polk continued to favor a policy of intervention, and the caste war soon erupted again, bloodier than before the truce, but the expansionists did not try to revive the issue, for the public fear of British intervention had grown somewhat threadbare. As the Whigs surmised, Whitehall had no more desire to annex Yucatán than they. When Percy W. Doyle in Mexico City reported the caste war and American interest in the peninsula, Palmerston attached an uncompromising memorandum to the dispatch before filing it away: "State to any whom it may concern that H.M. Govt. have no intention whatever of taking advantage of the disturbed State of Yucatan in order to gain Possession of the Country."[53]

*　　*　　*　　*

Early in the summer of 1848 the Yucatán project had collapsed, but by then Polk had substituted another, much more tempting—the purchase of Cuba from Spain. Cuba had several advantages over Yucatán as a prospect for annexation. It was closer to the American coast, and its resources were much greater. Also, the American public knew more about the island and had feared British intervention there since the 1820s. Lastly, American ambitions for Cuba were not limited by the restraints of the Mexican peace treaty.

As with Yucatán, John L. O'Sullivan and Moses Y. Beach laid the groundwork of Polk's project. During 1843 and 1844 serious slave revolts in Cuba had stimulated thoughts of annexation both among Creole planters, who had little confidence in Spain's ability to keep order, and among American slaveowners, who feared that the Cuban uprisings might spread to their own plantations. O'Sullivan, a popularizer of expansion in general, had friends among the Cuban annexationists, and during the next two years he joined their cause. He happened to be in Havana during the spring of 1847, when Beach passed through on his way home from his Mexican reconnaissance venture (see Chapter 14). They dis-

53. Doyle to Palmerston, May 14, 1848, No. 51; memorandum by Palmerston, July 6, GB, FO 50/220, ff. 212–16. When Sierra first appeared in Washington, however, Palmerston told the British minister there that if Sierra approached him, he might comment that the nearness of British Honduras to Yucatán might be a good reason for not joining the United States. Memorandum by Palmerston, December 26, 1847, GB, FO 5/472, f. 92.

cussed annexation with local enthusiasts and with the United States consul, Robert B. Campbell. Beach went home to propagandize for annexation with bold editorials, declaring that Cuba would "complete our chain of territory, and give us the North American Continent."[54]

For a change, O'Sullivan preferred to work behind the scenes, approaching the Polk administration by way of Buchanan. In July 1847 he wrote a memorandum to the secretary, in which he suggested that the Cuban planters would be willing to pay as much as $150 million for Spain to facilitate annexation. He warned against seizure by the British and advised Buchanan to negotiate secretly for the purchase of the island and to order units of Scott's troops to stop there on their way home from Mexico. Soon afterward, actions of the British government seemed to reinforce O'Sullivan's warning. A member of Parliament had hinted that Britain should take Cuba and Puerto Rico in payment of defaulted Spanish bonds, and Palmerston replied that Britain would surely have a right to secure redress.[55] For the remainder of the year O'Sullivan continued to correspond with Buchanan, while Beach propagandized in the New York *Sun*, and Cuban annexationists plotted armed revolt.[56]

During the spring of 1848 O'Sullivan decided to propose his purchase plan directly to Polk. The Mexican treaty was out of the way; the congressional debate over Yucatán was arousing the public to the danger of European influence in the Gulf of Mexico; and Britain had recalled her ambassador to Spain, creating a sense of urgency. On May 10 O'Sullivan and the expansionist Senator Stephen A. Douglas talked to the President. Polk approved of the idea but not of O'Sullivan, whom he identified with a dissident

54. New York *Sun*, July 23, 1847. Clipping in Buchanan Papers, box 66, HSP. A slightly different version appears in Basil Rauch, *American Interest in Cuba, 1848–1855*, p. 59. Except where noted, this summary of the Cuban question is derived from Chaps. 2 and 3. For a shorter account, see Merk, *Monroe Doctrine and Expansionism*, pp. 233–69. A Cuban study of Polk's efforts, based largely on American sources, is Emeterio S. Santovenia, *El Presidente Polk y Cuba*.

55. The American press exaggerated the British comments. In reality Palmerston showed no desire to acquire Cuba and directed his remarks against

the idea that the British government was responsible for protecting British investments abroad. *Hansard Parliamentary Debates*, XCIII, cols. 1298–1306. For American comments, see *NNR*, 122 (August 7, 14, 1847), 353, 377–78.

56. In the spring of 1848 the Cuban conspirators sent an agent to Mexico to offer General Worth $3 million if he would aid the rebellion with 5,000 of his men. The agent failed to see Worth, who had returned to the United States, but he did carry on inconclusive talks with General Franklin Pierce. Santovenia, *Polk y Cuba*, p. 45.

New York faction of the Democratic party.[57] For nearly three weeks he let the matter rest.

At the end of the month Polk finally laid the purchase project before the cabinet. Walker was immediately enthusiastic and declared that it would be worth while to offer Spain $100 million. Buchanan doubted that the government should raise such a controversial subject during the campaign, but when Cass, now the Democratic nominee, supported Walker's view, Buchanan soon became enthusiastic for the project.[58] Polk entrusted the negotiations to his minister to Spain, Romulus M. Saunders. The instructions to Saunders combined all arguments for annexation. Since Spain seemed in danger of losing Cuba to Britain, she might welcome the opportunity to sell the island to another power. Although of relatively little value to Spain, Cuba would flourish under American institutions. After an estimate of the probable revenues to be derived from the island, the instructions stated that the United States was willing to offer as much as $100 million for it. Saunders was warned to proceed with great caution, to conduct only oral negotiations, and to assure the government of Spain that, whatever its decision, the United States would continue its traditional policy of resisting the acquisition of Cuba by any other nation.[59]

Polk's bid for Cuba was doomed from the start. In the first place, Spanish pride and economic interests in the island were far too great to permit any voluntary cession. Also, the American negotiations revealed a woeful lack of diplomatic skill and coordination. Saunders was poorly fitted for his difficult assignment, being a party hack who could speak neither Spanish nor French. He made a timid gesture or two to carry out his instructions but was forestalled by a change in the Spanish cabinet. In August the new foreign minister asked him abruptly if he proposed to treat for the cession of Cuba and if Spain could count on earlier American assurances of support. Saunders replied that the United States would rather buy the island than fight Britain to preserve Spanish rule over it. The Spaniard then declared that he saw no likelihood of war with Britain and discouraged any idea of cession.[60]

57. Polk, *Diary*, III, 446, 476–81, 493. John L. O'Sullivan to Buchanan, March 19, 1848, Buchanan Papers, box 68, HSP. Rauch, *American Interest in Cuba*, pp. 48–51.

58. Polk, *Diary*, III, 469, 475, 477–79, 482–83, 485–88.

59. Buchanan to Romulus M. Saunders, June 17, 1848, No. 21, Manning, *IAA*, XI, 54–65. Polk, *Diary*, III, 487–88, 492–94.

60. Rauch, *American Interest in Cuba*, pp. 86–91. Santovenia, *Polk y Cuba*, pp. 101–19. Saunders to Buchanan, June

Events in the United States complicated the unfortunate minister's task. Buchanan, still reluctant to carry out the annexation project, undercut Saunders by reassuring the Spanish minister at Washington that Saunders had not been instructed to purchase Cuba. During September the New York *Herald* published a sensational rumor that negotiations for cession were in progress, and this rumor naturally excited the hostility of Spanish nationalists. At the same time the Spanish government became alarmed at a quarrel in Havana between American Consul Campbell and the Spanish authorities over the imprisonment of an American suspected of conspiracy. In December the foreign minister told Saunders decisively that he "believed such to be the feeling of the country, that sooner than see the Island transferred to *any power*, they would prefer seeing it sunk in the Ocean." [61]

Even without the strong Spanish negative, Taylor's victory in the November election would have killed Polk's annexation project. When Congress convened, a Whig senator tried to bring the Cuban negotiations out into the open with a resolution calling on Polk for information and diplomatic correspondence on the subject. The Democrats managed to table the resolution, 23 to 19, and one historian regards this vote as a fair measure of the Senate's attitude toward annexation.[62] The vote was both more partisan and more sectional than that on the Mexican peace treaty, for of the opposition votes, 14 were Whig and 12 represented free states. If this vote is an accurate indication of sentiments, the Senate would not have approved an annexation treaty.

The abortive projects to annex Yucatán and Cuba contained some of the elements observed in Polk's successful earlier annexations: his underestimation of Latin pride when confronted with an offer of money, his desire to share responsibility as widely as possible, and his elaborate rationalization with arguments of every idealistic and materialistic description. Improvised like much of his earlier diplomacy, these two projects were developed largely in response to expansionist sentiment at the end of the Mexican War. Unfortunately for Polk's plans, the opposition had come into balance with the expansionists. The public was tired of war and

27, July 29, August 18, 1848, Nos. 35, 37, 38, Manning, *IAA*, XI, 440–41, 443–50.

61. Santovenia, *Polk y Cuba*, pp. 50–51. Pedro J. Pidal to Angel Calderón de la Barca, September 16, 1848; Saunders to Buchanan, November 17, December 14, Nos. 42, 43, Manning, *IAA*,

XI, 452–53, 456–59. The quotation appears on p. 458. Concerning Campbell's quarrel with the Cuban authorities, see Santovenia, *Polk y Cuba*, pp. 129–40.

62. Rauch, *American Interest in Cuba*, pp. 99–100.

the acquisition of new lands. The Whigs, having incongruously mounted a military hero on their old antiexpansionist platform, were on their way to the White House, where they would temporize on the question for four years. Until the spring of 1848 Polk's program of territorial additions had won success unique in American history, but then his magical powers deserted him, and his charms would no longer work.

18

The Diplomacy of Annexation
An Appraisal

Shortly after the Mexican War the American Peace Society offered a $500 prize for the best study of the recent conflict "on the principles of Christianity, and an enlightened statesmanship." Abiel A. Livermore, a Unitarian minister from New Hampshire, won the prize with a manuscript setting forth the thesis that the war and the preceding annexation of Texas had been parts of a plot by Polk, Tyler, Calhoun, and the South for the extension of slavery.[1] Another entry in the contest by the Rev. Mr. Philip Berry, a Presbyterian, was less to the judges' liking, perhaps because it criticized the war not as immoral but as unnecessary: "Tested by the principles which have ordinarily governed the civilized world in its international relations [it] was . . . one of the most *just* wars that have blotted with gore the history of man—a war that might nevertheless have been avoided by the United States, had they been so disposed, probably without diminution of an inch of territory."[2]

Livermore's blast was an opening gun in a long historiographical battle over the legal and moral validity of American actions, which lasted well into the twentieth century, but Berry's arresting statement drew no answering fire from the defenders of the war and the annexations. Was the war, in fact, necessary? More broadly expressed, did Tyler, Polk, and other policy makers of the mid-1840s carry through their program of territorial expansion in such a way as to minimize dangers, loss, and general tension? Did the annexations cost the United States too much? Speculative questions such as these cannot be finally answered, but they may serve as a point of departure for appraising policies and actions.

* * * *

The first step in such an appraisal is to draw up a balance sheet of American gains and losses resulting from the war and from the Texas and Oregon treaties. Some gains are obvious to

1. Abiel Abbot Livermore, *The War with Mexico Reviewed*, p. v, Chap. 3, et passim.

2. Philip Berry, *A Review of the War on Christian Principles*, p. 19.

anyone who can read a map. Between 1845 and 1848 the United States acquired more than 1,200,000 square miles of territory, just over a third of its present area, including Alaska and Hawaii—a vast domain almost as large as all the countries of Free Europe after World War II. During the Mexican War some Whigs were inclined to write off California and Oregon as worthless, save for a few Pacific harbors, but the gold rush of 1849 quickly put an end to such skepticism. After the news of the gold strikes reached Mexico City, Consul John Black, once more at his old post, overheard a Mexican in a restaurant remark bitterly, "Ah, . . . the Yankees knew full well before they commenced the war, what they were going to fight for, they knew the value of that country better than we did."[3]

Other American gains were more intangible—for example, the increasing respect of Europeans. Impressed by the show of power, Old World statesmen and publicists recognized that the United States would now dominate the north Pacific coast and the Gulf of Mexico. After the American occupation of California was confirmed, the London *Times* commented, "From so favourable a harbour the course lies straight and obvious to Polynesia, the Philippines, New Holland, and China, and it is not extravagant to suppose that the merchants of this future emporium may open the commerce of Japan."[4]

To be sure, European efforts against American expansion did not entirely cease after 1848, but never again did their agents act so boldly and so close to American borders as had Captain Charles Elliot, the British consul in Texas. Indeed, in 1848, as revolution spread over Europe, the democratic republicanism that most persons identified with the United States seemed close to a final triumph on both sides of the Atlantic. The irrepressible George Bancroft rejoiced that "the struggles of Europe . . . will not rest, till every vestige of feudal nobility is effaced; and the power of the people shall have superseded that of hereditary princes." In these struggles, he added, the United States would be the model.[5] To Bancroft's dismay, reaction soon triumphed over the Revolution of 1848, but American successes in the New World remained to raise the discouraged spirits of Old World liberals and democrats.

More immediately important to the United States, the Mexican War helped to shift the balance of power in the Western Hemi-

3. John Black to James Buchanan, January 12, 1849, No. 2, US, DS, CD, Mexico, IX.

4. London *Times*, August 11, 1847, p. 5.

5. George Bancroft to James K. Polk, August 5, 1848, Bancroft Papers, MHS.

sphere. In January 1848 the Earl of Ellenborough, who had wanted San Francisco for a British naval base, wrote gloomily to his former chief, Sir Robert Peel, that the only hope for Anglo–American peace was the indefinite occupation of Mexico by the United States, since this would keep the Americans too busy to seize Canada. Probably to his surprise, when the war ended a few weeks later the troops were immediately brought home and mustered out.[6] Nevertheless, the American lodgement on Puget Sound and the American performance in the Mexican War emphasized more firmly to succeeding British administrations that Her Majesty's Canadian subjects were hostages to American good will.

As a result of the war, the British government also gave up any remaining hopes of political influence around the Gulf of Mexico. In 1848 it declined to guarantee the new Mexican boundaries, sponsor a Tehuantepec transit route, or set up a protectorate over Yucatán.[7] The Americans then pursued the British into Central America, which became a field of intrigue for rival diplomatic agents during the late 1840s. Both sides accepted a temporary stalemate in the Clayton–Bulwer Treaty of 1850, which placed the United States for the first time on an equal basis with Great Britain in that area. During the following decade the British gradually abandoned political aspirations in Central America too, content to compete for economic gains with the potent but unmilitary weapons of their factory system and their merchant marine.[8] If the Mexican War alone did not accomplish this contraction of British influence in the Western Hemisphere, it surely hastened the process.

Against these American gains of territory and prestige, how-

6. Earl of Ellenborough to Sir Robert Peel, January 5, 1848, Peel Papers, BM, AM, vol. 40473, ff. 368–71.

7. On the Mexican boundaries, see Viscount Palmerston to José María Luis Mora, June 30, 1848, GB, FO 50/224, ff. 105–7. On Tehuantepec, see Palmerston to Percy W. Doyle, August 31, 1848, No. 38; G. R. Porter to Lord Eddisbury, August 12, GB, FO 50/218, ff. 77–79; 50/225, ff. 201–5. On Yucatán, see Palmerston memoranda of June 7 and July 2, 1848; and Palmerston to Doyle, August 31, 1849, GB, FO 50/220, ff. 75, 216; 50/226, ff. 91–92.

8. Kenneth Bourne, *Britain and the Balance of Power in North America, 1815–1908*, Chap. 6. Mary W. Williams, *Anglo-American Isthmian Diplomacy,*

1815–1951, Chaps. 1–8. Richard W. Van Alstyne, "The Central American Policy of Lord Palmerston, 1846–1848," *Hispanic American Historical Review*, 16 (August 1936), 339–59. Robert A. Naylor, "The British Role in Central America Prior to the Clayton-Bulwer Treaty of 1850," ibid., 40 (August 1960), 361–82. Richard W. Van Alstyne, "British Diplomacy and the Clayton-Bulwer Treaty, 1850–1860," *Journal of Modern History*, 11 (June 1939), 149–83. Van Alstyne says of the treaty: "It made the United States an American power, equal in every respect to the only other first-class American power, Great Britain. To it, rather than to the Monroe Doctrine, the United States owes this position." Ibid., p. 168.

ever, the appraising historian must charge certain losses. Some of these were the familiar costs of all wars: about 12,800 men dead out of 90,000 under arms and about $100 million in expenses, to which might be added the $15 million paid to Mexico under the peace treaty.[9] The families and friends of the dead soldiers were the chief sufferers, for the growing nation hardly felt the expenditure of men and money. But, as with the gains, some of the most serious losses caused by the Western annexations and the war are impossible to measure exactly.

One part of this intangible deficit was a rising spirit of "lick all creation," an overblown chauvinism with strong hints of militarism and racism that coarsened democratic sensibilities and laid American ideologues open to charges of hypocrisy. Two examples of this national hubris will suffice. The last Texan secretary of state, Ashbel Smith, who had opposed annexation in 1845, saw in the Mexican peace treaty three years later only the first chapter of a long story:

> The Mexican War is part of the mission, of the destiny allotted to the Anglo Saxon race on this continent. It is our destiny, our mission to Americanize this continent. No nation once degenerate has ever been regenerated but by foreign conquest; and such is the predestined fate of degenerate Mexico. The sword is the great civilizer, it clears the way for commerce, education, religion and all the harmonizing influences of morality and humanity.... Palo Alto and Buena Vista, Cerro Gordo and Churubusco . . . will be the talismanic watchwords of freedom and security.[10]

A little later, as Lieutenant Raphael Semmes USN looked back on his wartime service, he agreed:

> The passage of our race into Texas, New Mexico, and California, was but the first step in that great movement southward, which forms a part of our destiny. An all-wise Providence has placed us in juxtaposition with an inferior people, in order, without doubt, that we may sweep over them, and remove them (as a people) and their worn-out institutions from the face of the earth. We are the northern hordes of the Alani, spreading ourselves over fairer and sunnier fields, and carrying along with us, beside the newness of life, and the energy and courage of our prototypes, letters, arts, and civilization.[11]

9. Justin H. Smith, *The War with Mexico*, II, 266–67, 318–19, 488–89.

10. Ashbel Smith, *An Address Delivered in the City of Galveston on the 22d of February, 1848, the Anniversary of the Birth Day of Washington and of the Battle of Buena Vista*, pp. 12–13 *et passim*.

11. Raphael Semmes, *Service Afloat and Ashore during the Mexican War*, p. 67.

The rest of the world, long accustomed to American strutting, might well have discounted these predictions but for the amazing victories of Zachary Taylor and Winfield Scott and the persistent filibustering expeditions that Americans launched during the 1850s against Mexico, Cuba, and Central America. To Latin Americans the events of 1843–1848 revealed, perhaps for the first time, the aggressive potential of the United States. Sympathy for Mexico encouraged a widespread but disorganized sentiment for some sort of congress to unite Spanish-speaking peoples against their external enemies. The press of many South American countries reprinted the Whigs' speeches and editorials attacking Polk as evidence that the war was unpopular with the American people, but the onward march of the troops suggested that even public opinion could not halt the *yanqui* government. A stereotype began to take shape in Latin American writing about the United States—the Colossus of the North.[12]

But the most alarming effects of Western annexations and the Mexican War developed within the United States. By the early 1840s many Whigs had come to believe that further expansion in any direction would place intolerable strains on national unity. For that reason Daniel Webster opposed acquiring Texas, and even the expansionist James Buchanan eventually came to think of it as a Trojan horse, for its annexation widened the sectional gap between North and South. To abolitionists Texas became a moral issue; as Charles Sumner put it, "By welcoming Texas as a Slave State we make slavery our own original sin."[13]

In debating the Oregon question, Webster's Whigs also discouraged annexation, expecting that the American emigrants would form an independent, friendly nation on the Pacific coast. To annex it would be as preposterous as annexing Ireland.[14] Nev-

12. The Argentine reaction to the war is described in W. A. Harris to Polk, June 27, 1847, Polk Papers, CXVII, LC. In July 1847 the government of Honduras sent to the Mexican foreign ministry a number of declarations and circulars expressing sympathy and advocating defense. US, LC, /270. A long, thoughtful Chilean editorial of 1860 analyzing United States policy of that day with backward glances at the Mexican War appears in Manning, *IAA*, V, 311–13n3. During the war a Madrid newspaper predicted this Latin American reaction and urged the Spanish government to exploit it and regain lost prestige. *El heraldo*, n.d., reprinted in London *Times*, November 13, 1847, pp. 8–9.

13. Quoted from a speech of November 4, 1845, in David Donald, *Charles Sumner and the Coming of the Civil War*, p. 140. For Webster's views, see Daniel Webster, *The Letters of Daniel Webster*, ed. C. H. Van Tyne, pp. 289–94. The effect of the Texas question on the Democratic party is discussed in James C. N. Paul, *Rift in the Democracy*, pp. 181–83 *et passim*.

14. Philadelphia *United States Gazette*, n.d., quoted in New York *Evening Post*, April 25, 1845, p. 3.

ertheless, the Democratic platform of 1844 and Polk's inaugural address reassured Northern and Western expansionists that the "clear and unquestionable" American title to all Oregon would maintain the balance of sections. The compromise at 49°, however reasonable in legal and practical argument, struck many of them as betrayal by the South. "We have been duped . . .," declared an Ohioan. "Oregon & Texas should have went [*sic*] hand in hand, Oregon first."[15]

Northern sectionalism undoubtedly encouraged the nation's desire for California, thereby reinforcing the prowar group within the Democratic party. But it also strengthened Whigs' opposition to the war, especially as the progress of Taylor's army suggested the annexation of territory to the southwest. The Northerners' feeling of betrayal crystallized in the Wilmot Proviso, first introduced by one of Polk's own Democrats, which completed the association of slavery and expansion and made the war seem, like Texas and Oregon before it, both a sectional and a moral issue. "It was conceived in sin . . .," proclaimed the Albany *Evening Standard*, "not to promote any great principle; . . . but to conquer a neighboring republic to acquiesce in an attempt to extend the borders of slavery." "When the foreign war ends, *the domestic war will begin*," warned the New York *Gazette and Times*.[16] Ralph Waldo Emerson compared the Mexican War to a dose of arsenic, and he might well have applied the term to the acquisition of Texas and Oregon too.[17]

No one would be so bold as to attribute Latin American Yankeephobia and the Civil War wholly or mainly to the annexations of the 1840s. It would be safer to argue that Texas, Oregon, and the Mexican War hastened and intensified trends that might have led to the same results eventually. But insofar as these annexations inflated American arrogance and spread hemispheric and national disunity, they exacted a heavy price, which a fair appraisal must somehow balance against the material gains and the rise in national prestige.

*　　*　　*　　*

One may next ask whether the nation might have secured substantially the same territory at smaller cost. Brief examination of

15. William L. Henderson to William Allen, Findlay, Ohio, February 6, 1846, William Allen Papers, XI, ff. 42179–80.
16. Albany *Evening Standard*, n.d., and New York *Gazette and Times*, n.d., as quoted in Washington *National Intelligencer*, May 13, 1847, p. 2.
17. Ralph Waldo Emerson, *Journals of Ralph Waldo Emerson*, eds. E. W. Emerson and W. E. Forbes, VII, 206.

this question suggests that the alternatives multiplied as the expansion progressed. Given the situation of the early 1840s, the only way for the United States to acquire Texas was to negotiate an acceptable settlement with the Texan government. After the annexation, the United States had the choice of conciliating Mexico, perhaps by paying a disguised indemnity, or of ignoring her claims to the lost province, secure in the confidence that she would not or could not back them with force.

In the Oregon question the United States faced the alternatives of fighting Britain, negotiating with her, or waiting for American settlers to overrun the disputed territory. Controlling elements in both the American and British governments regarded the first option as a last resort, the unthinkable result of blundering rather than of a deliberate decision by either side. The other two options, both highly plausible, will be discussed later.

In the case of the Mexican War the choice was the most complicated of all, for at various points in their relations with Mexico, American leaders contemplated four different lines of action. One was the course actually followed, that of invading Mexico, compelling her to cede the desired territory in a treaty, and then withdrawing American troops at once. A second was the establishment of a temporary protectorate over all Mexico to regenerate that unhappy nation while the United States detached her northern provinces or even prepared her for total absorption. A third was passive military occupation of California, New Mexico, and parts of Chihuahua, Coahuila, Nuevo León, and Tamaulipas, the Army maintaining a chain of forts along the line of the Sierra Madre until Mexico gave up and recognized the *fait accompli*. The last course of action was not to declare war at all but to wait until American settlers could form a majority in California and possibly also in New Mexico, rebel, create an independent state, and enter the Union in the manner of Texas.

The alternative of establishing a protectorate and regenerating Mexico was a most unlikely one. In the first place, its plausibility was muddied by Americans' envy of Mexican natural resources, so that many who espoused it did so only as a rationalization for annexation. But even if the protectorate plan had been more fully worked out and less burdened with hypocrisy, it would still have been wholly impracticable on several counts. At the most abstract level, no one has ever convincingly demonstrated that democracy can be imposed from above. Waddy Thompson, ex-minister to Mexico and a comparatively enlightened commentator on the war, asked, "But of what avail are free institutions without the spirit of liberty amongst the people; or what avail are both without general intelligence and virtue?" Many Americans believed Mexicans to be sunk so deep in ignorance and reaction that if the United States tried to do more than set a good example, the effort would end by endangering this country's free institutions through militarism, bureaucracy, and executive tyranny.[18]

Descending to more concrete levels, opponents of a protectorate could reasonably doubt that it would command the support of many Mexicans. To be sure, a group of *puros* expressed admiration for American institutions, especially control by the civil government over the military. But at the same time, another part of this faction, the followers of Valentín Gómez Farías, were proclaiming undying hatred of the *yanqui*. Assuming that a sizable group of Mexican liberals had initially supported a protectorate, the detachment of California and New Mexico would have disillusioned many of them.

Also, if a protectorate had been established, the American officials in charge of Mexico would quickly have had to deal with deep-seated internal problems—the powers of the Church, the ownership of land, the role of the army, and others. Whatever they did, these officials would have alienated large blocs of influential citizens. A cursory glance at the French protectorate of the 1860s, the well-meant but blundering leadership of Maximilian, and the everlasting guerrilla warfare fought by the *juaristas* suggests the staggering obstacles confronting even a temporary administration of Mexico. Finally, the protectorate plan would have done nothing to abate destructive sectionalism in the United States. Indeed, the rivalry of conservative and liberal policies in Mexico might have exacerbated the quarrels of North and South.

Another plan of action, somewhat less ambitious than the regeneration of all Mexico, was to occupy the northern territory which the United States wished to annex, establish a line of forts along the proposed new boundary, and wait for Mexico to abandon her efforts at reconquest. This idea seems to have occurred to many Americans at about the same time during the early autumn of 1846. By then Taylor had established his control along the lower Rio Grande, and Stockton and Frémont had taken over the principal settlements along the California coast. Although various

18. Waddy Thompson, *Recollections of Mexico*, p. 186. A good sample of articles denigrating Mexico during the war is *DeBow's Review*, 1 (February 1846), 116–32.

versions of the partial occupation plan differed in details, most of them specified a line from Tampico to Mazatlán or San Blas, including several cities such as Monterrey and San Luis Potosí as well as many important silver mines. During the invasion of central Mexico and especially after the impasse had developed at Mexico City, some generals and civilians suggested withdrawal to a northern line. But by this time such a policy would have been most difficult to execute, for the evacuation of any territory whatever would have affronted American patriots, spread war weariness, and encouraged Mexican resistance.

Even if undertaken earlier in the war, the indefinite passive military occupation of northern Mexico would have presented serious obstacles. The advocates of this strategy counted heavily on local separatism and growing friendliness between the inhabitants and the occupying forces. But cities such as Tampico, Monterrey, and San Luis Potosí comprised fully developed Mexican societies and culture, as contrasted to the conglomerate, shallowly rooted settlements of California and the Rio Grande Valley. Sooner or later the relations of long-established Mexican groups with the Protestant, Anglo–Saxon Americans, each despising the strangeness of the other, would surely have produced chronic instability. Arguments over the introduction of slaves, economic and social rivalry between the lower classes of both countries, and differences concerning the position of the Church would probably have intensified sectional and partisan divisions within the United States. At the same time, the indefinite continuation of the war would have stimulated Polk's opposition—Whigs, abolitionists, and those who impatiently demanded bold attack and speedy victory.[19] Once the war had gotten under way, it was hard to refute Thomas Hart Benton's argument that an overwhelming offensive was the surest route to peace.

But was it necessary to fight for the territory at all? The last alternative under consideration was for the United States to maintain "a wise and masterly inactivity"[20] following the annexation of Texas—to parry British proposals for ending joint occupation in Oregon, station a defensive force at the western edge of effective Texan settlement, and wait for the movement of American pio-

---

19. Samples of demands for more action are two excerpts from New Orleans *Picayune* and New Orleans *Bulletin*, reprinted in London *Times*, December 18, 1846, p. 5.

20. The phrase was originally used by John C. Calhoun in a speech of January 31, 1843, with respect to Oregon. Charles M. Wiltse, *John C. Calhoun, Sectionalist, 1840–1850*, pp. 107–8.

neers to fill up the desired areas. If left to themselves, Californians would presumably declare their independence of Mexico, and the settlers in the Willamette Valley would expand northward to Puget Sound. Meanwhile, in both areas bonds of trade and kinship with the United States would develop. Eventually, the United States government would negotiate an annexation treaty with California; Britain would recognize the *fait accompli* in Oregon by splitting the territory at 49°; and Mexico would abandon her claims, perhaps in return for an indemnity.

This policy assumed that American expansion was inevitable and that the past would continue to repeat itself. Politicians and journalists were fond of proclaiming this assumption; as one of them declared in 1846, "No power on earth . . . can check the swelling tide of American population. . . . Every portion of this continent, from the sunny south to the frozen north, will be, in a very few years, filled with industrious and thriving Anglo–Saxons. . . . This is the irresistible progress of our people. Like the flow of the ocean, it overcomes all opposition."[21] Since its independence the United States had developed a flexible, effective procedure for acquiring territory with a minimum of risk. This procedure was to reinforce the "irresistible progress" with diplomatic and economic pressure or perhaps veiled threats and to exploit fully the disunity among European powers and their tepid interest in North America. In this manner the Americans had won first the navigation of the lower Mississippi, then Louisiana, then the Floridas, and finally Texas without an open declaration of war or serious fighting except against the Indians.

Why not use the time-proven procedure in Oregon and California? In 1843 Calhoun advocated exactly this strategy in Oregon, and he conducted cordial but indeterminate negotiations with Britain during his year in the State Department.[22] The outstanding exponent of the same policy in California was Thomas O. Larkin, the leading American merchant and, after 1843, American consul in Monterey. Always maintaining friendly relations with

21. *Merchants' Magazine*, 14 (May 1846), 436. For other examples of this argument, see Albert K. Weinberg, *Manifest Destiny, a Study of Nationalist Expansionism in American History*, Chaps. 2, 7, *passim*. The *Times* recognized the effectiveness of this process when it anticipated the annexation of Texas: "Without a negotiation and without a war, by a mere coarse artifice and a fair share of private audacity, the United States will see their frontier extended to the Rio Grande, quite as effectively as if they had marched an army to the spot." London *Times*, December 22, 1843, p. 4.

22. Wiltse, *Calhoun, Sectionalist*, pp. 107–8, 204–6. John C. Calhoun to John Y. Mason, May 30, 1845, John C. Calhoun, *Correspondence of John C. Calhoun*, pp. 659–62.

native inhabitants and local governments, Larkin encouraged a movement for an independent republic in which natives, Europeans, and Americans would enjoy equal status. Eventually, he believed, all three groups would find it to their interest to enter the American Union. For a time Polk approved this policy. After the war began, he experimented with secessionism in northeastern Mexico, hoping to attract the inhabitants peaceably into the United States.[23]

The policy of relying on migration and gradual assimilation of thinly populated areas faced certain obstacles. In northeastern Mexico the boisterousness of the new American arrivals irrevocably antagonized most upper-class Mexicans. In California the Bear Flag revolt showed that many pro-American inhabitants preferred action to persuasion; sometimes Larkin himself leaned in that direction.[24] Another obstacle to gradualism was certain to be the stubbornness of the Mexican government. After resisting the recognition of Texan independence for nine years, it had yielded in 1845 only through British persuasion and in the desperate hope of preventing annexation by the United States. The Mexicans might have resisted for a longer time if California had pulled away from their grasp, and subsequent annexation by the United States might have created a chronic, festering diplomatic problem. Polk might not have come to terms even with the independent Californian republic during his four years as President. Had gradualism won California to the Union, New Mexico might not have attracted enough American settlers to repeat the process, thereby leaving an inconvenient Mexican salient between Texas and the Pacific coast. The chances of delay and of creating an awkward boundary must be weighed against the dangers and cost of precipitate action.

From the viewpoint of Polk and his generation the most serious drawback to gradualism was the risk of British intervention. Persistent rumors throughout 1845 declared that the Mexican government would sell or mortgage California to Britain. British residents were said to be planning an invitation for a protectorate. The British warships that regularly visited the Oregon coast might be carrying on reconnaissance to the south at the same time. Even if Britain did not interfere with an independence movement in

23. William L. Marcy to Taylor, July 9, 1846, US, 30C, 1S, HED 60, pp. 333–36. Justin H. Smith, "La República de Río Grande," *American Historical Review*, 25 (July 1920), 660–75.

24. Larkin to Jacob P. Leese, Abel Stearns, and Jonathan Trumbull Warner, April 17; Larkin to Moses Y. Beach, April, Thomas O. Larkin, *The Larkin Papers*, IV, 295–97, 355–56.

California, the partly known story of her activities in Texas furnished a precedent for fearing subsequent intrigue on the Pacific coast. To many Americans a short, decisive war seemed greatly preferable to another long series of negotiations with some Californian Sam Houston, "coquetting" at the same time with the wily Aberdeen or the daredevil Palmerston.

*　　*　　*　　*

The feasibility of gradually attracting California into the Union, therefore, depended on British policies and actions along the Pacific coast of North America, and these, in turn, depended on the outcome of the negotiations for Oregon. An analysis of these negotiations will shed considerable light in the dark corners of American suspicions.

No other part of the diplomacy of annexation has been so often or so thoroughly studied by American historians as the settlement of the Oregon question. Most writers concede that both sides were influenced by a variety of forces, while differing as to their relative importance. In the judgments concerning British motives one may summarize the majority opinion in this manner: Aberdeen and a vaguely defined but considerable group of Yankeephiles in both parties were early convinced that the material value of Oregon to Britain was not enough to justify shattering the fragile Anglo–American truce established by the Webster–Ashburton Treaty. They therefore set for themselves the two tasks of finding a formula for a treaty that would satisfy Britain's national honor and of justifying that formula to the opposition, which included powerful members of the Peel cabinet and, to some extent, Peel himself.[25] Twentieth-century writings on Oregon have disagreed principally on the importance of individual factors, in particular the Hudson's Bay Company, the British fear of war with France, the desire for free trade and grain imports from America, and the northward movement of American settlers.

The Hudson's Bay Company influenced the development of the Oregon question at a number of points. Its activities in western North America formed an important basis of the British legal claim; it furnished Americans with a symbol of British aggressive-

25. The best statement of this thesis is Frederick Merk, *The Oregon Question, Essays in Anglo-American Diplomacy and Politics,* Essays IX, X, and especially pp. 255–57, 284–85. For an example of Aberdeen's deprecating attitude on Oregon, see Earl of Aberdeen to Peel, October 22, 1844, No. 290, reprinted in Robert C. Clark, ed., "Aberdeen and Peel on Oregon, 1844," *Oregon Historical Quarterly,* 34 (1933), 240.

ness and deceit on which to focus dislike; and at the same time it aroused criticism in Britain as a "monopoly against the English people," maintaining an artificially high price for furs and actually preventing British settlement of the area.[26] Its closest connection with the final treaty seems to have been the decision of its field governor, Sir George Simpson, to shift its main depot from Fort Vancouver on the north bank of the Columbia River to the newly constructed Fort Victoria on the southern tip of Vancouver Island. This decision, taken at the beginning of 1845, indicated that the Company no longer valued the Columbia River as a major trade channel or felt certain of defending its supplies at the old depot from the oncoming American settlers. By implication, it regarded the territory between the river and Puget Sound as expendable. Although the Company still maintained a subsidiary land-and-cattle outfit on the Sound, Simpson's decision to move the headquarters reinforced Aberdeen's view of Oregon's limited value and helped him to convince others.[27]

Anglo–French relations also conditioned the thinking of British government leaders and publicists on the Oregon question. The *entente cordiale* was the cornerstone of Aberdeen's foreign policy, and at times, as in Texas, he was willing to jeopardize friendship with the United States in order to create fields for joint Anglo–French action. There was no question of such a choice in Oregon, for the French government had no interest in the north Pacific, and the French opposition was united in its sympathy with the Americans. The Duke of Wellington, Sir Charles Napier, and even Peel expected France to join the United States in case of Anglo–American war over Oregon, and despite Aberdeen's objections they intensified rearmament against the possibility of a cross-Channel attack. Always concerned about the budget, Peel resisted expensive preparations for an additional war with the United States. The French question thus made him susceptible to Aberdeen's arguments for a negotiated Oregon settlement.[28] Probably British rearmament also contributed to a settlement by convincing the Polk administration that Britain would fight if pushed too far.[29]

26. New York *Evening Post*, January 8, 1844, p. 2. For British criticism, see London *Examiner*, April 26, 1845, quoted in Merk, *Oregon Question*, p. 290; and London *Morning Chronicle*, November 27, 1845, p. 4.

27. Merk, *Oregon Question*, pp. 245–53. Other arguments were the declining

fur trade in the river valley and the sandbar at its mouth.

28. John S. Galbraith, "France As a Factor in the Oregon Negotiations," *Pacific Northwest Quarterly*, 44 (April 1953), 69–73. Merk, *Oregon Question*, pp. 347–56.

29. This interpretation is perhaps

Among economic influences on the Oregon settlement undoubtedly the most important were the many Anglo–American business and financial undertakings: the cotton trade, the export of manufactures, and investments by British citizens in American enterprises. These undertakings would certainly suffer from war or another long diplomatic crisis like that before 1842. Consequently, representatives of these interests, such as Joshua Bates and Thomas Wren Ward of Baring Brothers and Company, joined with economics-minded publicists, such as Nassau Senior, to further Aberdeen's campaign of persuasion. After the Oregon question became deadlocked in the summer of 1845, Bates, Ward, and other business-oriented pacifists maintained a channel of extra-official communication between the two governments.

The role of these economic interests has caused little controversy among historians. More disagreement surrounds the importance of parallel Anglo–American free-trade discussions and in particular of the British food crisis during the autumn of 1845. To be sure, some publicists in 1845 and 1846 combined free trade and Oregon into a "package deal" through which Britain might exchange several thousand square miles of forest for a larger market in manufactured goods.[30] The prospect of free trade no doubt confirmed Calhoun and his Southern bloc in their opposition to an immediate crisis over Oregon, but it would be difficult to prove that this argument had much effect on Western expansionists. While the crop failures in England and Ireland and the resultant food crisis occurred at precisely the right time for maximum influence, Frederick Merk has shown convincingly that American shipments during this period never displaced Britain's usual supply of grain from the Continent, so that Britain neither depended on American grain nor considered that she did. Merk admits that the hope of tariff reform contributed in general to a conciliatory atmosphere. Also, and more important, the "Whig abortion" and Peel's informal alliance with Russell to repeal the corn laws—both occasioned by the food crisis—undoubtedly helped to create bipartisan support in Britain for a compromise Oregon settlement as well.[31]

overemphasized in Julius W. Pratt, "James Knox Polk and John Bull," *Canadian Historical Review*, 24 (December 1943), 341–49. See also Wilbur Devereux Jones and J. Chal. Vinson, "British Preparedness and the Oregon Settlement," *Pacific Historical Review*, 22 (1953), 353–64.

30. *NNR*, 69 (November 1, 1845; February 14, 1846), 132, 370; and London *Morning Chronicle*, November 6, 1845, p. 4; November 20, p. 4; December 27, p. 4.
31. Merk, *Oregon Question*, Essay XI. Wiltse, *Calhoun, Sectionalist*, pp. 255–56, 524–25*n*20. An important statement

The contributions of American settlers have called forth sharp differences of opinion among historians. Under the influence of the "frontier thesis" many of them have assumed that the waves of emigrants swept aside British resistance in the disputed area and that the treaty of 1846 was simply another triumph of the Western movement.[32] In fact, however, the role of the settlers was probably less direct. As Merk has shown, they settled south of the Columbia River in territory which (for that very reason) Britain was quite willing to relinquish to the United States. Before the treaty few Americans crossed the river. But this is not the whole story, as he admits. The great migrations of 1843 and 1844 impressed Simpson and other Hudson's Bay Company officials and contributed materially to their withdrawal from the river to Vancouver Island. At the height of the Oregon controversy, in February 1846, the British cabinet received unimpeachable information from its agents on the spot that the Americans had established a government in the Columbia Valley and that prospects for British dominance there were hopeless. Thus the migrations also supported Aberdeen's campaign for a negotiated compromise.[33]

Whatever the relative importance of these contributing factors, the pivotal British figure in the Oregon settlement was Peel's foreign secretary, the Earl of Aberdeen. His writings indicate that by the end of 1843 he had drawn up his own terms for a compromise: a boundary at 49° and all of Vancouver Island to Britain, together with free ports south of the line and the free navigation of the Columbia River—in other words the settlement of 1846 plus two nominal concessions of no practical value to Britain.[34]

Why, then, did agreement require two and a half years of diplomatic sparring and a major war crisis? No settlement was likely during 1844 and early 1845, while Americans were intent

---

of the opposite thesis is Thomas P. Martin, "Free Trade and the Oregon Question, 1842–1846," in *Facts and Factors in Economic History: Articles by Former Students of Edwin Francis Gay*, pp. 470–91.

32. Joseph Schafer, *A History of the Pacific Northwest*, pp. 181–84. Schafer, "Oregon Pioneers and American Diplomacy," in Guy Stanton Ford, ed., *Essays Dedicated to Frederick Jackson Turner*, pp. 35–55. Merk, *Oregon Question*, p. 236n6.

33. Merk, *Oregon Question*, Essay VIII. A more emphatic statement of the indirect contributions is Leslie M.

Scott, "Influence of American Settlement upon the Oregon Boundary Treaty of 1846," *Oregon Historical Quarterly*, 29 (March 1928), 13–19. Scott, "Report of Lieutenant Peel on Oregon in 1845–46," ibid., 66–71.

34. Aberdeen to Richard Pakenham, March 4, 1844; Pakenham to Aberdeen, March 28, Aberdeen Papers, BM, AM, vol. 43123, ff. 233–38. These private notes considerably modified the more restricted official instructions Pakenham carried with him to Washington. Aberdeen to Pakenham, December 28, 1843, No. 10, GB, FO 115/83, ff. 187–95.

on conducting a presidential campaign and annexing Texas. Calhoun's tactics during this period properly kept the question in abeyance. In the spring of 1845, however, the advent of a new American administration and Peel's increasing uneasiness over Oregon created a situation favorable to renewal of negotiations. Then, if ever before 1846, a compromise treaty was possible. Aberdeen's instructions to Pakenham in March and April show that he was alarmed at the evidence of hostility in the American Congress but willing to consider a compromise if it were offered without threats.[35]

Instead, there followed a series of misunderstandings and blunders, the most serious of which must be ascribed to Polk. He overstated the American case in his inaugural address. He also failed to explain his policy to the American minister in London, Edward Everett, so that Everett might counter the predictable British reaction.[36] Having touched off a series of explosions in the British and American press, Polk could yet have redeemed the situation by composing for Pakenham a brief, moderate statement of the American position. Instead, he had Buchanan reconstruct the whole ramshackle legal case and patronizingly offer to concede some of what the British held to be rightfully theirs. At that point Pakenham contributed his own error to the confusion by rejecting the American terms without referring them to London. Pakenham's was a relatively minor blunder, since it involved an agent rather than a policy maker. With patience and a little probing Polk might still have exploited the British alarm to determine whether Pakenham had acted on instructions. Allowing Aberdeen to explain and excuse his minister's fault might even have given Polk a psychological advantage.

Instead he yielded to his suspicions of British treachery, withdrew his offer, and produced an impasse. In subsequent weeks he permitted—if he did not encourage—talk of hostilities.[37] Nine

35. Aberdeen to Pakenham, March 3, April 6, 18, 1845, Nos. 8, 21, 22, GB, FO 115/88, ff. 63–65, 153–55, 157–59. Same, April 2, 18, Aberdeen Papers, BM, AM, vol. 43123, ff. 247–50.

36. Edward Everett to Aberdeen, July 1, 1846, BM, AM, vol. 43123, f. 447.

37. Richard Rush, a knowledgeable but anti-British elder statesman who had been minister to Britain in the Monroe administration, approved Buchanan's reply to Pakenham in August and Polk's stiff policy in general. He particularly praised the annual message of December 1845. Richard Rush to Buchanan, December 16, 1845, George Ticknor Curtis, *Life of James Buchanan, Fifteenth President of the United States*, I, 572–73. Same, August 26, 1846, Buchanan Papers, box 63, HSP. Rush to Nicholas P. Trist, September 21, Trist Papers, XXII, ff. 59760–61, LC. Sellers follows Rush's views and defends Polk's strong stand as necessary to jolt Peel into supporting Aberdeen's compromise proposal.

months later, when negotiations finally took place, Polk managed to end a war crisis that was largely of his own creation and secured terms which he might have had earlier with more sophisticated diplomacy.

*　　*　　*　　*

The supposition that the Anglo–American war crisis over Oregon was avoidable, however, does not utterly rule out the possibility of British designs on California. Indeed, a few historians have seen some substance in the widespread rumors of 1845 and 1846 that Britain intended to intervene and preserve Mexican rule in California or even appropriate the province for herself.[38] But in 1909 Ephraim D. Adams, having searched through the newly opened British archives for the 1840s, categorically denied that the Peel government had any such intent, and most subsequent writers on the subject have simply added evidence to support this view.[39]

Undoubtedly, the British government considered intervention in California on several occasions. In 1841 Richard Pakenham, then Britain's minister to Mexico, suggested that a British colonizing company might profitably settle the area with Europeans and eventually secure political control. The Colonial Office replied through Aberdeen, discouraging the project.[40] In 1844 British consuls on the Pacific coast reported popular sentiment in favor of a British protectorate over the province. Aberdeen, however, quashed this idea in comprehensive policy statements of December 31. As long as Mexico retained sovereignty over California, he declared, the British government would not entertain proposals for a protectorate. If an independence movement developed there, Britain would take no part, but it would "view with much dissatisfaction" a protectorate in California under any other nation.[41]

Charles Grier Sellers, *James K. Polk, Continentalist: 1843–1846*, pp. 244–46, 257–58. The evidence suggests, however, that Polk and his Western allies actually complicated Aberdeen's task by affronting British honor.

38. Robert Glass Cleland, *A History of California: the American Period*, p. 188. Ernest A. Wiltsee, "The British Vice Consul in California and the Events of 1846," *California Historical Society Quarterly*, 10 (June 1931), 117–18. Wiltsee, *The Truth about Frémont:*

An Inquiry, pp. 42–48.

39. Ephraim Douglass Adams, *British Interests and Activities in Texas, 1838–1846*, Chap. 11. This chapter was originally published in *American Historical Review*, 14 (July 1909), 744–63.

40. G. W. Hope to Viscount Canning, November 23, 1841, GB, CO 43/100, pp. 34–36. Adams, *British Interests*, pp. 236–40.

41. Aberdeen to Bankhead, December 31, 1844, No. 53; Aberdeen to Eustace Barron, December 31, No. 3, GB, FO

During the Oregon crisis Aberdeen was tempted several times to abandon this self-denying policy. In the fall of 1845 he briefly considered joint Anglo–French intervention of some sort in California to strengthen the *entente cordiale*. At the same time he learned of a new colonization plan developed by the British consul in Mexico City, Ewen C. Mackintosh, and supported by many British holders of Mexican bonds.[42] Late in May 1846, after the first Mexican defeats in the war, President Paredes himself proposed California as security for a British loan—an "indirect offer of sale." At the same time the First Lord of the Admiralty, the aggressive Earl of Ellenborough, was pressing Peel to acquire San Francisco as a naval base.[43]

None of these temptations moved Aberdeen. Peel showed some interest in Ellenborough's proposal, but the foreign secretary pointed out that acquiring San Francisco would be tantamount to a declaration of war against the United States, and Ellenborough's subordinates warned Peel that reinforcement of the Pacific Squadron would dangerously weaken defenses against France at home. *Entente cordiale* or not, France was the real enemy. On June 1, 1846, Aberdeen restated the British policy of noninterference in California and refused to extend to Mexico any help beyond mediation.[44] When Palmerston returned to the Foreign Office, he saw no reason to change this policy.

It is not enough, however, to demonstrate that the British government had no designs on California in 1846. Did the Polk administration have any way of knowing this policy? Talk of war was rife in the press of both countries through the winter and spring. No one could predict the movements of British troops in Canada, of British warships in the north Pacific, or of British dip-

---

50/172, ff. 148–52; 50/179, ff. 9–12. Adams, *British Interests*, pp. 247–50, reprints most of both dispatches. Lester G. Engelson, "Proposals for the Colonization of California by England in Connection with the Mexican Debt to British Bondholders, 1837–1846," *California Historical Society Quarterly*, 18 (June 1939), 145.

42. Wilbur Devereux Jones, *Lord Aberdeen and the Americas*, pp. 68–71. Bankhead to Aberdeen, July 30, 1845, No. 74, with enclosed memorandum, GB, FO 50/186, ff. 18–22, 28–30.

43. Engelson, "Proposals for Colonization," pp. 145–46. Bankhead to Aberdeen, May 30, 1846, No. 73, GB, FO

50/197, ff. 120–23. Ellenborough to Aberdeen, May 16, 1846, Ellenborough Papers, PRO 30/12/34/7.

44. Arthur Hamilton-Gordon Stanmore, *The Earl of Aberdeen*, pp. 183–84. H. T. L. Corry to Undersecretary of State for Foreign Affairs, June 9, 1846, GB, A 1/5568. Peel to Ellenborough, May 30, 1846, Peel Papers, BM, AM, vol. 40473, ff. 334–35. H. U. Addington to Corry, June 19, GB, A 1/5568. Aberdeen to Bankhead, June 1, No. 15, GB, FO 50/194, ff. 32–37. Largely reprinted in George Lockhart Rives, *The United States and Mexico*, II, 162–63.

lomats and promoters in Mexico. Many Americans feared that they would wake up some morning to find a British squadron anchored in San Francisco Bay and a puppet regime ruling the compliant Californians.

Nevertheless, certain considerations, discernible by careful observation and thought, might have suggested to the Polk administration that if the Oregon question were peaceably settled, Britain would not further provoke the United States by intervening elsewhere in the north Pacific. First, California did not involve British honor or legal rights as did Oregon, where British explorations and the activities of the Hudson's Bay Company had created a well-substantiated claim. The British government never tried to set up a claim to California. A second indication was recent British policy concerning the Hawaiian Islands, where British explorers and merchants had also established a vested interest without legal title. In February 1843 Lord George Paulet, acting without instructions, raised the British flag over Honolulu and proclaimed a British protectorate, but his government disavowed him at once and fully explained its nonimperialist intentions to the United States.[45] Three years later it was reasonable to suppose that Admiral Seymour would not make the same mistake in California that Lord Paulet had made in Hawaii.

The precedent which Britain had established in Texas was a third indication. That province was more important to British economic interests than California, and the British government was completely opposed to American annexation. Nevertheless, the irascible *Times* distinguished sharply between Oregon, where "the thing attacked is *our own*," and Texas, where "the interests of Mexico are not so closely identified with our own. . . . The results of the annexation of Texas," it concluded, "are not so prejudicial to the welfare of England or her dependencies, as to constitute a just cause of war."[46] British agents might try to persuade the Texan government to remain independent or to patch up a settlement with Mexico, but when the situation became critical in the spring of 1845 and the Mexican government appealed for military aid to prevent annexation, Britain held aloof.[47]

If all these considerations were not enough, another reason for expecting Britain to keep her armed forces out of California

45. Ralph S. Kuykendall, *The Hawaiian Kingdom, 1778–1854: Foundation and Transformation*, pp. 199–202, Chap. 13. Aberdeen to H. S. Fox, June 3, 1843, No. 23, GB, FO 115/81, ff. 124–25.

46. London *Times*, April 10, 1845, p. 4.

47. The reports of Mexican Minister Murphy on his efforts to obtain a promise of aid from Aberdeen are in An-

was to be found in the many official and private British expressions of desire for friendship with the United States. At every twist and turn of the Oregon crisis Aberdeen and Pakenham repeated their concern for peace. The American minister to Britain, Louis Mc-Lane, reported much antiwar sentiment in England. Representatives of British business and financial interests maintained a steady flow of soothing, conciliatory statements to correspondents in New England. To be sure, many of these American correspondents were suspect as Whigs, but the conciliators had a respectable Democratic outlet in Polk's cabinet—Secretary of the Navy George Bancroft.[48]

British pacifism arose at least partly from economic considerations and was reinforced by British hope that the Polk administration would lower the American tariff. In a long dispatch of February 3, 1846, at a time when Britain's rearmament was most alarming, McLane plainly stated that the desire for American friendship was an important motive behind Peel's campaign to repeal the Corn Laws. He added, "They would adopt the proposed scheme to very little purpose, if, for the sake of a degree of latitude on the Pacific, they should destroy the commercial intercourse of Great Britain with all the Atlantic states."[49] McLane was referring to Oregon, but his reasoning applied with equal logic to California.

What is more, the accurate assessment of Anglo–French relations during the early 1840s might have revealed that the *entente cordiale* was not truly cordial and might thus have reassured the American government concerning the British threat to California. During 1842 and 1843 Britain and France had experienced a serious crisis over Tahiti, followed by disagreements over Greece and Spain. As late as the autumn of 1845 the newspapers of both countries were filled with rumors of war, although the two governments tried to paper over the cracks in their relationship with ceremonial court visits and inspired editorials. American diplomats kept their

tonio de la Peña y Reyes, ed., *Lord Aberdeen, Texas y California, passim.*

48. Bancroft was not always receptive to their suggestions. Bancroft to Louis McLane, December 12, 1845, M. A. de Wolfe Howe, *The Life and Letters of George Bancroft*, I, 281.

49. McLane to Buchanan, February 3, 1846, No. 34, US, DS, D, Britain, LVI. This passage is not included in Manning, *CR.* As early as 1845 and as far

away as California the merchant Larkin had appreciated the importance of British exports to the United States: "This will cause her [Britain] to pause before she drives from her market her best & greatest customer, and in case of war perforce, thousands of [*sic*] more factories will go up in the states that a future peace will not put down." Larkin to James Alexander Forbes, June 9, 1845, Larkin, *Papers*, III, 230.

government informed about the main outlines of Anglo–French disputes, and Minister William R. King in Paris repeatedly described as conciliatory the French attitude toward the United States. On January 30, 1846, for example, he wrote that public opinion would prevent any joint Franco–British action in questions affecting Texas or Mexico: "There is nothing to apprehend from this government and country. The latter is with us and will restrain the former from being against us."[50]

Thus, even though the British Whigs were expected to return to power in the spring of 1846, there were good reasons why British intervention in California should not have seemed very likely. Probably the reappearance of the rambunctious Palmerston at the Foreign Office would not change the situation radically. Polk was unaware that Palmerston's Whig colleagues had clipped his wings after Russell's vain effort to form a cabinet, but the President and Buchanan might have observed that even in Palmerston's most jingoist days, during the Canadian border crises of the late 1830s, the noble lord had been given more to attitudes than to action. In any case, his return to office could only complicate Anglo–French relations and thus increase the Continental deterrent to hostilities in North America.[51]

Polk could or should have understood many of these considerations—which does not mean that he did understand them. But it is difficult to avoid the conclusion that during his first year in office he not only cut short unnecessarily an excellent opportunity for peaceful negotiations over Oregon but also exaggerated the British threat to California and the need for prompt American action there. Above all, he failed to appreciate properly the connection between the two questions. An Anglo–American war over Oregon would almost certainly have led to an alliance between Britain and Mexico, and the price of such an alliance might well have been the cession of San Francisco or of the whole territory.[52] Pushing the doubtful American claim to 54°40′ might have precipitated the very disaster in California the United States sought to avoid.

50. William R. King to Buchanan, January 30, 1846, No. 25, Manning, *IAA*, VI, 562–64. The quotation is on p. 564. As Waddy Thompson pointed out in his memoirs (published in 1846), Britain was more hostile to Russia than to the United States and would probably want American sympathy in case of a crisis with the Tsar. Thompson, *Recollections of Mexico*, pp. 237–38.

51. Merk, *Oregon Question*, pp. 270–80.

52. Murphy to Ministerio de Relaciones Exteriores, February 1, 1846, No. 4, Peña y Reyes, *Aberdeen, Texas y California*, pp. 62–64. Bankhead to Aberdeen, May 30, No. 73, GB, FO 50/197, ff. 120–23. Stanmore, *Aberdeen*, p. 184.

Polk also jeopardized the nation's aims in California by risking an army on the Rio Grande, hundreds of miles away in northeastern Mexico. According to McLane, if Taylor had met defeat, Mexican agents would probably have been able to float loans in London.[53] Had stalemate followed such a defeat, the Polk administration, facing a divided nation, might have had to accept mediation by the British and postpone indefinitely its ambitions on the Pacific coast. How could Polk be sure that the Mexican army's outrageously bad leadership would offset its numerical superiority? The erratic performance of the American Army in the recent Seminole War should have emphasized the risk of Taylor's maneuvers.[54] From the viewpoint of California, hostilities on the Rio Grande would seem to have been, in General Omar Bradley's phrase, "the wrong war, at the wrong place, at the wrong time, and with the wrong enemy."

*   *   *   *

If the Mexican War was indeed an unnecessary gamble, why did Polk undertake it? He and his supporters explained that he did so only as a last resort, in defense of American interests and honor after Mexico had ignored claims, rejected negotiation, and hurled insult and defiance at the United States. Many historians have applied their scholarship to defense of this viewpoint.[55] But a considerable segment of antiwar opinion at the time proclaimed that Polk was waging a war of conquest, pure and simple, which he rationalized with sophistical arguments, so as to legalize the American occupation of California under the law of nations and set up such a barrier as the British would not dare cross.[56] Pursuing the matter further, some of Polk's opponents accused him of "a deliberate contrivance to bring the war about in such a manner as to throw on Mexico the odium of its commencement."[57] Since the

53. McLane to Buchanan, June 3, 1846, No. 54, Manning, *IAA*, VII, 278.
54. Edwin C. McReynolds, *The Seminoles*, Chaps. 10–13. Mark F. Boyd, "The Seminole War: Its Background and Onset," *Florida Historical Quarterly*, 30 (July 1951), 3–115. Charles Winslow Elliott, *Winfield Scott, the Soldier and the Man*, Chaps. 24–26.
55. The classic statement is Smith, *War with Mexico*, especially I, Chaps. 4, 5. See also Eugene C. Barker, "California As a Cause of the Mexican War," *Texas Review*, 2 (January 1917), 213–21.

56. For example, Washington *National Intelligencer*, December 9, 1846, p. 3; December 12, pp. 3–4; December 15, p. 3. For a convenient summary of the bibliography on the relationship between the California question and the Mexican War, see Frank A. Knapp, Jr., "The Mexican Fear of Manifest Destiny in California," in Thomas E. Cotner and Charles E. Castañeda, eds., *Essays in Mexican History*, pp. 192–94.
57. Charles T. Porter, *A Review of the Mexican War*, pp. 95–96. See also William Jay, *A Review of the Causes and Consequences of the Mexican War*,

1880s a few historians have accepted this "plot thesis" and have applied it to all his policies from his inauguration to the beginning of the war.[58]

None of these explanations is wholly convincing. The list of American claims and the story of the Slidell mission suggest that American grievances were bearable and that the United States government had not exhausted the possibilities of negotiation.[59] Also, the opening hostilities took place on disputed ground to which Mexico had an arguable claim. But if Polk was waging simply a war of conquest, it is hard to understand why he did not plan it more comprehensively from the beginning and why he conducted it with spurts of action followed by long periods of stagnant delay. As for the "plot thesis," its supporters offer too little evidence and too much surmise in its defense. They ignore the administration's repeated predictions that war was neither likely nor desirable and the administration's failure to enlarge or overhaul the inadequate army until war had begun.[60] Also, they fail to make clear why Polk should have provoked Britain to a war crisis at the same time that he planned to fight Mexico.

A more consistent explanation of Polk's foreign policies appears in several revealing statements he made about Britain and Oregon. Note his account of a conversation with a minor Democratic Congressman on January 4, 1846, during the Oregon debate:

> I remarked to him that the only way to treat John Bull was to look him straight in the eye; that I considered a bold & firm course on our part the pacific one; that if Congress faultered [*sic*] or hesitated

---

Chap. 20 *et passim*. During the debate on the Texas annexation treaty Benton accused Tyler of trying to force the United States into a war with Mexico so as to be reelected. US, 28C, 1S, *CG*, Appendix, pp. 474–86, especially pp. 482–83.

58. Hubert H. Bancroft, *History of Mexico*, V, 307–8. Richard R. Stenberg, "The Texas Schemes of Jackson and Houston," *Southwestern Social Science Quarterly*, 15 (December 1934), 229–50. Stenberg, "The Failure of Polk's Mexican War Intrigue of 1845," *Pacific Historical Review*, 4 (March 1935), 39–68. Stenberg, "Polk and Frémont, 1845–1846," ibid., 7 (1938), 211–27. Stenberg, "President Polk and California: Additional Documents," ibid., 10 (June 1941), 217–19. Glenn W. Price, *Origins*

of the *War with Mexico: the Polk-Stockton Intrigue, passim.*

59. On the American claims, see Clayton Charles Kohl, *Claims As a Cause of the Mexican War*, pp. 58–79.

60. See, for example, Bancroft to Henry Wikoff, May 12, 1845, Howe, *Life and Letters of Bancroft*, I, 288. Bancroft to Robert F. Stockton, June 2, 15, C. T. Neu, "The Annexation of Texas," in *New Spain and the Anglo-American West*, II, 88–89, 90–91. Buchanan to Andrew J. Donelson, June 15, No. 9, Manning, *IAA*, XII, 94–97. Marcy to P. M. Wetmore, July 6, Marcy Papers, ff. 34478–79, LC. Polk to A. O. P. Nicholson, July 28, Polk Papers, NYHS. Ivor Debenham Spencer, *The Victor and the Spoils, a Life of William L. Marcy*, pp. 141–42, 144–45.

in their course, John Bull would immediately become arrogant and more grasping in his demands; & that such had been the history of the Brittish [*sic*] Nation in all their contests with other Powers for the last two hundred years.[61]

He put it even more succinctly to a friend: "Great Brittain [*sic*] was never known to do justice to any country—with which she had a controversy, when that country was in an attitude of supplication or on her knees before her."[62] Accordingly, when he sent Buchanan or McLane to approach Pakenham or Aberdeen, Polk took a high hand, exaggerated his legal case and his demands, and regarded all suggestions of compromise as probes from Britain or American Anglophiles to find weak points in his armor.

Polk applied the same policy of aggressive negotiation to American–Mexican relations, with the difference that, instead of respectful suspicion toward a tough, tenacious power, he felt contemptuous impatience toward a weak, corrupt, disorganized government, much given to delay and evasion. Tight-mouthed, he let slip no revealing private remarks about the Mexican character such as his comments on Britain, but his public statements in his annual message of 1845 and especially in the war message give some idea of his underlying feelings. "A continued and unprovoked series of wrongs," hope for "a returning sense of justice," "frivolous pretexts," "the subsisting constitutional authorities . . . subverted," a "manifest breach of faith," "a government either unable or unwilling . . . to perform one of its plainest duties," a "system of outrage and extortion"—all these phrases suggest Polk's distaste for Mexico.[63] Such a government, like that of Britain, would respond only to strong words and a show of force. He declared to his cabinet during the last weeks before the declaration of war that "we must treat all nations, whether great or small, strong or weak, alike, and that we should take a bold and firm course toward Mexico."[64]

Thus, when Polk became President, he set forth on a foreign policy of strong stands, overstated arguments, and menacing public pronouncements, not because he wanted war but because he

---

61. James K. Polk, *The Diary of James K. Polk during His Presidency, 1845 to 1849,* ed. Milo M. Quaife, I, 155.

62. Polk to Nicholson, April 2, 1846, Polk Papers, NYHS. See also Polk to Gideon J. Pillow, February 4; and Polk to William J. Polk, March 27, Letterbook, 1845–1846, pp. 320–25, 378–83, Polk Papers, LC.

63. James D. Richardson, ed., *A Compilation of the Messages and Papers of the Presidents, 1789–1897,* IV, 388–92, 437–43.

64. Polk, *Diary,* I, 354. Polk made this statement on April 25. He had used the same words to Calhoun a week earlier. *Ibid.,* p. 337.

felt that this was the only language which his foreign adversaries would understand. Faced at his inauguration with the delicate final arrangements for the annexation of Texas, Polk had no desire to precipitate an immediate crisis with either Mexico or Britain. Accordingly, he sent a special agent to reconnoiter in Mexico City for a renewal of diplomatic relations and agreed to exchange views on Oregon with Britain. When Pakenham cut short this exchange, Polk, overreacting, jumped to the conclusion that he had been tricked. Breaking off the dialogue, he stiffly notified the British government that it must now make a concrete proposal which he might treat as he chose.

The strong stand toward Mexico was slower to develop. During the summer and autumn of 1845 rumors of Mexico's intentions to attack in the Rio Grande Valley or to reconquer California with British aid provoked Polk to station troops and ships where they would be useful in case of war and also to inaugurate a program of propaganda and intrigue among the natives of California. These preparations made, he sent Slidell to Mexico, with instructions to press Herrera not only for recognition of Texan boundaries but for the sale of California and New Mexico as well. In December his annual message summarized the strong stands toward both Britain and Mexico and added new arguments, such as the Monroe Doctrine, to earlier rationalizations.

Events during the winter of 1845–1846 forced Polk to modify his original plans. He had called on Congress to demonstrate unified support by quickly passing a firm resolution of notice to Britain on Oregon. But before doing so, in late April, the legislators spent four months in rancorous debate, thus threatening Polk's whole legislative program and the unity of his party. Meanwhile, the Mexican government refused even to receive Slidell, who finally returned home empty-handed. At some time during the last stages of the Oregon debate Polk became convinced that an actual war with Mexico would be necessary—not a major conflict, but a limited, short, decisive engagement in the Rio Grande Valley which would convince Mexico that the United States meant business.[65] If the Mexicans began the fighting, their attack could be used to unify the Democratic party and confound the Whigs. If American forces could then occupy California and New Mexico, Mexico would be forced to negotiate and the United States could

---

65. Benton aptly summarized this viewpoint in Thomas Hart Benton, *Thirty Years View*, II, 680. Polk's statements on the subject after the war began were more restrained but also indicated limited military objectives. Polk, *Diary*, I, 400, 403-4, 437-38.

obtain title to the provinces, perhaps in return for a disguised indemnity to Mexico. By this time Britain would have decided to propose an Oregon settlement which the Senate would accept.

This version of Polk's policies explains his episodic method of waging war. During May and June he carried out much of his program through Taylor's victories in the Rio Grande Valley, the Oregon settlement, and the occupation of California—so much that, when the Mexicans continued to resist, Polk was firmly convinced that one more crushing victory would cause their collapse and bring peace. First, the Americans advanced to Monterrey, then to Tampico, while he let the apparently pliant Santa Anna slip through the blockade to return home. He then pressed Congress for a special fund of $3 million, which might be used as an inducement to Mexico to sign a proper peace treaty.

After waiting in vain for Santa Anna to negotiate, Polk decided to occupy Veracruz and then to advance into the fever-free interior, sending a minor diplomat, Nicholas P. Trist, to accompany the army and transmit correspondence. But even Scott's victory at Cerro Gordo, the most impressive of the entire war, failed to break the Mexicans' amazing will to resist. After pausing three months at Puebla, Scott moved into the Valley of Mexico—a dangerous advance, for he risked being cut off from his base.[66] At this point one setback would have undone the effect of all previous victories. But the Americans continued to win battles. At one point peace talks actually got under way, but again Santa Anna did not choose or dare to submit, and Scott had to occupy Mexico City.

The war now threatened to get out of hand altogether, as a movement spread through the United States for extensive annexations in central Mexico or rule over the entire country as the only acceptable return for American losses. But Polk gave no evidence that he had lost his nerve or had changed his plans. Instead, learning of the fruitless peace talks, he recalled Trist. Apparently the President intended to take over direct control of negotiations and perhaps force the Mexicans to come to Washington if they wanted peace. However, his repudiated envoy spared him the need of testing his assumptions further by an act of courageous insubordination. Urged by British diplomats and merchants, Trist remained in Mexico and with their aid obtained a treaty along the lines of

66. When the Duke of Wellington learned that the Americans had entered the Valley of Mexico, he declared, "Scott is lost! He cannot capture the city and he cannot fall back upon his base!" Quoted in Elliott, *Scott*, pp. 501–2.

his original instructions. One might add that Polk's luck continued to hold, even in his failure to acquire Yucatán and Cuba after the war, for he was able to leave office without bequeathing to his successor half-realized annexations which were beyond the country's capacity at that time.

* * * *

To the retrospective eye of the historian Polk's alarums and excursions present an astonishing spectacle. Impelled by his conviction that successful diplomacy could rest only on a threat of force, he made his way, step by step, down the path to war. Then, viewing the war as a mere extension of his diplomatic scheme, he proceeded as confidently as a sleepwalker through a maze of obstacles and hazards to the peace settlement he had calmly intended from the beginning.

Despite his boldness and his unshakable determination, Polk was at heart a cautious leader. His apparently most impetuous acts —the withdrawal of the Oregon offer to Pakenham, the bold stands of his first annual message, the declaration of war, and the occupation of Veracruz—were undertaken only after weeks or even months of meditation and discussion with his advisers. If he thought long and hard about his country's interests, he was even more careful when the interests of his party and himself were concerned, for he tried to associate Congress in some way with every important decision he made, in order to divert and disperse the wrathful lightning of his many opponents.

Nevertheless, for all his prudence, he clearly did not anticipate the rigors of a war crisis with Britain or a long-drawn-out invasion of Mexico. Why did he miscalculate so grossly? One reason was simple lack of up-to-date, accurate information. Dispatches from London or Mexico City required at least three or four weeks to reach Washington, and news from Oregon and California five or six months. Even the most experienced, trusted observers were sometimes highly unreliable. While Everett and McLane presented fairly exact pictures of British attitudes, Consul Black in Mexico City consistently misled the United States government about the Mexicans' support of the war, and Larkin's important dispatch of July 10, 1845, about the British threat to California was wrong on every count.[67] During the critical weeks of April and

67. For samples of misleading dispatches by Black, see Manning, *IAA*, VIII, 728–29, 738–39, 853–54, 863–64, 881–82. Larkin's dispatch is ibid., pp. 735–36.

May 1846 Polk and his cabinet learned about Mexican troop movements from rumors in the New Orleans newspapers or hearsay dispatches from Mexico City and Veracruz. When Taylor marched into the lower Rio Grande Valley, his superiors provided him with an almost useless topographical map put together in Washington and with little more.[68] In effect, both the administration and the general were feeling their way into unknown territory.

Polk's rigid determination to follow a course of aggressive diplomacy and war also rose from traits of his personality. His diary reveals that he could be insensitive to the ideals and convictions of others; this characteristic was dominant when he looked outward toward Europe or Latin America. He lacked a primary qualification of the diplomat—the ability to appreciate a foreign people's hopes, fears, and driving impulses and to see America and himself through their eyes. To him, Britain was a thieving bully, British appeals to national honor mere rationalizations, and British sentiments of democracy and friendship no more than traps for the unwary. Similarly, the Mexicans were a people hardly worthy of self government, unable to develop the borderlands that stood in the way of American expansion, and their clamorous boasts and appeals to patriotism mere mouth honor.

Polk's insensitivity toward Britain, though dangerous to American interests, was eventually nullified by countervailing factors. The more sophisticated Britons understood the President's personality, having seen its traits in some of their own politicians, and they made allowances for it, although they found it distasteful. Webster, Everett, Sturgis, and other American conciliators well known in London assured them by their demeanor that Polk represented only one aspect of the American character. Most important, perhaps, British leaders were perceptive enough to sense some of the possibilities for future Anglo–American cooperation and strong enough to defend British national honor with patience rather than with passion.

If such countervailing factors existed in American–Mexican relations, they are hard to discern. Mexicans had long regarded the United States with a combination of admiration and suspicion, and in the 1840s their rising anger was both complicated and frustrated by profound ignorance concerning American political

68. Brantz Mayer, *History of the War between Mexico and the United States, with a Preliminary View of Its Origin,* pp. 91–93. More than once Polk complained of Scott's irregular correspondence.

and social institutions.[69] Weak, disunited, repeatedly humiliated by revolutions, penury, and foreign slights, the Mexicans seemed to have nothing further to lose but national integrity. Remembering his experiences in Mexico City, Pakenham predicted that the Mexicans' sense of honor would require stubborn defense of their boundaries and that an American offer of money would probably intensify their resistance. A high British official, well acquainted with the Spanish character, once observed, "The Mexican is like a mule—if you spur him too much he will back off the precipice with you."[70]

The most enlightened leaders of this quixotic people were far behind Peel and Aberdeen in training, perception, and firmness of purpose. Some, like Herrera and Cuevas, saw the need to restrain a national impulse toward self-immolation but did not know how. Others, like Gómez Farías, plunged into the flames with the rest. The master of Mexico during most of the war, Santa Anna, was even more inscrutable than Polk. Despite his postwar apologies and reams of Mexican writings, no convincing evidence has emerged to indicate that he ever seriously intended to reach an agreement with the United States. The record of his words and deeds suggests only that he was an incorrigible opportunist who improvised his plans from day to day without any guiding principle more sophisticated than self preservation.[71]

Whatever the qualities of the Mexican leaders, their view of Polk and the United States was as simplistic as Polk's view of them, and the intermediaries between the two nations did little to correct the fault. Almonte's abilities might have been comparable to

69. In some respects Mexican historiography has made little progress since the 1840s. The most recent and comprehensive Mexican account of relations with the United States identifies the American Whigs as a Northern party opposed to slavery and Southern expansion and the Democrats as Southern proslavery expansionists. Luis G. Zorrilla, *Historia de las relaciones entre México y los Estados Unidos de América, 1800–1958*, I, 5–6, 186.

70. H. U. Addington, the British foreign undersecretary, who had served in Madrid, made a statement to this effect to the Texan Ashbel Smith, who paraphrased it in a letter of July 1, 1844, to Anson Jones. Anson Jones, *Memoranda and Official Correspon-dence Relating to the Republic of Texas, Its History and Annexation*, p. 370. See also Pakenham to Palmerston, March 29, 1847, No. 40, GB, FO 5/469, ff. 229–33.

71. Mexican writers have characterized Santa Anna as brave, patriotic, resourceful, cowardly, traitorous, calculating, impulsive, and venal. His fiercest critics are to be found among both proclerical nationalists and liberal antimilitarists. The most complete survey of these views is Homer C. Chaney, Jr., "The Mexican-United States War, As Seen by Mexican Intellectuals, 1846–1956," Ph.D. diss., Stanford University, 1959, pp. 22–25, 36–37, 39–40, 77–78, 115–16, 149–51, 159, 183–86, 189–93, 198, 275–76.

Pakenham's, but the Mexicans recalled him in 1845. Slidell might have been as persuasive as McLane, but the Mexicans would not receive him. As for unofficial go-betweens, Atocha and Beach are not comparable with Everett, Sturgis, or the Baring agents.

Polk's myopia and lack of empathy in relations with Britain and Mexico can also be attributed in large measure to his training and environment. From his mentor Andrew Jackson, he may have derived the models for his British and Mexican policies—the peremptory Jacksonian challenge to France over unpaid debts and the conniving mission of Anthony Butler to Mexico. In the challenge to France the threat of force, though later modified, had brought action; while the heavy-handed Butler was unsuccessful, Polk might reasonably have supposed that a more suave agent would prevail.

In a broader sense, whether Polk received from Jackson his suspicions of other nations and his techniques for dealing with them, he may be said to have epitomized the self-centered, aggressive nationalism prevalent in the Mississippi Valley during much of the nineteenth century.[72] Remembering British–Indian intrigues and the War of 1812, Midwesterners easily envisaged the Hudson's Bay Company, the governor general of Canada, and the cabinet in London as deceitful bullies. Remembering how Spanish dons in Madrid and New Orleans had opposed American expansion, the inhabitants of the lower valley and their cousins, the transplanted Texans, easily attributed to Mexico the same sly, ceremonious evasion they had experienced earlier. During the first fifty years of the United States' national existence Presidents and secretaries of state had frequently displayed a sophisticated cosmopolitanism that mitigated or, in some instances, nullified American xenophobia. This restraining factor, however, almost disappeared with the generation of Madison and Monroe. Post-Jacksonian leaders were not always more free from international involvements than their predecessors, but with few exceptions they were certainly less citizens of the world.

If Polk shared the *Weltanschauung* of his people and times, what may be said of his other blind spot—failure to anticipate the disunity Oregon and the Mexican War spread among the American people? Ideological and sectional rivalry arising from the Texas question had nearly torn the Democratic party asunder in

72. Stenberg called Polk "the grasping hand of a nation infected with the expansionist urge." Stenberg, "Polk and Frémont," p. 227.

the campaign of 1844. Once in office, Polk could not avoid carrying through the immediate annexation of Texas, since Congress and Tyler had precipitated the action. But why did he not realize that internal suspicions and resentments made it expedient to halt the pressure on Britain and Mexico for the time being?

Polk's abolitionist opponents and some later pro-Northern historians answered this question by labeling him the tool of the blind, recklessly imperialist Southern "slaveocracy." Years ago, American scholars punctured the thesis that the South monopolized or was even united behind southwest expansionism, although many Mexican writers still accept it as sound.[73] Might Polk have wished to avoid a repetition of the sectional struggle over Texas and therefore set out to acquire Oregon, California, and New Mexico directly and quickly, so as to give sectionalism no time to develop? There is no evidence in his correspondence or diary to indicate this line of thought. Like many other Southerners, Polk regarded the "local institutions" of Texas as a matter of concern to the Texans alone.[74] In his diary he had nothing to say about sectional agitation over slavery until the introduction of the Wilmot Proviso in the summer of 1846, when the war had already begun. Thereafter, he clearly looked on all attempts to link slavery and expansion as mischievous, wicked, and foolish—mischievous and wicked because his opponents were using the issues for partisan gain, foolish because the territory to be acquired would never support slavery.[75]

Polk was not alone in his shallow, unenlightened view of the nation's most threatening problem, for other statesmen of the mid-1840s, older and more experienced than he, failed also to understand that sectionalism and expansion had formed a new, explo-

73. For samples of the Southern conspiracy thesis, see Hermann Von Holst, *The Constitutional and Political History of the United States*, III, Chaps. 9–11; and James Ford Rhodes, *History of the United States from the Compromise of 1850*, I, 87–93. For refutation, see Chauncey W. Boucher, "In Re That Aggressive Slaveocracy," *Mississippi Valley Historical Review*, 8 (June-September 1921), 13–19. Barker has performed a similar service for the movement into Texas. Eugene C. Barker, "The Influence of Slavery in the Colonization of Texas," ibid., 11 (June 1924), 3–36. An example of the persistence of the conspiracy thesis in even moderate Mexican writing is Agustín Cue Cánovas, *Historia social y económica de México (1521–1854)*, pp. 382–408, *passim*.

74. See, for example, his inaugural address. Richardson, *Papers of the Presidents*, IV, 381.

75. The most succinct statement of his attitude appears in an entry of January 5, 1847: "Slavery has no possible connection with the Mexican War, and with making peace with that country. . . . There is no probability that any territory will ever be acquired from Mexico in which slavery could ever exist." Polk, *Diary*, II, 308. See also II, 75–76, 283–84, 305, 350, 458; IV, 33–34.

sive compound. John C. Calhoun, deliberate and canny where Oregon was concerned, acted with reckless abandon in the Texas question when he answered Aberdeen's mild defense of abolitionism with a note gratuitously proclaiming what the North already suspected—that Calhoun wanted annexation in order to preserve slavery as a positive good.[76] John Quincy Adams, who had reluctantly surrendered American claims to Texas in the Spanish treaty of 1819, threatened a secessionist movement in 1843 if Texas were annexed. Three years later he shifted back to expansionism and invoked *Genesis* to support the American claim to 54°40'.[77] When one sees elder statesmen like these playing ducks and drakes with American passions, the insensitivity of younger men becomes more understandable.

*　　*　　*　　*

In the effort to explain and appraise Polk's policies, one final element remains to be considered—his freedom of choice. To what extent were his decisions shaped or forced on him by circumstances beyond his control?

From 1845 to 1848 Polk seems to have experienced a phenomenon that diplomatic and military strategists of the mid-twentieth century have called *escalation*. This phenomenon is a process by which an initial set of decisions starts a chain of causes and effects, each more difficult to control than its predecessor. At the beginning of the chain the decision maker may have been presented with a fairly wide range of acceptable choices. The range is gradually reduced until at the end he has—or seems to have—none. In other words, events close in on him until he finds himself surrounded with dilemmas, all exits blocked.

Even at the beginning of his administration Polk did not have complete freedom of choice, for his party platform, the joint resolution of Congress, and Tyler's last-minute offer to Texas committed him to immediate annexation. This action, in turn, brought an unavoidable break in formal diplomatic relations with Mexico. Nevertheless, since that nation was in no position to launch a concerted attack, Polk could take stock of the situation, send a private observer to Mexico, and wait for the Mexicans' anger to subside. In the Oregon question he was limited only by

76. Calhoun to Pakenham, April 18, 1844, Manning, *IAA*, VII, 18–22.
77. Washington *National Intelligen-cer*, n.d., as reprinted in *NNR*, 64 (May 13, 1843), 173–75. US, 29C, 1S, *CG*, pp. 339–42.

an extremist plank in the Democratic platform and by the statements of Democratic congressmen during the winter debate of 1844–1845.

Polk might have taken stock of this question too, and perhaps he intended to do so. But he committed his first serious tactical error when he inserted into his inaugural address a restatement of the "clear and unquestionable" United States title—by implication to all Oregon—and thereby stirred up violent argument in Britain and in the American West. After this address, postponement of action was no longer possible, but for a time he considered private negotiations with Britain on the basis laid down by Calhoun in 1844. Pakenham rebuffed him; then, yielding to his own convictions about Britain, Polk committed his second major error by breaking off negotiations altogether and insisting that Britain must take the initiative to resume them. In less than six months he had abdicated nearly all choice concerning Oregon.

Until November 1845 Polk retained, almost unhampered, the power to determine the direction and timing of his Mexican policy. During the next two months, however, he seriously restricted his freedom of choice here as well. His instructions to Slidell and his annual message to Congress announced to Mexico and to the world at large that the United States would take an extreme position regarding its claims and objectives to the southwest. By thus proclaiming his intentions and by sending Taylor's army to the Rio Grande, Polk destroyed any hope of privately persuading Mexico. Meanwhile, his annual message again stimulated Western expectations for all of Oregon and formally transferred to Congress much of the responsibility for settling the question.

After January 1846 events began to drive Polk irresistibly. The long, raucous debate on Oregon encouraged the British government to postpone any useful initiative to resume negotiations. The debate and Mexico's rejection of Slidell induced Polk to plan for a short war with Mexico. But a short war turned into a long one, for the Mexicans now held the power of decision, and although repulsed or routed in every major battle, they determined to resist the invaders, supported by their formidable topography and climate.

Once war had been declared, Polk's policy choices were limited to alternate military strategies, attack of some sort versus a holding action. After the landing at Veracruz there remained only one way forward—up the foothills and across the mountains into the Valley of Mexico. When Scott captured Mexico City, Polk had exhausted the acceptable choices available to him, for further conquest, indefinite occupation, and retreat to a line across northern Mexico all presented insuperable difficulties. Fortunately, at this point conciliation and compromise, so foreign to Polk's nature, saved him.

* * * *

All in all, an appraisal of the diplomacy of annexation brings the realization that annexation might have been less painful and costly if skillful diplomacy had been allowed to play a more vital role at several points. Diplomats drew up the basic terms for the incorporation of Texas, and the climactic victory of Donelson over Elliot was in large measure a diplomatic one. After a serious Anglo–American war crisis, it was the diplomacy of McLane that pointed the way to a settlement of the Oregon question. Similarly, after nearly two years of costly war with Mexico, it was the diplomacy of Trist, aided by British representatives, that laboriously untied the Gordian knot in Mexico City.

Could Polk have avoided the Oregon and Mexican crises by placing his chief reliance on conventional, professional diplomacy in the spring of 1845? The evidence suggests that he might have done so. In one of Tyler's last special messages, the outgoing President had reassured Congress about Oregon: "Considerable progress has been made in the discussion, . . . [and] there is reason to hope that it may be terminated and the negotiation brought to a close within a short period."[78] Some such bromide, inserted into Polk's inaugural address, would probably have mollified most Western expansionists for the time being and would have allowed him opportunity to examine the files of the diplomatic correspondence before taking a stand.

At Polk's inauguration he had a nine-month period of grace before facing Congress—a period in which distribution of patronage, internal problems, and the Texas question were certain to occupy the public's attention. If he had set diplomats to work privately during this period, he might have been able to announce a viable solution of the Oregon question in his first annual message. The prospect of a peaceful settlement with Britain would then have immeasurably strengthened his hand in further diplomacy with Mexico. As the urgency of the Oregon question

78. Richardson, *Papers of the Presidents*, IV, 362.

faded, Polk might have sent Slidell to Mexico as a special envoy, nominally to discuss Texan annexation but actually to present a confidential offer for boundary adjustments, while Taylor's army, still at Corpus Christi, mounted guard over the disputed zone without offering an overt threat that would goad the Mexicans to cross the Rio Grande.

By avoiding a crisis, Polk might have maintained this indeterminate but not uncomfortable position for a year or more, while the emigrants of 1845 and 1846 settled in central California. Tactful private warnings to Britain and the presence of Sloat's squadron cruising off the Mexican coast could have shielded an independence movement in California, which would establish a new state. At the least, an independent California could have maintained friendly relations for an indefinite period with the government at Washington. Eventually, the United States might have opened negotiations for annexation, choosing a time when Britain was fully involved in European affairs. As events developed, the revolutions of 1848 provided just such an opportunity, and there were others during the succeeding years.

Would this gradualism have satisfied Western expansionists? Probably not, but it is inconceivable that their protests could have been as divisive as the debates that took place over Oregon and the Mexican War. Indeed, their impatient outbursts might have been put to good use, for diplomats such as McLane or Slidell, their cunning sharpened by experience in American politics, would have known how to invoke Western extremism as a stimulus for lagging negotiations. If expansionist pressure became too great to resist, Polk would yet have retained his freedom to speak out; after initiating bona fide efforts toward peaceful settlement, his stirring pronouncements would probably have had more effect than they actually did. They might indeed have strengthened moderates in Britain or Mexico instead of repelling them.

Polk's background and character militated against such reliance on conventional diplomacy. Instead of carefully exploring issues and interests, he chose a policy based on bluff and a show of force. At the time it seemed an easier policy. In its constant appeals to Congress and the people it seemed more democratic. By goading British and Mexican nationalists, however, this policy raised obstacles, and as these obstacles increased, it proved impossible to reverse. No one can deny that Polk achieved his goals, but he was favored by good luck, by the steadfastness of American soldiers, and, at the end, by the long-neglected skill of his diplomats. For many persons his achievements justified themselves. But later generations might reasonably complain that he served his country ill by paying an unnecessarily high price in money, in lives, and in national disunity.

List of Maps

Bibliography

I. MANUSCRIPT SOURCES

1. UNITED STATES OFFICIAL PAPERS, NATIONAL ARCHIVES

Department of State, Foreign Affairs Section (Record Group 59)
 Instructions to United States Ministers
 Despatches from United States Ministers
 Consular Instructions
 Consular Despatches
 Post Records
 Notes to Foreign Legations
 Notes from Foreign Legations
 Special Agents
 Special Missions

Department of War, Office of Judge Advocate General (Record Group 153)
 General Courts Martial, 1812–1938, Box FF–300. "Proceedings of a Court of Inquiry Held in Mexico and the United States under Confidential Instructions from the Secretary of War, 17th March 1848 in Regard to the Use of Secret Service Money for the Purchase of a Peace."

Department of Navy (Record Group 45)
 Letters Received by the Secretary of the Navy from Commanding Officers of Squadrons (file microcopy 89)
 Letters Received by the Secretary of the Navy from Officers below the Rank of Commander (file microcopy 148)

2. GREAT BRITAIN OFFICIAL PAPERS, PUBLIC RECORD OFFICE, LONDON

Foreign Office
 Series 5, 115 (United States). Photostats, Library of Congress
 Series 27 (France)
 Series 50, 203, 204, 207 (Mexico)
 Series 72 (Spain)
 Series 75 (Texas)

Admiralty
 Series 1, 50

Colonial Office
    Series 43, 100

3. FRANCE OFFICIAL PAPERS, ARCHIVES DU MINISTÈRE DES AFFAIRES
    ÉTRANGÈRES, PARIS

Correspondence Politique
    États Unis
    Mexique
    Texas
Correspondence Consulaire et Commerciale
    Veracruz
Mémoires et Documents
    Amérique

4. SPAIN OFFICIAL PAPERS, MADRID

Biblioteca de Asuntos Exteriores
    Legajos 1649–1651, 2545
Archivo Histórico Nacional
    Legajos 5585, 5655, 5867, 5869, 5870

5. MEXICO OFFICIAL PAPERS

United States, Library of Congress, Photostats, H/252 (73:72)
University of Texas Libraries, Austin. Eugene C. Barker Transcripts

6. PRIVATE PAPERS

Earl of Aberdeen (George Hamilton-Gordon) Papers. British Museum,
    Additional Manuscripts
William Allen Papers. Library of Congress
George Bancroft Papers. Massachusetts Historical Society, Boston
George Bancroft Papers. New York Public Library
Blair Family Papers. Library of Congress
Baron Brougham (Henry Peter Brougham) Papers. University College,
    London
James Buchanan Papers. Historical Society of Pennsylvania, Philadel-
    phia
James Buchanan Papers. Library of Congress
Henry Clay Papers. Library of Congress
David E. Conner Papers. Library of Congress
David E. Conner Papers. New York Public Library
Earl Cowley (Henry Richard Wellesley) Papers. Public Record Office,
    London. Series 519
John J. Crittenden Papers. Library of Congress
George M. Dallas Papers. Historical Society of Pennsylvania

Andrew J. Donelson Papers. Library of Congress
Earl of Ellenborough (Edward Law) Papers. Public Record Office
Edward Everett Papers. Massachusetts Historical Society
Valentín Gómez Farías Papers. University of Texas Libraries, Austin
Duff Green Papers. Library of Congress
Ethan Allen Hitchcock Papers. Library of Congress
William Huskisson Papers. British Museum, Additional Manuscripts
Andrew Jackson-William B. Lewis Correspondence. New York Public
    Library
Thomas S. Jesup Papers. Library of Congress
Louis McLane Papers. University of Delaware Library, Newark
Manning and Mackintosh Papers. University of Texas Libraries
William L. Marcy Papers. Library of Congress
Viscount Palmerston (Henry John Temple) Papers. British Museum,
    Additional Manuscripts
Sir Robert Peel Papers. British Museum, Additional Manuscripts
Franklin Pierce Papers. Library of Congress
Joel Poinsett Papers. Historical Society of Pennsylvania
James K. Polk Papers. Library of Congress
James K. Polk Papers. New York Historical Society
Earl of Ripon (Frederick John Robinson) Papers. British Museum,
    Additional Manuscripts
Antonio López de Santa Anna Papers. Library of Congress
Benjamin Tappan Papers. Library of Congress
Waddy Thompson Papers. Library of Congress
Nicholas P. Trist Papers. Library of Congress
Martin Van Buren Papers. Library of Congress
Sir Charles R. Vaughan Papers. All Souls College, Oxford University
Robert J. Walker Papers. Library of Congress
Robert J. Walker Papers. New York Historical Society
Thomas Wren Ward Papers. Massachusetts Historical Society

7. DISSERTATIONS

Bennett, Margaret L. "British Interests in Mexico, 1830–1845." M.A.
    thesis, University of California (Berkeley), 1930.
Berge, Dennis E. "Mexican Response to United States Expansionism,
    1841–1848." Ph.D. dissertation, University of California (Berke-
    ley), 1965.
Brent, Robert Arthur. "Nicholas Philip Trist, Biography of a Disobe-
    dient Diplomat." Ph.D. dissertation, University of Virginia,
    1950.
Chaney, Homer C., Jr. "The Mexican–United States War, As Seen by
    Mexican Intellectuals, 1846–1956." Ph.D. dissertation, Stan-
    ford University, 1959.

Cody, William Frederick. "British Interest in the Independence of Mexico, 1808–1827." Ph.D. dissertation, University of London, 1954.

Delalande, Guy. "La légation de France auprès de la République du Texas (1839–1846)." Doctorat de l'Université, Université de Paris, n.d.

Dooley, Oscar S. "The Presidential Campaign and Election of 1844." Ph. D. dissertation, Indiana University, 1942.

Farabee, Ethel Sadie. "The Career of William Stuart Parrott, Business Man and Diplomat in Mexico." M.A. thesis, University of Texas, 1944.

Florstedt, Robert Frederick. "The Liberal Role of José María Luis Mora in the Early History of Independent Mexico." Ph.D. dissertation, University of Texas, 1950.

Graebner, Norman A. "The Treaty of Guadalupe Hidalgo: Its Background and Formation." Ph.D. dissertation, University of Chicago, 1949.

Hammond, William Jackson. "The History of British Commercial Activity in Mexico, 1820–1830." Ph.D. dissertation, University of California (Berkeley), 1929.

Harris, Helen Willits. "The Public Life of Juan Nepomuceno Almonte." Ph.D. dissertation, University of Texas, 1935.

Hillman, Franklin Powell. "The Diplomatic Career of James Buchanan." Ph.D. dissertation, George Washington University, 1953.

Hutchinson, Cecil Alan. "Valentín Gómez Farías: A Bibliographical Study." Ph. D. dissertation, University of Texas, 1948.

Robertson, Frank Delbert. "The Military and Political Career of Mariano Paredes y Arrillaga, 1797–1849." Ph. D. dissertation, University of Texas, 1955.

Schuster, Alice K. "Nicholas Philip Trist: Peace Mission to Mexico, April 17, 1847, to February 2, 1848." Ph. D. dissertation, University of Pittsburgh, 1947.

Spence, Mary Lee. "British Interests and Attitudes Regarding the Republic of Texas and Its Annexation by the United States." Ph. D. dissertation, University of Minnesota, 1956–1957.

Vigness, David Martell. "The Republic of the Rio Grande: An Example of Separatism in Northern Mexico." Ph. D. dissertation, University of Texas, 1951.

Wickman, John E. "Political Aspects of Charles Wilkes's Work and Testimony, 1842–1849." Ph. D. dissertation, Indiana University, 1964.

Wozencroft, Gordon. "The Relations between England and France during the Aberdeen–Guizot Ministries (1841–6)." Ph. D. dissertation, University of London, 1932.

II. PUBLISHED SOURCES—PRIMARY

1. OFFICIAL PAPERS

United States

27th Congress, 3d Session, House Executive Document 166
28th Congress, 1st Session, House Executive Document 291
29th Congress, 1st Session, Senate Document 1
                Senate Document 2
29th Congress, 2d Session, House Executive Document 4
30th Congress, 1st Session, Senate Executive Document 52
                House Executive Document 60
34th Congress, 1st Session, Senate Executive Document 34
41st Congress, 2d Session, Senate Report 261
Congressional Globe
Department of Commerce, Bureau of the Census, *Historical Statistics of the United States, Colonial Times to 1957.* Washington, 1960.
William R. Manning, ed. *Diplomatic Correspondence of the United States: Canadian Relations, 1784–1860.* 4 vols. Washington, 1940–1945.
———. *Diplomatic Correspondence of the United States: Inter-American Affairs, 1831–1860.* 12 vols. Washington, 1932–1939.
———. *Diplomatic Correspondence of the United States Concerning Latin-American Independence.* 3 vols. New York, 1925.
David Hunter Miller, ed. *Treaties and Other International Acts of the United States of America.* 8 vols. Washington, 1931–1948.
James D. Richardson, ed. *A Compilation of the Messages and Papers of the Presidents, 1789–1897.* 10 vols. Washington, 1896–1899.
Senate, *Journal of the Executive Proceedings of the Senate of the United States.*

Great Britain

Hansard Parliamentary Debates (3d Series).
Ephraim Douglass Adams, ed. *British Diplomatic Correspondence Concerning the Republic of Texas, 1838–1846.* Austin, n.d.
Robin A. Humphreys, ed. *British Consular Reports on the Trade and Politics of Latin America, 1824–1826.* London, 1940.
Charles K. Webster, ed. *Britain and the Independence of Latin America, 1812–1820.* 2 vols. London, 1938.

France

Luis Weckmann, ed. *Las relaciones franco-mexicanas.* 2 vols. México, 1961–1962.

Spain

Javier Malagón Bárcelo, Enriqueta Lópezlira, and José María Miquel i Vergès, eds. *Relaciones diplomáticas hispano-mexicanas (1839–1898). Documentos procedentes del archivo de la Embajada de España en México. Serie I, Despachos generales.* 4 vols. México, 1949–1968.

Mexico

Balanza general del comercio marítimo por los puertos de la República mexicana en el año de 1827. México, 1829.

Cámara de diputados. *Dictamen de la comisión de industria de la Cámara de diputados sobre el nuevo arbitrio para dar un gran aumento a la hacienda federal, y para proporcionar al mismo tiempo ocupación y medios de subsistir a la clase de gentes pobres de la República mexicana.* México, 1829.

Secretaría de Relaciones Exteriores. *La diplomacia mexicana.* 3 vols. México, 1910–1913.

―――. *Memoria del Secretario de estado y del despacho de relaciones exteriores y gobernación de la República mexicana correspondiente a la administración provisional, en los años de 1841, 42 y 43. Leida en las cámaras del Congreso constitucional desde el dia 12 al 17 de enero de 1844.* México, 1844.

―――. *Memoria del Ministro de relaciones exteriores y gobernación leida en el Senado el 11 y en la Cámara de diputados el 12 de marzo de 1845.* [México, 1845].

―――. *Memoria de la Primera secretaría de estado y del despacho de relaciones interiores y esteriores de los Estados-unidos mexicanos, leida al Soberano congreso constituyente en los días 14, 15 y 16 de diciembre de 1846, por el ministro del ramo, C. José María Lafragua.* México, 1847.

[Tampico, Ayuntamiento]. *Esposición del Ayuntamiento constitucional de Tampico de Tamaulipas, al Congreso de la Unión, sobre reforma del arancel de aduanas y de todas las leyes comerciales.* Tampico, 1833.

Carlos Bosch García, ed. *Material para la historia diplomática de México.* México, 1957.

Luis Chávez Orozco, ed. *La gestión diplomática del Doctor Mora.* México, 1931.

Manuel Dublán, José María Lozano, Adolfo Dublán, and A. A. Esteva, eds. *Legislación mexicana, ó Colección completa de las disposiciones legislativas expedidas desde la independencia de la República* [etc.]. 50 vols. México, 1876–1912.

Antonio de la Peña y Reyes, ed. *Algunos documentos sobre el tratado de Guadalupe y la situación de México durante la invasión americana.* México, 1930.

————. *Don Manuel Eduardo de Gorostiza y la cuestión de Texas; Documentos históricos precedidos de una noticia biográfica.* México, 1924.

————. *El Barón Alleye de Cyprey y el Baño de las Delicias; Colección de documentos precedida de una introducción.* México, 1926.

————. *Incidente diplomático con Inglaterra en 1843.* México, 1923.

————. *La primera guerra entre México y Francia.* México, 1927.

————. *Lord Aberdeen, Texas y California.* México, 1925.

Texas

George Pierce Garrison, ed. *Diplomatic Correspondence of the Republic of Texas.* Annual Report of the American Historical Association for the Years 1907, 1908. 3 vols. Washington, 1908–1911.

2. MEMOIRS, PRIVATE CORRESPONDENCE, PAMPHLETS, ETC.

Aberdeen, Earl of. "Letter of Aberdeen to Pakenham, March 4, 1844, Concerning the Oregon Question." Edited by Robert C. Clark. *Oregon Historical Quarterly,* 39 (1938), 74–76.

Adams, John Quincy. *Memoirs of John Quincy Adams.* Edited by Charles Francis Adams. 12 vols. Philadelphia, 1874–1877.

Adams, Sir William. *The Actual State of the Mexican Mines, and the ... Expectations of the Shareholders of the Anglo-Mexican Mine Association* [etc.]. London, 1825.

Anderson, Robert. *An Artillery Officer in the Mexican War, 1846–7.* New York, 1911.

Anonymous. *Le Mexique et l'Europe ou Exposé de la situation actuelle du Mexique et des dangers qui peuvent en résulter pour l'Europe si elle ne prend des mesures efficaces pour y remédier.* Paris, 1847.

————. *The Mexican War.* "Published by the Green Mountain Liberty Association." N.p., n.d.

Austin, Stephen F. "The 'Prison Journal' of Stephen F. Austin." *Texas Historical Quarterly,* 2 (January 1899), 183–210.

Beach, M. S. "A Secret Mission to Mexico. Origin of the Treaty of Guadalupe Hidalgo." *Scribner's Monthly,* 17 (December 1878), 299–300; 18 (May 1879), 136–40.

Beaumont, Baron Joseph-Gabriel-Marie de. *Lettre à M. le comte Molé sur la question mexicaine* [etc.]. Paris, 1839.

————. *Résumé et solution de la question mexicaine, pour servir à la discussion sur les crédits supplementaires.* Paris, 1839.

Benton, Thomas Hart. *Thirty Years View: or a History of the Working of the American Government for Thirty Years, from 1820 to 1850.* 2 vols. New York, 1854–1859.

Berry, Philip. *A Review of the Mexican War on Christian Principles.* Columbia, S. C., 1849.

Blanchard, P., and A. Dauzats. *San Juan de Ulua, ou Rélation de l'Expédition française au Mexique sous les ordres de M. le contreamiral Baudin.* Paris, 1839.

Boucher, Chauncey S., and Robert P. Brooks, eds. *Correspondence Addressed to John C. Calhoun, 1837–1849.* Annual Report of the American Historical Association, 1929. Washington, 1931.

Brooks, N. C. *A Complete History of the Mexican War.* Philadelphia and Baltimore, 1849.

Buchanan, James. *The Works of James Buchanan.* Edited by John Bassett Moore. 12 vols. Philadelphia, 1908–1911.

Bustamante, Carlos María de. *El nuevo Bernal Díaz ó sea Historia de la invasión de los Anglo-Americanos en México.* 2 vols. México, 1847; reprinted, México, 1949.

Calderón de la Barca, Frances. *Life in Mexico during a Residence of Two Years in That Country.* New York, 1931.

Calhoun, John C. *Correspondence of John C. Calhoun.* Edited by J. Franklin Jameson. Annual Report of the American Historical Association for the Year 1899. Vol. II. Washington, 1900.

"Californiana." *Century Magazine,* 40 (September 1890), 792–97.

Capen, Nahum. *The Republic of the United States of America: Its Duties to Itself, and Its Responsible Relations to Other Countries. Embracing Also a Review of the Late War between the United States and Mexico.* Philadelphia, 1848.

Carta de un ciudadano mexicano a un oficial del ejército norteamericano, en respuesta a las observaciones a los habitantes de la República, que escribió hace pocas días en Puebla, y corren impresas. Atlixco, 1847.

Channing, William E. *A Letter to the Hon. Henry Clay, on the Annexation of Texas to the United States.* 2d ed. Boston, 1937.

Claiborne, J. F. H. *Life and Correspondence of John A. Quitman, Major-General, U. S. A., and Governor of the State of Mississippi.* 2 vols. New York, 1860.

Clark, Robert C., ed. "Aberdeen and Peel on Oregon, 1844." *Oregon Historical Quarterly,* 34 (1933), 236–40.

The Complaint of Mexico, and Conspiracy against Liberty. Boston, 1843.

Corral, Juan José del. *Esposición acerca de los perjuicios que ha causado al erario de la República y a su administración, el agiotaje sobre sus fondos, y reflexiones sobre los medios de remediar aquellos males.* México, 1834.

Coxe, Richard S. *Review of the Relations between the United States and Mexico and of the Claims of Citizens of the United States against Mexico.* New York, 1846.

De la Granja, Juan. *Epistolario,* preliminary biographical study by Luis Castillo Ledón, notes by Nereo Rodríguez Barragán. México, 1937.

Downey, Joseph T. *The Cruise of the Portsmouth, 1845–1847. A Sailor's View of the Naval Conquest of California.* Edited by Howard Lamar. New Haven, 1958.

Dubouchet, C. *La Goatzacoalcos, colonie de MM. Laisné de Villévêque et Giordin, ou les horreurs dévoilées de cette colonie.* Paris, 1830.

Emerson, Ralph Waldo. *Journals of Ralph Waldo Emerson.* Edited by E. W. Emerson and W. E. Forbes. 10 vols. Boston, 1912.

English, Henry. *A General Guide to the Companies Formed for Working Foreign Mines with Their Prospectuses, Amount of Capital, Number of Shares, Names of Directors, &c.* London, 1825.

Exposición de una persona residente en la República mexicana sobre la guerra que actualmente sostiene con los Estados unidos del norte. México, 1847.

Flores D., Jorge, ed. *Lorenzo de Zavala y su misión diplomática en Francia, 1834–1835.* México, 1951.

Forbes, Alexander. *California: A History of Upper and Lower California from Their First Discovery to the Present Time, Comprising an Account of the Climate, Soil, Natural Productions, Agriculture, Commerce.* London, 1839.

Frémont, John Charles. "The Conquest of California." *Century Magazine,* 41 (April 1891), 917–28.

Gannett, E. S. "The Mexican War." *Christian Examiner,* 44 (January 1848), 124–42.

García, Genaro, and Carlos Pereyra, eds. *Documentos inéditos ó muy raros para la historia de México.* 36 vols. México, 1905–1911.

Grant, Ulysses S. *Personal Memoirs of U. S. Grant.* 2 vols. New York, 1885–1886.

[Green, Duff]. "Duff Green's 'England and the United States,' with an Introductory Study of American Opposition to the Quintuple Treaty of 1841." Edited by St. George L. Sioussat, *Proceedings of the American Antiquarian Society,* new series, 40 (October 1930), 175–276.

Greenhow, Robert. *Memoir, Historical and Political, on the Northwest Coast of North America, and the Adjacent Territories.* Washington, 1840.

Greville, Charles C. F. *A Journal of the Reign of Queen Victoria from 1837 to 1852.* Edited by Henry Reeve. 2 vols. New York, 1885.

Hart, Burdette. *The Mexican War. A Discourse Delivered at the Con-*

gregational Church in Fair Haven, on the Annual Fast of 1847. New Haven, 1847.

Hitchcock, Ethan Allen. *Fifty Years in Camp and Field.* Edited by W. A. Croffut. New York, 1909.

Hone, Philip. *Diary of Philip Hone, 1828–1851.* Edited by Allan Nevins. 2 vols. New York, 1936.

Houston, Sam. *Autobiography of Sam Houston.* Edited by Donald Day and Harry H. Ullon. Norman, Okla., 1954.

———. *The Writings of Sam Houston.* Edited by Amelia W. Williams and Eugene C. Barker. 6 vols. Austin, 1938–1941.

Howe, M. A. de Wolfe. *The Life and Letters of George Bancroft.* 2 vols. New York, 1908.

An Inquiry into the Plans, Progress, and Policy of the American Mining Companies. 3d ed. London, 1825.

Jackson, Andrew. *The Correspondence of Andrew Jackson.* Edited by John Spencer Bassett. 7 vols. Washington, 1926–1935.

James, Edward. *Remarks on the Mines, Management, Ores &c &c of the District of Guanaxuato, Belonging to the Anglo–Mexican Mining Association.* London, 1827.

Jay, William. *A Review of the Causes and Consequences of the Mexican War.* 2d ed. Boston, 1849.

Jones, Anson. *Memoranda and Official Correspondence Relating to the Republic of Texas, Its History and Annexation.* New York, 1859.

Kenly, John Reese. *Memoirs of a Maryland Volunteer.* Philadelphia, 1873.

Larkin, Thomas O. *The Larkin Papers.* Edited by George P. Hammond. 10 vols. and index. Berkeley and Los Angeles, 1951–1968.

Latrobe, Charles J. *The Rambler in Mexico.* London, 1836.

Lawyers and Legislators: or Notes on the American Mining Companies. London, 1825.

Livermore, Abiel Abbot. *The War with Mexico Reviewed.* Boston, 1850.

Lowell, James Russell. *The Complete Writings of James Russell Lowell.* 16 vols. Boston, 1904.

Löwenstern, Isidore. *Le Mexique, Souvenirs d'un voyageur.* Paris, 1843.

McLoughlin, John. *The Letters of John McLoughlin from Fort Vancouver to the Governor and Committee: Second Series, 1839–1844.* Edited by E. E. Rich. Toronto, 1943.

———. *Third Series, 1844–46.* Toronto, 1944.

Mangum, Willie P. *The Papers of Willie Person Mangum.* Edited by Henry Thomas Shanks. 5 vols. Raleigh, N.C., 1950–1956.

Martineau, Harriet. *Society in America.* 2 vols. London, 1839.

Mayer, Brantz. *History of the War between Mexico and the United*

States, with a Preliminary View of Its Origin. New York and London, 1848.

Meade, George Gordon. *The Life and Letters of George Gordon Meade, Major-General United States Army.* 2 vols. New York, 1913.

Mofras, Eugène Duflot de. *Exploration du territoire de l'Orégon, des Californies et de la Mer Vermeille, éxecutée pendant les années 1840, 1841 et 1842.* Translated and edited by Marguerite Eyer Wilbur. 2 vols. Santa Ana, Calif., 1937.

Nance, Joseph Milton, ed. "A Letter Book of Joseph Eve, United States Chargé d'Affaires to Texas." *Southwestern Historical Quarterly,* 43 (October 1939), 196–221, (January 1940), 365–77, (April 1940), 486–510; 44 (July 1940), 96–116.

Nasatir, Abraham P., ed. "The French Consulate in California, 1843–1846." *California Historical Society Quarterly,* 11 (September, December 1932), 195–223, 339–57; 12 (March, June, December 1933), 35–64, 155–72, 331–57; 13 (March, June, September, December 1934), 56–79, 159–75, 262–80, 355–85.

Otero, Mariano. *Obras.* Edited by Jesús Reyes Heroles. México, 1967.

Owen, Robert Dale. "Recallings from a Public Life." *Scribner's Monthly,* 16 (October 1878), 868–78.

Parker, Charles Stuart, ed. *Sir Robert Peel, from His Private Papers.* 3 vols. London, 1891–1899.

Poinsett, Joel. "The Mexican War." *DeBow's Review,* 2 (July 1846), 21–24. "The Republic of Mexico." Ibid., 2 (July 1846), 27–42. "Mexico and the Mexicans." Ibid., 2 (September 1846), 164–77. "Our Army in Mexico." Ibid., 2 (December 1846), 425–30.

———. *Notes on Mexico, Made in the Autumn of 1822* [etc.]. Philadelphia, 1824.

Polk, James K. *Diario del Presidente Polk.* Edited by Milo Milton Quaife; translation and Introduction by Luis Cabrera. 2 vols. México, 1948.

———. *Polk, the Diary of a President.* Edited by Allan Nevins. New York, 1929.

———. *The Diary of James K. Polk during His Presidency, 1845 to 1849.* Edited by Milo Milton Quaife. 4 vols. Chicago, 1910.

———. "Letters of James K. Polk to Andrew J. Donelson, 1843–1848." Edited, with Introduction and notes by St. George L. Sioussat. *Tennessee Historical Magazine,* 3 (1919), 51–73.

Porter, Charles T. *A Review of the Mexican War.* Auburn, N.Y., 1849.

Powles, J. D. *A Letter to Alexander Baring, Esq., M.P., on the Subject of Some Observations Reported to Have Been Made by Him in the House of Commons, on the 16th March, 1825, in Relation to the Foreign Mining Associations.* London, 1825.

Prieto, Guillermo. *Memorias de mis tiempos, 1840 a 1853.* Paris and México, 1906.

Ramírez, José Fernando. *Mexico during the War with the United States.* Edited by Walter V. Scholes, translated by Elliott B. Scherr. University of Missouri Studies, 23:1. Columbia, 1950.

Rejón, Manuel Crescencio. *Correspondencia inédita de Manuel Crescencio Rejón.* Edited by Carlos A. Echanove Trujillo. México, 1948.

———. *Pensamiento política.* Edited by Daniel Moreno. México, 1968.

"Representación de los mexicanos al Soberano congreso para la espulsión de estrangeros." Broadside, México, January 28, 1835. British Museum.

Ripley, R. S. *The War with Mexico.* 2 vols. New York, 1849.

Rivero, Luis Manuel del. *Méjico en 1842.* Madrid, 1844.

Robertson, Alexander. *Reflexions on the Present Difficulties of the Country; and on Relieving Them, by Opening New Markets to Our Commerce, and Removing All Injurious Restrictions.* London, 1820.

Russell, Lord John. *The Later Correspondence of Lord John Russell, 1840–1878.* Edited by G. P. Gooch. 2 vols. London, 1925.

Santa Anna, Antonio López de. *Apelación al buen criterio de los nacionales y estangeros. Informe que el Ecsmo. General de división, Benemérito de la patria D. Antonio López de Santa-Anna, dió por acuerdo de la Sección del gran jurado, sobre las acusaciones presentadas por el Sr. diputado Don Ramón Gamboa.* México, 1849.

———. *The Eagle, the Autobiography of Santa Anna.* Edited by Ann Fears Crawford. Austin, 1967.

———. "Letter of Antonio López de Santa Anna to Manuel Reyes Veramendi, President of the *Ayuntamiento* of Mexico City, Guadalupe, September 15, 1847." Edited by Robert S. Chamberlain. *Hispanic American Historical Review,* 24 (November 1944), 614–17.

———. "Letters of General Antonio López de Santa Anna Relating to the War between the United States and Mexico, 1846–1848." Edited by Justin H. Smith. *Annual Report of the American Historical Association for the Year 1917.* Pages 357–431. Washington, 1920.

Schafer, Joseph, ed. "Documents Relative to Warre and Vavasour's Military Reconnoissance in Oregon, 1845–46." *Oregon Historical Quarterly,* 10 (March 1909), 1–99.

Scott, Leslie M., ed. "Report of Lieutenant Peel on Oregon in 1845–46." *Oregon Historical Quarterly,* 29 (March 1928), 51–76.

Scott, Winfield. *Memoirs of Lieut.-General Scott, Ll.D.* 2 vols. New York, 1864.

[Sedgwick, Theodore, Jr.]. *Thoughts on the Proposed Annexation of Texas.* New York, 1844.

Semmes, Raphael. *Service Afloat and Ashore during the Mexican War.* Cincinnati, 1851.

[Senior, Nassau W.]. "The Oregon Question." *Edinburgh Review,* 82 (July 1845), 123–37.

Sierra O'Reilly, Justo. *Diario de nuestro viaje a los Estados Unidos (La pretendida anexión de Yucatán).* Edited by Héctor Pérez Martínez. México, 1938.

Simpson, Sir George. "Letters of Sir George Simpson, 1841–1843." Edited by Joseph Schafer. *American Historical Review,* 14 (October 1908), 70–94.

———. *Narrative of a Journey Round the World, during the Years 1841, and 1842.* 2 vols. London, 1847.

Sioussat, St. George L., ed. "Selected Letters, from the Donelson Papers." *Tennessee Historical Magazine,* 3 (1917), 134–63.

A Sketch of the Customs and Society of Mexico, in a Series of Familiar Letters; and a Journal of Travels in the Interior, during the Years 1824, 1825, 1826. London, 1828.

Smith, Ashbel. *An Address Delivered in the City of Galveston on the 22d of February, 1848, the Anniversary of the Birth Day of Washington, and of the Battle of Buena Vista.* Galveston, [1848].

———. *Reminiscences of the Texas Republic.* Galveston, 1872.

Sturgis, William. *The Oregon Question.* Boston, 1845.

Tayloe, Edward Thornton. *Mexico, 1825–1828, the Journal and Correspondence of Edward Thornton Tayloe.* Edited by C. Harvey Gardiner. Chapel Hill, N.C., 1959.

Taylor, John. *Selections from the Works of the Baron de [sic] Humboldt, Relating to the Climate, Inhabitants, Productions and Mines of Mexico.* London, 1824.

———. *Statements Respecting the Profits of Mining in England Considered in Relation to the Prospects of Mining in Mexico. In a Letter to Thomas Fowell Buxton, Esq., M.P.* London, 1825.

Taylor, Zachary. *Letters of Zachary Taylor from the Battle-fields of the Mexican War.* Rochester, N.Y., 1908.

Thompson, Waddy. *Recollections of Mexico.* New York and London, 1846.

Thümmel, A. R. *Mexiko und die Mexikaner, in physischer, socialer und politischer Beziehung, ein vollständiges Gemälde des alten und neuen Mexiko* [etc.]. [Erlangen, 1848].

Tocqueville, Alexis de. *Democracy in America.* Translated by Henry Reeves. 2 vols. in 1. New York, 1851.

Tyler, Lyon G. *The Letters and Times of the Tylers*. 3 vols. Richmond and Williamsburg, 1884–1896.

Walker, Robert J. *Letter of Mr. Walker, of Mississippi, Relative to the Annexation of Texas in Reply to the Call of the People of Carroll County, Kentucky, to Communicate His Views on That Subject*. Washington, 1844.

Ward, Henry George. *Mexico*. 2d ed. 2 vols. London, 1829.

Webster, Daniel. *The Letters of Daniel Webster from Documents Owned Principally by the New Hampshire Historical Society*. Edited by C. H. Van Tyne. New York, 1902.

——. *The Private Correspondence of Daniel Webster*. Edited by Fletcher Webster. 2 vols. Boston, 1857.

——. *The Works of Daniel Webster*. 6 vols. Boston, 1872.

Wilkes, Charles. *Narrative of the United States Exploring Expedition during the Years 1838, 1839, 1840, 1841, and 1842*. 5 vols. Philadelphia, 1845.

——. "Report on the Territory of Oregon." *Quarterly of the Oregon Historical Society*, 12 (1911), 269–99.

Wise, Henry A. *Los Gringos: or An Inside View of Mexico and California, with Wanderings in Peru, Chili, and Polynesia*. New York, 1850.

Wyllie, Robert Crichton. *Mexico. Report on its Finances under the Spanish Government; since Its Independence, and Prospects of Their Improvement; with Calculations on the Public Debt, Foreign and Domestic*. London, 1844.

3. DAILY NEWSPAPERS

United States

New York *Evening Post*
New York *Herald*
New York *Journal of Commerce*
New York *Sun*
Washington *Madisonian*
Washington *National Intelligencer*
Washington *Union*

Great Britain

London *Examiner*
London *Morning Chronicle*
London *Times*

France

Le constitutionnel (Paris)
Le journal des débats (Paris)
Le national (Paris)
La presse (Paris)

Mexico

El boletín de noticias (Mexico City)
El monitor republicano (Mexico City)
El razonador (Mexico City)
El republicano (Mexico City)
El siglo diez y nueve (Mexico City)
El tiempo (Mexico City)

4. OTHER PERIODICALS

American Review
Anglo-American
British Quarterly Review
Le correspondent
DeBow's Commercial Review
Dublin University Magazine
L'Illustration
Merchants' Magazine and Commercial Review
Niles' National Register
North American Review
Quarterly Mining Review
Quarterly Review
Southern Quarterly Review
United States Magazine and Democratic Review
Additional newspapers and periodicals not listed were used through clippings in public or private papers and reprints in other publications.

III. PUBLISHED SOURCES—SECONDARY

1. BOOKS

Adams, Ephraim Douglass. *British Interests and Activities in Texas, 1838–1846.* Baltimore, 1910.
Alamán, Lucas. *Historia de México desde los primeros movimientos que prepararon su independencia en el año de 1808, hasta la época presente.* 5 vols. México, 1885.
Alcaraz, Ramón, et al. *Apuntes para la historia de la guerra entre*

México y los Estados-Unidos. México, 1848; reprinted, México, 1952.

Alessio Robles, Vito. *Coahuila y Texas, desde la consumación de la Independencia hasta el Tratado de paz de Guadalupe Hidalgo.* 2 vols. México, 1946.

Allen, H. C. *Great Britain and the United States, a History of Anglo–American Relations (1783–1952).* New York, 1955.

Ambler, Charles H. *Life and Diary of John Floyd.* Richmond, 1918.

Arrangoiz y Berzábal, Francisco de P. de. *México desde 1808 hasta 1867.* 4 vols. Madrid, 1871–1872.

Bancroft, George. *History of the United States from the Discovery of the American Continent.* 10 vols. New York, 1834–1874.

Bancroft, Hubert H. *History of California.* 7 vols. San Francisco, 1884–1890.

————. *History of Mexico.* 6 vols. San Francisco, 1883–1888.

————. *History of the North Mexican States and Texas.* 2 vols. San Francisco, 1883–1889.

Barker, Eugene C. *Mexico and Texas, 1821–1835.* Dallas, 1928.

Barnes, Donald Grove. *A History of the English Corn Laws from 1660 to 1846.* London, 1930.

Barnes, Gilbert Hobbs. *The Anti-Slavery Impulse, 1830–1844.* New York, 1933.

Bartlett, C. J. *Great Britain and Sea Power, 1815–1853.* Oxford, 1963.

Bauer, K. Jack. *Surfboats and Horse Marines: U. S. Naval Operations in the Mexican War, 1846–48.* Annapolis, Md., 1969.

Bazant, Jan. *Historia de la deuda exterior de México (1823–1946).* México, 1968.

Bell, Herbert C. F. *Lord Palmerston.* 2 vols. London, 1936.

Bell, James C. *Opening a Highway to the Pacific, 1838–1846.* New York, 1921.

Bemis, Samuel F., ed. *American Secretaries of State and Their Diplomacy.* 10 vols. New York, 1927–1929.

————. *John Quincy Adams and the Foundations of American Foreign Policy.* New York, 1949.

————. *John Quincy Adams and the Union.* New York, 1956.

Benson, Nettie Lee. *La diputación provincial y el federalismo mexicano.* México, 1955.

Bill, Alfred Hoyt. *Rehearsal for Conflict, the War with Mexico, 1846–1848.* New York, 1947.

Binkley, William Campbell. *The Expansionist Movement in Texas, 1836–1850.* Berkeley, 1925.

————. *The Texas Revolution.* Baton Rouge, La., 1952.

Blake, Clagette. *Charles Elliot, R.N., 1801–1875, a Servant of Britain Overseas.* London, 1960.

Blumenthal, Henry. *A Reappraisal of Franco-American Relations, 1830–1871*. Chapel Hill, N.C., 1959.

Bosch García, Carlos. *Historia de las relaciones entre México y los Estados Unidos, 1819–1848*. México, 1961.

———. *Problemas diplomáticas de México independiente*. México, 1947.

Bourne, Kenneth. *Britain and the Balance of Power in North America, 1815–1908*. Berkeley and Los Angeles, 1967.

Brauer, Kinley J. *Cotton versus Conscience: Massachusetts Whig Politics and Southwestern Expansion, 1843–1848*. Lexington, Ky., 1967.

Bravo Ugarte, José. *Historia de México*. 4 vols. México, 1941–1959.

Brookes, Jean Ingram. *International Rivalry in the Pacific Islands, 1800–1875*. Berkeley and Los Angeles, 1941.

Buck, Norman Sydney. *The Development of the Organization of Anglo–American Trade, 1800–1850*. New Haven, 1925.

Cady, John F. *Foreign Interventions in the Rio de la Plata, 1838–1850*. Philadelphia, 1929.

Callahan, James Morton. *American Foreign Policy in Mexican Relations*. New York, 1932.

Callcott, Wilfrid Hardy. *Church and State in Mexico, 1822–1857*. Durham, N.C., 1926.

———. *Santa Anna, the Story of an Enigma Who Once Was Mexico*. Norman, Okla., 1936.

Carey, Charles H. *A General History of Oregon Prior to 1861*. Portland, Ore., 1936.

Carreño, Alberto María. *La diplomacia extraordinaria entre México y Estados Unidos, 1789–1947*. 2 vols. México, 1951.

Caughey, John W. *California*. New York, 1940.

Chambers, William Nisbet. *Old Bullion Benton, Senator from the New West*. Boston, 1956.

Chase, Mary Katherine. *Négociations de la République du Texas en Europe, 1837–1845*. Paris, 1932.

Christian, Asa Kyrus. *Mirabeau Buonaparte Lamar*. Austin, 1922.

Clapham, J. H. *An Economic History of Modern Britain*. 3 vols. Cambridge, 1926–1938.

Clark, Robert C. *History of the Willamette Valley, Oregon*. Chicago, 1927.

Clarke, Dwight L. *Stephen Watts Kearny, Soldier of the West*. Norman, Okla., 1961.

Cleland, Robert Glass. *From Wilderness to Empire: a History of California, 1542–1900*. New York, 1944.

———. *A History of California: the American Period*. New York, 1922.

Cole, Arthur Charles. *The Whig Party in the South*. Washington, 1914.

Connor, Seymour V., and Odie B. Faulk. *North America Divided. The Mexican War, 1846–1848*. New York, 1971.

Corey, Albert B. *The Crisis of 1830–1842 in Canadian-American Relations*. New Haven, 1941.

Cotner, Thomas Ewing. *The Military and Political Career of José Joaquín de Herrera, 1792–1854*. Austin, 1949.

Cue Cánovas, Agustín. *Historia social y económica de México (1521–1854)*. 3d ed. México, 1967.

Cuevas, Mariano. *Historia de la nación mexicana*. México, 1940.

Curtis, George Ticknor. *Life of James Buchanan, Fifteenth President of the United States*. 2 vols. New York, 1883.

Dangerfield, George. *The Era of Good Feelings*. New York, 1953.

Delgado, Jaime. *España y México en el siglo XIX*. 3 vols. Madrid, 1950.

DeVoto, Bernard. *The Year of Decision, 1846*. Boston, 1942.

Dictionary of National Biography. Edited by L. Stephen, Sir S. Lee, *et al*. Rev. ed. 22 vols. Oxford, 1921–1922.

Dillon, Richard. *Fool's Gold. The Decline and Fall of Captain John Sutter of California*. New York, 1967.

Donald, David. *Charles Sumner and the Coming of the Civil War*. New York, 1960.

Downey, Joseph T. *The Cruise of the Portsmouth, 1845–1847. A Sailor's View of the Naval Conquest of California*. Edited by Howard Lamar. New Haven, 1958.

Dyer, Brainerd. *Zachary Taylor*. Baton Rouge, La., 1946.

Elliott, Charles Winslow. *Winfield Scott, the Soldier and the Man*. New York, 1937.

Estep, Raymond. *Lorenzo de Zavala, profeta del liberalismo mexicano*. México, 1952.

Favre, Jean-Paul. *L'éxpansion française dans le Pacifique de 1800 à 1842*. Paris, 1953.

Fehrenbacher, Don E. *Chicago Giant, a Biography of "Long John" Wentworth*. Madison, 1957.

Foner, Philip S. *Business and Slavery; the New York Merchants and the Irrepressible Conflict*. Chapel Hill, N.C., 1941.

Friend, Llerena. *Sam Houston, the Great Designer*. Austin, 1954.

Fuentes Díaz, Vicente. *Gómez Farías, padre de la reforma*. México, 1948.

———. *La intervención norteamericana en Mexico (1847)*. México, 1947.

Fuentes Mares, José. *Poinsett, historia de una gran intriga*. 3d ed. México, 1960.

———. *Santa Anna, aurora y ocaso de un comediante*. México, 1956.

Fuller, George W. *A History of the Pacific Northwest*. 2d ed. New York, 1938.

Fuller, John Douglas Pitts. *The Movement for the Acquisition of All Mexico, 1846–1848.* Baltimore, 1936.

Galbraith, John S. *The Hudson's Bay Company As an Imperial Factor, 1821–1869.* Berkeley, 1957.

Gambrell, Herbert. *Anson Jones, the Last President of Texas.* New York, 1948.

————. *Mirabeau Buonaparte Lamar, Troubadour and Crusader.* Dallas, 1934.

Gaxiola, F. Jorge. *Mariano Otero (Creador del juicio del amparo).* México, 1937.

Gayarré, Charles. *History of Louisiana, the French Domination.* 4 vols. New Orleans, 1885.

Génin, Auguste. *Les français au Mexique du XVIᵉ siècle à nos jours.* Paris, [1933].

Goetzmann, William H. *Army Exploration in the American West, 1803–1863.* New Haven, 1959.

————. *Exploration and Empire: the Explorer and the Scientist in the Winning of the American West.* New York, 1966.

Going, Charles Buxton. *David Wilmot, Free-Soiler.* New York, 1924.

González Navarro, Moisés. *El pensamiento político de Lucas Alamán.* México, [1952].

Goodwin, Cardinal. *John Charles Frémont, an Explanation of His Career.* Palo Alto, 1930.

————. *The Trans-Mississippi West (1803–1853).* New York, 1922.

Govan, Thomas Payne. *Nicholas Biddle, Nationalist and Public Banker, 1786–1844.* Chicago, 1959.

Graebner, Norman A. *Empire on the Pacific; a Study in American Continental Expansion.* New York, 1955.

Greenberg, Michael. *British Trade and the Opening of China, 1800–42.* Cambridge, 1951.

Guedalla, Philip. *Palmerston, 1784–1865.* London, 1927.

Hale, Charles A. *Mexican Liberalism in the Age of Mora, 1821–1853.* New Haven, 1968.

Halévy, Élie. *The Age of Peel and Cobden, a History of the English People, 1841–1852.* New York, 1948.

————. *The Triumph of Reform, a History of the English People, 1830–1841.* 2d ed. London, 1950.

Hall, Claude H. *Abel Parker Upshur, Conservative Virginian.* Madison, 1963.

Hall, John. *England and the Orleans Monarchy.* London, 1912.

Hamilton, Holman. *Zachary Taylor.* 2 vols. Indianapolis and New York, 1941–1951.

Hammond, Bray. *Banks and Politics in America from the Revolution to the Civil War.* Princeton, 1957.

Hawgood, John A. *First and Last Consul: Thomas Oliver Larkin and the Americanization of California.* San Marino, Calif., 1952.

Henry, Robert Selph. *The Story of the Mexican War.* New York, 1950.

Hidy, Ralph W. *The House of Baring in American Trade and Finance. English Merchant Bankers at Work, 1763–1861.* Cambridge, Mass., 1949.

Hill, Jim Dan. *The Texas Navy in Forgotten Battles and Shirtsleeve Diplomacy.* Chicago, 1937.

Hittell, John S. *History of the City of San Francisco.* San Francisco, 1878.

Holt, Edgar. *The Opium Wars in China.* Chester Springs, Pennsylvania, 1964.

Howay, F. W., W. N. Sage, and H. F. Angus. *British Columbia and the United States.* Edited by H. F. Angus. Toronto, 1942.

Hunt, Rockwell D. *John Bidwell, a Prince of California Pioneers.* Caldwell, Ida., 1942.

Hutchinson, C. Alan. *Frontier Settlement in Mexican California: the Hijar-Padres Colony and Its Origins, 1769–1835.* New Haven, 1969.

Imlah, Albert H. *Economic Elements in the Pax Britannica: Studies in British Foreign Trade in the Nineteenth Century.* Cambridge, Mass., 1958.

———. *Lord Ellenborough, a Biography of Edward Law, Earl of Ellenborough, Governor-General of India.* Cambridge, Mass., 1939.

Jenks, Leland Hamilton. *The Migration of British Capital to 1875.* New York, 1927.

Johanson, Dorothy O., and Charles M. Gates. *Empire of the Columbia. A History of the Pacific Northwest.* 2d ed. New York, 1967.

Jones, Wilbur Devereux. *Lord Aberdeen and the Americas.* Athens, Ga., 1958.

Klein, Philip Shriver. *President James Buchanan, a Biography.* University Park, Pa., 1962.

Kohl, Clayton Charles. *Claims As a Cause of the Mexican War.* New York, 1914.

Kuykendall, Ralph S. *The Hawaiian Kingdom, 1778–1854: Foundation and Transformation.* Honolulu, 1947.

Lambert, Oscar Doane. *Presidential Politics in the United States, 1841–1844.* Durham, N.C., 1936.

Lavender, David. *Climax at Buena Vista: the American Campaigns in Northeastern Mexico, 1846–47.* Philadelphia and New York, 1966.

Lewis, Charles Lee. *David Glasgow Farragut, Admiral in the Making.* Annapolis, Md., 1941.

Logan, John A., Jr. *No Transfer, an American Security Principle*. New Haven, 1961.

Loomis, Noel M. *The Texan-Santa Fe Pioneers*. Norman, Okla., 1958.

López Cámara, Francisco. *La estructura económica y social de México en la época de la Reforma*. México, 1967.

Lyman, George D. *John Marsh, Pioneer*. New York, 1930.

McCabe, James O. *The San Juan Water Boundary Question*. Toronto, 1964.

McCormac, Eugene Irving. *James K. Polk, a Political Biography*. Berkeley, 1922.

McCoy, Charles A. *Polk and the Presidency*. Austin, 1960.

McGrane, Reginald Charles. *Foreign Bondholders and American State Debts*. New York, 1935.

————. *The Panic of 1837, Some Financial Problems of the Jacksonian Era*. Chicago, 1924.

————. *William Allen, a Study in Western Democracy*. Columbus, 1925.

McLemore, Richard Aubrey. *Franco-American Diplomatic Relations, 1816–1836*. University, La., 1941.

McMaster, John Bach. *A History of the People of the United States, from the Revolution to the Civil War*. 8 vols. New York, 1883–1913.

McReynolds, Edwin C. *The Seminoles*. Norman, Okla., 1957.

Marshall, Thomas Maitland. *A History of the Western Boundary of the Louisiana Purchase, 1819–1841*. Berkeley, 1914.

Marti, Werner H. *Messenger of Destiny: the California Adventures, 1846–1847, of Archibald Gillespie, U. S. Marine Corps*. San Francisco, 1960.

Merk, Frederick, *Fruits of Propaganda in the Tyler Administration*, with the collaboration of Lois Bannister Merk. Cambridge, Mass., 1971.

————. *Manifest Destiny and Mission in American History, a Reinterpretation*. With the collaboration of Lois Bannister Merk. New York, 1963.

————. *The Monroe Doctrine and American Expansionism, 1843–1849*. With the collaboration of Lois Bannister Merk. New York, 1966.

————. *The Oregon Question, Essays in Anglo-American Diplomacy and Politics*. Cambridge, Mass., 1967.

————. *Slavery and the Annexation of Texas*. With the collaboration of Lois Bannister Merk. New York, 1972.

Micard, Etienne. *La France au Mexique, étude sur les expéditions militaires, l'influence, le rôle économique de la France au Mexique*. Paris, 1927.

633

Morison, Samuel Eliot. *"Old Bruin," Commodore Matthew Calbraith Perry, 1794–1858.* Boston, 1967.

Morrison, Chaplain W. *Democratic Politics and Sectionalism: the Wilmot Proviso Controversy.* Chapel Hill, N.C., 1967.

Morton, Ohland. *Terán and Texas: a Chapter in Texas-Mexican Relations.* Austin, 1948.

Mowat, R. B. *Americans in England.* Boston, 1935.

Muñoz, Rafael F. *Santa Anna, el que todo lo ganó y todo lo perdió.* Madrid, 1936.

Nance, Joseph Milton. *Attack and Counter-attack, the Texas-Mexican Frontier, 1842.* Austin, 1964.

————. *After San Jacinto, the Texas-Mexican Frontier, 1836–1841.* Austin, 1963.

Nasatir, Abraham P. *French Activities in California, an Archival Calendar-Guide.* Stanford, 1945.

Nevins, Allan. *The Emergence of Lincoln.* 2 vols. New York, 1950.

————. *Frémont, Pathmarker of the West.* New York, 1939.

————. *Frémont, the World's Greatest Adventurer.* 2 vols. New York, 1928.

————. *Ordeal of the Union.* 2 vols. New York, 1947.

————, ed. *America through British Eyes.* New York, 1948.

Nichols, Edward J. *Zach Taylor's Little Army.* New York, 1963.

Nye, Russell B. *George Bancroft, Brahmin Rebel.* New York, 1944.

O'Connor, Thomas H. *Lords of the Loom: The Cotton Whigs and the Coming of the Civil War.* New York, 1968.

Ogden, Adele. *The California Sea Otter Trade, 1784–1848.* Berkeley and Los Angeles, 1941.

Parkes, Henry Bamford. *A History of Mexico.* Boston, 1938.

Paul, James C. N. *Rift in the Democracy.* Philadelphia, 1951.

Pereyra, Carlos. *Tejas, la primera dismembración de Méjico.* Madrid, [1917?].

Perkins, Bradford. *Castlereagh and Adams: England and the United States, 1812–1823.* Berkeley and Los Angeles, 1964.

Perkins, Dexter. *The Monroe Doctrine, 1826–1867.* Baltimore, 1933.

Poage, George Rawlings. *Henry Clay and the Whig Party.* Chapel Hill, N.C., 1936.

Potash, Robert A. *El banco de avío de México. El fomento de la industria, 1821–1846.* México, 1959.

Price, Glenn W. *Origins of the War with Mexico: the Polk-Stockton Intrigue.* Austin, 1967.

Randall, Robert W. *Real del Monte, A British Mining Venture in Mexico.* Austin, 1972.

Rauch, Basil. *American Interest in Cuba, 1848–1855.* New York, 1948.

Reeves, Jesse. *American Diplomacy under Tyler and Polk.* Baltimore, 1907.

Rhodes, James Ford. *History of the United States from the Compromise of 1850.* 7 vols. New York, 1892–1922.

Rich, E. E. *The History of the Hudson's Bay Company, 1670–1870.* 2 vols. London, 1959.

Richman, Irving Berdine. *California under Spain and Mexico, 1535–1847.* Boston and New York, 1911.

Rippy, J. Fred. *Rivalry of the United States and Great Britain over Latin America (1808–1830).* Baltimore, 1929.

———. *The United States and Mexico.* Rev. ed. New York, 1931.

Riva Palacio, Vicente. *México a través de los siglos. Historia general y completa del desenvolvimiento social, político, religioso, militar, artístico, científico y literario de México desde la antigüedad más remota hasta la época actual.* 5 vols. México, [1887–1889].

Rivera Cambas, Manuel. *Los gobernantes de México.* 2 vols. México, 1872–1873.

Rives, George Lockhart. *The United States and Mexico, 1821–1848.* 2 vols. New York, 1913.

Roa Bárcena, José María. *Recuerdos de la invasión norteamericana (1846–1848).* Edited by Antonio Castro Leal. Rev. ed. 3 vols. México, 1883; reprinted, México, 1947.

Robertson, William Spence. *France and Latin American Independence.* Baltimore, 1939.

———. *Iturbide of Mexico.* Durham, N.C., 1952.

Rogers, Fred Blackburn. *Montgomery and the Portsmouth.* San Francisco, 1958.

Royce, Josiah. *California from the Conquest in 1846 to the Second Vigilance Committee in San Francisco, a Study of American Character.* Edited by R. G. Cleland. New York, 1948.

Russel, Robert R. *Improvement of Communications with the Pacific Coast As an Issue in American Politics, 1783–1864.* Cedar Rapids, Iowa, 1948.

Sage, W. N. *Sir James Douglas and British Columbia.* Toronto, 1930.

Santovenia, Emeterio S. *El Presidente Polk y Cuba.* 2d ed. La Habana, 1936.

Schafer, Joseph. *A History of the Pacific Northwest.* Rev. ed. New York, 1918.

Schefer, Christian. *La France moderne et le problème coloniale.* Paris, 1907.

Schlesinger, Arthur M., Jr. *A Thousand Days.* Boston, 1965.

———. *The Age of Jackson.* New York, 1945.

Schmitz, Joseph William. *Texan Statecraft, 1836–1845.* San Antonio, 1941.

Schouler, James. *History of the United States of America under the Constitution.* 7 vols. New York, 1880–1913.

Schuyler, Robert Livingston. *The Fall of the Old Colonial System, a Study in British Free Trade, 1770–1870.* New York, 1945.

Seager, Robert, II. *and Tyler Too, a Biography of John & Julia Gardiner Tyler.* New York, 1963.

Sears, Louis M. *John Slidell.* Durham, N.C., 1925.

Sellers, Charles Grier. *James K. Polk, Continentalist: 1843–1846.* Princeton, 1966.

——. *James K. Polk, Jacksonian: 1795–1843.* Princeton, 1957.

Shenton, James Patrick. *Robert John Walker, a Politician from Jackson to Lincoln.* New York, 1961.

Sherman, Edwin A. *Life of the Late Rear Admiral John Drake Sloat of the United States Navy* [etc.]. Oakland, Calif., 1902.

Siegel, Stanley. *A Political History of the Texas Republic, 1836–1845.* Austin, 1956.

Silbey, Joel H. *The Shrine of Party: Congressional Voting Behavior, 1841–1852.* Pittsburgh, 1967.

Silver, James W. *Edmund Pendleton Gaines, Frontier General.* Baton Rouge, La., 1949.

Smith, Justin H. *The Annexation of Texas.* Rev. ed. New York, 1941.

——. *The War with Mexico.* 2 vols. New York, 1919.

Sosa, Francisco, *Biografías de mexicanos distinguidos.* México, 1884.

Soulsby, Hugh G. *The Right of Search and the Slave Trade in Anglo-American Relations, 1814–1862.* Baltimore, 1933.

Southgate, Donald. *"The Most English Minister . . . ," the Policies and Politics of Palmerston.* London, 1966.

Spencer, Ivor Debenham. *The Victor and the Spoils, a Life of William L. Marcy.* Providence, R.I., 1959.

Stacey, Charles P. *Canada and the British Army, 1846–1871.* London, 1936.

Stanmore, Arthur Hamilton-Gordon. *The Earl of Aberdeen.* London, 1905.

Stanwood, Edward. *American Tariff Controversies in the Nineteenth Century.* 2 vols. Boston, 1903.

Stapleton, Augustus Granville. *George Canning and His Times.* London, 1859.

Swain, James Edgar. *The Struggle for the Control of the Mediterranean Prior to 1848, a Study in Anglo-French Relations.* Boston, 1933.

Sydnor, Charles S. *The Development of Southern Sectionalism, 1819–1848.* Baton Rouge, La., 1948.

Taylor, George Rogers. *The Transportation Revolution, 1815–1860.* New York, 1951.

Temperley, Harold W. V. *The Foreign Policy of Canning, 1822–1827: England, the Neo-Holy Alliance and the New World.* London, 1925.

Thistlethwaite, Frank. *The Anglo-American Connection in the Early Nineteenth Century*. Philadelphia, 1959.

Toro, Alfonso. *La Iglesia y el estado en México (Estudio sobre los conflictos entre el clero católico y los gobiernos mexicanos desde la Independencia hasta nuestros dias)*. México, 1927.

Turlington, Edgar. *Mexico and Her Foreign Creditors*. New York, 1930.

Tyler, Alice Felt. *Freedom's Ferment: Phases of American Social History from the Colonial Period to the Outbreak of the Civil War*. Minneapolis, 1944.

Tyler, David B. *The Wilkes Expedition: the First United States Exploring Expedition (1838–1842)*. Philadelphia, 1968.

Underhill, Reuben L. *From Cowhides to Golden Fleece*. 2d ed. Stanford, 1946.

Valadés, José C. *Breve historia de la guerra con los Estados Unidos*. México, 1947.

———. *Santa Anna y la guerra de Texas*. 3d ed. México, 1965.

Van Alstyne, Richard W. *The Rising American Empire*. New York, 1960.

Van Deusen, Glyndon G. *The Jacksonian Era, 1828–1848*. New York, 1959.

Vasconcelos, José. *Breve historia de México*. México, 1956.

Von Holst, Hermann. *The Constitutional and Political History of the United States*. 8 vols. Chicago, 1881–1892.

Wallace, Edward S. *Destiny and Glory*. New York, 1957.

———. *General William Jenkins Worth, Monterey's Forgotten Hero*. Dallas, 1953.

Ward, A. W., and G. P. Gooch, eds. *The Cambridge History of British Foreign Policy, 1783–1919*. 3 vols. New York, 1923.

Weinberg, Albert K. *Manifest Destiny, a Study of Nationalist Expansionism in American History*. Baltimore, 1935.

Wells, Tom Henderson. *Commodore Moore and the Texas Navy*. Austin, 1960.

Williams, Elgin. *The Animating Pursuits of Speculation: Land Traffic in the Annexation of Texas*. New York, 1949.

Williams, Mary W. *Anglo-American Isthmian Diplomacy, 1815–1915*. Washington, 1916.

Willson, Beckles. *America's Ambassadors to England (1785–1920), a Narrative of Anglo-American Diplomatic Relations*. London, 1928.

———. *Friendly Relations, a Narrative of Britain's Ministers and Ambassadors to America (1791–1930)*. London, 1934.

———. *The Paris Embassy, a Narrative of Franco-British Diplomatic Relations, 1814–1920*. London, 1927.

Wiltse, Charles M. *John C. Calhoun, Sectionalist, 1840–1850.* Indianapolis, 1951.

Wiltsee, Ernest A. *The Truth about Frémont: an Inquiry.* San Francisco, 1936.

Winther, Oscar Osburn. *The Great Northwest: a History.* New York, 1947.

Wisehart, M. K. *Sam Houston, American Giant.* Washington, 1962.

Woodford, Frank B. *Lewis Cass, the Last Jeffersonian.* New Brunswick, N.J., 1950.

Woodham-Smith, Blanche Cecil. *The Great Hunger, Ireland, 1845–9.* London, 1962.

Woodward, E. L. *The Age of Reform, 1815–1870.* Oxford, 1938.

Zamacois, Niceto de. *Historia de Méjico desde sus tiempos más remotas hasta nuestros días.* 22 vols. Barcelona and México, 1878–1902.

Zollinger, James P. *Sutter: the Man and His Empire.* New York, 1939.

Zorrilla, Luis G. *Historia de las relaciones entre México y los Estados Unidos de América, 1800–1958.* 2 vols. México, 1965–1966.

2. ARTICLES

Adams, Ephraim D. "English Interest in the Annexation of California." *American Historical Review,* 14 (July 1909), 744–63.

Armond, Louis de. "Justo Sierra O'Reilly and Yucatecan-United States Relations, 1847–1848." *Hispanic American Historical Review,* 31 (August 1951), 420–36.

Barker, Eugene C. "The Annexation of Texas." *Southwestern Historical Quarterly,* 50 (July 1946), 49–74.

———. "California As a Cause of the Mexican War." *Texas Review,* 2 (January 1917), 213–21.

———. "The Finances of the Texas Revolution." *Political Science Quarterly,* 19 (December 1904), 612–35.

———. "The Influence of Slavery in the Colonization of Texas." *Mississippi Valley Historical Review,* 11 (June 1924), 3–36.

———. "Land Speculation As a Cause of the Texas Revolution." *Texas Historical Quarterly,* 10 (July 1906), 76–95.

———. "On the Historiography of American Territorial Expansion." In *The Trans-Mississippi West,* edited by James F. Willard and Colin B. Goodykoontz, pp. 219–47. Boulder, Colo., 1930.

———. "President Jackson and the Texas Revolution." *American Historical Review,* 12 (July 1907), 788–809.

———. "The United States and Mexico, 1835–1837." *Mississippi Valley Historical Review,* 1 (June 1914), 3–30.

Bauer, K. Jack. "The United States Navy and Texan Independence: a Study in Jacksonian Integrity." *Military Affairs,* 35 (April 1970), 44–48.

Baur, John E. "The Evolution of a Mexican Foreign Trade Policy, 1821–1828." *The Americas*, 19 (January 1963), 225–61.

Berge, Dennis E. "A Mexican Dilemma: the Mexico City Ayuntamiento and the Question of Loyalty, 1846–1848." *Hispanic American Historical Review*, 50 (May 1970), 229–56.

Blue, [George] Verne. "The Oregon Question—1818–1828." *Quarterly of the Oregon Historical Society*, 23 (1922), 193–219.

Bosch García, Carlos. "Dos diplomacias y un problema." *Historia mexicana*, 2 (1952), 46–65.

Boucher, Chauncey W. "In Re That Aggressive Slaveocracy." *Mississippi Valley Historical Review*, 8 (June–September 1921), 13–79.

Bourne, Edward G. "The Proposed Absorption of Mexico in 1847–48." *Annual Report of the American Historical Association for the Year 1899* (Washington, 1900), 157–69.

Boyd, Mark F. "The Seminole War: Its Background and Onset." *Florida Historical Quarterly*, 30 (July 1951), 3–115.

Brack, Gene M. "Mexican Opinion, American Racism, and the War of 1846." *Western Historical Quarterly*, 1 (April 1970), 161–74.

Brauer, Kinley J. "The Massachusetts State Texas Committee: a Last Stand against the Annexation of Texas." *Journal of American History*, 51 (September 1964), 214–31.

Bravo Ugarte, José. "La misión confidencial de Moses Y. Beach en 1847 y el clero mexicano." *Abside*, 12 (1948), 476–96.

Brooke, George M., Jr. "The Vest Pocket War of Commodore Jones." *Pacific Historical Review*, 31 (August 1962), 217–33.

Castañeda, Carlos E. "Relations of General Scott with Santa Anna." *Hispanic American Historical Review*, 29 (November 1949), 455–73.

Chamberlin, Eugene K. "Nicholas Trist and Baja California." *Pacific Historical Review*, 32 (February 1963), 49–63.

Clark, Robert C. "How British and American Subjects United in a Common Government for Oregon Territory in 1844." *Quarterly of the Oregon Historical Society*, 13 (1912), 140–59.

Cleaves, W. S. "Lorenzo de Zavala in Texas." *Southwestern Historical Quarterly*, 35 (July 1932), 29–40.

Cleland, Robert Glass. "The Early Sentiment for the Annexation of California: an Account of the Growth of American Interest in California, 1835–1846." *Southwestern Historical Quarterly*, 18 (July, October 1914), 1–40, 231–60.

Commager, Henry S. "England and [the] Oregon Treaty of 1846." *Oregon Historical Quarterly*, 28 (March 1927), 18–38.

Costeloe, Michael P. "The Mexican Church and the Rebellion of the Polkos." *Hispanic American Historical Review*, 46 (May 1966), 170–78.

Coughlin, Sister Magdalen. "California Ports: a Key to Diplomacy for the West Coast, 1820–1845." *Journal of the West*, 5 (April 1966), 153–72.

Cramer, Richard S. "British Magazines and the Oregon Question." *Pacific Historical Review*, 32 (May 1963), 369–82.

Cunningham, A. B. "Peel, Aberdeen and the *Entente Cordiale*." *Bulletin of the Institute of Historical Research*, 30 (November 1957), 189–206.

Current, Richard N. "Webster's Propaganda and the Ashburton Treaty." *Mississippi Valley Historical Review*, 34 (September 1947), 187–200.

Davies, Thomas M., Jr. "Assessments during the Mexican War: an Exercise in Futility." *New Mexico Historical Review*, 41 (July 1966), 197–216.

Delgado, Jaime. "España y el monarquismo mexicano en 1840." *Revista de Indias*, 13 (1953), 57–80.

Denton, Bernice Barnett. "Count Alphonse de Saligny and the Franco-Texienne Bill." *Southwestern Historical Quarterly*, 45 (October 1941), 136–46.

Dodd, William E. "The West and the War with Mexico." *Journal of the Illinois State Historical Society*, 5 (July 1912).

D'Olwer, Luis Nicolau. "Santa Anna y la invasión vistos por Bermúdez de Castro." *Historia mexicana*, 4 (Julio–Septiembre 1954), 47–65.

Duniway, C. A. "Daniel Webster and the West." *Minnesota History*, 9 (March 1928), 3–15.

Edwards, Herbert Rook. "Diplomatic Relations between France and the Republic of Texas." *Southwestern Historical Quarterly*, 20 (January, April 1917), 209–41, 341–47.

Ellison, Joseph. "The Sentiment for a Pacific Republic, 1843–1862." *Proceedings of the Pacific Coast Branch of the American Historical Association, 1929*, [Los Angeles(?) 1930(?)], pp. 94–118.

Ellsworth, C. S. "The American Churches and the Mexican War." *American Historical Review*, 45 (January 1940), 301–26.

Engelson, Lester G. "Proposals for the Colonization of California by England in Connection with the Mexican Debt to British Bondholders, 1837–1846." *California Historical Society Quarterly*, 18 (June 1939), 136–48.

Esquenazi-Mayo, Roberto. "Historiografía de la guerra entre México y los EE. UU." *Duquesne Hispanic Review*, 1 (Fall, Winter 1962), 33–48, 7–35.

Farnham, Thomas J. "Nicholas Trist & James Freaner and the Mission to Mexico." *Arizona and the West*, 11 (Autumn 1969), 247–60.

Flaccus, Elmer W. "Guadalupe Victoria, the Good Neighbor." In *Essays in Mexican History*, edited by Thomas E. Cotner and Carlos E. Castañeda, pp. 104–12. Austin, 1958.

Foner, Eric. "The Wilmot Proviso Revisited." *Journal of American History*, 56 (September 1969), 262–79.

Franklin, John Hope. "The Southern Expansionists of 1846." *Journal of Southern History*, 25 (August 1959), 323–38.

Frantz, Joe B. "The Mercantile House of McKinney and Williams, Underwriters of the Texas Revolution." *Bulletin of the Business Historical Society*, 26 (March 1952), 1–18.

Galbraith, John S. "France As a Factor in the Oregon Negotiations." *Pacific Northwest Quarterly*, 44 (April 1953), 69–73.

———. "A Note on the British Fur Trade in California, 1821–1846." *Pacific Historical Review*, 24 (August 1955), 253–60.

García Gutiérrez, Jesús. "El clero durante la guerra de 1847." *Abside*, 5 (1941), 264–69, 391–95.

Garrison, George Pierce. "The First Stage of the Movement for the Annexation of Texas." *American Historical Review*, 10 (October 1904), 72–96.

Gerhard, Peter. "Baja California in the Mexican War, 1846–1848." *Pacific Historical Review*, 14 (December 1945), 418–24.

Goldin, Gurston. "Business Sentiment and the Mexican War with Particular Emphasis on the New York Businessman." *New York History*, 33 (January 1952), 54–70.

Gough, Barry M. "H.M.S. *America* on the North Pacific Coast." *Oregon Historical Quarterly*, 70 (December 1969), 293–311.

Graebner, Norman A. "American Interest in California, 1845." *Pacific Historical Review*, 22 (February 1953), 13–27.

———. "Maritime Factors in the Oregon Compromise." *Pacific Historical Review*, 20 (1951), 331–45.

———. "Party Politics and the Trist Mission." *Journal of Southern History*, 19 (May 1953), 137–56.

Green, Fletcher M. "Duff Green, Militant Journalist of the Old School." *American Historical Review*, 52 (January 1947), 247–54.

Hale, Charles A. "The War with the United States and the Crisis in Mexican Thought." *The Americas*, 14 (October 1957), 153–73.

Harstad, Peter T., and Richard W. Resh. "The Causes of the Mexican War, a Note on Changing Interpretations." *Arizona and the West*, 6 (Winter 1964), 289–302.

Hatheway, C. G. "Commodore Jones's War." *History Today*, 16 (March 1966), 194–201.

Hawgood, John A. "Friedrich von Roenne—a German Tocqueville, and His Reports from the United States in 1848 and 1849." *University of Birmingham Historical Journal*, 3 (1951), 79–94.

———. "The Pattern of Yankee Infiltration in Mexican Alta California, 1821–1846." *Pacific Historical Review*, 27 (1958), 27–37.

High, James. "Jones at Monterey, 1842." *Journal of the West*, 5 (April 1966), 173–86.

Hinckley, Ted C. "American Anti-Catholicism during the Mexican War." *Pacific Historical Review*, 31 (May 1962), 121–37.

Howren, Alleine. "Causes and Origin of the Decree of April 6, 1830." *Southwestern Historical Quarterly*, 16 (April 1913), 378–422.

Husband, Michael B. "Senator Lewis F. Linn and the Oregon Question." *Missouri Historical Review*, 66 (October 1971), 1–19.

Hussey, John Adam. "The Origin of the Gillespie Mission." *California Historical Society Quarterly*, 19 (March 1940), 43–58.

Hutchinson, C. Alan. "Mexican Federalists in New Orleans and the Texas Revolution." *Louisiana Historical Quarterly*, 39 (1956), 1–47.

———. "Valentín Gómez Farías and the Movement for the Return of General Santa Anna to Texas in 1846." In *Essays in Mexican History*, edited by Thomas E. Cotner and Carlos E. Castañeda, pp. 169–91. Austin, 1958.

———. "Valentín Gómez Farías and the 'Secret Pact of New Orleans'." *Hispanic American Historical Review*, 36 (November 1956), 471–89.

Johnson, C. T. "Daniel Webster and Old Oregon." *Washington Historical Quarterly*, 2 (1907–1908), 6–11.

———. "Daniel Webster, Lord Ashburton and Old Oregon." *Washington Historical Quarterly*, 1 (1906–1907), 208–16.

Jones, Okah L. "The Pacific Squadron and the Conquest of California, 1846–1847." *Journal of the West*, 5 (April 1966), 187–202.

Jones, Wilbur Devereux. "Lord Ashburton and the Maine Boundary Negotiations." *Mississippi Valley Historical Review*, 40 (December 1953), 477–90.

Jones, Wilbur Devereux, and J. Chal. Vinson. "British Preparedness and the Oregon Settlement." *Pacific Historical Review*, 22 (1953), 353–64.

Jordon, H. D. "A Politician of Expansion: Robert J. Walker." *Mississippi Valley Historical Review*, 19 (1932–1933), 362–81.

Kelsey, Rayner Wickersham. "The United States Consulate in California." *Academy of Pacific Coast History*, 1 (1910), 161–267.

Knapp, Frank A., Jr. "John Quincy Adams, ¿Defensor de México?" *Historia mexicana*, 7 (July–September 1957), 116–23.

———. "The Mexican Fear of Manifest Destiny in California." In *Essays in Mexican History*, edited by Thomas E. Cotner and Carlos E. Castañeda, pp. 192–208. Austin, 1958.

———. "Preludios de la pérdida de California." *Historia mexicana*, 4 (October–December 1954), 235–49.

Le Duc, Thomas. "The Maine Frontier and the Northeastern Boundary Controversy." *American Historical Review*, 53 (October 1947), 30–41.

———. "The Webster-Ashburton Treaty and the Minnesota Iron Ranges." *Journal of American History*, 51 (December 1964), 476–81.

Lofgren, Charles A. "Force and Diplomacy, 1846–1848: the View from Washington." *Military Affairs*, 31 (Summer 1967), 57–64.

McCabe, James O. "Arbitration and the Oregon Compromise." *Canadian Historical Review*, 41 (December 1960), 308–27.

McCornack, Richard Blaine. "The San Patricio Deserters in the Mexican War." *The Americas*, 8 (October 1951), 131–42.

McElhannon, Joseph Carl. "Relations between Imperial Mexico and the United States, 1821–1823." In *Essays in Mexican History*, edited by Thomas E. Cotner and Carlos E. Castañeda, pp. 127–41. Austin, 1958.

McLemore, Richard Aubrey. "The Influence of French Diplomatic Policy on the Annexation of Texas." *Southwestern Historical Quarterly*, 43 (January 1940), 342–47.

Mannix, Richard. "Albert Gallatin and the Movement for Peace with Mexico." *Social Studies*, 60 (December 1969), 310–18.

Marshall, Thomas Maitland. "Commercial Aspects of the Texan Santa Fe Expedition." *Southwestern Historical Quarterly*, 20 (January 1917), 242–59.

———. "The Southwestern Boundary of Texas, 1821–1840." *Texas Historical Quarterly*, 14 (April 1911), 155–63.

Martin, Thomas P. "Cotton and Wheat in Anglo-American Trade and Politics, 1846–1852." *Journal of Southern History*, 1 (August 1935), 293–319.

———. "Free Trade and the Oregon Question, 1842–1846." In *Facts and Factors in Economic History: Articles by Former Students of Edwin Francis Gay*, pp. 470–91. Cambridge, Mass., 1932.

———. "New Alignments in Anglo-American Politics, 1842–1843." Louisville *Courier-Journal*, April 15, 1923, section 3, pp. 11–12.

———. "The Upper Mississippi Valley in Anglo-American Anti-Slavery and Free Trade Relations: 1837–1842." *Mississippi Valley Historical Review*, 15 (September 1928), 204–20.

Merk, Frederick. "Dissent in the Mexican War." In Samuel Eliot Morison *et al.*, *Dissent in Three American Wars*, pp. 35–63. Cambridge, Mass., 1970.

Middleton, Annie. "Donelson's Mission to Texas in Behalf of Annexation." *Southwestern Historical Quarterly*, 24 (April 1921), 247–91.

Miles, Edwin A. " 'Fifty-Four Forty or Fight'—an American Political Legend." *Mississippi Valley Historical Review*, 44 (September 1957), 291–309.

Naylor, Robert A. "The British Role in Central America Prior to the Clayton-Bulwer Treaty of 1850." *Hispanic American Historical Review*, 40 (August 1960), 361–82.

Neu, C. T. "The Annexation of Texas." In *New Spain and the Anglo-American West, Historical Contributions Presented to Herbert Eugene Bolton*, II, 71–102. 2 vols. Los Angeles, 1932.

Northup, Jack. "Nicholas Trist's Mission to Mexico: a Reinterpretation." *Southwestern Historical Quarterly*, 71 (January 1968), 321–46.

Ogden, Adele. "Alfred Robinson, New England Merchant in Mexican California." *California Historical Society Quarterly*, 23 (September 1944), 193–202.

Pratt, Julius W. "James Knox Polk and John Bull." *Canadian Historical Review*, 24 (December 1943), 341–49.

———. "John L. O'Sullivan and Manifest Destiny." *Proceedings of the New York State Historical Association*, 14 (July 1933), 213–34.

Rippy, J. Fred. "Diplomacy of the United States and Mexico Regarding the Isthmus of Tehuantepec, 1848–1865." *Mississippi Valley Historical Review*, 6 (March 1920), 503–21.

Rives, George Lockhart. "Mexican Diplomacy on the Eve of War with the United States." *American Historical Review*, 8 (January 1913), 275–94.

Robertson, William Spence. "French Intervention in Mexico in 1838." *Hispanic American Historical Review*, 24 (May 1944), 222–52.

Schafer, Joseph. "The British Attitude toward the Oregon Question, 1815–1846." *American Historical Review*, 16 (January 1911), 273–99.

———. "Oregon Pioneers and American Diplomacy." In *Essays in American History Dedicated to Frederick Jackson Turner*, pp. 35–55. New York, 1910.

Scheina, Robert L. "The Forgotten Fleet: the Mexican Navy on the Eve of the War, 1845." *American Neptune*, 30 (January 1970), 46–55.

Scott, Leslie M. "Influence of American Settlement upon the Oregon Boundary Treaty of 1846." *Oregon Historical Quarterly*, 29 (March 1928), 1–19.

Sears, Louis M. "Nicholas P. Trist, a Diplomat with Ideals." *Mississippi Valley Historical Review*, 11 (June 1924), 85–98.

Smith, Justin H. "Great Britain and Our War of 1846–1848," *Massachusetts Historical Society Proceedings*, 47 (June 1914), 451–62.

———. "La República de Río Grande." *American Historical Review*, 25 (July 1920), 660–75.

———. "The Mexican Recognition of Texas." *American Historical Review*, 16 (October 1910), 36–55.

Smither, Harriet. "English Abolitionism and the Annexation of Texas." *Southwestern Historical Quarterly*, 32 (January 1929), 193–205.

Spell, Lota M. "Gorostiza and Texas." *Hispanic American Historical Review*, 37 (November 1957), 425–62.

Sperber, Hans. "Fifty-four Forty or Fight: Facts and Fictions." *American Speech*, 32 (February 1957), 5–11.

Stenberg, Richard R. "The Failure of Polk's Mexican War Intrigue of 1845." *Pacific Historical Review*, 4 (March 1935), 39–68.

––––––. "The Motivation of the Wilmot Proviso." *Mississippi Valley Historical Review*, 18 (March 1932), 535–41.

––––––. "Polk and Frémont, 1845–1846." *Pacific Historical Review*, 7 (1938), 211–27.

––––––. "President Polk and California: Additional Documents." *Pacific Historical Review*, 10 (June 1941), 217–19.

––––––. "The Texas Schemes of Jackson and Houston." *Southwestern Social Science Quarterly*, 15 (December 1934), 229–50.

Stewart, Watt. "George Bancroft." In William T. Hutchinson, ed., *The Marcus W. Jernegan Essays in American Historiography*, pp. 1–24. Chicago, 1937.

Tade, George T. "The Anti-Texas Address: John Quincy Adams' Personal Filibuster." *Southern Speech Journal*, 30 (Spring 1965), 185–98.

Tays, George. "Frémont Had No Secret Instructions." *Pacific Historical Review*, 9 (June 1940), 157–72.

Tuterow, Norman E. "Whigs of the Old Northwest and Texas Annexation, 1836–April 1844." *Indiana Magazine of History*, 66 (March 1970), 56–69.

Van Alstyne, Richard W. "British Diplomacy and the Clayton-Bulwer Treaty, 1850–1860." *Journal of Modern History*, 11 (June 1939), 149–83.

––––––. "The Central American Policy of Lord Palmerston." *Hispanic American Historical Review*, 16 (August 1936), 339–59.

––––––. "International Rivalries in [the] Pacific Northwest." *Oregon Historical Quarterly*, 46 (September 1945), 185–218.

Van Horn, James. "Trends in Historical Interpretation: James K. Polk." *North Carolina Historical Review*, 42 (October 1965), 454–64.

Watt, Alastair. "The Case of Alexander McLeod." *Canadian Historical Review*, 12 (June 1931), 145–67.

Webster, Charles K. "British Mediation between France and the United States in 1834–1836." *English Historical Review*, 42 (1927), 58–78.

Wiltsee, Ernest A. "The British Vice Consul in California and the

Events of 1846." *California Historical Society Quarterly*, 10 (June 1931), 99–128.

Winston, James E. "The Attitude of the Newspapers of the United States towards Texan Independence." *Proceedings of the Mississippi Valley Historical Association for the Year 1914–1915*, 8, 160–75.

———. "New Orleans Newspapers and the Texas Question, 1835–1837." *Southwestern Historical Quarterly*, 36 (October 1932), 109–29.

———. "Notes on Commercial Relations between New Orleans and Texas Ports, 1838–1839." *Southwestern Historical Quarterly*, 34 (October 1930), 91–105.

———. "Robert J. Walker, Annexationist." *The Texas Review*, 2 (April 1917), 293–312.

Worley, J. L. "The Diplomatic Relations of England and the Republic of Texas." *Texas Historical Quarterly*, 9 (July 1905), 1–40.

Wyllys, Rufus K. "French Imperialists in California." *California Historical Society Quarterly*, 8 (June 1929), 116–29.

Yañez, Agustín. "Santa Anna y la guerra con los Estados Unidos." *Filosofía y letras*, No. 27 (July–September 1947), pp. 133–60.

Index